THE STUDY
OF AMERICAN
FOLKLORE

An Introduction
THIRD EDITION

THE STUDY
OF AMERICAN
FOLKLORE

An Introduction
THIRD EDITION

Jan Harold Brunvand
UNIVERSITY OF UTAH

W · W · NORTON & COMPANY
New York · London

Published simultaneously in Canada by Penguin Books Canada Ltd, 2801 John Street,
Markham, Ontario L3R 1B4.
PRINTED IN THE UNITED STATES OF AMERICA.

Library of Congress Cataloging-in-Publication Data

Brunvand, Jan Harold.
  The study of American folklore: An introduction.

  Bibliography: p.
  Includes index.
  1. Folklore—United States.   2. United States—Social life and customs.   I. Title.
GR105.B7 1986   398.07   85–29650

ISBN 0-393-95495-1

W. W. Norton & Company, Inc., 500 Fifth Avenue, New York, N.Y. 10110
W. W. Norton & Company Ltd., 10 Coptic Street, London WC1A 1PU
  5 6 7 8 9 0

To Richard Mercer Dorson
1916–1981
from whom I received my own
introduction to American folklore

Contents

IV. MATERIAL FOLK TRADITIONS

Preface

Since the publication of the first edition of this textbook in 1968, the study of folklore in the United States has advanced greatly. Changes in the second edition (1978) reflected this growth in American folklore studies; the third edition brings the book into line with the latest scholarship and enhances both its pedagogic and reference uses.

The purpose of *The Study of American Folklore* is to pave the way for deeper studies of the subject by clearly and systematically presenting the types of folklore found in the United States. It is a basic guidebook for beginning students to genres of American folklore, to theories and methods of research, and to major publications in the field. The book is organized around three large groupings of folk materials—oral, customary, and material. Each chapter begins with definitions of the type involved and continues with a delineation of subtypes, a selection of examples, and discussion of research methods or theories appropriate to that type. Although the bulk of the examples are Anglo-American, often *modern* folklore, for many categories some older lore or representative traditions of ethnic and racial minorities are included.

The philosophy behind these features retained from the first edition is that Anglo-American folklore is a coherent and familiar body of material with a vast bibliography of studies behind it. Once understood, the Anglo-American material provides a basis for further studies of the folklore of other groups, either in the United States or elsewhere. In other words, I expect the majority of students using this book to approach American folklore via their own traditions, without losing sight of American history or of the diversity of subcultures that this country embraces. As for theory, I have provided an eclectic overview of modern theories rather than narrowing the book by following a single contemporary approach.

Professional folklorists will find (as in earlier editions) that I have generalized freely from their studies, citing sources in the text or in the Bibliographic Notes. I do not list the same works more times than necessary, although certainly many publications have a bearing on more than one kind of folklore. For ease of reference, the major generic and theoretical terms introduced appear in boldface or italicized type, and a new Glossarial Index refers to these primary definitions. For the third edition the bibliographic entries are updated through 1982.

While retaining the general organization of *The Study of American Folklore,* I have made many important changes for this edition. Besides replacing some of the examples, correcting errors, and introducing new analytical approaches, I have added a number of subtopics, introduced subheads in the chapters, and rewritten several sections completely. For example, in the introductory section there is a new capsule summary of the history of folklore study in the United States (Chapter 1), a broader discussion of folklore theory with a description of several "schools" (Chapter 2), and an outline of a fourth folk group— the "gender-differentiated" (Chapter 3). The treatment of riddle-jokes, a popular form of modern folklore, has been consolidated in Chapter 6. Chapter 8, "Myths and Motifs," is new, drawing some of its material from the previous "Myths and Legends" chapter and adding a discussion of native American narratives, along with a section on mythic traditions in American history and an enlarged treatment of the *Motif-Index of Folk Literature.* The discussions of family stories, personal-experience narratives, and urban legends have been expanded in the new Chapter 9, "Legends and Anecdotes." Chapter 19, "Folklife," is a new one that introduces concepts and research methods useful for all the categories of material tradition that follow.

Readers will discover for themselves many other alterations and additions, such as some foreign-language proverbs in

Chapter 5, a better discussion of neck riddles and graphic puzzles in Chapter 6, a mention of sampler verse in Chapter 7, joke fables and fractured fairy tales along with two illustrated examples of pictorial folktales in Chapter 10, the swamp holler in Chapter 11, recent findings about an American murder ballad in Chapter 12, folk religion in Chapter 14, legend tripping and "small group festive gatherings" in Chapter 15, some better descriptions of house and barn types in Chapter 20, and "women's art" in Chapter 21.

The last important change to note in the book is the replacement in the Appendix of the first sample study ("The Taming of the Shrew Tale in the United States") with a new essay on American urban legends, a subject that I have researched intensively for the past few years. For the second study, Barre Toelken has thoroughly rewritten his popular essay composed in 1968, "The Folklore of Academe." Also, corrections and additions to the references were made in the studies by Professors Glassie and Evans. In order to tie these four sample studies more closely to the text itself, I have provided a new introductory section to the Appendix called "Putting It All Together: Research in American Folklore."

Three recent books supplement this one in various ways and should be the next readings in a student's introduction to folklore. First, *Folklore and Folklife: An Introduction* (Chicago, 1972), edited by Richard M. Dorson, expands the survey of folklore types internationally. Folklorists from several countries contributed to this collection, and Dorson provided the introduction on folklore definition, theory, and method. A second important reading supplementary to this textbook is Barre Toelken's *The Dynamics of Folklore* (Boston, 1979), a well-written and illustrated work on behavioral, contextual, communicative, and functional aspects of folklore analysis, which draws examples largely from American folklore, including immigrant and native American. The third recommended work is my own *Readings in American Folklore* (New York, 1979), a collection of thirty-six essays selected from folklore journals and provided with introductory headnotes. These readings are grouped as collectanea, studies in context, interpretations, and essays in theory; items in the Bibliographic Notes to the present work that are reprinted in the *Readings* are so indicated.

Many years of planning the original book, using it myself in the classroom, collecting comments from other teachers and students, revising, rewriting, and supplementing the text, updating the bibliographies, and endlessly cutting, pasting, and tinkering have gone into this edition, which I trust (since the third's the charm) will be found by teachers and students of American folklore to be the best yet in the ongoing series. A study guide for instructors using this book is forthcoming.

Salt Lake City, Utah
August 1985

Abbreviations Used in the Bibliographic Notes and Appendix

AA   *American Anthropologist*

AFFWord   (journal of "Arizona Friends of Folklore"; replaced by *SWF* in 1977)

AQ   *American Quarterly*

ArQ   *Arizona Quarterly*

AS   *American Speech*

BJA   *British Journal of Aesthetics*

CA   *Current Anthropology*

C&T   *Culture and Tradition*

CFQ   *California Folklore Quarterly*

CL   *Comparative Literature*

EM   *Ethnomusicology*

FF   *Folklore Forum*

FFC   *Folklore Fellows Communications* (Helsinki)

FFemC   *Folklore Feminists Communication* (after 1977, *FWC*)

FFMA   *The Folklore and Folk Music Archivist*

FFV   *Folklore and Folklife in Virginia*

FMS   *Folklore and Mythology Studies* (UCLA)

Folk Life   (full title of the journal of the [English] Society for Folk Life Studies)

Folklore   (full title of the journal of the [English] Folklore Society)

FWC   *Folklore Women's Communication* (until 1977, *FFemC*)

GR   *Geographical Review*

HF   *Hoosier Folklore*

HFB   *Hoosier Folklore Bulletin*

IF   *Indiana Folklore*

IFR   *International Folklore Review*

IMH   Indiana Magazine of History

IY   Idaho Yesterdays

JAC   Journal of American Culture

JAF   Journal of American Folklore

JAMS   Journal of the American Musicological Society

JEGP   Journal of English and Germanic Philology

JFI   Journal of the Folklore Institute (after 1982, JFR)

JFR   Journal of Folklore Research (before 1982, JFI)

JGLS   Journal of the Gypsy Lore Society

JIFMC   Journal of the International Folk Music Council

JOFS   Journal of the Ohio Folklore Society

JPC   Journal of Popular Culture

JSP   Journal of Social Psychology

KF   Keystone Folklore (until 1973, KFQ; in 1982 began a new series with vol. 1)

KFQ   Keystone Folklore Quarterly (after 1973, KF)

KFR   Kentucky Folklore Record

KR   Kenyon Review

LFM   Louisiana Folklore Miscellany

MAF   Mid-American Folklore (until 1978, MSF)

MF   Midwest Folklore

MFR   Mississippi Folklore Register

MFSJ   Missouri Folklore Society Journal

MH   Minnesota History

MJLF   Midwestern Journal of Language and Folklore

MLN   Modern Language Notes

MLQ   Modern Language Quarterly

MLW   Mountain Life and Work

MP   Modern Philology

MQ   Musical Quarterly

MSF   Mid-South Folklore (after 1978, MAF)

NCF   North Carolina Folklore (after 1973, NCFJ)

NCFJ   North Carolina Folklore Journal (until 1973, NCF)

NEF   Northeast Folklore

NEQ   New England Quarterly

NH   Nebraska History

NJF   New Jersey Folklore

NMFR   New Mexico Folklore Record

NWF   Northwest Folklore

NYF   New York Folklore (until 1975, NYFQ)

NYFQ   New York Folklore Quarterly (after 1975, NYF)

OFB   Oregon Folklore Bulletin

PA   *Pioneer America*
PADS *Publications of the*
      American Dialect So-
      ciety
PF   *Pennsylvania Folklife*
PMLA *Publications of the*
      Modern Language
      Association
PTFS *Publications of the*
      Texas Folklore
      Society
SFQ   *Southern Folklore*
      Quarterly
SWF   *Southwest Folklore*
      (replaced *AFFWord*
      in 1977)

TAW   *The American West*
TFSB *Tennessee Folklore*
      Society Bulletin
TQ   *Texas Quarterly*
TSL   *Tennessee Studies in*
      Literature
TSLL *Texas Studies in*
      Literature and Lan-
      guage
UHQ   *Utah Historical*
      Quarterly
UHR   *Utah Humanities*
      Review
WAL   *Western American*
      Literature
WF   *Western Folklore*

Basic Bibliography: Collections Cited in Notes by Title Only

Beck, Horace P., ed. *Folklore in Action: Essays for Discussion in Honor of MacEdward Leach.* Vol. 14. Philadelphia: American Folklore Society Bibliographical and Special Series, 1962.

Brunvand, Jan Harold. *Readings in American Folklore.* New York: Norton, 1979.

Dorson, Richard M. *American Folklore and the Historian.* Chicago: University of Chicago Press, 1971.

———. *Folklore: Selected Essays.* Bloomington: Indiana University Press, 1972.

———. *Folklore and Fakelore: Essays toward a Discipline of Folk Studies.* Cambridge: Harvard University Press, 1976.

Dundes, Alan. *The Study of Folklore.* Englewood Cliffs, N.J.: Prentice-Hall, 1965.

———. *Analytic Essays in Folklore.* The Hague and Paris: Mouton, 1975.

———. *Interpreting Folklore.* Bloomington: Indiana University Press, 1980.

Pound, Louise. *Nebraska Folklore.* Lincoln: University of Nebraska Press, 1959.

Richmond, W. Edson, ed. *Studies in Folklore.* No. 9. Bloomington: Indiana University Folklore Series, 1957.

I · INTRODUCTION

1
The Field of Folklore

What Is Folklore?

Folklore comprises the unrecorded traditions of a people; it includes both the form and content of these traditions and their style or technique of communication from person to person. The study of folklore (or "folkloristics") attempts to analyze these traditions (both content and process) so as to reveal the common life of the human mind apart from what is contained in the formal records of culture that compose the heritage of a people.

This type of research has been a respected academic specialty in Europe for generations. In the United States, however, the field of folklore is relatively new. Writing in the first issue of *The Folklore Historian*, a newsletter begun in 1984, folklorist W. K. McNeil gave this capsule account of the founding of the American Folklore Society (AFS) nearly a century before:

> In the summer of 1887 several scholars resident in the United States received a letter proposing the formation of an American folklore society modeled somewhat on the organization established in England nine years earlier. A few months later, in October, a second letter containing 104 names from different areas of the United States and Canada was distributed. As a result, a number of people gathered in University Hall at Harvard University on January 4, 1888, to

officially establish the American Folklore Society. . . . Although the new organization selected the eminent ballad scholar Francis James Child president, the real moving force behind the Society was William Wells Newell, the secretary and, for many years, editor of the *Journal of American Folklore*.

The goals of the society were well expressed in the description of "a journal of a scientific character" which appeared in the first number of the journal itself:

(1) For the collection of the fast-vanishing remains of Folk-Lore in America, namely:
    (*a*) Relics of Old English Folk-Lore (ballads, tales, superstitions, dialect, etc.).
    (*b*) Lore of Negroes in the Southern States of the Union.
    (*c*) Lore of the Indian Tribes of North America (myths, tales, etc.).
    (*d*) Lore of French Canada, Mexico, etc.
(2) For the study of the general subject, and publication of the results of special students in this department.

The accomplishments of some of the founders and early leaders of American folklore study are discussed in appropriate chapters of this book: Child in Chapter 12, Newell in Chapter 18, Archer Taylor's work on riddles in Chapter 6, Stith Thompson's motif and tale-type indexes in Chapters 8 and 10, Wayland D. Hand's studies of superstitions in Chapter 14, and so forth. Still other American folklorists' names come up in briefer notices: see, for example, the index references to John Lomax, A. H. Krappe, Louise Pound, Olive Dame Campbell and Cecil J. Sharp, Vance Randolph, and others. Thanks to these and many other scholars whose works are mentioned in the Bibliographic Notes, the study of American folklore (borrowing from international folklore studies) grew from the concern of a handful of enthusiasts to a secure place today in the academic scene, although it was not until the 1950s that advanced degrees in folklore began to be offered at American universities. The original goals of the founders of AFS remain primary—to collect and study folklore in America and to publish it in the *Journal of American Folklore* (*JAF*) and elsewhere. The notion that folklore is "fast vanishing" has proven false, however, as this book amply documents. The creation and dissemination of folklore are still thriving, and, as the 1988 centennial of AFS approaches, folklore study is vigorous.

Unfortunately, the field tends to be narrowly understood by many people who may have been attracted to it through treatments in the popular media, where the word "folklore" is loosely applied, or who may know the word only with reference to children's literature or in the sense of rumor, hearsay, or error. However, it is in the scholarly sense of "oral and customary tradition" that we are employing the word "folklore" here. Archer Taylor put it succinctly in 1948: "Folklore is the material that is handed on by tradition, either by word of mouth or by custom and practice."

The chief difficulty in defining "folklore" more completely and scientifically is that the word has acquired varying meanings among the different scholars and writers who use it. The word was coined by a nineteenth-century English scholar, W. J. Thoms, to supply an Anglo-Saxon word to replace the Latinate term "popular antiquities," or the intellectual "remains" of earlier cultures surviving in the traditions of the peasant class. Modern folklorists have tried to avoid the peasant connotations of the term, but they still use it partly in the original sense to signify that portion of any culture that is passed on in oral or customary tradition. Folklorists tend to exclude as spurious or contaminated any supposed folklore that is transmitted largely by print, broadcasting, or other commercial and organized means without an equally strong interpersonal circulation. American folklorists sometimes use the term "fakelore" (coined by Richard M. Dorson in 1950) to disparage the professional writers' contrived inventions and rewritings—like many Paul Bunyan stories—which are foisted on the public as genuine examples of native folk traditions, but which have only a thin basis of real tradition underlying them.

"Folk" is a somewhat misleading term in an academic context, which has led some folklorists to suggest substitutes for "folklore" such as "hominology" or simply "lore." But "hominology" is just another word for "anthropology" and has achieved no currency; the term "lore" itself is no improvement, since it is hard to justify including behavioral and material data under that heading, and it is still necessary to differentiate *traditional* "lore" from other aspects of culture. The anthropological terms "folk culture" and "verbal arts" have also been proposed as better names for folklore, but neither seems adequate for the full range of topics studied by folklorists; furthermore, "folk culture" implies specific social and economic conditions that are not found in most of the settings folklorists study. The best approach, still, for understanding the scholarly field of American folklore seems to be to state as clearly as possible the concepts folklorists themselves hold, for, as one frustrated definer of the term finally put it, "Folklore is what folklorists study."

Folk, Normative, Elite

Folklore is the traditional, unofficial, noninstitutional part of culture. It encompasses all knowledge, understandings, values, attitudes, assumptions, feelings, and beliefs transmitted in traditional forms by word of mouth or by customary examples. Many of these habits of thought are common to all human beings, but they always interact with and are influenced by the whole cultural context that surrounds them. Folklore manifests itself in many oral and verbal forms ("mentifacts"), in kinesiological forms (customary behavior, or "sociofacts"), and in material forms ("artifacts"), but folklore itself is the whole traditional complex of thought, content, and process which ultimately can never be fixed or recorded in its entirety; it lives only in its performance or communication as people interact with one another. It is instructive to represent these generalizations and terms as a chart, with typical labels for the supposed levels of culture (or behavior) on one axis and the kinds of traditional materials (or products) on the other. The result is as follows:

Products:

Levels	ORAL (Mentifacts)	CUSTOMARY (Sociofacts)	MATERIAL (Artifacts)
Elite (academic, progressive, etc.)			
Normative (popular, mass, mainstream, etc.)			
Folk (conservative, traditional, etc.)			

In general, the elite and normative traditions are transmitted in print or by other formal means, while the folk tradition relies on oral or customary circulation, although there are always exceptions. If we try now to isolate one specific human need or desire for each level and its typical products, we arrive at a set of samples like this:

	ORAL (entertainment)	CUSTOMARY (cure)	MATERIAL (housing)
Elite	serious novel	doctor's care	architect's design
Normative	popular romance	nonprescription drug	tract develop- ment house
Folk	tall tale or joke	home remedy	log cabin or saltbox house

Such a chart and samples are oversimplifications of very complex phenomena, and an important part of many research projects in folklore is sorting out the various threads of influence and the interweavings in one level from another. For example, while most movies are popular art, some serious works of "cinema" tend to be elite; musical comedy would seem to be a mass-culture variant of opera. Similarly, bluegrass music has roots in folk music, but most of its development is in popular music; and Paul Bunyan stories span the same two categories. In general, the movement of ideas tends to be from top to bottom, as when Greek Revival architecture became a popular style for banks and survived later as a traditional decorative style on houses. Other materials and ideas, however, have stayed in place (many barn types), or moved upward ("'folk" clothing becoming "fashionable"), or skipped steps ("folk" arts appealing to "elite" art critics). The study of folklore itself is, of course, "elite." Most important to bear in mind is that individuals may be aware of, influenced by, and participate in any level of culture during their lifetime, or even during the course of a particular day.

Oral, Customary, Material

The materials and manifestations of folklore are extremely wide-ranging and diverse; their genres may be identified as either *ethnic* (or *native*) *categories,* those of the people themselves (like "old-wive's tales"), or *analytical categories,* those of research scholars (like "Child ballads"). For the purpose of an orderly presentation of American folklorists' practices, we will treat the types of folklore here, using typical analytical categories, in three groups, according to their modes of existence: *oral, customary,* or *material.*

Oral folklore, the type most commonly studied until recently in the United States, may be conveniently arranged and listed from the simplest to the most complex varieties. At the level of the individual word is folk *speech,* including dialect and naming. Traditional phrases and sentences make up the area of folk *proverbs* and *proverbial sayings,* while traditional questions are folk *riddles.* Next are folk *rhymes* and other traditional poetry, then folk *narratives* of all kinds, and finally folk *songs* and folk *ballads* with their *music.*

Customary folklore, which often involves both verbal and nonverbal elements, includes folk *beliefs* and *superstitions,* folk *customs* and *festivals,* folk *dances* and *dramas, gestures,* and folk *games.*

Material folk traditions include folk *architecture, crafts, arts, costumes,* and *food.*

These categories and subcategories overlap, but such a three-part classification emphasizes elements that comprise folklore and shows how individual items and performances may be roughly sorted on the basis of their major modes of existence. Placing a folk singer's lyrics in one category, his or her guitar-playing style and melody in another, and the call and figures of a dance done to the same song in a third is not intended to lead to fragmentation either of the tradition involved or the study of it. The classification is only a means of clarifying and organizing the processes and materials that are to be observed and analyzed. Without an awareness of these elements of a traditional performance, there would be a tendency simply to tape-record "the song" without capturing its context or the nonverbal nuances. Similarly, because folktales are basically verbal folklore, folklorists should not overlook collecting and studying such nonverbal elements as facial expressions, gestures, and audience reactions while tales are being told. The ideal study is one that takes into account the entire traditional event, which is what we are referring to as a "performance."

Definitions: What Folklore Is and What It Isn't

The foregoing discussion identifies mainly the *materials* that circulate in folk tradition; we can extract from these materials some common qualities that will provide us with a good general *definition* of the subject. Folklorists generally associate five qualities with true folklore: (1) its content is oral (usually verbal), or custom-related or material; (2) it is traditional in form and transmission; (3) it exists in different versions; (4) it is usually anonymous; (5) it tends to become formularized. Each of these terms is used in a fairly broad sense, and the first three qualities are the primary ones to be considered in arriving at a definition.

Folklore is oral or custom-related in that it passes by word of mouth and informal demonstration or imitation from one person to another and from one generation to the next. Much folklore is "aural," reaching the ear either from voices or from musical instruments. While written folklore (such as graffiti or autograph rhymes) is verbal without being oral, its transmission is customary, not institutionalized. The same is true for learning to produce or use folk artifacts, such as whittled wooden chains, hand-sewn quilts, or traditional log cabins. Folklore is never transmitted *entirely* in a formal manner through printed books, phonograph records, school classes, church sermons, or by other learned, sophisticated, and commercial means.

Folklore is traditional in two senses in that it is passed on repeatedly in a relatively fixed or standard form, and it circulates among members of a particular group. Traditional form or structure allows us to recognize corresponding bits of folklore in different guises. The characters in a story, the setting, the length, the style, even the language may vary, but we can still call it the "same" story if it maintains a basic underlying form. Think, for example, of "Cinderella," which would probably be recognizable even in a comic-strip parody if the characters were made modern teen-agers, or in the movies if the parts were acted by Hollywood stars in a big-city setting.

But comic strips and movies are not folklore, and this leads to the observation that the first two qualities must be found together to define folklore. For example, some things, like conversations, are oral, but not traditional. (Entire conversations are not passed on between members of a group in a relatively fixed or standard form and repeated over and over again.) Other things, like legal processes, are largely traditional, but not oral. (The proceedings in courts of law are preserved in print, not by word of mouth. Law precedents must be followed precisely, but folk performers [sometimes called "informants"] seldom refer to printed collections of folklore.) Only those aspects of culture that are both oral or customary and traditional may be folklore; thus, there may be traditional folk stories, proverbs, or gestures passed on either in conversations or in courtroom arguments and testimony. These items are legitimate examples of folklore. The American "folk groups" that possess major bodies of tradition are discussed in Chapter 3. Much controversy has centered on the meaning of the "folk" in "folklore," but it is sufficient to say here that one should not think only of quaint, rustic tradition-bearers, but rather of any group that has distinctive oral traditions, which is to say, just about *any* group.

Oral transmission invariably creates different versions of the same text, and these versions or "variants" are the third defining characteristic of folklore. Folklorists often speak of individual recordings of folklore as either "texts" or "versions," reserving the term "variants" for texts that deviate more widely from the common standard. A story, proverb, or other text is living folklore only as long as it continues to circulate orally in different traditional variations. "The Three Bears," for instance, except in oral parodies, has always been more a literary tale than a folktale; "Home on the Range" was collected as an oral folksong but, after the influence of wide reprinting, is now learned from books or sheet music in a standardized form.

Generally speaking, then, folklore may be defined as *those materials in culture that circulate traditionally among members of any group in different versions, whether in oral form or by means of customary example, as well as the processes of traditional performance and communication.*

Although oral or customary tradition and the presence of different versions serve to define folklore, the two other qualities, anonymity and formularization, are important enough to belong in a complete description. Folklore is usually anonymous simply because authors' names are seldom part of texts that are orally transmitted and folk artifacts are seldom signed, although occasionally a ballad may contain the supposed name or initials of its composer in the last verse and sometimes local tradition preserves the name of a notable folk composer or artisan. On occasion, too, research has unearthed the identity of a creator of folklore, but the majority of folklore bears no trace of its authorship, and even the time and place of its origin may be a mystery.

Most folklore tends to become formularized—that is, it is expressed partly in commonplace terms. These may range in complexity from simple set phrases and patterns of repetition to elaborate opening and closing devices or whole passages of traditional verbal stereotypes. Furthermore, there are different bodies of formularized language in different countries and for different kinds of folklore, so that we can distinguish between

English and American ballads, for example, partly on the basis of the different formulas used in each. Nonverbal folklore, too, makes use of stereotyped habits, gestures, patterns, designs, and the like. One interesting area of folklore research is the identification and attempted explanation of this recurring formularization.

The criteria for identifying authentic folklore and the specific definition of "folklore" given in this chapter are not meant to exclude other views or other formulations by different folklorists. There is something to be learned both about folklore and the history of its study in the United States from every definition, ranging from C. F. Potter's metaphorical one, "a lively fossil which refuses to die" (1949), and Alan Dundes's "definition consisting of an itemized list of the forms of folklore" (1965) to Dan Ben-Amos's elegant and concise "performance" definition of folklore as "artistic communication in small groups" (1971). Recent definitional statements attempt to reconcile the older generic approach to folklore with the current emphasis on context. Thus we have Barre Toelken's cautious statement: "We might characterize or describe the materials of folklore as 'tradition-based communicative units informally exchanged in dynamic variation through space and time' " (1979). And we also have Robert Georges's similar careful reference to folkloristics as the study that concentrates on "continuities and consistencies in human behavior . . . what human beings express and the ways they express themselves during face-to-face interaction" (1980).

The boundaries of the field of folklore laid out in this chapter do not take in all of the various recent uses to which the term "folk" and "lore" have been put. They do, however, delimit rather broadly the scholarly area that folklorists have staked out for their studies. It bears repeating that this study is one of prime significance for our fuller understanding of human behavior and culture. Certainly the current popularization and sometimes banalization of folklore, the appearance of fakelore, and even utter misapplication of the term "folklore," also reveal important things about culture and behavior, and these deserve study, too. But this is subject matter for another kind of book,

one for which a survey like the present one is probably a necessary prerequisite.

BIBLIOGRAPHIC NOTES

The Victorian gentleman-scholar W. J. Thoms suggested the term
"folklore" in a letter, signed "Ambrose Merton," to *The Athenaeum* in
1846; see Duncan Emrich, " 'Folk-Lore': William John Thoms," *CFQ* 5
(1946): 355–74. The twenty-one definitions by modern folklorists are
gathered in *Funk & Wagnalls Standard Dictionary of Folklore, Mythology, and Legend*, 2 vols. (New York: Funk & Wagnalls, 1949; rev. 1 vol.
ed., 1972). The Thoms letter and a discussion of the dictionary definitions are reprinted in Dundes's *The Study of Folklore*, which contains
other important articles (including Archer Taylor's, quoted in this
chapter) on the problem of defining folklore. Richard M. Dorson introduced the word "fakelore" in an article in *The American Mercury* 70
(March 1950): 335–43, and he furnished the background for his coinage
in an article in *Zeitschrift für Volkskunde* 65 (1969): 56–64 (reprinted in
American Folklore and the Historian, pp. 3–14). Writing "In Defense of
Paul Bunyan" in *NYF* 5 (1979): 43–51, Edith Fowke criticized writings
(including earlier editions of this textbook) that branded Paul Bunyan a
complete fakelore invention, pointing out that there are reliable
sources dated before 1910 from at least eight locations proving a Bunyan oral tradition before popularizing began. Fowke likened the early
popularizers' works to the printed sheets ("broadsides") that once
helped to disseminate ballads. However, this reasonable argument
does not obviate the need for the term "fakelore" itself.

Three addresses by former presidents of the American Folklore Society are important statements on the field of folklore. They are Herbert
Halpert's "Folklore: Breadth versus Depth," *JAF* 71 (1958): 97–103;
Wayland D. Hand's "American Folklore after Seventy Years: Survey
and Prospect," *JAF* 73 (1960): 1–11; and William Bascom's "Folklore,
Verbal Art, and Culture," *JAF* 86 (1973): 374–81. Three professional as-
sessments of the state of American folklore studies are Tristram P. Coffin's "Folklore in the American Twentieth Century," *AQ* 13 (1961):
526–33; Francis Lee Utley's "The Academic Status of Folklore in the
United States," *JFI* 7 (1970): 110–15; and Richard M. Dorson's "Is Folklore a Discipline?" *Folklore* 84 (1973): 177–205.

The history of American folklore study itself and how it bears on ongoing research was taken up in the special "American Folklore Histor-
iography" issue of *JFI* 10 (June/August 1973): 1–128, which had essays
on figures like William Wells Newell, A. L. Kroeber, George Lyman
Kittredge, and Phillips Barry, as well as theoretical and bibliographical
articles. Important backgrounds to American folklore studies in the

work of their English predecessors are contained in Richard M. Dorson's book *The British Folklorists: A History* (Chicago: University of Chicago Press, 1968). Individual folklorists' works are evaluated in such studies as Dudley C. Gordon's "Charles F. Lummis: Pioneer American Folklorist," *WF* 28 (1969): 175–81; Dorson's "Elsie Clews Parsons: Feminist and Folklorist," *AFFWord* 1 (1971): 1–4 (reprinted in *FFemC* 2 [1974]: 4 ff.); Keith S. Chambers, "The Indefatigable Elsie Clews Parsons—Folklorist," *WF* 32 (1973): 180–98; and Jeanne Patten Whitten, "Fannie Hardy Eckstorm: A Descriptive Bibliography of Her Writings, Published and Unpublished," *NEF* 16 (1975). The title of Angus K. Gillespie's *Folklorist of the Coal Fields: George Korson's Life and Work* (University Park: Pennsylvania State University Press, 1980) speaks for itself. The special issue of *JFI* (vol. 16, nos. 1–2 [1979]) dedicated to Harry Middleton Hyatt contains a good analysis of the work of the compiler (with his sister Minnie Hyatt Small) of *Folklore from Adams County, Illinois* and other works. Doubtless of great future interest for historians of American folkloristics will be *Roads into Folklore*, no. 14 in the *Folklore Forum* "Bibliographic and Special Series" (Bloomington, Ind.: 1975), which contains anecdotal accounts of how they got into folklore by forty of Richard M. Dorson's students with a bonus of one parody entry credited to "Gregor Isomotif." *The Folklore Historian*, a newsletter directed to students of the history of folkloristics, appeared in early 1984, just in time to be noted here, and was doubtless in part inspired by the upcoming centennial of the American Folklore Society in 1988, organized planning for which began in late 1983.

For statements on the discipline of folklore in the United States made two decades apart by the dean of American folklore scholars see Stith Thompson's "American Folklore after Fifty Years," *JAF* 51 (1938): 1–9, and "Folklore at Midcentury," in *MF* 1 (1951): 5–12. Jan Harold Brunvand reviewed Thompson's evaluations in the light of another twenty years' progress in "New Directions for the Study of American Folklore," *Folklore* 82 (1971): 25–35 (repr. in *Readings in American Folklore*, pp. 416–26). A politically oriented critique by John Alexander Williams entitled "Radicalism and Professionalism in Folklore Studies: A Comparative Perspective" was published in *JFI* 11 (1974 [misdated 1975]): 211–34, and answered by Richard M. Dorson in the same journal, 235–39. And a philosophical critique, mainly of American folklore studies, is Kenneth Laine Ketner's "Identity and Existence in the Study of Human Traditions" published in *Folklore* 87 (1976): 192–200. Invoking Plato, Wittgenstein, and others, Ketner finds so many logical flaws in the assumptions underlying folklore studies that one wonders how the field has managed to survive at all.

In "American Folklore vs. Folklore in America," *JFI* 15 (1978): 97–111, Richard M. Dorson urged scholars to "relate folkstuff to the American historical experience," as he found most earlier studies sadly lacking in this regard. His particular demand for a chronological framework for true "American folklore" studies drew a rebuttal from Stephen Stern and Simon J. Bronner entitled "Comment—American Folklore vs. Folklore in America: A Fixed Fight?" *JFI* 17 (1980): 76–84; Dorson replied in the same journal (85–89) that such scholars "lock themselves into a parochial present and blind themselves to the buried treasure in America's past." Dorson edited a special double issue of *JFI* (vol. 17, nos. 2–3, 1980) on "The American Theme in American Folklore," with articles on American outlaws, biography, folklore in literature, folk religion, sports, urban legends, and (inevitably) fakelore.

One gains a clear impression of older European attitudes toward folklore from *The Handbook of Irish Folklore* (Dublin, 1942; rpr. Hatboro, Pa., 1963) and Krappe's *The Science of Folklore* (1930; rpr. New York: Norton, 1964), and also from *The Handbook of Folklore* published by the [English] Folk-Lore Society in 1890 and revised and enlarged in 1957. Especially pertinent in the *Handbook* is the first chapter, "What Folklore Is," in which it is declared that folklore is "the expression of the psychology of early man" and comprises "the traditional Beliefs, Customs, Stories, Songs, and Sayings current among backward peoples, or retained by the uncultured classes of more advanced peoples." A grudging nod toward "folklife" was inserted in an addendum to the 1913 edition of the *Handbook*, but this was qualified by the insistence that "by no stretch of definition can the word *lore* be taken to include the material objects to which it may be attached." To redress the balance at last, the Society for Folk Life Studies was formed in England in 1961, and their yearbook, *Folk Life*, first appeared in 1963.

Alan Dundes has presented "The American Concept of Folklore" in *JFI* 3 (1966): 226–45, repr. in *Analytic Essays in Folklore*, pp. 3–16. The same author speaks for many, perhaps most, of his compatriots in his 1977 essay "Who Are the Folk?" (reprinted in *Interpreting Folklore*, pp. 1–19) when he answers the question "Among others, *we* are!" Taking a comparative approach, Américo Paredes discussed "Concepts about Folklore in Latin America and the United States" in *JFI* 6 (1969): 20–38. An important exegesis is Paulo de Carvalho Neto's *Concepto de Folklore* (Montevideo, Uruguay: 1955), first translated into English as *The Concept of Folklore* (Coral Gables, Fla.: University of Miami Press, 1971).

That North American folklorists have widened their traditional view of folklore as oral literature and are embracing the concept of folklore as including "folklife"—the totality of traditional life—is indicated by the greatly expanded coverage of folklife topics possible in this textbook since its first publication in 1968. The journal *Pioneer America* devoted to American material-culture studies spanned about the same period, having started in 1969; the cumulative index for volumes 1 through 10, published in volume 11 (1979), shows a great number and variety of studies in this periodical alone. (In 1984 the title of the journal was changed to *Material Culture*.) Henry Glassie, a prime mover among American material-culture scholars, wrote a study presented in the Appendix of this book; it has become a classic of the field since its first publication in 1968. Glassie's general appraisal of the cultural roles of handmade things appears in "Artifacts: Folk, Popular, Imaginary, and Real," published in Marshall Fishwick and Ray B. Browne's *Icons of Popular Culture* (Bowling Green, Ohio: Bowling Green University Popular Press, 1970), pp. 103–22.

Theoretical problems in distinguishing folklore types and categories are taken up in a "Symposium on Folk Genres" conducted by Dan Ben-Amos in the journal *Genre* 2 (1969): 1–301; of particular importance is Ben-Amos's own essay there, "Analytical Categories and Ethnic Genres," 275–301. These essays were reprinted in book form as *Folklore Genres*, ed. Dan Ben-Amos, American Folklore Society Bibliographic and Special Series, no. 26 (Austin, Texas: 1976). Alan Dundes identifies "Some Minor Genres of American Folklore" (envelope sealers, evasive answers, feigned apologies, etc.) in *SFQ* 31 (1967): 20–36. A good example of how the social context in which a folkloric item is communicated determines its genre is Ronald L. Baker's note " 'Hogs Are Playing with Sticks—Bound to Be Bad Weather': Folk Belief or Proverb?" *MJLF* 1 (1975): 65–67 (repr. in *Readings in American Folklore*, pp. 199–202).

Richard M. Dorson's 1973 paper "Folklore in the Modern World," reprinted in *Folklore and Fakelore*, pp. 33–73, outlines the traditional versus "revised" concept of what folklore is, putting the emphasis in the "new" definition on the influences of industry and technology, the mass media, nationalism, and the like. In an essay entitled " 'For Want of a Nail': A Synthesis of Metaphorical Definitions" in *TFSB* 46 (1980): 1–15, Mariella Hartsfield proves with multiple examples how folklorists have drawn on metaphors of warfare, flowing water, mirrors, fields, games, and especially plants—particularly *trees* and their wooden products—in conceptualizing the subject matter and methodology of folklore and its study. (For example, this textbook and the accompanying *Reader* have a wood-grained dust-jacket design, Dorson's *American Folklore* cover shows a rail fence, Krappe's *The Science of Folklore* uses twiglike lettering, and so forth; the *language* of folklore definitions is often similarly treelike.)

Probably the most influential publication directed to the strong desire to redefine "folklore" along contextual or behavioristic lines is Dan Ben-Amos's "Toward a Definition of Folklore in Context," pp. 3–15, in "Toward New Perspectives in Folklore," ed. Américo Paredes and Richard Bauman, *JAF* 84 (1971): iii–172, and in the American Folklore Society Bibliographic and Special Series, no. 23 (1972). This essay (also repr. in *Readings in American Folklore,* pp. 427–43), originally a paper delivered orally at an AFS meeting, was debated in print even before it reached print itself; see Roger L. Welsch, "A Note on Definitions," *JAF* 81 (1968): 262–64; Richard Bauman, "Towards a Behavioral Theory of Folklore: A Reply to Roger Welsch," *JAF* 82 (1969): 167–70; Roger D. Abrahams, "On Meaning and Gaming," *JAF* 82 (1969): 268–70; and Jan Harold Brunvand, "On Abrahams' Besom," *JAF* 83 (1970): 81. Roger Welsch leaped back into the fray with "Beating a Live Horse: Yet Another Note on Definitions and Defining" in *Perspectives on American Folk Art,* ed. M. G. Quimby and Scott T. Swank (Winterthur, Del.: Winterthur Museum, 1980), pp. 218–33.

Folklore Forum devoted its "Bibliographic and Special Series" no. 12 to fourteen articles on "Conceptual Problems in Contemporary Folklore Study"; the most lucid of these (despite its title) was Gerald Cashion's "Folklore, Kinesiological Folklore, and the Macro-Folklore Complex," 24–35. An equally well-written and clarifying essay is Kay L. Cothran's "Participation in Tradition," *KF* 18 (1973): 7–13 (repr. in *Readings in American Folklore,* pp. 444–48). Identifying "folklore about folklore" as a traditional practice worthy of more study, Alan Dundes proposed "Metafolklore and Oral Literary Criticism," a concept quickly seized upon by folklorists, in *The Monist* 50 (1966): 505–16 (repr. in *Analytic Essays in Folklore,* pp. 50–58, and in *Readings in American Folklore,* pp. 404–15).

The further definitions of "folklore" quoted in this chapter are from the *Standard Dictionary of Folklore* (Potter), *The Study of Folklore* (Dundes; see the Basic Bibliography in this book), Ben-Amos's article cited above, *The Dynamics of Folklore* (Toelken; see the Preface), and Georges's 1980 article on the text/context controversy cited in the notes to Chapter 2.

2
The Study of Folklore

Folklore is fascinating to study because people are fascinating creatures. It is a diversified and complex subject because it reflects the whole intricate mosaic of the rest of human culture. Folklore is part of culture, but it is elusive, flowing along separately from the mainstream of the major intellectual attainments of humanity. In traditional lore, however, there are counterparts for literary and representational art, philosophical speculations, scientific inquiries, historical records, social attitudes, and psychological insights. Thus, the study of folklore is a subdivision of the broader study of people and their works, and as such, folklore research has much in common with both the humanities and the social sciences.

From the humanistic point of view folklore research has tended to emphasize the "lore," usually taking a literary approach to the recorded "texts" of verbal traditions; from the social-science point of view folklore research has emphasized the "folk," taking an anthropological (or "functional") approach to the full cultural significance of traditions. Thus, to a humanist, proverbs may be "folk philosophy," riddles may be "traditional metaphorical questions," and folktales may be "oral literature," but to an anthropologist these forms may be considered more as educational tools, social controls, or status markers. Seen from either viewpoint, the materials of folklore afford the unique opportunity of studying what exists and persists in culture largely without the support of established learning, religion, government, and other formal institutions. Folklore represents what people preserve in their culture through the generations by custom and word of mouth when few other means exist to preserve it. The discovery of the historical depth and the geographical breadth of some of these traditional "survivals" (as they were once called) is what first gave the study of folklore much of its fascination. Nowadays, however, there is much more interest in the *present* functions and meanings of folk traditions, and the literary and anthropological approaches to folklore study are merging as a new "folkloristic" study develops.

What humanists and social scientists share when they study folklore is an interest in finding out how, why, and which traditional cultural mentifacts, sociofacts, and artifacts develop, vary, and are passed on. From observations and records of these materials they hope to reconstruct something of the unrecorded intellectual life of people of the past and present. The findings of such folklore research are applicable to many fields. Some literary scholars are interested, for instance, in the folk roots of epic and other narrative poetry and in the stylistic or thematic use of folklore in literature. Students of the fine arts may similarly consider the background of their subjects in folk music and folk art. Historians find that oral traditions, although seldom factually accurate, furnish insights into grass-roots attitudes toward historical events. Psychologists have long held that folklore, in common with dreams and other manifestations of fantasy, contains clues to the subconscious. Sociologists may study folklore (especially protest lore) along with other data on group life and behavior. While such applications of folklore study to other fields (such as the natural sciences) are still in an early stage, other and new applications (such as studying the efficacy of folk medicine) are also emerging. In fact, probably every field of study involving people and their works will in some way eventually make use of evidence from folklore as folklorists continue to refine and publicize their work. And the unified (or holistic) approach of recent folklore research holds even more promise for the application of findings to other fields.

Some Fundamental Questions

Modern folklore study embraces oral, customary, and material aspects of tradition equally, and it makes eclectic use of theoretical and methodological approaches from anthropology, linguistics, communications, psychology, and other relevant areas. While several distinct theoretical approaches and schools of thought have developed within folklore studies, most folklore research may still be thought of as an attempt to answer only a few of the fundamental questions:

> *definition* (what folklore is)
> *classification* (what the genres of folklore are)
> *source* (who "the folk" are)
> *origin* (who composed folklore)
> *transmission* (how folklore is carried, how fast, and how far)
> *variation* (how folklore changes and for what reasons)
> *structure* (what the underlying form of folklore is and the relation of form to content)
> *function* (what folklore means to its carriers and how it serves them)
> *meaning* and *purpose* (what the performer intends to convey and the intended effect)
> *use* and *application* (what should be done with folklore and in what other areas of study it is useful).

Ideally, no folk product or performance would be considered fully understood until answers had at least been suggested for all such questions. In practice, however, because past folklorists have tended to be specialists in one genre or region or technique, studies seldom considered more than one or two of these matters at a time, and very few aspects of folklore have been subjected to more comprehensive research. The assumption that underlies all research in folklore is that, since nothing in culture is meaningless or random, folklore—as a part of culture —inevitably has some function or meaning for those who create it and transmit it. Often the key to unlocking the meanings of folklore is the identification of habits of thought or formal patterns that both the *items* and the *performances* of folklore display.

The linguist Allen Walker Read described the process of studying folklore concisely in an essay on graffiti as a field for research: "[The folklorist] can take unpromising, trivial details, organize them into an orderly body of material, and from them derive significant findings in the interpretation of human life." This statement introduces the three traditional stages of folklore research which give us a convenient framework to survey this scholarship—*collection, classification,* and *analysis.*

Collecting Folklore

The raw materials of oral folklore research are texts (or "records of mentifacts"). It is axiomatic that these texts must be collected verbatim from oral sources; editorial additions to or "improvements" in the texts have no part in honest research. Most folklorists today seek out promising informants and use tape recorders to collect the exact words of the informants, practicing a variety of interview techniques to achieve a relaxed atmosphere and a natural response. Not only the most skilled "active" informants are sought, but also the relatively "passive" informants who may remember interesting lore, although they impart it only in garbled or fragmentary form. Often collectors will make several visits to their best informants, sometimes over a long span of time, recording familiar material and asking for new items.

Besides verbatim texts, folklorists record data about the informants themselves (age, occupation, national origin, etc.) and gather background on the families and communities of the informants. An informant's gestures and facial expressions should be described as an integral part of the performance, and these aspects of style (or "texture") may be captured with candid photographs, movie films, or video tapes.

The texts and texture of folklore always exist in a specific context, and this, too, needs to be carefully documented. Field workers must note the setting for the performance (time, place, and situation), the participants and their responses to the performer, and the "frame" for the folk event (what preceded and followed the performance of folklore). Contexts may be natural —just something that happened in a traditional way—or they

may be induced by the collector who sets up a more or less artificial situation of "collecting folklore." Probably the closer collectors are to blending in with the folk as participant-observers
themselves, the better and less self-conscious the performances
will be. Contexts may be summarized in general terms ("Where
do you usually tell this kind of story?" etc.) or may be described
from immediate observation ("How the children played jump
rope this afternoon . . ."). In the most penetrating studies, informants may be asked to discuss or interpret their texts (providing "oral-literary" criticism), and experiments using
"planted" folk materials have been attempted with some informants and their audiences.

Questionnaires are successfully used for folklore collecting in
Europe, generally with trained semiprofessional field workers
asking the questions of residents in their own region. Mailed
questionnaires allow researchers to cover a wider area than they
might conveniently visit in person, but this technique also limits
the inquiry to a specific subject and eliminates the free association that is often the most productive part of direct collecting.
Only a few studies of American folklore have thus far made use
of questionnaires, but they seem to hold promise, particularly
for accurate distributional and variation studies of folk speech,
customs, and artifacts.

Folklore texts or descriptions of customs and artifacts may
sometimes be collected from handwritten sources, such as
diaries, letters, and notebooks, or from printed matter, such as
books, magazines, and newspapers. For instance, many colonial
"divine providences" collected and printed by Puritan writers
were probably old popular beliefs and superstitions, some Civil
War folksongs survived in soldiers' writings, and American regional newspapers in the nineteenth century preserved much
traditional native humor that has not been fully explored. Current popular periodicals also occasionally print items of folklore
that have been reported either as rumors or as actual events.
(See "Urban Legends" in Chapter 9.)

A beginning folklore collector can learn much about field
problems and techniques by reading accounts of field work by
veteran collectors. For example, the works of Richard M. Dor-

son, one of the most active and successful American collectors, are rich in anecdotes and suggestions. In his *Negro Folktales in Michigan* (Cambridge, Mass.: 1956) two prefatory chapters analyze the communities and informants visited and include several photographs of narrators in action. He recalled that it was the leather patches on his jacket sleeves that convinced one informant that he was really a "writer feller" and not, as some others in the town thought, an FBI agent.

In *Bloodstoppers and Bearwalkers* (Cambridge, Mass.: 1952) Dorson described how he pieced together the Upper Peninsula legend of "The Lynching of the McDonald Boys" from numerous incomplete reports and offhand allusions. "Old-timers have spun the grisly yarn . . . to pop-eyed youngsters for more than sixty years . . . [but] no two granddads tell quite the same story, for this is strictly a family tradition, never frozen in print, and unceasingly distorted with the vagaries that grow from hearsay and surmise." Turning to a completely different subject near the end of his life—the urban center as a field for folklore collecting—Dorson described his techniques for "doing fieldwork in the city." He located informants by haunting the same hangouts as his sources, and by following the leads of people he called "bridge contacts" who introduced him to good performers. With his equipment always at the ready, Dorson tape-recorded numerous everyday conversations, life histories, and personal experiences; he supplemented these sound records by keeping a daily field diary in which he recorded "ethnographic observations of the urban scene." The results of his field work appeared in the book *Land of the Millrats* (Cambridge, Mass.: 1981).

The Ozark collector Vance Randolph was as industrious and successful in the field as Dorson, but more casual in his approach; he generally included in his books a prefatory note something like the following from his collection of Ozark jokes, *Hot Springs and Hell* (Hatboro, Pa.: 1965):

> Some of these items were recorded on aluminum discs, but most of them were set down in longhand and typed a few hours later while the details were still fresh in my mind. They are not verbatim transcripts, but every one of them is pretty

close to the mark. They are not literary adaptations. I did not add any characters or incidents, or try to improve the narrator's style. I did not combine different versions, or use material from more than one informant in the same tale. Many backwoods jokes are nonverbal anyhow, and some folk humor is too subtle for print, just as certain folk tunes cannot be compassed by the conventional notation. I just set down each item as accurately as I could and let it go at that.

Unorthodox collecting methods sometimes yield good results when conventional approaches fail. Some folklorists, for instance, have tried rocking an empty rocking chair, opening an umbrella in the house, or violating some other superstitious taboo in order to elicit a response about bad luck. Others have had success singing a song or telling a tale in garbled form so that intended informants will correct them. Kenneth S. Goldstein once devised a field experiment that led two Scottish women unself-consciously to tell their versions of a previously tape-recorded family legend in the presence of the other. He later asked them to retell the legend on the pretense that he had accidentally erased the tape. He discovered that each storyteller had somewhat modified her own telling, influenced by what she had heard from the other narrator. An excellent collection of Norwegian tall tales was made by a paint company through a contest advertised in popular periodicals. Similarly, I found a rich stock of shaggy-dog stories that had been collected by a network radio program devoted to answering listeners' questions. A student based a fascinating term project on the following topic, presented with teachers' cooperation to several classes of elementary-school children: "Write down your favorite jump-rope rhyme and tell why you like it." (Some specific hints on tape-recorder technique are included in Chapter 13, and on collecting with camera or sketch pad in Chapter 19.)

Whatever the collecting methods employed, and however ingenious or well prepared the collector may be, persistence and a willingness to adapt to the informants' habits and moods will pay off in the long run. The following quotation from John A. Lomax's autobiographical *Adventures of a Ballad Hunter* (New York: 1947) is illustrative:

It was cowboy songs I most wished. . . . These I jotted down on a table in a saloon back room, scrawled on an envelope while squatting about a campfire near a chuck wagon, or caught behind the scenes of a broncho-busting outfit or rodeo. To capture the cowboy music proved an almost impossible task. The cowboys would simply wave away the large horn I carried and refused to sing into it! Not one song did I ever get from them except through the influence of generous amounts of whiskey, raw and straight from the bottle or jug.

An important, but often neglected, aspect of field work in folklore is the ethical dimension—the responsibilities and liabilities of a folklorist with regard to informants and their material, especially when embarrassing, antisocial, or illegal material is involved. Unless clear legal limits of access to and liability for collected information are established (and this is seldom done), the folklorist would do well to code or to give pseudonyms to his human sources of such lore—for example, that concerning drug use, moonshining, telephone or machine fraud, tax evasion, and the like. But even less criminal subjects may raise ethical questions, such as whether informants should be compensated for their cooperation, by whom collected material may be used and for what purposes, and whether published material should be specifically credited to informants. It is never a good idea to record folklore surreptitiously unless the informants are advised of the act later and allowed to review the material, and archives should always insist upon some kind of informants' and collectors' release forms accompanying any filed material and clearly outlining any conditions to be imposed on it.

Classifying Folklore

Collected folklore texts, descriptions of customs, or artifacts are of little use to a scholar until identified by category and arranged systematically in an archive (or museum) or published. Classification of the myriad forms of folklore facilitates their study just as classification systems do for the natural sciences: without standardized terminology and arrangement, we could not communicate effectively or gather data from archives and published collections. The difficulty (as pointed out in Chapter 1) is that ethnic or "native" categories differ a great deal from culture to culture or even from person to person. The more abstract "analytical" categories devised by scholars have not always yielded mutually exclusive systems, nor have they won universal scholarly acceptance. Any classification, it should be borne in mind, is always for a purpose; and, for the purpose of organizing data for analysis, certain traditional categories have become established in the voluminous reference works for motifs, tales, ballads, superstitions, riddles, proverbs, and other forms. These classification systems, whatever their shortcomings, have yet to be superseded; they structure the balance of this book and are cited in the appropriate bibliographic notes.

Folklore materials are usually arranged by genre and subgenre within a regional or folk-group framework in the published or archived collections. Thus, the proverbs of Illinois might be divided into full sentences ("true proverbs") versus phrases ("proverbial phrases and comparisons") and then listed alphabetically by the first noun or other significant word if there is no noun (see Chapter 5). Superstitions collected from fishermen might be divided as "signs or magic" and then subdivided into such categories as "equipment," "good luck," "winds and weather," and "taboos" (see Chapter 14). Such systems of organization are useful for bringing like materials together, and with proper cross references other groupings are possible. But for the needs of analysis or interpretation the folklorist may wish to sort the data by other criteria, using headings such as recreational traditions (games, dances, and so forth), educational lore (instructive stories, songs, or sayings), practical skills (crafts, cooking, and the like), and artistic creations (folk arts, crafts, music, etc.). The specific manner of classifying a folklore collection depends entirely on the interests and needs of researchers, which, when we start using publications and archives, usually means simply being able to find what we need to carry the research further.

Since much American folklore has been collected by university folklorists or by their students, the largest folklore archives in this country are on campuses. Although there is no national folklore archive in the United States, nor even a uniform archiving system in use, individual archivists can still consult the standard reference works to arrange and annotate their materials. Folklore journals and other publications rely on the same indexes. Most archivists and editors also make some attempt to cross-index materials by region and by ethnic background and sometimes even by collector. But since no one can anticipate all the possible research needs future users of an archive may have, the chief frustration of archivists is probably locating among their varied holdings all the materials potentially useful for a particular project. Some archives have tried to increase their flexibility and usefulness by publishing catalogues of their holdings or by computerizing materials. To their tasks of acquisition, cataloguing, storage, and retrieval, folk museums must add the challenges of display and interpretation for the public, which few folklore archives even attempt to meet.

Analyzing: Comparative Study

In the past it was assumed that only when folklore had been collected in some quantity, classified in considerable detail, and made generally available to scholars could any significant analysis take place. In general, for historical and transmission studies, this still holds true. The oldest and perhaps still the most common technique of folklore analysis is comparison, usually of different versions of the same item. This approach requires many recorded examples arranged in workable categories by type. The most elaborated form of this kind of research, the **historic-geographic method** (or "Finnish Method"), introduced into American folklore study by Archer Taylor and Stith Thompson, is described in Chapter 10 as it applies to folktale analysis.

Another avenue of comparative research followed by some American folklorists is to bring their viewpoint to bear on other closely related scholarly fields. For example, such material traditions in the United States as homemade cabins, houses, and barns have been investigated for some time by American folklorists and cultural geographers, the former concerning themselves mainly with the survival and variation of traditional patterns, and the latter with regional distribution and the explanations for it. To some degree, architectural historians have also been involved, fitting "vernacular" styles in with the sequence of high or academic design. Henry Glassie, an eclectic American folklorist (see Chapter 19 and the Appendix), has some acquaintance with all three fields, plus solid field experience. He attempts to frame a unified explanation for certain kinds of traditional buildings, adding to this his **cross-cultural comparisons** to prototypical building types found in Europe.

Even a beginning student not specializing in folklore might, for example, comparatively study common attitudes toward geography as found in folk speech, proverbs, place names, legends, tall tales, jokes, folksongs, or other genres. A student trying this project might consider the cartographic suggestions of such expressions as "*up* North" and "*down* South," the historical suggestions of "*out* West," and the difference between "*back* East" and "*down* East"; then one might assemble variant folk sayings referring to geographic features—"to be sold down the *river*" as opposed to "to cross that *river* when we come to it"; and "as old as the *hills*" versus "over the *hill*." Such an approach could be revealing of regional culture in relation to physical geography. Other geographic lore would seem to derive from old schoolroom drills. There is one orally collected song, for instance, that describes numerous geographic features of oceans and shorelines, always returning in the refrain to "Green Little Islands." Another song, collected in the Ozarks, names and accurately characterizes thirteen Texas rivers and streams. Probably from the schoolroom come several variants of a sentence for remembering how to spell the word "geography" itself: "*George Elliot's old grandmother rode a pig home yesterday.*" Similar comparative research projects could be done with folklore references to such fields as journalism, law, business, or politics.

Analyzing: Some Major Schools

While students' own research in folklore may be limited by time or unavailability of published references, the folklore student should at least become aware of the range and diversity of recent scholarship as it extends far beyond collection, classification, and comparative analysis. For a guide to some major scholarly trends as they have affected the study of American folklore, see the notes to this chapter. The following summary descriptions of schools of folklore analysis refer to some specific parts of this book in which theory and method are demonstrated in concise practical applications, but to understand folklore theory well there is no substitute for reading the works of analysis themselves.

A **literary or esthetic approach** to folklore, typical of humanists, may take the form either of analyzing the poetics of oral style or of charting the influence of folk traditions upon works of literature and the fine arts. A taste of the first application is provided in Chapters 11 ("Folksongs") and 12 ("Ballads"), where art songs are distinguished from popular and folk songs. The second application of an esthetic approach is best represented in longer studies (such as the essays and books on folklore in American literature mentioned in the notes). The broader relation of American folklore to American studies and cultural history, what Richard Dorson called "**the hemispheric approach,**" is demonstrated in this book in connection with local and historical legends in Chapter 9. Also see the discussions of historic American folk costumes and foods in Chapters 22 and 23.

The **functional or anthropological approach** to American folklore, typical of scholars with a background in the social sciences, examines the roles of folklore in culture in order to determine meanings and functions. Barre Toelken's discussion of college folk speech, songs, and customs in the Appendix is functionalist in part because the emphasis is less on the traditions themselves than on how they serve tradition-bearers in their everyday campus life. Building upon earlier **anthropological approaches,** most folklorists now agree that "folklore" exists not just as a fixed set of abstract genres, verbal or otherwise, but as traditional patterns of thought and behavior manifested in various ways during acts of communication between people. This constitutes an entirely new approach, variously called **contextual, behavioral, rhetorical,** or **performance-oriented.** The works of several champions of this theoretical orientation are listed in the notes, and one good example of a specific application is the conclusion of David Evans's study (see the Appendix) of Afro-American blues songs in their natural performance context.

The **psychological approach** to interpreting meanings in folklore, often Freudian or Jungian in orientation, has been advocated by David Hufford and Alan Dundes, among others. Here either the habits of mind underlying folk belief may be investigated (see Chapter 14, "Superstitions") or the symbolic and metaphorical patterns in folk traditions are decoded (as with urban legends in Chapter 9). What Dorson called an **ideological approach** to the symbolic interpretation of folklore (Marxist, capitalistic, Christian, etc.) so far has not had many adherents in American folklore, but this may change.

Another interpretive method advocated by Alan Dundes is the **formal or structural** one. Linguistic structuralism (the analysis of grammar according to patterns of speech) flowered into several approaches toward a true folkloristic structuralism based on the patterns in folklore, rather than those in language itself. This is touched on in Chapter 5, with a simple fixed-phrase oral form (proverbs), and in Chapter 10, with more complex oral narratives (folktales). Another brand of formal text analysis—the **oral-formulaic theory**—was developed by Harvard University folklorists Milman Parry and Albert B. Lord. Although the "Parry-Lord" system of analyzing thematic formulas and rhythmic patterns was invented for the study of Balkan epic songs, it was also applied to Anglo-American ballads (see notes to Chapter 12) and to American folk sermons (see Rosenberg's work mentioned in the notes to this chapter).

Besides these well-established theories and methodologies of folklore research are a number of approaches still evolving at the time of this writing. **A mass-cultural school,** for instance, may develop out of the work of several American folklorists studying interrelations of oral and customary traditions with the mass media and advertising. The particular interests and scholarly styles of specialists in **material culture** (those with a "**folk-cultural approach**") should eventually result in a coherent body of research with distinctive goals and techniques. **Applied folklore**—the viewpoint that folklore study can make specific contributions to knowledge and progress in other scholarly fields—has had advocates for some time and will probably constitute a "school" at some point. The same is true of what might be called **feminist folkloristics**—American women folklorists with a special approach both to women's folklore as such and to countering the male biases evident in some earlier studies.

The study of American folklore, either in its own boundaries or as applied to outside subjects, is still a relatively young and flexible academic discipline. Almost every new folklore journal or conference suggests some new approaches or theories for future research, and even the categories of folklore themselves are being continually expanded. The history of American folklore studies has only begun to be compiled, and the dimensions of such fields as urban folklore, obscene folklore, and women's folklore have barely been sketched out. The appointment of several "state folklorists" holds great promise for future regional research, just as the passage of the American Folklife Preservation Act in 1976 (creating the American Folklife Center in the Library of Congress) does for national study. To keep abreast of such developments, the reader may follow current publications and use the bibliographic tools listed following these chapters.

BIBLIOGRAPHIC NOTES

E. J. Lindgren's essay "The Collection and Analysis of Folk-Lore," although outdated, is still worth reading; see *The Study of Society*, ed. F.C. Bartlett and others (London: Routledge and Kegan Paul, 1939), pp. 328–78. Discussions by an international group of folklore scholars on the collecting, archiving, publicizing, and study of folklore were edited by Stith Thompson in *Four Symposia on Folklore*; the talks were held at Indiana University in 1950 and published as No. 8 in the Indiana

University Folklore Series (Bloomington: 1953). Martha Warren Beckwith's *Folklore in America: Its Scope and Method* (Poughkeepsie, N.Y.: Vassar College Folklore Foundation, 1931) was an early survey of the field. In *Our Living Traditions: An Introduction to American Folklore* (New York: Basic Books, 1968) Tristram P. Coffin gathers twenty-five essays by American folklorists that cover a wide variety of approaches; the chapters were originally written as Voice of America broadcasts.

Richard M. Dorson surveyed "Current Folklore Theories" in *CA* 4 (1963): 93–112. His essay is updated and expanded as the introduction to the excellent general textbook *Folklore and Folklife: An Introduction* (Chicago: University of Chicago Press, 1972), which contains specialized chapters by folklorists mostly associated somehow with the graduate program at Indiana University. The various collections of essays listed as "Basic Bibliography" in this book—particularly those by Brunvand, Dorson, and Dundes—contain discussions of folklore theory, methodology, interpretation, and the like. Similar useful surveys are contained in Dorson's compilation of many scholars, the *Handbook of American Folklore* (Bloomington: Indiana University Press, 1983); these essays are not cited in the Bibliographic Notes to this book. Thirteen articles by another major American folklorist are included in *Mody Boatright: Folklorist. A Collection of Essays*, ed. Ernest B. Speck (Austin: University of Texas Press, 1973). A somewhat idiosyncratic but intriguing approach is taken by Munro S. Edmonson in *Lore: An Introduction to the Science of Folklore and Literature* (New York: Holt, Rinehart and Winston, 1971); the author identifies his subject matter as "connotative semantics and analogic systems of thought" and pursues it widely through world literature and oral tradition.

Archer Taylor outlined "The Problems of Folklore" in *JAF* 59 (1946): 101–7. Louise Pound's thorough survey "The Scholarly Study of Folklore," *WF* 11 (1952): 100–8, was reprinted in *Nebraska Folklore*, 222–33. Stanley Edgar Hyman defined the questions of origin, structure, and function in folklore studies and criticized some popularized anthologies in "Some Bankrupt Treasuries," *KR* 10 (1948): 484–500. Other general discussions of approaches to folklore are reprinted in Dundes's *The Study of Folklore*.

Techniques of collecting folklore are expertly treated in the Introduction to Richard M. Dorson's *Buying the Wind* (Chicago: University of Chicago Press, 1964). Rosalie H. Wax's *Doing Fieldwork: Warnings and Advice* (Chicago: University of Chicago Press, 1971), although written for anthropologists, offers good examples and advice for folklorists as well. Kenneth S. Goldstein's manual *A Guide for Field Workers in Folklore* was published by the *American Folklore Society* (Philadelphia: Memoirs of AFS, vol. 52, 1964). An important supplement to Goldstein's book is *People Studying People: The Human Element in Fieldwork*, by Robert A. Georges and Michael O. Jones (Berkeley and Los Angeles: University of California Press, 1980). William R. Ferris, Jr., takes up some special interviewing problems in "The Collection of Racial Lore: Approaches and Problems," *NYFQ* 27 (1971): 261–79.

A local field-work guide that may be useful even outside the region it deals with is Jan Harold Brunvand, *A Guide for Collectors of Folklore in Utah* (Salt Lake City: University of Utah Press, 1971). Other compact manuals are Richard and Laurna Tallman's *Country Folks: A Handbook for Student Folklore Collectors* (Batesville: Arkansas College Folklore Archive Publications, 1978) and a pamphlet published by the American Folklife Center, written by Peter Bartis, called *Folklife and Fieldwork: A Layman's Introduction to Field Techniques* (Washington, D.C.: 1979). A detailed and useful survey is Eleanor Fein Reishtein's "Bibliography on Questionnaires as a Folklife Fieldwork Technique," *KFQ* 13 (1968): 45–69, 121–66, 219–32.

Edward D. Ives's *The Tape-recorded Interview: A Manual for Field Workers in Folklore and Oral History* (Knoxville: University of Tennessee Press, 1980) is an expansion of a widely used work originally published in 1974 mainly for folklorists working in the Northeast. Considering its purpose—to dispense technical information and helpful advice to inexperienced field workers using tape recorders—this book is surprisingly engaging and encouraging. It covers basic information, often overlooked in other manuals, such as how a tape recorder works, how to interview people with a tape recorder, and the "processing" of the collected material (transcription, archiving, analysis, etc.) after field research is finished. Two studies from the Northeast that are clearly in the Ives tradition of research are Ives and others' *Argyle Boom . . .*, *NEF* 17 (1976), a study of rafting logs on the Penobscot River in Maine; and Roger E. Mitchell's *"I'm a Man That Works": The Biography of Don Mitchell of Merrill, Maine*, *NEF* 19 (1978), a book about the father of its author.

The field experiences of two folksong collectors are preserved in W. Roy Mackenzie's *The Quest of the Ballad* (Princeton, N.J.: Princeton University Press, 1919) and John A. Lomax's *Adventures of a Ballad Hunter* (New York: Macmillan, 1947). The results of many years of devoted collecting in the Ozarks are gathered in the numerous books edited by Vance Randolph, in the prefaces and notes to which are many insightful comments on the art of unobtrusive collecting. Experiences collecting urban folklore are presented in two works based on the same project: "Folklorists in the City: The Urban Field Experience," ed. Inta Gale Carpenter, a special issue of *FF* (vol. 11, no. 3, 1978) which contains eight articles by members of "The Gary [Indiana] Gang" of field workers; and Richard M. Dorson's "Doing Fieldwork in the City," in *Folklore* 92 (1981): 149–54.

My own manual for folklore researchers, called *Folklore: A Study and*

Research Guide (New York: St. Martins, 1976), is directed more to the library than to field work. It contains selected bibliography; a history and survey of folkloristics; directions for taking notes, outlining, and actually writing a research paper; and a sample folklore paper written by an undergraduate student in one of my classes. Her subject was folk narratives from a southern Utah town.

The chief example of a comprehensive American regional collection, fully classified and annotated, is the seven-volume *The Frank C. Brown Collection of North Carolina Folklore*, edited by a committee of specialists (Durham, N.C.: Duke University Press, 1952–64). Analyses of folklore in a specific regional tradition are found in such books as Emelyn E. Gardner's *Folklore from the Schoharie Hills* (Ann Arbor: University of Michigan Press, 1937); and Richard M. Dorson's *Negro Folktales in Michigan* (Cambridge, Mass.: Harvard University Press, 1956). The last, for instance, contains not only the verbatim texts, classified and fully identified with background data, but also chapters on "The Communities and the Storytellers" and "The Art of Negro Storytelling" as well as four pages of photographs.

From 1958 to 1968, *The Folklore and Folk Music Archivist*, published by Indiana University, provided a quarterly forum for articles on collecting, documenting, indexing, and cataloguing folklore. The editor, George List, published "A Statement on Archiving" in *JFI* 6 (1969): 222–31. A finding list, *Folklore Archives of the World*, ed. Peter Aceves and Magnus Einarsson-Mullarký, constituted the first number of the *Folklore Forum* "Bibliographic and Special Series" (Bloomington, Ind.: 1968). One model for catalogues of folklore archival holdings is Florence Ireland's "The Northeast Archives of Folklore and Oral History," *NEF* 13 (1972). Important legal questions were raised in an American Folklore Society symposium of 1971 published as "Folklore Archives: Ethics and the Law," *FF* 6 (1973): 197–210. Directions for modernizing archival techniques are discussed by Robert A. Georges, Beth Blumenreich, and Kathie O'Reilly in "Two Mechanical Indexing Systems for Folklore Archives: A Preliminary Report," *JAF* 87 (1974): 39–52.

A necessary skill of the folklorist—identifying folklore lodged in print—is demonstrated in George G. Carey's "Folklore from the Printed Sources of Essex County, Massachusetts," *SFQ* 32 (1968): 17–43. An important methodological essay on studying folklore in literature is Alan Dundes's "The Study of Folklore in Literature and Culture: Identification and Interpretation," *JAF* 78 (1965): 136–42, repr. in *Analytic Essays in Folklore*, pp. 28–34. MacEdward Leach surveyed "Folklore in American Regional Literature" in *JFI* 3 (1966): 376–97; but Roger D. Abrahams found the "lore-in-literature" approach insufficient and proposed other kinds of analysis in "Folklore and Literature as Performance," *JFI* 9 (1972): 75–94. Essays on folklore in individual American authors abound in the journals; two examples are Karl P. Wentersdorf's "The Element of Witchcraft in *The Scarlet Letter*," *Folklore* 83 (1972): 132–53; and Sandra Bennett's "Thurber and Traditional Comic Modes," *JOFS* 2 (1973): 1–11. A book-length study admirable for its sound approach and full details is Ronald L. Baker's *Folklore in the Writings of Rowland E. Robinson* (Bowling Green, Ohio: Bowling Green University Popular Press, 1973). Two attempts at a wider synthesis are Daniel Hoffman's *Form and Fable in American Fiction* (New York: Oxford University Press, 1961; Norton paperback edn., 1973) and Gene Bluestein's *The Voice of the Folk: Folklore and American Literary Theory* (Amherst: University of Massachusetts Press, 1972).

Two recent special issues of folklore journals have expanded the horizons in American folklore/literature studies. "Folklore and Literature" in *FF* 11, no. 2 (1978), edited by Eleanor Wachs, contains six articles and reviews, the most generally useful one being Carl Lindahl's "On the Borders of Oral and Written Art" (94–123). The special double issue of *SFQ* was vol. 43, nos. 1–2 (1979), with an introduction and ten articles. Here Daniel R. Barnes's "Toward the Establishment of Principles for the Study of Folklore and Literature" (5–16) and Neil R. Grobman's "A Schema for the Study of the Sources and Literary Simulations of Folkloric Phenomena" (17–37) are the specifically theoretical pieces. Grobman was also editor of the issue.

Richard M. Dorson suggests projects involving "Folklore and Cultural History" in *Research Opportunities in American Cultural History*, ed. John Francis McDermott (Lexington: University of Kentucky Press, 1961), pp. 102–23. An important theoretical discussion of folklore and history, citing mostly African examples, is Jan Vansina, *Oral Tradition*, trans. H. M. Wright (Chicago: Aldine, 1965). Articles on folklore and history appeared in *JFI* 1 (1964). Richard M. Dorson collected a dozen of his essays from journals in *American Folklore and the Historian*, including the important "A Theory for American Folklore" from 1959 and his thoughts on the "Theory . . . Reviewed" from 1969, both originally published in *JAF*. William A. Wilson takes a western perspective in "Folklore and History: Fact amid the Legends," *UHQ* 41 (1973): 40–58 (repr. in *Readings in American Folklore*, pp. 449–66). Two exemplary books on the subject are William Lynwood Montell's *The Saga of Coe Ridge: A Study in Oral History* (Knoxville: University of Tennessee Press, 1970) and Gladys-Marie Fry's *Night Riders in Black Folk History* from the same publisher (1975).

An important handbook for American folklore/history studies was published in 1981: Barbara Allen and William Lynwood Montell's *From Memory to History: Using Oral Sources in Local Historical Research* (Nashville, Tenn.: American Association for State and Local History). Montell's latest book at the time of this writing is *Don't Go up Kettle Creek: Verbal Legacy of the Upper Cumberland* (Knoxville: University of Tennessee Press, 1983), another fine Midwestern study of oral tradition and folk history. In the rapidly emerging field of family folklore research, Margaret R. Yocom's "Family Folklore and Oral History Interviews," *WF* 41 (1982): 251–74, gives excellent guidance and advice.

A bibliographic survey on "American Folklore and American Studies" by Richard Bauman, Roger Abrahams, and Susan Kalčik in *AQ* 28 (1976): 360–77, has a historical framework and strives to "delineate the conceptual organizing principles of the field" rather than simply listing major sources. Consequently, this is a useful introduction to the subject as well as a guide to published sources.

Kenneth S. Goldstein described his innovative research methods in "Experimental Folklore: Laboratory vs. Field," in *Folklore International*, ed. D. K. Wilgus (Hatboro, Pa.: Folklore Associates, 1967), pp. 71–82. Theoretical backgrounds for such studies are given in Kenneth Laine Ketner's "The Role of Hypotheses in Folkloristics," *JAF* 86 (1973): 114–30; an opposing view appears in Anne Cohen and Norm Cohen, "A Word on Hypotheses," *JAF* 87 (1974): 156–60. Alan Dundes pointed to what he saw as a limiting mind-set for research in "The Devolutionary Premise in Folklore Theory," *JFI* 6 (1969): 5–19; reprinted in *Analytic Essays in Folklore*, pp. 17–27. Responses to this have come from Ronald Grambo in *FF* 3 (1970): 57–58; William M. Clements in *NYFQ* 29 (1973): 243–53; and Elliott Oring in *WF* 34 (1975): 36–44, among others. Oring discussed "Three Functions of Folklore: Traditional Functionalism as Explanation in Folkloristics" in *JAF* 89 (1976): 67–80; comments and a response then appeared in *JAF* 90 (1977): 68–77.

David J. Hufford provides an overview of another analytic approach in "Psychology, Psychoanalysis, and Folklore," *SFQ* 38 (1974): 187–97. Paulo de Carvalho-Neto's *Folklore and Psychoanalysis*, originally published in 1956, was issued in its first English translation in 1972 (Coral Gables, Fla.: University of Miami Press) with a foreword by Alan Dundes, a leading North American advocate of psychoanalytic interpretations of folk tradition; see for example, Dundes's 1976 article "Projection in Folklore: A Plea for Psychoanalytic Semiotics," in *Interpreting Folklore*, pp. 33–61. A representative psychological analysis is illustrated in Eric Berne's "The Mythology of Dark and Fair: Psychiatric Use of Folklore," *JAF* 72 (1959): 1–13. A sociopsychological study is Brian Sutton-Smith's "A Formal Analysis of Game Meaning," *WF* 18 (1959): 13–24. A sociological approach to folk belief and behavior is *Water Witching U.S.A.* by Evon Z. Vogt and Ray Hyman (Chicago: University of Chicago Press, 1959).

Two pacesetting early treatments of folklore in its cultural context were by William Hugh Jansen, "A Culture's Stereotypes and Their Expression in Folk Clichés," *Southwestern Journal of Anthropology* 13 (1957): 184–200; and "The Esoteric-Exoteric Factor in Folklore," *Fabula* 2 (1959): 205–11, which was reprinted in *The Study of Folklore*, pp.

43–51. A chief advocate of this "contextual" or "behavioral" approach
to folklore is Roger D. Abrahams, three of whose influential articles are
the following: "Folklore in Culture: Notes toward an Analytic
Method," *TSLL* 5 (1963): 98–110 (repr. in *Readings in American Folklore*, pp. 390–403); "Introductory Remarks to a Rhetorical Theory of
Folklore," *JAF* 81 (1968): 143–58; and "A Rhetoric of Everyday Life:
Traditional Conversational Genres," *SFQ* 32 (1968): 44–59. Abraham's
pioneering study *Deep Down in the Jungle: Negro Narrative Folklore
from the Streets of Philadelphia* appeared in 1964 (Hatboro, Pa.: Folklore Associates) and in a revised edition in 1970 (Chicago: Aldine
Press). Another representative study from this viewpoint is Richard
Bauman's "Verbal Art as Performance," *AA* 77 (1975): 290–311. A group
of articles on folklore and culture appeared in *JFI* 2 (1965).

One of the most enduring early articles advocating more attention to
the contexts in which folklore is performed is Alan Dundes's 1964 essay
"Texture, Text, and Context," reprinted in *Interpreting Folklore*, pp.
20–32. A published debate—typical of much of the oral debate conducted at professional conferences—concerning the contextual approach to folklore pitted Steven Jones against Dan Ben-Amos in the
"Topics and Comments" section of *WF* 38 (1979): 42–55; much depends upon just what the scholars mean by the term "traditional" in
analyzing folklore. Robert A. Georges attempted ". . . A Resolution of
the Text/Context Controversy," in *WF* 39 (1980): 34–40; he prefers to
be called a "behaviorist," and he denies that there is any "war" between factions of contextualist and noncontextualist schools. Rebutting
Georges is Yigal Zan's "The Text/Context Controversy: An Explanatory Perspective," *WF* 41 (1982): 1–27. More interesting, perhaps, to a
beginning folklore student than these abstract essays would be
Georges's article "Feedback and Response in Storytelling," *WF* 38
(1979): 104–10, in which a specific instance of context affecting text and
performance is described in concrete terms.

A useful general discussion of the structural approach to folklore is
Butler Waugh's "Structural Analysis in Literature and Folklore," *WF*
25 (1966): 153–64. In *Structural Models in Folklore and Transforma-
tional Essays* (The Hague: Mouton, "Approaches to Semiotics" 10,
1971), Pierre and Elli [Köngäs] Maranda provide a systematic presentation of an important structural theory and method. This is a revised
version of an essay first published *MF* (1962) supplemented by new
studies of myth and riddle. The Marandas' anthology *Structural Analysis of Oral Tradition* (Philadelphia: University of Pennsylvania Press,
1971) contains eleven essays by various scholars analyzing myth, ritual,
drama, folktale, riddle, and folksong. The contributors include most of
the leading contemporary structuralists who are doing folklore studies.

An imaginative application of the oral-formulaic theory to American
materials is found in Bruce A. Rosenberg's *The Art of the American Folk*

Preacher (New York: Oxford University Press, 1970). A related analytic approach is found in Bennison Gray's "Repetition in Oral Literature," *JAF* 84 (1971): 289–303; and another is William M. Clements's "The Rhetoric of the Radio Ministry," *JAF* 87 (1974): 318–27.

Brief notes on traditional "Geographic Sayings from Louisiana" were published in *JAF* 67 (1954): 78, by Fred Kniffen. He distinguished those sayings that "attribute qualities to specific areas" ("the ozone belt") from those "based on a striking natural process in geography" ("My grandfather crossed there on a plank"). One is reminded of numerous sayings elsewhere in the United States that fall into the same classes, "the banana belt," for instance, for unusually mild climates in northern regions, and "You can set your watch by it," referring to Old Faithful. Two discussions of general relationships for cooperation are Roger T. Trindell's "American Folklore Studies and Geography," *SFQ* 34 (1970): 1–11; and W. F. H. Nicolaisen's "Folklore and Geography: Towards an Atlas of American Folk Culture," *NYFQ* 29 (1973): 3–20. An excellent example of a specific application of geographic and folkloristic methods is E. Joan Wilson Miller's study "Ozark Superstitions as Geographic Documentation," *The Professional Geographer* 24 (1972): 223–26.

A groundbreaking panel, "Folk Literature and the Obscene," sponsored by the American Folklore Society, was published in a special issue of *JAF* (75 [1962]: 189–282) edited by Frank A. Hoffmann; speakers included Herbert Halpert, Horace Beck, Alan Dundes, and Gershon Legman. *The Horn Book: Studies in Erotic Folklore and Bibliography* (New Hyde Park, N.Y.: University Books, 1964) by Legman is a basic scholarly reference in this area. Kenneth S. Goldstein discusses a process common to handling of obscene folk materials in "Bowdlerization and Expurgation: Academic and Folk," *JAF* 80 (1967): 374–86; and Mac E. Barrick presents some traditional erotic materials that appear in written form as "The Typescript Broadside," *KFQ* 17 (1972): 27–38.

The interrelations of folklore with mass culture have begun to be discussed by scholars. Priscilla Denby surveys "Folklore in the Mass Media" in *FF* 4 (1971): 113–25. Alan Dundes's "Advertising and Folklore," *NYFQ* 19 (1963): 143–51, may be compared with Tom E. Sullenberger's "Ajax Meets the Jolly Green Giant: Some Observations on the Use of Folklore in American Mass Marketing," *JAF* 87 (1974): 53–65. Other mass-cultural studies are Tom Burns's "Folklore in the Mass Media: Television," *FF* 2 (1969): 90–106, and John T. Flanagan's "Grim Stories: Folklore in Cartoons," *MJLF* 1 (1975): 20–26.

Dick Sweterlitsch edited nine "Papers on Applied Folklore" in *FF*, Bibliographic and Special Series, no. 8 (1971). See also Mary Ellen B. Lewis's "The Feminists Have Done It: Applied Folklore," *JAF* 87 (1974): 85–87. The most common application of folklorists' studies is in teaching, for which see "Folklore and Education: A Selected Annotated Bibliography of Periodical Literature" (by five compilers) in *KF* 22 (1978): 53–85; Dorson's *Handbook of American Folklore* also has several chapters on teaching folklore.

The invaluable bibliographic notes in Richard M. Dorson's *American Folklore* (pp. 282–300) should be supplemented in any search for references to a particular topic in American folklore by the analytic indexes to folklore journals *(FF, JAF, JFI, WF, PTFS,* etc.) and the annual AFS bibliography published in the Supplement to *JAF* until 1963, when it was shifted to the new journal *Abstracts of Folklore Studies.* When *Abstracts* ceased publication in 1969 its important bibliographic function was filled by the expanded folklore section of the huge Modern Language Association bibliography appearing annually in *PMLA.* Perhaps the most important American folklore bibliography was that published annually in *SFQ* from 1937 to 1973, then continued in book form by Merle E. Simmons for two years by the Folklore Institute, Bloomington, Indiana, and thereafter by the Institute for the Study of Human Issues (Philadelphia). This bibliography's founder, Ralph Steele Boggs, also published the useful *Bibliography of Latin American Folklore* (New York: H. W. Wilson Co., 1940). Charles Haywood's *A Bibliography of North American Folklore and Folksong* is unusual in that it includes much North American Indian material; originally published in 1951, it was reprinted in two volumes by Dover Books in 1961, but unfortunately none of the numerous factual errors in citations of the first edition was corrected. Another guide to check for references is Cathleen C. Flanagan and John T. Flanagan's *American Folklore: A Bibliography, 1950–1974* (Metuchen, N.J.: Scarecrow Press, 1977), but for most purposes, the beginning student's best bibliographic aid will simply be the notes to each chapter of this textbook itself.

3

Folk Groups: Bearers of American Folk Tradition

Does America Have a Folklore?

Depending upon how it is defined, "American" folklore may be pictured as nonexistent, relatively rare, or extremely common. As late as 1930 Alexander H. Krappe, a prominent American folklorist, was still European-oriented enough to take the extreme position that there was no such thing as American folklore, but only a few folkloric importations that eventually lost themselves in our mechanized age. The American Folklore Society itself, as described in Chapter 1, was formed in 1888 partly to collect the "fast-vanishing remains" of foreign (including black) folklore in the United States; as for the phrase "American Folklore," that referred to the Indians, or to the nationality of members of the society. Published collections of American folklore still appear prefaced with gloomy essays about disappearing traditions and the rapid loss of our meager folklore. The other extreme is reached by the many popular books and records that try to boost every scrap of Americana in sight—old or new—as another example of our profuse national folklore. Most of these publications are very heavy on fakelore—that is, imitation folklore attributed to a group that never possessed it.

One should not be dogmatic about whether American folklore exists in abundance until the terms "American" and "folklore" are explained. Our criteria for "folklore" are "oral, customary, and material tradition," while for "American" an inclusive definition would be *"found* in the United States," and a restrictive one *"originated* in the United States." Most American folklorists incline toward the inclusive view, as far as theory is concerned, although their field-collecting emphasizes older American, or at least Americanized, material. For example, while some American folklore collectors have realized that there exist traditional native songs (most of them relatively recent) of protest, industries, parodies, pornography, and the like, what they have collected most vigorously are old British traditional ballads and lyrical songs.

American folklore research has amply demonstrated that there is a substantial body of oral, customary, and material tradition circulating in the United States, some of it home-grown, and some transplanted from other cultures. Of course, individual folk practices do fade away, but new ones are constantly appearing, so that the report of the demise of American folklore, as Mark Twain said about the report of his own death, "has been greatly exaggerated." In a general sense we can say that some types of folklore (such as folk drama) are nearly extinct in the United States; some types survive vigorously in quite ancient forms (such as superstitions); some types have been revived for a popular audience (folk dances and songs); and some types are still being invented along contemporary lines (jokes).

To assert that folklore is regularly being created and transmitted in modern American culture is to suggest that "the folk" must now exist in a modern guise. While most attempts to characterize the sources of folklore have emphasized isolation, lack of sophistication, and groups with relative homogeneity, judging from the materials that folklorists collect and study, such qualities are certainly not essential to fostering folklore. On the contrary, folklore flourishes among some of the most sophisticated and mobile Americans—teen-agers, entertainers, athletes, professors, and members of the armed forces. Strict preconceived notions of who "the folk" are have led to much disputing in folklore research when energy might better have been devoted to field work and comparative studies to learn just how folklore actually is developed and put into circulation. To begin such studies, no better definition of "folk" would seem necessary than "anyone who has folklore."

Theories of the Folk and Folk Groups

On the broad general level, four basic theories have been offered to explain who the folk are and how their lore originates. The **communal theory** holds that the folk are unsophisticated peasants who compose folklore as a group effort. The **survivals theory** pushes the origin of folklore back to a "savage stage" of civilization and maintains that modern folklore is an inheritance or "survival" from the past. The theory of *gesunkenes Kulturgut* (German for "debased elements of culture") reverses the direction of diffusion—folklore has sunk from a high origin, such as "learning," to become tradition among the common people. Finally, the theory of **individual origins and communal re-creation** holds that an item of folklore has a single inventor at any level of society, but that it is repeatedly made over as it is transmitted by word of mouth. Each of these theories has been applied to specific types of American folklore, and each has some validity in particular cases, as is pointed out in later chapters. (See, for example, the arguments about communal origins versus re-creation of ballads in Chapter 12, survivals of myths discussed in Chapter 8, and *gesunkenes Kulturgut* in superstitions in Chapter 14).

The focus on specific creators and performers of traditions usually involves identifying these individuals with what have been called **folk groups**. The acceptance of traditions by these groups usually implies some degree of conformity with group tastes and values. (There are exceptions, however, both in individual traditional creators with no strong group affiliation and in lore that is subversive of group values.) While some such groups may be identified simply in terms of obvious social, political, or geographic factors, they are often identified for folklore purposes first by their distinctive folk speech and other traditions —the lingo and lore which set one group apart from others. Thus, among themselves, loggers talk about "widow makers" (dangerous dangling limbs) and may sing ballads about woods disasters; children playing independently from adult supervision may cry "King's-X" (a "truce term" in a game like "Tag") and play a game like Anthony Over (a ball game played around a garage or other small building); girls may know the terms for playing jacks ("taps," "baskets," etc.) or the variations of playing jump rope better than the boys, who may themselves be better informed about marble terms ("fudgies," "changies," etc.) and mumbletypeg (a game played with a pocketknife); residents of southern Illinois speak of themselves as living in "Egypt" and give varying legendary explanations for the name based on supposed parallels to the history of the old-world country in Biblical times; and Finns in America tell stories from both the old country and the new, mixing their native tongue with English into "Finglish."

The examples summarized above suggest five major kinds of American folk groups—*occupational groups, age groups, gender-differentiated groups, regional groups,* and *ethnic or nationality groups.* It is also possible to distinguish folk groups that are set apart by religion, education, hobbies, neighborhood, or family. Viewed from this point, it is clear that folk groups need not be composed only of hillbillies, and that a person may also belong to several folk groups at the same time. A Polish steelworker in Gary, Indiana, for instance, may know distinct types of ethnic, industrial, and regional lore, and if he happens to be a second-generation American he may also know immigrant lore unknown to his own parents. As a child he surely participated in different traditions than he has as a man, and as a man he likely knows some folklore that is not familiar to or popular with his mother, sisters, or wife. The first test a folklorist could make of membership in a folk group is the members' awareness of shared folklore; then the background of this conformity can be investigated.

Occupational Groups

Among **occupational groups** in the United States, we immediately associate the old rugged callings with vigorous oral traditions: ax logging, raft and barge freighting, sailing before the mast, and running cattle were all activities rich in folklore. The long exposure of small bands of toughened men to the elements led them to fall back on their stocks of stories and songs for entertainment, and the dangers inherent in the work produced superstitions like the "Flying Dutchman" and the "ghost herd." But the present has its comparable groups, too, with their own folklore, as studies of mining, railroading, oil pumping, and other industries have shown. To some degree, the modern armed forces retain typical traditions of the older all-male labor groups, as do prisons, but physical strain is no necessary accompaniment to occupational folklore; jet pilots, journalists, and even clergymen (including seminarians) have esoteric oral traditions of language and lore that are little known outside these groups. Nor are the domestic scene and the other usual workplaces of American women lacking in folklore; folk traditions surround cooking, childbearing and child raising, and household crafts as well as the traditional jobs for women in schools, offices, or libraries. The folklore of women in professional fields where they have often had some starring roles—such as sports and entertainment—is probably no less rich than for the comparable positions held by men, but it has been less often collected and studied.

So rapidly does folklore develop around new jobs and products that there is already a considerable cycle of exoteric (told by outsiders) oral stories circulating about computers and their designers or programmers, as well as a rich set of esoteric (inside) terms, stories, and pranks that are known to the "hackers" (computer buffs) themselves. The whole computer industry is loaded with rumors and legends, mostly about future products and their alleged features, a kind of lore that once characterized the American automobile industry when the technology was evolving and annual major model changes were highly publicized. The folklore of many other modern occupations has barely been recognized; this includes most factory lore of assembly and processing plants, folklore of government service, of science, and of academic life. Merely to suggest the possibilities of the latter, there are the ubiquitous campus stories of eccentric and absent-minded professors, of master cheaters in the student body, of prudish deans of women, and of administrators and their vagaries. These topics and others are discussed by Toelken in the Appendix, "The Folklore of Academe."

Age Groups

The distinctive folklore of different **age groups** is another area that is little understood, beyond the general notion of children growing from one stage to another, shedding layers of folklore as they go and acquiring new ones. Probably the study of this material will have to consider the differing folklore of sexes at the same time, for the rigid patterns of child behavior (who plays which games when or tells which stories to whom or uses which terms) are bound by both age and sex. Children's folklore offers a particularly interesting field for research, for here we have almost a pure field situation in which some items are transmitted completely by word of mouth in an atmosphere of great textual conservatism, as any adult who has changed the wording of a bedtime story or tried to instruct a child in the "right way" to play a game like Kick the Can knows. While American children's folklore has been collected in some quantity, little analysis has been made until recently of such factors as its distribution, variants, or function. Even the collecting tends to be from grownups recalling their youth instead of from the youths themselves, and it tends to be spotty; we have the singing games, but few of the jokes of small children; the jargon, but little of the sexual or alcoholic lore of teen-agers; and so forth. Probably beyond adolescence people cease to have much significant age-group lore and instead participate in other folk groups, but even this is a supposition that has never been systematically examined.

Gender-differentiated Groups

The specific folklore of **gender-differentiated groups** is strongly influenced by the typical roles assigned to each gender by the culture. Thus, American women were the midwives in pioneer communities and may have told more supernatural legends or sung the lullabies, while men were expected to be the blacksmiths and may have swapped mostly brags and tall tales among themselves. Women's versus men's folklore repertoires seem fairly fixed in the published collections, but to some extent this reflects the biases of collectors who *expected* women to know the charms or to do the needlework and men to know the hunting lore and to do heavy outdoor work. Research has failed to reveal the extent to which people crossed the barriers—such as when men participated in quilting and cooking or women related bawdy jokes and songs. Study also needs to be done on the functional aspects of traditional gender-related lore—for instance, how quilting bees were the settings for exchanging supportive women's lore, while men met their cronies and got positive reinforcement at livery stables or barbershops. Both kinds of groupings prefigured the encounter groups and "rap sessions" advocated by present-day psychologists and spokespersons for women's liberation. The functions of gender-related *modern* stories also need more documentation; these would probably include men boosting their egos with memories from military or sports experiences, and women warning other women by describing encounters with male "putdowns" or experiences with street crimes. Along with changing attitudes toward such folklore and new avenues for research, there are gradual changes in the very language of discussing the subject —we speak of "spokespersons" and "chairpersons," of "women" (not "girls") and "artisans" (not "craftsmen").

Besides the subject of women's folklore as such, the negative views of many men (who were often the folklorists) regarding these traditions are revealed in a number of ways. At a folk level, male chauvinism takes such forms as antifeminist proverbs ("Keep her barefoot and pregnant") or proverbial warnings to women ("A whistling woman and a crowing hen will always come to some bad end"). Or the community might brand some women with supposed special powers as "witches," and call some of women's traditional talk mere (malicious?) "gossip"; but at the same time men who are gifted with alleged supernatural skills might be called "wizards" or "healers," and some men's talk might be regarded as mere (harmless?) "windies" or "yarns." It is also necessary to study how certain traditional tale or ballad themes—such as bride tests versus hero tests or seductions versus faithful love—were altered in the American oral tradition. When folklore is presented to mass audiences, sex-role stereotypes are perpetuated by such matters as which European fairy tales are usually translated (and how) and which ones are turned into popular films. Not to be ignored when gender-differentiated folklore is considered is the lore of homosexuals in American society, which until recently was known only to insiders or in the form of exaggerated stereotypes of gay speech and behavior.

Regional Groups

Regional groups have yielded some of the most bountiful harvests of folklore material in this country because geographic features tend to create relative isolation and encourage a community spirit that sustains long-standing traditions. The major folklore regions that American folklorists have described so far are New England, the southern Appalachians, the Midwest, the Ozarks, and the Southwest. Some folkloristic subregions that have been studied are Schoharie County, New York; Brown County, Indiana; the Upper Peninsula of Michigan, and the Mormon-settled Great Basin. State and other political boundaries have little effect on the types of folklore and its distribution, although many state collections have been brought together, mostly as a convenience for publishing. Studies of regional folk groups offer an excellent chance for cooperative projects by folklorists working with historians, geographers, linguists, and others; certainly a thorough understanding of settlement history and the national backgrounds of immigrants should underlie any study of their folklore. Although such cross-disciplinary research has been unusual in this country, it has been done for some time in Europe. Soviet folklorists, in particular, have organized collective expeditions to gather the lore of one region or of one craft in depth. The results have been far richer than the random gatherings of pre-Revolutionary field workers, but they have contained the predictable overlay of propaganda applications as well.

Several American folklorists began working at the regional level and later branched out to broader comparative studies, just as some regional folklore journals have expanded their coverage. Thus *Midwest Folklore* (1951), formerly *Hoosier Folklore Bulletin* (1942), and *Hoosier Folklore* (1946), became the more international *Journal of the Folklore Institute* (1964), which was renamed *Journal of Folklore Research* in 1982; and in 1968 a new journal, *Indiana Folklore*, began. The *California Folklore Quarterly* (1942) became *Western Folklore* (1947), and *Southern Folklore Quarterly* (1937) no longer has any particular southern slant. On the other hand, new regional journals have sprung up: *Northeast Folklore* (1958) and *Mid-South Folklore* (1973, changing to *Mid-American Folklore* in 1978), for example.

Ethnic or Nationality Groups

Ethnic or nationality groups have a folklore as rich and varied as the American population itself. Again, only a fraction of it has been recorded or studied. The folktales, songs, proverbs, and other folklore of American Indians, however, have been intensively studied for generations, partly by folklorists but mostly by anthropologists with special linguistic and ethnographic training. There has been very active folklore collecting and research among American blacks, both in the Deep South and in the northern ghettos and other settlements, as black folk music, then tales and other lore have interested scholars. The early studies were concerned mainly with tracing African survivals in America, but now folklorists increasingly deal with the psychological and sociological functions of folklore among blacks. The best-documented nationality group in the United States is also an important regional group—the so-called "Dutch" of German Pennsylvania, about whom there are numerous articles and books. Fewer studies are available about the folklore of other groups such as the Jews in big cities, the Spanish in the Southwest, the Cajuns in Louisiana, and the Scandinavians in the Midwest. Some other urban nationality groups that have been approached are the Greeks in Tarpon Springs, Florida, the Finns in Astoria, Oregon, the Poles in Hamtramck, Michigan, and the Spanish in Denver, Colorado. All these and many other groups await more attention; to mention only a few more, consider the Basques in the Far West, the Puerto Ricans in New York City, the Norwegians in the Northwest (including Alaska), the Bohemians in Nebraska, the Cubans in Florida, and the Southeast Asians in many cities.

Often the study of immigrant folklore has resulted from the devoted work of a scholar who is himself a fairly recent arrival. One such notable collector is the Lithuanian-American Jonas Balys. Another is the Hungarian-American Linda Dégh. In other groups an American-born descendant of immigrants takes up folklore collecting such as Warren Kliewer among Low-German speaking Mennonites, Robert Georges among Greeks, and Larry Danielson among Swedes. Non-European groups have been studied very little, but they could be; one good possibility is in the "Chinatowns" of several cities, and another is the Japanese of California. In a sense, the United States is the world's greatest meeting ground of foreign folklores and an ideal arena for observing the survival of old traditions and the assimilation of new ones. American Christmas customs, for example, are a curious blend of several European sources, while immigrant folksong repertoires tend to be influenced by hillbilly, Tin Pan Alley, blues, and even cowboy songs. The scope of possibilities can be imagined when the largest nationality groups are considered—Irish, Italian, German, Scandinavian, and especially the most prominent group, the Anglo-Americans.

This chapter has only sketched in rough outline some few American folk groups, and it has only referred to a fraction of their folklore. To treat fully the oral traditions of even one such group would require at least a book in itself, preceded by extensive field work. Essentially, the following chapters should be regarded as only a survey of English-language folklore in America. Most of it, naturally, is Anglo-American in character if not in origin, but many of the groups mentioned above have been referred to and their traditions sampled.

BIBLIOGRAPHIC NOTES

Alexander H. Krappe discussed "'American' Folklore" in *Folk-Say: A Regional Miscellany* in 1930 (Norman: University of Oklahoma Press), pp. 291–97, but he strongly denied that there really was any; Krappe maintained that there were only imported traditions in this country and that the culture of the immigrant was lost after he or she became Americanized.

Three studies of contemporary individual creators of folk traditions (from New York, Maine, and Newfoundland) are printed in *Folksongs and Their Makers* (Bowling Green, Ohio: Bowling Green University Popular Press, 1970). Two fine examples of dictated life stories published by *Northeast Folklore* are "Fleetwood Pride, 1864–1960: The Autobiography of a Maine Woodsman" (9 [1967]); and "Me and Fannie: The Oral Autobiography of Ralph Thornton of Topsfield, Maine" (14 [1973]). Five studies of "Creativity in Southern Folklore" constituted a special issue of *Studies in the Literary Imagination* (3 [April 1970]: 1–107), compiled by John A. Burrison. Gregory Gizelis discussed the same point—namely, real individual creation as an aspect of folk tradition—in his note "A Neglected Aspect of Creativity of Folklore Performers," *JAF* 86 (1973): 167–72.

American folklore arranged in an occupational group context is collected in Tristram Potter Coffin and Hennig Cohen's *Folklore from the Working Folk of America* (New York: Doubleday, 1973; Anchor paperback, 1974). The "occupational folklore" issue of *JOFS* is 3 (1974): 1–67. Following are some representative articles on the folklore of specific occupations: Marcello Truzzi, "The American Circus as a Source of Folklore: An Introduction," *SFQ* 30 (1966): 289–300; Joyce Gibson Roach, "Diesel Smoke and Dangerous Curves: Folklore of the Trucking Industry," *PTFS* 35 (1971): 45–53; Lois A. Monteiro, "Nursing-Lore," *NYFQ* 29 (1973): 97–110; William R. Ferris, "Railroad Folklore: An Overview," *NCFJ* 22 (1974): 169–76; Mary C. Fields, "The View from the Water Table: Folklore of the Offshore Oilfield Workers," *MSF* 2 (1975): 63–76; and William R. Ferris, Jr., "The Enlisted Man: Army Folklore," *NYF* 2 (1976): 229–34.

In 1978 two special issues of folklore journals concentrated on occupational folklore. "Working Americans: Contemporary Approaches to Occupational Folklore" was *WF* 37, no. 3 (1978), edited by Robert H. Byington and containing five articles; and "Occupational Folklore and the Folklore of Working" was *FF* 11, no. 1 (1978), edited by Catherine Swanson and Philip Nusbaum, and containing seven articles. Individual articles continue: Michael T. Spooner, "Lookout Lore: A Study in Occupational Folklore," *SWF* 2 (1978): 1–17; Joyce A. Ice, "Folklore among the Employees at Grand Canyon National Park," *SWF* 3 (1979): 18–30; Jack Santino, "'Flew the Ocean in a Plane': An Investigation of Airline Occupational Narrative," *JFI* 15 (1978): 189–208; William H. Beezley, "Locker Rumors: Folklore and Football," *JFI* 17 (1980): 196–221; two articles on folklore among medical personnel in *LFM* 5 (1981): 38–47; Carolyn Lipson-Walker, "Black-robed Folklore: The Oral and Customary Traditions of the Supreme Court," *SWF* 5 (1981): 21–41;

Rosemary O. Joyce, "Wall Street Wags: Uses of Humor in the Financial Community," *WF* 41 (1982): 292–303; and B. S. Barnes, "Policelore," *LFM* 5 (1982): 34–47.

Book-length studies of the lore of occupational groups are Mody C. Boatright's *Folklore of the Oil Industry* (Dallas: Southern Methodist University Press, 1963), George Korson's *Black Rock: Mining Folklore of the Pennsylvania Dutch* (Baltimore: Johns Hopkins Press, 1960), Horace Beck's *Folklore and the Sea* (Middletown, Conn.: Wesleyan University Press, 1973), Patrick B. Mullen, *I Heard the Old Fishermen Say: Folklore of the Texas Gulf Coast* (Austin: University of Texas Press, 1978), and Howard W. Marshall and Richard E. Ahlborn, *Buckaroos in Paradise: Cowboy Life in Northern Nevada* (Washington, D.C.: Library of Congress, 1980), essentially a catalogue of an exhibit of cowboy artifacts. See also the works on occupational customs listed in the notes to Chapter 14.

American children's lore is gathered mostly in journal articles, such as Nancy C. Leventhal and Ed Cray, "Depth Collecting from a Sixth-Grade Class," *WF* 22 (1963): 159–63, and 231–57. (Articles dealing with individual genres of childlore are listed in the appropriate bibliographic notes that follow.) An excellent book-length treatment drawn from research among English children reveals many parallels in American lore. See Iona Opie and Peter Opie's *The Lore and Language of Schoolchildren* (New York: Oxford University Press, 1959); for a comparison based on the Opies' work see Loman D. Cansler, "Midwestern and British Children's Lore Compared," *WF* 27 (1968): 1–18. Finally, a comprehensive book on American children's folklore appeared: Mary and Herbert Knapp's *One Potato, Two Potato: The Secret Education of American Children* (New York: Norton, 1978). The autobiographical book *Dorothy's World* (Englewood Cliffs, N.J.: Prentice-Hall, 1977) by the American children's folklorist Dorothy Howard includes lore from her childhood in the Sabine bottom area of Texas in the early twentieth century. In 1980 two folklore journals published important special issues on children's folklore: *SWF* 4, nos. 3–4, had twelve articles, and *WF* 39, no. 3, had six articles and a good bibliography.

Brian Sutton-Smith, who has published many good studies of children's games, discusses "Psychology of Childlore: The Triviality Barrier," in *WF* 29 (1970): 1–8. An interesting analysis based on a verbatim ninety-minute tape-recorded storytelling session with five boys is given in Steve Bartlett's "Social Interaction Patterns of Adolescents in a Folklore Performance," *FF* 4 (1971): 39–67. In "Teaching and Collecting Folklore at a Boys' Prep School," *KFQ* 15 (1970): 55–113, the folklore of adolescents was collected and studied by themselves, and edited by Angus K. Gillespie.

A special issue of *JAF* (88, no. 347 [1975]) highlighted "Women and Folklore"; Claire R. Farrer was the editor. A critical response to the material and its handling by Rosan A. Jordan was published in *FFemC* no. 8 (Winter 1976): 4–5. In the renamed version of this journal—*FWC* —Elizabeth Starr commented "On Sexism in Folklore Scholarship" (no. 20, Winter 1980: 16–22), citing specific examples from the publications of several male American folklorists. Alan Dundes's essay "The Crowing Hen and the Easter Bunny: Male Chauvinism in American Folklore," first published in 1976, was reprinted in *Interpreting Folklore,* pp. 160–75; it is not surprising to find here that American folklore reflects the traditional biases of American history and culture. Specific categories and styles of women's folklore as such have slowly been emerging to view in scholarly studies such as Susan Kalčik's " '. . . Like Ann's Gynecologist or The Time I Was Almost Raped': Personal Narratives in Women's Rap Groups" in the "Women and Folklore" issue of *JAF* mentioned above, 3–11. A related kind of warning story, in a similarly entitled essay, is found in Eleanor Wachs's " 'With My Heart in My Throat and My Whistle in My Hand': Women's Crime-Victim Narratives from the Urban Setting," *NYF* 6 (1980): 11–26. Kathryn L. Morgan's autobiographical study *Children of Strangers: The Stories of a Black Family* (Philadelphia: Temple University Press, 1980) demonstrates how her family stories—particularly those about a resolute female ancestor—served as "buffers" against the forces of racial prejudice in the modern world.

A good example of the data of cultural geography used to differentiate a regional folk group is found in E. J. Wilhelm, Jr., "Folk Settlement Types in the Blue Ridge Mountains," *KFQ* 12 (1967): 151–74. The Ozarks, a prime American folk enclave, is discussed in E. Joan Wilson Miller's "The Ozark Culture Region as Revealed by Traditional Materials," *Annals of the Association of American Geographers* 58 (1968): 51–77. The riches of material already collected there are indexed in Vance Randolph's *Ozark Folklore: A Bibliography,* Folklore Institute Monograph Series, vol. 24 (Bloomington: Indiana University Press, 1972); it extends only up to 1964 and yet lists 2,489 items. Volume 3, no. 3 (Winter 1975), of *MSF* was a special issue dedicated to Vance Randolph, with essays about and dedicated to the regional folklorist.

One model study of a region and its folk groups, prefaced by a discussion of "the folk" in the United States, is Richard M. Dorson's *Bloodstoppers and Bearwalkers: Folk Traditions in the Upper Peninsula* (Cambridge, Mass.: Harvard University Press, 1952; paperback repr., 1972). A fine Western counterpart is Austin and Alta Fife's *Saints of Sage and Saddle: Folklore among the Mormons* (Bloomington: Indiana University Press, 1956).

There are many large popularized anthologies of American folklore, most of them either arranged or cross-indexed by regional groups, and many of them probably trading on the success of B. A. Botkin's inclusive but somewhat unscholarly *A Treasury of American Folklore* (New

York: Crown Publishers, 1944) and Botkin's several regional "treasuries." Tristram P. Coffin and Hennig Cohen's *Folklore in America* (Garden City, N. Y.: Doubleday, 1966; Anchor paperback, 1970) draws all of its examples from *JAF*, but often without the annotations or analyses originally provided there. Duncan Emrich's *Folklore on the American Land* (Boston: Little, Brown and Company, 1972) includes some extraneous editorializing by the compiler, but the sources and bibliography are clearly stated, and the illustrative photographs of Americans from the 1930s and 1940s are excellent.

A popularized anthology from one important region is Richard Chase's *American Folk Tales and Songs . . . as Preserved in the Appalachian Mountains . . .* (New York: New American Library, 1956; Dover Books repr., 1971). John Greenway's *Folklore of the Great West* (Palo Alto, Calif.: The American West Publishing Co., 1969) is drawn from the pages of *JAF* but presented in an essentially nonscholarly format. Similarly, Jan Harold Brunvand's "Folklore of the Great Basin," *NWF* 3 (1968): 17–32, is written for a nonprofessional audience, although based on scholarly sources and field work. Perhaps the best introduction to regional American folklore is Dorson's *Buying the Wind*, which presents folklore from seven regions to illustrate the corresponding discussion in Chapter 3 in his *American Folklore* (Chicago: University of Chicago Press, 1959).

Supplementary to Frank C. Brown's collection of North Carolina folklore mentioned in the notes to Chapter 2 is Charles Bond's article "Unpublished Folklore in the Brown Collection," *NCF* 20 (1972): 11–20, which catalogues and offers a few samples from materials on file in the Duke University Library (repr. in *Readings in American Folklore*, pp. 5–15). Other state anthologies include Earl J. Stout's *Folklore from Iowa*, American Folklore Society Memoir, vol. 29 (New York, 1936); Harold W. Thompson's *Body, Boots and Britches* (on New York State) (Philadelphia: J. P. Lippincott, 1940); George Korson's *Pennsylvania Songs and Legends* (Philadelphia: University of Pennsylvania Press, 1949); Samuel J. Sackett's *Kansas Folklore* (Lincoln: University of Nebraska Press, 1961); Roger L. Welsch's *A Treasury of Nebraska Pioneer Folklore* (Lincoln: University of Nebraska Press, 1966); and three works by George G. Carey: *Maryland Folklore and Folklife* (Cambridge, Md.: Tidewater Publishers, 1970), *Maryland Folk Legends and Folk Songs* (Cambridge, Md.: Tidewater Publishers, 1971), and *A Faraway Time and Place: Lore of the Eastern Shore* (on Chesapeake Bay) (Washington, D.C., and New York: Robert B. Luce, 1971). In *Sang Branch Settlers: Folksongs and Tales of a Kentucky Mountain Family*, American Folklore Society Memoir, vol. 61 (Austin, Tex., 1974), Leonard Roberts presents a family tradition within a regional context.

Three recent studies in regional folklore are Robert D. Bethke's *Adirondack Voices: Woodsmen and Woods Lore* (Urbana: University of

Illinois Press, 1981), Francis Harper and Delma E. Presley's *Okefinokee Album* (Athens: University of Georgia Press, 1981), and the Wisconsin folklore issue of *MJLF* (8, no. 1) published in 1982 and edited by James P. Leary, who provided a bibliography of more than 200 items.

Three theoretical discussions of regionalism are Suzi Jones's "Regionalization: A Rhetorical Strategy," *JFI* 13 (1976): 105–20; W. F. H. Nicolaisen's "The Folk and the Region," *NYF* 2 (1976): 143–49; and William M. Clements's "The Folklorist, the Folk, and the Region," *MFSJ* 1 (1979): 44–54, in which "region" is viewed either as an analytical category, in terms of ethnic constraint, or as an administrative unit.

A useful index to *HFB* (1942–45) and *HF* (1946–50) was published by *FF* as their Bibliographic and Special Series, no. 10 (1973). Other regional folklore journals include *Tennessee Folklore Society Bulletin* (1934), *New York Folklore Quarterly* (1945–74, *New York Folklore* thereafter), *Keystone Folklore Quarterly* (1956–73, *Keystone Folklore* thereafter), *Kentucky Folklore Record* (1955), *New Mexico Folklore Record* (1946), *AFFWord* ("Arizona Friends of Folklore," 1971–75, *Southwest Folklore* thereafter), *Journal of the Ohio Folklore Society* (new series begun in 1972), *Louisiana Folklore Miscellany* (1960), *Midwestern Journal of Language and Folklore* (1975), *Northwest Folklore* (1965–68), and *North Carolina Folklore* (1952–72, *North Carolina Folklore Journal* thereafter). The *Publications of the Texas Folklore Society* have appeared in annual volumes since 1924, and there were sporadic folklore journals in Illinois, New Hampshire, Wisconsin, and several other states. For information about these, see an article in yet another regional journal: William J. Griffin's "The *TFS Bulletin* and Other Folklore Serials in the United States: A Preliminary Survey," *TFSB* 25 (1959) 91–96. More recently established regional journals appear in the complete list of abbreviations for periodicals that are cited in these notes, following the Preface. *Indiana Folklore: A Reader,* edited by Linda Dégh (Bloomington: Indiana University Press, 1980), contains fifteen essays from the pages of the journal *Indiana Folklore.*

Publications on American Indian folklore, including the vast anthropological literature, are far too numerous and varied to be represented here by a few citations. The bibliography *Native American Folklore, 1879–1979,* by William M. Clements and Frances M. Malpezzi (Athens, Ohio, London, and Chicago: Swallow Press and Ohio University Press, 1984), contains more than 5,000 entries. The notes to Chapter 8 on mythology and motifs list some key works on native American oral narratives.

For backgrounds to Afro-American folklore see Ruth Finnegan's comprehensive survey *Oral Literature in Africa* (New York: Oxford University Press, 1970). *Afro-American Folk Culture: An Annotated Bibliography* (Philadelphia: Institute for the Study of Human Issues, 1978), compiled by John F. Szwed, Roger D. Abrahams, and others, has volume 1 devoted to North America, volume 2 to the West Indies and

Central and South America. Papers of the African Folklore Conference held at Indiana University in 1970 were published in *African Folklore,* ed. Richard M. Dorson (Bloomington: Indiana University Press, 1972). A particularly valuable collection that places Afro-American folklore in a historical context is Bruce Jackson's *The Negro and His Folklore in Nineteenth-Century Periodicals,* American Folklore Society Bibliographic and Special Series, vol. 18 (Austin, Tex., 1967). *African Folklore in the New World,* ed. Daniel J. Crowley (Austin: University of Texas Press, 1977), contains five essays on the topic and reveals some spirited debate among the contributors. Roger D. Abraham's *Positively Black* (Englewood Cliffs, N.J.: Prentice-Hall, 1970) offers interpretive social and cultural comments on his own and others' recent studies. Alan Dundes's *Mother Wit from the Laughing Barrel: Readings in the Interpretation of Afro-American Folklore* (Englewood Cliffs, N.J.: Prentice-Hall, 1973) anthologizes many important essays on the subject. An often unappreciated cross-ethnic pattern of borrowing is treated in Alan Dundes's "African Tales among the North American Indians," *SFQ* 29 (1965): 207–19. Lawrence W. Levine's *Black Culture and Black Consciousness: Afro-American Folk Thought from Slavery to Freedom* (New York: Oxford University Press, 1977) is a successful application of Afro-American folklore studies to writing the history of this people.

The distinguished Canadian folklorist C. Marius Barbeau discussed "The Field of European Folk-Lore in America" in *JAF* 32 (1919): 185–97; Reidar Th. Christiansen, while professor of folklore at the University of Oslo, wrote "A European Folklorist Looks at American Folklore," *PTFS* 28 (1958): 18–44. Christiansen's full discussion, *European Folklore in America,* was published as number 12 of *Studia Norvegica* (Oslo, 1962). W. John Rowe placed more emphasis on material traditions than verbal folklore in "Old-World Legacies in America," *Folk Life* 6 (1968): 68–82. *The Folklore of Texas Cultures,* ed. Francis Edward Abernethy, *PTFS* 38 (1974), is a good compilation of lore from two dozen groups found in the Lone Star State, with illustrations drawn from both old and recent photographs of each group. An important aid to immigrant-American folklore studies is Robert A. Georges and Stephen Stern's *American and Canadian Immigrant and Ethnic Folklore: An Annotated Bibliography* (New York: Garland, 1982), classified by groups (Armenian through Yugoslavian in alphabetical order) and cross-indexed by folklore forms, regions, and authors. There are about 1,900 entries, though some are multiple listings.

The only older book-length work on an immigrant group's folklore to be recommended is Phyllis H. Williams's *South Italian Folkways in Europe and America* (New Haven, Conn.: Yale University Press, 1938); a worthy recent counterpart is Carla Bianco's *The Two Rosetos* (Bloomington: Indiana University Press, 1974), a comparison of folkways in Roseto Valfortore, Italy, and Roseto, Pennsylvania.

Representative journal articles on immigrant folklore are Henry R.

Lang, "The Portuguese Element in New England," *JAF* 5 (1892): 9–18; Jay K. Ditchy, ed., "Early Louisiana French Life and Folklore from the Anonymous Breaux Manuscript," *LFM* 2 (May 1966); Robert A. Georges, "Matiasma: Living Folk Belief [Greek]," *MF* 12 (1962): 69–74; Warren Kliewer, "Collecting Folklore among Mennonites," *Mennonite Life* 14 (July 1961): 109–12 (repr. in *Readings in American Folklore*, pp. 22–30); Arthur L. Campa, "Spanish Folksongs in Metropolitan Denver," *SFQ* 24 (1960): 179–92; Rosan Jordan DeCaro, "Language Loyalty and Folklore Studies: The Mexican-Americans," *WF* 31 (1972): 77–86; Pat Bieter, "Folklore of the Boise Basques," *WF* 24 (1965): 263–70; Alixa Neff, "Belief in the Evil Eye among the Christian Syrian-Lebanese in America," *JAF* 78 (1965): 46–51; Erik Wahlgren, "Scandinavian Folklore and Folk Culture in the Trans-Mississippi West," *NWF* 3 (1969): 1–16; Yvonne R. Lockwood, "The Sauna: An Expression of Finnish-American Identity," *WF* 36 (1977): 71–84; and Dennis J. Clark, "Our Own Kind: Irish Folk Life in an Urban Setting" [Philadelphia], *KF* 23 (1979): 28–40.

Theoretical and methodological matters underlying immigrant folklore studies are taken up in Elli Kaija Köngäs, "Immigrant Folklore [Finnish]: Survival or Living Tradition?" *MF* 10 (1960): 117–23; and Linda Dégh, "Approaches to Folklore Research among Immigrant Groups," *JAF* 79 (1966): 551–56. A special issue of *WF* (36, no. 1), "Studies in Folklore and Ethnicity," edited by Larry Danielson, was published in 1977 and contains an introduction and five articles.

An aural anthology of Indian, immigrant, and Anglo-American folk music from one state is the record *Folk Voices of Iowa*, collected and edited by Harry Oster (Iowa City: University of Iowa Press, 1965).

The long tradition of folklore studies among Canada's diverse ethnic and regional groups has been continued and consolidated lately in the Canadian Centre for Folk Cultural Studies at the National Museum of Man in Ottawa. A useful introduction to their research is provided by Carmen Roy in Paper No. 7 of their Mercury Series (Ottawa, 1973); a representative commissioned report is Jan Harold Brunvand, *Norwegian Settlers in Alberta*, Mercury Series, Paper No. 8 (Ottawa, 1974). Robert B. Klymasz's *An Introduction to the Ukranian-Canadian Immigrant Folksong Cycle* (Ottawa: National Museums of Canada, Bulletin no. 234, Folklore Series no. 8, 1970) is a model study with texts in two languages, music, illustrations, and three small discs of recorded examples. An essay with implications for the future of this research is Klymasz's "From Immigrant to Ethnic Folklore: A Canadian View of Process and Tradition," *JFI* 10 (1973): 131–39.

Until very recently American folklore continued to be thought of only in a rural or small-town setting; a special issue of *JAF* devoted to "The Urban Experience and Folk Tradition" (83, no. 328 [April–June, 1970]; Bibliographical and Special Series no. 22 [1971]), ed. Américo Paredes and Ellen J. Stekert, indicated changes in attitude that were developing. Richard M. Dorson's contribution to this publication, "Is There a Folk in the City?" 185–228, elicited much discussion along with the eventual expansion of his thesis in Bruce E. Nickerson's "Is There a Folk in the Factory?" *JAF* 87 (1974): 133–39. A special issue of *NYF* (4, nos. 1–4, 1978), edited by Susan G. Davis, described "The Utica Project" in which a number of folklorists analyzed traditions of that city. The urban folklore research of Richard Dorson's Indiana University folklore graduate students in the Calumet Region of the north of the state is described in a special issue of *IF* (10, no. 2 [1977]). Dorson's full treatment of the results of the project is given in his *Land of the Millrats* (Cambridge: Harvard University Press, 1981).

An unsuspected field for modern folklore studies is revealed in Mac E. Barrick's "Folktales from the Institute at Duke," *NCFJ* 23 (1975): 75–81, which contains traditional material heard from some fifty scholars assembled for the Sixth Southeastern Institute of Medieval and Renaissance Studies. That modern and urban folklore is by no means exclusively an American phenomenon is indicated by Stewart Sanderson's article "The Folklore of the Motor-Car," in *Folklore* 80 (1969): 241–52. A useful reference is Camilla Collins's "Bibliography of Urban Folklore," *FF* 8 (1975): 57–125. See also the discussion of urban legends in Chapter 9.

Modern technology spawns folklore rather than replacing it or rendering it obsolete. Among others, Michael J. Preston has published examples of "Xerox-lore" in *KF* 19 (1974): 11–26; and in *JOFS* 3 (1975): 27–30. The first book-length collection and commentary is offered in Alan Dundes and Carl R. Pagter, *Urban Folklore from the Paperwork Empire*, American Folklore Society Memoirs, vol. 62 (Austin, Tex.: 1975), republished by Indiana University Press as *Work Hard and You Shall Be Rewarded* (1978). Two even larger collections were published in actual photocopy format by Xerox University Microfilms of Ann Arbor, Michigan: *Urban Folklore from Colorado: Typescript Broadsides*, ed. Cathy M. Orr and Michael J. Preston, and *Urban Folklore from Colorado: Photocopy Cartoons*, ed. Cathy M. Orr and Michael J. Preston, both 1976.

Alan Dundes documents an old but prevailing mindset of Americans (reflected frequently even in this textbook!) in an essay first published in 1968: "The Number Three in American Culture," reprinted in *Interpreting Folklore*, pp. 134–159. The sometimes quick reaction of modern folklore to current events is shown in Yvonne J. Milspaw's "Folklore and the Nuclear Age: 'The Harrisburg Disaster' at Three Mile Island," *IFR* 1 (1981): 57–65.

Contemporary social concerns reflected in folklore are the subjects of such essays as Norine Dresser's "'The Boys in the Band Is Not Another Musical': Male Homosexuals and Their Folklore," *WF* 33 (1974):

205–18; Eve Mitchell's "Folklore of Marijuana Smoking," *SFQ* 34 (1970): 127–30; and many others listed in the bibliographic notes to subsequent chapters.

Folklore collected from the folk group of folklorists themselves makes one wonder where it will all end. See Richard A. Reuss, "'That Can't Be Alan Dundes! Alan Dundes is Taller Than That!' The Folklore of Folklorists," *JAF* 87 (1974): 303–17.

II · ORAL FOLKLORE

The lore that circulates from person to person by word of mouth includes most traditions originally associated with the term "folklore." Most of it is *oral* (one may quibble about exactly how human speech is produced, and we make an exception for instrumental music); a good part of it is *verbal*. But all of it is *aural*. Calling it all "oral folklore" is something of a simplification, but to do so has been traditional for a long time in folklore studies. In an analogy with literary and language studies, these types of folklore are set up in collections, archives, and studies usually in terms of their relative linguistic or stylistic complexity—from words, names, phrases, and sentences, to questions (i.e., "riddles"), rhymes, stories, songs, and ballads. While beginning students should find this a convenient approach (especially as they peruse older folklore studies), they should always bear in mind that any given folklore performance is more than the automatic transmission of "text," more even than text-in-context, but is in fact a complex communicative event in which "oral folklore" items are only one conspicuous component.

Music is included in this section because so often in American folk tradition it coexists and interacts with words. Instead of separating purely instrumental tradition for discussion purposes, Chapter 13 sketches out the whole topic of folk music.

4
Folk Speech and Naming

The simplest level of verbal folklore is the traditional word, expression, usage, or name that is current in a folk group or in a particular region. When a Southerner says "y'all," or a Missourian pronounces his state name ending in "uh" [məz′ərə],* or an Easterner differs with a Midwesterner over what a *soda* and a *cruller* are, or a child names a puppy *Rex, Prince,* or *Queenie,* we have instances of what the folklorist calls **folk speech.** Strictly speaking, these subjects are in the domain of *linguistics* (especially dialect study or "linguistic geography") and of *onomastics* (the study of names), but the folklorist has a legitimate and somewhat specialized interest in them, too.

Dialects and Speech Variations

Dialect—the traditional deviation from standard speech—includes variations in *grammar* (both morphology and syntax), *pronunciation,* and *vocabulary.* While only trained linguists have the special ability and techniques needed to collect and study dialect in a rigorously scientific manner, they usually focus their attention on typical informants in one region who are interviewed on the basis of a formal questionnaire. Then "isoglosses" or dialect boundaries may be mapped to show the distribution of certain usages, and these maps are potential guides for folklore collecting. But a "linguistic atlas" does not serve all the needs of research in folk speech. For one thing, some dis-

* The International Phonetic Alphabet (IPA) spelling to indicate pronunciation.

tinction should be made between standard regional dialects and special regional or social folk dialects.

Folklorists also concern themselves with the dialects of different groups, but they usually study deviations from standard speech only as they are embedded in folktales, songs, rhymes, and other traditional contexts. Folklorists are interested in the use of dialect within groups, the retention of outmoded dialect forms in folk texts, and in the linguistic changes that take place as texts are transmitted orally. Similarly, the *naming* that a folklorist studies is that which is traditional and which appears in the context of other folklore. Whatever their separate specialties, then, folklorists should be aware of some terms and techniques for collecting and studying folk speech, while students of dialect or names may benefit from an awareness of folklore research methods and of folk materials.

Variations of grammar in folk speech may consist of nonstandard word forms (morphology) or word order (syntax); collectors of folklore should carefully record both kinds without exaggerating their occurrence. Also they should note whether some expressions used in folklore are missing in everyday speech. There are countless variations possible, but space permits illustrating only a few. The past tense of verbs, for instance, is frequently nonstandard in regional folk speech, so that informants may say "It *snew* yesterday," "I *seen* him," or "He *drownded*"; the past tense of *climb* may be *clim* or *clum*, and such distinctions as *hung/hanged* or *lay/laid* made in polite speech may be disregarded. Some speech forms such as *boughten, enthused, being as,* or *different than* have become so common as to be almost respectable now, while others such as *fotch* (past of *fetch*) and *hit* (for *it*) linger only in isolated regions like the southern Appalachians. Many modern folk expressions such as *I could care less* and *Tell it like it is,* although "ungrammatical," are heard in daily usage.

Dialect forms may be coined to fit a familiar pattern: the Ozark hillman has his combined verbs *house-clean, target-practice,* and many others like them, while the college student has *proficiency-out* (to substitute a proficiency examination for a course) and *brown-nose* (to flatter an instructor). The combinations with *-ify* follow another favorite pattern; they range from *prettify* and *speechify* to *rectify* (to correct school homework) and *witchify* (to apply witchcraft to). Accounts of children's talk may qualify as folklore when they achieve oral circulation as part of a family's anecdotes: "It's *winding*" (on the analogy of *raining* and *snowing*), "I *hood* it from you" (nonstandard past tense of *hide*), and "We're *undusting*" (i.e., removing the dust).

Syntactical variations are often heard in the speech of nonnative-speaker groups, such as the Pennsylvania Germans, who are credited (in what is sometimes referred to as "ferhoodled English") with sentences like "Make the window up," "Don't eat yourself done, there's a pie back," "The off is on" (i.e., "The vacation has begun"), "Throw Mama from the train a kiss," and "Outen the lights." Often vocabulary plus word form or syntax vary simultaneously, as shown in the last example and in a sentence based on the word *liver-out* for "hired girl"—"Is your liver-out in?" Anecdotes based on expressions such as these are a form of folklore themselves, and they are more likely traditional tales than authentic incidents. Nevertheless, such speech does occur, and even in relatively sophisticated American circles one may occasionally hear syntactical oddities learned by imitation, not classroom instruction, such as "I can't remember things like I used to could." (The author once heard a professor shout, in an outburst of unreflective "folk speech," "Where you stayin' at, Jack?" in an elevator that was crowded with delegates to a national Modern Language Association convention.)

For a folklore collector untrained in linguistics, the phonetic transcription of **dialect pronunciations** may be too demanding, but a satisfactory substitute for most purposes is the use of rhyming words. Thus, for local community names, the pronunciation of *Moscow* [máskow] in Idaho may be reported as rhyming with *toe; Spokane* [spowkǽn] in Washington rhymes with *can* rather than *cane; residents of Indiana call their city of *Brazil* [bréyzəl] by a name rhyming with *hazel* (which may be closer to *gray zeal*, with almost no syllable accent), and *Versailles*, Indiana (also Kentucky), rhymes with *curtails*. Berlin, New Hampshire, is accented on the first syllable, and the Thames River in Connecticut is pronounced *Thayms*, not *Temms*. The people of Utah speak of *Zion's Park* instead of Zion National Park. Such pronunciations as these for place names may prove useful for defining the boundaries of folk regions.

Sometimes a dialect pronunciation may creep into spelling, as in the sign painted by a Southerner peddling "Red Haven" peaches who wrote "*Raid Haven* Peaches." Or the college freshman frequently must be taught not to spell *athlete* as he carelessly pronounces it—*athalete*. A lengthy "manuscript of the folk language" laboriously typed out by an uneducated man for folklorist Duncan Emrich began in this manner:

> In Writing This Book I Have Carictorized It In The Best Manner Posible For Me To Remember As I Am A Man of 66. Years Of Age And Did Nevver Keep No Dairie Of The Dayley Happenings As I Should Of Did But Nevver Thinking Of Writing This Book, I Just Have To Go Back In Memory As Fare As Posible And Give The Facts As Best I Can Remember. . . .

Especially when the point of a folk story turns on a certain pronunciation, it is important for the collector to record sounds carefully; such texts indicate folk recognition of dialect. Examples of this are jokes about Swedes confusing *jail* with *Yale,* or Finns praising the two American cars that begin with *P*—"the *Puiks* and the *Packards.*" (The last instance might also be dated by the demise of the Packard.)

Vocabularies

Regional variations in **dialect vocabulary** such as *earthworm, angleworm, night crawler, night walker, mud worm,* and *fish worm;* or *root-beer float, black cow, Boston cooler,* and *Alaskan milkshake,* have been extensively mapped by linguistic geographers. Workers on the *Dictionary of American Regional English* (DARE), a project now of some twenty years duration, have found more than 175 ways that Americans describe a downpour, including *hay rotter, duck drencher, tree bender, chunk floater, sewer clogger, clod roller, toad strangler, stumpwasher,* and *goosedrowner.*

Folklorists tend to concern themselves less with the language of regions than with that of occupational and social folk groups. As a result, numerous glossaries have been compiled from such groups as actors, children, construction workers, homosexuals, jazz musicians, miners, railroad workers, and truck drivers, to name but a few. Euphemisms (for diarrhea or pregnancy, for instance) are a form of folk speech, as are intensifiers like *hogwash, tarnation,* and *oh, fudge,* or such sham-swearing expressions as "Cheese and rice got damp in the cellar." Actual profanity, blasphemy, cursing, and other "maledicta" are, of course, largely folk language, learned orally and practiced traditionally as well as varying according to time, place, and social situation.

The easiest test of a folk group's existence is to identify a specialized informal vocabulary; an important early step in any field-work project is to compile a glossary of the distinctive terminology of the group under study. By way of example, consider college students, who may at first appear not to have any significant oral traditions but from whom in a short time one might easily collect such terms (heard in the Northwest in 1961–63) as *high-school Harry, pasture function* (night picnic with beer), *pig pot* (money collected for the escort of the ugliest partner at an "exchange party"), *troll* (plain or ugly girl), and *wimp* (coward). These examples are possibly all now forgotten, but such language is being updated constantly, and students of folklore should collect their own current slang.

Even highly technical and specialized fields have their in-group folk expressions. Among themselves medical personnel speak of *gomers* (difficult and uncooperative patients, usually elderly), *blue bloaters* (sufferers from chronic emphysema), *crispy critters* (burn victims), and cases of *NAT* ("nonaccidental trauma," such as physical abuse by family members). A sick child, as yet undiagnosed, may be dubbed an *FLK,* or "funny-looking kid," in folk-medical shorthand. Such usages, it seems clear, are partly mechanisms for negating, via humor, some of the stresses of working daily with the sick and wounded. Traditional terminology of modern drug use includes *turn on, trip, speed, grass, pot,* and *roach clip* (a holder for a marijuana cigarette). Folk language of space flight includes *A-OK*, *blast off* (or *lift off*), *cherry picker*, *gantry*, *docking*, and nicknames for crewmen, rockets, and moon-exploration vehicles. Computers have yielded a rich new vocabulary of *bits*, *bytes*, *glitches*, *crashes*, *hackers*, and the acronym *GIGO* (the programmer's maxim for "garbage in, garbage out").

The supposed explanations of acronyms for common short words are usually pure fantasy, unprovable at best; these include "port out, starboard home" (for *posh*), "constable on patrol" (for *cop*), "for unlawful carnal knowledge" (not hard to figure out), and "boys' ventilated drawers" for the trade-name *BVDs*). Sets of initials not forming words used as signals in family folklore are *FHB* (for "family hold back"—i.e., abstain from eating too much when guests are present), *LKF* ("lick and keep fork"), and *PMIK* ("plenty more in the kitchen").

Not uncommonly, a traditional folk term acquires a new meaning as times change. The word *twofer*, for example, long used to mean "two tickets for the price of one" in theater lore, has lately been employed as bureaucratic personnel jargon for the appointment of a black woman to a government position. And *longhair*, once widely applied to lovers or performers of classical music, currently is more likely to refer to long-haired youth with rebellious or antisocial attitudes.

Military servicemen in general quickly learn to converse in the terms traditional in their group, such as *KP* ("Kitchen Police"), *SOP* (standard operating procedure), *no sweat*, *deuce and a half* (for a two-and-a-half-ton truck), and *the old man*. When folk jokes based on a specialized vocabulary occur, we again have the phenomenon of folk commenting on their own distinctiveness. One such GI (Government Issue) story concerns a USO (United Service Organizations) entertainer who was asked whether she preferred "to *mess* with the officers or the men"; she responded, "Makes no difference, but can I eat first?"

Among nationality groups in the United States a whole conglomerate dialect language sometimes develops in the first generation. Norwegians tell about an emigrant joyfully greeting his mother back in the old country with "How's my *gamle mor*?" (The Norwegian words mean "old mother," the only words she would understand in the sentence.) Another Norwegian-American is supposed to have remarked, describing a disastrous drought, *"Jeg luse hele kroppen,"* meaning, to him, "I lost my whole crop"; but in Norwegian the sentence sounds more like "I have lice on my entire body." In "Finglish" the word *nafiksi* frequently occurs—nonexistent in native Finnish but derived in the United States from the English "enough." A Finnish-American storyteller might also end a text with the sentence *"Ne sanot että se oli tosi stori"* ("They said it was a true story"), using the final English word in an otherwise Finnish context. In the "Tex-Mex" spoken in the bilingual Southwest, one might hear *"Dame mi pokebuk"* ("Give me my pocketbook") or *"Es un eswamp"* ("It's a swamp").

"Pig Latin" and other secret languages of children deserve study. These include "backwards talk," "Double Dutch," "G-talk," "King Tut," sign languages, and certain orthographic codes for writing secret messages. Even more peculiar is a regional "slanguage" discovered in Boonville, California, and dubbed "Boontling." Here a language of apparently nonsensical words was invented by children, but later spread to adults of the community. At first, the parents picked up the expressions in an attempt to understand and communicate with their children. Then others found in them a way to express what they felt was the uniqueness of Boonville, unrecognized and unappreciated by outsiders. The language includes many nouns, such as *gannow* ("apple"), *beemsh* ("show"), and *higg* ("money"); verbs such as *dehigg* ("spend money") and *deek* ("learn"); and a few adjectives, such as *ball* ("fine"). The "Boontling" terms, together with local nicknames, are used in oral communication only and intermixed with otherwise conventional English. The following passage is typical:

> We have *ball gannows* here in *Boont*. Why don't we *dehigg* ourselves and have a *beemsh* so people will *deek* how *ball* our *gannows* are?

Folklorists' studies of American folk speech have usually been mere collections, although sometimes these have been imaginative ones. George W. Boswell extracted folk etymologies from folksong diction, finding such onomatopoetic terms as *trinkling* ("Her life's blood came *trinkling* down"), oral mistakes like "He dressed himself in *a tie* [for *attire*] of blue," and irregular verb forms: "I *tuck* her by her yellow hair / I *drug* her 'round and 'round." In a closer analysis of traditional speech patterns, Alan Dundes recognized three kinds of reduplicative phrases, identical (*din din* or *goody goody*), ablaut (*zigzag*), and rhyming (*mumbo jumbo*) with a marked preference in American English for the third type. The "Henny Penny phenomenon" of initial consonant alternation appears in many verbal folk forms, often as /h/:/p/ (*henpecked*), or /t/:/l/ (*Turkey Lurkey, toodle-loo*), and even in such commercial brand names as Hotpoint and Hush Puppies (already a folk term).

Naming

Folk naming practices present a broad field for collecting as well as some interesting possibilities for interpretation, since there are certain traditional names or nicknames for almost anything that can be given a name, ranging from family members and domestic animals to vacation cottages, apartment houses, family cars and hot rods, rifles, and elusive game fish. As in some primitive cultures in which one's "real" name is earned by a great deed or perhaps even a shortcoming, American folk practice is to name children for some notable man or woman, to give names of positive connotation, to avoid giving names thought inappropriate for the child's sex, or to award one's nickname because of his appearance, behavior, or background.

Place names—both for geographic features and for communities—have been more thoroughly researched than any other branch of name lore, but even here vast areas remain unexplored. From the folklorist's point of view (but not the historian's or the cartographer's) the legendary folk etymologies for place names are of prime concern. Thus the folk imagination can be counted on to concoct a story about gnawing on bones to explain a town name like *Gnawbone* (Indiana), whereas the likely origin is a corruption of the displaced French name *Narbonne*.

Also having traditional roots are regional nicknames like *Hoosier, Sooner,* or *Webfoot.*

Studies have been made of such subjects as folk names for cats (*Tabby, Tom,* etc.), for plants (*piss fir, spear grass,* etc.), for pioneer foods (*hush puppies, hoe cakes, pluck and plunder stew,* etc.), and even for teen-ager's automobiles (*Blue Boy, Magnificent Six, Little White Dove, Travellin' Man,* etc.). Traditional variations in a folk name are demonstrated in those used for a favorite picnic dessert made from toasted marshmallows, graham crackers, and a chocolate bar: *some-mores, Brownie Delights, angels on horseback, angels with dirty faces, heavenly hoboes,* and *heavenly hash.* (The latter is also sometimes applied to a whipped-cream and fruit-cocktail salad and it has been used as a name for a commercial ice-cream flavor.) In using traditional names like these, people are sometimes only following tradition or habit (*Tabby*); other times they may be rendering judgment (*piss fir*), alluding to a legend (*hush puppies*), revealing a mood (*Blue Boy*), or creating metaphysical images (*angels with dirty faces*).

Names play a traditional role—though not always an apparent one—in such folk sayings as "robbing *Peter* to pay *Paul,*" "every *Tom, Dick, and Harry,*" and "quicker than you can say '*Jack Robinson.*'" Certain names recur in folk ballads (*Pretty Polly*), folktales (*Jack*), and legends (*Old Scratch*), while other names creep into everyday usage in remarks like "sign your *John Hancock*" (or, unreasonably, "your *John Henry*") and in sample addresses to *John Doe* or *John Q. Citizen.* Finally, ethnic and place names are employed as slurring adjectives in such terms as *Dutch treat, Irish lace* (spider webs), *Mexican credit card* (a hose for stealing gasoline), *Indian giver, Puerto Rico Pendleton* (an old work shirt), *Swedish fiddle* (either a crosscut saw or an accordian), *French screw driver* (a hammer), *Jewish penicillin* (chicken soup), and *Vatican roulette* (the "rhythm" birth-control method).

The vocabulary and traditional naming habits of one folk group can be a fascinating subject for a limited folklore study. Northwest loggers offer a convenient example, for nearly every aspect of their life and work has acquired a distinctive folk term.

There are terms for pieces of equipment (*A-frame, bells and buttons, gut wrappers*), terms of particular jobs (*cat skinner, choker setter, pond monkey*), terms for trees and logs (*widow maker*—a dangerously leaning or hanging tree or limb, *barber chair*—a split-cut stump), and even special terms for some foods (*saddle blankets* for hotcakes, *chokum* for cheese, *excelsior* for noodles, *bear sign* for blackberry jam).

Some of these loggers' terms have either penetrated to more general usage by other groups, or have acquired specialized meanings in the woods, and it is often impossible to tell which way a term has gone. *Haywire*, for instance, has long been used by loggers to refer to any lightweight wire (also called *straw wire*), and when such wire was frequently used for general camp repairs, it became a *haywire outfit*—a patched-together and mixed-up camp. An alternative explanation is that when one cuts baling wire loose from a bale, the wire goes every which way in a tangled mess. These may be either the origins of or only offshoots from the generally used expression "to go haywire." Similarly, the logger uses *hoosier* not for a resident of Indiana, necessarily, but for any greenhorn in the woods. A *gypo outfit* in loggers' parlance is not a company that "gyps" customers, but simply a company, especially a small one, that logs on contract. The term *skid road*, used originally for a log-skidding road, then for the tough streets in West Coast towns, has been altered to *skid row* in general usage. (The loggers consider the term as phony as *lumberjack*, the term applied to the loggers by almost everyone but themselves.)

Names and naming contribute further to the flavor of woods terminology. Corn bread may be designated *Arkansaw wedding cake;* a homemade lantern is a *palouser* (from the "Palouse" region of eastern Washington and northern Idaho); the Chinook word *Potlatch* (a gift-exchange festival) appears in the company name "Potlatch Forests Incorporated" (called *P.F.I.* or "Pin Feathers, Inc." locally), as well as in place names and in such terms as *Potlatch turkey* (crow) and *Potlatch tram* (a type of logging tramway). The American loggers' *peavey*, used all over the country, supposedly was developed by J. H. Peavey of Bangor, Maine, but a *Jacob's staff* and a *Johnson bar* are other tools not clearly traceable to sources. Loggers have christened their trucks and other modern equipment with such nicknames as *The Monster, Old Asthma, Road Runner,* or *Widow Maker,* just as fellow workers bear such descriptive nicknames as *White Pine Joe, The Galvanized Swede, Cruel-Jimmy Holmes,* and *Greasy Pete.*

A similar collecting project might successfully focus on any occupational group. Thus, the house painter's "haywire outfit" is a *Joe McGee rig,* although just why this name refers to make-shift equipment is unclear. (From the term come the verbs *Joe McGee it* or simply *McGee it.*) Paint cans are always *pots;* thinner of any kind is *turps;* the last coat of paint applied is *the third coat,* and so forth. With the popularity of Citizens' Band two-way radios spreading from truckers to the general public, the eso-teric "CB" language became better known: the *dirty side* refers to the eastern United States, *clean side* to the West. A highway patrolman is *Smoky the Bear,* and when he is checking traffic speeds, "Smoky's in the woods taking pictures." Furniture trucks are *bedbug haulers,* and a truckload of new cars is a *future junk yard.* In the folk language of some college students the course names may be humorously replaced: Abnormal Psychol-ogy becomes *Nuts and Sluts;* Introductory Geology is *Rocks for Jocks;* Military History is *Tanks and Jeeps; Play a Day* refers to English Drama; and *Darkness at Noon* fits an art-history class held in the middle of the day and largely devoted to showing slides of the works studied.

Every trade, every hobby, every age group, and every region has a dialect of its own, most still awaiting the thorough collec-tor of folk speech. When such linguistic strayings from the stan-dard speech are purely ephemeral or technical, they may be regarded as *slang* or *jargon,* respectively; but when such lan-guage is longer-lived and more generally used, it becomes tra-ditional speech of prime interest to the folklorist.

BIBLIOGRAPHIC NOTES

Linguistic, onomastic, and folkloristic studies of folk speech are scat-tered through the professional books and journals of all three disci-plines. A good general survey of the subject is Raven I. McDavid's chapter "The Dialects of American English," in W. Nelson Francis's *The Structure of American English* (New York: Ronald Press, 1958), pp. 480–543. McDavid also provides a comprehensive view of the two related disciplines in "Linguistic Geography and the Study of Folklore," *NYFQ* 14 (1958): 242–62. From the folklorist's point of view, see Louis Pound's "Folklore and Dialect," *CFQ* 4 (1945): 146–53, reprinted in *Nebraska Folklore*, pp. 211–21. More recently, Jay Robert Reese has made specific suggestions for cooperative studies in "Dialectology and Folklore: Woodscolts in Search of Kin," *TFSB* 45 (1979): 48–60.

Two useful general reference works are *A Dictionary of Americanisms on Historical Principles*, ed. M. M. Mathews (Chicago: University of Chicago Press, 1951), and *Dictionary of American Slang*, ed. Harold Wentworth and Stuart Berg Flexner (New York: Crowell, 1960; reissued with supplement, 1967). The basic background study for all such research is H. L. Mencken's *The American Language*, first published in 1919, issued in a rewritten and enlarged edition in 1936, with supplements added in 1945 and 1948, and subsequently many times reprinted (New York: Alfred A. Knopf).

Linguistic geographer Frederic G. Cassidy reviews the history of a proposed "Dictionary of American Regional English" in "The ADS Dictionary—How Soon?" *PADS* no. 39 (1963): 1–7. (The *DARE* project was accepted in 1964 as a cooperative research project of the Department of Health, Education, and Welfare; the American Dialect Society; and the University of Wisconsin.) James W. Hartman summarizes "Some Preliminary Findings from *DARE*" in *AS* 44 (1969): 191–99. Technical and detailed studies of the kind that will feed into such a project include Gary N. Underwood, "Midwestern Terms for the Ground Squirrel," *WF* 29 (1970): 167–74; James E. Spears, "Southern Folk By-Words, Intensifiers, and Reinforcement Phrases," *MFR* 6 (1972): 115–17; and a thorough study in one state, E. Bagby Atwood's *The Regional Vocabulary of Texas* (Austin: University of Texas Press, 1962).

Most folk-speech studies by folklorists concern vocabulary; three exceptions are Gordon Wilson's "Some Folk Grammar," *TFSB* 33 (1967): 27–35; George W. Boswell's "The Operation of Popular Etymology in Folksong Diction," *TFSB* 39 (1973): 37–58; and Alan Dundes's "The Henny Penny Phenomenon: A Study of Folk Phonological Esthetics in American Speech," *SFQ* 38 (1974): 1–9.

Dundes documents what he calls "future orientation in American worldview" largely from folk speech in an essay entitled "Thinking Ahead" (in *Interpreting Folklore*, pp. 69–85). Yet another approach was taken by Duncan Emrich in "A Manuscript of the Folk Language," *WF* 11 (1952): 266–83: he presents a verbatim transcript of a "folk" speaker just as he wrote (or rather typed) out his reminiscences, spelling and punctuating the words and sentences exactly as they sounded to him.

An imaginative study by Howard Wight Marshall and John Michael

Vlach demonstrates the relationship between folk dialect and folk architecture; see "Toward a Folklife Approach to American Dialects," *AS* 48 (1973): 163–91. In Wayland D. Hand's "From Idea to Word" (*AS* 48 [1973]: 67–76), several folk words and expressions that derive from folk beliefs and customs are explained.

The best dialect survey of an American folklore region is Vance Randolph and George P. Wilson's *Down in the Holler: A Gallery of Ozark Folk Speech* (Norman: University of Oklahoma Press, 1953; paperback repr., 1979). Ramon Adams's three books on western folk speech, *Cowboy Lingo* (Boston: Houghton Mifflin, 1936), *Western Words* (Norman: University of Oklahoma Press, 1944: rev. edn., 1968), and *The Cowboy Says It Salty* (Tucson: University of Arizona Press, 1971) are authoritative and highly readable. On Western American folk speech see also Richard Poulsen, "Black George, Black Harris, and the Mountain Man Vernacular," *Rendezvous* 8 (Summer 1973): 15–23.

For a discussion of "Spanglish" in Puerto Rico see Rose Nash in *AS* 45 (1970): 223–33; the same author discusses "Englañol" [Spanishized English] in *AS* 46 (1971): 106–22.

Children's folk speech, a neglected subject, is treated in Rochele Berkovits's "Secret Languages of Schoolchildren," *NYFQ* 26 (1970): 127–52; her examples include sign languages, bop talk, pig Latin, girl talk, boy talk, and an orthographic code traceable back to sixteenth-century Italian practice. Mary and Herbert Knapp discuss "Tradition and Change in American Playground Language" in *JAF* 86 (1973): 131–41; they analyze truce terms, terminology in games of tag, and a ceremony when children accidentally say the same thing and shout "jinx."

"Boontling," first reported in a folklore journal in the 1940s, has been widely discussed since. Charles C. Adams gathers most references and presents a detailed study in *Boontling: An American Lingo* (Austin: University of Texas Press, 1971), which should be supplemented with E. N. Anderson, Jr., and Marja C. Anderson, "The Social Context of a Local 'Lingo,'" *WF* 29 (1970): 153–65.

Fully documented historical studies of individual expressions are well represented by Allen Walker Read's "The Folklore of O.K.," *AS* 39 (1964): 5–25; and Peter Tamony's "'Hootenanny': The Word, Its Content and Continuum," *WF* 22 (1963): 165–70. The general language of American labor is glossed in an appendix to Archie Green's article "John Neuhaus: Wobbly Folklorist," *JAF* 73 (1960): 189–217. The following works are only a few of the many that deal with vocabulary in a particular occupation: Walter F. McCulloch, *Woods Words: A Comprehensive Dictionary of Loggers' Terms* (Portland: Oregon Historical Society, 1958); Roberta Hanley, "Truck Drivers' Language in the Northwest," *AS* 36 (1961): 271–74; John F. Runice, "Truck Drivers' Jargon," *AS* 44 (1969): 200–9; Terry L. McIntyre, "The Language of Railroading," *AS* 44 (1969): 243–62; T. G. Lish, "Word List of Construction Terms," *PADS* no. 36 (1961): 25–31; Barbara P. Harris and Joseph F. Kess, "Salmon Fishing Terms in British Columbia," *Names* 23 (1975): 61–66; Gerald E. Warshaver, "*Schlop* Scholarship: A Survey of Folkloristic Studies of Lunchcounter and Soda Jerk Operatives," *FF* 4 (1971): 134–45; Marvin Carmony, "The Speech of CB Radio: Observations on Its Past, Present, and Future," *MJLF* 4 (1978): 5–17; Roberta Krell, ". . . The Technical Language of Pitchmen," *FMS* 4 (1980): 26–32; and two by Kelsie B. Harder: "The Vocabulary of Hog-Killing," *TFSB* 25 (1959): 111–15; and "Hay-Making Terms in Perry County," *TFSB* 33 (1967): 41–48.

Further references suggest some folk speech topics outside of strictly regional or labor terminology: S. J. Sackett, "Marble Words from Hays, Kansas," *PADS* no. 37 (1962): 1–3; R. T. Prescott, "Calls to Animals," *SFQ* 2 (1938): 39–42; Gertrude Churchill Whitney, "New England Bird Language," *WF* 20 (1961): 113–14; C. Douglas Chrétien, "Comments on Naval Slang," *WF* 6 (1947): 157–62; Richard K. Seymour, "Collegiate Slang: Aspects of Word Formation and Semantic Change," *PADS* no. 51 (1969): 13–22; Paul A. Eschholz and Alfred F. Rosa, "Course Names: Another Aspect of College Slang," *AS* 45 (1970): 85–90; Julia P. Stanley, "Homosexual Slang," *AS* 45 (1970): 45–59; Sterling Eisiminger, "Acronyms and Folk Etymology," *JAF* 9 (1978): 582–84; and Sidney I. Landau, "Popular Meanings of Scientific and Technical Terms," *AS* 55 (1980): 204–9.

The folk speech of medical personnel is the focus of three recent publications: Victoria George and Alan Dundes's "The Gomer: A Figure of American Hospital Folk Speech," *JAF* 91 (1978): 568–81; C. J. Scheiner, "Common Patient-directed Pejoratives Used by Medical Personnel," *Maledicta* 2 (1978): 67–70; and Lois Monteiro, "Not Sticks and Stones, but Names: More Medical Pejoratives," *Maledicta* 4 (1980): 53–58.

Names, published quarterly as the journal of the American Name Society, since 1953, is the major organ for onomastic activities and studies in this country. The society's pamphlet publication, *Theory of Names*, by Ernst Pulgram (Berkeley: 1954), is a solid introduction to the field.

George R. Stewart's frequently reprinted book *Names on the Land* (New York: Random House, 1945; 4th edn., San Francisco: Lexikos, 1982) is the basic introduction for American place-name studies, many of which have been carried out in great detail for individual states; two good ones that have been recently revised are Lewis A. McArthur's *Oregon Geographic Names* (1928), 3rd edn. (Portland: 1952), and Will C. Barnes's *Arizona Place Names* (1935), rev. and enl. Byrd H. Granger (Tucson: University of Arizona Press, 1960). E. Joan Wilson Miller, a geographer with folklore training, discusses "The Naming of the Land in the Arkansas Ozarks: A Study in Cultural Processes" in *Annals of the Association of American Geographers* 59 (1969): 240–51. Terry L. Alford's article "An Interesting American Place-Name" in *MFR* 2 (1968): 76–78, concerns the name "Indianola," seventeen examples of which in the United States he attributes to the origin in Texas, renamed from "Powderhorn" in 1849 and *not* because of an Indian maiden named "Ola," as is sometimes reported. W. F. H. Nicolaisen treated "Some Humorous Folk-Etymological Narratives" in *NYF* 3 (1977): 1–13. Robert M. Rennick discussed in general "The Folklore of Place-Naming in Indiana" in *IF* 3 (1970): 35–94, while Ronald L. Baker discusses the Indiana place named "Monsterville" in *Names* 20 (1972): 186–92. Audrey R. Duckert identifies eight varieties of "Place Nicknames" in *Names* 21 (1973): 153–60. An article by Hazel E. Mills, "The Constant Webfoot," in *WF* 11 (1952): 153–64, traces the history of Oregon's state nickname.

The general role of names and naming in folklore is taken up by Robert M. Rennick in "The Folklore of Curious and Unusual Names (A Brief Introduction to the Folklore of Onomastics)," *NYFQ* 22 (1966): 5–14, and by Jan Harold Brunvand in the introduction to a special folklore issue of *Names*: 16 (Sept. 1968): 197–206. Byrd Howell Granger surveys a subarea in her article "Naming: In Customs, Beliefs, and Folktales," *WF* 20 (1961): 27–37. Warren E. Roberts, in a review of P. H. Reaney's book *The Origin of English Surnames* (*FF* 14 [1981]: 41–50), provides a good argument and excellent examples for folklorists' interest in this category of naming. See also Robert M. Rennick, "Successive Name-Changing: A Popular Theme in Onomastic Folklore and Literature," *NYFQ* 25 (1969): 119–28; O. Paul Straubinger, "Names in Popular Sayings," *Names* 3 (1955): 157–64; and Archer Taylor, "The Use of Proper Names in Wellerisms and Folktales," *WF* 18 (1959): 287–93. Nicknames (among Amish) are the subject of studies by Maurice A. Mook in *Names* 15 (1967): 111–18; (among prison inmates) by Bruce Jackson in *WF* 26 (1967), 48–54; and (in an immigrant community) by Rosemary Hyde Thomas in "Traditional Types of Nicknames in a Missouri French Creole Community," *MFSJ* 2 (1980): 15–25.

J. L. Dillard's *Black Names* (Contributions to the Sociology of Language 13 [The Hague and Paris: Mouton, 1976]) traces patterns of African usage in black American naming. He considers personal names, musical-group names, church names, vehicle names, and names in trade and business.

A study of the term preferred by an ethnic group for self-reference is José E. Limón's "The Folk Performance of 'Chicano' and the Cultural Limits of Political Ideology" included in *"And Other Neighborly Names . . . ,"* ed. Richard Bauman and Roger D. Abrahams (Austin: University of Texas Press, 1981), pp. 197–225.

A miscellany of name studies for specific subjects includes: *blooming plants*—Lalia Phipps Boone in *SFQ* 19 (1955): 230–36; *cats*—Wendell S. Hadlock and Anna K. Stimson in *JAF* 59 (1946): 529–30, and Archer Taylor in *JAF* 60 (1947): 86; *cars*—Jan Harold Brunvand in *Names* 10

(1962): 279–84, and *WF* 23 (1964): 264–65; *apartment houses*—Elli Kaija Köngäs in *JAF* 77 (1964): 80–81; *tobacco*—Kathrine T. Kell in *JAF* 79 (1966): 590–99.

House painters' jargon of the kind quoted at the end of this chapter is collected by Donald M. Hines in *AS* 44 (1969): 5–32, and by John Michael Bennett in *SFQ* 33 (1969): 313–16.

Ed Cray discusses "Ethnic and Place Names as Derisive Adjectives" and gives numerous examples in *WF* 21 (1962): 27–34. David J. Winslow takes a more specialized approach in "Children's Derogatory Epithets," *JAF* 82 (1969): 255–63. George Monteiro's examples are "Chinese Fire Drill," "French Screw Driver" (a hammer), and "Jewish Penicillin" (chicken soup) in his note published in *WF* 34 (1975): 244–46. The best summary of scholarship and most systematic approach to this whole subject is found in Alan Dundes's "Slurs International: Folk Comparisons of Ethnicity and National Character," *SFQ* 39 (1975): 15–38.

The founding of the journal *Maledicta* in 1977 specifically to publish studies of cursing and other aggressive language signaled a new wave of interest in this area of research. Some samples of essays published there are Reinhold Aman's (editor of *Maledicta*) "An Onomastic Questionnaire" in 1 (1977): 83–101; David L. Closson's "The Onomastics of the Rabble" (nicknames in a predominantly black male liberal arts college) in 1 (1977): 215–33; Sterling Eisiminger's "A Glossary of Ethnic Slurs in American English" in 3 (1979): 153–74; and Gary Alan Fine's "Rude Words: Insults and Narratives in Preadolescent Obscene Talk" in 5 (1981): 51–68. Of related interest is Sandra K. D. Stahl's "Cursing and Its Euphemisms: Power, Irreverence, and the Unpardonable Sin," *MJLF* 3 (1977): 54–68. (The unpardonable sin, she finds, is blasphemy directed against the Holy Spirit.)

5

Proverbs and Proverbial Lore

One step up from folk speech on the scale of complexity in verbal folklore is the proverb—the popular *saying* in a relatively *fixed form* which is, or has been, in *oral circulation*. Many attempts have been made to define proverbs more precisely than this, usually in terms of their origin ("the wisdom of many, the wit of one"), their nature (sayings that "sum up a situation . . . characterize its essence"), or their function (". . . to provide an argument for a course of action which conforms to community values"); but the three qualities italicized above are basic to all. First, the proverb must be a saying, not merely a traditional word like "fiddlesticks" or "phooey." Second, the proverb exists in a somewhat standardized form; "sour grapes" is proverbial, but not "bitter grapes," or "acid grapes," or "sweet grapes." Third, a proverb must have had some oral vitality as distinguished from the written clichés of poetry, advertising, sports reporting, and the like. The combination of all three features is what makes "Waste not, want not!" or "Keep your eye upon the donut and not upon the hole" proverbs.

Proverbs

Proverbs are perhaps the most common and familiar form of *conversational folklore* (oral traditions that occur frequently in everyday situations of communication); but proverbs are much more than mere quotable quotes, wise sayings, or memorable phrases. People employ proverbial expressions to pass judgment on events, to give advice, to rationalize their own actions, or to criticize and praise others. Proverbs provide a "name" or a category for situations that recur in life, saying, in effect, something like "That's a matter of a little knowledge being a dangerous thing" or "You shouldn't judge a book by its cover, you know." And proverbs come to mind not only when speaking conversationally, but also in teaching, preaching, counseling, political persuasion, advertising, and many other situations of communication and personal interaction. Both the events that we recognize as being part of the common human experience and the sayings that we traditionally draw upon to describe these situations have become "proverbial."

For not quite fully explainable reasons, some authored epigrams, like "I'd rather be right than be President" or "History is bunk," have never become proverbial, while many others, like "Pride goeth before a fall" or "Something is rotten in Denmark," have, though these are generally misquoted. Four major categories of proverbs and proverbial lore with several subdivisions, plus a broad classification of miscellaneous sayings may be distinguished in American tradition, and most of these are paralleled in folk sayings throughout the world.

The **true proverb** is always a complete sentence, varies slightly in form, and usually expresses some general truth or wisdom. Such sayings are termed "fixed phrase" kinds of oral folklore, and the variation comes in their meanings and uses in particular contexts. Some true proverbs are simple sententious comments such as "Live and let live," "Absence makes the heart grow fonder," and "Accidents will happen." A few of these leave part of the sentence (here the verb) unstated but understood: "No fool like an old fool," "Penny-wise and pound-foolish," etc. Other true proverbs are based on Aesop's fables or similar old stories—for example, "Don't count your chickens before they hatch" and "Don't kill the goose that lays the golden egg." But the majority of true proverbs are metaphorical descriptions of an act or event applied as a general truth; examples are numerous: "A burnt child dreads the fire," "A new broom sweeps clean," "A rolling stone gathers no moss." The "wisdom" expressed in a true proverb, rather than being in the form of a serious adage, may employ irony or other wit, as in "Marry in haste, repent at leisure" or "Be true to your teeth or they will be false to you."

Proverbial Phrases and Sayings

Proverbial phrases, on the other hand, are never complete sentences, regularly vary in form as they are used, and seldom express any generalized wisdom; nearly all of them are metaphorical. Proverbial verb phrases vary in number and tense and permit the addition of adverbial modifications. Such traditional phrases are often anthologized as infinitives ("to be in hot water," "to raise the roof," "to cut off one's nose to spite one's face"), although they do not occur in speech that way ("He's in hot water now!" or "You're going to get in hot water doing that!"). Phrases without a verb are equally common, such as "behind the eight ball," "from A to Z" (a modernization of "from Alpha to Omega"), and "a song and dance." Some proverbial phrases allow for extensions, either of images or applications. For instance, "up a creek" may add "without a paddle," and the creek may be named.

While proverbial phrases are traditional metaphors, proverbial comparisons are traditional similes, usually expressed in the "like" or "as" form. A proverbial comparison may be logical and direct ("red as a beet," "go like blazes," "greedy as a pig"), or it may be ironical ("as clear as mud," "a face like a can full of worms," "as little chance as a snowball in Hell"). Often there is humorous particularization or exaggeration in American proverbial comparisons; "go like blazes," for instance, becomes "go like *blue* blazes," or a person's luck is described in terms of the chances of "a celluloid cat chased by an asbestos dog in Hell." Some comparisons are grammatical ("cool as a cucumber"), but others are not ("quick like a bunny"). Many American proverbial comparisons are graphic and quite variable: "slick as snot," for example, though meaningful enough as it stands, gains even more effect when further terms are added. It becomes "slick as snot on an ax handle" (or "on a *new* ax handle"), "slick as snot on a doorknob" (or "a *brass* doorknob"), and, in its ultimate slickness, "slick as snot on a *new glass* door-knob." Sayings may be stated in comparative form ("tighter than a drum," "lower than a snake's belly," "blacker than a stack of black cats") or in the "so . . . that" or "more . . . than" pattern: "so tight he screaks," "so slow you have to set a stake to see him move," "more nerve than Carter has Little Liver Pills," "more troubles than you can shake a stick at," and so on. Doubtless there are more typical patterns yet to be identified, because the collection and classification of proverbial comparisons are still in a pioneer stage.

The **Wellerism** (or "Quotation Proverb"), named for Charles Dickens's character Sam Weller, in *Pickwick Papers,* who often used them, is a fourth major kind of proverb. Wellerisms—actually much older than their nineteenth-century namesake—are easy to identify but harder to imagine from their definition: "a saying in the form of a quotation followed by a phrase ascribing the quotation to someone who has done something humorous and appropriate." For example: " 'Everyone to his own taste,' [quotation] as the old lady said [ascription] when she kissed the cow [action]." A subvariant involves someone spoken to: " 'There's always a first time,' as the actress said to the bishop." Other familiar Wellerisms are " 'Neat but not gaudy,' said the Devil, as he painted his tail blue," and " 'It won't be long now,' as the monkey said when he backed into the electric fan." Some Wellerisms involve puns, sometimes with grammatical change (" 'I see,' said the blind man, as he picked up his hammer and saw"), and a few of them are completely obscure in meaning (" 'Aha!' she cried, as she waved her wooden leg and died.") Another curious fact about Wellerisms is that the speaker in them is frequently an old woman, the Devil, a monkey, or a blind man.

Variations of **miscellaneous proverbial sayings** seem to be innumerable, and they tend to come in and go out of fashion quickly. A few long-term popular types may be represented as follows: *Insults, retorts, and wisecracks* (sometimes called "slam sayings")—"He's all right in his place, but that hasn't been dug yet," "You make a better door than you do a window," and "He couldn't be elected dogcatcher in a ward full of cats." *Sarcastic* _interrogatives_—"Does a dog have fleas?", "Is the pope a Catholic?" _Euphemisms_—"It's snowing down south" (meaning, "Your slip is showing"), "There's a star in the East" (meaning, "Your fly is unzipped"). _National and ethnic slurs_—"The British have taken to Scotch; the French have taken to cognac; the Italians have taken to port." _Authors and titles_—"_School Dinners_, by Major Sick." (A related category is _Records and artists_ —" 'On the Sunken Side of the Street,' by the Earthquakes.") _Confucius say_—"Girl in stretch pants get stern look." _She was only_—"the stableman's daughter, but all the horsemen knew her." _Tom Swifties_ (Wellerism-like often-adverbial puns based on a familiar expression in the old _Tom Swift_ boys' books)— " 'Only seven more days,' Tom said weakly."

Analyzing and Researching Proverbs

Because they are short, pithy, common, and extremely varied, proverbs offer many interesting possibilities for analysis which often lead to better understanding of other aspects of culture. The contents of proverbs, for instance, which may suggest their origin, are wide-ranging. There are proverbs based on beliefs ("Rats leave a sinking ship"), proverbs based on weather signs ("All signs fail in a dry season"), proverbs based on medical lore ("An apple a day keeps the doctor away"), proverbs based on business ("Out of debt, out of danger"), proverbs based on folk law ("Two wrongs don't make a right"), proverbs deriving from historical events or slogans ("Old soldiers never die; they just fade away"), and many proverbs referring to household or farm tasks ("A watched pot never boils," "Make hay while the sun shines," etc.). America's pioneer past is suggested by such proverbs as "to come down like Davy Crockett's coon," "to see the elephant" (a popular frontier expression meaning "to see everything worth seeing"), "dry as a powder horn," "to play possum," "to go on the warpath," and "The only good Indian is a dead Indian."

Numerous proverbs are really familiar quotations, usually misquoted, especially from the Bible, from Shakespeare, or from other literary sources. These are called *geflügelte Worte* or "winged words" in German, and they often are used by people without reference to any source. Biblical proverbs include "Money is the root of all evil" (misquoted from 1 Timothy 6:10) and the phrase "to cast bread upon the waters" (from Ecclesiastes 11:1). Shakespeare has given us "What's in a name," "The wish is father to the thought," and scores of other proverbs, while other important literary sources include Alexander Pope ("Fools rush in where angels fear to tread"), William Congreve ("Hell hath no fury like a woman scorned"), Samuel Johnson ("Patriotism is the last resort of a scoundrel"), and William Wordsworth ("The child is father to the man"). The extent to which our daily speech may be colored by such literary borrowings, often with some traditional variation, is indicated by the following common sayings, all of which gained their currency from *Hamlet* and probably take their origin from that play as well: "A method in his madness," "brevity is the soul of wit," "to know a hawk from a handsaw," "suit the action to the words," "sweets to the sweet."

Many proverbs come from classical Greek and Roman sources ("Love is blind," "The die is cast," "Many men, many minds"), or they contain references to classical mythology and history ("to cross the Rubicon," "as rich as Croesus," "Rome was not built in a day"). Similarly, there are proverbs which refer to Biblical or legendary characters, including "Adam's off ox," "poor as Job's turkey," " 'round Robin Hood's barn," and "as bare as Mother Hubbard's cupboard." However, many personal references in proverbs are irretrievably lost in history; who, we may wonder, are "Sam Hill," "Jack Robinson," "George" (as in "Let George do it"), and the trio "Tom, Dick, and Harry"? ("George" may refer to the tradition of calling railroad conductors by this name.) There may be an echo of saints' names in expressions such as "for the love of Mike," "for Pete's sake," and "rob Peter to pay Paul," but conclusive evidence for such origins has yet to be presented.

Proverbs exhibit most of the stylistic devices of poetry. They have *meter* ("You can leád a horse to wáter, but you cán't máke him drínk"), *rhyme* ("Haste makes waste"), *slant rhyme* ("A stitch in time saves nine"), *alliteration* ("Live and let live"), *assonance* ("A rolling stone gathers no moss"), *personification* ("Necessity is the mother of invention"), *paradox* ("No news is good news"), *parallelism* ("Man proposes; God disposes"), and several other poetic characteristics. Many figures of speech occur not only in proverbial phrases and proverbial comparisons, but also in true proverbs.

The philosophy expressed in proverbs introduces yet another area of inquiry. In the first place, it is easy to think of proverbs that contradict one another yet are current simultaneously: "Look before you leap" versus "He who hesitates is lost." Many proverbs offer conservative advice such as "Don't bite off more than you can chew" or "Experience is the best teacher," while others are more cynically inclined, such as "It's not what you know, but who you know" or "If you can't be good, be careful." On the whole, judging from several representative collections, the subjects of well-known American proverbs tend to come from homey, simple, familiar, natural, and domestic topics. Nouns such as "dog," "man," "cat," "bird," "wind," "bear," and "day" appear more frequently than any others; a somewhat contradictory fact, however, is that references to the Devil in American proverbs usually outnumber those to God in collections by about four to one. The most popular individual proverbs in American sayings tend to create a picture of optimism and a Puritanical social code; in nineteenth-century Indiana novels, for instance, the chief favorites were "to build castles in the air," "Honesty is the best policy," and "to turn over a new leaf."

Although all of these topics (and many more) challenge the student of proverbs, most past studies have consisted only of collecting, and too often only from literary or other printed sources. Gradually, oral proverbs are also being collected, sometimes to be printed in regional folklore journals or in book-length dictionaries of proverbs. Oral collections are important for several reasons. They help to validate supposed proverbs from print, they are the only way to include off-color proverbs, they show which ancient proverbs still live in tradition, and they may allow us to capture the process of proverb making as it occurs.

Fully documented collections both from print and from oral tradition are needed before folklorists will be able to evaluate the numerous and often highly imaginative explanations that have been proposed for some proverbs. The expression "Mind your P's and Q's," for example, has had at least five different explanations; it is said to refer to penmanship, typesetting, measurements ("pints and quarts"), dancing instruction *("pied et queue,"* that is, "foot and pigtail"), and religion (Puritan and Quaker). Without full collections of dated texts, it is impossible to evaluate such etymologies.

Another such puzzle, a proverbial saying with internal rhyme, containing a national slur, has now been identified as an immigrant-American coinage. The saying is "Ten thousand Swedes ran through the weeds, chased by one Norwegian" (sometimes continued as a quatrain with "It weren't no use, 'cause they had no snoose at the battle of Copenhagen" or "Ten thousand Jews jumped out of their shoes; they smelled them frying bacon"). Norwegian-American informants associated the saying with a seventeenth-century military engagement against Sweden, but, significantly, they never quoted the rhyme in Norwegian; as a matter of fact, the saying would not form a rhyme in Norwegian. One scholar concluded that most likely the rhyme was invented in the United States by Norwegians carrying on the traditional Old World rivalry with Swedes; they probably patterned it after the similar Anglo-Irish rhyme "Ten thousand micks [Irishmen] got killed with picks at the Battle of Boyne Water."

Individual English proverbs may be traced through several historical dictionaries of them, sometimes even back to the Middle Ages (see the bibliographic notes for references). A sampling of these shows how deceptively "modern" an old saying might sound; the still-current "penny-wise and pound-foolish," for example, was already recorded in the seventeenth century. "The coast is clear" and "Beggars cannot be choosers" were both known in the sixteenth century, "To eat one out of house and home" in the fifteenth century, "A short horse is soon curried" and "Look before you leap" in the fourteenth century, and the proverb about leading a horse to water but failing to make him drink in the late twelfth century.

Other dictionaries of proverbs allow us to compare the sayings of different cultures concerning the same theme. S. G. Champion's *Racial Proverbs*, for instance, lists these, among others, under the heading "Celibacy": "old maids lead apes in Hell" (English), "old maids and young dogs should be drowned" (Romanian), "a bachelor and a dog may do everything" (Polish), "an old spinster is not worth more than an unposted letter" (Hungarian), "a bachelor is never sent as a 'go-between' " (Russian), "no man too old for old maid" (Jamaican), and "an old bachelor compares life to a shirt-button, because it so often hangs by a thread" (Chinese).

Another avenue of research is to collect proverbs in foreign languages that are still current among immigrant Americans. Sometimes these, too, have their parallels in English sayings. For instance, there is an American Mennonite proverb in a Low-German dialect *"Waut dee Maun met dem Ladawoage nenbringe kaun, daut kaun dee Fru met dem Schaldoak erut droage"* ("What the husband can bring in with the wagon, the wife can carry out with her apron"). This is matched by Anglo-American sayings in which the man uses a wheelbarrow or shovel and the wife a spoon. (The wife might find her rejoinder, then, in a proverb like "A man may work from sun to sun, but woman's work is never done!") One of my mother's favorite Norwegian sayings is *"Fra barn og fyllefolk skal du høre sannheten"* ("From children and drunks you hear the truth"). This is partly matched in English by "Kids say the darndest things" and "Out of the mouths of babes."

A comprehensive study of the interest of American authors in proverbs and their use of them would provide some new insights into American literature. From the beginning, American authors have cited proverbs; William Bradford's *Of Plymouth Plantation*, begun in 1630 and chronicling the Pilgrims' first settlement, contained "last and not least," "tide stops for no man," "one swallow makes no summer," and others. Benjamin Franklin was famous for the proverbs he employed in *Poor Richard's Almanack* and *The Way to Wealth*, although he seems to have coined only one that passed into oral circulation on its own— "Three removes [that is, *moves* to a new household] is worse than a fire." James Fenimore Cooper's novels were rich in proverbs; Ralph Waldo Emerson quoted proverbs, altered them, and even tried to invent them; and Carl Sandburg wove proverbs, wisecracks, and other folk speech into *The People Yes*.

Of course, proverbs derived from authors' coinages may change as they enter oral tradition. The last time I saw Franklin's "three removes" saying quoted, it was in the form "Three moves are equal to one fire" and attributed to a popular newspaper advice columnist. Similarly, when proverbs are used commercially, they may be altered or merely alluded to. A reply card querying about the quality of service on a Volkswagen car was headed "Thanks for letting us fix your wagen." The television sitcom title "Three's Company" varies the old proverb "Two's company, three's a crowd," while the title "All in the Family" takes the proverbial phrase straight. The "Rolling Stones" rock band alludes to a true proverb, using just two of its words.

Structures and Contexts of Proverbs

Alan Dundes advocates study of the "folkloristic structure" of proverbs (as distinguished from the linguistic structure of their grammar). Such patterning is independent of the various languages in which a proverb may appear, and its analysis should allow eventually for a true structural definition of the proverb and its subtypes. Dundes begins with the observation that all proverbs contain a topic (A) and a comment (B), so that simple equational proverbs such as "Boys will be boys," "Business is business," or "Coffee boiled is coffee spoiled" might all be represented as an $A = B$ equation. Other proverbs are oppositional, asserting a contrast or a lack of equivalence, such as "A fair exchange is no robbery," "One swallow does not make a summer," or "Two wrongs don't make a right," all of which suggest the $A \neq B$ formula. Still other patterns are possible: "His eyes are bigger than his stomach" is $A > B$; "Half a loaf is better than no bread" might be $A/2 > (B)$, and "Two heads are better than one" $2A > B$, although *essentially* both are still $A > B$. Many multidescriptive element proverbs (whether oppositional or nonoppositional) are based on traditional semantic contrastive pairs (few-many, young-old, before-after, etc.): "Like father, like son" is a nonoppositional example, and "Man works from sun to sun, but woman's work is never done" is oppositional. A limited number of such structural types exist, with some types being more popular in one culture than in another.

The functions or uses of proverbs, although seldom studied in American folklore, would offer a fruitful field for research. As Roger Abrahams has pointed out, "The strategy of the proverb . . . is to direct by appearing to clarify; this is engineered by simplifying the problem and resorting to traditional solutions." The philosophy of a single prolific informant might be investigated by means of his proverbial stock. The use of proverbs in advertising ("When it rains it pours," etc.) could be studied. Parodies of proverbs are specially popular nowadays, either as separate utterances ("Absence makes the heart go wander," "Don't enumerate your fowl until the process of incubation has materialized," "Familiarity breeds attempt," "A stitch in time gathers no moss," "You've buttered your bread, now lie in it") or as the punch lines of so-called "shaggy-dog stories" ("People who live in grass houses shouldn't stow thrones"). Generally the proverb parody seems to mock the very notion of giving "good advice" in a sententious form, but sometimes (as in "An ounce of contraception is worth a pound of cure") the old reliable advice is simply updated and rephrased.

The specific meanings and functions of particular proverbs should always be determined within the individual contexts where the sayings occur. Something like "Apple pie without some cheese is like a kiss without a squeeze" may be used to *justify* one's preference for a food combination, to *request* that particular combination, or to *offer* these foods to a diner. When printed on a restaurant napkin or placemat, the proverb notifies customers that such a food preference may indeed be satisfied here; and when the proverb is alluded to ("I'll have to give you the kiss without the squeeze"), the speaker assumes common knowledge of the food preference and the related saying, but might also be making a flirtatious remark.

Even international relations and political tensions might be better understood, one scholar has suggested, through *pare-miology*—the study of proverbs. The former Soviet premier Nikita S. Khrushchev was inclined to pass judgment on events in terms of proverbs; his belief in peaceful coexistence with the United States, for instance, was once expressed with the Russian proverb "When you live with a goat, you must get used to the bad smell." Other world leaders may quote "old proverbs" of their peoples in order to justify policy or characterize a viewpoint on some international issue. Thus, proverbs and proverbial lore reach from the common folk to the elite political leader, all of whom, to some extent, behave very traditionally when speaking proverbially.

BIBLIOGRAPHIC NOTES

An excellent introduction to the nature and study of proverbs is Margaret M. Bryant's "Proverbs and How to Collect Them," *PADS* no. 4 (1954), a handbook prepared for the collectors in the (now defunct?) ADS project to compile a *Dictionary of American Proverbs*. It is instructive to compare Archer Taylor's older survey, "Problems in the Study of Proverbs," *JAF* 47 (1934): 1–21, with his new foreword to the second edition of his 1931 classic, *The Proverb* (Hatboro, Pa.: Folklore Associates, 1962). Taylor, the chief American authority on proverbs, also outlined "The Study of Proverbs" in *Proverbium* no. 1 (1965): 1–10. This bulletin was distributed free by the Society of Finnish Literature to libraries, institutes, and active proverb scholars until no. 25 (1975). *Proverbium* was revived as a yearbook of paremiological research in 1984, published by the Ohio State University. Archer Taylor's other contributions to the original *Proverbium* included "The Collection and Study of Proverbs" in no. 8 (1967): 161–76, and "Method in the History and Interpretation of a Proverb" in no. 10 (1968): 235–38 (repr. in *Readings in American Folklore*, pp. 263–66). The fifteenth number of *Proverbium* (1970) was "Essays in Honor of Archer Taylor on his Eightieth Birthday" with a bibliography of Taylor's writings on proverbial lore. *Selected Writings on Proverbs by Archer Taylor* (*FFC* 216 [1975]) was edited by Wolfgang Mieder, editor of the new *Proverbium*.

The basic American proverb dictionary is Archer Taylor and Bartlett Jere Whiting's *A Dictionary of American Proverbs and Proverbial Phrases, 1820–1880* (Cambridge, Mass.: Harvard University Press, 1958); the introduction to this work is very useful, and the reference bibliography includes all of the important American collections in book or periodical form at the time of publication. Three inclusive state collections are B. J. Whiting's "Proverbs and Proverbial Sayings," in *The Frank C. Brown Collection of North Carolina Folklore*, vol. I (Durham, N.C.: Duke University Press, 1952), pp. 331–501; Jan Harold Brunvand's *Proverbs and Proverbial Phrases from Indiana Books Published before 1890*, Indiana University Folklore Series no. 15 (Bloomington, 1961); and Frances M. Barbour's *Proverbs and Proverbial Phrases of Illinois* (Carbondale and Edwardsville: Southern Illinois University Press, 1965). The bibliographies in these works may now be supplemented with F. A. DeCaro and W. K. McNeil's *American Proverb Literature: A Bibliography*, Bibliographic and Special Series no. 6, *Folklore Forum* (1970).

Proverbs circulating in the United States in languages other than English may be found in such journal articles as Rubén Cobos, "New Mexican Spanish Proverbs," *NMFR* 12 (1969–70): 7–11; Anna Mary Boudreux, "Proverbs, Metaphors and Sayings of the Kaplan Area [Vermillion Parish, Louisiana]," *LFM* 3 (April 1970): 16–24; and those in a special issue of *NJF* (vol. 1, no. 1) published in 1976. (The latter includes Polish, Italian, Hungarian, Gaelic, German, and Russian examples.)

In "The Proverbial Three Wise Monkeys," *MJLF* 7 (1981): 5–38, Wolfgang Mieder traces a familiar saying, often illustrated ("See no evil, hear no evil, speak no evil"), to its apparent Japanese source and through its Western circulation since at least the 1920s.

The only book-length collection of proverbial comparisons is Archer Taylor's *Proverbial Comparisons and Similes from California*, Folklore Studies no. 3 (Berkeley, 1954). More California comparisons are printed in *WF* 17 (1958): 12–20. James N. Tidwell discusses the special language of American proverbial comparisons in "Adam's Off Ox: A Study in the Exactness of the Inexact," *JAF* 66 (1953): 291–94; and in "Folk Comparisons from Colorado," *WF* 35 (1976): 175–208, Cathy M. Orr presents a computer-aided study of some 4,500 items coded by age and sex.

C. Grant Loomis gathered various miscellaneous kinds of nineteenth-century proverbial sayings in three articles in *Western Folklore*: Wellerisms and Yankeeisms are in *WF* 8 (1949): 1–21; epigrams and perverted proverbs in *WF* 8 (1949), 348–57; and such types as definitions, literal clichés, naming, and occupational punning are in *WF* 9 (1950): 147–52. Wayland D. Hand lists more perverted proverbs in *WF* 27 (1968): 263–64: "Familiarity breeds attempt," "A stitch in time gathers no moss," and so forth. In Charles Clay Doyle's "Title-Author Jokes, Now and Long Ago," *JAF* 86 (1973): 52–54, this minor proverbial genre is related to a mid–seventeenth-century English fashion for book-title jokes. The same author comments on "Sarcastic Interrogative Affirmations and Negatives ['Is the Pope a Catholic?' or 'Does a chicken have lips?'],'' in *MJLF* 1 (1975): 33–34, and in *Maledicta* 1 (1977): 77–82.

Besides sources of proverbs described in Taylor's *The Proverb*, Frances M. Barbour gave examples of three more in *MF* 13 (1963): 97–100; these are from songs (i.e., "Babes in the Woods"), from echoes of other proverbs (i.e., "easy as falling off a diet"), and from advertising (i.e., "good to the last drop"). C. Grant Loomis discussed other "Proverbs in Business" in *WF* 23 (1964): 91–94. In *Names* 6 (1958): 51–54, Archer Taylor concluded that the phrase "Tom, Dick, and Harry" was an Americanism of the early nineteenth century based upon antecedents reaching back three centuries; later, however, he found the same expression in earlier sources from England.

The relationships of proverbs to poetry are analyzed in detail by S. J. Sackett in "Poetry and Folklore: Some Points of Affinity," *JAF* 77 (1964): 143–53. B. J. Whiting extracted the proverbial material from the popular ballads for an article in *JAF* 47 (1934): 22–44. The unraveling of the background of "Ten Thousand Swedes" was accomplished by the Norwegian-American sociologist Peter A. Munch, who published his findings in *MF* 10 (1960): 61–69.

Two good reference works for tracing English proverbs are G. L. Apperson's *English Proverbs and Proverbial Phrases: A Historical Dictionary* (London: J. M. Dent, 1929; repr. Detroit: Gale Research Co., 1969) and W. G. Smith and J. E. Heseltine's *The Oxford Dictionary of English Proverbs* (Oxford, England: Oxford University Press, 1935, 3d ed. rev. by F. P. Wilson, 1970). S. G. Champion's *Racial Proverbs* (London: Routledge, 1938; rev. 1950) is perhaps the most reliable of several similar compilations of proverbs from many lands to be found in most large libraries.

On proverbs in literature, see Wolfgang Mieder, "The Essence of Literary Proverb Studies," *NYFQ* 30 (1974): 66–76 (also published in *Proverbium* no. 23 [1974]: 888–94). Mieder surveyed "The Proverb and Anglo-American Literature" in *SFQ* 38 (1974): 49–62. Four good individual studies are Stuart A. Gallacher's "Franklin's *Way to Wealth*: A Florilegium of Proverbs and Wise Sayings," *JEGP* 48 (1949): 229–51; Warren S. Walker's "Proverbs in the Novels of James Fenimore Cooper," *MF* 3 (1953): 99–107; J. Russell Reaver's "Emerson's Use of Proverbs," *SFQ* 27 (1963): 280–99; and Joseph Moldenhauer's "The Rhetorical Function of Proverbs in *Walden*," *JAF* 80 (1967): 151–59.

Structural analysis of proverbs was suggested by Alan Dundes in *MF* 12 (1962): 31–38, in a review of *Trends in Content Analysis* (1959), ed. Ithiel de Sola Pool. Another approach was taken by G. B. Milner in "Quadripartite Structures," *Proverbium* no. 14 (1969): 379–83; Dundes subsequently reconsidered the matter and expanded upon his own proposal in "On the Structure of the Proverb," *Proverbium* no. 25 (1975): 961–73, repr. in *Analytic Essays in Folklore*, pp. 103–18.

The majority of past studies of proverbs by literary folklorists have been collections or source searches, an exception that deals with functions being Joseph Raymond's "Tensions in Proverbs: More Light on International Understanding," in *WF* 15 (1956): 153–58. Representative of the functional or communications approach taken by some anthropological folklorists is E. Ojo Arewa and Alan Dundes's "Proverbs and the Ethnography of Speaking Folklore," in *AA* 66 (1964): 70–85. Recent studies with more attention paid to the contexts of proverbs' uses and meanings are Richard Bauman and Neil McCabe's "Proverbs in an LSD Cult," *JAF* 83 (1970): 318–24; James P. Leary's " 'The Land Won't Burn': An Esoteric American Proverb and Its Significance," *MJLF* 1 (1975): 27–32; and Rosan A. Jordan's "Five Proverbs [Mexican-American ones] in Context," *MJLF* 8 (1982): 109–15.

In an essay entitled "The Use of Proverbs in Psychological Testing," *JFI* 15 (1978): 45–55, Wolfgang Mieder provides a bibliography of forty-nine items, discusses how proverbs have been used in this way, outlines hazards of such uses, and calls for better communication between folklorists and psychologists in testing. In "Proverbial Speech in the Air," *MJLF* 7 (1981): 39–48, Robert A. Georges draws on examples of proverbial speech overheard during a cross-country airplane trip to illustrate persuasive uses of proverbs in a conversational context.

Alan Dundes's discussion of the proverb "Seeing is believing" (1972), reprinted in *Interpreting Folklore* (pp. 86–92), stresses the apparent primacy of sight data in American world view as revealed in traditional speech patterns. However, Simon J. Bronner disputes the point in an essay entitled from the traditional completion of the proverb " . . . Feeling's the Truth," *TFSB* 48 (1982): 117–24; the sense of touch, he says, is sometimes primary. Bronner presents the theoretical background for his argument in "The Haptic Experience of Culture," published in *Anthropos* 77 (1982): 351–62.

6
Riddles and Other Verbal Puzzles

Folk riddles are traditional questions with unexpected (albeit traditional) answers—verbal puzzles (although some involve writing) that demonstrate the cleverness of the questioner and challenge the wit of the audience. The practice of riddling can be traced to the dawn of literary expression; it is referred to in the most ancient Oriental and Sanskrit writings, in the Bible, in classical legends and myths, in European folktales and ballads, and in some of the earliest manuscripts of medieval literature. Compilations of riddles were among the first printed books in the Middle Ages, and books of literary riddles remained popular well into the Renaissance. Since the beginning of professional interest in folklore in the nineteenth century, massive collections of folk riddles have been published in most European countries and in many other countries. Riddles have been found in the native cultures of most peoples, including the American Indians, who were once thought to possess only a few that had been borrowed from Europeans.

Not only is riddling widespread, but the variety of actual riddles in collections is dazzling. Yet the basic forms that riddles take seem to be relatively limited, and many individual riddles have persisted with little essential change for centuries. A striking example is the "Sphinx riddle" from the Greek legend of Oedipus—"What walks on four legs in the morning, on two in the afternoon, and on three in the evening?" This riddle, with the answer "man" (who crawls in infancy, walks upright in adulthood, and leans on a cane when aged), is only the best-known of many with the same answer based on related puzzling questions that are common in Western tradition and scattered through the rest of the world. Literature has helped to keep the riddle of the Sphinx alive from the beginning, but its oral circulation has never ceased. It has been found in English in Great Britain, Canada, the United States, and the West Indies. One collected from a fifteen-year-old schoolgirl in Scotland is rendered in rhyme without the metaphor of times of day, but with the added detail of man's decreasing vigor; yet it is still clearly recognizable as the same enigma that challenged Oedipus on the outskirts of Thebes:

> Walks on four feet,
> On two feet, on three.
> The more feet it walks on,
> The weaker it be.

Studies of riddles date from the late 1800s in European languages and emerged in English with the pioneering work of the American folklorist Archer Taylor, which began in the 1930s and culminated in the publication of his *English Riddles from Oral Tradition* in 1951. Taylor gave us the basic bibliography and methodology for riddle studies as well as the important distinctions between the "true riddle" and others, and an ingenious scheme of classification.

True Riddles

The **true riddle** is essentially a comparison between the unstated answer and something else that is described in the question. This description usually has two parts, a general and straightforward part, such as "Little Nancy Eddicote, in a white petticoat, and a red nose," followed by a more precise, but apparently contradictory part: "The longer she stands, the shorter she grows." The answer to this common English riddle is "a candle," and the riddle can be regarded as a *comparison* of a candle to a little girl or a *description* of a candle in terms of a little girl.

An American variant of this riddle adds a further contradictory detail but retains the same descriptive method:

> Little Miss Etticoat in a white petticoat
> Shorter and shorter she grows.
> Oh, how she suffers while we with the snuffers
> Are nipping her little red nose.

These two basic parts of a true riddle were called by Taylor the *description* and the *block,* and they may be observed in a great variety of texts. Many riddles have only these two parts plus an answer, as in the following:

> Robbers came to our house and we were all in; [description]
> the house leapt out the windows and we were all taken. [block]
> Answer: Fish in a net (The "house" is the water; "windows" are holes in the net).

It is possible for a true riddle to have fully six distinct parts which may be designated this way:

Introduction	As I went over London Bridge
Description	I met my sister
Name	Jenny;
Block	I broke her neck and drank her blood And left her standing empty.
Close	Answer me if you can.
Answer	A bottle of wine.

Few riddles collected from oral tradition, however, have all six parts.

Attempts to classify true riddles by their answers long frustrated folklorists because the answers may vary considerably from text to text, and quite different riddles may have the same answers. Instead, Archer Taylor's system classifies riddles by the nature of the item described in the question, using seven general categories:

    I.   Comparisons to a Living Creature (e.g., the Sphinx riddle)

II.   Comparisons to an Animal
III. Comparisons to Several Animals
IV.   Comparisons to a Person (e.g., "Little Nancy
      Eddicote," "Sister Jenny," and "Humpty
      Dumpty")
V.   Comparisons to Several Persons (e.g., the
      fish-in-a-net riddle)
VI.   Comparisons to Plants
VII. Comparisons to Things
            The man who made the coat didn't use
                it; the man who bought it didn't
                want it; the man who used it
                didn't know it.—A coffin.

There are four further categories in Taylor's classification in which the principle behind the puzzling question is an enumeration of details rather than the description of a recognizable item. With examples for each, these are:

VIII. Enumerations of Comparisons
            Round as a hoop, deep as a cup; all the
                king's oxen can't pull it up.—A well.
IX.   Enumerations in Terms of Form or of Form
       and Function
            Patch on patch and has no seams.—
                Cabbage. [form]
X.   Enumerations in Terms of Color
            Throw it up green, comes down red.—
                A watermelon.
XI.   Enumerations in Terms of Acts
            With what vegetable do you throw
                away the outside, then cook the inside,
                then eat the outside, and throw the
                inside away?—Corn.
            I went into the woods and got it; I set
                me down on a log to look for it; and
                then I brought it along home with me
                because I couldn't find it.—A splinter.

Most English true riddles are very old, and their counterparts may be found somewhere among Taylor's 1,749 individual types. The following, for example, learned in San Francisco about 1932 and collected in Idaho in 1964, is Taylor's riddle type number 1,727 (category XI), first reported from the British West Indies in 1921:

> What does a man love more than life, hate more than death or mortal strife? That which contented men desire, the poor have, the rich require. The miser spends, the spendthrift saves, and all men carry to their graves?—Nothing!

Occasionally a new riddle will be invented, such as the following:

> What is round and has squares [the *block*]; it lived once upon a time. You see it every day, and most every home has it?—A roll of toilet paper.

One riddle based on comparisons (category VIII) refers to a unique American animal, and so far has been reported only from the state of Mississippi:

> Hands like a man, ears like a bat, tail like a rat; guess what it is and I'll give you my hat.—An opossum.

Two special categories, sometimes included with true riddles, should be distinguished. The first of these, the **neck riddle,** is so called because it is usually attributed in folktales and legends to a condemned prisoner who to "save his neck" must pose a riddle that no one can solve. His riddle refers to a scene which he, and he only, has observed and can identify from the cryptic description given. Samson's riddle in the Bible (Judges 14:14) is a neck riddle of this kind:

> Out of the eater came forth meat, and out of the strong came forth sweetness.—Honeycomb in a lion's carcass.

One American counterpart of this "living in the dead" neck riddle is this one from Texas:

> Six set and seven sprung, from the dead they live and run.
> What is it?—One quail that hatched six quails out of a dead
> cow's skull.

One of the most common story riddles in the United States concerns a desperate prisoner—a Confederate captive during the Civil War, according to an Ozark version—who declared:

> Corn et corn in a high oak tree, if you guess this riddle, you
> kin hang me!

The Union captors, however, could not guess that his name was Corn and that he had been eating parched corn while sitting up in a tree before being captured. (In other versions, his name is Horn, he had gnawed on a cow's horn, and his riddle begins "Horn ate horn. . . .") In another favorite American story riddle, the prisoner has had his dog named "Love" killed; its skin is made into leather for use in a glove, a shoe, and part of his saddle. The riddle he poses is "On love I ride, on love I stand, and I hold love in my right hand."

There are two other story-riddle types, both involving tricky language—the first kind substituting the part for the whole (synechdoche) and the second using "queer words" or nonsense syllables that approximate the sound of the answer. An example of the first, from Southern black tradition:

> Two legs sat on three legs; up jumped four legs and grabs one
> leg.—Man sitting on a three-legged stool; up jumps a dog and
> grabs ham on the table.

And a version of the second, from Indiana:

> My mother went over to your mother's house to borrow a
> wim babble, wam bobble, a hind body, fore body, whirl-a-kin
> nibble.—A spinning wheel.

The **pretended obscene** riddle is another special subtype, often of the comparative or enumerative variety. Here the description suggests something risqué, usually sexual, but the correct answer is quite tame. For example, the question "What is a man called who marries another man?" has the bland solution "a minister." Other pretended obscene riddles seem to be describing sexual intercourse, but actually refer to scrubbing clothes, chewing gum, picking fruit, making a bed, and other innocuous acts. Compare, too, this attempt to lead a listener into speaking a taboo word: "What has four letters, starts with an *F,* gives old folks a backache and young folks pleasure?"—A Ford (car).

A variation of the old "Ford" riddle, above, usually appears with three other pretended obscene riddles on membership cards for the so-called "Turtle Club," an American riddling mock organization that is popular in the military services. Knowledge of the "right" answers is required of members to riddles such as these: "What is a four letter word ending in K that means the same as intercourse?" (Answer: talk); "What is it a man can do standing up, a woman sitting down, and a dog on three legs?" (Answer: shake hands). Once a new Turtle is initiated into the mysteries of such riddles, he or she is given a personal membership card signed by the poser of the riddles and then required to answer the question "Are you a Turtle?" with the invariable answer "You bet your sweet ass I am." Failure to give the proper answer requires the member asked to provide a beverage of choice to the asker. The whole routine of asking the riddles, issuing the cards, and quizzing others for their membership is often performed in bars.

In all of the riddle types presented thus far, the facts for answering are well contained within the questions themselves; when one understands how true riddles operate, he or she can learn to solve them. But there are many traditional riddles that do not follow such a predictable pattern, and they can only be solved by means of special knowledge or wit. These can be placed in several distinct categories.

Riddling Questions and Other Nonpredictable Riddles

The **riddling question** (or "clever question") is the general type of nonpredictable riddle. The "Riddle Song" of British balladry is made up of these: the first question in it, "How can there be a cherry without a stone?" is answered, "A cherry when it's

blooming, it has no stone." There are countless other such riddles: "How deep is the ocean?—A stone's throw"; "How many
balls of string to reach the moon?—One, if it's long enough";
"Where was Moses when the lights went out?—In the dark";
"What do they call little black cats in England?—Kittens";
"What lives in a stable, eats oats, and can see as well out of one
end as the other?—A blind horse"; and so forth. One riddling
question is answered with a sound rather than a word: "What
makes a horse go, a dog come, and a man stay?" For the answer,
the sound of a kiss is made.

The **conundrum** is a riddle based on punning or other wordplay. The pun may occur in the answer ("When is a ship not a
ship?—When it's *afloat*") or in the question ("What has four
wheels and *flies*?—A garbage truck"). Often the conundrum
asks why one thing is like another—"Why is a thief in the attic
like an honest man?—Because he's above doing a mean thing."
Some conundrums develop double or larger multiple puns:
"What's the difference between a ball and a prince?—One is
thrown in the air; the other is heir to the throne." Or "What
would happen, geographically speaking, if a black waiter
dropped a roasted turkey?—The fall of Turkey, the destruction
of China, the overthrow of Greece, and the humiliation of
Africa." A few that form a spoonerism* in the answer may be
termed *spooneristic conundrums:* "What's the difference between the clown at the circus and a guilty conscience?—One is
a cute amuser, the other a mute accuser."

The general terms **puzzle** or **problem** may be applied to a host
of traditional questions involving special biblical, arithmetical,
genealogical, or practical knowledge for an answer. These may
be posed seriously for an attempted solution, or they may be
completely whimsical. For example, there are serious arithmetical riddles involving weights and measures, ages, or monetary
figures that can be solved by an acute mind, but the following
Ozark text is pure whimsy:

> If it takes a peckerwood eight months t' peck a four-inch hole
> in a gum-tree that would make 250 bundles o' good shingles,

---

* Named for Rev. W. A. Spooner (1844–1930), an Englishman famous for unintentionally interchanging the sounds of words in sayings.

how long would it take a wooden-legged grasshopper t' kick
all th' seeds out'n a dill pickle seven inches long an' an inch
and a quarter thick?—There ain't no answer, you fool!

Some problems involve the practical enigmas of transporting in-
compatible creatures across a river in a small boat, or picking a
matched set of socks out of a drawer in the dark, and the like.
But one is a sort of anagrammatic problem, requiring the solver
to find four letters that will make five words to fill the blanks:

> An _____ old woman of _____ intent
> Put on her _____ and away she went.
> "Come _____ my son," she was heard to say.
> "We'll _____ on the fat of the land today."

(As soon as it is recognized that the fourth line of the verse incorporates a variation of a familiar proverbial phrase, the puzzle
is easily solved.)

Some traditional questions are really not intended to be answered at all; they are merely **catch questions,** designed to em-
barrass the unwary. A boy asks a girl, "Do you know what
virgins eat for breakfast?" and all she need do is respond "No,
what?" to bring his laugh and her blush. A child asks, "What
comes after seventy-five?" and if one is gullible enough to say
"seventy-six," he gleefully shouts, "That's the spirit!" In a more
elaborate catch someone asks, "What's the first sign of insanity?—Hair growing on your knuckles." Then, as the dupe
sneaks a look at the back of his hand, the riddler asks, "What's
the second sign?—Looking for it."

A prolific modern form of riddle, usually just termed a "joke"
in folk tradition, is the **riddle-joke.** Riddle-jokes come and go in
fad cycles, usually centering on a single theme while they last.
Popular in the 1950s were the so-called *moron jokes* with their
outrageous puns: "Why did the little moron cut a hole in the
rug?—To see the floorshow." Another favorite cycle dwelt
upon foods—grapes, pickles, bananas, etc. ("What's purple and
conquers continents?—Alexander the Grape"; "What's green,
bumpy, and floats around in the ocean?—Moby Pickle.") A
Mormon variant of the fruit joke asks, "What's purple and has
twenty-seven wives?—Brigham Plum." Dialogue riddle-jokes
called *knock-knocks* were the rage for a while, and then it was

elephant jokes, sick jokes (macabre humor), *wind-up–doll jokes, celebrity riddle-jokes, AIDS jokes, Ethiopian jokes,* and on and on.

Numskull riddle-jokes often center on particular ethnic or regional groups ("Aggies," "Newfies," "Italians," etc.), but huge cycles such as the light-bulb jokes may be aimed ("beamed?") at just about anybody: "How many psychologists does it take to change a light bulb?—Just one, but the light bulb has to *want* to change." An even larger group of recent riddle-jokes had the Polish-American as its target: "How do you tell the groom at a Polish wedding?—He's the one with a clean bowling shirt on." Then with the election of a pope who came from Poland, we began to hear Polish-pope riddle-jokes: "Did you hear about the new pope's first miracle?—He made a blind man lame." And "Did you hear about his second one?—He bowled a three-oh-five." Yet another joke on this theme claimed that the Polish pope built a tavern behind the Vatican palace so he would have a place to cash his paycheck. A few Polish jokes (which most people seem to tell without any specific denigration of Polish-Americans in mind) have some narrative content, and some are based on a photocopied sketch or diagram, such as the "Polish Computer System" for "output processing," an elaborate drawing that folds down to a picture of a simple toilet. At this point the riddle-joke form has overlapped both with folktale and Xerox lore.

Non-Oral Riddles

Two special kinds of riddles are "non-oral," involving as they do either gestures or drawings. The **non-oral riddle** itself (or sometimes "facial droodle") has only the question "What's this?" accompanied by a gesture, such as waving the hand and snapping fingers (a butterfly with hiccups), or holding fingertips of both hands together palm to palm with fingers flexing (a spider doing pushups on a mirror). The *droodle,* which was briefly syndicated in many newspapers but was initially derived from folklore, asks "What's this?" about sketches like these:

—A man
practicing his
trombone in a
telephone booth.

—A girl with a pony
tail in a bubble bath
practicing the trumpet.

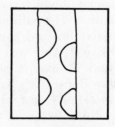

—A bear climbing
a tree. (Variant:
a giraffe's neck.)

As in most oral riddles, the droodle basically involves seeing
something from an unusual point of view. The persistence of
this principle in droodle art across a span of some three hundred
years is illustrated in the two examples below, the right-hand
one from an Italian source of 1678, and the left-hand one from
the United States about 1950:

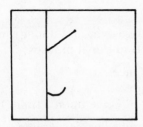

—A soldier and his dog,
just disappearing around
a corner.

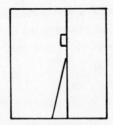

—A blind beggar with cup
and stick, just coming around
a corner.

The complicated riddlelike *question guessing* game that John F. Kennedy's aides reportedly played during dull moments in the 1960 presidential campaign is also based on taking an unusual viewpoint. Here the quizzer gave an *answer* and the players tried to find a question to match. To the answer "9–W," for example, the proper question was "Is your name spelled with a 'V,' Mr. Wagner?" The answer—"Nein, 'W.'"

There are several other types of traditional verbal puzzles and tricks, some of which require a written rather than purely oral presentation. The **palindrome** is a sentence that reads the same backward or forward, such as "Madam, I'm Adam" (what Adam said to Eve), "Able was I ere I saw Elba" (referring to Napoleon), and "A man, a plan, a canal: Panama" (an allusion to Theodore Roosevelt's backing for the Panama Canal). The **all-letter** sentence is just what its name implies—a sentence containing all the letters of the alphabet, such as "William F. Jex quickly caught seven dozen Republicans." Such sentences are used by teletype operators and typewriter repairmen to test their equipment, and many people immediately rap out "The quick brown fox jumps over the lazy dog" when trying out a new typewriter. A sentence that contains all the letters only once each is "J. Q. Vandz struck my big fox whelp." The **over-and-under sentence** depends upon written position for its meaning; the following allegedly used as an address, is translated "John Underwood, Andover, Massachusetts."

> Wood
> John
> Mass.

Analogous to this are the following two over-and-under renderings (and there are many more) of traditional phrases:

> Well   Once
> My word   4 P.M.
> ("Well upon my word")   ("Once upon a time")

Other written puzzles employ different positional clues:

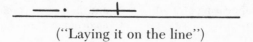

("Laying it on the line")

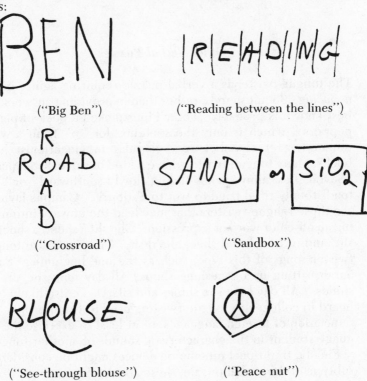

("Grapes in season")

Such graphic and orthographic puzzles have proliferated in recent years (or perhaps folklorists have just begun to notice them). Examples like the following are sometimes set up on sheets labeled "Entrance Exam" or "Brain Teasers" containing about one or two dozen such enigmas, but seldom the explanations:

("Big Ben")   ("Reading between the lines")

("Crossroad")   ("Sandbox")

("See-through blouse")   ("Peace nut")

Another variety of puzzle/test, often duplicated, involves cryptic letter-and-number statements like these:

26 = L. of the A. (26 letters of the alphabet)
88 = P. K. (88 piano keys)

200 = D. for P. G. (200 dollars for passing Go [in
    Monopoly])
  8 = S. on a S. S. ([you figure it out])

One very curious traditional guessing item is based on the following numbers and letters written on a sheet of paper: 3909
Ǝ H T. The question is then asked, "If this many nuns went to
Rome, who would be the happiest?" The answer is discovered
by holding the paper up to the light backward and reading
through it—"The Pope."

Other Verbal Puzzles

The **tongue-twister** is a verbal puzzle requiring agility in *pro-
nouncing* difficult sounds, rather than in providing answers. The
best known is probably "Peter Piper picked a peck of pickled
peppers," which is only the sentence for "p" from a whole
tongue-twister alphabet once popular in elocutionist handbooks. Many tongue-twisters have a kind of surrealistic quality:
"Seven slick slimy snakes sliding slowly southward" or "Two
toads totally tired tried to trot to Tadbury." Campus favorites
are those tongue-twisters that may lead the unwary into utter-
ing an off-color word or expression: "She slit a sheet, a sheet she
slit, and in her slitted sheet she'd sit." There are also tongue-
twister songs of this type, such as the one beginning "Sarah,
Sarah, sitting in a shoeshine shop. / All day long she sits and
shines, / All day long she shines and sits. . . ." Also likely to be
heard in college are tongue-twisters used to teach proper pronunciation of foreign languages, or at least to exercise the language student in the characteristic sounds of another tongue.

Finally, traditional **mnemonic devices** might be considered a
subtype of the verbal puzzle; these are rhymes, sayings, words,
or other expressions intended to aid the memory. There are
mnemonic devices for remembering spellings, geographic facts,
scientific principles, navigational rules, and many other matters.
Some are very simple, such as the acronym "Roy G. Biv" for remembering the colors in the spectrum in order (*R*ed, *O*range,

Yellow, Green, Blue, Indigo, and Violet), while some are more complex, as in the sentences used for remembering the twelve cranial nerves from "olfactory" to "hypoglossal" ("*On old Olympus' towering tops, a Finn and German viewed some hops*") or for the scale of hardness for geological analysis from "talc" to "diamond" ("*Troy girls can flirt and other queer things can do*").

Analyzing Riddles

Many English and American riddles of all varieties have been collected and published, providing rich possibilities for analysis. One interesting observation that can be verified simply from the index of answers in Taylor's classification is that the subjects of true riddles tend to come from the world of a farm woman looking out of her kitchen window; thus, the most characteristic answers to riddles are berries, fruits, garden vegetables, the stars and the moon, the well, a needle and thread, cooking utensils, clothing, and the like. Furthermore, in common with many proverbs, riddles are essentially metaphorical, and they exhibit other stylistic features of poetry, especially meter and rhyme. Sometimes, too, archaic words and expressions are preserved in riddle texts.

The structure of true riddles interested folklorists Robert Georges and Alan Dundes, who pointed out that the same basic "topic-comment" form exists in them as in some proverbs. They defined the riddle structurally as containing "one or more descriptive elements . . . the referent [to which] is to be guessed." They determined that the description may be either *oppositional* or *nonoppositional* (that is, may or may not contain the "block" element), and either *literal* or *metaphorical*. Riddles with blocks (oppositional) are almost always metaphorical and may exhibit one of three kinds of opposition: *antithetical* (only one part can be true); *privational* (the second part denies a logical or natural attribute of the first); or *causal* (the first part consists of an action that is denied by the second). To this Roger Abrahams has added the identification of three techniques employed in riddling: *incomplete detail* (not enough information provided for the parts to fit together clearly); *too much detail* (inconsequential details that bury the important traits); and *false Gestalt* (commonly leading to off-color answers in catches and pretended obscene riddles). These approaches (and others have extended them) help to tie up loose ends of earlier definitions, furnishing more concrete and specific descriptions of what riddles really are.

The symbolism and functions of riddles in folk tradition raise further questions. Do riddles mask meanings not immediately apparent in their literal wording? How can these meanings be discovered? What roles do riddles play in folk groups as entertainment and as educational devices? Are riddles primarily children's folklore, and how long do *they* circulate them? What are the favorite times for asking riddles, besides parties, dances, "bees," wakes, and other social occasions during which they have previously been observed? Is riddling usually engaged in as a "concert" (one riddler performing for the others) or as a "contest" (riddlers taking turns and matching question for question)? What are the usual practices of guessing riddles? Do these matters all vary from region to region, family to family, period to period? Do the uses of riddles in folktales and ballads reflect their earlier functions in courtship, initiation, legal processes, and the like?

One study of the riddles included in British and Anglo-American traditional ballads concluded that there is thinly veiled sexual symbolism in all of them. The sequence of answers in the widely known "Riddle Song," for instance—cherry, egg, ring, baby—suggests impregnation, an interpretation also supported by both context and variants of the ballad. Another pioneering field study carried out in the United States and Scotland resulted in the first systematic observations of riddling customs in these areas. While riddles in American tradition tended to occur only incidentally, the riddle session or contest was still occasionally discovered in Scotland; in one such session the collector recorded sixty-five riddles from five persons during an evening. Such studies begin to answer questions about riddles and riddling, and they point the way for many other possible analyses of these eternally fascinating enigmas. The continued popularity of trivia books and games and of TV quiz and game shows proves how durable the charm is of trying to solve (or guess at) the puzzling problems and queries posed by others.

BIBLIOGRAPHIC NOTES

Archer Taylor surveyed "Problems in the Study of Riddles" in *SFQ* 2 (1938): 1–9; and he compiled "A Bibliography of Riddles" in *FFC* no. 126 in 1939. His *English Riddles from Oral Tradition* was published in 1951 (Berkeley: University of California Press) and established the basic corpus of English and Anglo-American true riddles. A succinct essay on the types of riddles is Taylor's "The Riddle" in *CFQ* 2 (1943): 129–47. A similar statement is his "The Riddle as a Primary Form," published in *Folklore in Action*, pp. 200–7. An article in a popular vein that incorporates folkloristic concepts is Duncan Emrich's "Riddle Me, Riddle Me, What Is That?" in *American Heritage* 7 (Dec. 1955): 116–19.

In recent years several American folklorists have explored new definitions and analytic approaches for riddles. The special issue "Riddles and Riddling" of *JAF* 89, no. 352 (1976), edited by Elli Köngäs-Maranda, contains six articles, among them an important study of riddles in context by David Evans (166–88). Thomas A. Green and W. J. Pepicello proposed a strictly linguistic approach in "The Folk Riddle: A Redefinition of Terms," *WF* 38 (1979): 3–20, one that Pepicello pursued further in "Linguistic Strategies in Riddling," *WF* 39 (1980): 1–16.

The supposed nonexistence of American Indian riddles was challenged in three articles in *JAF*: Archer Taylor's "American Indian Riddles" in 57 (1944): 1–15; Charles T. Scott's "New Evidence of American Indian Riddles" in 76 (1963): 236–41; and David P. McAllester's "Riddles and Other Verbal Play among the Comanches," in 77 (1964): 251–57.

The riddles themselves from collections in English up to 1951 are all included in Archer Taylor's classification, but three representative articles from mid-America might be listed for reference to their original publication with notes. Vance Randolph and Isabel Spradley published "Ozark Mountain Riddles" in *JAF* 47 (1934): 81–89; Randolph and Taylor published more "Riddles in the Ozarks" in *SFQ* 7 (1944): 1–10; and Paul G. Brewster published "Riddles from Southern Indiana" in *SFQ* 3 (1939): 93–105. A group of 143 items of riddling lore, including 48 true riddles, from the state of Mississippi was analyzed in George W. Boswell's "Riddles in the WPA-collected Folklore Archives," *MFR* 3 (1969): 33–52.

Various riddle types are often intermixed in the published collections such as Catherine Harris Ainsworth's "Black and White and Said

All Over" in *SFQ* 26 (1962): 263–95, containing 535 miscellaneous texts collected by mail from ninth-grade and tenth-grade students in seven states. The conundrum alluded to in Ainsworth's title is discussed in many different contexts, variants, and offshoots in Mac E. Barrick's note "The Newspaper Riddle Joke," *JAF* 87 (1974): 253–57. Another large riddle collection from schoolchildren is Meryl Weiner's "The Riddle Repertoire of a Massachusetts Elementary School," *FF* 3 (1970): 7–38, in which about 260 students from first through fifth grades contributed examples.

Roger D. Abrahams's monograph "Between the Living and the Dead," *FFC* 225 (1980), the completion of a work begun by Archer Taylor, contains a survey and analysis of neck riddles with a catalogue of 423 types arranged in the three subcategories described in this chapter. The quoted examples come from this study as well.

Two articles explored the dynamics of the so-called "pretended obscene" riddles with particular attention paid to what a culture senses as being obscene and how a particular folklore genre operates with these assumptions: see Jan Hullum, "The 'Catch' Riddle: Perspectives from Goffman and Metafolklore," *Folklore Annual* 4–5 (1972–73), 52–59; and Waln K. Brown, "Cognitive Ambiguity and the 'Pretended Obscene Riddle,' " *KF* 18 (1973): 89–101. Use of pretended obscene riddles in a prank or initiation context is discussed by Richard Bauman in "The Turtles: An American Riddling Institution," *WF* 29 (1970): 21–25.

Conundrums from nineteenth-century American newspapers were compiled by Archer Taylor in *CFQ* 5 (1946): 273–76, and by C. Grant Loomis in *WF* 8 (1949): 235–47. Donald M. Hines culled 230 examples from regional newspaper files in "Rare Blooms from a Rude Land: Frontier Riddles from the Inland Pacific Northwest," *IF* 6 (1973): 205–40; he discovered only 19 that were "true riddles."

In "American Numskull Tales: The Polack Joke," *WF* 26 (1967): 183–86, Roger L. Welsch directed folklorists' attention to a new popular cycle of ethnic riddle-jokes. In 1969 William M. Clements published *The Types of the Polack Joke*, a comprehensive catalogue, as Bibliographical and Special Series no. 3 of *FF* (a supplementary list appeared in *FF* 4 [1971] : 19–29). Mac E. Barrick compared "Racial Riddles and the Polack Joke," in *KFQ* 15 (1970): 3–15; and Kathleen A. Preston and Michael J. Preston discussed the "Visual Polack Joke," in *JAF* 86 (1973): 175–77.

Reports on two large collections of ethnic riddle-jokes are Michael J. Preston's "A Typescript Ethnic Joke Anthology," *NYF* 1 (1975): 223–34; and Linda T. Humphrey, " 'It Ain't Funny, Buster': The Ethnic Riddle-Joke at Citrus Community College," *SWF* 4 (1980): 20–25, concerning a collection of over 500 individual jokes.

Three articles which concentrate on interpretive analysis of more than one cycle of racial or ethnic joke are Jan Harold Brunvand, "Some Thoughts on the Ethnic-Regional Riddle Jokes," *IF* 3 (1970): 128–142;

Nathan Hurvitz, "Blacks and Jews in American Folklore," *WF* 33 (1974): 301–25; and Alan Dundes, "A Study of Ethnic Slurs: The Jew and the Polack in the United States," *JAF* 84 (1971): 186–203.

Another cycle of numskull jokes in riddle form which may denigrate ethnic minorities is introduced in Judith B. Kerman's "The Light-Bulb Jokes: Americans Look at Social Action Processes," *JAF* 93 (1980): 454–58, and Alan Dundes's "Many Hands Make Light Work, or Caught in the Act of Screwing in Light Bulbs," *WF* 40 (1981): 261–66. Dundes assets that these jokes are essentially about sexual and political impotence. Yet another cycle of numskull/ethnic/riddle-jokes is the subject of Alan Dundes's "Polish Pope Jokes," *JAF* 92 (1979): 219–22, and Lydia Fish's "Is the Pope Polish? Some Notes on the Polack Joke in Transition," *JAF* 93 (1980): 450–54. The pope referred to was elected in October 1978, the first Pole to hold the office and thus the most obvious target for a new round of "Polack" jokes. ("Why does the pope have 'TGIF' embroidered onto his slippers?" "It means 'Toes go in first,' " and so forth.)

The first article in a folklore journal on another recent popular riddle-joke genre was Alan Dundes's "The Elephant Joking Question," *TFSB* 29 (1963): 40–42. More analysis was offered in Roger D. Abrahams's "The Bigger They Are the Harder They Fall," *TFSB* 29 (1963): 94–102. A brief list of examples was printed in *WF* 23 (1964): 198–99, and a gathering of them was made by Mac E. Barrick in "The Shaggy Elephant Riddle," *SFQ* 28 (1964): 266–90. Another large collection was Ed Cray and Marilyn Eisenberg Herzog's "The Absurd Elephant: A Recent Riddle Fad," *WF* 26 (1967): 27–36. Roger D. Abrahams and Alan Dundes offered further interpretive suggestions in "On Elephantasy and Elephanticide," *The Psychoanalytic Review* 56 (1969): 225–41, reprinted in *Analytic Essays in Folklore*, pp. 192–205.

Two folklorists subjected the "sick joke" of the late 1950s to some analysis; Brian Sutton-Smith published " 'Shut Up and Keep Digging': The Cruel Joke Series," *MF* 10 (1960): 11–22; and Roger D. Abrahams published "Ghastly Commands: The Cruel Joke Revisited," *MF* 11 (Winter 1961–62): 235–46. Then as further sick-joke subgenres emerged, folklorists were quick to study them. See Alan Dundes, "The Dead Baby Joke Cycle," *WF* 38 (1979): 145–57; Mac E. Barrick, "The Helen Keller Joke Cycle," *JAF* 93 (1980): 441–49; and Barrick, "Celebrity Sick Jokes," *Maledicta* 6 (1982): 57–62 (Dolly Parton, Natalie Wood, John Belushi, and others). Maurice D. Schmaier discussed "The Doll Joke Pattern in Contemporary American Oral Humor," in *MF* 13 (Winter 1963–64): 205–16. Robin Hirsch also treated this form in an article in *WF* 23 (1964), 107–10.

A small collection largely of arithmetical puzzles gathered by a radio station in Lafayette, Indiana, was annotated by Ray B. Browne for *MF* 11 (1961), 155–60. A page of short written "Verbal Puzzles" appeared in *NCFJ* 23 (1975): 112. Sixteen examples of what some people call "logic problems," short puzzling narratives with cryptic solutions, were published by Danny W. Moore in "The Deductive Riddle: An Adaptation to Modern Society," *NCFJ* 22 (1974): 119–25.

Non-oral riddles were printed in *WF* 17 (1958): 279–80, and *WF* 19 (1960): 132–33. David Bowman asks the questions: "Whatever Happened to Droodles? Whatever happened to Roger Price?" in *JPC* 9 (1975): 20–25. He provides useful information about their popularization in the United States during the early 1950s by Roger Price's publications, but he fails to identify the droodle itself (not the name) as a much older form. Four examples of "pictorial riddles" drawn for amusement by seventeenth-century Italian painters are reproduced as Figure 55 and mentioned on pp. 65–66 in Donald Posner, *Annibale Carracci*, vol. I (London: Phaidon Press, 1971). These were originally published by Carlo Cesare Malvasia in Bologna in 1678. A semiotic analysis of droodles ("visual descriptive riddles") was published by Danielle M. Roemer in *JAF* 95 (1982): 173–99. Other riddles involving writing or drawing are the subjects of articles by Thomas A. Green and W. J. Pepicello, "Sight and Spelling Riddles," *JAF* 93 (1980): 23–34, and Michael J. Preston, "The English Literal Rebus and the Graphic Riddle Tradition," *WF* 41 (1982): 104–38.

Tongue-twisters are sometimes printed as fillers in folklore journals or in general folklore anthologies. One specialized article, however, is Maurice A. Mook's "Tongue Tanglers from Central Pennsylvania," *JAF* 72 (1959): 291–96; the article is followed by a tongue-twister song from collegiate tradition (296–97). Another popular article, by Duncan Emrich, is "The Ancient Game of Tongue-Twisters," *American Heritage* 6 (Feb. 1955): 119–20. A children's book of tongue-twisters, but with a useful bibliography, is Alvin Schwartz's, *A Twister of Twists, a Tangler of Tongues* (Philadelphia and New York: J. B. Lippincott, 1972). An article by Marilyn Jorgensen, "The Tickled, Tangled, Tripped, and Twisted Tongue: A Linguistic Study of Factors Relating to Difficulty in the Performance of Tongue Twisters," *NYF* 7 (1981): 67–81, offers not only a technical analysis, but also some strategies for reciting tongue-twisters correctly. A richly annotated article on mnemonic devices was published by Alan Dundes in *MF* 11 (1961): 139–47.

A structural analysis of true riddles was made by Robert A. Georges and Alan Dundes and published in *JAF* 76 (1963): 111–18, reprinted in *Analytic Essays in Folklore*, pp. 95–102. Dundes and Roger D. Abrahams survey riddles from a structural and typological viewpoint in their chapter "Riddles" in Dorson's textbook *Folklore and Folklife: An Introduction* (Chicago, 1972), pp. 129–43.

J. Barre Toelken examined the riddle ballads in "Riddles Wisely Expounded," *WF* 25 (1966): 1–16. "Riddling Traditions in Northeastern Scotland" were described by Kenneth S. Goldstein in *JAF* 76 (1963): 330–36.

7

Rhymes and Folk Poetry

_____

Rhyme is a basic stylistic device of verbal folklore, and it occurs in many types beside the rhyming proverbs and riddles already mentioned. There are some rhymes in folktales—the dialogues in "The Three Little Pigs" and the giant's threats in "Jack and the Beanstalk" for example. Folk beliefs may be expressed in rhyme, for instance:

> Mole on the neck, trouble by the peck,
> Mole on the face, suffers disgrace.

or the card players' rule:

> Cut 'em thin, sure to win,
> Cut 'em deep, sure to weep.

A traditional rhyme may serve as a characterizing or mnemonic device:

> Low and lazy,
> High and crazy,
> Broad and hazy.

This refers to the Episcopal Church services, "low" (no kneeling, hence "lazy"), "high" (formal and full of symbolism), and "broad" (a "hazy" mixture of low and high). A schoolroom mnemonic rhyme combines information with commentary:

> Ours is not to reason why,
> Just invert and multiply.
> (How to divide by a fraction)

A belief-rhyme that is regarded as having magical power is called a _verbal charm_, the best known being the "Star light, star bright" verse used in wishing on a star. Many charms are intended to affect the transference of some ailment:

> Sty, sty, leave my eye;
> Take the next one passing by.

Other charms may make butter come in a churn, remove warts, stop bleeding in a wound, or drive the rain away to "come again another day." Good advice is sometimes transmitted in a rhyme, such as the following one for hours of sleep:

> Nature needs but five.
> Custom gives thee seven.
> Laziness takes nine,
> And wickedness eleven.

Besides such uses of rhyme in other kinds of folklore, there are numerous independent rhymes, largely circulated by children, that are chanted, whined, sung, shouted, muttered, or otherwise recited as suitable occasions appear. These bits of fluid folklore are highly elusive and have not been systematically collected or arranged on a large scale in the United States; thus, this chapter can only indicate some basic types of folk rhymes and suggest possible subdivisions. In general, there are four major categories of American folk rhymes—*nursery rhymes; rhymes of play, games, and fun* (including "the dozens" or "jiving"); *rhymes of work* and *written traditional rhymes*. A few longer rhymed texts (including epic toasts or "toasties") qualify for the rather vague title *folk poetry*.

Nursery Rhymes

Nursery rhymes, although usually British in origin and often printed in their transmission, still play a role in American oral folklore. Parents may read "Mother Goose" to children out of books, but book versions vary significantly from text to text, and children alter them further as they repeat them.

At first, as children learn the rhymes by heart, they will rebel at any variation that is introduced into their favorites. Later, however, they delight in **parodies of nursery rhymes,** which range from such innocent humor as the spider saying to Miss Muffet, "Pardon me, is this seat taken?" or "Mary Mary, quite contrary" finding in her garden "one lousy petunia," all the way to obscene parodies and grotesqueries such as:

> Little Jack Horner
> Sat in a corner
> Eating his sister.

What may be the best-known verse in the English language, "Mary Had a Little Lamb," is also probably the most often parodied. It was composed by Mrs. Sarah Josepha Hale of Boston in 1830. It appeared in journalistic parodies by 1871 in the United States and by 1886 in England—a sure sign that readers were expected to be familiar with it. The themes of printed parodies clustered around subjects like Mary having different pets or new clothes, desiring special food or drink, and the like; only a few suggested the risqué twist that oral parodies have taken. The following, for example, is from a college humor magazine of 1928:

> Mary had a little dress
> It was so light and airy;
> It never showed a speck of dust,
> But it showed just lots of Mary.

This has its counterpart in the oral parody:

> Mary had a little lamb,
> She also had a bear;
> I've often seen her little lamb,
> But I've never seen her bear [bare].

Persistence of tradition is illustrated in the "Mary" parodies. The earliest recorded reference to the rhyme was a note in *Harper's Weekly* in 1869, discovered by folklorist C. Grant Loomis, in which a child was reported to be confused about the "fleas as white as snow." Still known in oral tradition is the parody:

> Some folks say that fleas are black,
> But I'm not sure they know.

> Cause Mary had a little lamb,
> Whose fleas were white as snow.

A full collection of children's oral parodies of "Mary" would reveal some of their preoccupations. For instance, delight in wordplay and a dawning awareness of the facts of life are suggested in:

> Mary had a little lamb
> (Boy was the doctor surprised!)

Or observe the abrupt shift from playing with a pet at home to the real business of going off to school (initiated by the domineering figure of a parent and supported by vigorous vernacular language) in this one:

> Mary had a little lamb,
> Her father shot it dead.
> Now Mary takes her lamb to school,
> Between two hunks of bread.

The contents of Mother Goose rhymes, as Archer Taylor has pointed out, are extremely broad, reflecting a great range of traditional sources that include lullabies ("Bye Baby Bunting"), finger rhymes ("Pat a Cake"), bouncing rhymes ("To Market, to Market, to Buy a Fat Pig"), story rhymes ("Old Mother Hubbard"), games ("Here We Go 'round the Mulberry Bush"), riddles ("Humpty Dumpty"), limericks ("Hickory Dickory Dock"), and even such types as charms, street cries, mnemonic devices, and traditional prayers. Ingenious and sometimes fantastic theories and interpretations have been offered for the origin and meaning of nursery rhymes, but about all that might be safely said is that many of them are very old, and some of them were certainly used (and perhaps invented) for political and social satire in Great Britain.

Most of the "explanations" offered for English nursery rhymes turn out to be what the best authorities on the genre (Iona and Peter Opie) characterize as "the work of the happy guessers." For instance, "Mary, Mary, quite contrary" is said to refer to Mary, Queen of Scots, and her ladies-in-waiting (the "four Marys" of balladry); the "cockleshells" are said to be decorations on a particular dress of the queen's. One problem with this theory is that no version of the rhyme was found until some 150 years after Mary's beheading. On the other hand, there are some examples of "political squibs" in nursery rhymes, such as the use of "Jack Spratt" to ridicule an Archdeacon Pratt in the seventeenth century and a popular rhyme that emerged in 1914 as a political cartoon with this text:

Kaiser, Kaiser-gander, where do your men wander?
Upstairs, downstairs, in my lady's chamber,
Burning their cathedrals till they couldn't say their prayers,
Then there came the British troops who flung them down the stairs.

Rhymes of Play, Games, and Fun

Play rhymes begin a baby's social life with such highly amusing (to infants) activities as bouncing, finger and toe counting, and tickling to the accompaniment of chants such as "This Is the Way the Farmer Rides," "Here Is the Church; Here Is the Steeple," "This Little Piggy," and

> Ticklee, ticklee on the knee,
> If you laugh, you don't love me.

All these rhymes are performed in connection with gestures or other actions, thus combining simple motor activity with a rhythmic verse. The parent chants, "Round a bit, round a bit, like a wee mouse," while circling his finger in baby's palm; then he says, "Up a bit, up a bit, into the house," while running his fingers up baby's arm to tickle him under the chin. Later, the baby learns to perform the rhyme on himself or others. Another favorite group of rhymes assigns comical names to the features of the face—"chinchopper" and "eyewinker." In finger-and-toe-counting rhymes, with their simple narrative plots, the child probably is expected to identify with the smallest digit, who not only "cried 'wee, wee, wee,' all the way home," but in other versions and other lands may be chastised as a glutton, a crybaby, a tattletale, a prig, or a noisy nuisance who wakes up the big, strong thumb. As children grow more adept in their mo-tions, they master the more complex gestures that accompany rhymes like "Pease Porridge Hot," "Two Little Blackbirds," or "Eensy Weensy Spider."

Next, what one collector has called "the *ars poetica* of children" manifests itself in **game rhymes.** Simplest is the basic amphimacric beat (unstressed syllable between two stressed syllables) of a bounce-ball-catch rhyme ("Ívorў sóap/ Seé ĭt flóat . . ."), followed in complexity by the rhymes that involve both bouncing and patting the ball, then making leg-lifting movements ("O Leary") and pantomime gestures or bouncing the ball to another child. The word "a-lery" (i.e., holding one's leg crooked so as to appear crippled) has been found in a fourteenth-century manuscript, leading one American folklorist to remark about the "O Leary" rhyme that "although children obviously use [the word] correctly, not one of them can say what it means."

When competitive games begin, the **counting-out rhyme** appears for choosing "it." The one beginning "Eeny, meeny, miney, mo" is at once the most common and the most obscure in meaning of all counting-out rhymes, and no convincing origin for it has yet been proposed. The rhyme has changed to suit the times, so that the offensive word "nigger" has yielded to "chigger," "tiger," "froggy," or "lawyer," who is caught by the toe. Children of many countries know variants fully as complicated as this American one:

> Eentery, meentery, cutery corn
> Apple seed and apple thorn
> Wire, briar, limber lock,
> Three geese in a flock.
> One flew east, and one flew west.
> One flew over the cuckoo's nest.
> O-U-T spells "out goes she!"

Jump-rope rhymes exhibit astonishing variety within a limited number of basic forms, and they frequently contain perceptive commentaries from a child's-eye view of the world. The simplest pattern is the *plain jump* game in which a child simply chants a rhyme to the rhythm of her jumping. More demanding is the *endurance jump* based on an open-end rhyme which continues until the jumper misses:

> I love coffee; I love tea,
> How many boys are stuck on me?
> One, two, three, four . . .

Endurance jumps frequently use *prophetic rhymes,* as above, or end "Yes-no-maybe," or with a series of colors, or with the alphabet. Social comment is specific in the following example in which the young jumper is watching her older sister primp:

> Grace, Grace, dressed in lace,
> Went upstairs to powder her face.
> How many boxes did she use?
> One, two, three, four . . .

The game of *speed jump* is set off by such words as "pepper," "hot," or "fire" in a rhyme; then the rope is twirled with ever-increasing speed until the jumper misses. Most complicated of all are *action rhymes* which require the jumper to imitate the behavior of the subject of the verse—usually "Teddy Bear"—as he touches the ground, turns around, goes upstairs, says his prayers, and so forth. Finally, there are *call-in, call-out rhymes* to signal changing jumper during a group game.

The list of characters frequently mentioned in jump-rope rhymes is peculiar. While "Mickey Mouse" and "Teddy Bear" (or sometimes "Yogi Bear") seem suitable for the context, what is the reason for the continuing popularity of "Shirley Temple," "Betty Grable," and that shadowy figure in popular rhymes, "the lady with the alligator purse"? Several past motion-picture stars and other historical personages, too early for most of today's rope-jumpers to remember in action, live on in their rhymes:

> Charlie Chaplin went to France,
> To teach the ladies how to dance;

It is clear that "Teddy Bear," originally referring to Theodore Roosevelt, is now to the jump-rope rhymes what the littlest pig is to the toe-counting verse. The child sees himself and his be-

loved stuffed toy suppressed in a world that is tyrannically ruled
by harsh adults, in a rhyme like the following:

> Teddy on the railroad, pickin' up stones,
> Along came a train and broke Teddy's bones.
> "Oh," said Teddy, "that's not fair!"
> "Oh," said the engineer, "I don't care!"

And for a nutshell summary of the course of life, what could be
clearer than this:

> First comes love, then comes marriage,
> Then comes Judy with a baby carriage.

Rhymes too numerous to list accompany other games and recreations; they are usually gathered and studied in connection
with the games themselves. A typical game of Hide and Seek illustrates this. First there is a counting-out rhyme to select "it."
The designated child then covers his eyes and counts in a formula manner to a specified number before calling out "Bushel
of wheat, bushel of rye / Who's not ready holler 'I' " or "Bushel
of wheat, bushel of clover / Who's not ready can't hide over."
When he tags a hider, "it" calls out one saying or rhyme; but if a
hider slips in safely, he can cry a rhyme of his own, calling the
others in "free." Other games may have more or less rhyme
content than this, but nearly all active folk games have some
rhyme attached to them; amusements like the following are little more than a rhyme followed by appropriate behavior:

> Order in the courtroom, monkey wants to speak.
> First one to speak is a monkey for a week.

A vast number of rhymes have no connection with organized
play or games at all, but are simply recited for the pure fun of it.
Even so, there may be some underlying sense to the most non-
sensical of them:

> I sent my boy to college,
> With a pat on the back.
> I spent ten thousand dollars,
> But I got a quarterback.

*

> Marriage for me in '83
> Marriage for sure in '84
> Anything alive in '85

Many are **topical rhymes:**

> Reagan's in the White House
> Waiting to be elected.
> Mondale's in the garbage can,
> Waiting to be collected.

Some fun rhymes are **parody rhymes,** often of religious texts such as prayers, hymns, and blessings:

> Good food, good meat,
> Good God, let's eat!
>
> *
>
> Now I lay me down to sleep,
> Bedbugs all around me creep.
> If they bite before I wake,
> I pray the Lord their jaws will break.

Some parodies of old school recitations are in rhyme:

> The boy stood on the burning deck,
> Melting with the heat.
> His big blue eyes were filled with tears,
> And his shoes were full of feet.

Other rhymed recitations are pure nonsense rather than parodies:

> Ladies and gentlemen, hoboes and tramps,
> Crosseyed mosquitoes, bowlegged ants,
> I now tell you something I know nothing about.
> Last night about 3 o'clock this morning,
> An empty truckload of bricks drove up my front back alley,
> And ran over my poor dead cat and half killed her.
> I rushed her to the hospital as slow as I could go,
> And there I saw Gene Autry eating vinegar with a pitchfork.

But most **nonsense orations** are composed in a sort of surrealistic free verse:

> Ladies and jellyfish, I come here not to dress you or undress you, but to address you as to how Christopher Cockeyed Cu-

cumber crossed the Missisloppi River with the Declaration of Indigestion in one hand and the Star Speckled bannaner in the other. . . .

Missionaries for the Latter-day Saints (Mormon) church have made a sort of nonsense oration out of a parody of the rhetoric of their typical opening statement used when going door-to-door with the church's message. They call it "A Poor Green Missionary's First Day," and it begins:

> Good Madam Morning! How do you do? I'm Joseph Smith from Salt Lake City. I mean, I'm a mission mormonary representing the church of Jesus Christ of Rattle-Day Snakes. I'm traveling without body parts or passions, and I represent a God without a purse or script.

Athletic cheers form a pattern for further rhyme parodies, such as this effete revision of a popular one, "Retard them, retard them / Make them relinquish the ball," or this bilingual gem from Wisconsin:

> *Lutefisk, lefse,*
> *Takk skal du ha.*
> Stoughton High School
> Rah! Rah! Rah!

Many fun rhymes reflect nothing more than pure boredom, daydreaming, and release:

> Spring is sprung, the grass is riz,
> I wonder where the birdies is.
>
> *
>
> Squirrel, squirrel on the ground,
> You don't make a single sound
> I know why so still you are,
> You've been flattened by a car.
>
> *
>
> Said Aaron to Moses,
> "Let's cut off our noses."
> Said Moses to Aaron,
> "It's the fashion to wear 'em."

Other nonsense rhymes are **circular rhymes**. Among the best known are the dialect pieces beginning "My name is Yon Yon-

son" and "Where do you worka John?" which advance a story
for a few lines that lead right back to the opening line and repetitions *ad infinitum.*

A curious form of nonsense rhyme is the so-called **spelling-
riddle**, really only another fun rhyme. "How do you spell 'snapping turtle'?"

> Snopey, snappin'
> Fat an' tickin'
> Tortle, tortle,
> Snappin' turtle.

Rhymes of derision may be classified as fun rhymes, fun at
least for the ones who chant them against fat kids, skinny kids,
weak kids, foreign kids, kids who wear glasses, sissies, tattle-
tales, and all the other unfortunates of a child's world. Let a
youngster acquire a sweetheart, and someone is sure to amuse
himself with "Johnny's got a girlfriend" sung to a well-known
tune, or the rhyme:

> Johnny's mad, and I'm glad,
> And I know what'll please him.
> A bottle of ink to make him stink
> And _____ to squeeze him.

Similarly, **rhymed retorts** (compare "catches" in Chapter 6)
are delivered:

> What's your name?
> —Puddin-tane
> Ask me again and I'll tell you the same.
>
> *
>
> Do you like Jelly?
> —I'll punch you in the belly.
>
> *
>
> See my finger?
> See my thumb?
> See my fist?
> You better run!

Ritualized **rhymed insults,** usually directed at another's
mother, are common in the black tradition of "sounding" or
"playing the dozens." Lately, such verses have also been col-

lected from whites. Mild examples of dozens, which are often quite obscene (the "dirty dozens"), are:

> I can tell by your eyes,
> You've been eatin' welfare pies.
>
> *
>
> I can tell by your hair,
> Your father was a grizzly bear.
>
> *
>
> Fee, fie, fo, fum,
> Your mother's a bum.
>
> *
>
> I can tell by your toes,
> Your mother wears brogues.

A second type of mostly black folk verse is the "toast," not primarily a drinking stanza or compliment as much as a longer narrative or editorial rhymed recitation.

Of course the **drinking toast** itself is also folklore, whether it be the simple compliment "Cheers!" or "Bottoms up!" or the longer verse. Analogous to rhymed toasts are verses like the following, used when a particular product is served:

> Carnation Milk in a little red can,
> Best tasting milk in the whole wide land.
> No tits to squeeze, no tail to twitch,
> Just punch a little hole in the son of a bitch.

Work Rhymes

What might be called **work rhymes** are gradually disappearing from American life, and they have always tended to shade off into folksongs. This category includes various rhymes associated with a particular trade, craft, or calling; they function as advertising, or for retaining useful information, for maintaining the rhythm of work, or simply to ease strain and weariness.

Peddlers' cries (or "street cries") and newsboys' calls—chanted or sung—were once heard regularly on many American streets from fresh fruit and vegetable men, rag and bone collectors, fishmongers, refreshment dispensers, and other wandering hawkers. But now most street vendors, except for ice-cream salespeople, have been replaced by supermarkets; even the "Good Humor Man" or other street sellers rely on bells or recorded music to announce their arrival. Old-time peddlers' cries are rarely heard, but an occasional informant may recall how they used to sound. The words were generally very simple—mere lists of the goods offered:

> Green corn and tomatoes
> Sweet and Irish potatoes.
>
> *
>
> Blackberries, blackberries,
> Fresh and fine,
> Just off the vine.

The rhymes were often imperfect, the form loose, and the words improvised from a stock of commonplaces. Sometimes a claim for the product's qualities was included in the cry:

> Hot tamales, floatin' in gravy,
> Suit your taste and I don't mean maybe.
>
> *
>
> Watermelons, come and see,
> Every one sold with a guarantee.
>
> *
>
> Ice cold lemonade!
> Freeze your teeth, curl your hair,
> Make you feel like a millionaire.

In Texas, and perhaps elsewhere, the story was told of an Italian street peddler who was weak in English and so followed an American hawker around calling out, "Same-a-ting! Same-a-ting!"

Planting rhymes have also been driven aside by automation; no powered corn drill needs anyone to chant "One for the blackbird / One for the crow . . ." or any of its numerous continuations and variants. Other such rhymes contained the traditional dates for planting certain crops, information now secured from a government bulletin or a county farm adviser:

> Plant pumpkin seeds in May,
> And they will all run away.

> Plant pumpkin seeds in June,
> And they will come soon.

Verses for rhythmic group work—sea chanteys, chain-gang hollers, chopping and pounding songs, and so forth—usually were delivered in a two-part call-and-response pattern, with a leader initiating the call or song and the community of workers chorusing back the response. One Afro-American rhyme for shifting railroad ties went:

> Oh, shove 'em up solid,
> Up solid and sound,
> So the big Nine-Hundred, boys,
> Cannot whop him down.

Although many of these types are dead or dying now, circus roustabouts used them until recently when hoisting the big tops. And one such practice remains in **military cadence chants:**

> *Leader:* You had a good home but you left.
> *Chorus:* You're right!
> *Leader:* Jody was there when you left.
> *Chorus:* You're right!

The "left-rights," of course, must fall on the proper feet for the march; the name "Jody," which occurs frequently, represents the civilian men back home who enjoy the good life that soliders secure for them. Comments on army life and discipline are also popular:

> Ain't no need in lookin' down,
> Ain't no discharge on the ground.

(A more recent version, heard in Joseph Wiseman's film *Basic Training:*

> Uncle Dicky, drop the bomb—
> I don't want to go to "Nam.")
>   *
> Airborne, airborne, where you been?
> Round the world and gone again.
> What you gonna do when you get back?
> Run again with a full field pack.

Some traditional admonitions in rhyme (often incorporating folk beliefs) might simply be termed **rhymed advice:**

> If he has one white foot, buy him,
> If two, try him,
> Three, deny him,
> Four white feet and a white nose,
> Take off his hide and feed him to the crows.
> —(Advice for buying horses)

Written Traditional Rhymes

Although they are seldom transmitted orally, certain **written rhymes** qualify as folklore on the grounds of traditionality, variation, and anonymity. For example, verses found carved on old powder horns often turn out to be variants of this one:

> I powder with my brother ball,
> A hero like I conquer all.
> The rose is red, the grass is green,
> The years are past which I have seen.

Other powder-horn rhymes commemorate the designer or owner of the horn and may advertise the latter's prowess:

> The man who steals this horn,
> Will go to Hell, so sure as he is born.
> I James Fenwick of Ogdensburg
> Did the year of 1817 kill 30 wolf,
> 10 bear, 15 deer
> And 46 partridges.

Similar traditional verses are sometimes found on hope chests, jewel boxes, snuffboxes, and the like.

Epitaphs, especially humorously facetious or ironical ones, may be traditional, as is the following:

> Pass on stranger, don't waste your time,
> O'er bad biography or bitter rhyme,
> For what I am this crumbling clay insures,
> And what I was is no concern of yours.

Sometimes the verses stitched into old samplers (needlework exercises for girls) resembled epitaphs in their pious and sententious language, as in this example from England, which has counterparts in American sampler verse:

> Mary Purmtum is my name.
> And England is my nation.
> Danvers is my dwelling place,
> And Christ is my salvation.
> When I am dead and laid in my grave,
> And all my bones are rotten,
> When this you see, remember me,
> That I may not be forgotten.

Another and simpler piece of sampler verse is this:

> This I have done
> To let you see
> What care my parents
> Took of me.

The flyleaves of old textbooks are another source of written traditional rhymes; **flyleaf inscriptions** may be simple statements like "In case of flood, stand on this; it's dry"; but often they are traditional admonitions in rhyme:

> If by chance this book should roam,
> Box its ears and send it home.

*

> Don't steal this book,
> My little lad,
> For fifty cents
> It cost my dad;
> And when you die
> The lord will say,
> "Where is that book,
> You stole one day?"
> And when you say
> You do not know,
> The lord will say,
> "Go down below!"

One curious inscription found written over the Ten Commandments in a school book dated 1832 reveals its rhymed message when a letter "e" is inserted for each dot:

P.RS.V.R.Y.P.RF.CTM.N
.V.RK..PTH.S.PR.C.PTST.N

Sometimes envelope sealers and inscriptions have a similar form. The familiar "SWAK" (sealed with a kiss) may be expanded to "SWALCAKWS" (sealed with a lick 'cause a kiss won't stick). An admonition to the postman is "PMPMDBS / BLEGMG" (Postman, postman, don't be slow, / Be like Elvis, "Go, man, go!"). And even more complicated is this one:

D-liver
D-letter
D-sooner
D-better
D-later
D-letter
D-madder
I-getter

Graffiti—writings on public walls—are frequently traditional, sometimes rhymed, but most often take the form of witty prose commentaries:

> Death is nature's way of telling you to slow down.
>
> *
>
> Ask God in prayer and she will answer.

Public-restroom graffiti ("latrinalia"), a common form in more ways than one (they tend to be profane, sexual, and scatological), have been widely collected and studied. Their earthy language led linguist Allen Walker Read to comment: "That anyone should pass up the well-established colloquial words of the language and have recourse to the Latin *defecate*, *urinate*, and *have sexual intercourse*, is indicative of grave mental unhealth."

A related form, **desk-top inscriptions** (or "horizontal graffiti"), may comment on the school or college situation:

I came, I saw, I laughed.

*

Professional absentee sits here.

or involve some whimsical trick writing:

THGUAC M'I PLEH
REDNU GNIHTEMOS NO
KSED SIHT

Autograph rhymes (or "friendship verses") constitute the largest, most varied, and most enduring category of written American folk rhymes. Enjoying a great vogue in the late nineteenth century, autograph books then were elegant; the writings in them tended to be pious and sentimental:

Remember well and bear in mind,
A constant friend is hard to find,
But when you get one kind and true,
Forsake not the old one for the new.

*

Our lives are albums written through,
With good or ill, with false or true,
And as the blessed Angels turn,
The pages of your years,
God grant they read the good with smiles,
And blot the bad with tears.

But even then whimsical verses began to appear—often comments on the writing of such verses or on marriage:

Some write for pleasure,
Some write for fame,
But I write simply,
To sign my name.

*

When you get married and cannot see,
Put on your specks and think of me!

*

As you slide down the bannister of life,
I hope you don't get a splinter in your career.

The "When you get married" verse with the "Yours 'til . . ." signoff is still a favorite autograph gimmick, rivaled recently by such novelty inscriptions as these:

I'd cross the hottest desert,
I'd swim the deepest sea,
I'd climb the highest mountain,
But I can't come over tonite, 'cause it's raining.

*

Two sat in a hammock
About to kiss,
When all of a sudden,
It went like sıɥʇ

*

Don't be #
Don't be ♭
Just be ♮

*

YYUR
YYUB
ICUR
YY4Me

*

UR 2 good 2B 4 got 10

The enduring long-term favorite autograph-book rhyme, whether "straight" or in parody, is "Roses are red / Violets are blue. . . ."

Folk Poetry

Folk Poetry is a term that has been very broadly applied, ranging from a description of the proverb as "a one-line folk poem" to consideration of lengthy folksong texts as poems. A reasonable limitation of the term might be to use it for "longer" folk rhymes (usually more than one stanza), especially those that are not connected with a specific game or work, such as many Afro-American toasts which, like "Shine" or "The Titanic," reach nearly epic proportions. The traditional *limerick,* which is usually off-color and hence circulated orally, is a familiar example of folk poetry:

There was an old lady from Kent,
Whose nose was most awfully bent,
She followed her nose,
One day I suppose,
And nobody knows where she went.

The Spanish-American *memoria*—newspaper verses memoria-
lizing the dead—are also considered folk poetry, leading folklorist T. M. Pearce, an investigator of this and other local verse,
to propose this definition of a folk poet:

> He writes often of community events and personalities asso-
> ciated with them and of manifestations of natural forces with
> effects upon society. He writes of the experiences of individ-
> uals when such happenings offer occasion for joy or sorrow to
> groups of relatives and friends or acquaintances. His poetic
> forms (metrical and stanzaic) are traditional, sometimes ir-
> regular or modified in the direction of informal and freer
> communication. His poetic idiom is stamped with expressions
> describing group feeling and thought.

This definition could embrace the soldiers of the First World
War who composed rhymed chronicles of their experiences,
such as the following fragments of a long piece written in a notebook by a retired Indiana railroad man:

> In the year of 1918, April the 26th day,
> I joined the American army to help whip Germany.
> I spent four weeks at camp Taylor in the city of Louisville,
> There they dressed me in khaki and taught me how to drill.
>
> *
>
> In fourteen days I had eight meals,
> And most of them, I fed the seals.
> Most of the way it was very cool.
> July the 10th we arrived at Liverpool.
>
> *
>
> There we seen hard fighting, also done our bits,
> Sending over three-inch shells, making each one a good hit.
> For two weeks we advanced continually through the Hin-
>   denburg line,
> And our intentions were very great for reaching the River
>   Rhine.
> The huns made no resistance, they knew they couldn't win.
> They kept right on retreating away from us fighting men.
>
> *
>
> The 11th of November we had them on the hop
> When they gave us orders at eleven o'clock to stop.
> But we were not sorry, a happy bunch were we,
> To know the war was over and we had won the victory.

This poem ended with a reference to returning to the job back home:

> I'm no poet, just a railroad man,
> And I work between Lafayette and Bloomington.
> When I am back home you'll find me without doubt,
> Someplace up and down the dear old Monon route.

That compositions like this one are traditional is suggested by parallels such as these lines from a Pennsylvania logger's recitation:

> I'm only just a raftsman
> From up Clearfield way
> I been up in the mountains
> E'r since the last o' May.
> Peelin' oak and hemlock
> And skiddin' yeller pine
> And I just come down the river
> To have a little 'shine. . . .
> And off we go once more
> Gellahootin' through the chute
> Bound for Jersey Shore.

One long poetic text in free verse—the Twenty-third Psalm—has inspired many full-length parodies. Certainly there is a traditional process operating when so many different versions of this verse circulate around themes such as the Model-T Ford ("The Ford is my auto, I shall not want another / It maketh me to lie down in mud puddles . . ."), the Great Depression ("Mr. Roosevelt is my shepherd, I am in want / he maketh me to lie down on park benches . . ." or "The Welfare Board is my shepherd, I shall not want another / It maketh me work in the road ditches . . ."), and so forth. Most of the Twenty-third Psalm parodies are conservative, pious, and anti–big government in tone; several of them are commentaries on recent American presidents.

Clearly the folk poets of our culture, whoever they are, in common with the recognized art poets, respond to both personal emotions and social conditions in their works. And at the present, when formal poetry has discarded most restraints of the past masters and Tin Pan Alley composers—often employing folksong forms—may touch upon the most serious and immediate problems, it becomes virtually impossible to draw hard and fast lines around art, popular, or folk poetry.

BIBLIOGRAPHIC NOTES

There is no book-length collection of general American folk rhymes to compare with Thomas Talley's specialized work *Negro Folk Rhymes* (New York: Macmillan, 1922). Duncan Emrich's *American Folk Poetry* (Boston: Little, Brown, 1974) is really an anthology of the lyrics of American folksongs. Interesting popular collections are Carl Withers's *A Rocket in My Pocket: The Rhymes and Chants of Young America* (New York: Henry Holt, 1948). Lillian Morison's *A Diller a Dollar: Rhymes and Sayings for the Ten o'Clock Scholar* (New York: Crowell, 1955), and Ian Turner, *Cinderella Dressed in Yella: Australian Children's Play-Rhymes* (Melbourne: Heinemann Educational Publications, 1969), which has a good introduction, thorough annotation, and a surprising number of parallels to American rhymes.

Some general compendiums of folklore have sections of rhymes; Paul G. Brewster edited them for the *Frank C. Brown Collection of North Carolina Folklore*, vol. I (Durham, N.C.: Duke University Press, 1952), pp. 160–219. *Kansas Folklore* (Lincoln: University of Nebraska Press, 1961), edited by Samuel J. Sackett and William E. Koch, has two chapters of folk verse (pp. 116–37). A representative special collection is Ruth Ann Musick and Vance Randolph's "Children's Rhymes from Missouri," *JAF* 63 (1950): 425–37.

Mary Anne Spiller offers "Some Contrasts in Rhymes Related by Children and Remembered by Adults in the San Gabriel Valley" in *FMS* 3 (1979): 47–64. She presents fifty-three examples, comparing those collected from children and adults. In a chapter co-authored with Mary Sanches, Barbara Kirshenblatt-Gimblett discusses "Children's Traditional Speech Play and Child Language," which appears in a book edited by Kirshenblatt-Gimblett, *Speech Play* (Philadelphia: University of Pennsylvania Press, 1976), pp. 65–110. An appendix identifies thirteen classic rhetorical patterns in children's folk rhymes.

Iona and Peter Opie's *The Oxford Dictionary of Nursery Rhymes* (New York: Oxford University Press, 1951) is the standard work on that genre, providing bibliography and evaluations of the many interpretations of Mother Goose. Archer Taylor's succinct and useful survey "What Is 'Mother Goose'?" appeared in *NMFR* 2 (1947–48): 7–13. Nursery-rhyme parodies are discussed by C. Grant Loomis in "Mary Had a Parody: A Rhyme of Childhood in Folk Tradition," *WF* 17 (1958): 45–51; and by Joseph Hickerson and Alan Dundes in "Mother Goose Vice Verse," *JAF* 75 (1962): 249–59.

Sam M. Shiver's "Finger Rhymes" in *SFQ* 5 (1941): 221–34, presents an interesting comparative survey of foreign, mostly German, and some English texts. Marian Hansen gathers "Children's Rhymes Accompanied by Gestures" in *WF* 7 (1948): 50–53. Dorothy Howard has written many fine articles on children's folklore, among them "The Rhythms of Ball-Bouncing and Ball-Bouncing Rhymes," *JAF* 62 (1949): 166–72.

Counting-out rhymes held the interest of some early folklorists in America, among them Henry Carrington Bolton, who published a classic book, *The Counting-Out Rhymes of Children* (New York: Appleton, 1888; repr. Detroit: Singing Tree Press, 1969); Bolton published an article with the same title during the same year in Volume 1 of *JAF* (31–37). Later notes on counting-out rhymes appeared in *JAF* 2 (1889): 113–16, and *JAF* 10 (1897): 313–21. Still later, an important midwestern collector, Emelyn E. Gardner, published "Some Counting-Out Rhymes in Michigan," *JAF* 31 (1918): 521–36. These and many other sources were consulted for Roger D. Abrahams and Lois Rankin's invaluable *Counting-Out Rhymes: A Dictionary* (Austin, Texas: AFS Bibliographic and Special Series, vol. 31, 1980).

Roger D. Abrahams's *Jump-Rope Rhymes: A Dictionary* (Austin, Texas: AFS Bibliographic and Special Series, vol. 20, 1969) gathers numerous examples and compiles a thorough bibliography of previously published sources which need not be listed here again. The classification of jump-rope rhymes used in this chapter was suggested by Bruce R. Buckley in *KFQ* 11 (1966): 99–111. Ed Cray includes previously unpublished variants (which, therefore, are not listed in Abrahams's work) in "Jump-Rope Rhymes from Los Angeles," *WF* 29 (1970): 119–27.

Paul G. Brewster collected " 'Spelling Riddles' from the Ozarks," in *SFQ* 8 (1944): 301–3. Kenneth W. Porter collected references from earlier published notes, and he classified various texts of "Circular Jingles and Repetitious Rhymes" in *WF* 17 (1958): 107–11; George Monteiro performed the same service for "Parodies of Scripture, Prayer, and Hymn," in *JAF* 77 (1964): 45–52. See also Kenneth W. Porter, "Humor, Blasphemy, and Criticism in the Grace before Meat," *NYFQ* 21 (1965): 3–18, and Monteiro's "Religious and Scriptural Parodies," *NYF* 2 (1976): 150–66.

The game of playing the dozens is discussed by Roger D. Abrahams in *JAF* 75 (1962): 209–20, and by Guy Owen in *NCFJ* 21 (1973): 53–54. Some similar material from white informants was included in Anna K. Stimson's "Cries of Defiance and Derision, and Rhythmic Chants of West Side New York City, 1893–1903." *JAF* 58 (1945): 124–29, and in Millicent R. Ayoub and Stephen A. Barnett's "Ritualized Verbal Insult in White High School Culture," *JAF* 78 (1965): 337–44. The publications dealing with toasts are listed in the bibliography of Bruce Jackson's collection and study entitled *Get Your Ass in the Water and Swim*

Like Me: Narrative Poetry from Black Oral Tradition (Cambridge, Mass.: Harvard University Press, 1974). Jackson wrote a negative response to the article by Dennis Wepman, Ronald B. Newman, and Murray B. Binderman, "Toasts: The Black Urban Folk Poetry" in *JAF* 87 (1974): 208–24, which appeared in the next volume of *JAF* along with a rejoinder by the original authors. The first article to get much beyond toast texts and functions is David Evans's "The Toast in Context," *JAF* 90 (1977): 129–48.

Street cries have been published in numerous scattered sources. Among them are Elizabeth Hurley's Texas collection "Come Buy, Come Buy" in *PTFS* 25 (1953): 115–38; Edward Pinkowski's "Philadelphia Street Cries" in *KFQ* 5 (1960): 10–12; Laurilynn McGill's "The Street Cry as an Artistic Verbal Performance," *Folklore Annual* 3 (1971): 17–25: Richardson L. Wright's *Hawkers and Walkers in Early America* (New York: Ungar, 1927; repr. 1965), ch. XV; Simon J. Bronner's "Street Cries and Peddler Traditions in Contemporary Perspective," *NYF* 2 (1976): 2–15; and Anne Warner's, "Fresh Peanuts Is the Best of All: A Street Cry from Suffolk, Virginia," *FFV* 1 (1979): 68–72.

Kenneth Porter discusses the familiar "Corn-planting Rhyme" ["One for the blackbird . . ."] in *WF* 17 (1958): 205–7. A collection of Afro-American work chants is William R. Ferris, Jr., "Railroad Chants: Form and Function," *MFR* 4 (1970): 1–14. George G. Carey, himself a former paratrooper, prepared "A Collection of Airborne Cadence Chants" for *JAF* 78 (1965): 52–61.

Rhymes from old powder horns were illustrated and discussed by W. M. Beauchamp in *JAF* 2 (1889): 117–22, and *JAF* 5 (1892): 284–90. Epitaphs were discussed by D. P. Penhallow in *JAF* 5 (1892): 305–17; northern California epitaphs were printed by Kenneth W. Clarke in *WF* 20 (1961): 238, and *WF* 21 (1962), 146. An interesting chapter on "Flyleaf Scribblings" was included in Clifton Johnson's *Old-Time Schools and School-Books* (New York: Macmillan, 1904, reissued in paperback by Dover, 1963); the chapter was also reprinted in *What They Say in New England*, edited from Clifton Johnson's various folklore publications by Carl Withers (New York: Columbia University Press, 1963), pp. 196–206. An early note on the same subject was Fanny D. Bergen's "Flyleaf Rhymes and Decorations," *New England Magazine*, n.s. 23 (1901): 505–11, which contains variants of several references quoted by Johnson. A more recent discussion is Robert H. Woodward's "Folklore Marginalia in Old Textbooks," *NYFQ* 18 (1962): 24–27.

Graffiti have been the subject of both scholarly and popularized treatments. A casual survey of much typical wall writing is Norton Mockridge's *The Scrawl of the Wild: What People Write on Walls—and Why* (Cleveland and New York: World, 1968). A lavish production with examples in color and an interpretation written by Norman Mailer is *The Faith of Graffiti* (New York: Praeger, 1974). Alan Dundes studied just toilet graffiti, coining a new term for them, in "Here I Sit—a Study of American *Latrinalia,*" *Kroeber Anthropological Society Papers* no. 34 (Spring 1966): 91–94, reprinted in *Analytic Essays in Folklore*, pp. 177–91. In "The Growth of Graffiti," *FF* 7 (1974): 273–75, Mac E. Barrick analyzes thirty-two additions to a single graffito written in a men's room of the Duke University library; further campus examples are discussed in Patricia A. Mastick, "The Function of Political Graffiti as Artistic Creativity," *NYFQ* 27 (1971): 280–96; Charlene Gates, "Graffiti and Environment of the Folk Group: University Music Majors," *FF* 9 (1976): 35–42; Gregory J. Longenecker, "Sequential Parody Graffiti," *WF* 36 (1977): 354–64; and Don L. F. Nilsen, "Sigma Epsilon XI: Sex in the Typical University Classroom" (desk-top graffiti), *Maledicta* 5 (1981): 79–91.

Terrance L. Stocker, Linda W. Dutcher, Stephen M. Hargrove, and Edwin A. Cook present a comprehensive bibliography of studies and a most ambitious analysis in their article "Social Analysis of Graffiti" in *JAF* 85 (1972): 356–66. Introducing a category of graffiti neither obscene nor humorous is Sylvia Ann Grider, "*Con Safos:* Mexican-Americans, Names and Graffiti," *JAF* 88 (1975): 132–42, reprinted in *Readings in American Folklore*, pp. 138–51. The pioneering work by Allen Walker Read originally entitled *Lexical Evidence from Folk Epigraphy in Western North America* (1935) was reissued with the straightforward title *Classic American Graffiti* by Maledicta Press (Waukesha, Wis., 1977). Read's excellent statement "Graffiti as a Field of Folklore" was published in *Maledicta* 2 (1978): 15–31. A theoretical advance in studies of graffiti is represented by George Gonos, Virginia Mulhern, and Nicholas Poushinsky's "Anonymous Expression: A Structural View of Graffiti," *JAF* 89 (1976): 40–48. Notes on male versus female graffiti (mostly latrinalia) are found in *JAF* 90 (1977): 188–91, and *Maledicta* 2 (1978): 42–59. In "Folk Epigraphy by Subtraction," Charles Clay Doyle reveals how latrinalia may be formed by scraping away letters on a set of stenciled instructions found on hand dryers. ("Push Button" becomes "Push Butt," etc.) See *MJLF* 7 (1981): 49–50. A sort of roadside graffiti is described by Thomas H. King in "Roadside Rock Art," *JAF* 93 (1980): 60; desert stones are arranged along a Utah freeway to spell out names and inscriptions.

Alan Dundes has thoroughly surveyed the bibliography of friendship verses in "Some Examples of Infrequently Reported Autograph Verse," *SFQ* 26 (1962): 127–30. Two representative older collections are Vance Randolph and May Kennedy McCord's "Autograph Albums in the Ozarks," *JAF* 61 (1948): 182–93, in which a useful classification of these rhymes is offered; and Lelah Allison's "Traditional Verse from Autograph Books," *HF* 8 (1949): 87–94, in which Gay Nineties and modern verse are compared. W. K. McNeil has published three important articles on the subject: "The Autograph Album Custom: A Tradition and Its Scholarly Treatment," *KFQ* 13 (1968): 29–40; "From Advice to Laments: New York Autograph Album Verse: 1820–1850," *NYFQ* 25 (1969): 175–94; and the continuation of the latter article to 1850–1900 in *NYFQ* 26 (1970): 163–203. Stephen Stern reports on interviews with those who write in and collect autograph books in his article "Autograph Memorabilia as an Output of Social Interactions and Communication," *NYFQ* 29 (1973): 219–39. Two other articles on the subject are Sylvia C. Henricks, "The Gentle Pastime," *IF* 11 (1978): 161–73, and Meguido Zola, "'By Hook or by Crook': New Look at the Autograph Book," *NYF* 6 (1980): 185–94. Related areas of tradition are described in Steven J. Zeitlin's "As Sweet As You Are: The Structural Elements in the Signed High School Yearbook," *NYFQ* 30 (1974): 83–100, and Toni Flores Fratto, "'Remember Me': The Sources of American Sampler Verses," *NYF* 2 (1976): 205–22.

Jeanne Soileau makes a case for "Children's Cheers as Folklore" in *WF* 39 (1980): 232–47; her texts come from black and white children in Louisiana in 1975–76. Susan Gelman has an impressive collection of what she calls "postal graffiti" (envelope sealers, etc.) in an article in *WF* 36 (1977): 102–18.

The quotation from T. M. Pearce in this chapter comes from his "What Is a Folk Poet?" published in *WF* 12 (1953): 242–48; Rubén Cobos supplemented some of Pearce's assertions in "The New Mexican *memoria,* or In Memoriam Poem," in *WF* 18 (1959): 25–30. Further examples of Mexican-American folk poetry appear in Inez Cardozo-Freeman, "Arnulfo Castillo, Mexican Folk Poet in Ohio," *JOFS* 1 (1972): 2–28, and John Donald Robb, "H. V. Gonzales: Folk Poet of New Mexico," *NMFR* 13 (1973–74): 1–6.

The passages quoted above from the World War I rhymed chronicle were collected by me from Clarence E. ("Old Hickory") Pierson in Bloomington, Indiana, on August 8, 1959; Elsie Clews Parsons discussed similar folk poems in her note "War Verses," in *JAF* 47 (1934): 395. Américo Paredes reviewed the concept of folk poetry in his article "Some Aspects of Folk Poetry" in *TSLL* 6 (1964): 213–25; he saw the subject as ranging from the proverb to the folksong and drew comparisons between "The Maid Freed from the Gallows" and Shakespeare's Sonnet 73 ("That time of year thou mayst in me behold") to illustrate his points. Two studies of individual folk-poetry composers are Edward D. Ives's *Laurence Doyle, the Farmer Poet of Prince Edward Island* (Orno, Me.: University of Maine Studies, no. 92, 1971) and Steven A. Schulman, "Howess Dewey Winfrey: The Rejected Songmaker," *JAF* 87 (1974): 72–84.

An example of the traditional recitation, long a neglected genre of folk poetry, was given in *AffWord* 2 (1972): 38–39—the piece was "The Volunteer Organist." The same journal, renamed *Southwest Folklore,* devoted an entire issue (vol. 2, no. 4 [1978]: 63 pp.) to "Uncle

Horace's Recitations," a set of notes to accompany a recording of a dozen texts from one informant. The subject had come into its own as an area for study with the "Monologues and Folk Recitations Special Issue" of *SFQ* (vol. 40, nos. 1–2 [1976]), edited by Kenneth S. Goldstein and Robert D. Bethke.

G. Legman published his essay "The Limerick: A History in Brief" in *The Horn Book* (New Hyde Park, N.Y.: University Books, 1964), pp. 427–53. Legman's definitive collection *The Limerick: 1700 Examples, with Notes, Variants, and Index*, originally published in France and long a rare book, was reprinted recently (New York: Bell, 1974). A most engagingly written popular survey is William S. Baring-Gould's *The Lure of the Limerick: An Uninhibited History* (New York: Clarkson N. Potter, 1967).

The presidential parody of the Twenty-third Psalm appears in Ed Cray, "The Quadrennial Perennials," *WF* 24 (1965): 199–201. Further examples appear in Gary Alan Fine, "In Search of the Quadrennial Perennials," *FF* 7 (1974): 203–5, and in Mac E. Barrick, "The Presidential Psalm," *FF* 8 (1975): 357–60. Fine mentions this and other pieces of typescript political satire in an article in *Maledicta* 6 (1982): 71–74.

8
Myths and Motifs

Traditional prose narratives in oral circulation, often loosely termed "folktales," constitute one of the largest and most complex branches of folklore. These narratives include stories that are regarded as true, called "myths" and "legends," and stories that are regarded as fictional, properly called by the term "folktales." Myths are distinguished from legends (as anthropologist William Bascom formulated it) by the attitudes of storytellers toward them, the settings described in them, and their principal characters. Myths are regarded as sacred and legends as either sacred or secular; myths are set in the remote past, in the otherworld, or an earlier world, and legends in the historical past; myths have as their principal characters gods or animals, while legends (which will be discussed in Chapter 9) generally have humans in the major roles.

Myths, then, may be defined as "traditional prose narratives, which, in the society in which they are told, are considered to be truthful accounts of what happened in the remote past." Typically, they deal with the activities of gods and demigods, the creation of the world and its inhabitants, and the origins of religious rituals. Whenever myths purport to explain such matters as origins of geographic features, animal traits, rites, taboos, and customs, they are known as *explanatory* or *etiological* narratives.

Native American Myths and Tales: Problems in Categorization

There is some difficulty in using these terms and distinctions because the word "myth" has acquired other specialized meanings among literary critics, historians, and philosophers. Furthermore, it is not always possible to establish clearly whether a given narrative should be termed myth, legend, or folktale. With traditions outside our own, it is particularly artificial to make such distinctions. Native American narratives, for instance, which have been collected in large numbers over a long period of time, constitute an impressive body of what is often loosely termed "myth"; but such a designation takes little account of the tellers' actual attitudes, their oral style, or even of the stories' typical elements. American Indian narratives often freely mix human and animal characters, and the animals may have both human and godlike qualities. The stories tend to combine believable and fantastic elements, and even when they seem to be explanatory in purpose, the specific facts of life that are "explained" may not be as apparent to the non-Indian reader of collected stories as they were to the original audiences. These stories were often performed in a dramatic oratorical or poetic manner, employing some language forms used only in storytelling. What we have, then, in our older compilations of English prose translations of Native American myths—as numerous and varied as they are—is only an approximation of a rich and diverse repertoire of poetic texts.

Three short excerpts from English prose translations of Indian narratives in Stith Thompson's *Tales of the North American Indians* (1929)—all of them involving animals—demonstrate both the applicability of the myth/legend/folktale categories and the problems associated with them. This was collected from Pacific Coast Indians (Tahltan) and published in *JAF* in 1919:

> Once Porcupine and Beaver quarreled about the seasons. Porcupine wanted five winter months. He held up one hand and showed his five fingers. He said, "Let the winter months be the same in number as the fingers on my hand." Beaver said, 'No," and held up his tail, which had many cracks or scratches on it. He said, "Let the winter months be the same in number as the scratches on my tail." Now they quarreled and argued. Porcupine got angry and bit off his thumb. Then, holding up his hand with the four fingers, he said emphatically, "There must be only four winter months." Beaver be-

came a little afraid, and gave in. For this reason porcupines have four claws on each foot now.

[The story continues to explain how Raven came to consider the arguments and decided that Porcupine had been right, though the number of winter months was then set to be only approximately four months henceforth.]

This story is a typically "mythic" one, serving to explain features of nature as supposedly determined by the actions of primeval animals.

The next story was collected from Central Woodland Indians (Menomini) and published in a Bureau of American Ethnology report in 1896:

There was a large settlement on the shore of a lake, and among its people were two very old blind men. It was decided to remove these men to the opposite side of the lake, where they might live in safety, as the settlement was exposed to the attack of enemies, when they might easily be captured and killed. So the relations of the old men got a canoe, some food, a kettle, and a bowl and started across the lake, where they built for them a wigwam in a grove some distance from the water. A line was stretched from the door of the wigwam to a post in the water, so they would have no difficulty in helping themselves. . . .One day a raccoon, which was following the water's edge looking for crawfish, came to the line which had been stretched from the lake to the wigwam. The raccoon thought it rather curious to find a cord where he had not before observed one. . . .Wishing to deceive the old men, [the racoon] untied the cord from the post, and carried it to a clump of bushes.

[The story continues with the raccoon continuing to shift the cord around and to play tricks on the two blind men until they accuse each other of stealing food. Then the raccoon criticizes the blind men for finding fault with each other so easily, and returns to his crawfish hunting along the shore.]

This is more characteristically "legendary," since it deals with a realistic human problem solved in a nonsupernatural way, although an oddly anthropomorphic (humanlike) animal enters the story as a trickster.

The third is an Eskimo tale published in *JAF* in 1899:

A man who was walking, once upon a time, came to a pond, where there were a number of geese. These geese had taken off their garments and had become women, and were now swimming in the pond. The man came up to them without being seen, and seized their feather-garments. He gave them all back but two, whereupon the women put them on and flew away. Finally he gave one of the two remaining ones hers, whereupon she also flew off. The last woman, however, he kept with him, took to his house, and married. Soon she became pregnant and gave birth to two children.

[The story continues with the wife and children putting on feathers and flying away, the husband going on a long quest to find them, and his eventual killing of the wife and driving off of the children.]

This story has the "folktale" qualities (indicated by the translator's use of "once upon a time") of magical themes that are treated fictionally.

The original texture, or style, of such ancient stories, once told widely by the native Americans, is lost to us in these renderings into standard written English. (The situation is worse with literary treatments like Longfellow's "Hiawatha," or storybook versions given in pseudo-scriptural prose.) An even greater loss in our appreciation of Indian narrative tradition is any clear sense of the ultimate meanings of the stories to their owners. Just how literally are we expected to take the adventures of these animals? Are the plots merely vehicles for various "lessons" rather than accounts of events that were really believed in? Thus, it has become crucially important in the study of native American narratives to work with the few remaining speakers of the hundreds of aboriginal languages and dialects of the continent, and to uncover through close linguistic and ethnographic analysis the layers of meaning that the stories contain. This study is complicated because the themes and plots of American Indian narratives are often close enough to European folk stories to raise the possibility of borrowing. (Oral stories about the deception of blind persons and the existence of "Swan Maidens," for example, have international distribution.)

Because of the extremely wide range of native American customs, languages, and traditions, plus the sheer numbers of collected narratives, it is difficult to generalize about their themes and plots. It *is* possible to say, however, that all Indian groups used stories to explain the creation of the world and its transformation into the condition in which we know it. Most groups, too, had stories of heroes and the tests they underwent, of supernatural journeys, and of animal husbands and wives. Comparing the many bodies of native American narratives, scholars have also distinguished cycles of stories with widespread variants across the continent and sometimes beyond; these are referred to with such conventional titles as "The Earth Diver," "The Theft of Fire," "The Star Husband," "The Arrow Chain," and "The Sun Snarer."

The most characteristic group of North American Indian narratives is the trickster cycle, a lengthy series of adventures experienced by a sort of combined man/animal, god/human, benefactor/enemy figure known by the general name of "Trickster." The trickster appears in various different forms, such as the human Manabozho in the Central Woodlands region, Coyote in the Plains and Western regions, and Raven, Mink, or Blue Jay in the North Pacific. (Some of these figures are creators or transformers as well, and their specific names and epithets vary a good deal from group to group.) Tricksters engage in all manner of outrageous, dangerous, and even obscene behavior, often injuring themselves as well as others. Their antisocial behavior provides negative models for conduct and the release of tensions via fantasy—that is, the Indian audiences are shown in the stories how *not* to behave, but they are also afforded a release through humor from the strain of maintaining proper behavior. The consequences of the trickster's acts are often simple enough realities of everyday life, as in this Uintah Ute coyote story published in *JAF* in 1910:

> Long ago Wildcat had a long nose and tail. One day he was sleeping on a rock when Coyote came along. He pushed Wildcat's nose and tail in, and then went home. At noon Wildcat woke up, and noticed his short nose and tail. "What's the matter with me?" he asked. Then he guessed the cause. "Oh! Coyote did that," he said, and he hunted for him.
>
> Now, Coyote was sleepy and had lain down. Wildcat came

and sat down beside him. He pulled Coyote's nose and tail
and made them long. They were short before. Then he ran
off. After a while Coyote woke up and saw his long nose and
tail.

Probably a non-Indian reader of this story would conclude,
"So that's how the Indians thought these animals' appearances
got that way." But a Paiute Indian woman, telling another version of the same story, remarked, "This story carried an admonition for us not to do things to our brothers and sisters out of
anger. Fights between brothers and sisters ended by grandfather saying, 'All right, Coyote and Bobcat!' That stopped
everything."

Another interesting aspect of native American storytellers is
their occasional adoption into the repertoire of a story told by
missionaries, or their adaptation into a satiric commentary upon
the invading whites of a traditional Indian story. Here are two
short examples of such stories:

Almost everything was Coyote's way. The Indian planted
the apple. When he planted it, he said for all the Indians to
come and eat. When he told them that, all the people came.
The white man was a rattlesnake then, and he was on the tree.
The white people have eyes just like the rattlesnake. When
the Indians tried to eat the apples, that snake tried to bite
them. That's why the white people took everything away
from the Indian; because they were snakes. If that snake
hadn't been on that tree, everything would have belonged to
the Indians. Just because they were snakes and came here,
the white people took everything away. They asked the Indians where they had come from. That's why they took everything and told the Indians to go way out in the mountains
and live.
[A Northern Paiute telling of the Adam and Eve story,
published in *JAF* in 1938]

Once they were making a railroad through Coyote's place.
"I don't want it. Take it away; take your tools and go away,"
he said. "Don't pay any attention to him." the people said.
"Just go ahead and lay the tracks." The workers paid no attention to Coyote and laid the tracks. When Coyote saw it, he

said, "Oh, there's a train going through my place now."
"Stay right where you are," he said to the train. Then the
train and all the people inside it turned into a rock right on
the spot. "You must stay there forever; you will never move
again," Coyote said.

[A Northern Pacific (Coast Salish) story collected in the
early twentieth century and published in 1934]

Motifs and the Motif-Index

Despite the remoteness of myths, in both time and cultural distance, from mainstream modern folklore, there are good reasons for American folklorists to be concerned with myths,
whether the so-called *primitive myths* of prehistoric cultures
and modern preliterate peoples, the *Oriental myths* of India and
the Far East, or the familiar *Occidental myths* of the classical
world and ancient northern Europe. Among these three bodies
of world myth there are themes that recur again and again, raising difficult questions of origin and dissemination. These include the creation of the world and the shaping of it to the
present form, the origin of death or of fire, the consequences of
rivalries between individuals and peoples, the arrival of heroes
who save their people from enemies or disasters, and the resurrection of slain gods or kings to become mythic personalities.

Fantastic and grotesque elements that have widespread distribution in myths are especially puzzling, such as cannibalism,
shape shifting, marriage between different species, and many
kinds of mutants and monsters. Another enigma is the relatively
limited number of distinct *forms* of myths, the texts of which
may vary greatly in their specific details. For example, the story
of a destruction of the world's creatures by a flood and the beginning of a new cycle of life after one remaining creature
enters the void and returns with a scrap of the old world has international circulation in myths, though the specifics (cause of
the flood, nature of the creature, method of restoring life, etc.)
are extremely variable.

This variety is demonstrated by turning to one of the most comprehensive general reference works in folklore studies, Stith Thompson's *Motif-Index of Folk-Literature*. The contents and the broad scope of this encyclopedic six-volume work are indicated in its subtitle, *A Classification of Narrative Elements in Folktales, Ballads, Myths, Fables, Mediaeval Romances, Exempla, Fabliaux, Jest-Books and Local Legends*. A **motif,** or "narrative element," from these traditional texts is any striking or unusual unit recurring in them; it may be an object (such as a magic wand), a marvelous animal (such as a speaking horse), a concept (such as a taboo or forbidden act), an action (such as a test or a deception), a character (such as a giant, an ogre, or a fairy god-mother), a character type (such as a fool or a prophet), or a structural quality (such as formulistic numbers or cumulative repetition). Thousands of such elements are arranged in the *Motif-Index* according to a systematic plan, along with biblio-graphic references to their occurrences in collected texts. (A fair number, however, exist as separate oral narratives, some-times termed one-motif tales.) Use of the work is facilitated by detailed synopses before each of the twenty-three lettered chapters, numerous cross references to the numbered individ-ual motifs throughout it, and an alphabetical "index to the *Index,* in the sixth volume. Although the *Motif-Index* is primarily used in studies of folktales (see Chapter 10), it is introduced here because it has important applications for analyzing myths.

Motifs from myths are scattered throughout the *Index,* but the predominantly "Mythological Motifs" are contained in Chapter "A" under the following broad divisions:

A0–	A99.	Creator
A100–	A499.	Gods
A500–	A599.	Demigods and culture heroes
A600–	A899.	Cosmogony and cosmology
A900–	A999.	Topographical features of the earth
A1000–	A1099.	World calamities
A1100–	A1199.	Establishment of natural order
A1200–	A1699.	Creation and ordering of human life
A1700–	A2199.	Creation of animal life

A2200–A2599. Animal characteristics
A2600–A2699. Origin of trees and plants
A2700–A2799. Origin of plant characteristics
A2800–A2899. Miscellaneous explanations

These thirteen general categories of mythological motifs are subdivided into numerous specific categories that are numbered in groups of tens. For example, A1200–A1299, "Creation of man," is broken down as follows in the synopsis:

A1210. Creation of man by creator
A1220. Creation of man through evolution
A1230. Emergence or descent of first man to earth
A1240. Man made from mineral substance
A1250. Man made from vegetable substance
A1260. Mankind made from miscellaneous materials
A1270. Primeval human pair
A1290. Creation of man—other motifs

As can be seen above between A1270. and A1290., Thompson sometimes skipped numbers in the *Motif-Index* to allow for adding further groups of motifs. Also, within each chapter (which in this instance contains 279 pages of closely printed motif entries) the subdivisions are made infinitely expandable by a system of "points." Thus motif A1226. is "Man created after series of unsuccessful experiments," and A1226.1. is the more specific motif "Creator makes man out of butter first; it would not stand up and melted." If a new myth were discovered in which man were made out of margarine first, then, considering this as a variant of butter, the number *A1226.1.1. could be added; but if a new material, say chocolate, were used for a succession of creations, number *A1226.2. would be appropriate. (Whenever a new motif number is created, it is designated with an asterisk until it appears in a revised edition of the master index.) It might also be noted that two cross references appear under A1226.: numbers A630., "Series of creations," and A1401., "Culture originated by previous race of man." Thompson's bibliographic references indicate that the concept of a series of unsuccessful experiments to create man is found in myths from Greece, Latin America, and the Banks Islands in the Pacific New Hebrides; the unsuccessful creation out of butter is found in a myth from India. These references do not establish that there is any historical relationship between these similar myth motifs, although further research may suggest that there is.

The varied and sometimes fantastic nature of mythological motifs is shown in the *Motif-Index* in the materials out of which man is said to have been made. The mineral substances include sand sprinkled with water, earth reddened with animal blood, stones, ice, shells, and metals. Vegetable substances indexed include trees and wood, fruit, nuts, seeds, sugar-cane stalks, ears of corn, herbs, and grass. In some mythological explanations of the creation of man, the raw material comes from the body of the creator himself—his sweat (the Lithuanians); his spittle (the Lithuanians and in Oceanic myths); or even a broken-off toenail (the Indians of Brazil). The *Motif-Index* lists parallels for the Judaic-Christian explanation that man was made from clay or other earth in Hindu, Babylonian, Greek, Irish, Siberian, Chinese, Polynesian, Indonesian, Australian, Eskimo, North and South American Indian, and Aztec mythology. Again, it must be borne in mind that listing such parallels does not presuppose any necessary historical connection between these bodies of mythology. Some of these particular parallels, in fact, must predate Judaism and Christianity, while others were probably influenced directly by missionaries.

Using the Motif-Index

The *Motif-Index*, less a theoretical work than simply a massive catalogue of traditional narrative elements, has applications in folklore study far beyond myth comparisons. The term "motif," it should be remembered, refers in this special folkloristic sense only to traditional *narratives*. Motifs are often international in distribution, but not necessarily related historically, and usually somewhat generalized and simplified for their *Index* listings. Mastery of the *Motif-Index* is important to much folklore scholarship, and this skill may be acquired best through working with the *Index* listings and references, and by observing how motif numbers are applied in studies such as those in the Appendix of this book. As a guide for approaching the *Index* itself, here is a synopsis of the twenty-three lettered chapters,* with one or more examples of motifs from each and a few parenthetical comments:

A. Mythological Motifs
    A1150. Determination of seasons. [See a story quoted earlier.]
    A2214.3. Unicorn thrown from ark and drowned; hence no longer exists.

B. Animals
    B422. Helpful cat. [As in "Puss in Boots"]

C. Tabus
    C480.1.1. Tabu: whistling in mine.

D. Magic
    D361.1. Swan Maidens [See a story quoted earlier.]
    D1323.1. Magic clairvoyant mirror. [As in "Snow White"]

E. The Dead
    E332.3.3.1. The Vanishing Hitchhiker.
    E332.3.3.2. Deity as ghostly rider. [I.e., Jesus as the hitchhiker]

F. Marvels
    F511.2.2. Person with ass's (horse's) ears. [I.e., King Midas]

G. Ogres
    G303.4.5.3.1. Devil detected by his hoofs.

H. Tests
    H542. Death sentence escaped by propounding riddle a king (judge) cannot solve. [I.e., a neck riddle]

J. The Wise and the Foolish
    J1741.3.1. Stupid scholar memorizes set answers to oral examination in Latin. The questions are not given in the order he expects; comic results. [Told in the Northwest about an Indian trying to pass an exam given orally in English]

* There are no chapters for the letters "I," "O," and "Y."

K. Deceptions
 K333. Theft from blind person. [See a story quoted earlier.]
 K581.1. Briar-patch punishment for rabbit.
 K581.2. Burying the mole as punishment.
 K584. Throwing the thief over the fence.
L. Reversal of fortune
 L50. Victorious youngest daughter.
 L100–199. Unpromising hero (heroine). [I.e., the Cinderella figure]
M. Ordaining the Future
 M312.0.1. Dream of future greatness.
N. Chance and Fate
 N338.3. Son killed because mistaken for someone else.
P. Society
 P314. Combat of disguised friends. [Found in one Civil War ballad, for example]
Q. Rewards and Punishments
 Q386. Dancing punished.
R. Captives and Fugitives
 R41. Captivity in tower (castle, prison). [I.e., as in "Rapunzel"]
S. Unnatural Cruelty
 S262. Periodic sacrifices to a monster.
T. Sex
 T554. Woman gives birth to animal.
 T562. White woman bears black child.
U. The Nature of Life
 U111. Many books do not make a scholar. [A "folk idea"]
 U147. Animals try unsuccessfully to exchange food. [As in the fable of the fox and heron]
V. Religion
 V81.2. Tails fall off mountain spirits when they are baptized.
 V221.3. Saint cures leprosy.
W. Traits of Character
 W111. Laziness.
 W111.3.6. "Who will not work, shall not eat."
 W111.5.4. Lazy dog wakes only for his meals.
 W111.5.13. Man weeds garden from cushioned rocking chair, using fire tongs to reach weeds.

X. Humor
    X900–1899. Humor of lies and exaggeration.
    X905.4. The liar: "I have no time to lie today"; lies nev-
        ertheless. [A very popular one-motif tall tale]
    X115.1. Fisherman catches fish with amazing contents.
Z. Miscellaneous groups of motifs
    Z13.2. Catch tale: teller is killed in his own story.
    Z71.1. Formulistic number : three.

"Our Own" Myths

The study of myths and motifs raises the question of how to regard "our own" myths, such as the Biblical accounts of the Creation, the Great Flood, the Last Supper, and the Resurrection,
or the various written and traditional backgrounds of practices
and beliefs among Christians, Jews, Moslems, and members of
other major religions. On the one hand, the unvarying scriptural
basis for "organized religions" would argue against regarding
them as folk-related; yet the cross-cultural and cross-denomina-
tional variations that exist do remind us of folk tradition. (See
also the discussions of "religious legends" in Chapter 9 and of
"folk religion" in Chapter 14.) Furthermore, to some extent
even modern children learn the sacred stories of their culture
by traditional means, such as family conversations or celebrations of religious holidays, rather than by strictly institutionalized means, such as Sunday-school lessons or Bible-study
classes. Another consideration must be the uses to which people
put their religious narratives—as guides for living, charters for
belief, means of evaluating others' actions, and the like. These
functions and attitudes are not unlike those related to myths in
primitive cultures, and it ought not to damage the religious
convictions of students of American folklore to regard their own
system as part of a continuum of world-wide tradition rather
than a set of unique literal and inviolable truths. Only the culturally naïve could regard "our" beliefs and religious narratives
as true but the beliefs of "others" as myths, superstitions, and
mere folklore. As the folklorist Dell Hymes wrote, after years of
study of Northwestern Indian myths and their counterparts

elsewhere, "The shaping of deeply felt values into meaningful, apposite form, is present in all communities, and will find some means of expression among all." In other words, with regard to contemplating their relationship to a larger reality, the world's people are all "folk."

Another aspect of modern folk thought that resembles myth-making is what might be called "mythic traditions" in American history. Archetypal images found in our culture, such as the country bumpkin (Brother Jonathan in colonial times), the city slicker (for example, in "The Arkansas Traveler"), and the national symbol (Uncle Sam) are metaphors for concepts about our past. The same is true for the "myths" surrounding events, like the fall of the Alamo, Custer's Last Stand, and the assassination of presidents. Also mythic are the stereotyped plots of romance and legend—"from rags to riches" or "virtue is rewarded." To a large extent, myth- and image-making of this kind underlie our sense of national identity, and even influence our social and political decisions.

Theories and the Origin of Myths

The history of scholarly theories of traditional myth origins is essentially the history of attempts to account for similar elements in different bodies of mythology and similarities between myths and folktales. In story after story, whether myth or tale, heroes are set difficult tasks to perform—they slay monsters, and they receive royal gifts as rewards; women sometimes marry animals that often turn out to be transformed humans; food or other necessities are magically provided; and characters go on long voyages and sometimes return unrecognized. Basically, only two explanations are possible for such parallels: they may be the result of *polygenesis*, the independent invention of the same materials in different places, or of *diffusion*, the single invention at one place of an item that was then transmitted to other regions.

It is noteworthy that those pioneer folktale scholars, Jacob and Wilhelm Grimm of nineteenth-century Germany, perceived both possibilities and selected diffusion, which still has more favor among folklorists, as the better explanation. The Brothers Grimm theorized that folktales, such as those they collected in Germany, were *broken-down myths* that had originated among the prehistoric Indo-European tribes and had been disseminated during their migrations throughout Europe.

A second nineteenth-century theory drew further on the advancing study of comparative linguistics for its evidence. It was championed by a German "philologist," or what we would now call a linguist, Max Müller, an Oxford University professor. When Sanskrit came to be recognized as the key language of the Indo-European family, Müller compared the names of gods in various bodies of mythology with the names of heavenly bodies in Sanskrit; he concluded that all of the principal gods' names had originally stood for solar phenomena. His theory, which came to be called *solar mythology,* regarded myths as essentially accounts of the recurrence of day and night; the European folktales presumably were descended from myths and conveyed the same symbolism.

Followers of Max Müller, both in England and in the United States, carried solar (and also lunar) explanations of myths to great lengths, applying them to texts from around the world. Similar research also produced a "zoological" interpretation that read animal symbolism into myths, and a sweeping "Indianist" theory that traced all European folktales back to India.

The solar mythologists were opposed by the so-called *English anthropological school* of comparative mythologists. Their theoretical foundation was the idea of *cultural evolution,* patterned on the biological evolution which Charles Darwin had described in *The Origin of Species* in 1859. Assuming that all cultures, like plants and animals, had evolved in stages from lower to higher forms, these anthropologists postulated that the primitive and peasant cultures of today retain "survivals" of the "savage stage" of modern civilization. E. B. Tylor's landmark book *Primitive Culture* (1871) articulated this *theory of survivals,* and the following passage from Andrew Lang's *Custom and Myth* (1884) describes the method by which it was applied.

The student of folklore is led to examine the usages, myths, and ideas of savages, which are still retained, in rude enough shape, by the European peasantry. . . .

The method is, when an apparently irrational and anomalous custom is found in any country, to look for a country where a similar practice is found, and where the practice is no longer irrational and anomalous, but in harmony with the manners and ideas of the people among whom it prevails. . . . Folklore represents, in the midst of a civilised race, the savage ideas out of which civilisation has been evolved.

With Lang as their standard-bearer, the English anthropologists waged a devastating campaign against the solar mythologists, even to the extent of using Müller's own method to prove that Müller himself was a sun god. One monument of Victorian scholarship, Sir James G. Frazer's *The Golden Bough* (first published in 1890 and expanded to twelve volumes by its final revision in 1915), was essentially a massive assemblage of evidence of the world-wide persistence of folk beliefs, myths, and customs that was taken by some readers to support the theory of survivals of culture.

The suggestion of several nineteenth-century German scholars that the fantasy world of dreams might have given rise to myths anticipated the *psychoanalytical approach to myths* introduced by Sigmund Freud. This schoool, like that of the English anthropologists, assumed that polygenesis explained widespread myth parallels. The Freudian explanation drew on the study of dreams, neuroses, and complexes to unravel the workings of the unconscious and subconscious minds with their Oedipal, phallic, and other symbolism. Carl Jung, who introduced the term "collective unconscious" for generalized human patterns of culture, and Otto Rank, author of *The Myth of the Birth of the Hero* (1914), made major contributions to this type of interpretation.

As early as the fourth century B.C. the idea arose that myths were actually based on historical traditions, and myth heroes were real people. The theory was known as *euhemerism* after the Sicilian philosopher Euhemerus who proposed it; he held, in effect, that man had made gods in his own image. A kind of "new euhemerism" constituted the *heroic-age theory* set forth by H. M. and N. K. Chadwick in their work *The Growth of Literature* (3 volumes, 1932–40). They asserted that mythical heroes such as England's Beowulf, Germany's Siegfried, France's Roland, and Ireland's Cuchulain were based on actual chieftains who had led roving bands of warriors across prehistoric Europe; historical accounts of their deeds had been passed down as heroic legends and myths. Recently the theory was applied by Richard M. Dorson to the American frontier, with Davy Crockett as a heroic-age figure.

Exactly the opposite assumption—that the basis of myth is *never* history—underlies the *myth-ritual theory* advanced by Lord Raglan in his work *The Hero* (1936). Like Otto Rank and others before him, Lord Raglan schematized a large number of mythical biographies into a *monomyth*. Raglan's analysis then held that no myth, legend, or folktale that significantly matched this pattern could preserve any history. Instead, religious ritual was the source of all myths, and myths preceded all genuine folklore. The myth-ritual theory has been strongly criticized in the United States but has also had a vigorous defense in the writings of Stanley Edgar Hyman.

Although all of these theories of myth origins once had their firm adherents, most of them claim only a few serious advocates among folklorists today. But the theories introduced in these early studies continue to influence folklore scholarship. The question of polygenesis versus diffusion must still be dealt with; the concepts of folktales as "broken-down myths" and of all folklore as cultural "survivals" are far from dead. Psychoanalytical theory has gained recent disciples among professionally trained folklorists, as has euhemerism. Many terms introduced in the nineteenth-century studies are still employed by writers, and several anthropological-folklorists have tried to combine what they consider to be the best features of several schools of analysis and interpretation into new, more comprehensive explanations of myths.

The materials outlined and sampled in this chapter, together with the bibliographic notes that follow, give only a skeletal idea of *myths* in the fullness of their narrative and symbolic development and *motifs* in the fineness of their distinctions among myriad narrative elements. Because myth and motif are fundamental aspects of folklore material and analysis, the student should explore these subjects further both by reading the scholarly literature and by using reference works.

BIBLIOGRAPHIC NOTES

J. R. Rayfield's "What Is a Story?" in *AA* 74 (1972): 1085–1106, establishes criteria by which listeners accept or reject a telling as conforming to their idea of what constitutes a story. There is a voluminous literature devoted to the same question. For two recent works that make generous reference to it, see Margaret K. Brady, "Narrative Competence: A Navajo Example of Peer Group Evaluation," *JAF* 93 (1980): 158–81, and Brian Sutton-Smith and collaborators, *The Folkstories of Children*, AFS Publications, New Series, Vol. 3 (Philadelphia, 1981).

William Bascom's formulation of definitions for "The Forms of Folklore: Prose Narratives" (quoted in this chapter) appeared in *JAF* 78 (1965): 3–20. Stith Thompson's *The Folktale* (New York: Dryden Press, 1946) is a basic older survey of traditional prose narratives and their study; part 3, "The Folktale in a Primitive Culture," surveys North American Indian traditional narratives. J. L. Fisher's article "The Sociopsychological Analysis of Folktales," *CA* 4 (1963): 235–95, is important, with a valuable bibliography and comments by seventeen anthropologists and folklorists. Like Thompson, Fischer and others use the general term "folktale" for all traditional prose narratives. The introduction by Bødker in *European Folk Tales*, ed. Laurits Bødker, Christina Hole, and G. D'Aronco (Copenhagen: Rosenkilde and Bagger; and Hatboro, Pa.: Folklore Associates, 1963), compares similar motifs in folktales and myths.

For nearly one hundred examples of native American traditional prose narratives taken from the older collections and with voluminous notes, see Stith Thompson's *Tales of the North American Indians* (Cambridge, Mass.: Harvard University Press, 1929; paperback edn. Bloomington: Indiana University Press, 1966). The first four stories quoted in this chapter come from Thompson's anthology. Alan Dundes's "The Morphology of North American Indian Folktales," in *FCC* no. 195 (1964) discusses the structural approach to myths and establishes some basic forms of Indian narratives. Levette J. Davidson quotes some interesting examples of "White Versions of Indian Myths and Legends" in *WF* 7 (1948): 115–28. Links between Asiatic and American Indian mythology were considered in Gudmund Hatt's monograph *Asiatic Influ-*

ences in American Folklore, Det. Kgl. Danske Videnskabernes Selskab, Historisk-Filologiske Meddelelser, 31:6 (Copenhagen, 1949). Another specific case is taken up in E. Adamson Hoebel's "The Asiatic Origin of a Myth of the Northwest Coast," *JAF* 54 (1941): 1–9. I make reference to an Old Norse myth to explain a recent American joke in a note "Thor, the Cheechako and the Initiates' Tasks: A Modern Parallel for an Old Jest," *SFQ* 24 (1960): 235–38.

"Myth: A Symposium," edited by Thomas A. Sebeok for *JAF* (October–December 1955), reprinted in 1958 by Indiana University Press, contains nine important articles on theories of myth, including Richard M. Dorson's "The Eclipse of Solar Mythology" and Thompson's "Myths and Folktales." William Bascom discussed "The Myth-Ritual Theory" in *JAF* 70 (1957): 103–14, and set off a wave of responses, favorable and hostile, in the following issues of the journal. Two later important contributions to evaluating the myth-ritual and other monomyth theories are Archer Taylor's "The Biographical Pattern in Traditional Narrative," *JFI* 1 (1964): 114–29 and Herbert Weisinger's "Before Myth," *JFI* 2 (1965): 120–31. Two other good anthologies of myth studies are "Myth and Mythmaking," ed. Henry A. Murray in *Daedalus* (Spring 1959), and the January–March 1966 special issue of *JAF,* ed. Melville Jacobs, called "The Anthropologist Looks at Myth." Jacobs's methods of myth analysis were criticized in a review of *The People Are Coming Soon: Analyses of Clackamas Chinook Myths and Tales* (Seattle, 1960), by Sven Liljeblad in *MF* 12 (1962): 93–103. In "Five Interpretations of a Melanesian Myth," *JAF* 86 (1973): 3–13, Elli Köngäs-Maranda subjects the same text to analysis in terms of (1) Myth and Ritual, (2) Reflection of Culture, (3) Charter of Society, (4) Freudian and Jungian Symbolism, and (5) Structure.

Although there was a wealth of native American narrative texts available in government reports, museum bulletins, journals of folklore and anthropology, etc. since the late nineteenth century, the integration of these traditions with mainstream American folklore studies has been poor. (Only the third edition of this textbook has even introduced the subject, drawing inspiration from the new "ethnopoetics" and awareness of native American narratives as poetic/dramatic art forms.) In older collections like Harold W. Thompson's *Body, Boots, and Britches* (1940), for example, the chapter "Injun-Fighters" is *about* New York State Indians rather than based on their own traditions. In George Korson's *Pennsylvania Songs and Legends* (1949), one chapter concerns a single Indian personality—the Seneca chief "Cornplanter"—and the traditions surrounding his people. Richard M. Dorson's *Bloodstoppers and Bearwalkers* (1952) devoted one section (three chapters) to "The Indian Tradition" of Michigan's Upper Peninsula, contrasting the "stuffed" Indian of tourist-promotional literature and other published sources with the "live" Indians of everyday Peninsular life and history.

(Full references to these three collections are given in the notes to Chapter 3.) Roger L. Welsch provides twenty-three Plains Indian texts in English translations in his *Treasury of Nebraska Pioneer Folklore* (Lincoln: University of Nebraska Press, 1966), pp. 176–238. But better than any of these sources—and considerably cheaper as well—is the paperback collection of fifty-two texts, selected from the vast anthropological literature, in Susan Feldman's *The Storytelling Stone: Myths and Tales of the American Indians* (New York: Dell-Laurel, 1965). This handy volume also contains a bibliography.

Two examples of articles containing Indian stories from the *Journal of American Folklore* are included in *Readings in American Folklore*. Roland B. Dixon's "Some Coyote Stories from the Maidu Indians of California" (pp. 16–21), containing four texts in English without comment, came from *JAF* for 1900; Judy Trejo's "Coyote Tales: A Paiute Commentary" (pp. 192–198), from *JAF* for 1974, also has four tales but includes an insider's comments on their style, performance, and meaning. (One of Trejo's comments is included in this chapter, following the story of Wildcat and Coyote.)

Stith Thompson's "The Star Husband Tale," a classic study of a widespread native American narrative first published in 1953, is conveniently reprinted in Dundes's *The Study of Folklore*, pp. 414–74. Two studies reviewing the same material are George W. Rich's "Rethinking the Star Husbands," *JAF* 84 (1971): 436–41, and Frank W. Young, "Folktales and Social Structure: A Comparison of Three Analyses of the Star Husband Tale," *JAF* 91 (1978): 691–99.

The Indian "Adam and Eve" story quoted in this chapter comes from Jarold Ramsey's article "The Bible in Western Indian Mythology," *JAF* 90 (1977): 442–54, quoted there from *JAF* of 1938. The quoted adaptation of a Coyote story to criticize the white man comes from Madronna Holden's article "'Making All the Crooked Ways Straight': The Satirical Portrait of Whites in Coast Salish Folklore," *JAF* 89 (1976): 271–93, quoted there from an earlier book. A study of related material is Keith H. Basso's *Portraits of "The Whiteman": Linguistic Play and Cultural Symbols among the Western Apache* (London and Cambridge: Cambridge University Press, 1979).

Two essays in Richard M. Dorson's recent *Handbook of American Folklore* (see the Preface) briefly discuss the shortcomings of previous scholarship in this area and some promises for the future. Elaine Jahner, in "Finding the Way Home: The Interpretation of American Indian Folklore" (pp. 11–17), demonstrates "micro-analysis" of texts with a Sioux story of a rescue aided by wolves. George Lankford, in "The Unfulfilled Promise of North American American Indian Folklore" (pp. 18–23), advocates an exhaustive study of "local rules for tale-telling" among Indian groups.

Barre Toelken's work with Navajo storytelling offers an excellent example of current folklorists' concern with close reading of texts plus full attention to contexts and styles. Toelken's essay *"Ma'i Jaldloshi: Legendary Styles and Navaho Myth"* appeared in *American Folk Legend: A Symposium*, ed. Wayland D. Hand (Berkeley and Los Angeles: University of California Press, 1971), pp. 203–11. The next stage of Toelken's analysis resulted in the essay "The 'Pretty Languages' of Yellowman: Genre, Mode, and Texture in Navaho Coyote Narratives," included in *Folklore Genres*, ed. Dan Ben-Amos, American Folklore Society Bibliographic and Special Series, Vol. 26 (Austin: University of Texas Press, 1976), pp. 145–70. Then Toelken's retranslation and re-evaluation of Yellowman's stories appeared as an essay cowritten with Tacheeni Scott in the collection *Traditional American Indian Literatures: Texts and Interpretations*, ed. Karl Kroeber (Lincoln: University of Nebraska Press, 1981), pp. 65–116. (This same volume contains important chapters by Kroeber, Jarold Ramsey, Dennis Tedlock, and Dell Hymes.)

At the forefront of scholars and critics promoting a fresh awareness of the artistic qualities of native American narratives is Jarold Ramsey. His essay "The Wife Who Goes Out Like a Man, Comes Back as a Hero: The Art of Two Oregon Indian Narratives" broke new ground by appearing in the leading American journal of literary scholarship, *PMLA* 92 (1977): 9–18. The same year Ramsey published a volume of texts, *Coyote Was Going There: Indian Literature of the Oregon Country* (Seattle: University of Washington Press). Related writings by other scholars are John Bierhorst's "American Indian Verbal Art and the Role of the Literary Critic," *JAF* 88 (1975): 401–8, and "Folklore and Literary Criticism: A Dialogue," *JFI* 18 (1981): 97–156, which contains a study of two English renderings of a single story by Karl Kroeber with commentary by five scholars and a rejoinder by Kroeber.

An excellent introduction to the problem of the translation of Indian texts is Dennis Tedlock's "On the Translation of Style in Oral Narrative," *JAF* 84 (1971): 114–33. Tedlock points out specific shortcomings in the translations given in classic collections of Zuñi narratives such as Ruth Benedict's *Zuñi Mythology* (1935), and then he presents principles for retranslating texts as dramatic poetry, with a few passages of example. More of Tedlock's translations are given in his anthology *Finding the Center: Narrative Poetry of the Zuñi Indians* (1972; repr. with a new preface in Bison Books, University of Nebraska Press, 1978).

The most impressive body of recent work on native American texts —both in subtlety of analysis and in sheer volume—is that of Dell Hymes on Northwest Indian material. Hymes's essay "Folklore's Nature and the Sun's Myth" (quoted in this chapter), originally a presidential address to the American Folklore Society, was published in *JAF* 88 (1975): 345–69. It presents Hymes's conception of the discipline of folklore set forth partly in the form of an Oregon Indian text as rendered into poetic lines. Dell Hymes's book *In Vain I Tried to Tell You* (Philadelphia: University of Pennsylvania Press, 1981) reprints ten of his earlier "Essays in Native American Ethnopoetics" (the subtitle) and contains a good bibliography of the new ethnopoetics.

Some materials relating to mythic traditions in American history and culture are contained in E. McClung Fleming's essay "Symbols of the United States: From Indian Queen to Uncle Sam" in *Frontiers of American Culture*, ed. Ray B. Browne, Richard H. Crowder, and Virgil L. Stafford (Lafayette, Ind.: Purdue University Studies, 1968), pp. 1–24. See also the section "American Cultural Myths" in Dorson's *Handbook of America Folklore*. Perry McWilliams, in "The Alamo Story: From Fact to Fable," *JFI* 15 (1978): 221–33, delineates what he terms "the process of enfablement." Karl G. Heider shows how three generals of the American Revolution were transformed into mythic figures in folk and popular sources in his essay "The Gamecock, the Swamp Fox, and the Wizard Owl: The Development of Good Form in an American Totemic Set," *JAF* 93 (1980): 1–22. Daryl Dance considers some mythic aspects of Afro-American narratives in an essay entitled "In the Beginning: A New View of Black American Etiological Tales," *SFQ* 40 (1977): 53–64.

Stith Thompson's *Motif-Index of Folk-Literature* appeared in its revised definitive six-volume edition between 1955 and 1958 (Copenhagen and Bloomington, Ind.: Indiana University Press).

9
Legends and Anecdotes

Myth, Legend, Anecdote

Legends, the second large category of traditional prose narratives are like myths in that they are stories regarded by their tellers as true, despite being partly based on traditional motifs or concepts. Unlike myths, however, legends are generally secular and are set in the less remote past in a conventional earthly locale. Legends are sometimes referred to as *folk history*, although history is soon distorted by oral transmission. Because many legends reflect folk beliefs, the term *belief tale* is also applied to them; and just as myths serve the function of validating religious rites in a primitive culture, legends are often told to validate superstitions in modern folklore. Since the spread of legends is analogous to the dissemination of *rumors* (unverifiable reports of supposed events), some sociological rumor theories have been applied to legends as well. Rumors may swell to legend proportions as they develop a specific narrative content. Single-episode belief tales, especially those centering on individuals, are termed *anecdotes* and constitute a large and common genre of legendary lore in modern America.

Rumors, anecdotes, and legends alike are concerned with remarkable, even bizarre, events that allegedly happened to ordinary people in everyday situations. These reports and stories are recounted, usually in conversation, as a way of explaining strange things that occur—or are thought to have occurred— and they are passed on in order to warn or inform others about these unprovable events. The structure of legends is loose. In effect, each version is a re-creation of the story by the teller using the basic elements of its traditional content. Often legends and their kin are given the added support of certain "validating formulas," such as "This happened in our neighborhood" or "I heard this from a friend of mine who knows the person it really happened to" or "I read this in the paper once" or "I think I heard about this on the radio." Indeed, the subject matter of legends is the same sort of event that makes news; so in modern folklore the mass media sometimes contribute to the spread of rumors and legends.

Legends are usually *migratory*—widely known in different places—but when texts become rooted and adapted to a particular place, they are said to be *localized*. For example, the widespread legend about a new member of a college secret society accidentally killed during an initiation has been localized on many campuses to a particular fraternity and a specific kind of ceremony or prank. The motif that a Judas figure within a group was responsible for the betrayal and death of the hero gets attached to every outlaw whom the folk admire from Robin Hood to Jesse James and beyond.

Often legends are circulated in *cycles,* or groups of narratives relating to one event, person, or theme. Among these stories there may be both long, well-developed accounts and mere fragments of rumor and hearsay. For this reason the classification of legends has been a vexing matter; as the folklorist Wayland D. Hand, who has wrestled with the problem, wrote, "For the systematizer, folk legends seem endless in bulk and variety, and they are often so short and formless as to defy classification." For discussion purposes, however, five groups of legends may be established on the basis of their primary concern with religion, the supernatural, urban settings, individual persons, or localities and their histories.

Religious Legends

Religious legends include the narratives to which the term "legend" originally applied exclusively—stories of the lives of Christian saints. Such stories belong to religious literature when they have been attested by an official investigation and are entered in printed accounts, but they remain folklore while they circulate orally in traditional versions. Even the sanctioned "lives of saints" in print contain numerous traditional motifs from folk sources, and saintly influences continue to be manifested, according to folk accounts both from Europe and the United States, in many cases never validated by the Church. A counterpart tradition in a native American sect is that of the miraculous appearances of the three "Nephites" who have aided Mormons in time of need by bringing them food, comforting them, rescuing them, and sometimes healing them.

"Legend" now refers to many more kinds of stories than just *saints' legends,* and even the term "religious legends" includes other types. Traditional stories about miracles, revelations, answers to prayers, marvelous icons, and blessings bestowed upon the faithful may all be called religious legends if their dissemination is largely oral and some of their motifs are traditional. To say that such stories are legendary is not necessarily to say that they are of doubtful veracity, for folklore may be true as well as false. Thus, a legend about a group of nuns who retreat to prayerful sanctuary before an advancing forest fire and emerge later to find that the fire has miraculously bypassed them may be believed, but unprovable, or it may be supported by historical record. In either case, however, it is a religious legend as long as traditional oral versions continue to circulate.

A third category of religious legends is "the Bible of the folk" —a cycle of stories that fill the blanks of, or extend, Biblical narratives. For example, the term "Adam's apple" refers to legendary accounts of the apple sticking in Adam's throat when he took it from Eve and ate it. The dog is said to have a cold nose because he was late coming to the ark and had to ride next to the rail. Gypsies are allowed to roam the whole earth, according to legend, because one of them stole the nail forged for Christ's heart when He was nailed to the cross. Various animals or plants are rewarded or formed as they are because of some legendary connection with the life of the Saviour. Flies that gathered on the body of Christ at His crucifixion looked like nails and prevented more nails from being driven—therefore they may dine at kings' tables—while various trees (the aspen, poplar, and others) are said to be "cursed" for supplying wood for His cross. All of these examples, it should be noted, are etiological legends and to many tellers may even function as myths—that is, as charters for religious faith. The folklorist Francis Lee Utley referred to this area of religious legends as "an uncharted wilderness" that requires the use of numerous sources, both written and oral, for its successful exploration.

Supernatural Legends

Supernatural legends generally take the form of supposedly factual accounts of occurrences and experiences which seem to validate folk beliefs and superstitions. For the simplest of these, a kind of prelegend that is merely a "narrative of a personal happening," the useful term *memorate* was coined by the Swedish folklorist C. W. von Sydow. Memorates are firsthand descriptions of personal experiences with the supernatural, although a story about a remarkable (nonsupernatural) personal experience could be thought of as a "secular memorate." While a memorate might be repeated by a second or third person, more commonly the story would either remain with its original subject as a personal narrative or become detached, acquire further traditional elements, and grow into a legend proper.

The Hungarian-American folklorists Linda Dégh and Andrew Vázsonyi have isolated an even more basic unit they call the *proto-memorate*, referring to any "credibility-seeking utterance like folk belief itself" which may precede or provide background for legend formation. The true legend must be a traditional rather than just a personal narrative, but the proto-memorate and memorate, though influenced by folk belief, mainly describe a purely personal experience of the narrator's. All such stories are told, at least in part, to give credence to folk beliefs. Yet, as Patrick B. Mullen points out, sometimes the "basic narrative value" of a legend may keep it alive in tradition long after anyone seriously believes it. Supernatural legends may be grouped according to such categories of superstition as beliefs in supernatural creatures, in returning spirits of the dead, in magic, and in supernatural signs.

European legendry is full of stories of supernatural creatures, both evil ones, such as vampires, werewolves, trolls, and other monsters, and the partly helpful ones, such as elves, brownies, fairies, *nisser*, and other "little people." But very few of these creatures migrated to the New World where immigrant life lacked the settings and family traditions to maintain this lore. We can collect legends of "bearwalkers" and other shape shifters, and of occasional zombies, deformed maniacs, ape men, "Bigfoots," and other monsters, but usually just in isolated pockets of folk culture, especially where Indian, Afro-American, or certain immigrant tradition is strong. A hotbed of creaturelore is the adolescent summer camp, where stories of fearsome folk figures are told to wide-eyed campers gathered around the nightly bonfire.

Legends of witchcraft, a staple of colonial American folklore, are still circulated in modern America, though mostly in the backwoods or rural towns. The following slightly condensed account collected by Leonard Roberts in Kentucky shows a typical mix of community beliefs and personal narrative. The first episode is essentially a memorate.

> When I was a small girl there was an old man named George. The folks around home said he was a witch. . . .
>
> One day I was in the barn milking when I suddenly heard a noise. I went to see what it was, of course. There stood George with his old crooked cane pointing at our old red cow. . . . She turned around and walked right up the ladder into the barn loft. Well, we had a time getting her down from there.
>
> A while after that my mother was churning but was not getting much butter to come. George came along and wanted to churn, so mother let him take the dasher. Well, he churned about five minutes and he had that churn full of butter. My mother was afraid to use the butter, so she gave it to our twelve hogs and they everyone died as dead as a wedge.
>
> Old George used to tell people how he become a witch. He said that he went to the top of the mountain before the sun rose and prayed to the Devil and cursed the Lord.

Magically influencing animals, preventing butter from forming, and praying to the Devil are all typical motifs of witchcraft.

Supernatural legends concerning the returning spirits of the dead, a major category in world folklore, are equally common and varied in the United States. The term *ghost stories* for such narratives suggests blood-curdling scare tales about white-sheeted or invisible spooks who are out to destroy humankind. But most ghosts in American legends are lifelike in appearance and come back from the dead only to set right an error or finish a task. A better term for these creatures is *revenants,* or "re-turners"—those who return from the world of the dead, usually only temporarily. Their reasons for coming back are numerous, and harmless to anyone with a clear conscience. Only a few spirits return for revenge, and they always have justification; more commonly they return for such a purpose as to reveal hidden treasure, to ask that a crooked limb in the coffin be straightened, or to reveal the cause of death. A common motif in these legends is E402: "Mysterious ghostlike noises heard." These sounds include calls, moans, snores, sobs, sighs, footsteps, and sometimes even that old standby of Hollywood horror films, chain rattling. Often a brave person can communicate with the spirit by means of these noises, asking for one for "yes," and two for "no" to discover the reason for the haunting. Besides humans, even the ghosts of animals may come back to torment the living, but more often they come to assist. The ways by which ghosts may be summoned, the reasons they come, their appearance, the attempts to placate them, and the variants of tales about encounters with them can make up a fascinating study within a region or for a particular folk group, but only a few such studies have been completed.

An approach to legend research suggested by John M. Vlach is to distinguish from actual supernatural belief tales the *humorous anti-legends* told mostly by children and adolescents to evoke simultaneous fear and laughter. Serving a more sinister purpose were the stories of *"Night Riders"* and *"Night Doctors"* told by Southern whites to intimidate their black slaves by encouraging superstitious fear of ghosts and bogies. A study by Gladys-Marie Fry based on ex-slave narratives and oral history interviews reveals how actual mounted white patrols and the Ku Klux Klan served to lend credence among blacks to the rumors spread by whites about ghostly spirits and human body-snatchers who would capture them if they ventured forth after dark. Thus a cycle of created legends was used for social control and racial suppression.

Memorates of supernatural signs and magic are probably more common than full-scale legends concerning them, although memorates have not been collected as frequently as legends have by American folklorists. Yet, one often hears first-person accounts of folk cures that worked, wishes that came true, warnings of death that were fulfilled, bad luck that followed a traditional omen, prophetic dreams, and so forth. As one analysis has described the forming sequence, "primary stimuli," such as folk superstitions (i.e., "Bad luck comes in threes") encounter the "releasing stimuli" involved in an actual situation (three unlucky things happen to someone); the event is interpreted ("That saying is *true!*"), and then that happening is narrated to others as a memorate. Repeated transmissions of the memorate in turn support the folk belief.

Personal narratives of supposed cases of prenatal influence demonstrate this process at work. One informant stated the well-known belief "If you are suddenly startled by something while you are pregnant and then touch your body, your baby will be marked in that same spot." Then she related this second-hand memorate as evidence:

> My aunt had this experience. She was startled by a rabbit while working in her garden one day. The rabbit suddenly jumped out near her and she hit herself quite hard on the thigh in reaction to the scare. Her baby girl was born with a birthmark on her thigh in the shape of a rabbit in the exact spot where she had hit herself.

But not every story with similar content is a memorate. The following, though told in a serious manner and referring to the same belief, is really a parody of a belief tale:

> Many people today don't believe when a pregnant woman gets scared that an imprint of this goes on the child. But I

know of an actual case. This lady was at the Bronx Zoo just before she was to have her baby, and she got scared by a bear. And sure enough when the child was born, it had bare feet!

Urban Legends

The most convenient subject in which the student might observe the growth of legends is the so-called **urban legend**— stories in a contemporary setting (not necessarily a big city) that are reported as true individual experiences but that have traditional variants that indicate their legendary character. Urban legends typically have three good reasons for their popularity: a suspenseful story line, an element of actual belief, and a warning or moral that is either stated or implied. Only a few urban legends contain *super*natural motifs, but all of them include at least highly *un*natural details. This fact shakes popular belief in them not a bit, for people in all walks of life credit such stories, and various publications frequently reprint them—or radio commentators report them—as the truth.

One of the oldest American urban legends, and a rare supernatural example, is "The Vanishing Hitchhiker" (Motif E332.3.3.1.), in which the spirit of a young girl tries to hitchhike home annually on the anniversary of her death. More recently the hitchhiker who vanishes suddenly is said to be a wholesome-looking young man who announces that Jesus is coming soon. Another favorite car story based on presumed facts concerns "The Death Car," a late-model automobile selling for a song because the smell of a corpse cannot be eradicated from it. Still other modern car legends play on possible dangers met with while driving (i.e., "The Hook" [maniac's hook hand torn off by car doorhandle] and "The Killer in the Backseat" [assailant hidden in car]) or else on the theme of inexpensive cars (i.e., "The Economical Carburetor" and "The Fifty-Dollar Car" [man's car sold cheaply by his spurned wife]).

In some urban legends an original supernatural element was rationalized. "The Robber Who Was Hurt," for example, is told nowadays about a would-be intruder who is badly burned when he tries to enter a woman's home and she thrusts a hot iron or poker against his hand. When she asks a neighbor woman for help, the neighbor says that she has to tend to her husband who just returned home with a burned hand. This legend seems to be a revision of an old witchcraft story about a supernatural intruder in animal form who is injured in the paw; later a neighbor found to have a hand that is cut or burned is detected as the culprit. Another supernatural connection is found in recent rumors and legends about the Procter & Gamble company trademark —a man in the moon and thirteen stars enclosed in a circle. This innocent design was claimed by some to be a satanic symbol adopted by the company when the founder made a Faustlike pact with the Devil to secure his financial success.

Many urban legends, though they may display the coloration of other national folklore, are international in their distribution. The story of "The Hairy-armed Hitchhiker," known in England during the 1977–1978 "Yorkshire Ripper" scares (ultimately springing from a tale known there for more than a century), migrated to the United States by spring 1983. Rather than being recognized as a man in woman's clothing by his hairy arms or hands, as in England, the threatening figure now was unmasked when his wig fell off during a struggle with a shopping-mall security guard. In either version a hatchet or an ax is later found in the stranger's handbag left in the intended victim's car. This legend adapted easily to the American scene, where stories of crime in shopping centers are common.

Occasionally it may appear that an urban legend has sprung from verifiable history. Richard M. Dorson thought he had traced "The Death Car" to a 1938 incident in the small town of Mecosta, Michigan, but later study turned up prototypical elements earlier in Europe. Similarly, the legend about a husband who fills a Cadillac parked in front of his house with cement, thinking that the owner is seducing his wife, seemed to have been verified by a newspaper article. Folklorist Louie W. Attebery found such an event reported in a Denver, Colorado, newspaper in 1960; the cemented vehicle in this instance was a 1946 DeSoto, but there was no jealousy motive. The same legend, however, had been heard in Texas some four months earlier, suggesting that life may at times imitate folklore.

The urban legend about a lady's dead cat wrapped in a neat package for burial, which is then pilfered by a shoplifter while the owner pauses in a department store on the way to meet a friend, has been reported by newspapers in different cities for at least twenty-five years. Possibly such an event *did* happen somewhere once, but not all the times and in all the places to which it has been attributed. Besides, once again, oral tradition has carried the same story for several decades longer than the news media have known it. For example, the legend about a grandmother's corpse stolen from the car-top rack when a vacationing family was driving her back home from Mexico for burial seems to be a mere re-creation of the same stolen-corpse plot, but with different details. ("The Runaway Grandmother" was also originally a European story.)

A variation on the dead-cat theme involves guests at a dinner party who rush to a hospital to have their stomachs pumped when the family pet, earlier caught nibbling at the fish course, is found dead on the back porch. The next day a neighbor confesses that he ran over the cat in the driveway and left the corpse on the porch rather than interrupting the party. (A variation of this "Poisoned Pussycat" story involves a family testing some mushrooms they have picked by feeding them to their pet.) Yet another treatment of the suffering-pet idea involves an animal put into a microwave oven to be dried after a bath, whereupon the creature explodes. (In a horrific variation, a baby is put into the microwave by a babysitter who has taken drugs.) Still other suffering pets are eaten in Chinese-American restaurants, or served to their owners in a Hong Kong restaurant, or pounded flat under a newly laid carpet (a parakeet or a gerbil), or flushed down the toilet in New York City (baby pet alligators). Probably all of these creatures of legend to some degree represent mistreated family members, an idea made explicit in the grandmother-heist story.

Basic modern anxieties often lie behind popular urban legends. An instance of this is fear of contamination from manufactured goods. A favorite story in this category is about a girl who sickens and sometimes dies because black-widow spiders have infested her sprayed hairdo; there are counterpart tales of insects living under plaster casts or in the sinus cavities. A similar story describes a girl who is embalmed alive in a "poisoned dress" which had been taken from a corpse and resold. Vague rumors about foreign matter contaminating food, another frequent motif, may develop into narratives about a mouse in a soda bottle, worms in hamburgers, a dead rat floating in a chocolate company's vats, a batter-fried rat, and so forth. That successful lawsuits have been brought against companies for selling food or drink contaminated in similar ways does not prevent the stories from qualifying as folklore, for the traditional versions are highly stylized in both form and content, and they seldom concern specific documented cases. Instead, the legends rely on the familiar and unreliable "friend of a friend" validation of other urban lore.

An antibusiness viewpoint may be revealed in urban legends, such as the Procter & Gamble story mentioned above. Defective or accidentally released experimental products (like the economical carburetor) crop up repeatedly—a bathing suit becomes transparent, a light bulb or razor blade never wears out, a tin-can speedometer casing is found on an early Japanese car, and so forth. Well-known establishments may become associated with a particular legend. The Waldorf Astoria hotel, for example, is named as the place where a secret recipe for "Red Velvet Cake" was sold to a woman for an outrageous price. In revenge, she distributed the "secret" ("Add one-quarter cup of red food coloring to the batter") widely among her friends. The management of the Waldorf cannot explain why, but this legend has stuck with them for decades, though no such cake was ever featured on their menus. Recently, the story has applied to Mrs. Fields Chocolate Chip Cookies.

In another business-legend cycle, one of a particular chain of discount stores (often K mart) is said to be the place where a woman was bitten by a poisonous snake sewn into the sleeve or lining of an imported coat. Or it may be misuse of a product, rather than a defect or other shortcoming, that causes an accident. This idea appears in legends about contact lenses sticking to the cornea after a welding accident, superglue bonding parts of the body together, power-lawnmower blades hacking off fingers when the running mower is lifted to trim a hedge, or butane cigarette lighters exploding in a pocket and injuring someone.

Anxiety about being caught in the nude or otherwise embarrassed is projected in several migratory legends of wide circulation in the United States. In a railroading version, a traveling businessman wearing only pajamas is enticed into a young woman's Pullman compartment, where he awakens alone the next morning; his clothes and luggage are back in his own Pullman car which had been disconnected from the train during the night. In a mobile-home variation, the man is napping nude in the trailer while his wife drives; at a sudden stop for a traffic light he groggily arises and steps outside, only to be left behind when the light changes. A cycle of "nude surprise party" stories describes a serviceman or businessman misunderstanding the secretive arrangements of his girlfriend or secretary for a dinner party at her home; he removes his clothes in anticipation of love-making only to discover that the event is really a surprise welcome-home party or an office party in his honor. Another surpriser-surprised tale describes a housewife caught doing her laundry in the nude by the gas-meter reader, or a babysitter and her boyfriend caught frolicking in the nude. There is a flatulent form of the same theme in which a girl breaks wind in the front seat of her date's car, unaware that the couple they are double-dating with are already sitting in the back seat.

Aspects of modern technology (microwave ovens, contact lenses, etc.) sometimes seem to substitute in urban legends for the supernatural threats of older belief tales. In one favorite story among teen-agers, an assailant threatens a babysitter by calling her from the extension telephone in the same home she is working in, but she foils him by having the calls traced and then escaping. Other telephone legends involve a celebrity offering his credit-card number for fans to make unlimited free calls on, and a woman unable to report a fire in her home because she cannot find the number 11 on her dial in order to call the 911 emergency code. Plots like these—as well as others involving computers—can generally be shown to be unverifiable and probably fictional.

Research on the "new" urban legends that crop up usually reveals older prototypes. A prime instance involves the "Choking Doberman" story that raced across the country beginning in 1981. Here a guard dog was discovered with two or three fingers stuck in its throat, and an injured intruder was found hiding in the house. Comparisons with many other legends about dogs, fingers, assailants, and the like linked the Doberman story with centuries-old traditional plots involving similar motifs, as well as with several other new legends in simultaneous circulation. Central in this history of an urban legend was the notion of a pet found in puzzling or compromising circumstances which were later explained as proving the pet's heroic defense against an intruder in the master's home (e.g., a guard dog with a bloody mouth has really killed an attacking wolf, *not* the master's child). The hidden burglar in the modern story replaced an attacking beast (usually a snake or a wolf) that was repelled by the dog in the earlier versions. The severed-fingers (or hand) motif had been lifted without alteration from other older narratives. Only the recombination of traits and the addition of some contemporary themes (often racial, sexist, or technical) could be said to distinguish the "new" story of the choking guard dog from the older versions.

Personal Legends

Personal legends are stories attached to individuals and told as true. In Old World tradition, cycles of ancient *hero legends* described an impressive catalogue of national champions such as Roland, Charlemagne, Saint Patrick, King Arthur, and Robin Hood; in American folklore the hero legend has been manifested first in such frontier figures as Davy Crockett and the keelboatman and scout Mike Fink, later in regional characters like Johnny Appleseed and Billy the Kid, and in the twentieth century in the largely fakelore elaboration of Paul Bunyan and the characters created in imitation of him. Scattered narratives, sometimes heroic, also circulate about gangsters (John Dillinger), sports stars (Babe Ruth, John L. Sullivan, Jim Thorpe), martyrs (Martin Luther King, John F. Kennedy), and military leaders (Generals Doolittle, Patton, MacArthur), as well as others. But the stories concerning such figures do not compare in number and national folk circulation to the European heroic-legend cycles, and no greater misconception exists about American folklore than the notion that we are a people who have continually created and celebrated epic folk heroes. The vaunted "heroes" of juvenile literature and chamber-of-commerce boosting are often inventions of professional writers and public-relations people, not of the folk groups to which they are attributed.

The typical hero of genuine indigenous *oral* tradition in the United States is not the brawling frontier trailblazer or the giant mythical laborer, but rather the local tall-tale specialist who has gathered a repertoire of traditional exaggerations and attached them all to his own career. Figures like John Darling of New York State, Abraham "Oregon" Smith of southern Indiana and Illinois, and Len Henry of northern Idaho were famous yarn-spinners in their own regions who have been the subjects of study by folklorists but who have no popular reputations beyond their own communities, where they were celebrated fondly as "the biggest liars in seven counties." These figures might, like John Darling, be pictured mainly as powerful men or great hunters, or they might possess a special repertoire, like Oregon Smith's travel yarns. Smith also had a reputation as a folk doctor, hence his other nickname, "Sassafras," from his favorite source of a curative potion. Almost invariably the story is told about someone approaching the local liar to ask him to "Tell the biggest lie you know!" The vaunted liar, however, says he is too busy to tell a lie; "old man so-and-so just died and I have to go order a coffin for him." When people call on the widow, they discover that the liar has indeed told them a big one, for there is old so-and-so, rocking on the front porch. Although this story is reported as a tribute to the yarnspinner's quick wit, actually it is a traditional tale that has been widely collected both in Europe and America.

First-person reminiscences and *family stories* have long puzzled American folklore collectors and scholars. How many repetitions are needed, or how widely must a personal narrative be spread for it to qualify as folklore? How can we distinguish between unstructured musings, polished retellings of events, memorates, personal narratives, and personal legends? Every folklorist who has tape-recorded good informants has had to deal with such questions. It has been asserted, with some convincing examples, that family traditions constitute a traditional category with subcategories, including courtship stories, misfortune stories, favorite anecdotes about eccentric relatives, and often-repeated—and somewhat embellished—experiences. Such stories tend to develop specific themes: family-misfortune stories might explain "Why we are not a rich family today," "How Grandpa lost his fortune or failed to capitalize on his invention," or "The time someone failed to marry money." Courtship stories may follow such themes as "love at first sight," or "meant for each other," or to be interlarded with fairy tale or romance conventions.

Nicknames and distinctive verbal expressions used within a family group might be the subject of other stories. Jimmy Durante's famous sign-off, for instance, "Good night, Mrs. Calabash, wherever you are!" is said to refer to a pet name he used for his first wife. In one family a whining child was always called "Ransey Sniffle." Why do children in one family say "We need a tombstone, Mom!" when they need to find a restroom on an auto trip? The family's oral tradition preserves the answer: because one time on a trip they were sent into a roadside cemetery to "find a tombstone" behind which to relieve themselves. In another family the expression "off towards Kelsey's" is used to describe having a coverlet or tablecloth on crooked; the story explains that one time they lived across the street at a diagonal ("kitty-corner") from a family named Kelsey.

Longer narrative traditions than these bits and pieces may preserve a good deal of family history. In some Texas families, the folklorist Mody Boatright reported, members cherish traditional accounts (which he proposed calling "family sagas") of how their pioneer forebears behaved and why they came to Texas. Richard M. Dorson suggested the term "sagaman" for the old-timer who spins long, fantastic yarns about his own exploits, in which "he plays an heroic role, overmastering the hazards and outwitting the dangers presented by vicious men, ferocious beasts, and implacable nature." Personal reminiscences of these kinds furnish background for the other folklore texts of gifted informants, and for this reason also they ought to be collected.

Not all personal experiences that become "folklorized" during retellings into personal narratives are necessarily family stories. Individuals may repeat, embellish, and dramatically perform stories about close calls, embarrassing situations, coincidences, lucky occurrences, accidents, crimes directed against them, run-ins with government authorities, and a host of other topics common to everyday conversation. As such narratives enter the teller's repertoire of set pieces, they may be drawn forth time and again at the requests of his or her acquaintances, who will listen for the pleasure the *performance* gives, long after any suspense about the outcome of the story is gone. And when traditional groupings of tellers and listeners form, the topics of personal narratives tend to fall into patterns. For example, Susan Kalčik found that the narratives told in women's rap groups (consciousness-raising groups developed by the women's liberation movement) usually drew from four subjects —men in general, other women, mothers, and male doctors. These stories, Kalčik felt, served usually as strategies to cope with the oppression of women or else as devices of self-discovery.

The *anecdote* proper is a short personal legend, supposedly true but generally apocryphal, told about an episode in the life of either a famous individual or a local character. (Sometimes the term "anecdote" is also applied to single-episode stories about a place or event.) The anecdote about George Washington and the cherry tree ("I cannot tell a lie; I did it with my little hatchet!"), though concocted by Parson Weems, an early Washington biographer, remains a traditional story to illustrate the first president's perfect honesty, and it is repeated both in print and orally. An anecdote about a famous intellectual and a chorus girl has the folkloric credentials of being attached to various individuals. In one version it is George Bernard Shaw who is propositioned thus: "You have the greatest brain in the world. I have the most graceful body. Let us then produce the perfect child." Shaw responded, "But suppose the child had my body and your brain!" In other accounts Albert Einstein is the man named, but the episode has ultimately been found in an Old French manuscript dated 1319, and it was reprinted several times in the eighteenth and nineteenth centuries.

Another persistent anecdote about a famous person deals with the supposed derivation of John Philip Sousa's name from his initials "S.O." (for "Siegfried" or "Sigismund Ochs," presumably German) and the "U.S.A." stenciled on his baggage when he traveled to (or from) the United States; another version claims that "John Phillipso USA" was the baggage marking. Sousa was actually born in Washington, D.C., and the family name was Sousa (a Portuguese name) from the start. Tales of this sort circulate especially about political figures, scientists, gangsters, show-business personalities, professional athletes, and military men. They should be distinguished from *jokes* about personalities, which are obviously false, though revealing of popular attitudes toward public figures; anecdotes always have the air of truth about them, and they supposedly demonstrate how people have revealed their own personalities.

Anecdotes of local characters emphasize supposed character and personality traits of their subjects in stories presumed to be true by the local populace, but they are often made up of motifs found in other regions as well. The local miser pays his son a penny for going to bed without supper, and then charges him a penny for breakfast; the town's laziest man wins a load of corn in a contest and asks, "Is it shelled?" The village dolt is eating his first banana on a train ride; the train goes through a tunnel, and he cries out that the fruit has blinded him. The clever rascal, on the other hand, plays dumb and always picks the big coin (nickkel) instead of the little one (dime) because, "Otherwise those smart alecks would quit asking me to choose." The absent-minded professor is a frequent target of local-character anecdotes of college campuses. He forgets that he has driven to the campus and walks home; when he gives a speech, he sometimes reads both the original and the carbon-copy of each page; and when he reaches into his pocket for the frog he caught for dissection class, he finds instead the sandwich he thought he had eaten for lunch. (Such academic anecdotes are discussed in the Appendix).

The comical Indian, sometimes foolish but more often shrewd, was the subject of a long cycle of racist anecdotes from early American history that still echoes through modern jokebooks and in oral folklore. The white man shivers in his heavy winter clothing while the Indian is comfortable in only a blanket, because, as he explains it, "Me all face." (This story has been traced to a late classical Greek source which came via French and English literary versions to the United States.) In other anecdotes Indians turn the tables on whites by using their own law and their religion against them, or the white settler may frighten the Indians by removing his wig, wooden leg, glass eye, or other artificial body part. A common theme in these anecdotes is feeding the Indians; the Indians arrive at a farm or ranch to beg for food, and the settler watches in dismay as a whole platter of fried eggs disappears down the gullet of one brave, while all of the others demand the same size serving. The Indians may stand around the molasses barrel, dipping their fingers into it and licking off the sweet. One brave is said to have eaten a whole pot of half-cooked beans one day; he was found dead the next day with his stomach distended. An anecdote about Indians offering to trade many horses or other valuables for a blonde white girl is related as true in several accounts of early Western travel, but a historian's study of them indicates that "Goldilocks on the Oregon Trail" is a legendary story stemming from traditional sources rather than from firsthand experience. An old Navajo living on the tribal reservation in Arizona is the subject of another local-character anecdote. He walks to town to pick up his monthly government check, stopping overnight at several hogans of kinsmen on the way. By the time he has gone in and back, it is time to begin going in again for the next check.

Local Legends

Local Legends are closely associated with specific places, either with their names, their geographic features, or their histories. Presumably these legends are unique regional creations, but in reality many of them are simply localized versions of migratory legends; even one that originates from a local feature or event tends to spread outward, changing and being localized as it moves. A good example of the transplanted migratory legend is the Maine-woods story of "The Man Who Plucked the Gorbey" (Canada jay), who later was plucked of his own hair while he slept. This tale evidently goes back to a Scottish and North-Country English legend about plucking a sparrow, but it has become solidly entrenched in Maine and New Brunswick, being locally credited there to some thirty different characters.

A good example of a legend spawned by technology that became localized as a historical tradition is "The Image on Glass" story analyzed by folklorist Barbara Allen. Evidently the idea that a flash of lightning could cause a photographic image to form on an ordinary windowpane or a mirror arose from people's misunderstanding in the late nineteenth century of the nature of the emerging science of photography. Stories that grew out of this concept usually referred to criminals, murder victims, or even Christ leaving an image on the glass. Specific rootings of these general accounts became local legends, as illustrated by the version from Carrollton, Alabama, about a black prisoner whose face was allegedly engraved by lightning onto a window while he awaited trial in 1878 for burning a courthouse. The name of the prisoner, the date, and the facts of his crime are matters of record, but the oral legend developed numerous variations of detail as it circulated in and around Carrollton, and the lightning-image motif appeared in local legends in other regions, eventually fading away in the late 1880s as photography became less of a novelty and as flexible films were introduced to replace glass plates.

Sometimes stories that seem to be reliable accounts of local incidents, even being carried by newspapers, have legendary plots with a long history in tradition. A good example is the urban legend about a child that is nearly abducted or is actually mutilated or killed by a group of assailants in the restroom of a department store or shopping center. The earliest known version of the story circulated in Rome in the second and third centuries A.D., claiming that the Christians were ceremonially murdering non-Christian children in their initiation rites. (Possibly the legend grew from misunderstanding the nature of the Holy Eucharist in Christian belief and practice.) By the fifth century there is evidence of a revision of the story: in Syria, it was said, a group of Jews had tortured and murdered a Christian child in mockery of Christ. This accusation against the Jews in the form of legend was common in the Middle Ages, and it has been revived frequently ever since. (The British-American traditional ballad "Little Sir Hugh" is one variant, and Chaucer's "Prioress's Tale" is another.) In Nazi Germany it was a common piece of anti-Semitic propaganda, and by 1933 it had turned up in American hate literature. In the 1960s the plot took a new twist in the urban legend in which an assault upon a white child was attributed either to blacks or Mexicans. Reports of the story, often detailed as to supposed time, place, and result, are circulated by print and word of mouth; they serve to reinforce prejudice and encourage persecution of the falsely accused minority group.

Local place-name etymologies (mentioned in Chapter 4) often have their parallels and close variants in other places. Numerous puzzling town names, for example, are explained as being made up on the basis of early settlers' initials, or as coming from some final-desperation act like pointing out a name from a map of Europe while blindfolded or taking a name from the side of a provisions box. Also, folk etymologies often disagree about the origin of the same name. One version may try to make sense out of the name spelled backward, while another maintains that United States Post Office officials either misread the handwritten name that townspeople submitted or made an error while taking it down.

Several of these processes are illustrated in Idaho place-name stories collected by students. *Emida* is said to be derived from the names of three early settlers, *E*ast, *Mi*ller, and *Da*wson; but other informants point out that "It's 'a dime' spelled backwards, and that's about what it's worth!" *Moscow* is usually associated with the Russian capital, leading to the mistaken notion that many Russians settled that part of Idaho, but sometimes stories are developed around phrases such as "Ma's cow" or "the moss cow." *Tensed,* Idaho, is near the old *Desmet* mission, named for its founding father; one folk etymology maintains that spelling the mission name backward for the village name was not acceptable to the Post Office, so officials in Washington changed the "m" to "n" on their own. Other people say that a telegraph operator or a writer mistook the letter while sending the name in for registry. Stories like these abound in every region, and the collector can usually assume that hardly any oral explanation for a place name will actually convey historical truth.

Striking geographical features are frequently the subjects of local legends. Scores of deep, dark, cold lakes are supposed to be bottomless, and a number of them are also said to have monsters lurking in them. Some lakes have underground connections with other lakes, complete with currents strong enough to pull a drowned person from one to the other. Most large caves were robber hideouts and have treasure stashed away inside somewhere, or else someone was trapped there once and starved to death before rescuers arrived. Western deserts are said to contain hidden oases, known to early explorers but never found since. Mountain ranges are sprinkled liberally with "lost mines" or, in California and the Southwest, with lost Spanish missions that are crammed with treasure.

Even outstanding man-made features like bridges, tunnels, dams, and mountain highways acquire legendary lore about such things as their designers' methods ("His six-year-old son really drew the original plans") or accidents during construction ("There's a workman's body inside that concrete!"). The "haunted house" tradition, which includes many other kinds of buildings besides houses, is a good example of a migratory supernatural motif which becomes localized in regional legends; another is "The Graveyard Wager" (Motif N384.2. "Death in the graveyard; person's clothing is caught; Tale Type 1676B, "Clothing caught in graveyard"), which is generally attached to a specific local cemetery. In the vicinities of mental institutions, legends often circulate concerning maniac escapees who were never recaptured but who still live as wild men in a woods or swamp.

Local *historical legends* are a largely still-uncollected aspect of American narrative folklore, although folk ballads based on historical events have long interested folksong scholars. Such occurrences as lynchings, feuds, sensational crimes, scandals, fires and other natural disasters, Indian massacres, and labor disputes have generated legends that become formularized in characteristic ways as they pass in oral tradition and that eventually accumulate supernatural and other motifs. Probably because of their preoccupation with other forms of folklore or because such legends may seem to be simply garbled local history of little value, few collectors have awarded them the attention, for example, that Dorson did in the Upper Peninsula of Michigan with "The Lynching of the McDonald Boys" and "How Crystal Falls Stole the Courthouse from Iron River," or that William Ivey did in the same region with "The 1913 Disaster," a legend from the community of Calumet. Countless other legends based on local history could be collected and studied elsewhere.

Cycles of national legends tend to cluster around the most dramatic events in the country's history. Thus, in Norway for example, the most numerous historical legends are about the miracles of Saint Olaf, the medieval Great Plagues, the wars with Sweden, and the Nazi occupation. In the United States, legend cycles have developed about the Revolution, the Civil War (particularly in the South), the Indian wars, and the settlement of the frontier.

BIBLIOGRAPHIC NOTES

For the analysis of legends, a basic survey is Wayland D. Hand's "Status of European and American Legend Study," *CA* 6 (1965): 439–46. Fourteen important papers from a conference on legends were edited by Hand as *American Folk Legend: A Symposium* (Berkeley and Los Angeles: University of California Press, 1971). Richard M. Dorson gathered American legends in a historical context in his anthology *America in Legend: Folklore from the Colonial Period to the Present* (New York: Pantheon Books, 1973).

Reidar Th. Christensen proposed a list of international legend types and catalogued the Norwegian variants in his work "The Migratory Legends," *FFC* no. 175 (1958). Another important classification of widespread legends is Barbara Allen Woods's *The Devil in Dog Form: A Partial Type-Index of Devil Legends,* University of California Folklore Studies no. 11 (Berkeley, 1959). Wayland D. Hand surveyed "European Fairy Lore in the New World" in *Folklore* 92 (1981): 141–48, including such specific creatures as the leprechauns and such generalized forms as the "tooth fairy." A specific European story that appears as both folk tale and legend is studied in terms of its special American adaptations in Butler H. Waugh's, "The Child and the Snake in North America," *Norveg* 7 (1960): 153–82.

Frederic C. Tubach's "Index Exemplorum: A Handbook of Medieval Religious Tales," in *FFC* no. 204 (1969), is a basic reference work on religious legends and tales with some 5,400 examples identified in thirty-seven central collections. *White Magic: An Introduction to the Folklore of Christian Legend* (Cambridge, Mass.: Harvard University Press, 1948), by C. Grant Loomis, is a good folkloristic discussion of saints' legends; Loomis also wrote on "Legend and Folklore" in *CFQ* 2 (1943): 279–97. A Jewish-American folk group is studied largely in terms of its legendry in Jerome R. Mintz's *Legends of the Hasidim* (Chicago: University of Chicago Press, 1968). An international religious-legend complex is traced in George K. Anderson's *The Legend of the Wandering Jew* (Providence, R.I.: Brown University Press, 1965). A distinctly American religious-legend cycle is the subject of such studies as Hector Lee's *The Three Nephites: The Substance and Significance of the Legend in Folklore,* University of New Mexico Publications in Language and Literature, no. 2 (Albuquerque, 1949), and William A. Wilson's "Mormon Legends of the Three Nephites Collected at Indiana University," *IF* 2 (1969): 3–35. F. L. Utley's "The Bible of the Folk" appeared in *CFQ* 4 (1945): 1–17.

Louis C. Jones analyzed "The Ghosts of New York" in *JAF* 57 (1944): 237–54. The same was done for California ghosts by Rosalie Hankey in *CFQ* 1 (1942): 155–77. Jones's anthology *Things That Go Bump in the Night* (New York: Hill and Wang, 1959) presents ghost beliefs and legends from New York. Two other anthologies of ghost stories from individual states are Ruth Ann Musick's *The Telltale Lilac Bush and Other West Virginia Ghost Tales* (Lexington, Ky.: University of Kentucky Press, 1965), and William Lynwood Montell's *Ghosts along the Cumberland: Deathlore in the Kentucky Foothills* (Knoxville: University of Tennessee Press, 1975). A good collection of Canadian ghost legends is Helen Creighton's *Bluenose Ghosts* (Toronto: Ryerson Press, 1957). Ghost stories told by juveniles held in correctional facilities are found in Bess Lomax Hawes's "La Llorona in Juvenile Hall," *WF* 27 (1968): 153–70, and Craig Soland's two-part article "Ghost Stories from Cottage II," *AFFWord* 3 (July 1973): 1–24; 3 (January 1974): 1–33. A good survey of scholarship on the famous "weeping woman" legend of Hispanic Americans is Shirley L. Arora's "La Llorona: The Naturalization of a Legend," *SWF* 5 (1981): 23–40.

Roger E. Mitchell studies a woodsman alleged to have sold his soul to the Devil in *George Knox: From Man to Legend*, no. 11 of *NEF* (1969). In a related vein, Christine Goldberg compiled a catalogue of "Traditional American Witch Legends" published in *IF* 7 (1974): 77–108. William E. Lightfoot, in "Witchcraft Memorates from Eastern Kentucky," *IF* 11 (1978): 47–62, reports examples of all eight story types listed by Goldberg in 1974. Examining thirteen West Virginia witchcraft stories, Yvonne J. Milspaw shows how women called "witches" could use their supposed powers to manipulate people and gain certain benefits; see "Witchcraft in Appalachia: Protection for the Poor," *IF* 11 (1978): 71–86. Further references to witchcraft beliefs are cited in the notes to Chapter 14.

An important analysis of the formation of legendary narratives is Lauri Honko, "Memorates and the Study of Folk Beliefs," *JFI* 1 (1964): 5–19, which should be supplemented by Linda Dégh and Andrew Vázsonyi's article "The Memorate and the Proto-Memorate," *JAF* 87 (1974): 225–39. Patrick B. Mullen made two important contributions to the study of legend forms: "The Relationship of Legend and Folk Belief," *JAF* 84 (1971): 406–13, and "Modern Legend and Rumor Theory," *JFI* 9 (1972): 95–109. On rumor itself, see Tomotsu Shibutani, *Improvised News: A Sociological Study of Rumor* (Indianapolis: Bobbs-Merrill, 1966), and Ralph C. Rosnow and Gary Alan Fine, *Rumor and Gossip: The Social Psychology of Hearsay* (New York: Elsevier, 1976), both with good case studies and bibliographies. Joe Graham's "The *Caso:* An Emic Genre of Folk Narrative," in *"And Other Neighborly Names,"* ed. Richard Bauman and Roger D. Abrahams (Austin: University of Texas Press, 1981), pp. 11–43, shows how certain personal-experience stories told by Chicanos are used to illustrate that "this kind of thing [often a supernatural event] happens."

Roger E. Mitchell studied folk and mass-cultural aspects of the accounts of the dreadful deeds of Wisconsinite Ed Gein (arrested in 1957 for murder, cannibalism, and other crimes) in "The Press, Rumor, and Legend Formation," *MJLF* 5, nos. 1–2 (1979). Other studies of legend formation are Helen Gilbert's "The Crack in the Abbey Floor: A Laboratory Analysis of a Legend," *IF* 8 (1975): 61–78; James Wise's "Tugging on Superman's Cape: The Making of a College Legend," *WF* 36 (1977): 227–38; and Bill Ellis's " 'Ralph and Rudy': The Audience's Role in Recreating a Camp Legend," *WF* 41 (1982): 169–91. For the use of rumor and legend to control black slaves, see Gladys-Marie Fry, *Night Riders in Black Folk History* (Knoxville: University of Tennessee Press, 1975).

The journal *Indiana Folklore* began with a volume devoted to studies of current legends (1 [1968]: 9–109); this interest continues with regular publication of such articles as John M. Vlach's "One Black Eye and Other Horrors: A Case for the Humorous Anti-Legend," *IF* 4 (1971): 95–140. Other studies of the legendary lore of American adolescents are Gary Alan Fine and Bruce Noel Johnson, "The Promiscuous Cheerleaders: An Adolescent Male Belief Legend," *WF* 39 (1980): 120–29, and Charlie Seemann, "The 'Char-Man': A Local Legend of the Ojai Valley," *WF* 40 (1981): 252–60.

The sizable scholarly and popular literature on urban legends is cited in three books of mine that also include numerous urban-legend texts along with comparative and historical notes plus a modicum of interpretation: see *The Vanishing Hitchhiker: American Urban Legends and Their Meanings* (New York: Norton, 1981), *The Choking Doberman and Other "New" Urban Legends* (New York: Norton, 1984), and *The Mexican Pet: More "New" Urban Legends and Some Old Favorites* (New York: Norton, 1986).

Hero legends of European traditional literature are surveyed in Jan deVries's *Heroic Song and Heroic Legend* (paperback ed., London and New York: Oxford, 1963). The authentic versus the ersatz aspects of American heroic legendry have been discussed thoroughly in many publications, which are referred to in Dorson's *American Folklore*, pp. 199–243. The basic story of Paul Bunyan's origins is detailed in Daniel G. Hoffman's study *Paul Bunyan, Last of the Frontier Demigods* (Philadelphia: University of Pennsylvania Press, 1952; reissued by Columbia University Press, 1966, and repr. as a University of Nebraska Press paperback in 1983 with some updating and added illustrations). Howard W. Marshall documents the invention of a farmer's hero on the Paul Bunyan model in "The Heroic Urge in Kansas: The Creation of Johnny Kaw," *AFFWord* 1 (Oct. 1971): 11–21.

Older traditional aspects of the frontier boast are discussed in two articles in *AS*, one by Dorothy Dondore in 6 (1930–31): 45–55, and the other by William F. Thompson in 9 (1934): 186–99. William Hugh Jansen's classic study of a Münchausen figure in America was reprinted from the original doctoral dissertation as *Abraham "Oregon" Smith: Pi-*

oneer, Folk Hero, and Tale-Teller (New York: Arno, 1977). An article of mine describes a local liar, "Len Henry: North Idaho Münchausen," *NWF* 1 (1965): 11–19. Roger D. Abrahams surveys "Some Varieties of Heroes in America" in *JFI* 3 (1966): 343–62, and Michael Owen Jones suggests a formula for the development of a heroic figure, using it as his title: "(PC + CB) × SD (R + I + E) = Hero," *NYFQ* 27 (1971): 243–60. Bruce A. Rosenberg views the mythologizing of a character in history in his *Custer and the Epic of Defeat* (University Park: Pennsylvania State University Press, 1974). William E. Lightfoot investigates a modern hipster hero in "Charlie Parker: A Contemporary Folk Hero," *KFQ* 17 (1972): 51–62.

An excellent collection of American local legends that are fully representative of the genuine oral lore of their vicinity is Ronald L. Baker's *Hoosier Folk Legends* (Bloomington: Indiana University Press, 1982), which ranges from traditional supernatural stories, place-name legends, and the like to modern legends and even UFO stories. Another good regional collection of legends is volume 3 in the *Publications of the Texas Folklore Society*, ed. J. Frank Dobie, *Legends of Texas* (1924; repr. 1964). Ronald L. Baker discusses "The Role of Folk Legends in Place-Name Research" in *JAF* 85 (1972): 367–73. Richard M. Dorson's *Bloodstoppers and Bearwalkers* (Cambridge, Mass.: Harvard University Press, 1952; repr. in paperback, 1972) contains personal and local legends from the Upper Peninsula of Michigan: "sagamen" are discussed on pp. 249–72.

Family legends are studied by Kim S. Garrett in "Family Stories and Sayings," *PTFS* 30 (1961): 273–81; Mody Boatright in the title essay of *The Family Saga and Other Phases of American Folklore* (Urbana: University of Illinois Press, 1958), pp. 1–19; Patrick B. Mullen, "Folk Songs and Family Traditions," *PTFS* 37 (1972): 49–63; and Stanley H. Brandes, "Family Misfortune Stories in American Folklore," *JFI* 12 (1975): 5–17. Two studies focus on a specific genre of family story: Steven J. Zeitlin's "'An Alchemy of Mind': The Family Courtship Story," *WF* 39 (1980): 17–33; and Patrick B. Mullen's "Two Courtship Stories from the Blue Ridge Mountains," *FFV* 2 (1980–81): 25–37. In "Did Great Grandpa Wood Really Talk about Tits in Church?" *SWF* 3 (1979): 29–35, Gordon S. Wood, Jr., examines a family anecdote about his ancestor and discovers it to be a well-traveled story, originally from Europe. A large collection of family folklore—rich in legends—is *A Celebration of American Family Folklore*, ed. Steven J. Zeitlin, Amy J. Kotkin, and Holly Cutting Baker (New York: Pantheon, 1982).

In recent years the personal-experience narrative has come into its own as a folklore phenomenon to be studied. A special double issue of *JFI* (vol. 14, nos. 1–2 [1977]), especially the opening essay by the editor, Sandra K. D. Stahl, is the best place to gain an acquaintanceship with these stories as folklorists have identified and analyzed them. Also basic is Stahl's article "The Oral Personal Narrative in Its Generic Context," *Fabula* 18 (1977): 18–39. Roger D. Abrahams discussed how "we represent, report, or replay" activities in "The Most Embarrassing Thing That Ever Happened: Conversational Stories in a Theory of Enactment," *FF* 10 (1977): 9–15. Yet another subcategory of the personal-experience story is introduced in Eleanor Wach's "The Crime-Victim Narrative as a Folkloric Genre," *JFI* 19 (1982): 17–30; some related material was included in James P. Leary's "Fists and Foul Mouths: Fights and Fight Stories in Contemporary Rural American Bars," *JAF* 89 (1976): 27–39. Further theoretical insights are contained in Barbara Allen's "Personal Experience Narratives: Use and Meaning in Interaction," *FMS* 2 (1978): 5–7, and William M. Clements's "Personal Narrative, the Interview Context, and the Question of Tradition," *WF* 39 (1980): 106–12. In "The Life Story," *JAF* 93 (1980): 276–92, Jeff Todd Titon distinguishes the life *history* (a record of events presumed accurate) and the more fictitious life *story* (which focuses on personality and dramatic events).

The Anatomy of the Anecdote (Chicago: University of Chicago Press, 1960), by Louis Brownlow, journalist, public servant, and educator, contains an informative discussion of the form and some good examples from the author's rich repertoire of family and political stories; the book was edited from tape-recorded talks by Brownlow. "Professor Einstein and the Chorus Girl" was traced by Jerah Johnson in *JAF* 73 (1960): 248–49. Sousa-name anecdotes were discussed by several correspondents, including Sousa's daughter, Helen Sousa Abert, in the "Letters to the Editor" columns of *Popular Mechanics* in July 1959. Other studies primarily of anecdotes are Wendy D. Caesar's " 'Asking a Mouse Who His Favorite Cat Is': Musicians' Stories about Conductors," *WF* 84 (1975): 83–116; Henry E. Anderson's "The Folklore of Draft Resistance," *NYFQ* 28 (1971): 135–50; and Harry Joe Jaffe's "The Welfare Letter," *WF* 34 (1975): 144–48. Sandra K. D. Stahl provides an illuminating discussion in "The Local Character Anecdote," *Genre* 8 (1975): 283–302. In "The Migratory Anecdote and the Folk Concept of Fame," *MSF* 4 (1976): 39–47, reprinted in *Readings in American Folklore*, pp. 279–88, Mac E. Barrick examines the human subjects of favorite anecdotes and concludes that they were often eccentric characters in real life, as well as being close to a "folk mentality" (like Lincoln, Truman, Davy Crockett, and so forth).

Legends about animals or about people who deal with animals are the subjects of three studies: David L. Wilson, "The Legend of the Pacing White Stallion," *Folklore* 90 (1979): 153–66; John W. Roberts, "Folklore of the Precocious Canine: Jim the Wonder Dog," *MFSJ* 3 (1981): 59–70; and Roger L. Welsch, *Mister, You Got Yourself a Horse: Tales of Old-Time Horse Trading* (Lincoln: University of Nebraska Press, 1981).

A general survey of "Comic Indian Anecdotes" by Richard M. Dorson appeared in *SFQ* 10 (1946): 113–28 (repr. in *Folklore and Fakelore*, pp. 269–82); see also Rayna D. Green, "Traits of Indian Character: The 'Indian' Anecdote in American Vernacular Tradition," *SFQ* 39 (1975): 233–62. The "Me All Face" story was traced in a note by Cecily Hancock in *JAF* 76 (1963): 340–42, and the "*Membra Disjuncta*" story was the subject of a note by Austin E. Fife in *WF* 22 (1963): 121–22. Colorado characters were treated in Levette J. Davidson's "'Gassy' Thompson—and Others: Stories of Local Characters," *CFQ* 5 (1946): 339–49. Anecdotes about a Utah Mormon local character are collected in Thomas E. Cheney's *The Golden Legacy: A Folk History of J. Golden Kimball* (Salt Lake City: Peregrine Smith, 1974). Francis Haines published his study "Goldilocks on the Oregon Trail" in *IY* 9 (Winter 1965–66): 26–30.

Dorson collected New England local legends of Indian tragedies, haunts, buried treasure, and place names in *Jonathan Draws the Long Bow* (Cambridge, Mass.; Harvard University Press, 1946), pp. 138–98. The Upper Peninsula historical legends appeared in Dorson's *Bloodstoppers and Bearwalkers*. See also William Ivey's "'The 1913 Disaster': Michigan Local Legend," *FF* 3 (1970): 100–14. "The Man Who Plucked the Gorbey" was studied by Edward D. Ives in *JAF* 74 (1961): 1–8. Barbara Allen's "The 'Image on Glass': Technology, Tradition, and the Emergence of Folklore" appeared in *WF* 41 (1982): 85–103. Other articles on local legends include Gerard T. Hurley's "Buried Treasure Tales in America," *WF* 10 (1951): 197–216; Patrick B. Mullen, "The Folk Idea of Unlimited Good in American Buried Treasure Legends," *JFI* 15 (1978): 209–20; Peter Gerhard's "The 'Lost Mission' of Baja California," *WF* 17 (1958): 97–106; Austin E. Fife's "The Bear Lake Monster," *UHR* 2 (1948): 99–106; and Henry A. Person's "Bottomless Lakes in the Pacific Northwest," *WF* 19 (1960): 278–80.

10
Folktales

If legends are folk history, then **folktales** are the prose fiction of
oral literature. Folktales are traditional narratives that are
strictly fictional and told primarily for entertainment, although
they may also illustrate a truth or a moral. Folktales range in
length and subject matter from some European stories about
fantastic wonders and magical events that take hours—even
days—of narration, to brief American topical jokes with concentrated plots and snappy punch lines that are told in minutes.
The term "folktale" usually connotes the complex, so-called
fairy tale, familiar in children's literature. But there is no valid
justification for ignoring recent tales that may have more realistic plots. Not only have these recent types of folktale replaced
fairy tales in most American and many foreign oral traditions,
but also, more often than not, these contemporary tales turn out
upon investigation to have ancient parallels.

The folktales of the world, like the myths and legends, en-
compass a great variety of different narrative elements contained in a fairly limited array of basic forms, and both the
details and the general outlines of specific folktales appear in
widespread cultures and through great reaches of time. The recognition of these similarities spurred attempts in Europe in the
early nineteenth century to organize comparative folktale research and to trace tales back to their origins. By the late nineteenth century a standard methodology had emerged, along
with the first of several important reference publications; since
analogous folktale *materials* and similar *methods* of study are
found in the United States, it is appropriate to review this European background.

Some Characteristics of Indo-European Folktales

A suitable general term for the "ordinary folktale" of broad Indo-European distribution is a basic problem, even though the characteristic style and form of such tales are easily recognized. Formularized openings and closings set off the items in this category; in English, they frequently begin with "Once upon a time . . ." and end "They lived happily ever after." The setting is often some unnamed kingdom in a remote age; the characters usually include royalty; the structure of the tales tends to be based on threefold repetition; and some of the typical motifs are imaginary creatures (ogres, dragons, and giants), transformations, magic objects, helpful animals, and supernatural powers or knowledge. The hero in these tales is frequently a poor stepchild who rises to wealth, power, and authority through a combination of supernatural aid, good luck, and his own ingenuity and perseverance. In short, these "ordinary folktales" are the kind of stories that most people know best from reading (or being read to from) books of "fairy tales."

But "fairy tales" is a poor term for such stories, because they almost never are concerned with the "little people," or fairies, of legendary narratives. "Nursery tales" is equally inappropriate, since mostly adults have circulated them. "Wonder tales" is a reasonable term that has some currency among folklorists, but the German word "*Märchen*" is the most widely adopted scholarly term. That is the name that the Brothers Grimm used for their famous fairy-tale collection, first published in 1812, the *Kinder- und Hausmärchen,* or "Children's and Household Folktales."

As the collection of *Märchen* and other folktales spread, encouraged by nationalism, and as the study of these tales progressed, it became increasingly desirable to devise a uniform system of referring to individual tale plots. In the beginning, "catchword titles" alone were sufficient—"Cinderella," "Puss in Boots," "Jack the Giant Killer," "Rumpelstiltzchen." In some early studies the numbers of the tales in the Grimm collection were used for reference purposes. But as large numbers of folktales were collected, serious drawbacks appeared in these systems. Titles vary greatly from country to country or even within an individual country. For instance, Cinderella is often a boy in Scandinavian tales with the nickname "Askeladden," or "the ash lad." The helpful dwarf Rumpelstiltzchen is "Tom-Tit-Tot" in English folktales and has a different local name in each of the many countries from which that tale has been collected. Most tales are collected from oral tradition without titles being given to them by informants, and often several distinct tale plots are intermixed in one oral text. Obviously, the use of the Grimm numbers for classification was limited to the tale types that the Grimms had collected.

The Type-Index

In Denmark, by the second half of the nineteenth century, the ballad scholar Svend Grundtvig had worked out a classification system for archiving Danish folktales for his own convenience in consulting them, but this was too narrow for general use. However, in Finland in the late nineteenth century a folklorist devised a catalogue based on most of the then-published European texts that introduced what has become the standard reference and classification system for *Märchen* and for some other kinds of European folktales as well. Kaarle Krohn, a founding father of modern folktale research, recognized the great need for an index of European folktale types when he experienced difficulties gathering from many countries variants of stories about the competition of a bear and a fox. He posed the problem to his student Antti Aarne, who undertook to solve it, producing in 1910 a catalogue called *Verzeichnis der Märchentypen* (*Folklore Fellows Communications* no. 3), which was translated and enlarged in 1928 by the American folklorist Stith Thompson as *The Types of the Folktale* (*FFC* no. 74). In its present second revision (*FFC* no. 184, 1961), the *Type-Index* is an essential tool for any collecting, archiving, or comparative analysis of Indo-European folktales throughout their present world-wide distribution.

The *Type-Index* should not be confused with the *Motif-Index*, introduced in Chapter 8. The two works are cross-indexed to each other, but they are distinctly different references. The *Type-Index*, theoretically, classifies only whole plots, while the *Motif-Index* is an index of narrative elements—actions, actors, objects, settings, and the like. ("Cinderella" is *Type* 510A, but "Identification by fitting of slipper" is *Motif* H36.1., and merely one narrative element of some versions of that tale.) In reference to the scholars who developed the *Type-Index*, tales catalogued therein are frequently cited as "Aarne-Thompson" types (or simply "AT" or "AaTh" types, and sometimes in Europe "MT" for "*Märchentypus*"). The *Motif-Index* was Thompson's creation alone and was separately compiled; motifs are simply cited by their lettered chapters in Thompson's system, and with their individual numbers. Both indexes may be used to identify tales and their elements, to arrange archives, and to collect bibliographic references. But the *Type-Index* deals mainly with Indo-European folktales, especially *Märchen*, while the *Motif-Index* is international in scope and contains narrative elements from many kinds of texts besides folktales. There is some overlapping of the two indexes in the area of single-motif tales, which properly seem to belong in the *Type-Index*. The most important basic distinction between the two indexes is that while the designation of a "type" in the folktale catalogue implies that all of the items listed there are historically related, *Motif-Index* entries make no such implication. To put it differently, it is assumed in the *Type-Index* that polygenesis of whole tales is impossible; in the *Motif-Index* it is assumed that polygenesis does explain parallels among some individual narrative elements that are widely known.

Even though it lacks many modern plots and variants of folktales, the *Type-Index* sets forth the basic kinds of tales found in Anglo-American folk tradition. This material is gathered under four major headings as follows:

I.   Animal Tales (Types 1 to 299)
II.   Ordinary Folktales (Types 300 to 1199)
III.   Jokes and Anecdotes (Types 1200 to 1999)
IV.   Formula Tales (Types 2000 to 2399)

Animal Tales and Fables

Animal tales have as their main characters domestic or wild animals that speak, reason, and otherwise behave like human beings. Usually these animals correspond to certain stock character types, such as the clever fox or rabbit, the stupid bear, the faithful dog, and the industrious ant. Frequently these tales describe conflicts between different animals or between animals and men. A few animal tales are etiological—for example, Type 2, "The Tail-Fisher," which explains that the bear now has a short tail because he was once tricked by the fox into fishing through the ice with his original long one. Several of the favorite stories printed in children's books are traditional animal tales. "The Bremen Town Musicians," for example, is Type 130: "The Animals in Night Quarters"; and "The Three Little Pigs" is Type 124: "Blowing the House In." Genuine oral versions of such tales, however, usually differ markedly from printed ones. For instance, in a Kentucky Mountain text of Type 124 the pigs are named "Mary, Martha, and Nancy" and they build their houses out of chips and clay, chips and hickory bark, and "steel and arn." When the wolf comes, he threatens "to get up on the house and fiddy, fiddy, faddy your house all down."

It must be conceded that popular published versions, at least in this country, now outnumber oral-traditional texts of animal tales, as well as of many other folktales. The best-known examples of animal tales in the United States come from Southern blacks, and these have been publicized mainly in the literary renderings of Joel Chandler Harris (the creator of "Uncle Remus") and in the cartoon treatments of Walt Disney. Both of these adaptations are somewhat removed from the actual oral specimens of such tales as Type 175, "The Tarbaby and the Rabbit," which has a wide international distribution.

Fables are sometimes regarded as a special subtype of animal tales, even though some fables have only human characters in them. A better term for fables might be *moral tales*, for their distinguishing quality is an explicit or implied lesson, often expressed as a proverbial moral to the story. Of the roughly 500 to 600 Greek and Indic fables that are known in literature, only about 50 have been collected from oral tradition. Such popular phrases as "the lion's share," "sour grapes," and "belling the cat" refer to such tales, these particular ones bearing the type numbers AT 51, 59, and 110, respectively.

Famous literary imitations of animal tales that have become children's classics should not be confused with stories in the oral tradition. Hans Christian Andersen's "The Ugly Duckling," for example, is not a folktale, although it might loosely be called a "fairy tale" in the popular or literary sense of the term. Similarly, "The Three Bears" was written by Robert Southey (1774–1843), the English Poet Laureate (from 1813 to 1843), probably in imitation of a folktale, and went through various literary revisions rather than oral changes. Parodies of "The Three Bears," however, do exist in modern folklore; in one of these, Mother Bear responds to the others' requests for their porridge, "Gripe, gripe, gripe, and I haven't even made breakfast yet!"

Joke fables (funny stories with a mock moral) and parodies of fables represent ways that the traditional folk fable adapts to the present. One such text, "The Fable of the Animal School" (often circulated as "Xeroxlore"), describes a group of animals determined "to do something heroic to meet the problems of a New World"; they decide to organize a school. The "activity curriculum" of their school includes all the means of animal movement (running, swimming, flying, etc.) but then all animals are required to take all the subjects, with the result that not one of them can master the school's demands. In the end the prairie dogs survive by fighting the tax levy because digging and burrowing are not in the curriculum, and they join the groundhogs and gophers to start a private school. The moral for modern educators is implied.

Ordinary Folktales

The **ordinary folktales** in part II of the Aarne-Thompson index include most of the *Märchen* proper, although the German term is sometimes used to refer to the entire contents of the *Type-Index*. But, as Thompson writes in the preface of his last revision, "there are certainly many things in the index which are by no means *Märchen.*" The "ordinary folktales," a poorly named category, constitute about one-half of the entire type catalogue and include almost all of the *Märchen* that are in it. Their characteristic features, as earlier stated, are formularized language and structure, supernatural motifs, and sympathy for the underdog or commoner.

All of the European immigrant groups in the United States, to some extent, carried their *Märchen* here with them, but these were seldom translated by the folk into English and thus have not usually persisted as oral tales in the second generation. The British wonder-tale tradition, however, with no language barrier to cross, became well established in this country, especially in the Southern Appalachian and Ozark mountains. There, distinctive American adaptations took place, and the collected texts sometimes seem almost like native stories. Type 313, "The Girl as Helper in the Hero's Flight," became "The Devil's Pretty Daughter" in the Ozarks. In Kentucky, Type 425A, "The Monster as Bridegroom," was collected as "The Girl that Married a Flop-Eared Hound-Dog," and Type 326, "The Youth Who Wanted to Learn What Fear Is," was collected as "Johnny That Never Seen a Fraid." A North Carolina text that is a combination of Type 330, "The Smith Outwits the Devil," and Type 332, "Godfather Death," is locally entitled "Whickety-Whack, Into My Sack." One cycle of Southern tales clustered around three brothers—Jack, Will, and Tom—with emphasis on the clever youngest one; these are known as "The Jack Tales."

Although the plots of Americanized *Märchen* may contain such unlikely motifs as royal characters, magical transportation, giants, ogres, and even unicorns, the language of the tellings is full of regional dialect. Expressions such as "bedads" (an exclamation), "bless me," "lit out," and "I reckon" are common; and terms such as "ash cake" (bread baked directly in fireplace ashes), "poke" (for a bag or sack), "riddle" (for a sieve), and "house plunder" (for the necessities of housekeeping) are freely introduced. As in the European versions of *Märchen,* the home life of royalty is described in very folksy terms: the hero may go down to "the king's house" and "holler him out"; and when the king summons the women in his family, he may call out, "Hey old woman and girls! Come on over here."

As was shown for animal tales, parodies of *Märchen* circulate among sophisticated modern folk, who base them on book versions they know. For example, Type 440, "The Frog King" (the first tale in the Grimm collection), ends in a parody version with a college coed saying to the prince in her room who has been transformed from a frog, "What is my housemother going to say?" Another form of "fractured fairy tale" found in modern tradition involves substituting sound-alike words for every word of the familiar old story. For example, the fractured version of "Ladle Rat Rotten Hut" (Little Red Riding Hood) begins "Wants pawn term, dare worsted ladle gull hoe lift wetter murder inner ladle cordage honor itch offer lodge dock florist." (Once upon a time there was a little girl who lived with her mother in a little cottage on the edge of a large dark forest.) As a tradition that requires writing for its transmission, this kind of parody belongs in the category of "Xeroxlore" as well.

Jokes and Anecdotes

The **jokes and anecdotes** section of the *Type-Index* also has a misleading title: no real difference between the two categories is established, and, as we have seen, the term "anecdotes" belongs to a subclass of personal legends. Simply "joke" seems the best term for short, funny, fictional folktales. Only a few of the countless jokes told in modern tradition are included here. This section of the index is essentially a classification of the older European *jests*, or *merry tales*—humorous stories characterized by short, fairly simple plots and by realistic settings. Some typical characters in the older jests were numskulls, married couples, and parsons; stories found in the *Type-Index* about such character types are still popular today in the United States.

Numskull jokes also called *noodle tales*, attribute absurd ignorance to people, often to a particular group. In Denmark, for example, the traditional fools are the *Molbos;* in England they are the "Wise Men of Gotham," and in the United States they may be two Irishmen named "Pat and Mike." Some old favorite examples that have been collected frequently in this country are Type 1240, "Man Sitting on Branch of Tree Cuts It Off"; Type 1278, "Marking the Place on the Boat [Where an Object was Lost Overboard]"; and Type 1319, "Pumpkin Sold as Ass's Egg."

Many of the joke fads of recent decades (moron jokes, Polish jokes, light-bulb jokes, etc.) contained numskull motifs, but in common with the many other fad jokes (elephant jokes, sick jokes, fruit jokes, etc.) they are really not narratives but question-and-answer routines. These have been treated under the heading "riddle-jokes" in Chapter 6.

The theme of stupidity manifests itself in many parallel jokes that are adapted to different groups. For instance, there is an airliner updating of the following characterization of how employees tell the time on four different divisions of the Illinois Central Railway:

> Iowa Division: "Fifteen hundred."
> Illinois Division: "Three o'clock."
> Kentucky Division: "The big hand's on the twelve and the little hand's on the three."
> Mississippi Division: "It's Tuesday."

In the airline version, the pilots reply similarly to the question:

> Pan American (or TWA): "Fifteen hundred."
> United (or American): "Three o'clock."
> Texas International: "The big hand's on the twelve . . ."

Stories about married couples, the next section of "Jokes and Anecdotes" in the *Index*, frequently deal with competition between husbands and their wives. For example, in Type 1351, "The Silence Wager," a husband and his wife become so angry that they refuse to speak to one another, even during a grave crisis. In Type 1365A, "Wife Falls into a Stream," the obstinate wife drowns, and her husband looks for the body upstream where he believes she would have drifted against the current. In a subtype of that tale the husband and wife had been arguing about whether to cut something with a knife or with scissors; the husband throws his wife into the stream, and as she drowns, she lifts her fingers out of the water and makes a clipping motion in order to have the last word in the dispute.

Jokes about parsons and religious orders make fools of churchmen. In Type 1791, "The Sexton Carries the Parson," one of the most popular anticlerical tales brought to the United States, thieves are overheard dividing their loot in a graveyard, and the two foolish listeners believe it is the Devil and the Lord dividing souls. In American versions, however, the listeners are not always specified as churchmen. In Type 1833, "The Boy Applies the Sermon," a parson's rhetorical question in a sermon receives a literal and absurd answer from someone in the congregation. For example, an American version has this dialogue:

> Parson: "How shall we get to heaven?"
> Baseball Player (just waking up): "Slide!"

Only a fraction of the oral jokes in American folk tradition are to be found in the Aarne-Thompson *Type-Index*. A few of them can be identified with Thompson's motif numbers, but the majority have not been entered in any catalogue. Some may be original American jests, but most of them probably have foreign parallels or counterparts. The histories of these stories cannot be written until workable reference systems are published. Thus, the indexing of jokes is a major future task for American folktale scholars. However, not even the basic framework for a classification has been developed. One possibility, employed in some college archives, is to arrange texts according to their general subjects under such headings as "Jokes about Religions," "Jokes about Nationalities," "Jokes about Sex." Another system is to group stories according to stock character types: "Jokes about Hillbillies," "Jokes about Musicians," "Jokes about Traveling Salesmen," "Jokes about Politicians." The difficulty with such plans is obvious: many jokes will fit several categories—for instance, a sexy joke about a hillbilly, or a joke about an Irish politician.

The immigrant *dialect story* has been identified as a distinctive American folk creation, and it may be grouped by nationalities or languages. The humorous point of such jokes is the immigrant's broken English and his resulting mistakes in using the language. The impetus for their circulation is not necessarily prejudice, for immigrants themselves are the best raconteurs, but generally a humorous reference to some of the group's problems in acculturation. Some dialect stories reproduce the actual linguistic quirks of a nationality group, such as the "l"-"r" confusion among Japanese speaking English. Other tales adhere to different groups, as does the story of the newly wealthy immigrant who orders a home built containing a "Halo Statue." He finally explains, "You know. It rings; you pick it up; you say, 'Halo, statue?'"

The consistent nature of immigrant problems with the English language, and the reworking of standard plot material in dialect stories about different languages, is illustrated by two versions of the same story from widely separated groups. In each joke the immigrant storytellers themselves display an awareness of the foolishness of some of their own language problems and solutions. The first example was told by a Norwegian settler in Alberta, Canada. The story concerns an old Norwegian woman who is trying to buy some matches in a store run by an Anglo-Canadian. Not knowing the word "matches," she pantomimes striking a match, lighting an invisible pipe, and holding up the burning match. "Oh," says the storekeeper, in fluent Norwegian, "*er det fyrestykker du vil ha?*" ("is it matches you want?"). The woman answers, astonished, "*Nei kan du snakke Norske? Og her staar jeg og snakker Engelsk!*" (No, do *you* speak Norwegian? And here I stand speaking English!"). In a Mexican-American version of this joke from Texas, as reported by Rosan A. Jordan (see the "Bibliographic Notes" to this chapter), two men speak to one another using English-accented Spanish until they discover that they are both Mexicans. "Then why are we speaking English?" they ask. Likely, the "speaking English" immigrant dialect story exists among other groups as well.

The *Jewish-American dialect story* is a particularly interesting subtype since it humorously crystallizes the esoteric and exoteric attitudes of Jews and gentiles toward themselves and each other (and also attitudes toward the others' attitudes toward *themselves*), adding the dialect flavoring of an exaggerated form of Yiddish-American speech. The best informants, usually

American-born offspring of European Jewish immigrants, become masters of the nasalized accent, stylized gesture, and dramatic role playing typical of the form. The Jewish-American businessman in a joke asks the headmaster of Eton College, "Mine Jake, he's speaking de King's English now?" Then the narrator assumes the part of the headmaster to deliver the punch line. He hunches his shoulders, spreads his upturned palms wide, and says, "Netchally, vat else?"

A study of the development of the *black dialect story* in America would yield insights into the psychology involved in the changing relationships between races. One group of jokes, now dying out, pictures the black as a comical old darky—slow-moving, dull-witted, usually named something like "Rastus" or "Liza," and always drawling in a thick Southern accent. (In the protest jokes of Southern blacks' own biracial folk humor, the same type of character—often "John," the slave or hired man—manages to outsmart the white man.) Another cycle of urban white stories creates a vicious stereotype of the black as a crude, oversexed, automobile-loving maniac. The latest development has been the *integration story* in which the effects of the civil rights movements are directly mirrored. In these jokes the white man seems to be jolted into a belated recognition of new patterns in American life. In one such story a white librarian refuses to censor books containing the word *nigger*, pointing out that offensive words like *bastard* appear in books, too. The black responds, "Yes, but us niggers is organized, and you bastards ain't." Another revealing story concerns the football coach in a Southern college who is forced to try out a black player. When the boy smashes through the team's best linemen, the coach shouts excitedly, "Will you look at that Mexican boy run!"

The whole complex of ethnic, religious, and racial folk humor in the United States deserves more investigation, but even separate studies of individual groups would not point up all of the interrelationships. For example, a Jewish dialect joke concerns the Jew converted to Catholicism who is put upon at once by his family and friends. He grumbles, "I've only been a gentile for twenty minutes, and already I hate those Jews." The same story is told as a black dialect joke. Here a little black boy has smeared his face with flour or cold cream, and he runs home shouting, "I's white! I's white!" He is criticized by his family, and he declares that he already hates blacks. This theme of role shifting is also found in the integration story about a Southern black boy allowed to join a white gang. When a tire on their car has a blow-out, he is the first to complain. "There's not a nigger for miles around to change it for us." The sometimes absurd basis for racial pride is illustrated in the joke about an Indian boy and a black boy arguing over who comes from the most notable race. The Indian wins the dispute when he points out that little white boys never play "cowboys and niggers." A related joke pits a white child in debate against a child from a black family that has just moved into the neighborhood. The black wins this round when he declares, "At least we don't live next door to no niggers."

One group of jokes, little collected or studied so far, involves children's misunderstandings of religious and patriotic texts. These not only allow for some criticism of these sensitive areas of life, but they also may demonstrate a basic joke-making process in action. First a child's inadvertent error in language is related as an anecdote by his amused parents, but eventually the incident is described often enough to become an anonymous joke. This sequence would seem to explain the origins of such stories as the one about a child who wants to name his teddy bear "Gladly," because the people sing in church "Gladly, the Cross-eyed Bear"; or the one about the child's recitation in the Pledge of Allegiance to the Flag: ". . . one nation, indigestible, with liver and juices for all."

A traditional story type usually told to children by adults—the *pictorial folktale*—has evolved mostly into joke form nowadays. In the older versions the storyteller would illustrate his or her tale with a simple sketch map of the locale of the tale. The last line which was added would turn the drawing into a picture of the animal being described or hunted in the story, such as a wildcat, a duck, or another animal. In modern pictorial jokes, usually told by children to other children, a group of grade-schoolers is asked by the teacher each to add a line to a drawing on the chalkboard. One draws an Indian teepee:

The next adds a smokehole (or decoration):

Another puts in the sun above:

But the fourth child draws an arc over the whole picture and calls it "My dad bending over the tub to wipe it out after he has taken a bath":

Another pictorial joke has one child drawing a simple representation of a lightbulb:

But another child turns the drawing around and says it is "My mom from the back pulling her girdle on":

A detailed classification has been published for just one modern joke type, the *shaggy-dog story*. Some 700 texts were secured from both printed and oral sources, including the entries mailed in response to a radio program's nationwide contest. The following definition, based on the stories' humorous twists, was worked out for their classification into three major groups and some 200 types and subtypes: "A nonsensical joke that employs in the punchline a psychological non sequitur, a punning variation of a familiar saying, or a hoax, to trick the listener who expects conventional wit or humor." On the basis of style, it was found that shaggy-dog stories "usually describe ridiculous characters and actions, and often are told (to heighten the effect of the final letdown) in a long drawn-out style with minute details, repetitions, and elaborations." The whole classification was lettered and numbered using decimal points, after the manner of the *Motif-Index*, so that new materials could be added at any point; but, like the *Type-Index*, it provided a brief summary of each plot, a list of known versions, cross references, and bibliographic and comparative notes. For example, the joke about a midget knight mounted on a large shaggy dog that has the punch line "I wouldn't send a knight out on a dog like that!" was classified C425., "The Midget Knight and his Mount," in a category with other stories that end with punning variations of popular sayings. Twenty-eight versions of the tale were reported, fifteen from the radio contest, six from a folklore archive, two from *Boys' Life* magazine, one each from a joke book, a mail-order catalogue, a comic strip, *Today's Health* magazine, and a newspaper political cartoon. Other jokes in the index were related to literature; to historical persons; to traditional myths, tale types, and motifs; to popular poems and songs; and one even to a Sumerian fable possibly 5,000 years old.

Shaggy-dog stories continue to be invented, often to incorporate new characters or to allude to newly popular phrases. For instance, a "shaggy-*frog* story" was popular in 1982 with Kermit the Frog (of the Muppet crew) entering a bank and asking a teller named Miss Paddywhack for a loan. As collateral he offers an odd triangular-shaped piece of polished wood with some wires connected to it. Miss Paddywhack takes the object in to the loan officer, who glances at it and then stamps Kermit's application "Approved." When the teller in puzzlement asks what the object is, her boss replies, "It's a knickknack, Paddywhack, give the frog a loan." (This time the phrase is an *old* one—a line from the English children's song "This Old Man.")

Tall Tales

Types 1875 to 1999 in the Aarne-Thompson index are *tales of lying*, commonly called **tall tales** or "windies" in the United States; this section is supplemented by a portion of Chapter "X" (Humor) in the *Motif-Index*, Motifs X900. to X1899., "Humor of Lies and Exaggerations." Americans think of the tall tale as a peculiarly American product, just as Turks, Germans, and Scandinavians each think of it as peculiarly *their* national invention, all of them forgetting that there were tall tales before any of their nations was thought of.

Some of the best-known American windies are found in the *Type-Index*, among them Type 1889F, "Frozen Words Thaw"; Type 1889L, "The Split Dog"; Types 1890A through F, "The Wonderful Hunt"; and Type 1920B, often called "Too Busy to Tell a Lie." Even though a good number of lying tales are included in the *Type-Index*, they were formerly not considered to be very numerous in most European countries. In the Norwegian standard type catalogue, for example, which was published in 1921, only 4 such tales were listed; but when a marine paint company in Norway offered prizes in 1959 for good "skipper tales," some 100 tall-tale texts were among the entries that sailors submitted. Some were Aarne-Thompson lying tales previously unlisted in the Norwegian catalogue; others could be identified with motif numbers; and most of the new discoveries are known in some form in American folklore as well.

Tall tales may not be original with Americans, but they are certainly popular in the United States and fully characteristic of American folklore. Mody Boatright has written that they represent a sort of reverse bragging about the hardships of settling the continent and an exaggeration of natural features of the frontier. They flourished among frontiersmen, Boatright suggested, as a buoyant reaction to the wilderness itself and against the Eastern tourists' version of what life out West was like. Men *were* tough there, though not as tough as the Eastern emphasis on eye-gouging fights made them seem, and the tall tales made men even tougher. Danger and death *were* familiar, so the tales laughed at death. Westerners *did* love to gamble, and in tall tales gambling was pictured as mania. A folk story about how a cowboy went about reporting a man's death to the bereaved wife indicates the proper climate for tall tales. He: "Howdy, Widow Jones." She: "I'm not a widow." He: "Bet you ten dollars you are!"

That illustration is really a local-character story, not a tall tale, but it is just that sort of narrator—the laconic, poker-faced, hardened, regional character—who specialized in telling tall tales (or "talking trash") to his cronies, youngsters, and tourists. Vance Randolph expresses the tone very well in the title of his book of Ozark tall tales: *We Always Lie to Strangers.* The success of tall tales does not depend on belief in the details of the story, but rather on a willingness to lie and be lied to while keeping a straight face. The humor of these tales consists of telling an outrageous falsehood in the sober accents of a truthful story. The best tall tales only improve upon reality: smart animals are made smarter, big mosquitoes are made bigger, bad weather is made worse, huge crops are made even larger. There is the smart dog that hunts all kinds of game and even starts to dig worms when its master gets out a fishing pole one morning. There are the mosquitoes that eat a team of horses and pitch horseshoes for the harness. There is the wind that blows a suspended log chain

out straight and snaps links off the end. And there is the strawberry so big that the cook won't cut one for only two orders of
strawberry shortcake. (Tall-tale humor of this kind is often captured in postcard art created by using pasteups or trick photography.)

Although these and numerous other tall tales have been frequently collected and printed, they retain an appeal in oral
transmission that quickly fades in reading printed versions. The
art of the tall tale, like the art of the anecdote and the joke, is
primarily a verbal one, deriving from the skill of the teller rather
than from the originality of his material. When stretching the
truth becomes second nature with a yarnspinner, he or she may
rework traditional materials to create personalized remarks at
the spur of the moment. A noted liar once got a jolt from a spark
plug when an automobile engine was running. Someone asked,
"Did it shock you, Len?" "Nope," the old-timer shot back, "I
was too quick for it." He was merely borrowing from an older
story about a person picking up and quickly dropping a hot
horseshoe in a blacksmith's shop: "Did it burn you?" he was
asked. "Nope, it just don't take me long to look at a horseshoe."

Formula Tales

The **formula tales** in the last section of the *Type-Index* represent
a very ancient category of folktales, those based on a strict pattern of development, usually involving repetition. Both *old* formula tales in several subclasses and *new* tales based on old
formulas are known in the United States.

Cumulative tales, or "chains" (Types 2000 to 2199), are often
based on the device of adding a further detail with each repetition of the plot. Familiar examples are Type 2030, "The Old
Woman and her Pig," and Type 2035, "House that Jack Built."
Another group contains a series of alternate responses, as in
Type 2014, "Chains Involving Contradictions or Extremes,"
which includes a dialogue based on the " 'That's good,' 'no,
that's bad' " formula. A popular American collegiate example
that has not been catalogued in any index of types contains se-

quences like the following, with the audience furnishing the responses:

> "We've just built a new fraternity house!"   (Yay!)
> "With only one bar."   (Boo!)
> "A mile long!"   (Yay!)

Catch tales (Types 2200 to 2205), like catch questions in riddling tradition, lead the listener on to be hoaxed; in this instance the trick consists of causing him or her to ask a question to which the storyteller returns a foolish answer. A favorite catch tale in the United States is Type 2205, "Teller is Killed in His Own Story," sometimes with the following variation, in a story about being surrounded by Indians—Listener: "What did you do?" Storyteller: "What could I do? I bought a blanket." Another recent favorite, not specifically listed in the *Type-Index,* is a long, boring story involving the repeated line "Patience, little burro, patience." When an exasperated listener finally demands the point of the story, the narrator admonishes, "Patience, little burro, patience."

Two catch tales have become part of American women's folklore; both of them are narrated in a serious manner as accounts of personal experiences. The first gives a long circumstantial account of being pursued by a man with a cane or umbrella who at some point in the story supposedly strikes the narrator across the chest. When a shocked listener asks "What happened?" the storyteller replies, "Well how do you suppose I got these two bumps here?" (A male version of the story says the blow caused "my big nose.") The second women's catch tale (which must be told to a woman) describes an encounter with another woman who in anger, because of some favor that is not granted, throws a strong perfume on the narrator's throat that will, supposedly, cause her to become a lesbian. This time the storyteller stresses how strong the odor was and that it still lingers, and when the listener leans forward to try to smell it, the narrator kisses her on the forehead.

Endless tales (Type 2300) are formula tales that might continue indefinitely if the narrator had the will and the breath for it. These stories set up an action that is then repeated ad infinitum—sheep jumping over a fence, geese quacking, locusts carrying corn from a barn one grain at a time. *Rounds* (Type 2320) are endless stories that come back to their own starting points and then begin again. Often the situation is a tale within a tale within a tale, theoretically without any ending. One example is: "I laughed so hard I thought I'd die. I did die. They buried me, and a flower grew on my grave. The roots grew down and tickled me. I laughed so hard I thought I'd die. I did die. . . ."

One final tale form does not appear in the Aarne-Thompson index as a separate type, although several different animal tales and *Märchen* display its characteristic device—a song or rhyme that is interspersed with the prose narration. This is the so-called *cante fable*, or "singing tale." The narratives in which neck riddles are embedded suggest the *cante fable* form. Two of the best-known examples are often printed as nursery tales— "The Three Little Pigs" (Type 124) and "Jack and the Beanstalk" (Type 328). Another European-American tale frequently collected as a *cante fable* is Type 1360C, "Old Hildebrand." In some versions a man bets his fiddle against a ship captain's cargo that his wife can resist seduction for two hours; the man sings:

> Be true, my lover, be true, my lover
> Be true for just two hours;
> Be true, my lover, be true, my lover,
> The cargo will soon be ours.

But the wife, from inside the captain's cabin, sings back:

> Too late, my lover, too late, my lover,
> He grabbed me round the middle;
> Too late my lover, too late my lover,
> You've lost your damned old fiddle.

An especially popular *cante fable* in the United States and Canada has to do with a man invited to supper who sees some very plain food replaced by better fare when the minister or other important guests arrive unexpectedly. The man then chants something like:

> The Lord be praised,
> But I'm amazed,

> To see how things are mended.
> Applesauce and pumpkin pie,
> When pudding and milk were intended.

Or a prairie preacher, subtly protesting the sameness of all his meals out, may pray:

> For rabbit roasted and rabbit fried,
> For rabbit cooked and rabbit dried,
> For rabbit young and rabbit old,
> For rabbit hot and rabbit cold,
> For rabbit tender and rabbit tough,
> We thank thee, Lord, that we have enough.

The humorous-grace *cante fable* involves more a curse than a blessing, a fact made clear in this verse collected from a Pennsylvania coal miner in the 1930s:

> May God above
> Send down a dove,
> With wings as sharp as razors;
> To cut the throats,
> Of those old bloats,
> Who cut the poor man's wages.

Using the Type-Index and the Motif-Index

The identification of different classes and subclasses of folktales as well as the cataloguing of types and motifs are only preliminary steps in the study of these narratives. The *Type-* and *Motif-Indexes* do not analyze tales, interpret them, or trace them to their origins; they simply organize the collected material in a systematic fashion, outline the usual forms, and provide bibliography. The two indexes used together render the tasks of identifying narratives, gathering variants, and analyzing them immeasurably easier than the process would be without such reference works. Thus, any folklorist working with traditional prose narratives should become familiar with these indexes. To illustrate their use, we might examine a verbatim entry from the *Type-Index:*

660 *The Three Doctors.* The hog's heart, the thief's hand, the cat's eye. The three doctors make a trial of their skill [H504]. One removes one of his eyes, one his heart, and the other a hand [F668.1.]. They are to replace them without injury the next morning [E782.]. During the night they are eaten and others substituted [X1721.2. E780.2.], and one of the doctors thus acquires a cat's eye which sees best at night, one a thief's hand that wants to steal [E782.1.1.], and one a hog's heart that makes him want to root in the ground [E786.].

    * BP II 552 (Grimm No. 118).—Finnish *50;* Finnish-Swedish *4;* Estonian *1;* Lithuanian *9;* Swedish *13* (Stockholm *2;* Göteborg *2,* Liungman *2,* misc. *7*); Norwegian *2;* Danish *3;* Irish *45;* French *7;* Flemish *3;* German: Ranke *6;* Czech: Tille Soupis II (2) 446f. *6;* Slovenian *3;* Polish *1;* Russian: Andrejev *1.*—Franco-American *4.*

    Like all descriptions in the Aarne-Thompson index, this one begins with a numerical designation, a conventional title, and condensed description of the tale type. The tale is summarized next, with the appropriate motif numbers indicated in brackets. (For the more complex tales, a separate motif list is used, and subtypes may be established.) Last come abbreviated bibliographic references, including the total numbers of variants contained in national folktale archives and collections. Turning to the motifs that are cited, we find the following entries in the *Motif-Index:*

H504.   Test of skill in handwork.

F668.1.   Skillful surgeon removes and replaces vital organs.

E782.   Limbs successfully replaced.

X1721.2.   Lie: man's organs replaced with animal's. He acts like animal.

E780.2.   Animal bodily member transferred to person or other animal retains animal powers and habits.

E782.1.1.   Substituted hand. Man exchanges his hand for that of another.

E786.   Heart successfully replaced.

For each of these motifs, cross references to other related motifs and to Type 660 are provided; also further bibliography is listed under most of them, although not all references will necessarily be related to the tale type in question. To save space and avoid repetition, only the numbers and descriptions are given with the motifs above, but the bibliographic references quoted with the Type 660 entry are typical items: The "°BP" refers to the voluminous notes by Bolte and Polivka for the Grimm tales (asterisks are used throughout to mark the best reference sources); in this instance the tale is number 118 in Grimm. Then follow a list of sixteen countries or national groups in which this tale has been found (including Swedes in Finland and French in America) and, in italics, the totals for each country (158 in all). The full references for each abbreviated item in the list are given in a bibliography at the beginning of the index.

Equipped with such indexes, folktale scholars are well prepared to identify and annotate the texts that they collect. Whether they begin searching for a whole tale plot, for a characteristic motif, or for details which may be in the alphabetical index to the *Motif-Index*, they should eventually be able to pin down parallels from narrative folklore that have already been identified and classified. To do this, however, they must not take type and motif entries too literally; the indexes work best when they are flexibly applied. After all, indexers cannot furnish the details of every text they have examined. In fact, they cannot usually even personally examine all of the relevant texts. Instead, for many items they must rely on catalogues and indexes made by others using their own collected materials.

Bearing these points in mind, it is not difficult to see that the following tale heard orally in the West in 1961 is related to this complex of Type 660 and its related motifs.

A cowboy is injured badly during a roundup, and a medical student is flagged down on a nearby highway to administer first aid. Finding an internal organ destroyed, the student calls for a wandering sheep to be dragged in, killed, and cut open. From the sheep's insides he borrows the parts to patch up the man. A year later the same student drives down the same road and sees the same crew rounding up cattle again. Inquiring about the injured man, he is told, "He's all right now. 'Course he had quite a lot of trouble this spring. He brought a nice pair of twin lambs, and we sheared him—he sheared eight pounds." That this tale is traditional and is related to Type 660 is suggested by other variants. In 1956, for example, an informant in Maine said that his uncle had sheep's intestines substituted for his own in a hospital operation, and "every spring they had to shear the old devil." In a volume of Civil War reminiscences, a doctor is described as removing the liver of a soldier wounded in the field. A dog eats it, so the physician substitutes a sheep's liver. The soldier recovers, but he has a "hankering after grass." If it seems that these American tales deviate too far from the outlined type description, consider this summary of a version from a medieval collection, the *Gesta Romanorum* (Tale LXXVI): Two physicians alternate in removing and replacing each other's eyes; a crow steals one, however, which must then be replaced with a goat's eye that thereafter persists in looking up at trees.

Researching and Analyzing Folktales

Until the early 1960s a typical form of folklore research was the gathering of all available variants of an international tale to try to discover, by means of comparative analysis, its most likely place of origin and its probable routes of dissemination. This approach is often called the "Finnish method," in reference to the late nineteenth-century Finns (Krohn, Aarne, and others) who developed it, or the **historic-geographic method,** in reference to the plan of tale arrangement employed in it. The ultimate goals of this method were to write "life histories" of individual folktales and to reconstruct an *archetype*, or a hypothetical original form, for each tale. The method was based on the assumption that complex folktales have a single origin in one time and one place (rather than having resulted from polygenesis), and that each tale then spread throughout its present area of distribution by *automigration*—that is, from person to person, without needing large-scale folk migrations to carry it.

Although scholars employing the historic-geographic method

were never able to make a definitive statement of exactly where a given tale began, their studies pointed to India as probably the most important center of folktale dissemination.

In essence, the historic-geographic method involved the following steps:

1. Gather all available texts (using the indexes, corresponding with archives, field collecting, etc.).
2. Label all texts (usually a letter code for the language group and a number for the specific text).
3. Arrange literary texts historically and oral texts geographically (often north to south within each country).
4. Identify the traits to be studied, and make a master outline of all traits found in the texts.
5. Summarize the traits in each individual text, referring to the outline of traits.
6. Compare all traits in texts, one by one, in order to:
   a. Establish subtypes (regional subclasses);
   b. Formulate the archetype (hypothetical original).
7. Reconstruct the life history of the tale that best explains all of the present texts and their variations.

Comparing the traits in families of folktales and reconstructing archetypal forms represent only one possible approach to studying the folktale. Another important method, the **structural approach to folktales,** seeks to establish a *synchronic* basis (viewed without reference to historical change) rather than a *diachronic* basis (viewed in terms of historical development) for comparing folktales. Following the method of structural linguistics, Alan Dundes, the chief proponent of this approach, begins by defining *minimal units* of folktales that are distinct from the specific contents of the tales. Whether a tale is about animals, ogres, or numskulls should make no difference in a structural analysis as long as the *form* of the narratives is parallel. (Several similar tale-forms are widely separated in the *Type-Index,* Dundes has pointed out, simply because their cast of characters and other details differ).

Borrowing terms from structural linguistics and adapting

them to the system of the Russian structuralist Vladimir Propp, Dundes further suggests that if the phonetic level of linguistic analysis is the equivalent of what he calls the "etic" (nonstructural) approach of motif indexing, then the "emic" level would be reached by an index of the structural units, or *motifemes*. The Proppian approach, which leaves folktale elements in their original linear sequence as the tales are told, Dundes terms "syntagmatic," or analogous to the analysis of syntax in languages. A "paradigmatic" approach, akin to the use of paradigms (sample patterns) in language analysis, rearranges the folktale elements so as to reveal their underlying structure, usually as sets of oppositions: life/death, raw/cooked, good/evil, and so forth. The leading exponent of this method is the French anthropologist Claude Lévi-Strauss. Structural approaches, it is emphasized, would not eliminate the comparative approach or its long-established reference tools. Rather, both synchronic and diachronic studies are needed to fully explore folktale form and development.

As a counterbalance to the highly schematized and often largely statistical nature of both historic-geographic and structural analyses of folktale texts, there is a need for more studies of the oral style of tale narrators. For this to be done requires first that collectors record much more than just the text and the informant's background. We would need to know *where* tales are told, *how* they are told, *when* they are told, and *to whom*. Probably photographs—preferably motion pictures or videotapes—are necessary to record gestures and facial expressions, and it is desirable to observe good informants retelling tales to different audiences. We should take note of the dramatic role-playing of the teller, use of repetitions and other verbal formulas, personal or local references and other improvisations, and the responses that come from the audience. When data of this sort are collected and have been analyzed, it is possible to differentiate the styles characteristic of a specific tale, of a taleteller, or of an individual culture. Moving beyond even these concerns, and rejecting past studies of story texts and their contents, Robert A. Georges, surely speaking for other "behavioral" folklorists, advocates instead a holistic analysis, not of "stories" but of "storytelling events"—which are "communicative events . . . social experiences, and . . . unique expressions of human behavior."

BIBLIOGRAPHIC NOTES

Stith Thompson's *The Folktale* (see Chapter 8) is the definitive survey of the field. Besides the *Type-* and *Motif-Indexes* discussed in Chapters 8 and 9, American folklorists should consult the satellite work by Ernest W. Baughman, *A Type and Motif-Index of the Folktales of England and North America* (The Hague: Indiana University Folklore Series no. 20, 1966). Advanced study of the folktale requires use of several reference works in foreign languages, especially Johannes Bolte and Georg Polívka, *Anmerkungen zu der Kinder- und Hausmärchen der Brüder Grimm*, 5 vols. (Leipzig, 1913–32). An important article translated from German for Alan Dundes's book *The Study of Folklore* is Axel Olrik's *Epische Gesetze der Volksdichtung* (Epic Laws of Folk Narrative) (1909). A good survey of older European folktale theories in English is in Emma Emily Kiefer's *Albert Wesselski and Recent Folktale Theories* (Bloomington: Indiana University Folklore Series no. 3, 1947).

European folktales in authentic texts, accurately translated and fully annotated, are available in the Folktales of the World series published under the general editorship of Richard M. Dorson by the University of Chicago Press. *Folktales of England*, edited for the series by Katharine M. Briggs and Ruth L. Tongue (Chicago, 1965), is of particular interest to American folklorists. Briggs also compiled the important new reference work entitled *A Dictionary of British Folktales in the English Language;* Part A covers folk narratives, Part B folk legends (Bloomington: Indiana University Press, 1970, 1971, 2 vols. each part).

Some representative non-English tales collected in the United States may be found in the following: Joseph Médard Carrière's *Tales from the French Folk-Lore of Missouri* (Evanston and Chicago, Ill.: Northwestern University Press, 1937); Thomas R. Brendle and William S. Troxell's *Pennsylvania German Folk-Tales, Legends, Once-Upon-a-Time Stories, Maxims, and Sayings* (Morristown: Pennsylvania German Society Publications no. 50, 1944); Richard M. Dorson's "Polish Wonder Tales of Joe Woods," *WF* 8 (1949): 25–52, 131–45; Rosemary Agonito's "Il Paisano: Immigrant Italian Folktales of Central New York," *NYFQ* 23 (1967): 52–64; Francine Pelly's "Gypsy Folktales from Philadelphia," *KFQ* 13 (1968): 83–102; Anthony Milanovich's "Serbian Tales from Blanford," *IF* 4 (1971): 1–60; and Elaine K. Miller's *Mexican Folk Narrative from the Los Angeles Area* (Austin, Tex.: AFS Memoir, vol. 56, 1973).

Robert B. Klymasz is only one field collector who has published non-English tales from Canada in such works as *Folk Narratives among*

Ukrainian-Canadians in Western Canada (Ottawa: Canadian Center for Folk Culture Studies, Paper no. 4, 1973) and "The Ethnic Joke in Canada Today," *KFQ* 15 (1970): 167–73.

In 1957 (vol. 70), the *Journal of American Folklore* published "The Folktale: A Symposium" with important articles by Warren E. Roberts, "Collections and Indexes: A Brief Review" (pp. 49–52); Richard M. Dorson, "Standards for Collecting and Publishing American Folktales" (pp. 53–57); and Herbert Halpert, "Problems and Projects in the American-English Folktale" (pp. 57–62). In a 1981 article, *"Märchen* to Fairy Tale: An Unmagical Transformation," *WF* 40, 232–44, Kay Stone shows how the reworkings of oral wonder tales in books and films have modified them for mass-media consumption. Her interviews with children and adults about such stories revealed that the stories seem more threatening to adults than to the children we are presumably protecting by the rewriting. See also Bruno Bettelheim's influential book *The Uses of Enchantment: The Meaning and Importance of Fairy Tales* (New York: Knopf, 1976).

The Library of Congress published the useful bibliography by Barbara Quinnam, *Fables: From Incunabula to Modern Picture Books* (Washington, D. C., 1966). "Southey and 'The Three Bears' " was discussed by Mary I. Shamburger and Vera R. Lachman in *JAF* 59 (1946): 400–3. Alan C. Elms, in " 'The Three Bears': Four Interpretations," *JAF* 90 (1977): 257–73, reviews ritual, structural, psychoanalytic, and anal readings of the familiar story.

There are many reliable book-length collections of American folktales. Richard Chase's two books, *The Jack Tales* (Cambridge, Mass.: Houghton Mifflin, 1943) and *Grandfather Tales* (Boston: Houghton Mifflin, 1948), are important Southern Appalachian collections, especially the first with its notes by Herbert Halpert. All of Vance Randolph's Ozark collections, which contain a variety of folktale types and forms, are outstanding; these (all published by Columbia University Press) are *Who Blowed Up the Church House?* (1953), *The Devil's Pretty Daughter* (1955), *The Talking Turtle* (1957)—all with notes by Halpert —and *Sticks in the Knapsack* (1958), with notes by Ernest W. Baughman. Marie Campbell's collection *Tales from the Cloud Walking Country* (Bloomington: Indiana University Press, 1958) contains folktales from Kentucky. Ruth Ann Musick's *Green Hills of Magic* (Lexington: University of Kentucky Press, 1970) is subtitled *West Virginia Folktales from Europe.*

Leonard W. Roberts, an excellent collector of Kentucky folktales, published numerous texts in journals such as *Mountain Life and Work, Kentucky Folklore Record,* and *Tennessee Folklore Society Bulletin.* His book, *South from Hell-fer-Sartin* (Lexington: University of Kentucky Press, 1955; reissued in paperback, Berea, Ky.: Council of the Southern Mountains, 1964), like his subsequent collections, is rendered in absolutely verbatim oral style and has complete notes for all tales. Roberts's *Old Greasybeard: Tales from the Cumberland Gap* (Detroit: Folklore Associates, 1969) contains fifty tales; his *Sang Branch Settlers: Folksongs and Tales of a Kentucky Mountain Family* (Austin, Tex.: AFS Memoir, vol. 61, 1974) incorporates all the material previously published in book and microcard form as *Up Cutshin and Down Greasy* (Lexington: University of Kentucky Press, 1959).

Numerous folktales have been published in journal articles, only a few of which may be cited here. A double "Folk Narrative Issue" of *Midwest Folklore* (6, 1956, 5–128) is a good example of such publications. Another is Helen Creighton and Edward D. Ives's "Eight Folktales from Miramichi as Told by Wilmot MacDonald," *NEF* 4 (1962): 3–70, a model of editing and annotation. Jan Harold Brunvand's "Folktales by Mail from Bond, Kentucky," *KFR* 6 (1960): 69–76, describes an unusual collecting method and provides several annotated texts. An excellent variety of folk-narrative types is represented in Donald Allport Bird and James R. Dow's "Benjamin Kuhn: Life and Narratives of a Hoosier Farmer," *IF* 5 (1972): 137–63. Horace P. Beck discussed "The Acculturation of Old World Tales by the American Indian" with the example of a "Jack Tale" in *MF* 8 (1958): 205–16.

Four "Jack Tales" were the focus of a special issue of *NCFJ* (vol. 26, 1978), which also featured four articles discussing the nature of the hero in the tales, and their structure, context, and style. W. F. H. Nicolaisen compared "English Jack and American Jack" in *MJLF* 4 (1978): 27–36, while Charles Thomas Davis III wrote of "The Changing World of the Jack Tales" in *TFSB* 45 (1979): 96–106.

It is essential that folktales be heard, not just read, if they are to be fully appreciated. For this purpose two fine recordings of North Carolina storytellers are available: *Jack Tales Told by Mrs. Maud Long of Hot Springs, N.C.*, ed. Duncan Emrich (Washington, D.C.: Library of Congress Disc no. AAFS L47, 1957), and *Ray Hicks of Beech Mountain, N.C., Telling Four Traditional "Jack Tales,"* ed. Sandy Paton, texts transcribed by Lee B. Haggerty (Sharon, Conn.: Folk-Legacy Records no. FTA-14, 1964). In *TFSB* 48 (1982): 68–82, W. J. McNeil and Kathy Nicol present "Folk Narratives of Jessie Hubert Wilkes," containing further stories and background on the narrator of seven folktales included on the recording *Not Far from Here: Traditional Tales and Songs Recorded in the Arkansas Ozarks* (Mt. View, Ark.: Arkansas Traditions, 1981).

A good selection of older European jests, some of which have modern oral counterparts, is *A Hundred Merry Tales and Other Jestbooks of the Fifteenth and Sixteenth Centuries*, ed. P. M. Zall (Lincoln: University of Nebraska Press, Bison Books paperback edn., 1963). A fully annotated collection of oral American jests is Vance Randolph's *Hot Springs and Hell* (Hatboro, Pa.: Folklore Associates, 1965), containing 460 brief items from the Ozarks and 130 pages of notes and bibliography. The erotic folktales collected by Vance Randolph, left out of his other books, were finally published in 1976 as *Pissing in the Snow and Other Ozark Folktales* (Urbana: University of Illinois Press, repr. as an Avon paperback), with annotations on the 101 texts by Frank A. Hoffman and an introduction by Rayna Green.

In "The Joke Fable," *SWF* 5 (1981): 1–10, Pack Carnes identifies a substantial group of oral narratives that mix two familiar forms; he quotes fables told as jokes, jokes with a moral, jokes masquerading as fables, and joking references to Aesop's fables.

Richard M. Dorson called attention to "Dialect Stories of the Upper Peninsula: A New Form of American Folklore" in *JAF* 61 (1948): 113–50, an essay reprinted in his *Folklore and Folklife* (Chicago, 1972), pp. 223–66. Two articles on dialect stories involving Mexican Americans are María Herrera-Sobek, "Verbal Play and Mexican Immigrant Jokes," *SWF* 4 (1980): 14–22, and Rosan A. Jordan, "Tension and Speech Play in Mexican-American Folklore," in *"And Other Neighborly Names,"* ed. Richard Bauman and Roger D. Abrahams (Austin: University of Texas Press, 1981), pp. 252–65. Keith Cunningham, in "Navajo Humor, Too," *SWF* 5 (1980): 1–15, gives examples of jokes told by Navajos, some of which he finds impossible to explain or appreciate.

Riddle-jokes, whether *ethnic* jokes or other numskull stories, are discussed in Chapter 6 with the bibliographic references placed there as well. Two articles by William M. Clements, however, take up larger issues of joking stereotypes and deserve mention here: "Cuing the Stereotype: The Verbal Strategy of the Ethnic Joke," *NYF* 5 (1979): 53–61; and "Braided Armpits, Clean Bowling Shirts, and the Feminine Mystique," *MJLF* 6 (1980): 34–40.

Richard M. Dorson presented "Jewish-American Dialect Stories on Tape," in *Studies in Biblical and Jewish Folklore,* ed. D. Noy, R. Patai, and F. L. Utley (Bloomington: Indiana University Folklore Series no. 13, 1960), pp. 111–74; further texts were published by *MF* 10 (1960): 133–46. The subclass of "Rabbi Trickster Tales" was the subject of an article by Ed Cray in *JAF* 77 (1964): 331–45. The following are analytical articles on Jewish dialect stories: Heda Jason, "The Jewish Joke: The Problem of Definition," *SFQ* 31 (1967): 48–54; Naomi and Eli Katz, "Tradition and Adaptation in American Jewish Humor," *JAF* 84 (1971): 215–20; and Dan Ben-Amos, "The 'Myth' of Jewish Humor," *WF* 32 (1973): 112–31.

The typical repertoire of Southern black folk narratives is surveyed by William R. Ferris, Jr., in "Black Prose Narrative in the Mississippi Delta," *JAF* 85 (1972): 140–51; a traditional vein of black jokelore is discussed by Harry Oster in "Negro Humor: John and Old Marster," *JFI* 5 (1968): 42–57. A brief discussion of some developments in dialect stories about blacks is in a note by Mac E. Barrick in *KFQ* 9 (1964): 166–68. Further study of black-white self-images and interrelationships as expressed in jokes may be found in such articles as Paulette Cross's "Jokes and Black Consciousness: A Collection with Interviews," *FF* 2 (1969): 140–61; Norine Dresser's "The Metamorphosis of the Humor of the Black Man," *NYFQ* 26 (1970): 216–28; and William R. Ferris, Jr.'s, "Racial Stereotypes in White Folklore," *KFQ* 15 (1970): 188–98. Two standard collections of black folk narratives with copious notes and bibliography are Richard M. Dorson's *Negro Folktales in Michigan* (Cambridge, Mass.: Harvard University Press, 1956) and *American Negro Folktales* (Greenwich, Conn.: Fawcett Premier Books, paperback, 1967), which incorporates part of the first-named collection.

G. Legman, the leading authority on sexual folklore, is the author of a combined collection, classification, and (mostly Freudian) analysis entitled *Rationale of the Dirty Joke: An Analysis of Sexual Humor*, First Series (New York: Grove Press, 1968); volume two, the "Second Series" is entitled *No Laughing Matter* (New York: Breaking Point, Inc., 1975). Vance Randolph's *Pissing in the Snow*, mentioned above, is a major collection of sexual jokes. Rosemary Zumwalt's "Plain and Fancy: A Content Analysis of Children's Jokes Dealing with Adult Sexuality," *WF* 35 (1976): 258–67, is reprinted in *Readings in American Folklore*, pp. 345–54. A related item is Sandra McCosh's "Aggression in Children's Jokes," *Maledicta* 1 (1977): 125–32. Carol A. Mitchell explores "The Sexual Perspective in the Appreciation and Interpretation of Jokes," in *WF* 36 (1977): 303–29.

Religious jokelore is studied in Jan Harold Brunvand's "As the Saints Go Marching By: Modern Jokelore Concerning Mormons," *JAF* 83 (1970): 53–60. See also Phyllis Potter's "St. Peter Jokes," *SWF* 3 (1979): 38–58. Mining another rich vein of modern oral humor, Michael J. Preston examines "A Year of Political Jokes (June 1973–June 1974); or, the Silent Majority Speaks Out," *WF* 34 (1975): 233–44.

My note on "Jokes about Misunderstood Religious Texts" appeared in *WF* 24 (1965): 199–200. A "pictorial folktale" was noted by Maud G. Early in *JAF* 10 (1897): 80. Others are given by Simon J. Bronner in "Pictorial Jokes: A Traditional Combination of Verbal and Graphic Processes," *TFSB* 44 (1978): 189–96. My own "Classification for Shaggy Dog Stories," appeared in *JAF* 76 (1963): 42–68.

Three essays dealing with studies of traditional jokes in a broad context are Francis Lee Utley and Dudley Flamm's "The Urban and the Rural Jest (With an Excursus on the Shaggy Dog)," *JPC* 2 (1969): 563–77; Jan Harold Brunvand's "The Study of Contemporary Folklore: Jokes," *Fabula* 13 (1972): 1–19; and Frank Hall's "Conversational Joking: A Look at Applied Humor," *Folklore Annual* 6 (1974): 26–45. In an essay on "The Curious Case of the Wide-Mouth Frog," first published in 1977 (reprinted in *Interpreting Folklore*, pp. 62–68), Alan Dundes suggests that a joke about an animal's speech patterns is really concerned with white attitudes toward blacks during the 1970s. Lois A. Monteiro introduces a new joke type in "The Electronic Pocket Calculator: Joke 1," *WF* 35 (1976): 75; the punch line "Shell Oil" is seemingly spelled out on the calculator when the device is viewed upside down.

There are, of course, numerous recordings of professional comedians telling jokes, and only a few of folk jokesters; a folklorist recites some good examples on the record *Folklore of the Mormon Country: J. Golden Kimball Stories, Together with the Brother Petersen Yarns, Told by Hector Lee* (Sharon, Conn.: Folk Legacy Records, Inc., FTA-25, 1964). The record has anecdotes on side 1 and dialect stories on side 2.

The Norwegian tall-tale contest referred to in this chapter was described by Gustav Henningsen in *Vestfold-Minne* in 1961 and was translated by Warren E. Roberts as "The Art of Perpendicular Lying" in *JFI* 2 (1965): 180–219. Mody Boatright's theory of frontier tall tales is contained in *Folk Laughter on the American Frontier* (New York: Macmillan, 1949; Collier Books paperback edn., 1961). A stylistic study of tall tales based on 233 texts of "The Wonderful Hunt" selected from a manuscript archive of more than 2,000 American tall tales is reported in J. Russell Reaver's "From Reality to Fantasy: Opening-Closing Formulas in the Structures of American Tall Tales," *SFQ* 36 (1972): 369–82. Examining the tellers, contexts, and attitudes involved in traditional joking and lying, Kay Cothran wrote of "Talking Trash in the Okefenokee Swamp Rim, Georgia," *JAF* 87 (1974): 340–56, reprinted in *Readings in American Folklore*, pp. 215–35.

Stan Hoig's *The Humor of the American Cowboy* (Caldwell, Idaho: Caxton Press, 1958; Signet paperback edn., 1960) contains a good selection of Western occupational tall tales. Mody Boatright's *Tall Tales from Texas* (Dallas: Southern Methodist University Press, 1934) selects examples from one state, as does Stephen Dow Beckham's *Tall Tales from Rogue River: The Yarns of Hathaway Jones* (Bloomington: Indiana University Press, 1974)—Oregon. Roger L. Welsch's *Shingling the Fog and Other Plains Lies: Tall Tales of the Great Plains* (Chicago: Swallow Press, 1972), the best annotated of this group, fills in part of the middle section of the West with tales from both oral and journalistic sources. Further examples from the Plains are in Welsch's *Catfish at the Pump: Humor and the Frontier* (Lincoln: Plains Heritage, 1982). *Man and Beast in American Comic Legend* by Richard M. Dorson (Bloomington: Indiana University Press, 1982) has ten chapters on fabulous animals in American folklore and eight chapters on tall-tale tellers.

Vance Randolph's classic *We Always Lie to Strangers* was published in New York (Columbia University Press) in 1951. Lowell Thomas, who collected tall tales from his huge radio audiences by mail for many years, published *Tall Stories* in 1931 (Funk & Wagnalls), and it has been frequently reprinted. *Hoosier Tall Stories* in the American Guide Series (Federal Writers' Project in Indiana, 1937) is a rare book but a comprehensive collection. More Indiana tall tales are in my article in *MF* 11 (1961): 5–14. Samuel T. Farquhar reprinted a 1904 pamphlet of tall tales from Maine in *CFQ* 3 (1944): 177–84. An excellent collection from the same state is C. Richard K. Lunt's "Jones Tracy: Tall-Tale Hero from Mount Desert Island," *NEF* to (1968): 1–75. An important older collection recently made available again is James R. Masterson's *Tall Tales from Arkansas* (Boston: Chapman and Grimes, 1942; republished as *Arkansas Folklore* by Rose Publishing Company, Little Rock, Ark., 1974). Roger L. Welsch explores an area of folk/popular overlapping in "Bigger 'n Life: The Tall-Tale Postcard," *SFQ* 38 (1974): 311–24, adapted from the introduction to his book *The Tall-Tale Postcard: A Pictorial History* (New York: A. S. Barnes, 1976).

The *cante fable* in America has been collected and discussed in a series of articles, including two by Herbert Halpert in *SFQ* 5 (1941): 191–200, and *JAF* 55 (1942): 133–43; one by Leonard Roberts in *MF* 6 (1956): 69–88; and one by Edward D. Ives in *NEQ* 32 (1959): 226–37. Halpert provides rich annotation for one popular category of *cante fables*, "The Humorous Grace," in *MSF* 3 (1975): 71–82; and has "More on the Humorous Grace Cante Fable" in *MSF* 4 (1976): 77–86.

The chief theoretical underpinning for the historic-geographic method of folktale analysis, Kaarle Krohn's *Die Folkloristische Arbeitsmethode* (Oslo, 1926) was translated by Roger L. Welsch as *Folklore Methodology* (Austin, Texas: AFS Bibliographic and Special Series no. 21, 1971). Archer Taylor identified "Precursors of the Finnish Method of Folklore Study" in *MP* 25 (1927–28): 481–91. Taylor wrote that the method "is only common sense codified into a rigid procedure and not applied at random." He also published "The Black Ox," *FFC* no. 70 (1927)—a historic-geographic study of Finnish variants alone—as an exemplification of the method. A full-length study of world-wide distribution of a tale is Warren E. Roberts's "The Tale of the Kind and the Unkind Girls: Aa-Th 480 and Related Tales," in *Fabula, Supplement, Series B*, no. 1 (Berlin, 1958). Edwin C. Kirkland's "The American Redaction of Tale Type 922" in *Fabula* 4 (1961): 248–59, is a comparative study of what is known here as "Pat and Mike and the Three Questions." Bruce A. Rosenberg and John B. Smith discuss "The Computer and the Finnish Historical-Geographical Method," marring their presentation with the questionable acronym FARTS (Folktale Analysis, Retrieval and Tabulating System) in *JAF* 87 (1974): 149–54.

Two older survey articles on folktale studies are Anna Birgitta Rooth's "Scholarly Tradition in Folktale Research," *Fabula* 1 (1958): 193–200; and Jan DeVries's "The Problem of the Fairy Tale," *Diogenes* no. 22 (1958): 1–15. Surveys that project sweeping changes in folktale studies are J. L. Fischer's "The Sociopsychological Analysis of Folktales," *CA* 4 (1963): 235–95; Melville Jacobs's "A Look Ahead in Oral

Literature Research," *JAF* 79 (1966): 413–27; and Heda Jason's "A Multidimensional Approach to Oral Literature," *CA* 10 (1969): 413–26.

V. Propp's *Morphology of the Folktale*, first published in Russia in 1928, the background for much modern structuralism in folklore, should be consulted in the second revised English translation (introduction by Alan Dundes) published both as AFS Bibliographical and Special Series vol. 9 (Austin, Texas, 1968) and as Indiana University Research Center in Anthropology, Folklore, and Linguistics, Publication no. 10 (Bloomington, 1968). Alan Dundes proposed the application of Propp's system to the structural study of tales in the Aarne-Thompson catalogue in an article in *JAF* 75 (1962): 95–105, reprinted in *Analytic Essays in Folklore*, pp. 61–72, and he demonstrated its application in "The Binary Structure of 'Unsuccessful Repetition' in Lithuanian Folktales," *WF* 21 (1962): 165–74. For other structural studies, refer to the "Bibliograhic Notes" to Chapter 2 and to those for individual genre chapters. Alsace Yen offers a comparison "On Vladimir Propp and Albert B. Lord: Their Theoretical Differences" and criticizes the English translation of Propp's work in *JAF* 86 (1973): 161–66.

Three recent articles discuss the distinctive American forms of European folktales: Wolfgang Mieder's "Modern Anglo-American Variants of the Frog Prince (AT 440)," *NYF* 6 (1980): 111–35; Yvonne J. Milspaw's "The Bride Test: Reflections on Changing Values in America," *KF*, NS vol. 1 (1982): 21–33; and Carl Lindahl's " 'Skallbone,' 'The Old Coon,' and the Persistence of Specialized Fantasy," *WF* 41 (1982): 192–204, a study of a black narrator retelling *Märchen* learned from her father.

The importance of studying story*telling* rather than simply story *plots* is emphasized in Linda Dégh's important study (published first in German in 1962) *Folktales and Society: Story-Telling in a Hungarian Peasant Community* (Bloomington: Indiana University Press, 1969). Another useful European study of a folk narrator, Mark Azadovskii's "*Eine Sibirische Märchenerzählerin*," *FFC* no. 68 (1926) has been translated by James R. Dow and published as "A Siberian Tale Teller" by the Center for Intercultural Studies in Folklore and Ethnomusicology, Monograph Series, no. 2 (Austin: University of Texas, 1974). The first influential and inclusive essay taking this approach by an American folklorist is Robert A. Georges's "Toward an Understanding of Storytelling Events," *JAF* 82 (1969): 313–28. Georges also asks "Do Narrators Really Digress?" in his article subtitled "A Reconsideration of 'Audience Asides' in Narrating," *WF* 40 (1981): 245–52.

John Ball's thoughts on "Style in the Folktale" appeared in *Folklore* 65 (1954): 170–72. William Hugh Jansen considered the problems of "Classifying Performance in the Study of Verbal Folklore" in *Studies in Folklore*, pp. 110–18. Richard M. Dorson analyzed the styles of six storytellers in "Oral Styles of American Folk Narrators," *Style in Language*, ed. Thomas A. Sebeok (Cambridge, Mass., New York, and London: Technology Press of MIT, 1960), pp. 27–51; the article was reprinted in *Folklore in Action*, pp. 77–100, and again (with four additional text samples) in Dorson's *Folklore: Selected Essays*, pp. 99–146. Dorson's 1961 study comparing the styles of two Maine storytellers, "Tales of Two Lobstermen," was reprinted in *Folklore and Fakelore*, pp. 212–22. Bruce A. Rosenberg considers the question of style in both written and oral storytelling in his essay "The Aesthetics of Traditional Narrative" in Stanley Weintraub and Philip Young's *Direction in Literary Criticism* (University Park: Pennsylvania State University Press, 1973), pp. 7–22. A practical example of the same subject is Willard B. Moore's "The Written and Oral Narratives of Sara Cowan," *IF* 10 (1977): 7–91, a good study of a writer for a weekly rural Kentucky newspaper using folk materials in her columns.

My Western text of Type 660, "The Two Doctors," with discussion of the variants that are mentioned in this chapter, appeared in "Some International Folktales from Northwest Tradition," *NWF* 1 (Winter 1966): 7–13. Luc Lacourcière studies nine French-Canadian texts of Type 660 in "Les Transplantations Fabuleuses: conte-Type 660," in *Cahiers d'Histoire* no. 22 (Québec: Archives de Folklore, Université Laval, 1970), pp. 194–204. A version from Italy retold as a sexy joke is reprinted in *European Anecdotes and Jests*, ed. Kurt Ranke (Copenhagen: Rosenkilde and Bagger, 1972), p. 10.

11
Folksongs

Problems in Defining the Folksong

Folksongs, although long a popular subject for collection and research, have seemed always to elude ventures at scholarly definition. The following attempt from A. H. Krappe's *The Science of Folklore* (1930) demonstrates the typical shortcomings of many in the past:

> The folksong is a song, i.e. a lyric poem with melody, which originated anonymously, among unlettered folk in times past and which remained in currency for a considerable time, as a rule for centuries.

Not only is the logic here neatly circular (folksong = song of the folk), but also the criteria of illiterate origins and "considerable" age will simply not apply to the greater part of the materials accepted as folksongs by folklorists of Krappe's time and later. American folksongs would be ruled out entirely; Krappe's own first example, named a few lines further on, does not fit:

> . . . the American *Kentucky Home*, though it is supposed to have originated in circles of a somewhat darker hue than is popular in certain sections of the country, is a genuine folksong of both coloured and white people.

Krappe's remark was a racist one, and "My Old Kentucky Home," of course, is a Stephen Foster composition that has never achieved any oral circulation in variants.

We have, on the one hand, the broad and vague popular concept that almost any folksy song performance is a folksong. On the other hand, we have narrow-minded antiquarian definitions such as Krappe's. But if we simply look at what the folk sing and what folklorists have collected and studied, we will discover that **folksongs** consist of words and music that circulate orally in traditional variants among members of a particular group. Like other kinds of oral traditions, folksongs have come from several sources, have appeared in many different media, and have sometimes been lifted out of folk circulation for various professional or artistic uses. But all of those that qualify as true *folk*-songs have variants found in oral transmission.

It is a common misconception that genuine folksongs can be detected by their style of performance, but non-folk performers may imitate a traditional style. Nor can the age of a song determine its status as folk or non-folk, for folksongs are still being created. Similarly, the specific origin of a song is not a reliable guide, because (as is shown in this chapter and the next) songs have entered the folk repertoire both from above (out of sophisticated music) and from below (rising from anonymous beginnings). Only the production of different variants via communal re-creation as a song remains for a time in the possession of a definite group can justify the label "folksong."

The words and music of folksongs belong together, of course, and should be gathered and analyzed together. However, to facilitate a systematic survey of the kinds of American folksongs and ballads, and because the research methods for words and music are so different, tunes of folksongs (as well as instrumental music) are discussed separately in Chapter 13.

Folksongs differ from non-folksongs by their fluidity of form and content. This is apparent in contrast to the two other basic bodies of song—art songs and popular songs. *Art songs* are learned from printed scores exactly as their composers originally wrote them. Professional singers are expected to perform art songs in a manner that is in keeping with the musical conventions of the composer's own time, and usually in the composer's own language. Such songs as Schubert's *Lieder,* "Drink to Me Only with Thine Eyes," "Ave Maria," favorite arias from operas, musical settings of well-known texts (including in the United States "The Lord's Prayer," "Trees," and Roy Harris's setting of Sandburg's "Fog,") are all familiar examples of art songs. They may follow any form the composer wishes to use, and they have a special, enduring intellectual or emotional "high-brow" appeal.

Popular songs are also printed or, more often, commercially recorded, and they, too, come from the pens of professional composers, sometimes more businessmen and -women than artists. Professional singers are expected to sing popular songs more or less as they were written and to pay royalties for their use. These songs are generally much more stereotyped in form than art songs are, tending either to fit a rigid ABA pattern (like that of most older pop standards) or following some current mode (like the AAB twelve-bar blues form and blues diction used for some rock pieces). Most popular songs enjoy only a short but a very intense existence, being enormously popular with a broad, mostly adolescent, audience for weeks or at most months and then disappearing for good from disk-jockey shows and music videos.

Folksongs as a group are even more widely accepted than art songs and popular songs, having circulated for generations, sometimes in different countries, among illiterate and semiliterate folk who had little knowledge of the other two bodies of song. Yet both middle-class and upper-class people know folksongs, too. Folksongs outlast most popular songs, and they may also be much older than art songs; for the latter generally go back to the eighteenth or nineteenth centuries at most, while some folksongs survive from the Middle Ages or earlier. Folksongs are unlimited in form and subject matter, ranging from very simple to relatively complex. But their chief distinction remains the manner by which they circulate and the resulting effect on their form: folksongs, unlike any other kind, are passed on mostly in oral tradition, and they develop traditional variants.

Since these song types are not defined primarily by their origin, folksongs may actually originate from either art songs or popular songs. As many scholars have emphasized, folksongs are *perpetuated* in oral tradition, but they need not have *originated* there. In fact, a song belonging to any one of the three groups may turn into one of the other two types, if we only apply our definitions a bit broadly.

Art songs, for instance, such as "O Promise Me" or the wedding march from *Lohengrin* reached a popular-song audience when they began to be regularly sung at weddings. The wedding march achieved oral circulation as a folksong when words like the following were fitted to it:

> Here comes the bride,
> Big, fat, and wide.
> See how she wobbles from side to side.

In another transformation the theme melody from a Rachmaninoff piano concerto became a popular song, "Full Moon and Empty Arms." But the "Toreador Song" from *Carmen* is a folksong when it is sung:

> Oh Theodora,
> Don't spit on the floor-a;
> Use the cuspidor-a,
> That's-a what it's for-a.

By the same token, some popular songs outlive their typical brief careers to survive for generations as "standards." This is true especially of songs closely associated with particular singers like Bing Crosby ("White Christmas"), Judy Garland ("Over the Rainbow"), or Frank Sinatra ("My Way"). Probably some popular songs also last because of the inherent high quality of their melodies and lyrics, and in a sense these are art songs in disguise. One thinks of "Stardust," "September Song," "Smoke Gets in Your Eyes," and such Beatles songs as "Eleanor Rigby" and "Yesterday," all of which have somewhat unconventional tunes and lyrics for popular songs. Other popular song hits seem to cloy the public's taste eventually and are then cynically parodied in oral tradition, thus becoming folksongs: "Jealousy" turned into "Leprosy" (". . . is making a mess of me"), and "It's Magic" turned into "It's Tragic" ("You smile, your teeth fall out; Your hair looks just like sauerkraut . . ."). The popular song "Davy Crockett" spawned at least a dozen folk parodies with lines like "Born on a table top in Joe's Cafe, / Dirtiest place in the U.S.A."

When folksongs are "arranged" and enter the repertoires of professional singers and singing groups, they cease to behave like folksongs and become art songs. This has been the case especially with Afro-American spirituals ("Go Down, Moses," "Swing Low, Sweet Chariot," etc.), with some folk lyrics ("Black is the Color of My True Love's Hair" and "Shenandoah"), and with many foreign folksongs, which like foreign art songs are generally sung in the parent language. When folksongs catch the ears of a broad sector of the public, they may become popular songs for a brief period, as happened in the 1950s with "Goodnight, Irene" and "Tom Dooley." More recently popular songs called "The Riddle Song" and "Scarborough Fair" were derived from Anglo-American folk ballads.

It should be evident now why folklorists cannot answer immediately when asked if "Barbara Allen" (or "Tom Dooley," or "Blue-tailed Fly") is a *folksong*. The only response they can give is "Which version?" Even knowing that, they might have to conclude, "Yes and no." The decision must ultimately rest on the singer's performance and source—in short, on the singer's folk tradition, if any—rather than on any features of text and tune themselves. If words and music were learned orally from other traditional singers, if the performance is natural, and if oral variants exist, then there is a likelihood that we are dealing with folksong. Thorny problems, of course, do exist—the city fad for singing country folksongs, for instance, or the deliberate composition of popular songs in the folk style, or a song like "Greensleeves," which is widely regarded as a folksong, but which was actually revived professionally from a non-folk tradition. Such problems, however, are legitimate ones for investigation by folklorists. An example of the findings of such a study is the case of "Home on the Range." That song was first a piece of Kansas newspaper verse (in 1873), then an anonymous, somewhat fluid, cowboy folksong. It was finally tracked back to its written source, and now it is a "standard" that is invariably sung just as it is printed in songbooks.

The various ways by which folksongs have been transmitted

are by no means limited solely to oral performance. Print, writing, sound recording, and broadcasting have all played a part in circulating folksongs among traditional singers. For example, many narrative songs now regarded as folksongs originated as *broadsides*—crudely printed single sheets containing the lyrics for a new song and the name of a familiar tune to which it might be sung. Broadsides flourished in England from about the sixteenth to the early nineteenth century. They were sold on the streets, usually for a penny. Broadsides were printed in the United States until somewhat later, and have occasionally been revived in the twentieth century for such gatherings as labor-union rallies and pacifist or civil rights demonstrations. (The general nature of Anglo-American broadside ballads is taken up in the next chapter.) *Songsters*—pamphlets of printed songs— became popular in the nineteenth century, and some are still printed now and then; their contents were generally miscellaneous, for they were compiled freely from all available sources, folk and otherwise. Songsters also were cheaply printed and sold, and, like broadsides, they were not preserved with any care either by their buyers or by early libraries. Today, however, intact broadsides and songsters are treasured library acquisitions. Countless American folksongs were also circulated in print by means of *periodicals*, especially local newspaper columns of old songs and poems. Sometimes readers were asked to submit the full texts for incomplete songs sent in by others, thus creating an informal folklore-collecting project. Some readers kept clippings of old song columns, and a few newspapers retained files of submitted songs for reference use; both kinds of collections can still occasionally be discovered.

Handwritten "*ballet books*" (*ballad* books, but spelled "ballet" to reflect a folk pronunciation) constitute another good source of folksongs ready-collected by informants themselves. The term "ballet book" has been applied to any notebook or scrapbook of songs kept by an individual for his own use. Some are in old copy books or ledgers, while others are made out of printed books with blank paper pasted over the pages; the songs they contain usually were selected from all the songs that happened to be known to their compilers, some of whom even kept track of their own printed and oral sources.

Finally, *commercial recordings* have played an important role in folksong transmission. Beginning in 1923, when a recording company first put a "hillbilly" singer on a commercial 78 rpm disk, folksongs have been borrowed from oral tradition and then fed back into it through recordings. Other songs such as Vernon Dalhart's version of "The Death of Floyd Collins" or the Carter Family's "Worried Man Blues" originated from recording artists and their writers, and then passed on to an oral life.

All that we have been describing here represents a liberal, modern scholarly concept of American folksong, but such has not always been the accepted view of the subject. In 1897, nine years after the American Folklore Society was founded, an early historian of American literature could write that we are a people "practically without folksongs." Nowadays, however, few anthologies of American literature do not contain a section devoted to native ballads and folksongs.

The first American folklorists in the late nineteenth century knew of almost no oral-traditional songs in the United States. Francis James Child, the great ballad editor, brought out his definitive edition of traditional British ballads at Harvard in the 1890s without doing any field work and including only a handful of American versions that others had sent him. But the famous English collector Cecil J. Sharp, together with the American Olive Dame Campbell, found English folksongs of all kinds in abundance in the Southern Appalachians beginning in 1917, and their writings encouraged others to seek them, too.

Pioneering American collectors like Phillips Barry in the Northeast and John A. Lomax in the West and South began to publish native American folksongs at about the same time, and gradually academic folklorists accepted their finds and had to revise their own ideas about folksong types and dissemination. Widely respected scholars such as Louise Pound of the University of Nebraska and H. M. Belden of the University of Missouri were instrumental in promoting a broadened definition of American folksong, while such industrious collectors as George

Korson, working among coal miners, and Vance Randolph, among Ozark mountaineers, gathered a widened spectrum of songs for analysis. In the 1950s and 1960s, John Greenway contended that American social-protest songs should be admitted into an inclusive definition of folksong:

> . . . folksong is any song concerned with the interests of the
> folk and in the complete possession of the folk, who in turn
> are members of a homogeneous, unsophisticated, enclave liv-
> ing in but isolated from a surrounding sophisticated society
> by such features as geography, topography, race, religion,
> economic and educational deprivation, social inferiority, or
> even choice.

The historian of Anglo-American folksong studies, D. K. Wilgus, along with Greenway and others, took a rationalistic view of folksong tradition and emphasized the importance of the hill-billy-record influence upon American folksongs.

Wordless Folksongs, Near-Songs, and Functional Folksongs

So broad is the field of folksong that Wilgus conceded in his history of its scholarship: "It is doubtful that there will ever be a complete, not to speak of a consistent, outline of the varieties of folksong." Yet, classify we must; and if we borrow terms freely from many editions and studies, and invent a few new ones to fill gaps, we come up with something like the following scheme, with the large divisions based on form (arranged from simple to complex) and the subclasses organized by subject matter or function.

Since folksongs consist of oral-traditional words and music, we can imagine examples in which one element is stronger than the other or even exists without the other's presence at all. Such *proto-folksongs* do in fact occur in folk tradition. Vocal music without words—what we might call **wordless folksong**—is found in American folklore in such traditions as "chin music" (or "Diddling," and in Ireland, "lilting"), when the voice imitates the sound of dance music played on a fiddle. The sound effect is similar to the nonsense refrains of some folk ballads, and it has a counterpart in jazz "scat singing." Some jazz instrumental styles derive from the early use of such partly vocal instruments as the Jew's harp, the jug, and the kazoo, developing into muted and "growl" effects produced on conventional band instruments. Yodeling, hollering, and Afro-American church "moaning," "humming," or "groaning," as it is variously called, are also examples of wordless folksong.

The musical as well as social aspects of a wordless folksong form are described in the following account of an Okefenokee swamp holler as observed by naturalist Francis Harper in 1912:

> Then I heard more of that strange music which always startles me—swamp hollering. I was unversed in the unwritten rules of the matter, and I assumed my friends at the upper end of the island were having fun. . . . [Later] Gator Joe asked me somewhat impatiently if I had heard them holler, and if so, why I hadn't answered. "When you hyear anybody hollerin', you holler back," he said with undisguised sternness. . . . And so Joe taught me rule one about the art of hollering. Even if I had been aware of what was required, I was . . . totally incapable of producing a sound at all akin to the marvelous swamp yodeling . . . the exquisite music made by two masters, Gator Joe Saunders and Bryant Lee.

Another type of wordless folksong, known either as "eeph-ing" or "hoodling," consists of breathy, grunting quasi-musical noises that sound somewhat like animal imitations. Wordless songs need not even necessarily be vocal; the "Johnny is a sissy!" three-note melody may be sung, hummed, whistled, or played on an instrument with the same insulting effect. The "wolf whistle" has an unmistakable meaning without any vocalizing of melody or words for it. However, the seven-stroke rhythmic pattern of one simple four-note melody does have traditional words associated with it: "Shave and a haircut, two bits." There can be no doubt that these items live orally, for no songbook contains them, yet everyone knows them. If you tap out the first five beats of "Shave and a haircut," someone will respond with "two bits"; if you hum "Johnny is a sissy" at a child, he will react. Similarly, the wolf whistle has no formal

support as a greeting from etiquette books, but it speaks eloquently just the same because of its folk denotation.

When *words* predominate and melody is weak, we have what
might be termed **near-songs**. The *cante fable*, as we have seen, is
half-and-half, and the verse may either be chanted or sung. The
peddlers' cries, discussed earlier as rhymes, are often delivered
in a singsong chant but sometimes are truly sung. Children's
play-and-game rhymes fall into the same twilight zone between
verse and song, as do many field hollers and work hollers.
Square-dance calls, auctioneers' chants, and "talking blues" are
all partly song, partly chant. For all of these materials, it could
be said in general that the texts are fully traditional and formularized, but the tunes are improvised and free. They are *nearly*
songs, but not quite.

The first group of true songs, with both traditional words and
music, are those which closely match the rhythm of some special activity, and thus they have been called **functional songs**.
Here we might classify *lullabies* that are smoothly rhythmical,
peaceful, or repetitious ("Hush, Little Baby" is all three) so that
they will induce sleep. Bess Lomax Hawes, who analyzed the
"peculiar melange" of songs used as lullabies, also identified
"happy vocalizing . . . a chatty style" and especially "the spatial
isolation of the baby" as typical traits of content and performance.

Work songs belong in the functional folksong category if they
are regulated by the repeated pulses of chopping, hammering,
marching, pulling on ropes, and so forth. Most American work
songs are either Afro-American slave songs ("Take This Hammer" is perhaps the best-known example) or sailors' "sea chanteys" ("Hangman Johnny" and "Away to Rio"). A few still
circulate as call-and-response songs or chants used when circus
workers hoist a tent:

> Every time (Heave it!)
> Ding, dong, ring (Heave it!)
> Look on the table (Heave it!)
> Same damn old thing!

Play-party songs, which could be classified as functional
songs, are discussed in Chapter 16 in connection with folk danc-

ing. Children's *game songs* belong in this category, for they are never sung apart from the playing of the game, and the words and melody closely follow the action of the game. A few songs are *mnemonic songs* used for remembering such lists as the presidents of the United States, the capitals of the states, or basic geographical terms. A Utah example simply versifies the names of all the state's counties to the tune of "Reuben and Rachel":

> Utah Train
> Beaver, Carbon, Davis, Morgan,
> Daggett, Millard, and Duchesne,
> Iron, Uintah, Rich, and Summit,
> Garfield, Cache, Piute, and Kane.
>
> Wasatch, Washington, and Weber,
> Sanpete, San Juan, Salt Lake, Wayne,
> Juab, Box Elder, Grand, Tooele,
> Sevier, Emery, Utah train.

Lyrical Folksongs

These first three broad divisions—wordless folksongs, near-songs, and functional folksongs—constitute clearly differentiated groups with easily recognizable contents. However, the folksongs that fit into them include only a small fraction of the whole. The last two divisions—lyrical folksongs and narrative folksongs—are much more complicated groups and involve many more texts. Narrative folksongs are discussed separately in the next chapter, leaving **lyrical folksongs** (the usual meaning of the simple term "folksongs") for the remainder of this one.

Some lyrical folksongs are true *folk lyrics*—that is, traditional songs devoted to expressing a mood or a feeling without telling any connected story. Many express despair for a lost or hopeless love, and these are sometimes developed as a series of impossible desires:

> Wisht I was a little fish,
> I'd swim to the bottom of the sea,
> And there I'd sing my sad little song,
> "There's nobody cares for me."

*

> I wish I was a little sparrow,
> Had wings, and oh! could fly so high.
> I'd fly away to my false lover
> And when he'd ask, I would deny.

Other folk lyrics have the thread of a story implied in them, as in "Down in the Valley" and "On Top of Old Smokey," while others simply take the form of warnings to lovers about the wiles of the opposite sex. Apart from the joys and sorrows of love, some folk lyrics refer to death ("Bury Me beneath the Willow"), homesickness ("The Indian Hunter" or "Let Me Go"), and general discontent ("Trouble in Mind"). One that is probably of literary origin complains about household toil:

> There's too much of worriment goes to a bonnet,
> There's too much of ironing goes to a shirt,
> There's nothing that pays for the time you waste on it,
> There's nothing that lasts us but trouble and dirt.

> Oh, life is toil and love is a trouble,
> And beauty will fade and riches will flee;
> And pleasures they dwindle and prices they double,
> And nothing is what I wish it to be.

A major category of American folk lyrical song is the Afro-American *blues*, a folk form based on field hollers and cries that developed countless fluid stanzas of emotional responses to life, entered a commercial and urban stage, and then profoundly influenced, both musically and textually, most of American popular music (see the Appendix). In its classic form, the blues consist of a three-line twelve-bar pattern based on repeating one line of four musical bars twice and then rhyming a third line containing a complementary or responsive idea with it. A famous published example, based on a folk verse, goes:

> I hate to see that evening sun go down,
> I hate to see that evening sun go down,
> Because my baby, she done left this town.

The spirit of the blues is often, although not necessarily, melancholy:

> Woke up this morning, blues all 'round my bed,
> Woke up this morning, blues all 'round my bed,
> Picked up my pillow, blues all under my head.

The subject matter is commonly disappointed love:

> I want to know, why did my baby go,
> I want to know, why did my baby go,
> I love that woman, love her 'til it hurts me so.

And blues imagery is often frankly sexual, as shown in this Bessie Smith lyric, typical of folk blues, although from a commercial recording:

> Bought me a coffee-grinder, got the best one I could find,
> Bought me a coffee-grinder, got the best one I could find,
> So he could grind my coffee, 'cause he has a brand new grind.

A black prisoner's blues, as recorded in Louisiana, is grippingly phrased:

> Wonder why they electrocute a man at the one o'clock hour
>   at night,
> Wonder why they electrocute a man at the one o'clock hour
>   at night,
> The current much stronger, people turn out all the light.

Spirituals and other traditional *religious songs* may sometimes allude to a Biblical story or a religious legend, or allegorize a lesson, but their narrative content is subordinate to their expression of strong feeling; they may be considered lyrical folksongs except for the relatively few that are "religious ballads." There are "white spirituals" as well as black ones, and the controversy over origins and precedence has filled several books. Religious songs exhibit much more variety than may be illustrated briefly, but the basic simplicity of many is seen in a stanza like "Where, oh, where are the good old patriarchs? [three times] / Safely over in the Promised Land." Some religious folksongs are infused with the imagery and fervor of revival meetings and fire-and-brimstone preaching. Frequent scenes depicted in others are crossing rivers, washing away sin, walking in heaven, and riding trains. Some folk hymns derive from English Protestant hymns, which later appeared in the old American "shape-note" collections like *The Sacred Harp* in which each tone of the scale was printed in one of four different shapes. The liveliest folk religious songs, such as "That Old Time Religion," anticipate the "gospel songs" that are still commercial country-music or bluegrass favorites on recordings and on the radio.

In the same spirit as religious songs are the *homiletic songs* that dispense advice like "Paddle Your Own Canoe," or ask embarrassing questions like "Why Do You Bob Your Hair, Girls?" But for every song that criticizes a life of "Puttin' on the Style," there are a dozen more that we might call *songs of gamblers, drinkers, ramblers, and prisoners.* Here the dissolute life, if not directly recommended for others, is often at least glorified by the singer. Witness "Old Rosin the Beau," who for his funeral wants to have his six pallbearers line up at the graveside and have one last drink to him, their burden. Some temperance songs circulate orally, like "Lips That Touch Liquor Must Never Touch Mine" and "I'll Never Get Drunk Anymore," but the more numerous variety of songs about drinking either describe the brewing process ("Moonshine" and "Mountain Dew") or revel in its product ("Pass 'round the Bottle" and "Pickle My Bones in Alcohol"). The most common song of the group is variously entitled "Jack of Diamonds," "Rye Whiskey," "On Top of Clinch Mountain," or "A Card-Player's Song." Typical verses, which may occur in any order, include:

> Jack of diamonds, Jack of diamonds
> I know you of old,
> You robbed my poor pockets
> Of silver and gold.
>
> For the work I'm too lazy
> And beggin's too low,
> Train robbin's too dangerous
> So to gamblin' I'll go.
>
> I eat when I'm hungry,
> I drink when I'm dry,
> And when I get thirsty,
> I lay down and cry.

> I've played cards in England,
> I've played cards in Spain,
> I'll bet you ten dollars,
> I'll beat you next game.

Folksongs of courtship and marriage form a distinct group. These include songs that describe a courtship ("The Quaker's Wooing" and "The Old Man's Courtship" or "Old Boots and Leggings"), those that represent a courting dialogue ("I'll Give to You a Paper of Pins" and "Soldier, Soldier, Will You Marry Me?"), a few that express a desire for marriage ("I Love Little Willie, I Do" and "The Old Bachelor"), but many more that celebrate the single life ("Wish I Was Single Again" and "I Am Determined to Be an Old Maid").

The logical sequel to songs of courting and marriage is the group of *nursery and children's songs*, many of which derive their appeal and their easy memorability from the use of a simple repeated pattern. This is true of "Go Tell Aunt Rhody," "The Barnyard Song" (or "I Bought Me a Cat"), "There Was an Old Woman Had a Little Pig," "There's a Hole in the Bottom of the Sea," and a host of others. The last named is a *cumulative song*, analogous to the cumulative folktales, and others involve imitations of animal sounds, dramatic dialogues (as in "Billy Boy"), gestures ("John Brown's Baby Had a Cold upon Its Chest"), and "jump" (or "scare") endings ("Old Woman All Skin and Bones"). This is also the place to mention three bodies of modern folksongs of childhood and adolescence that have not been collected or studied systematically—*summer-camp songs, high-school songs,* and *college songs.* A few representative examples of school and college songs are given in the Appendix; camp songs (which are sentimental, religious, homiletic, or simply funny) may be suggested by these two samples, one a parody and the other pure nonsense:

> Let me call you sweetheart,
>   I'm in love with your machine.
> Let me hear you whisper
>   that you'll buy the gasoline.
> Keep your headlights burning,
>   and your hands upon the wheel.

Let me call you sweetheart,
I'm in love with your automobile.

*

One bottle of pop, two bottles of pop
Three bottle of pop, four bottle of pop
[up to seven bottles]

Don't put your dust in my dustpan,
My dustpan, my dustpan,
Don't put your dust in my dustpan,
My dustpan's full

Fish and chips and vinegar,
Vinegar, vinegar,
Fish and chips and vinegar,
Pepper, pepper, pepper pot!

Although many folksongs (and a few ballads) are humorous, there are at least three kinds of funny songs that might be separately noted. First, *dialect songs*, like dialect stories, derive their humor from an exaggeration of racial or national speech peculiarities. Those in Southern black dialect often stem from blackface minstrel shows, while Chinese songs from the West and "Swede songs" from the upper Midwest reflect regional settlement patterns and local prejudices. Second, *nonsense songs* take their comedy from a stream of purely meaningless verbiage, often delivered at a rapid-fire pace. Examples include "The Barefoot Boy with Shoes On," "It Was Midnight on the Ocean, Not a Streetcar Was in Sight," "The Soft Side of a Brick," and "The Billboard Song." Third, *parody songs*, seldom collected and studied, seem to cluster to a few old popular numbers, "My Bonny Lies over the Ocean" being the apparent favorite and yielding versions like:

My Bonny has tuberculosis;
My Bonny has only one lung;
She coughs up the blood and corruption,
And rolls it around on her tongue.

Evidence for the folk status of "Happy Birthday" are the many parodies of the familiar words:

Happy Birthday to you,
Happy Birthday to you,
You act like a baby,
But you look ninety-two.

*

Happy Birthday to you
You live in a zoo,
We're sure that you'll live there,
On your next birthday, too.

Regional and occupational folksongs are numerous in this
country and offer insights into the history of labor and of settlement that few other sources give. *Cowboy songs* are now well
known, thanks largely to the early collecting efforts of N. Howard (Jack) Thorp and John A. Lomax, who first started to collect
and publish them after 1908. There are also songs of loggers,
railroaders, sailors, miners, military men, and other workers,
and of such hobby groups as mountain climbers, skiers, and
surfers.

Proof that the creation of occupational folksongs has not died
out lies in a group collected from American fighter pilots in
Southeast Asia in 1967 and 1968. Mostly parodies based on commercial hillbilly, folk, and popular songs, these were often
heavy with technical jargon and social protest, as this set of
words for two stanzas of "Wabash Cannonball" demonstrates:

"Hello, Cam Ranh Tower, this is Hammer 41;
My BLC light's glowing, I've just lost PC-1,
The engine's running roughly, the EGT is high,
Please clear me for a straight-in, this bird's about to die!"

"Hammer 41, this is Cam Ranh Tower here;
We'd like to let you in right now, but a senator is near;
He's here to please constituents, his plane is close at hand,
So please divert to Tuy Hoa, we can't clear you to land."

Verses from three songs of early American occupational
groups demonstrate how the working conditions and workers'
attitudes were mirrored in their singing then, too, and how the
general themes of songs, as well as details of texts, tended to be
passed on westward. One whalers' song contains this verse:

Some days we're catching whalefish, boys, and more days
   we're getting none,
With a twenty-foot oar placed in our hand from four
   o'clock in the morn.
But when the shade of night comes down we nod on our
   weary oar.
Oh, it's then I wished that I was dead, or back with the
   girls on shore!

A Northeast loggers' song describes similar conditions, even to the time of arising:

At four o'clock in the morning the boss he will shout,
"Heave out, my jolly teamsters; it's time to be on the route."
The teamsters they jump up all in a frightened way,
"Where is me boots? Where is me pants? Me socks is gone astray!"

And one cowboy song seems to be nothing more than a re-wording of the above.

Oh early every morning you will hear the boss say,
"Get out boys, it's the breakin' of day."
Slowly you rise with your little sleepy eyes,
And the bright dreamy night's passed away.

. . . The cowboy's life is a very dreary life,
It's a ridin' through the heat and the cold.

The most prominent group of regional songs are those of early Western travel and settlement, which, like tall tales, seem to laugh at hardships with an ironic tone. One song cheerfully concerns "Starvin' to Death on My Government Claim," another celebrates "The Dreary Black Hills," and a third begins:

I am looking rather seedy now,
While holding down my claim,
And my victuals are not always served the best;
And the mice play slyly round me,
As I nestle down to sleep
In my little old sod shanty in the West.

One ubiquitous Western song, sung to the tune of the old hymn "Beulah Land," has variants for many states—"Kansas

Land," "Dakota Land," "Nebraska Land," etc., all with verses like:

> I've reached the land of wind and heat,
> Where nothing grows for man to eat.
> The wind it blows with feverish heat,
> Across the plains so hard to beat.
>
> O Dakota land, sweet Dakota land,
> As on thy fiery soil I stand,
> I look away across the plains
> And wonder why it never rains,
> Till Gabriel blows his trumpet sound
> And says the rain's just gone around.

In the Northwest the same song appears as "Oregon, Wet Oregon" or "Webfoot Land."

Researching Folksongs

It would be an understatement to say that American folksongs have been collected and published with more energy than has been devoted to their classification and study; as a matter of fact, they have hardly been analyzed at all. The few categories for folksongs suggested in this chapter have counterparts in almost every published collection, but the specific songs placed under them vary widely. One person's "regional song" may be another's "comical song" and a third's "satirical song." Different terms entirely—including "historical songs," "jingles," "martial and political songs," and "dance songs"—appear in some collections, and every system has its "miscellaneous," under which usually appear what one scholar has called "sentimental balladlike pieces"—songs like "In the Baggage Coach Ahead," "Christmas at the Poor House," "Little Rosewood Casket," and "The Dream of the Miner's Child." The situation for folksong *studies* is even worse; in two exceptional examples only one Anglo-American lyric, "Green Grows the Laurel," was the subject of an exhaustive scholarly article, and only one type of American folksong—the regional and occupational—was the subject of a broad distributional survey.

American folksongs, therefore, seem to offer a particularly promising area for research. Hundreds of songs have been collected in possibly thousands of variants, and many of these are available in print. The broad outlines of a suitable classification system seem clear enough, but the details need to be worked out and published. Almost any song or song type that might be selected for study exists in enough variants from enough different regions to yield fascinating data, and both texts and tunes are usually intrinsically appealing in themselves. Questions of style, variation, function, and meaning would immediately present themselves in the study of any song. For all these reasons, and with the bibliographic aids and theoretical models now at hand and the many American folklorists interested in music, the study of American folksongs has the possibility of advancing quickly to the high level already achieved in the study of the Anglo-American ballad, which is discussed in the next chapter.

BIBLIOGRAPHIC NOTES

An excellent general introduction to the whole subject is George Herzog's essay "Song: Folk Song and the Music of Folk Song" in *Funk & Wagnalls Standard Dictionary of Folklore, Mythology, and Legend,* (1950) 2: 1032–50. Two comparable articles limited to the United States are Louise Pound's "American Folksong: Origins, Texts and Modes of Diffusion," *SFQ* 17 (1953): 114–21, reprinted in *Nebraska Folklore,* pp. 234–43, and Bruno Nettl's chapter "Words and Music: English Folksong in the United States" in Nettl, Charles Hamm, and Ronald Byrnside's *Contemporary Music and Music Cultures* (Englewood Cliffs, N.J.: Prentice-Hall, 1975), pp. 193–221. Among book-length surveys, Russell Ames's small *The Story of American Folksong* (New York: Grosset & Dunlap, 1955) is interestingly keyed to history, but the discussion is often too sketchy. Bruno Nettl's *An Introduction to Folk Music in the United States* (Detroit: Wayne State University Studies no. 7, paperback edn., 1960; rev. 1962; 3rd edn. rev. by Helen Myers, *Folk Music in the United States: An Introduction,* 1976) is comprehensive, though short, and well documented. Nettl and Myers consider both texts and tunes. Edith Fowke presents "Anglo-Canadian Folksong: A Survey" in *EM* 16 (1972): 335–50.

MacEdward Leach introduced a symposium of seven writers on folksong studies with a note, "Folksong and Ballad—a New Emphasis," *JAF* 70 (1957): 205–7. He identified the shift in interest from collecting to analysis. A second important collection of articles, originally in the *Texas Folklore Society Publications* (33, 1964), includes papers on the literary and esthetic approach, the anthropological approach, the comparative approach, and the rationalistic approach; see Roger Abrahams's *Folksong and Folksong Scholarship: Changing Approaches and Attitudes* (Dallas: Southern Methodist University Press, 1964). The definitive historical work is D. K. Wilgus's *Anglo-American Folksong Scholarship since 1898* (New Brunswick, N.J.: Rutgers University Press, 1959). Wilgus offered his assessment of folksong research and ventured a look ahead in two important articles: " 'The Text Is the Thing,' " *JAF* 86 (1973): 241–52, and "The Future of American Folksong Scholarship," *SFQ* 37 (1973): 315–29.

Herzog and Nettl, cited above, discuss art, folk, and popular songs; see also Frank Howes's "A Critique of Folk, Popular, and 'Art' Music," *BJA* 2 (1962): 239–48, and Peter Stadlen's "The Aesthetics of Popular Music," *BJA* 2 (1962): 351–61.

Most folksong collections contain some texts from broadsides, songsters, clippings, "ballet books," and occasionally even phonograph recordings. An interesting separate publication from a manuscript source is Harold W. Thompson and Edith E. Cutting's *A Pioneer Songster* (Ithaca, N.Y.: Cornell University Press, 1958); another is Ruth Ann Musick's "The Old Album of William A. Larkin," *JAF* 60 (1947): 201–51. In my article "Folk Song Studies in Idaho," *WF* 24 (1965): 231–48, a large Northwest newspaper collection of folksongs that goes back some thirty years is described.

Questions concerning the popularization and commercialization of folksongs have been discussed several times in folklore journals and meetings. William Hugh Hansen presented "The Folksinger's Defense" in *HF* 9 (1950): 65–75, in which he discussed the repertoires of three young Kentucky singers and their tastes and preferences in folksongs compared to folklorists' usual categories and theories. Sven Eric Molin touched off an exchange of opinions with his article "Lead Belly, Burl Ives, and Sam Hinton," in *JAF* 71 (1958): 58–79. Three folklorists criticized in the article replied with notes in the same issue, followed by a rejoinder by Molin and a "last word" by Sam Hinton. An amusing reaction to citybilly singing from a country singer is Eugene Haun's "Lares and Penates, Once Removed," *JAF* 72 (1959): 243–47. Oscar Brand, a popular performer of folksongs, has documented the rise of professional folksong singing in his book *The Ballad Mongers* (New York: Funk & Wagnalls, 1962). In a related vein, see Norman Cohen's "Tin Pan Alley's Contribution to Folk Music," *WF* 29 (1970): 9–20. Those wishing to study this movement more closely should also consult such popular periodicals as *Caravan, Sing Out,* and *Broadside.* R. Raymond Allen's "Old-Time Music and the Urban Folk Revival," *NYF* 7 (1981): 65–81, criticizes folklorists for disregarding the music of the revival and makes some good suggestions for scholarly directions to take.

John Greenway's thesis is backed by his *American Folksongs of Protest* (Philadelphia: University of Pennsylvania Press, 1953). It was attacked by Tristram P. Coffin in "Folksongs of Social Protest: A Musical Mirage," *NYFQ* 14 (1958): 3–9, with a brief rejoinder from Greenway, who then stated his position more fully in his article "Folksongs as Socio-Historical Documents," *WF* 19 (1960): 1–9, reprinted in *Folklore in Action,* pp. 112–19. A book that deals with some of the same materials without calling them folksongs is Josh Dunson's *Freedom in the Air: Song Movements of the Sixties* (New York: Little New World Paperbacks, LNW-7, 1965). Richard A. Reuss discusses a major figure in the social uses of folk and folklike music in his essay "Woody Guthrie and His Folk Tradition," *JAF* 83 (1970): 273–303, and provides an excellent historical survey in "American Folksongs and Left-Wing Politics: 1935–1956," *JFI* 12 (1975): 89–111. Reuss's essay on the "musical odyssey" of Charles Seeger appeared in *WF* 38 (1979): 221–38, the same year that Seeger died. A good survey is in Jens Lund and R. Serge Denisoff's "The Folk Music Revival and the Counter Culture: Contributions and Contradictions," *JAF* 84 (1971): 394–405. The other side of the coin is exposed in Marcello Truzzi's "The 100% American Songbag: Conservative Folksongs in America," *WF* 28 (1969): 27–40.

Wilgus and Greenway as co-editors blazed a new trail with the "Hillybilly Issue" of *JAF* (77 [July–September 1965]), which contains important articles and discography. Shortly thereafter the American Folklore Society published Bill C. Malone's book *Country Music: U.S.A.* as Volume 54 in the Memoir Series (Austin, Texas, 1968). Another folklore journal issue devoted to "commercialized folk music in general, and hillbilly music in particular" was *WF* 30 (1971): 171–246. Two separate articles of particular interest are Howard Wright Marshall's "'Keep on the Sunny Side of Life': Pattern and Religious Expression in Bluegrass Gospel Music," *NYFQ* 30 (1974): 3–43 (expanded from a 1971 publication in *FF*), and Frederick E. Danker's "The Repertory and Style of a Country Singer: Johnny Cash," *JAF* 85 (1972): 309–29. A good general article on the whole subject of folksong mass popularity is Samuel P. Bayard's "Decline and 'Revival' of Anglo-American Folk Music," in *Folklore in Action,* pp. 21–29. Bayard describes how folksongs change musically into art or popular songs as they are reproduced by city singers in a synthetic atmosphere of folksiness.

There are too many good general folksong collections to list them all, but Wilgus has a full bibliography. A few landmark volumes, however, may be mentioned. Olive Dame Campbell and Cecil J. Sharp's *English Folksongs from the Southern Appalachians* first appeared in 1917 (New

York and London: Oxford University Press). The two-volume edition, edited by Maud Karpeles, appeared in 1932 and was reissued in 1952. Louise Pound's anthology *American Ballads and Songs* (New York: Scribners, 1922) is a notable early book of native materials with a stunning introductory essay that manages to touch upon almost every important aspect of the pieces included. Midwestern states are well represented in collections such as Emelyn E. Gardner and Geraldine J. Chickering's *Ballads and Songs of Southern Michigan* (Ann Arbor: University of Michigan Press, 1939; repr. Hatboro, Pa.: Folklore Associates, 1967), Paul Brewster's *Ballads and Songs of Indiana* (Bloomington: Indiana University Folklore Series no. 1, 1940), and H. M. Belden's *Ballads and Songs Collected by the Missouri Folk-Lore Society* (Columbia: University of Missouri Studies vol. 15, 1940).

Vance Randolph's four-volume *Ozark Folksongs* (Columbia, Mo.: State Historical Society, 1946–50) is as indispensable as his many excellent folktale publications. (A revised edition with an introduction by W. K. McNeil was published by the University of Missouri Press in 1980.) The folksong texts in the *Frank C. Brown Collection of North Carolina Folklore* are edited in vol. 3 (1952) by H. M. Belden and Arthur Palmer Hudson; tunes are in vol. 5 (1962). Book-length collections published since Wilgus's history include two from the West: Lester A. Hubbard's *Ballads and Songs from Utah* (Salt Lake City: University of Utah Press, 1961), and Ethel and Chauncey O. Moore's *Ballads and Folk Songs of the Southwest* (Norman: University of Oklahoma Press, 1964).

The rich Afro-American folksong heritage has been well documented, earlier in such studies and anthologies as Dorothy Scarborough's *On the Trail of Negro Folksongs* (Cambridge, Mass.: Harvard University Press, 1925; repr. Hatboro, Pa.: Folklore Associates, 1963), and N. I. White's *American Negro Folksongs* (Cambridge, Mass.: Harvard University Press, 1928), and later in such works as Harold Courlander's *Negro Folk Music, U.S.A.* (New York: Columbia University Press, 1963). Dana J. Epstein's *Sinful Tunes and Spirituals* (Urbana: University of Illinois Press, 1977) traces Afro-American music up to the Civil War. Social backgrounds of an important Afro-American musical form, the blues, are given in Frederic Ramsey, Jr.'s *Been Here and Gone* (New Brunswick, N.J.: Rutgers University Press, 1960), and George Mitchell's *Blow My Blues Away* (Baton Rouge: Louisiana State University Press, 1971). For tracing further developments, see Samuel B. Charters's *The Country Blues* (New York: Rinehart, 1959), Harry Oster's *Living Country Blues* (Detroit: Folklore Associates, 1969), and Charles Keil's *Urban Blues* (Chicago: University of Chicago Press, 1966) and their discographies. Other aspects of blues tradition are discussed in William R. Ferris, Jr.'s, "Racial Repertoires among Blues Performers," *EM* 14 (1970): 439–49, and David Evans, "Techniques of Blues Composition among Black Folksingers," *JAF* 87 (1974): 240–49.

The special blues issue of *SFQ* (vol. 42 [1978]: 1–98), edited by Jeff Todd Titon, contained seven useful articles.

The popular-cultural effects of blues tradition are described in John M. Hellmann, Jr.'s, "'I'm a Monkey': The Influence of Black American Blues Argot on the Rolling Stones," *JAF* 86 (1973): 367–73. Another important aspect of black folksongs is treated by Bruce Jackson in articles and in his book *Wake Up Dead Man: Afro-American Worksongs From Texas Prisons* (Cambridge, Mass.: Harvard University Press, 1972).

Pioneering collections of American occupational and industrial folksongs were made by George Korson and published in such works of his as *Songs and Ballads of the Anthracite Miner* (New York: Grafton Press, 1927), *Minstrels of the Mine Patch* (Philadelphia: University of Pennsylvania Press, 1938; reissued Hatboro, Pa.: Folklore Associates, 1964), and *Coal Dust on the Fiddle* (Philadelphia: University of Pennsylvania Press, 1943; reissued Hatboro, Pa.: Folklore Associates, 1965). A companion work is Archie Green's *Only a Miner: Studies in Recorded Coal-Mining Songs* (Urbana: University of Illinois Press, 1972). Collections of sea songs include W. Roy Mackenzie's *Ballads and Sea Songs from Nova Scotia* (Cambridge, Mass.: Harvard University Press, 1928; reprinted Hatboro, Pa.: Folklore Associates, 1963), Elisabeth Bristol Greenleaf and Grace Yarrow Mansfield's *Ballads and Sea Songs of Newfoundland* (Cambridge, Mass.: Harvard University Press, 1933; reprinted Hatboro, Pa.: Folklore Associates, 1968), and Frederick Pease Harlow's *Chanteying aboard American Ships* (Barre, Mass.: Barre Publishing Co., 1962). See also Elliott Oring, "Whalemen and Their Songs: A Study of Folklore and Culture," *NYFQ* 27 (1971): 130–52.

The interplay between the songs of sailors and loggers is suggested in *Shantymen and Shantyboys* (New York: Macmillan, 1951) by William Main Doerflinger. For loggers' songs, see Edith Fowke, *Lumbering Songs from the Northern Woods* (Austin, Texas: AFS Memoir Series vol. 55, 1970). Hardrock miners' folksongs were first discussed by Duncan Emrich in *CFQ* 1 (1942): 213–32. A collection of "Songs of the Butte Miner" supplemented that pioneering article in *WF* 9 (1950): 1–49, by Wayland D. Hand, Charles Cutts, Robert C. Wylder, and Betty Wylder. S. Page Stegner discussed "Protest Songs from the Butte Mines" in *WF* 26 (1967): 157–67. Other articles on occupational folksong traditions are Ann Miller Carpenter, "The Railroad in American Folk Song, 1865–1920," *PTFS* 36 (1972): 103–19; "Big Tops Bloom, but Chanteys Disappear" reprinted from *Billboard* in *WF* 17 (1958): 57–60; and Marcello Truzzi, "Folksongs of the American Circus," *NYFQ* 24 (1968): 163–75. These and several other traditions deserve further attention from folklorists.

Folksong collector John A. Lomax with his son Alan produced some of the most widely read—and sometimes controversial—general anthologies of folksongs in this country. The publication of Alan Lomax's *The Folk Songs of North America in the English Language* (New York: Doubleday, 1960) was the occasion for several reviews in professional journals that variously damned and praised all of the Lomax books. See reviews by G. Legman and D. K. Wilgus in *JAF* 74 (1961): 265–69; by Gene Bluestein in *TQ* 5 (1962): 49–59; and by David P. McAllester in *EM* 6 (1962): 233–38.

John Lomax's *Cowboy Songs and Other Frontier Ballads* of 1910 (New York: Sturgis and Walton) has been reprinted and expanded several times. Jack Thorp's pamphlet *Songs of the Cowboys* of 1908 , to which Lomax was indebted for several of his texts, was reprinted with variants, commentary, notes, and a lexicon by Austin E. Fife and Alta Fife (New York: Clarkson N. Potter, 1966). In "Jack Thorp and John Lomax: Oral or Written Transmission?" *WF* 26 (1967): 113–18, John O. West reviews the evidence that Lomax had used nineteen out of the twenty-three songs Thorp earlier printed without giving credit. Professor and Mrs. Fife assembled at the Utah State University Library in Logan materials from print, recordings, and manuscripts for comprehensive analyses of most of the traditional songs of the cowboys. Two of their publications based on these data are *Cowboy and Western Songs: A Comprehensive Anthology* (New York: Clarkson N. Potter, 1969) with two hundred items, and *Heaven on Horseback: Revivalist Songs and Verse in the Cowboy Idiom* (Logan, Utah: Western Texts Society Series 1, 1970).

In an essay entitled "The Dying Cowboy Song," *WAL* 2 (1967): 50–57, John Barsness suggests that accounts of cowboy singing are greatly romanticized and that many collectors had little to do with real cowboys. The actual folksong repertoire of a real cowboy is given in Glenn Ohrlin's *The Hell-bound Train, a Cowboy Songbook* (Urbana: University of Illinois Press, 1973). John I. White, the composer of the song, gives the background for the Western-tinged "Great Grandma" in *WF* 27 (1968): 27–31. J. D. Robb provides examples in Spanish and English of another type of Western occupational song in "'Whereof I Speak,' or Songs of the Western Sheep Camps," *NMFR* 12 (1969–70): 17–28.

Folksongs in scholarly journals are beyond counting, but some representative examples may be cited. Edward D. Ives has held to an exceptionally high standard of editing in his "Twenty-one Folksongs from Prince Edward Island," *NEF* 5 (1963): 1–87; and "Folksongs from Maine," *NEF* 7 (1965): 1–104. Another collection from this region is Richard M. Dorson, George List, and Neil Rosenberg's "Folksongs of the Maine Woods: Annotated Transcriptions," *FFMA* 8 (1965): 1–33. From the Midwest and West come "Songs I Sang on an Iowa Farm," collected by Eleanor T. Rogers with notes by Tristram P. Coffin and Samuel P. Bayard, *WF* 17 (1958): 229–47 (repr. in *Readings in American Folklore*, pp. 31–52); and Ben Gray Lumpkin, "Colorado Folk Songs,"

WF 19 (1960): 77–97. A small collection of items of a kind often ignored is given in Gloria Dickens's "Childhood Songs from North Carolina," *NCFJ* 21 (1973): 4–9.

Edward D. Ives's book *Larry Gorman, the Man Who Made the Songs* (Bloomington: Indiana University Press, 1964) exhaustively traces and analyzes the work of a woods poet responsible for some of the best folksongs of the Northeast. Ives followed this with *Lawrence Doyle: The Farmer Poet of Prince Edward Island* (Orono, Maine: University of Maine Studies no. 92, 1971), and *Joe Scott: The Woodsman-Songmaker* (Urbana: University of Illinois Press, 1978). Other studies that focus on the singer rather than the songs exclusively are Roger D. Abrahams's *A Singer and Her Songs: Almeda Riddle's Book of Ballads* (Baton Rouge: Louisiana State University Press, 1970) and Henry Glassie, Edward D. Ives, and John F. Szwed's *Folksongs and Their Makers* (Bowling Green, Ohio: Bowling Green University Popular Press, 1970).

G. Legman deals with a long-neglected area of folksong in "The Bawdy Song in Fact and in Print," in *The Horn Book* (New Hyde Park, N.Y.: University Books, 1964), pp. 336–426. One such song is traced by Guthrie T. Meade, Jr., in "The Sea Crab," *MF* 8 (1958): 91–100; and Ed Cray has edited a sizeable anthology in *The Erotic Muse* (New York: Oak Publications, 1968).

Joseph Hickerson discusses college folksongs in two articles in *FFMA* 1 (1958): 2, and 6 (1963): 3–6. Some examples of camp songs are given by Linda Weaver in *NCFJ* 22 (1974): 75–79. Two nonsense songs ("The Soft Side of a Brick" and "She Was Built Like a Mississippi Shed") are given by Richard C. Poulsen in *AFFWord* 3 (1973): 11–15. Some military folksongs are given in an article by Gustave O. Arlt and Chandler Harris in *CFQ* 3 (1944): 36–40, and two by William Wallrich in *WF* 12 (1953): 270–82, and 13 (1954): 236–44. In the *FF* Bibliographic and Special Series no. 7 (1971), Major Joseph F. Tuso gathered thirty-three examples of "Folksongs of the American Fighter Pilot in Southeast Asia, 1967–68."

Good analytical studies of American folksongs (as opposed to studies of ballads) are still relatively uncommon. Some early ones by Phillips Barry are contained in the *Bulletin of the Folksong Society of the Northeast*, reprinted by the American Folklore Society with an introduction by Samuel P. Bayard (Philadelphia: Bibliographic and Special Series no. 11, 1960). An important work is Roger D. Abrahams and George Foss, *Anglo-American Folksong Style* (Englewood Cliffs, N.J.: Prentice-Hall, 1968). Levette J. Davidson first summarized the investigation of "Home on the Range" in *CFQ* 3 (1944): 208–11. John Lomax added his observations on the song in "Half-Million Dollar Song," *Southwest Review* 31 (1945): 1–8. Probably the definitive account is John I. White's article on it in *TAW* 12 (Sept. 1975): 10–15, a chapter from his book *Git Along Little Dogies: Songs and Songmakers of the American West* (Urbana: University of Illinois Press, 1975). My own study "'The Lane County Bachelor': Folksong or Not?" (the answer was "yes") appeared first in *Heritage of Kansas* 10 (1977) and was reprinted in *Readings in American Folklore*, pp. 289–308.

Tristram P. Coffin's "A Tentative Study of a Typical Folk Lyric: 'Green Grows the Laurel,'" *JAF* 65 (1952): 341–51, is unusual as a comparative study of a single nonnarrative song. Other approaches to specific genres of folksong are Peter T. Bartis's "An Examination of the Holler in North Carolina White Tradition," *SFQ* 39 (1975): 208–18; Bess Lomax Hawes, "Folksongs and Functions: Some Thoughts on the American Lullaby," *JAF* 87 (1974): 140–48 (repr. in *Readings in American Folklore*, pp. 203–14); D. K. Wilgus and Lynwood Montell, "Clure and Joe Williams: Legend and Blues Ballad," *JAF* 81 (1968): 295–315; and Américo Paredes, "The *Décima* on the Texas-Mexican Border: Folksong as an Adjunct to Legend," *JFI* 3 (1966): 154–67.

Two uncommon studies of the nature of folksong variation are John Quincy Wolf's "Folksingers and the Re-Creation of Folksongs," *WF* 26 (1967): 101–11, and Tom Burns's "A Model for Textual Variation in Folksong," *FF* 3 (1970): 49–56. Norman Cazden's article "Regional and Occupational Orientations of American Traditional Song," *JAF* 72 (1959): 310–44, offers an unusual statistical analysis of folksong distribution for various regions.

Sources of recordings of authentic American folksongs are identified in the notes to Chapter 13.

12
Ballads

Defining and Classifying Ballads

A traditional ballad is a narrative folksong—a folksong that tells a story. To carry the basic definition any further, as most ballad collectors and scholars have been inclined to do, is asking for trouble; every other quality that might be listed as characteristic of some ballads requires a balancing list of other ballads that are exceptions to the rule. But because they *all* tell stories, a traditional ballad *is* a narrative folksong.

We have defined "folksong" in Chapter 11. But how narrative is a "narrative"? At this point all folksong-versus-ballad distinctions become relative and arbitrary. For instance, the "folk lyric" called "On Top of Old Smokey," derived, in fact, from an English ballad "The Wagoner's Lad" and tells a reasonably clear story, as the following stanza illustrates:

> Your parents are against me
> And mine are the same;
> So farewell, my true love
> I'll be on my way.

The same thing is true of "Careless Love," "The Dreary Black Hills," "The Lane County Bachelor," "Old Dan Tucker," and a host of other American folksongs. Conversely, some accepted ballads occur in many variants that have confusing story lines or extremely scant narrative content.

Some 850-odd Anglo-American narrative folksongs have been arranged by scholarly indexers in three categories: *British traditional ballads*, *British broadside ballads*, and *native American ballads.* The idea that these ballad classifications are canonical has been exaggerated by some past scholars. Even in 1956 we find the noted Appalachian folklore collector Richard Chase declaring in his popular anthology *American Folk Tales and Songs* that "The genuine *ballad* is only one type of folksong. Your 'ballad' is not a true *folk* ballad unless it is closely kin to one of the 305—no more, no less!—in Professor Child's great collection." (Italics in original.)

Francis James Child wrote in 1882 that he had gathered "every valuable copy of every known ballad," but this was a good forty years before field collecting of ballads in America had gotten well under way. All that the twentieth-century ballad indexer G. Malcolm Laws, Jr., claimed to offer was a "guide" and "bibliographical syllabus"; it is the users of these collections and indexes who have elevated them into canons and treated their rough groupings as if they were systematic classifications. All of which is preliminary to a warning that in the discussion that follows, the "three kinds of ballads," as well as generalizations offered about them, are merely to be regarded as convenient scholarly concepts that facilitate description and analysis. The last word has certainly not been said on ballad definition or classification, although D. K. Wilgus seems to be making good progress toward an international Type Index with his proposal for a thematic catalogue of the narrative units of traditional songs based on such events or actions as seductions, murders, punishments, and bereavements.

British Traditional Ballads

The **British traditional ballads** are usually known as "the Child ballads," not because they are sung by children or have any connection whatever with children's folklore, but because they were gathered from hundreds of manuscript and printed sources in the late nineteenth century by Professor Francis James Child of Harvard and published, together with voluminous notes, in his monumental work, *The English and Scottish Popular Ballads* (5 volumes, 1882–1898). They are called "Child ballads," of course, by scholars and not by folk informants, who would no more call them that than they would call "Jack, Will, and Tom tales" *Märchen* or refer to such stories by their Aarne-Thompson type numbers.

The Child ballads have been the folksong collectors' prime finds and the literary anthologists' favorite set pieces. Collectors went to the extreme at one time in this country of periodically tallying-up, state by state and county by county, the Child ballad variants "recovered" from oral tradition, either in complete or in fragmentary texts. The anthologists continue to reprint some eight or ten selected ballad versions from Child as examples of medieval popular poetry, notwithstanding the fact that most of these selections came from manuscript sources no earlier than the seventeenth century and were probably revised by ballad editors in the eighteenth century or later. The veneration that has surrounded the Child canon—the mystique of the 305 ballads that he included—is also seen in the typical "Child and other" arrangements of printed folksong collections.

The editor's very choice of words in his title—*The* English and Scottish popular ballads—granted a false exclusiveness to his 305 ballads, when there are many other British popular ballads that he either would not admit on esthetic grounds or did not know. Yet his choices had considerable validity, too. These do constitute the oldest group of ballads in British tradition, and their basic *form* is found in medieval sources. These ballads are part of an international tradition in that they are related to corresponding narrative folksongs from the Continent, especially the Scandinavian ballads. The greatest influence upon Child was the edition of Danish ballads that came from the hand of Svend Grundtvig, beginning in 1853. Grundtvig's texts revealed numerous analogues to the English ballads. Furthermore, Grundtvig exerted direct influence on Child during their extended correspondence. Most important, these ballads serve as a norm against which other ballads are measured, for their treatments of subject matter, style, and narrative method are widely considered to be of a high poetic order, although within the limitations of a rigid set of traditional conventions.

Ballad Characteristics

The technique of comparing art songs and folksongs may be applied to literary poetry and ballad poetry. In literature we value originality—a fresh treatment of a universal theme, "What oft was thought, but ne'er so well expressed." But the traditional ballads, as Albert B. Friedman has written, are not literature but "illiterature"; they exist only in different oral performances, not in fixed written texts, and thus they abound in features that oral transmission creates and sustains. They use only a few simple stanza forms; their rhyme and meter seem irregular compared to conventional poetry; their language is stereotyped and cluttered with clichés; they freely repeat phrases, lines, and sometimes whole stanzas, often as refrains; and their texts are full of dialect terms, archaisms, and garbled usage. Despite all this, the best of the old traditional ballads have a unique charm and force that have not been equaled in literary imitations. Although no amount of description can ever replace *hearing* ballads sung by traditional performers, the characteristic features of ballad poetry may at least be illustrated in print.

The typical *ballad stanza* is the familiar one of many folk rhymes and jingles (including "Mary Had a Little Lamb") and of "common measure" in hymns. It is a quatrain rhyming "x, a, x, a" (that is, lines one and three do not rhyme), with lines measured "4, 3, 4, 3" (counting strong beats only), as shown in this typical opening verse from the ballad that Child called "James Harris" or "The Demon Lover" and that is frequently collected in this country as "The House Carpenter." It is Child's number 243:

> "Well mét, well mét," said an óld true lóve, (4, x)
> "Well mét, well mét," said hé; (3, a)
> "I've júst retúrned from a fár foreign lánd, (4, x)
> And it's áll for the lóve of thée." (3, a)

Other ballads, regarded by some scholars as the oldest ones, have a two-line stanza of four strong beats each, usually with refrain lines filling out a quatrain, such as in the following opening stanza from the Scottish ballad "Willie's Lyke-Wake" (Child 25):

> "O Wíllie my són, what mákes you so sád?"
> As the sun shines over the valley
> "I lýe sarely síck for the lóve of a máid."
> Amang the blue flowers and the yellow.

There are other kinds of ballad stanzas—some say as many as a dozen—but the various forms cannot be fully established without reference to ballad music.

The *refrains* in ballads are often lyrical lines interspersed with story lines, as in the last example quoted above, or they may involve both lyrical lines and repetition, as in this opening stanza from "The Two Sisters" (Child 10):

> There was an old man in the North Countree,
> Bow down!
> There was an old man in the North Countree,
> And a bow 'twas unto me
> There was an old man in the North Countree,
> And he had daughters one, two, three.
> I'll be true to my love if my love be true to me.

Refrains like this suggest dance movements or directions. Others are lists of plants, such as "Parsley, Sage, Rosemary and Thyme" (which sometimes appears in variants like "Every rose grows merry in time"). A number of refrains sound like pure nonsense, being merely strings of syllables such as "hey nonny no," "derry, derry, down," and "lillumwham, lillumwham."

Repetition alone in ballads may provide a refrain, usually through the repeating of the last two lines of each quatrain to form a six-line stanza, and there are numerous instances of repetition as a structural device in the plots themselves. Sometimes a question is repeated in an answer or a command is repeated in action, with very little change in wording, as shown in these typical commonplace lines found in numerous ballads:

> "Who will shoe your pretty little foot,
> And who will glove your hand?"
> ". . . mother will shoe my pretty little foot,
> And father will glove my hand."

*

"Go saddle me the black, the black,
Go saddle me the brown,
Go saddle me the fastest steed,
That ever ran through town."

She saddled him the black, the black,
She saddled him the brown . . .

The most typical form of ballad repetition is *incremental repetition*, in which several lines are repeated with a slight "increment" (addition or change). Some ballads like "The Maid Freed from the Gallows" (Child 95, also called "Hangman") and "Our Goodman" (or "Four Nights Drunk," Child 274) are developed entirely through this device. It is also seen in two stanzas from "The Bonny Earl of Murray" (Child 181):

He was a braw [fine] gallant,
And he rid at the ring
And the bonny Earl of Murray,
Oh he might have been a king!

The next stanza is the same, except that the second line becomes "And he played at the ba' [ball]," while the last is altered to "Was the flower among them a' [all]."

The oft-repeated "shoe your foot," "saddle my horse," and other stanzas ("Oh, make my bed, mother . . . ," "Go dig my grave, father . . . ," etc.) are one kind of *commonplace*, or stereotyped diction, found in ballads. These are "commonplace stanzas," and there are also repeated phrases. Wine is always "blood-red," steeds tend to be "milk-white," knives are usually "wee penknives" (perhaps an alteration of "weapon knife"), and a frequent courtly servant is the "little foot page." Child ballads often begin conventionally ("'Twas in the merry month of May . . .") and express times in commonplace phraseology ("Two [or three] hours before it was day"). Such expressions certainly aid ballad singers' memory, for the performers can fall back on these phrases easily if other words escape them; but whether the words indicate the spontaneous "formulaic composition" of ballads or are simply traditional poetic devices is debatable.

In the three opening stanzas of traditional ballads quoted, we can see two other characteristic devices—ballads, like epics, often begin abruptly, *in medias res* (in the middle of the story), and they are highly *dramatic* in that they are told largely in terms of dialogue and action. In "The House Carpenter," for instance, we do not know who the "old true love" is who has returned saying "Well met, well met" (a greeting like "Welcome," apparently). But as the ballad progresses in the dialogue of the next two stanzas, we can begin to piece the background together:

> "Come in, come in, my old true love,
> And have a seat with me.
> It's been three-fourths of a long, long, year
> Since together we have been."
>
> "Well I can't come in or I can't sit down,
> For I haven't but a moment's time.
> They say you're married to a house carpenter,
> And your heart will never be mine."

Two of the most popular ballads in literary anthologies, "Lord Randall" (Child 12) and "Edward" (Child 13), are told entirely in dialogue, as are several others. Most, however, have stanzas of dialogue alternated with stanzas of action, with an occasional bit of description. By this means ballads achieve the immediacy of real life, of plays, or, as one critic has suggested, of motion pictures. Another ballad characteristic that supports the film theory has been called *leaping and lingering*—the tendency to make abrupt scene changes and then "linger" in one place for several stanzas. The counterpart in film is the art of "montage," or selective cutting and splicing of long, middle, and close-up shots.

Perhaps the most striking aspect of traditional ballad style (or tone) is *impersonality*. Stories involving supernaturalism, stark tragedy, and bloody violence, often between lovers or family members, are narrated with little intrusion of editorial comment or sentimentality. (A pleasant and uncomplicated tune often supports this kind of tone.) Like modern newspaper stories, which often deal with the same kinds of subjects, the ballads tend to focus on the climax of an action and its result, relating the happenings in a straightforward, objective manner. In "Mary Hamilton" (Child 173), a lady of the Scottish court disposes of her illegitimate child thus:

> She's tyed it in her apron
> And she's thrown it in the sea;
> Says, "Sink ye, swim ye, bonny wee babe!
> You'll ne'er get mair o me."

In "Little Musgrave and the Lady Barnard" (Child 81, often "Little Matty Groves" in the United States) a duel is described thus:

> The first stroke that Little Musgrave stroke,
> He hurt Lord Barnard sore;
> The next stroke that Lord Barnard stroke
> Little Musgrave nere struck more.

Ballad Transmission and Changes

All of the ballad characteristics described so far are typical of English and Scottish texts, although the stanzas of "The House Carpenter" and "The Two Sisters" actually came from American variants. When we look more closely at traditional ballads collected in this country, a pattern of alteration becomes apparent. American versions of Child ballads tend to lose details of their stories, to slough off supernatural motifs, to become subjective in tone, to acquire local references, and to change their language.

The longer that ballads are transmitted orally, the more they tend to be reduced to what the folklorist Tristram P. Coffin has aptly termed the "emotional core" of the narrative; the focus is always on the climax of the story. Long ballads, originally sprinkled with circumstantial details, may eventually become lyrical folksongs. "Sir Lionel" (Child 18), for example, in older versions telling a complicated tale about a knight slaying a wild boar and a giant, becomes in the United States "Old Bangum and the

Boar," a comical song about a hunting expedition. "Little Sir Hugh" (Child 155), relating the same medieval legend as Chaucer's "Prioress's Tale" (part of the same tradition as the urban legend of "The Mutilated Boy"), loses its anti-Semitic plot in American versions and simply tells of a murder by a "Jeweler's daughter" or "gypsy lady." In "Mary Hamilton," Coffin's chief example of this process, the narrative is reduced to a five-stanza lament by the victim, and no story whatever is told.

Americans, presumably because they are hard-headed and practical, have tended especially to drop supernatural elements from British ballads. Little Sir Hugh no longer speaks miraculously after his murder; Sir Lionel faces no giant; James Harris is not a ghost (or the Devil) but merely a double-dealing sailor; and the ballad of "The Two Sisters" has lost its fascinating motif of a speaking harp being constructed from the dead girl's breastbone and strands of her hair. Ghosts, fairies, elves, and mermaids all drop out of most American texts. In the few variants in which the Devil still appears, he is a comic figure, not the Prince of Darkness.

American sentimentality and fundamentalist religion are credited with the alteration of the moral tone of many British traditional ballads. The most typical change is the addition of a concluding stanza that comments on the story. In "James Harris," the wife is persuaded to leave her husband and sail away with the returned lover. The ship sinks (in older British versions through magic), and this verse is then tacked on at the end:

> A curse be on the sea-faring men,
> Oh, curséd be their lives,
> For while they are robbing the House-Carpenter,
> And coaxing away their wives.

In some American versions of "Bonny Barbara Allen" (Child 84) the tragic heroine herself speaks:

> "Farewell ye virgins all," she said,
> "And shun the fault I've fell in;

> Henceforth take warning by the fall
> Of cruel Barbara Allen."

Unsavory subjects like incest are eliminated; cruel characters
in ballads may return later and apologize for their behavior. In
one of the most extreme examples of changed tone, the deeply
moving British ballad "The Three Ravens" (Child 26; in Scotland "The Twa Corbies") became in the United States a rolick-
ing nonsense song. The traditional British versions descend
from one that was first printed in 1611 that began:

> There were three ravens sat on a tree,
>   Downe a downe, hay downe, hay downe
> There were three ravens sat on a tree,
>   With a downe
> There were three ravens sat on a tree,
>   They were as blacke as they might be,
>   With a downe derrie, derrie, derrie, downe, downe.

The story continues as a dialogue between the ravens that reveals how a knight lying "slain under his shield" is guarded by
his hawks and hounds and is finally carried off for burial by a
fallow doe, "great with child," who perishes from the effort.
The ballad ends with the comment:

> God send every gentleman
> Such hawks, such hounds, and such a leman [sweetheart].

In the Scottish version the hawks and hounds desert the knight,
his lady takes another mate, and the ravens feast on his corpse.
However, the American versions ignore pathos entirely, so that
the song begins:

> There were three crows sat on a tree,
>   Oh Billy Magee Magaw!
> There were three crows sat on a tree,
>   Oh Billy Magee Magaw!
> There were three crows sat on a tree,
> And they were black as crows could be;
> And they all flapped their wings and cried,
>   "Caw! Caw! Caw!"

> And they all flapped their wings and cried,
> "Billy Magee Magaw!"

This time the two crows only pick out the eyes of an old dead horse, and the ballad sometimes ends:

> O maybe you think there's another verse,
> But there isn't.

Minor verbal variations in ballads may be the result of informants forgetting words, misunderstanding what they have heard, inserting a commonplace, or trying to improve on a story or expand it. A frequent result is the creation of near nonsense —"a parrot *sitting* on a willow tree" becomes "*exceeding* on a willow tree," or instead of characters calling out "*amain* [vigorously], 'Unworthy Barbara Allen,'" they do so "*amen.*" The first of these changes possibly came about as a result of misunderstood pronunciation, the latter from the use of an unfamiliar archaic word. Names in the British ballads are particularly subject to change in American tradition. In "The Gypsy Laddie" (Child 200), for example, many variants occur, including Gypsy Davey, Gypsum Davey, Black Jack Davey, and Harrison Brady.

In many instances, verbal changes in American versions of British traditional ballads serve to relocalize the setting. Thus, in a logger's version of the ballad called "The Farmer's Curst Wife" (Child 278), the subject is a "woodsman's wife"; and Lord Randall in Virginia may be "Johnny Randolph," picking up the name of a prominent local family. References to "deep blue sea" sometimes change to "Tennessee." One of the most amusing relocalizations has appeared in the commonplace stanza that attaches a "rose-briar" ending to a tragic love story:

> One was buried in the old churchyard,
> The other in the choir.
> And out of her grave grew a red, red, rose,
> And out of his a briar.
>
> They grew and they grew to the old church top,
> 'Til they couldn't grow any higher.
> And there they locked in a true-lover's knot,
> For all true lovers to admire.

A singer who did not recognize "choir" as a part of a church in which bodies might be interred changed it to "Ohio."

British Broadside Ballads

British broadside ballads are a more recent strain of balladry than the Child ballads, as noted in Chapter 11. Also, in contrast to Child's 305 ballads, the plots of broadsides are even more sensational, their attitudes are more subjective, their stanza forms are more varied, and their language is less poetic. Broadside diction tends even more heavily than that in Child ballads toward stereotypes, drawing both on the same commonplaces found in the older ballads and on some new ones. (The "Come all ye" opening stanza, for example, is frequent.) Broadsides not only are like newspapers in general style and narrative method, but also, in common with the most sensational modern tabloids, they often dwell upon murders, robberies, scandals, love-triangles, and like subjects.

Many thousands of such topical ballads were composed, printed on tens of thousands of broadside sheets, and sold on the streets, in both England and America, to a public eager for their lurid stories. But only a small number of these pieces passed into oral tradition and became folk ballads. The folk versions, in turn, continued to change in oral transmission in much the same way that Child ballads varied. Presumably, then, a broadside, too, can eventually be reduced to an "emotional core." Analysis of this whole process of ballad variation was greatly facilitated in 1957, when Professor G. Malcolm Laws, Jr., of the University of Pennsylvania published a classified bibliographic guide to some 290 common American ballads that had apparently derived from British broadsides, along with an illuminating discussion of their distribution, forms, and style. Laws's categories and some sample titles follow (letters "A" through "I" were reserved for the Laws native American ballad index, discussed next):

J. War Ballads (A small group with few American
        versions; "The Drummer Boy of
        Waterloo" is J 1.)

K.   Ballads of Sailors and the Sea ("The Sailor Boy" is K 12.)

L.   Ballads of Crime and Criminals ("The Boston Burglar" is L 16 B.)

M.   Ballads of Family Opposition to Lovers ("The Drowsy Sleeper" is M 4.)

N.   Ballads of Lovers' Disguises and Tricks ("Jack Monroe" is N 7.)

O.   Ballads of Faithful Lovers ("Molly Bawn" or "The Shooting of His Dear" is O 36.)

P.   Ballads of Unfaithful Lovers ("The Butcher Boy" is P 24.)

Q.   Humorous and Miscellaneous Ballads ("Father Grumble" is Q 1, and "The Babes in the Woods" is Q 34.)

Although ballads with broadside origins have not been so highly regarded by folklorists as have Child ballads, most traditional singers in America know more broadsides than any other kind of ballad. At any rate, in more than 1,800 folksong and ballad texts, Laws's analysis of the contents of six representative collections shows that the broadsides outnumber either Child or native American ballads by more than two to one. The fact that the collected *variants* of Child ballads outnumber either of the other two types in the same books is probably indicative of folklorists' rather than informants' preferences. In one other large and diversified printed collection, Frank C. Brown's *North Carolina Folklore,* a similar distribution among types is maintained. Among some 184 identifiable texts here, 49 are Child ballads, about 75 are broadsides, and about 60 are native American ballads. Another revealing statistic about this last collection is that the remaining printed texts—some 130 further ballads from North Carolina folk tradition—do not appear in any of the three published classifications of ballads in America, suggesting how incomplete these classifications still are.

Most other regional collections yield roughly similar figures. For example, when a miscellaneous group of some 730 folksongs and ballads (1,000 individual texts) from the Northwest was ana-

lyzed, about one-quarter of them were found to be ballads, and
these fell into the following groups:

	INDIVIDUAL BALLADS	INDIVIDUAL TEXTS
Child	19	49
Laws Broadsides	41	71
(Other, prob. British)	12	36
Laws native American	57	83
(Other, prob. American)	38	65

Such statistics suggest that non-Child ballads are more common than Child ballads in American folk tradition, that many
unclassified Anglo-American ballads still exist, and that, as a
group, ballads are outnumbered in tradition by nonnarrative
folksongs. Classifications, titles, and statistics, however, do not
tell us anything about ballads themselves. Selected stanzas from
the broadside ballads, whose titles and Laws numbers were
listed above, give some notion of their characteristics; the versions quoted in the following summary are all from *The Frank C.
Brown Collection of North Carolina Folklore.*

The broadside composers plodded grimly through their
stories, getting the maximum pathos out of every possible situation and always taking the easiest way out to provide the
rhymes. The following stanza of Laws J 1, given in the informant's own spelling, is typical:

> And when [his] lips his mother pressed
> And bid her noble boy adue
> With ringing hands and aching breast
> Behold a march for Waterloo.

Even when the characteristic rhetoric of the older ballads appears, it does little to elevate the general tone. The following
use of incremental repetition from Laws K 12, for instance, is
undistinguished:

> "Oh, father, go build me a boat,
> That over the ocean I may float."
> The father built her a boat
> And over the ocean she did float.

Further repetition appears in one later stanza of this ballad, from the beginning of which an alternate title is sometimes taken:

> "Oh, captain, captain, tell me true,
> Does my dear sailor boy sail with you?"
> "No, no, he does not sail with me;
> I fear he's drowned in the sea."

Frequently broadsides are narrated in the first person, but not usually with any improved poetic art. The burglar from Boston in Laws L 16B merely begins with an obvious bid for sympathy (addressing himself directly to listeners) and then reels out the sequence of events in a pedestrian manner:

> I was born in the town of Boston,
> A town you all know well,
> Raised up by honest parents—
> The truth to you I will tell—
> Raised up by honest parents,
> Raised up most tenderly,
> Until I became a sporting man
> At the age of twenty-three.
>
> My character was taken
> And I was sent to jail.
> The people tried, but all in vain,
> To keep me out on trail.
>   [probably should be "out on *bail*"]
> The juror found me guilty,
> The clerk he wrote it down,
> The judge he passed the sentence
> To send me to Charlestown.

At times, however, the language becomes more inspired, as in the usual opening phrases of Laws M 4. In this particular version the first stanza is muddled, but the second one rescues the story. It should also be noted that, like many fine old traditional ballads, things begin here *in medias res* and they are carried on entirely in dialogue:

> "Awake, arise, you drowsy sleeper!
> Awake, arise; it's near about day.

Awake, arise; go ask your father
If you're my bride to be.
And if you're not, come back and tell me;
It's the very last time I'll bother thee."

"I cannot go and ask my father,
For he is on his bed of rest
And in his hand he holds a weapon
To kill the one I love the best."

This ballad often merges with the American "Silver Dagger," a kind of "climax of suicides" folksong:

And he taken up that silver dagger
And plunged it in his snowy white breast,
Saying "Farewell, Bessie, farewell, darling;
Sometimes the best of friends must part."
And she taken up that bloody weapon
And plunged it in her lily-white breast . . .

Among the love ballads, external complications mar most romances, and tragic endings are the rule, with few exceptions. But lovers bring some problems on themselves, often as the result of their own attempts at tricks and disguises. One favorite device of broadsides is the return of a long-lost lover, in disguise, to his sweetheart. Another is the girl dressing in man's clothing in order to follow her lover into military service. From Laws N 7:

She stepped into the tailor shop and dressed in men's array
And enlisted with the captain to carry her away.
"Before you get on board, sir, your name I'd like to know."
She spoke with a pleasing countenance, "My name is Stephen
    Monroe."

"Your waist it is too slender, your fingers are too small,
Your cheeks too red and rosy to face a cannon ball."

"My waist is none too slender . . .

Generally the name in the above ballad is "Jack Monroe," and she is off to pursue "Jackie Frazier," from either of which characters the ballad may be named. Again in this passage, as well as the one quoted just before, we observe incremental repetition developing in the last partially quoted line.

An unintentional disguise led to the death of Molly Bawn (or "Bond," Laws O 36), who is called "Polly Bonn" in the North Carolina version. She threw her apron over her head against the rain, with this result:

> With her apron pinned around her
> The rain for to shun;
> Jimmy Randall he saw her
> And shot her for a swan.

In British versions Molly's ghost may return to defend Jimmy at his murder trial, but American texts characteristically lose the supernaturalism.

Broadside ballads of faithful lovers and unfaithful lovers run about even in Laws's index (forty to forty-one), but sometimes the classification of an individual piece is debatable. For instance, in Laws P 24 we have a faithful girl with an unfaithful sweetheart, and the ballad has been classified from her point of view:

> There lived a girl in that same town
> Where he would go and sit around.
> He'd take that girl upon his knee
> And tell her things that he wouldn't tell me.

Later she requests in her suicide note (using a commonplace stanza):

> "So bury me both wide and deep,
> Place a marble stone at my head and feet,
> And on my breast place a snow-white dove
> To show to the world that I died for love."

The saving grace of humor seems to raise some of the ballads in category Q a cut above most of the others in Laws's broadside index. "Devilish Mary" (Q 4) is a comical antifeminist (or at least antimarriage) piece; "The Love-of-God Shave" (Q 15) has some felicitous wording for a very funny situation; and "Finnegan's Wake" (Q 17) deserves the respectability and immortality

it achieved from James Joyce's use of it. Another humorous success is Laws Q 1, in which a farmer, variously named, takes an
ill-considered oath:

> Old Summerfield swore by the sun and the moon
> And the green leaves on the tree
> That he could do more work in one day
> Than his wife could do in three.

Teeny the cow has to be milked during the man's day at home,
and she proves to be only one source of exasperation to him:

> Teeny inched and Teeny winced
> And Teeny curled her tail;
> She gave the old man such a kick in the face
> It made him drop his pail.

At the other extreme in the last category are some of the "miscellaneous" ballads—sad, trite orphans with no home elsewhere in the index—like "The Babes in the Woods":

> Oh, don't you remember, a long time ago,
> Of two little children, their names I don't know.
> They were *stole on the way* on a bright summer day
>   [probably "*stolen away*"]
> And lost in the woods, I've heard people say.
>
> And when it was night so sad was their plight
> The moon went down and the stars gave no light.
> They sobbed and they sighed and they bitterly cried;
> Poor babes in the woods, they lay down and died.
>
> And when they were dead the robins so red
> Brought strawberry leaves and over them spread
> And sang a sweet song the whole day long.
> Poor babes in the woods, they lay down and died.

These three verses, all that usually remain in many American
versions, are based on a long and highly circumstantial ballad,
which seems to have inspired one of Emily Dickinson's best-
known poems. (It is number 9 in the standard numbering, and
begins, "Through lane it lay—thro' bramble— / Through
clearing and thro' wood—.") These verses also show that in

broadside as well as Child ballads, repeated oral transmission does tend to focus attention on the emotional core.

The broadsides have not stood up as good poetry under close examination, just as they did not under appraisal by Laws, who wrote, "The average or below average broadside is not so much composed as patched together from the materials at hand." However, we should bear in mind, as Laws also pointed out, that the poetic shortcomings of broadside ballads apply to them as printed literature only, not as oral folksongs. Most of these texts can be surprisingly appealing when they come from the lips of traditional singers. Such singers, at any rate, make no distinctions themselves between Child and non-Child ballads; they sing either kind (or nonnarrative folksongs) interchangeably.

Native American Ballads

The **native American ballads** are the most recent strain of all, coming largely from the last half of the nineteenth century. In style they are very similar to the British broadside ballads, and they have all of their stereotypes of attitude and situation and most of their poetic flaws. Current events, especially scandals and tragedies, still are common topics, but American history and development add new subjects, as the following summary of Professor Laws's categories shows (from the 1964 revision of his *Native American Balladry*):

A. War Ballads ("The Texas Rangers" is A 8.)
B. Ballads of Cowboys and Pioneers ("Joe Bowers" is B 14.)
C. Ballads of Lumberjacks ("Harry Bale" is C 13.)
D. Ballads of Sailors and the Sea ("The *Titanic*" is D 24.)
E. Ballads about Criminals and Outlaws ("Charles Guiteau" is E 11.)
F. Murder Ballads ("The Jealous Lover" is F 1.)
G. Ballads of Tragedies and Disasters ("Springfield Mountain" is G 16.)

H. Ballads on Various Topics ("The Young Man
Who Wouldn't Hoe Corn" is H 13.)
I. Ballads of the Negro ("Frankie and Albert" is I 3.)

Laws had indexed 256 native American ballads by 1964, far
too many to be discussed in detail here. But again we can survey
their characteristics by examining a group of sample stanzas.
This time all but one are quoted from H. M. Belden's *Ballads
and Songs Collected by the Missouri Folk-Lore Society.*

According to Laws's count, only two native American war
ballads have remained in tradition from the colonial period,
three from the Revolution, four from the War of 1812, two from
the Indian wars, about a dozen from the Civil War, and none
from World War I or later conflicts. This seems a very slim folk
inheritance, but any valid generalization about American history in folk music would have to take folk*songs* into account as
well; they survive in much greater numbers from all periods. A
typical war ballad is a highly stereotyped account of some notable conflict, set off by patriotic sentiments or memories of
mothers and sweethearts back home. The bare texts, as in the
following stanzas from Laws A 8, convey little real sense of battle:

> I saw the Indians coming,
> I heard them give a yell.
> My feelings at that moment
> No human tongue can tell.
>
> Our bugle it was sounded,
> Our captain gave command.
> "To arms, to arms!" he shouted,
> "And by your horses stand."

("No tongue can tell" is a frequent cliché of the more recent
ballads.)

The cowboy and pioneer ballads sometimes depict death and
suffering in the Wild West, especially accidents in the cow
camps—"When the Work's All Done This Fall" (B 3), "Utah
Carroll" (B 4), "Little Joe the Wrangler" (B 5), and so forth. But
many of the Western pieces laugh at the dangers instead, and

they picture a group of adventurers who are high-spirited and ready to tackle anything. Joe Bowers, for instance, risks security back East for the sake of his sweetheart Sally:

> "Oh Sally, dearest Sally,
> Oh Sally, for your sake
> I'll go to California
> And try to raise a stake."

> Says she to me, "Joe Bowers,
> You are the man to win;
> Here's a kiss to bind the bargain,"
> And she hove a dozen in.

Sally, however, proves false; when Joe next hears from her, she is married to a red-haired butcher, and she has a baby with red hair.

Missouri is a good state for Western subjects but would seem an unlikely place for loggers' ballads. Still, one does appear in Belden's collection (from an Arkansas informant), illustrating that the topics of ballads do not necessarily limit their distribution. In this example, the original ballad about a logger named Harry Bahel, who was killed in a sawmill accident in Arcadia Township, Lapeer County, Michigan, appears here as one about "Harry Dale," killed in "Arcadia, Laneer County," no state specified. As in all versions, the ballad begins with a commonplace "Come all ye":

> Come all kind friends and parents,
> Come brothers one and all;
> Attention pay to what I say;
> 'Twill make your blood run cold.
> 'Tis about a poor unfortunate boy,
> Who was known both far and near.
> His parents raised him tenderly,
> Not many miles from here.

Then the story advances to a gory description of the tragic accident:

> In lowering the Vantle wheel [The reference is unclear.]
> He threw the carriage in its gear.

It drew him into the saw
And it sawed him all severe.

It sawed him through the shoulder blade
And half-way down his back,
And he fell upon the floor
As the carriage it rolled back.

Woods accidents dominate the lumberjack ballads as a group, the most typical ones being drownings or deaths by crushing during a river drive. Probably the best known of these is number C 1, "The Jam on Gerry's Rock" or "Foreman Young Monroe."

For a ballad of the sea, we must turn to another anthology, for Belden has none that are indexed in Laws. From the Frank C. Brown collection, however, come these typical stanzas and chorus of "The *Titanic*" (as written out by an informant):

It was on one Monday morning about one o'clock
When the great Titanic began to reel and rock.
All the people began to cry saying lord I have to die.
It was sad when that great ship went down.

Oh it was sad when that great ship went down.
There were husbands and their wives,
Little children lost their lives.
It was sad when that great ship went down.

You know it was ofel out on the sea.
The people were singing nearer my god to thee.
Some were homeward bound, sixteen hundred had to dround.
It was sad when that great ship went down.

The sinkings of many ships—both salt-water and Great Lakes vessels—have been celebrated in balladry, but few have so gripped the folk imagination as did the sinking of the *Titanic* on her maiden voyage in 1912. Besides the serious version of the ballad, a comical version sung to a jolly tune still survives in American collegiate tradition, there are distinctive black variants (some of them recited as "toasts"), and there are at least four other *Titanic* ballads of more limited folk distribution.

Criminals and outlaws are the subjects of some of the most

popular and widely distributed of the native American ballads. Their typical motifs include the Robin Hood tradition, the tender-hearted criminal, the regretful "boy gone wrong," and sometimes the defiant captive. Perhaps the best known is "Jesse James," about whom there are two distinct ballads (E 1 and 2), as well as one about his cohort "Cole Younger" (E 3). President Garfield's assassin, like several other criminals of balladry, speaks for himself, using commonplace lines borrowed from older ballads and appealing for his listeners' sympathy.

> Come all ye Christian people,
> Wherever you may be,
> And likewise pay attention
> To these few words from me.
> For the murder of James A. Garfield
> I am condemned to die
> On the thirteenth of June
> Upon the scaffold high.
>
> For my name is Charles Guiteau,
> And the name I'll never deny,
> Tho I leave my aged parents
> In sorrow for to die.
> Oh! little did they think
> While in my youthful bloom
> I'd be taken to the scaffold
> To meet my fatal doom.

The favorite American ballad topic is the murder of an innocent girl. Naomi Wise, murdered in Randolph County, North Carolina, in 1808, has been described in Laws ballad number F 4. Laura Foster (Laws F 36) was stabbed to death in Wilkes county, North Carolina, in 1866 by Tom Dula, or "Tom Dooley," as the ballad tells it. Pearl Bryan of Greencastle, Indiana, was murdered by her lover, Scott Jackson, in 1896, and is celebrated in Laws F 2 and 3. Leo Frank, according to folk tradition, beat little Mary Phagan to death as she walked home from working at The National Pencil Company factory in Atlanta, Georgia, in 1913, and that is the subject of number F 20. (Frank, a Jewish pencilmaker, was convicted of the crime partly on the testimony of fourteen-year-old Alonzo Mann and was lynched by a mob in 1915. But in 1982 Mann, now eighty-three years old, came forward and said he was sure that Frank was innocent of the murder and that Jim Conley, the chief witness against Frank, had killed the girl. Conley had died in 1962.)

There are several other ballads associated with specific female victims, and many more that are generalized. Most of them, as a study by Anne B. Cohen shows, develop in stereotypic ways common also to sensational journalism. One of these ballads is about the killing of "fair Ellen," who is often called "Florella" or "Floella"; the ballad is usually entitled "The Jealous Lover":

> One evening when the moon shone brightly
> There fell a gentle dew,
> When out of a cottage
> A jealous lover drew.
>
> Says he to fair young Ellen:
> "Down on the sparkling brook
> We'll wait and watch and wonder
> Upon our wedding day."

This unfortunate girl, like so many others, is most cruelly murdered; yet she forgives the killer:

> "Oh Edward, I'll forgive thee,
> Though this be my last breath.
> I never was deceiving,
> Though I close my eyes in death."

The ballads in category G concern railroad accidents (like "Casey Jones," G 1), mine fires and other subterranean tragedies (like "The Avondale Disaster," G 6 and 7), floods (like "The Johnstown Flood," G 14), fires, suicides, explosions, cyclones, and even a spelunking accident ("Floyd Collins," G 22). One more example of a characteristic development in American balladry—stemming from one of the oldest native ballads—is seen in "Springfield Mountain." This once-serious ballad describing an agricultural accident in New England in 1761 has turned into

a funny song with a nonsense chorus, from which the following
sequence is typical:

> "Oh, Mollie dear, do come and see
> What a venomous viper did bite me."
>> With a bumble bumble dick a ri dum
>> Able de dinctum day

> "Oh, Johnnie dear, why did you go
> Away down yonder in the field to mow?"

> "Oh, Mollie, dear, I thought you knowed
> 'Twas Daddy's hay and it had to be mowed."

The miscellaneous classification includes ballads about wan-
derers, gamblers, and sportsmen, plus a few religious, romantic,
and humorous pieces. One ballad (Laws H 13), even comments
upon the unlikely poetic topic of hoeing corn. A lazy young man
never hoes his corn, with this result:

> He went to the fence and he peeped in.
> The grass and the weeds were up to his chin.
> The careless weeds they grow so high
> Caused this young man for to sigh.

Even worse, he finds that his sweetheart will no longer have
him:

> "Then what makes you ask me to wed
> When you can't raise your own corn bread?
> Single I am, single I'll remain.
> A lazy man I won't maintain."

In disgust—with *her* rather than with himself—the lazy farmer
takes his leave:

> He picked up his hat and he went away,
> Saying, "Madam, you'll rue the day,
> Rue the day as sure as you're born,
> Giving me the mitten 'cause I didn't hoe my corn."

Finally, the ballads in category I were segregated because of
their presumed Afro-American origin or their subject matter,
although many of them have become generally familiar

throughout the United States, including "John Henry" (I 1), "The Boll Weevil" (I 17), and "The Blue-tailed Fly" (I 19). The best known of all is, of course, "Frankie and Johnny" (I 3, "Albert" in older versions), which has passed into literary drama, popular song, and jazz. Repeated attempts to identify the principals in the story with real-life figures have met with failure. The ballad, with its familiar "He done her wrong" chorus, is too common to need quoting at any length; Belden's text, however, is an unusual one, being a long composite of various stanzas known to his informant, interspersed with lines of commentary and explanation. The informant at one point said, "Then they go to the city, and for a while all is lovely. But Albert gets 'onery' and don't work and spends money on other women." Then follows:

> "Frankie, she shot Albert,
> And I'll tell the reason why.
> Ever' dollar bill she give Albert,
> He'd give to Alice Blye. [Also "Nelly Bly" and "Alice Frye."]

"Frankie and Johnny" has developed a group of near-commonplaces of its own; these are the chorus, Frankie's "forty-four" that goes "roota toot toot," and this "graveyard stanza":

> They took him to that cemet'ry
> In a rubber-tired hack,
> They took him to that cemet'ry
> But they did not bring him back.

In many versions ten men go to the funeral in that "rubber-tired back," but only nine come back.

Researching and Studying Ballads

Ballads, especially the oldest British-American group, have attracted detailed and voluminous study since the beginning of British and American folklore research in the nineteenth century. Surveys of this scholarship by Sigurd B. Hustvedt, D. K. Wilgus, and Albert B. Friedman eliminate the necessity to do any more here than sketch out trends and rough outlines and indicate some areas for future studies.

One curious fact about ballad scholarship is that a "definitive" publication—the Child ballads—came before field collecting had been well established or had even been begun in this country. Then a period of broad theorizing about ballad origins followed, with the "communalists" (led by F. B. Gummere) disputing with the supporters of individual origins (dominated by Louise Pound). The Pound group eventually prevailed, but it was in the skirmishes of this "ballad war" that it first became fully apparent how important it was for more collecting and classification of American materials to be carried out before analyses were further pursued. It was then, too, that Phillips Barry's useful term "communal re-creation" was coined. (See "theories of the folk" in Chapter 3.) Subsequently, many brilliant collectors and editors of ballads emerged in the United States.

Child's notes for *The English and Scottish Popular Ballads* were themselves international studies of individual ballads, and further such studies followed, notably of "Edward," "The Two Sisters," and "Lady Isabel and the Elf Knight." Another approach, popular for generations, was the isolation of one particular aspect of many ballads—superstitions, place names, proverbs, commonplaces, and the like. As American collecting progressed, comparative studies of British and American versions of ballads followed, with results like tracing the descendants of "The Unfortunate Rake," a British broadside, in such new forms as "The Young Girl Cut Down in Her Prime" (Laws Q 26) and "The Cowboy's Lament" (Laws B 1). A favorite research topic has been searching for historical origins. Louise Pound, for instance, was able to show that John A. Stone, an early author of songster texts, probably composed "Joe Bowers." Austin E. Fife traced the cowboy ballad "The Trail to Mexico" from a seventeenth-century broadside, "The Seaman's Complaint," to its later evolution into "Early, Early in the Spring" (Laws M 1) and finally to numerous versions and parodies in the American West.

Generally speaking, ballad studies in the beginning were oriented toward literature and later were inclined to folkloristic and historic approaches. The strongest current trend is toward deeper studies of ballad music and the interdependence of texts and tunes (see Chapter 13). Interesting findings are also likely to come from the anthropological (or "functional") approach to ballads as "socio-historical documents" and from psychological or structural approaches to ballads. When these various possibilities are considered along with the continuing need for better and more inclusive classifications of ballads, it is apparent that, despite numerous ballad studies of the past, American folklorists may pursue their favorite subject for many years to come without running short of research topics. For the amateur or beginning folklorist, the history and the basic problems and broad approaches of ballad scholarship suggest many small-scale projects that are worth carrying out.

For example, students might teach themselves a great deal about ballad variation, and perhaps even make some original discoveries, by preparing an annotated edition of all readily available texts of a native or recent ballad. A good study of narrative method in ballads might also be done without any elaborate bibliographic materials. Another possibility is a full explication of the background, function, and meaning to the informant of a ballad that a student has collected from oral tradition. Psychological or structural discussions of ballads need not refer to every extant variant, but might be based on a fairly limited corpus from easily available library sources. There is also much to be learned from a close critical evaluation of a ballad study, an old 78 rpm "hillbilly" record of a ballad, or perhaps, a recent disk that purports to be "authentic" folk music.

BIBLIOGRAPHIC NOTES

General works on folksongs, cited in the notes to Chapter 11, by Herzog, Nettl, Pound, Ames, and Wilgus are all pertinent to ballads as well. The earlier history of ballad studies was treated in two books by Sigurd B. Hustvedt, *Ballad Criticism in Scandinavia and Great Britain during the Eighteenth Century* (New York: The American-Scandinavian Foundation, 1916), and *Ballad Books and Ballad Men* (Cambridge, Mass: Harvard University Press, 1930).

Two good general introductions are Gordon Hall Gerould's *The Ballad of Tradition* (Oxford: Oxford University Press, 1932; Galaxy paperback edn., 1957) and M. J. C. Hodgart's *The Ballads* (London: Hutchinson's University Library, 1950; Norton Library paperback edn., 1962).

MacEdward Leach and Tristram P. Coffin have edited *The Critics and the Ballad* (Carbondale, Ill: Southern Illinois University Press, 1961; paperback reprint, 1973), which contains fifteen articles (one a previously unpublished one by Philips Barry) concerning ballad origins, definitions, meter and music, and the literary tradition of ballads. Two of the most important articles included here are Thelma G. James's "The English and Scottish Popular Ballads of Francis J. Child" and Coffin's "'Mary Hamilton' and the Anglo-American Ballad as an Art Form" (repr. in *Readings in American Folklore*, pp. 309–18), both originally published in the *Journal of American Folklore*.

The three basic American ballad syllabi were all published by the American Folklore Society in the "Bibliographic and Special Series": Laws's *Native American Balladry* was volume 1 in the series (1950), revised in 1964; Coffin's *The British Traditional Ballad in North America* was volume 2 (1950), revised in 1963 (reissued with a supplement by Roger deV. Renwick in 1977); and Laws's *American Balladry from British Broadsides* was volume 8 (1957). D. K. Wilgus outlines problems and progress in improving ballad classifications in "A Type-Index of Anglo-American Traditional Narrative Songs," *JFI* 7 (1970): 161–76.

There are many general anthologies of ballads. Three easily available ones all have excellent introductions. Bartlett Jere Whiting has edited *Traditional British Ballads* for "Crofts Classics" (paperback; New York, 1955), containing forty Child texts with notes. MacEdward Leach's *The Ballad Book* (New York: Harper, 1955) and Albert B. Friedman's *The Viking Book of Folk Ballads of the English Speaking World* (New York: Viking Press, 1956; Compass Books paperback, 1963; reissued by Penguin in 1976) both contain many ballads, both Child and non-Child.

Folk ballads were gathered in volume 2 (1952) of the *Frank C. Brown Collection of North Carolina Folklore*, ed. H. M. Belden and Arthur Palmer Hudson. Ballad tunes are in volume 4 (1957). The Northwest ballad and folksong collection mentioned in this chapter are described in my article "Folk Song Studies in Idaho," *WF* 24 (1965): 231–48.

The thorny question of actual *oral* credentials for Child's selections is taken up in two articles: J. Barre Toelken, "An Oral Canon for the Child Ballads: Construction and Application," *JFI* 4 (1967): 75–101; and Kenneth A. Thigpen, Jr., "An Index to the Known Oral Sources of the Child Collection," *FF* 5 (1972): 55–69.

Literary aspects of the ballads have interested both folklorists and literary critics. Louise Pound examined the treatment of ballads in some popular anthologies of literature in her article of *SFQ* 6 (1942): 127–41. Arthur K. Moore took the literary point of view in an article in *CL* 10 (1958): 1–20. Holger Olof Nygard discussed a subject of importance to the question of literary ballad analogues in "Ballads and the Middle Ages," in *TSL* 5 (1960): 85–96. Central to the whole subject is Albert B. Friedman's book *The Ballad Revival: Studies in the Influence of Popular on Sophisticated Poetry* (Chicago: University of Chicago Press, 1961).

MacEdward Leach, an advocate of a literary approach to ballads, provided a good survey of the goals of such studies in "The Singer or the Song," *PTFS* 30 (1961): 30–45. His student, Tristram P. Coffin, has written many important articles from this point of view, including "The Folk Ballad and the Literary Ballad: An Essay in Classification," *MF* 9 (1959): 5–18 (reprinted in *Folklore in Action*, pp. 58–70), and "Remarks Preliminary to a Study of Ballad Meter and Ballad Singing," *JAF* 78 (1965): 149–53.

An important general introduction to the international body of ballads is W. J. Entwistle's *European Balladry* (Oxford: Oxford University Press, 1939). Archer Taylor discussed "The Themes Common to English and German Balladry" in *MLQ* 1 (1940): 23–35, and he published an important individual study of *"Edward" and "Sven i Rosengård"* (Chicago: University of Chicago Press, 1931). Paul G. Brewster studied "The Two Sisters" in *FFC* no. 147 (1953). The best study of "Lady Isabel" is by Holger Olof Nygard in *FFC* no. 169 (1958).

Three representative studies that draw material from many different ballads are L. C. Wimberly's *Folklore in the English and Scottish Ballads* (Chicago: University of Chicago Press, 1928); W. Edson Richmond's "Ballad Place Names," *JAF* 59 (1946): 263–67; and William E. Sellers's "Kinship in the British Ballads: The Historical Evidence," *SFQ* 20 (1956): 199–215.

There are a number of studies of variation in the American tradition of a particular ballad, including Foster B. Gresham's "The Jew's Daughter: An Example of Ballad Variation," *JAF* 47 (1934): 358–61; Frances C. Stamper and William Hugh Jansen's "'Water Birch': An American Variant of 'Hugh of Lincoln,'" *JAF* 71 (1958): 16–22; Tristram P. Coffin's "The Problem of Ballad-Story Variation and Eugene Haun's 'The Drowsy Sleeper,'" *SFQ* 14 (1950): 87–96; Alisoun Gardner-Medwin's "The Ancestry of 'The House Carpenter': A Study of the Family History of the American Forms of Child 243," *JAF* 84 (1971): 414–27; and a study that compares folk and popular traditions, Howard Wight Marshall's "'Black Jack David' on Wax: Child 200 and Recorded Hillbilly Music," *KFQ* 17 (1972): 133–43. Christine A. Cartwright, in "Johnny Faa and Black Jack Davey: Cultural Values and Change in

Scots and American Balladry," *JAF* 93 (1980): 397–416, demonstrates how changing concepts of an ideal marriage in the 1960s–1970s made the story told in Child 200 more acceptable to American singers.

A "formulaic improvisation" theory of ballad tradition was proposed by James H. Jones in *JAF* 74 (1961): 97–112, and opposed by Albert B. Friedman in the same issue of the journal, 113–15.

Journalistic reporting of news was compared to broadside ballad style in Winifred Johnston's article "Newspaper Balladry,' *AS* 10 (1935): 119–21. A longer and more detailed treatment of the same idea appeared in Helen MacGill Hughes's *News and the Human Interest Story* (Chicago: University of Chicago Press, 1940), pp. 126–49 and *passim*. For the developments based on the British broadside "The Unfortunate Rake" in American balladry, see references cited with the Folkways recording of the same title, edited by Kenneth S. Goldstein (*FS* 3805, 1960), which contains twenty versions and parodies of that ballad. Two books that have treated broadsides in general are Leslie Shepard's *The Broadside Ballad: A Study in Origins and Meaning* (London: Herbert Jenkins, 1962) and Claude M. Simpson's *The British Broadside Ballad and Its Music* (New Brunswick, N.J.: Rutgers University Press, 1966).

Phillips Barry, the best early student of American folksongs, discussed "Native Balladry in America" in *JAF* 22 (1909): 365–73. Louise Pound, another pioneer in this area, published a landmark essay, "The Southwestern Cowboy Songs and English and Scottish Popular Ballads," *MP* 11 (1913): 195–207; reprinted in *Nebraska Folklore*, pp. 156–70. Austin E. Fife provides a detailed study of 147 known versions of a cowboy ballad in "The Trail to Mexico," *MSF* 1 (1973): 85–102. Louise Pound's study of the composer of "Joe Bowers," originally published in *WF* 16 (1957): 111–20, was reprinted in *Nebraska Folklore*, pp. 171–83. A further study of the origin of that ballad was published by John Quincy Wolf in *WF* 29 (1970): 77–89. In " 'Rose Connoley': An Irish Ballad," *JAF* 92 (1979): 172–95, D. K. Wilgus establishes the foreign source of Laws F 6, also known as "Down in the Willow Garden." John Foster West provides the full history behind one of the most popular ballads of the folksong revival in *The Ballad of Tom Dula* (Durham, N. C.: Moore Publishing Co., 1977).

Bill Ellis, in two recent articles, studies sentimental ballads usually disregarded by American folklorists: " 'The "Blind" Girl' and the Rhetoric of Sentimental Heroism," *JAF* 91 (1978): 657–74, and " 'I Wonder, Wonder, Mother': Death and the Angels in Native American Balladry," *WF* 38 (1979): 170–85. The folk, Ellis points out, take the emotions of such ballads seriously, even if folklorists do not. Barton Levi St. Armand analyzes a major American poet's reworking of such a ballad in "Emily Dickinson's 'Babes in the Wood': A Ballad Reborn," *JAF* 90 (1977): 430–41.

Two general articles of interest to the study of native balladry are Robert D. Bethke's "Narrative Obituary Verse and Native American Balladry," *JAF* 83 (1970): 61–68, and Tristram P. Coffin's "American Balladry: The Term and the Canon," *KF* 19 (1974): 3–10.

Geraldine J. Chickering, in "The Origin of a Ballad," *MLN* 50 (1935): 465–68, reviewed the evidence for authorship of "Jack Haggerty" (Laws C 25). Arthur Field proposed some interesting interpretive answers to his question "Why Is the 'Murdered Girl' So Popular?" in *MF* 1 (1951): 113–19. But the definitive study in this genre is Anne B. Cohen's book *Poor Pearl, Poor Girl! The Murdered Girl Stereotype in Ballad and Newspaper* (Austin, Texas: AFS Memoir Series, vol. 58, 1973). Further studies of American ballad origins are Daniel G. Hoffman's "Historic Truth and Ballad Truth: Two Versions of the Capture of New Orleans," *JAF* 65 (1952): 295–303; Peter R. Aceves's "The Hillsville Tragedy in Court Record, Mass Media, and Folk Ballads: A Problem in Historical Documentation," *KFQ* 16 (1971): 1–38; Edward D. Ives's " 'Ben Deane' and Joe Scott: A Ballad and Its Probable Author," *JAF* 72 (1959): 52–66; and two articles by Norm Cohen: " 'Casey Jones': At the Crossroads of Two Ballad Traditions," *WF* 32 (1973): 77–103, and "Robert W. Gordon and the Second Wreck of 'Old 97,' " *JAF* 87 (1974): 12–38.

In " 'Railroad Bill' and the American Outlaw Tradition," *WF* 40 (1981): 315–28, John W. Roberts compares Afro-American with Anglo-American ballad tradition and finds it similar as to meaning but different in structure. The ballad story of Morris Slater, also known as "Railroad Bill," has some Robin Hood traits but pictures him more as an avenger—selling stolen goods to the poor at lower prices than those charged at the company store in Alabama—than as a noble robber in the Jesse James tradition.

A few non-English ballad traditions in the United States have been sampled in such works as Américo Paredes, *"With His Pistol in His Hand": A Border Ballad and Its Hero* (Austin: University of Texas Press, 1958), and Joan B. Purcell, "Traditional Ballads among the Portuguese in California," *WF* 28 (1969): 1–20 and 77–90.

For recordings of American ballads, see information in the notes to Chapter 13.

13
Folk Music

In 1898, when the publication of Francis James Child's edition of British traditional ballads was finally completed, the last section to leave the press (volume 5, part 10) contained the only reference in the entire work to folk music—a short index of published tunes for ballads, and fifty-five "Ballad Airs from Manuscript." Child made no analysis whatever of these melodies, in contrast to his erudite and extremely detailed comments that had accompanied each group of ballad texts. The proportion of space devoted to tunes as opposed to texts (20 pages out of about 2,500) is a good measure of the relative interest folklorists had in the words versus music of folksongs by the end of the nineteenth century.

In 1905, Phillips Barry, a forerunner of more diversified American folksong specialists of the twentieth century, delivered what he called later "the first shot fired in the thirty years' war for the rights of ballad music." He asserted then what has now become a commonplace in folklore scholarship—that "the words constitute but one-half of a folksong; the air is no less an essential part." While this generalization has long been accepted, the practice, especially by ballad editors, has changed slowly. As late as 1944, Bertrand H. Bronson, one of the most thorough and systematic of musical folklorists himself, warned again, "If the student of the ballad is not prepared to give equal attention to the musical, as to the verbal, side of his subject, his knowledge of it will in the end be only half-knowledge."

Barry's metaphor proved inappropriate. There never was any protracted "ballad war" over the issue of the significance of music. Instead, most folklorists in the past, while granting the importance of tunes, remained untrained either to collect or to study them. Editors of ballad and folksong collections continued to present mostly texts and published very little tune analysis. But by 1950 the study of traditional music had become sufficiently advanced to justify a special term for it—**ethnomusicology.**

Detailed technical research in folk music is complex; to master it requires devoting much time to developing the skills of a specialist. But anyone who desires more than a superficial understanding of American folklore and who wishes to avoid the kind of "half-knowledge" that Bronson cautioned against, should understand, in general terms at least, what the basic form and styles of American folk music are, how folk music is collected, and by what means it is analyzed.

Styles and Forms

In large part, with regard to *style*, American folk music is folk *singing.* Characteristically, in the oldest white tradition, it is solo singing, without accompaniment, of either lyrical or narrative matter (as "folksongs" or "ballads") by an amateur performer before a close-knit family or community audience. The songs are "strophic"—that is, arranged in stanzas—and the melody of the first stanza is used again and again with little conscious change until all the stanzas have been sung. A four-line stanza is common, but couplets, triplets, and stanzas of five, six, or more lines also occur. Many folksongs, as we have already observed in Chapters 11 and 12, have "refrains"—that is, regularly repeated independent elements attached to each stanza. The melodies to which folksongs are sung are not frozen to particular texts, so that one song text may be sung to several melodies or one melody may be attached to various songs. Furthermore, the general tone of a folksong text may seem to clash with the melodies sometimes used for it, so that what strikes us as a "jolly" tune may be employed for a tragic ballad. Whenever American folk singers have been known to make up new song texts, these generally have been sung to old folk tunes.

Singing style in Anglo-American tradition varies somewhat from region to region and group to group, but everywhere it differs radically both from concert-hall art-song style and popular singing. To the ear that is not accustomed to traditional singing, it may at first sound like merely an inept job of amateur vocalizing—the tone may be nasalized, the meter might not be maintained evenly, the pitch and tempo may waver in the first one or two stanzas or gradually shift from one point at the beginning of a song to another at the end. Unlike the professional singer, who tends to "act out" his material with appropriate facial expressions, gestures, and volume changes, traditional white American folk singers usually maintain an even volume level and are passive, sometimes even to the extent of tilting the head back, staring into space, and holding the face masklike. Black folk singers, in contrast, often perform in chorus and with instruments, may improvise more freely on the melodic or rhythmic base, introduce more personal feeling into their singing, and often slur words or notes and intersperse whoops, slides, or falsetto passages into the basic text, all of which are features probably derived from African tradition.

A broad sampling of genuine traditional folk singing will reveal that most of these techniques and mannerisms (or lack of mannerisms), as well as others, are regular features of a definite folk style that has been maintained by oral transmission through unself-conscious imitation of other singers. The practice of speaking the last phrase in a ballad instead of singing it, for instance, which is common in the Northeast, is not just an individual habit or the result of the singer running out of breath; it is a distinct characteristic of the regional style—a kind of traditional local custom. Similarly, the way some singers "lead up" to a note, using a nasalized slur ("Nnnh-It was in the merry month of May . . .") is a device passed in oral transmission from person to person, possibly influenced by traditional fiddle-playing technique. In general terms, singers who hold closely to an even meter—often with one note for each syllable of text—and with very few musical ornaments, are said to have a *tempo giusto* (strict tempo) style, while those who deviate widely from an established meter, and who ornament the melody freely with trills, slurs, and glides, are said to be using a *parlando rubato* (free, "speaking" rhythm) style.

The melodies themselves of old traditional songs may seem peculiar to non-folk listeners. That is because their ears are used to hearing music based only on a "diatonic scale"—that is, a series of tones separated by intervals of "seconds," or one-note jumps as represented by the white keys on the piano from C to C. Cultivated music, on the whole, is based on such scales in "major" and "minor" keys. But many old folksongs have melodies drawn from scales with larger intervals between some tones—the so-called "gapped scales"—or from scales with fewer than the usual seven tones ("do" to "do," as they are usually learned). These may be five-tone (*pentatonic*) or six-tone (*hexatonic*) scales. Even if a folksong is based on a seven-tone (*heptatonic*) scale, its intervals may be differently arranged so that its character is neither major nor minor, but "modal," or corresponding to the "church modes" of the Middle Ages that are generally referred to by Greek names. (As it happens, the original Greek names became scrambled between the classical period and the Middle Ages!) A folklorist without technical training in music may learn to recognize at least the general character of modal music by listening to the melodies of Gregorian chants or by playing the white keys of a piano as follows: C to C (*Ionian*, or "natural major"), D to D (*Dorian*), E to E (*Phrygian*), F to F (*Lydian*), G to G (*Mixolydian*), and A to A (*Aeolian*, or "natural minor").

The folk singing described so far has all been "monophonic," or single-toned, for in unaccompanied solo singing only one note of a melody can be produced at a time. But in group singing or when instruments are played to accompany songs, there occurs what may loosely be termed "polyphony," or more than one tone at a time. (This is not to be confused with formal polyphony in art music.) In American tradition, for instance, listeners may join in singing the refrain of a song, or a whole group may sing work songs, game songs, or party songs together— usually in unison rather than in harmony. Traditional religious songs, especially in the South, may be rendered in harmony or unison by the congregation, with a leader to "line out," or recite, each line of the text in advance, a procedure sometimes referred to as "deaconing." Black congregations still sometimes refer to certain hymns that are regularly "lined out" as "Doctor Watts," in reference to Isaac Watts (1674–1748), the English author of many still-popular hymns. The typical accompanying instruments in American folk-singing tradition are from the plucked-string family—the guitar, five-string banjo, and dulcimer—but sometimes the fiddle is also employed.

A bridge between vocal and purely instrumental music is formed by what were termed "wordless folksongs" in Chapter 11—"diddling" or chin music, nonsense chants, "scat singing," and so forth. From the other direction, we might think of clapping, "clogging" (rhythmic beating time with the feet), and rattling spoons or "bones" (polished slats of bone or wood) as the simplest kind of instrumental folk music, closely followed by the near-vocal effects produced on instruments such as the kazoo, "Jew's harp," and harmonica (or "French harp"). Highly complicated solo-instrumental music developed in American folk tradition on several of these instruments. For instance, harmonica players often perfected various "talking" pieces, fox chases, train sounds, and even narratives incorporating their "mouth organ" music. Early country string bands worked out solo techniques that later flowered in commercial country-western and bluegrass music, not only using the traditional fiddle, guitar, and banjo, but adding mandolins, autoharps, and electrified instruments of various kinds. Jazz instrumental virtuosity—along with blues-inspired jazz singing—provides another rich example of American folk-musical trends that reach much higher levels of achievement and much larger audiences than a pop or commercial style.

The student of instrumental American folk music should learn to approach the subject using its own terms and recognizing its own special techniques. For example, the "left-hand pizzicato" method of producing notes on a guitar or banjo by plucking strings with fingers of the upper, rather than the picking hand, has been called "pulling-off" in folk music, and its opposite is "hammering-on," or adding upper-hand notes by striking down sharply on selected strings. Folk guitar- and banjo-picking styles include patterns with names like "church lick," "lullaby lick," "Carter lick" (named for the Carter Family's hillbilly guitar style heard on 1920s and 1930s records), "double thumbing," "Cotton picking," "frailing," "clawhammer," and "Scruggs." Most folk instrumentalists play in several tunings besides the standard one for their instruments, and these have acquired such names as "mountain minor," "natural flat," "cross key," and "discord." Stringed instruments may be grouped for playing dance music, but the traditional melodies that are played are often called simply "fiddle tunes." The names of these tunes are wildly diverse, but their typical form is regular. There are two sections of eight-measures each, with a "first and second ending" so that one part is played twice, then the other part twice, then the first, and so on until the musicians or the dancers are tired. Then some kind of concluding figure (often "shave and a hair cut") is used for a sign-off. Some fiddlers will refer to one part of a fiddle tune as the "coarse" (played on lower strings) and the other as the "fine" (played on upper strings). Some players have learned instruments left-handed or "upside down." A final matter that may be taken up with instrumentalists is how they learned to play and how long they practiced to master their first tune. To such an inquiry, answers from one large group of traditional fiddlers ranged from "just picked up the fiddle and played it" to "I can't do very good even now."

Field Work: Using the Tape Recorder

The collector of folk music must develop a few more skills than just the ability to thread a tape recorder and adjust its sound level properly. Successful field work, as the ethnomusicologist Bruno Nettl has remarked, sometimes resembles "a combination of public relations and mental therapy." As in any folklore field project, the collector must be able to identify and locate good informants, to put them at their ease, and to encourage them to perform naturally and without inhibitions. The following advice applies to all collecting of folklore with a sound-recording device, but folk-*music* collecting also involves some special problems and techniques.

Folklorists of the past had to be technically trained in musical transcription before they could collect folk music; then they simply wrote out the tones they heard while a performer repeated his material several times. However, since different listeners tended to hear slightly different things, and standard musical notation cannot adequately represent all of the effects that occur in folk music anyway, these field transcripts were of uneven quality. Furthermore, there was no way to go back and verify field notes after an informant died.

The tape recorder is the standard—and the ideal—tool for field work in folk music, quickly replacing the cylinder, disk, and wire recorders that had preceded it. Modern high-fidelity recorders that operate from house current, batteries, or even from spring-wound motors are available today at prices that allow all folklorists either to have their own equipment or to have access to that belonging to universities, archives, and other institutions. But even the modern magnetic tape recorder has its quirks. Tapes may fade or the magnetic backing may crumble, destroying irreplaceable field data, and a tape recorder that is improperly handled may yield results that are nearly useless.

Collectors must become thoroughly familiar with the equipment they will use *before* they get into the field to use it, but a few general techniques apply to all machines. The slow speeds of 1⅞ and 3¾ inches per second found on many home recorders are suitable for recording the speaking voice alone, but nothing slower than 7½ ips should ever be used for music because the faster speed reproduces a wider range of "cycles" or sound waves. A speed of 15 ips, available on larger studio tape recorders, is even better for high-fidelity recording. The sound-level adjustment on the tape recorder should be set carefully for a trial recording at the normal volume for performance and then checked periodically to assure that the results are "loud and clear," but not overrecorded so that interference is created. If it is possible to do so without upsetting the informant, the collector should "label" items by announcing the facts of the session at the beginning of each tape and then identifying each selection with a title or description just before or after it is performed. To provide a reference point, a pitch-pipe A should be sounded just after each performance—*not* before, when it might predetermine an informant's choice of pitch. If instruments are played, the tuning of the individual strings should be recorded, with the order of strings announced as each one is played. It is also advisable to record an informant's actual tuning process from time to time. If the music is polyphonic, the microphone should be moved up to emphasize the role of each voice or instrument as a tune is repeated, keeping careful notes, of course, on where the microphone is situated at all times. Whenever possible, performers should be recorded several times on different days and perhaps before different audiences, in order to document their varying styles and techniques.

When the finished tapes are brought to an archive, copies should be made on separate reels of tape of any material that was recorded on "both sides" (really both "tracks") of tapes. In that way, cutting or splicing may be done without disturbing other items. Duplicate tapes might be "dubbed" for storage purposes, especially if one copy is to be played repeatedly for transcription or perhaps in the classroom. Some archives file disk dubbings of all tapes to guard against tape fading, but careful temperature and humidity control will assure reasonably long life for tape recordings if quality tapes are used at the start.

Transcribing Folk Music

The transcription of the field tapes—that is, the writing-out of them in musical notation—is a long and complicated process involving hours of careful listening and a firm technical grasp of music. The basic problems may be merely physical to begin with. For instance, Professor Jan Philip Schinhan, editor of the more than 1,000 tunes in the Frank C. Brown Collection from North Carolina, found that Brown had played his original wax cylinders over and over again for college classes until many of them were badly worn and scratched. Even the most sensitive job of dubbing in the sound lab retained all of the static and scratches that had been engraved into the originals. In addition, during the copying process, a number of labels were mixed up. These were hard errors to compensate for because in some instances even the texts of songs were nearly inaudible and the music was next to impossible to hear clearly.

The traditional folk singer's flexible style and unorthodox techniques make it difficult for even expert ethnomusicologists to reduce the sounds they hear to standard transcription. In order to stretch the possibilities of the system of notation, some special symbols have been introduced—a plus sign or arrow pointing upward for a tone slightly higher than notated, a minus sign or downward arrow for a slightly lower tone, small-head notes for indefinite pitches, and barring according to a melody's own internal structure rather than in a standard meter. The transcriber may find help in such mechanical devices as the oscillograph, which visually represents musical pitches on a graph; the stroboscope, which helps to identify individual pitches; and the "instantaneous musical notator," which produces a complete transcription from a sound recording, although a specially coded one that cannot substitute fully for standard notation.

Researching and Analyzing Folk Music

Any folklorist can learn to record folk music clearly enough for study purposes, and any collector with some basic musical ability and training can learn to produce a fair job of transcription from tapes. But when it comes to close technical analysis of folk music, we enter the true specialist's territory. Only the broad theoretical outlines need be sketched here. If collectors acquire some idea of what ethnomusicologists may wish to investigate, they can bring in the best possible field data for analysis.

Even preparing a complete transcription of a piece of folk music involves certain theoretical matters, such as how freely the modal scales should be interpreted, whether melodies should be transcribed to a common key signature, and how detailed a transcript need be for comparative purposes. Beyond such questions, the "first principles" of folk-musical analysis are generally as follows.

Tonality, determined by the kind of scale upon which a melody is based, may be indicated by a major or minor key signature or by one of the modal names, if applicable. "Gapped scales" are identified by the number of tones they contain—pentatonic, hexatonic, etc. The *range* of tones that occurs in a particular piece is sometimes indicated by the special terms "authentic" (all tones between the "tonic," or key-note, and the octave above) and "plagal" (some tones occur below the tonic). *Tempo* in a performance is represented in a transcription by the number of quarter-note beats per minute. *Meter* is stated as a standard "time signature" (4/4, 6/8, etc.) if appropriate, or simply by assigning time values to each tone, using the standard musical symbols, and then marking off musical phrases with bar lines. If the melody of a tune has been transcribed to a standard key, the original *pitch* of the tonic should stated.

Once a tune has been carefully transcribed, the *phrasal pattern* of the melody may be determined—that is, the musical "statements" may be counted and identified. (Some typical patterns in Anglo-American folksongs are AABA, AABB, ABAB, and ABBA.) The number of "bars" or measures in each melodic phrase is represented in parentheses, such as (4,3,4,3). Most ethnomusicologists have found it useful to go beyond this stage to define the *melodic contour* of a piece. This is done by removing all ornaments to the basic melody, then all repeated tones, until only a "skeletal melody" remains, which may be characterized (according to its shape on the page) as descending, ascending, arc (or "triangular"), undulating, or the like. From such skeletal abstracts of many melodies, combined with all of the other data, *tune families* may be recognized.

All of this technical data (which have been simplified above) lend themselves perfectly to computer analysis, a technique that was pioneered with the Child ballad melodies by Bertrand H. Bronson of the University of California. Bronson employed an IBM 5081 punch card, which provided twelve rows of eighty units each for data storage, with extra space for printed information. He coded into each card—representing one variant melody—nine categories of musicological information, and he imprinted on the cards certain bibliographic and historical notes. The cards were then sorted in various ways, thus greatly speeding comparisons and analyses of melodies. Perhaps the opposite approach is represented by the ethnomusicologist Samuel P. Bayard, who urges that "the investigator must, by immersing himself in the tunes, have impressed on his mind the identifying features of various members of perhaps many different tune families." Yet even Bronson has written that "the essence of melodic identity [is] . . . almost a metaphysical idea."

Classifying Anglo-American folksongs into meaningful categories is still progressing. However, as George Herzog, one of the earliest American ethnomusicologists, wrote in 1937, "The study of a melody *begins* after it has been placed in some system or index; it does not end there." Probably the next logical step is a return to the text—a close comparison of the "wedding" of folksong texts and tunes. But, as Herzog also wrote, "The marriage has often been rather modernistic; melodies as well as texts have frequently gone their own way."

Text-tune fit has already proved to be a fascinating subject for research, although few folklorists as yet have pursued it very far. Numerous questions suggest themselves. How much does verse meter alter a melody, and in what ways? Is there a corresponding effect the other way? Do the phrasal patterns of words and music match, or does one sometimes cross-cut the other? Can the wandering tunes as well as the floating verbal stanzas of folksongs help to explain their histories? What kinds of symbolic functions, if any, do tunes contribute to their texts? What aspects of conscious creative art may be identified in the whole text-tune relationship in folksongs? The full explication of folksongs, comparable to what is done with art songs, depends upon securing answers to such questions.

The most revolutionary ideas in Anglo-American ethnomusicology are those of Alan Lomax, who, backed by his years of field and editorial experience, proposed a "new science of musical ethnography." Lomax regards formal musical elements as merely one small and abstract segment of a total "folksong style," which, more importantly, includes such factors as the relationship between musicians and their audience, the physical behavior of musicians, the vocal timbre and pitch favored by different cultures, the social functions of music, and the psychological and emotional content of texts. Applying these criteria, Lomax first made a broad survey of world musical *styles* (in his enlarged sense of the term), listening to all available recordings of singers, until he could organize a rough grouping of musical families. From this background he listed fundamental factors in stylistic analysis, including the degree to which singing is communal or individualistic in a culture, the quality of voice and the mode of production used, the prevailing mood of the music, the content of texts, and the social and emotional factors present in the culture. Lomax next made field observations of these criteria in Spain in 1953 and tested his hypothesis concerning the relationship between culture and singing styles in Italy in 1955. Finding a "positive correlation between the musical style and the sexual mores of the communities," Lomax studied the mechanics of this relationship in Italian lullabies, noting the relationships between mothers and children, the roles in society of women and children, and the customs surrounding the singing of lullabies. He concluded that "In those societies considered, the sexual code, the position of women, and the treatment of children seem to be the social patterns most clearly linked with musical style." He explored these ideas further in the Introduction and notes of his anthology *The Folk Songs of North America in the English Language* (1960). Here he asserted that "after many years of collecting in both countries, I am profoundly impressed by the comparative paganism and resignation of Britain, as contrasted with the Puritanism and free aggressiveness of America."

Perhaps the "last word" on this stage of Anglo-American ethnomusicology may be quoted from Charles Seeger, who was one of the most specific critics of Lomax's proposal. Seeger suggested that for the present the task of studies might be to "refine music theory" and to "coarsen technological aids" until some kind of pragmatic middle ground is reached.

BIBLIOGRAPHIC NOTES

Many of the general works on folksongs and ballads cited fully in the notes to Chapters 11 and 12 contain discussions of music. The ballad anthologies edited by Leach and Friedman, for instance, treat ballad music briefly in their introductions. D. K. Wilgus surveys "Tune Scholarship" on pages 326 to 336 of his *Anglo-American Folksong Scholarship since 1898*. In Bruno Nettl and Helen Myers's *Folk Music in the United States: An Introduction*, the technical aspects of music are discussed throughout. Perhaps the best general survey of the subject is still George Herzog's article "Song: Folk Song and the Music of Folk Song" in *Funk & Wagnalls Standard Dictionary of Folklore, Mythology, and Legend*.

In Bruno Nettl's *Folk and Traditional Music of the Western Continents* (Englewood Cliffs, N.J.: Prentice-Hall, 1965), the most pertinent chapters are Chapter 2, "Studying the Structure of Folk Music" (pp. 15–32) and Chapter 3, "The General Character of European Folk Music" (pp. 33–52). Nettl has also written the introductory textbook *Theory and Method in Ethnomusicology* (London: Free Press of Glencoe, 1964), wherein he discusses field work, transcription, description of musical forms, style, instrumental music, and music in culture. He also provides guidance in bibliography and an appendix of exercises and problems designed for the reader with no advanced formal training in music.

Charles Seeger's essay "Professionalism and Amateurism in the Study of Folk Music" is recommended reading for any student embarking on such study for the first time. It appeared in *JAF* 62 (1949): 107–13, and was reprinted in *The Critics and the Ballad*, MacEdward Leach and Tristram P. Coffin (Carbondale: Southern Illinois University Press, 1961; paperback, Arcturus Books, 1973), pp. 151–60. Another good summary of studies and approaches is Samuel P. Bayard's essay "American Folksongs and Their Music," *SFQ* 17 (1953): 122–39.

A basis for studies of fiddle tunes is Ira W. Ford's collection *Traditional Music of America* (New York, 1940; reissued with an introduction by Judith McCulloh, Hatboro, Pa.: Folklore Associates, 1965). Vance Randolph listed "The Names of Ozark Fiddle Tunes" in *MF* 4 (1954): 81–86. Winston Wilkinson discussed some "Virginia Dance Tunes" in *SFQ* 6 (1942): 1–10. Samuel P. Bayard provided a detailed study of American fiddle tunes in his *Hill Country Tunes* (Philadelphia: AFS Memoir no. 39, 1944) and "Some Folk Fiddlers' Habits and Styles in Western Pennsylvania," *JIFMC* 8 (1956): 15–18. An interesting cross-genre analysis is Louie W. Attebery's article "The Fiddle Tune: An American Artifact," *NWF* 2 (1967): 22–29 (repr. in *Readings in American Folkore*, pp. 324–33). A questionnaire survey of traditional fiddlers was reported by Marion Unger Thede in *EM* 6 (1962): 19–24. Thede also published *The Fiddle Book* (New York: Oak Publications, 1967), a self-instructor for would-be folk fiddlers containing music for 150 traditional fiddle tunes, a chatty discussion of fiddling, and some very fine photographs. Linda C. Burman's article "The Technique of Variation in an American Fiddle Tune," *EM* 12 (1968): 49–71, provides a detailed transcription and analysis of a 1926 recording of "Sail Away Lady," comparing the variations to those of Elizabethan virginalists. Burt Feintuch's "Notes on a Fiddle Run: Formulaic Composition in the Music of an Old Time Fiddler," *KF* 21 (1976): 3–10, studies the role of memory and improvisation in learning and performing fiddle tunes. Eugene Wiggins discusses fiddlers' contests and folklore in literature in "Benéts' 'Mountain Whipoorwill': Folklore Atop Folklore," *TFSB* 41 (1975): 99–114.

Religious folk music in America has been studied by George P. Jackson, beginning with his *White Spirituals in the Southern Uplands* (Chapel Hill: University of North Carolina Press, 1933); see Wilgus for references to Jackson's other works as well as those of other scholars. Sacred-harp shape-note singing has attracted the major attention in this area. Richard D. Wetzel, for example, treats "Some Music Notation Systems in Early American Hymn-Tune Books," *KFQ* 12 (1967): 247–60. Brett Sutton, in "Shape-Note Tune Books and Primitive Hymns," *EM* 26 (1982): 11–26, shows the relationship between published books and the oral tradition of hymns in the rural South. A good description of sacred-harp singing in east Texas may be found in Francis Edward Abernethy's "Singing All Day & Dinner on the Grounds" in *PTFS* 37 (1972): 131–40. David Stanley's "The Gospel-singing Convention in South Georgia," *JAF* 95 (1982): 1–32, describes the setting and occasion for a gospel-singing convention in 1977 that has been held every July since 1893; the bibliography here is extensive. See also William H. Tallmadge, "Dr. Watts and Mahalia Jackson—the Development, Decline, and Survival of a Folk Style in America," *EM* 5 (1961): 95–99, and Joe Dan Boyd, "Negro Sacred Harp Songsters in Mississippi," *MFR* 5 (1971): 60–83.

For a useful recent assessment of the riches of black American folk music, see John F. Szwed, "Musical Adaptation among Afro-Americans," *JAF* 82 (1969): 112–21. Robert Ladner, Jr., classifies the major types of black traditional music and traces its adaptation and imitation by whites in "Folk Music, Pholk Music and the Angry Children of Malcolm X," *SFQ* 34 (1970): 131–45. Patrick B. Mullen describes "A Negro Street Performer: Tradition and Innovation" in *WF* 29 (1970): 91–103. For structure and meaning in the blues, see David Evans's essay in the Appendix; John Barnie's "Formulaic Lines and Stanzas in the Country Blues," *EM* 22 (1978): 457–473; and Harriet J. Ottenheimer, "Catharsis, Communication, and Evocation: Alternative Views of the Sociopsychological Functions of Blues Singing," *EM* 23 (1979): 75–86. The partially traditional music of the American minstrel show has been studied by Hans Nathan; see "The First Negro Minstrel Band and Its Origin," *SFQ* 16 (1952): 132–44, and "Early Banjo Tunes and American Syncopation," *MQ* 42 (1956): 455–72.

Richard Blaustein cites "musical punning" and the association of performances with lower-class musicians to answer the question raised in his article "Jugs, Washboards and Spoons: Why Improvised Musical Instruments Make Us Laugh," *TFSB* 47 (1981): 76–79. An inexpensive musical instrument much loved by folk but largely neglected by folklorists—the ten-hole diatonic harmonica—is the subject of Michael S. Licht's Study "Harmonica Magic: Virtuoso Display in American Folk Music," *EM* 24 (1980): 211–21. Articles on the history and construction of folk instruments are listed in the notes to Chapter 21.

Few publications deal specifically with the field recording of traditional music. Bruno Nettl has a useful note, "Recording Primitive and Folk Music in the Field," in *AA* 56 (1954): 1101–2, from which several suggestions in the present chapter were taken. Maud Karpeles has prepared a small and useful manual called *The Collecting of Folk Music and Other Ethnomusicological Material* (London: International Folk Music Council, 1958). George List discussed "Documenting Recordings," in *FFMA* 3 (Fall 1960): 2–3, and "The Reliability of Transcription," in *EM* 18 (1974): 353–77. The latter is accompanied by a small disk recording of the examples presented. Frances M. Farrell proposes another way to transcribe folk music in "Heightened Graphic Neumes," *FMS* 3 (1979): 33–38, illustrating the method with a transcription of a 1959 sacred song from Kentucky, "Lend Me a Hand, Dear Lord, and Guide Me." Charles Seeger evaluated the uses of an instantaneous music notator in "Prescriptive and Descriptive Music-Writing," *MQ* 44 (1958): 184–95, while various "Electronic Aids to Aural Transcription" are discussed by Nazir A. Jairazbhoy and Hal Balyoz in *EM* 21 (1977): 275–82.

Classic studies of American folk music are represented by the work of Cecil J. Sharp and Phillips Barry. Sharp's *English Folk-Song: Some Conclusions* (London: Simpkin and Co., 1907) still merits study, and Barry's approach may be seen in such articles as "Folk-Music in America," *JAF* 22 (1909): 72–81, "The Origin of Folk-Melodies," *JAF* 23 (1910): 440–45, and "American Folk Music," *SFQ* 1 (1937): 29–47.

An excellent summary of ethnomusicological approaches to analyzing American folksong is provided by George Foss in his essay "The Transcription and Analysis of Folk Music" in *Folksong and Folksong Scholarship*, ed. Roger D. Abrahams (Dallas: Southern Methodist University Press, 1964), pp. 39–71. In another valuable essay, Foss describes "A Methodology for the Description and Classification of Anglo-American Traditional Tunes," *JFI* 4 (1967): 102–26. Donald M. Winkleman's article "Musicological Techniques of Ballad Analysis," in

MF 10 (Winter 1960–61): 197–205, provides a clear introduction by means of generalizations and examples. The individual approaches of two major scholars are seen in Samuel P. Bayard's "Prolegomena to a Study of the Principal Melodic Families of British-American Folk Songs," *JAF* 63 (1950): 1–44, reprinted in *The Critics and the Ballad*, pp. 103–50, and Bertrand H. Bronson's "Some Observations about Melodic Variation in British-American Folk Tunes," *JAMS* 3 (1950): 120–34.

Bronson's theories and working methods may be traced through his important series of articles, eighteen of which are gathered in *The Ballad as Song* (Berkeley: University of California Press, 1969). The culmination of Bronson's work is appearing in his *The Traditional Tunes of the Child Ballads*, 4 vols. (Princeton, N.J.: Princeton University Press, 1959–72).

Two other folksong editions contain important technical studies of their music. Jan Philip Schinhan edited and analyzed "The Music of the Ballads" and "The Music of the Folksongs" for *The Frank C. Brown Collection of North Carolina Folklore* (4, 1957; 5, 1962). In Helen Hartness Flanders's *Ancient Ballads Traditionally Sung in New England*, 4 vols. (Philadelphia: University of Pennsylvania Press, 1960–65), the musical annotations are by Bruno Nettl.

An early discussion of the problems of folk-music classification was George Herzog's "Musical Typology in Folksong," in *SFQ* 1 (1937): 49–55. A practical system is described by George List in "An Approach to the Indexing of Ballad Tunes," *FFMA* 6 (Spring 1963): 7–16.

Bronson discussed text-tune relationships in two articles: "The Interdependence of Ballad Tunes and Texts," *CFQ* 3 (1944): 185–207, reprinted in *The Critics and The Ballad*, pp. 77–102, and *The Ballad as Song* (see above); and "On the Union of Words and Music in the 'Child' Ballads," *WF* 11 (1952): 233–49, reprinted in his *The Ballad as Song*, pp. 112–32. A detailed individual study is found in George Lists's "An Ideal Marriage of Ballad Text and Tune," *MF* 7 (1957): 95–112. George W. Boswell provides a good general discussion of the subject in Chapter 23 of his and J. Russell Reaver's *Fundamentals of Folk Literature* (Oosterhout, The Netherlands: Anthropological Publications, 1962), pp. 188–95, and he has a closer study of the matter in his article "Reciprocal Controls Exerted by Ballad Texts and Tunes," *JAF* 80 (1967): 169–74.

Musical analysis of commercial and popularized folk music has advanced in such articles as Judith McCulloh's "Hillbilly Records and Tune Transcriptions," *WF* 26 (1967): 225–44; Neil V. Rosenberg's "From Sound to Style: The Emergence of Bluegrass," *JAF* 80 (1967): 143–50; and especially Anne and Norm Cohen's "Tune Evolution as an Indicator of Traditional Musical Norms," *JAF* 86 (1973): 37–47. Documenting an interesting mix of musical traditions, W. H. Bass, in "McDonald Craig's Blues: Black and White Traditions in Context,"

TFSB 48 (1982): 46–61, writes of a black singer who has introduced songs learned from recordings by the white singer Jimmy Rodgers (who had himself incorporated black material) into his own oral tradition.

Alan Lomax proposed his concept of "Folk Song Style" in an article by that title published in *JIFMC* 8 (1956): 48–50. Charles Seeger offered a rebuttal and proposals of his own in "Singing Style," *WF* 17 (1958): 3–11. A more extended treatment of Lomax's ideas then appeared in his "Musical Style and Social Context," *AA* 61 (1959): 927–54, and in the introduction and notes to his anthology *The Folk Songs of North America in the English Language* (New York: Doubleday, 1960). Important reviews of that work are cited in the notes to Chapter 11. Alan Lomax's work in "cantometrics" yielded "The Good and the Beautiful in Folksong," *JAF* 80 (1967): 213–35 (an article replete with both field anecdotes and highly technical analysis of data), and the survey of world traditional song styles entitled *Folk Song Style and Culture* (Washington, D.C.: American Association for the Advancement of Science, publication no. 88, 1968). For the background of this work and a concise summary of its method, see William R. Ferris, Jr., "Folk Song and Culture: Charles Seeger and Alan Lomax," *NYFQ* 29 (1973): 206–18.

It is important that beginning students of folk music not confine themselves to studying printed materials alone, but also become familiar with recorded examples. A problem in this area, however, is caused by the great profusion of popularized or semi-original material on records, and the relative obscurity of companies that issue authentic recordings.

Several of the general books cited here and in Chapters 11 and 12 contain discographies. Wilgus offers an especially good annotated one on pages 365–82 of his work. The only catalogue entirely devoted to authentic American folk-music recordings offered for sale is published by the Library of Congress and may be obtained by mail from the Music Division, Recording Laboratory, LC Reference Department, Washington, D.C., 20402. Other companies with reliable folk-music recordings include Folkways Records (available from Scholastic A-V Materials, 906 Sylvan Ave., Englewood Cliffs, New Jersey, 07632), Folk-Legacy Records (Sharon, Connecticut, 06069), Arhoolie Records (incorporating the important Folk-Lyric Records, Box 9195, Berkeley, California, 94719), and Rounder Records (186 Willow Avenue, Somerville, Massachusetts, 02144). There are many other companies and series including folk-music recordings, and the interested reader should consult the record review columns of the various scholarly folklore periodicals.

Good individual recordings are too numerous to list here in any detail, but a few representative examples that are especially well suited for teaching purposes deserve notice. Charles Seeger's production of *Versions and Variants of "Barbara Allen"* for the Library of Congress (AAFS L54) contains thirty renditions of this favorite ballad by American folk singers; Alan Jabour's LC recording *American Fiddle Tunes from the Archive of Folk Song* (AFS L62) contains twenty-eight well-documented examples. On the Folk-Legacy label, one of the best examples available of a thoroughly annotated recorded collection is *Eleven Miramichi Songs Sung by Marie Hare* (FSC-9), which is accompanied by a booklet of background, textual, and musicological notes by Louise Manney and Edward Ives. An excellent two-record set from the same publishers is *The Traditional Music of Beech Mountain, North Carolina*, vol. 1, *The Older Ballads and Sacred Songs* (FSA-22) and vol. 2, *The Later Songs and Hymns* (FSA-23), both with notes by Sandy Paton. Among the numerous outstanding items in the Folkways catalogue is the *Anthology of American Folk Music* (FA 2951, 2952, 2953), six LP recordings containing early folk-music items from commercial disks, plus identifying notes.

A record surveying folk music in one state is *Green Fields of Illinois* (CFC 201), published by the Campus Folksong Club, University of Illinois, Urbana. Two records that sample the rich folk-music traditions of the state of Utah are *The New Beehive Songster*, vol. 1, *Early Recordings of Pioneer Folk Music* (OK 75003), vol. 2, recent field recordings (OK 75004), published by Okehdokee Records and the University of Utah Press in Salt Lake City, Utah, 84112 (1976).

III · CUSTOMARY FOLKLORE

While there is often a verbal component to the folk traditions described in this section, and sometimes even a material component, customary folklore is essentially a matter of traditional *behavior*. Some customs are characteristically employed for communicating directly to other individuals (as when gesturing in greeting or leave-taking); some are practiced by varisized family or community groups (as in folk festivals); and some may involve set numbers of performers (as in most folk dances). The "audiences" for such traditional performances may be participants themselves (as in a game), the community (folk dramas), or even, perhaps, "the gods" (superstitions). Customary folklore is typically regarded as "just entertainment," but often it has overtones of magic, ritual, or traditional science.

In some past studies, behavioral lore has been treated much like oral lore (collecting game "texts," etc.), but special approaches and techniques are needed to do the job of analysis more fully. Therefore, each type presented here is put into the framework of the most reliable recent studies, whatever direction they have taken.

14
Superstitions

What Are Superstitions?

Superstitions are often thought of as naïve popular beliefs, usually concerning chance, magic, or the supernatural, that are logically or scientifically untenable. Hence, the alternate term "folk belief" is often employed, carrying with it the negative connotations of unsophistication and ignorance that the word "folk" has in popular usage. Such a substitution is mistaken on three counts. First, superstitions include not only belief, but also behavior and experiences, sometimes equipment, and usually sayings or rhymes. Second, no one is immune from the assumptions that underlie superstition, nor from holding or practicing superstitions to some degree. Third, the term "superstition" is now so well entrenched in folklore study that it probably must continue to be tolerated, despite its traditional suggestions of ignorance and fear. While it may be more precise, as some folklorists have suggested, to speak of "folk (or 'traditional') science" or "conventional wisdom" rather than "superstition," it is under the latter name that most such items have been collected and published, and the habits of mind underlying them are the same in any case.

Superstitions involve beliefs, practices, and procedures based upon conscious or unconscious assumptions, usually concerned with the nature of cause and effect. Even though superstitions are not essentially just verbal statements, it is as such that they are usually transmitted and have often been collected by folklorists. Alan Dundes describes these characteristics in a typical compilation of "superstitious sayings." The sayings describe *conditions* (either *signs* or *causes*) and their supposed results: "If there's a ring around the moon (*sign*), it will rain (*result*)" or

"Turn a dead snake belly up (*cause*), and it will rain soon (*result*)." Superstitions like the last example, in which deliberate human actions "*cause*" the *result*, are termed *magic*. Other superstitious sayings describe *conversions*—that is, when a *sign* is right, a certain act will *convert* the conventionally expected *result:* "If you break a mirror (*sign*), you'll have seven years bad luck (*result*), unless you gather up the pieces and throw them into running water (*conversion*)." Another example is "If you see a shooting star (*sign*), you should say 'money' three times before it disappears (*conversion*), and then you'll have good luck (*result*)." Incorporating these characteristics into one description, Dundes proposes as a definition: "*Superstitions are traditional expressions of one or more conditions and one or more results with some of the conditions, signs and others causes.*"

While this definition seems more satisfactory than many older ones that simply branded superstitions as nonreligious beliefs, bad logic, or (in Sir James G. Frazer's term) "false science," there are other objections to it. Mainly, it is a definition of the "expressions" of superstition, not of superstitious beliefs and practices themselves. As Michael Owen Jones points out, Dundes's approach does not allow for considering "the meaning and function of the material or the nature of the folk mind." A better concept of superstition—much harder, however, to phrase in a concise description—would take into account the social contexts in which folk beliefs occur and also reflect the fact that informants themselves distinguish between useful traditional knowledge and harmful or foolish "superstitions." Dundes himself has suggested using the term *folk ideas* for simple statements of popular misconception that are neither signs, magic, or conversions, but which do appear in folklorists' collections of superstitions: "Lightning never strikes twice in the same place" or "Dragon flies feed [or cure] snakes," for example.

Superstitions in Modern Life

However unsound the assumptions underlying superstitious beliefs and behavior, they are generally couched in sound logic and are remarkably widespread at every level of society. (Some traditional superstitions have turned out to be fairly reliable, perhaps as cures, weather signs, planting lore, etc.) Since 1907, various American professors have investigated the degree of superstition found among their students. The published results of these surveys, which spanned the country geographically and reached students from a variety of backgrounds, indicated that many students are significantly superstitious, and that as a group they have become neither more nor less superstitious recently; only details of their belief and practice vary.

At the University of California at Berkeley in 1907, 900 psychology students were asked to list and comment upon their own superstitions. A total of 7,000 items was submitted: 4,000 were superstitions known but not believed, 2,000 were recognized as superstitions but still partly believed, and 1,000 were superstitions trusted fully. More than one-half of the test group believed in some superstitions, the most common being good- and bad-luck signs involving Friday the thirteenth (or other occurrences of thirteen), breaking mirrors, opening an umbrella in the house, finding a horseshoe, hearing a dog howl, seeing the moon over the left shoulder, or dropping silverware.

In 1923, forty-five students at Vassar College recorded 186 items of superstitious belief and practice from their personal knowledge. Most of the items had to do with good and bad luck, love and marriage, and wishing. Some unusual examples turned up: "Say the word 'hare' last on the last day of one month, and the word 'rabbit' first the next morning, and you will have good luck"; "A pause in conversation that occurs twenty minutes before or after an hour signifies that an angel is passing by"; "Count the cars in a passing freight train like daisy petals, 'Loves me, loves me not,' etc."

At about the same time as the Vassar collection, a Harvard professor of anthropology, who published his results in 1932, secured a large number of superstitions from students at Harvard and elsewhere. By having the students write papers about their personal superstitions, this investigator received comments as well as the items themselves. The results suggested that 70 to 75 percent of undergraduates "carried out certain acts or refrained from carrying them out in the hope that something good would follow or something evil would be prevented." About one-quarter of those questioned owned "fetishes"—lucky objects of some kind, such as coins, pens, clothing, or amulets. A large number of superstitions were associated with examinations, athletics, and "games of chance." Although some of the student writers strongly protested that superstition was dead in the twentieth century, and some even complained that college students should not be required to write such nonsense in an enlightened age, others described elaborate personal rituals that they were convinced had brought them luck. If they failed to practice these acts, the students suffered "a distinct feeling of uneasiness."

In 1950, an anthropologist at Indiana University submitted a questionnaire based on the Harvard study to 175 of his students and analyzed the results statistically. His conclusions were the most scientifically controlled yet reported, and showed that students were just as superstitious as ever. Some believed firmly in fully one-half of the total list of thirty-three items, but the average number of items believed by an individual was 5.1. Women seemed to be generally more superstitious than men, and the freshman-sophomore group more superstitious than juniors and seniors. Although the last finding seems to suggest that education erases superstition, the study also indicated that the more educated the parents, the *more* superstitious their children. Furthermore, there was no significant relationship indicated between the number of superstitions believed by urban versus rural students, who presumably should be closer to the roots of "folk wisdom."

In 1961, fifty freshmen in English composition at the University of Idaho were assigned to write papers on their personal superstitions, and not a single student lacked for subject matter. Not only did many of them admit to certain irrational practices to assure themselves good luck in examinations, athletics, or dangerous situations, but also most of the writers could cite personal experiences (that is, "memorates") that seemed to uphold the validity of their actions. The subjects included lucky items of clothing, ski accidents, wart cures, three on a match, logging and traffic dangers, farm and ranch work, and even a student wife's pregnancy, supposedly guaranteed by her residence in a lucky apartment and through the magic of the number 3.

Surveys in many undergraduate folklore courses continue to yield the same kind of information about students' superstitions (see, e.g., the Appendix), but one need not have a captive experimental group of college students to show that modern educated people are superstitious. The popular press is rich in examples. Winners of contests and athletic events are frequently quoted in news stories describing their good luck charms; medical and advice columnists regularly answer queries about common superstitions; victims of serious diseases, when publicized, often are sent numerous folk cures, which are later reported back to the press. When President John F. Kennedy was suffering from his back ailment, for example, it was reported that someone had written to him, "Just get an old pair of shoes and put them under your bed upside down." In 1964, Mrs. Kathryn O'Hay Granahan, treasurer of the United States, published a plea in a Sunday supplement magazine that had nationwide distribution, urging Americans to accept the two-dollar bill instead of rejecting it because of the bad luck that is supposed to attend that denomination, and not to tear off a corner to "let the bad luck drain out." In 1976, when printing and distribution of two-dollar bills was resumed, a spate of traditional and superstitious lore about them again appeared in the press. Just as this chapter was being first written, the following statements appeared in the health column of the St. Louis Post-Dispatch: "My son is a year old and has asthma. Several people have told me that if I get a Chihuahua it will cure the asthma. My husband won't get the dog until you answer."

Further examples of superstitions in modern life are easily multiplied. For example, when the popular newspaper advice columnist Ann Landers wrote that there was no way to guarantee the sex of a child that a woman would bear, an irate reader wrote:

> . . . you are wrong. My great-grandmother told me the secret of producing a boy or a girl baby . . . and it works! (I have two of each.)

The left ovary produces boys, the right ovary produces girls. The minute a woman discovers she is pregnant (or even suspects it) she should start to sleep on her left side if she wants a boy and her right side if she wants a girl. It's as easy as that!

—Lucky Me

But Landers had the right answer on this one:

Lucky is the word, all right. . . . The sex of a child is determined at the moment of conception. Once a woman is pregnant she can sleep on her head and it won't affect the sex of her unborn child.

(See also "the Drāno test" in Chapter 15.)

The survival of old superstitions, or at least the knowledge of them, is apparent in some familiar contemporary practices. Hotel owners will skip thirteen when numbering floors, or use that floor for storage only. Manufacturers of billfolds sometimes put a piece of imitation money in each one so that it may safely be given as a gift, for, "Giving an empty billfold or purse will spoil your friendship." People who believe that spitting, in certain situations, is good luck, or who belong to ethnic groups that may spit to avoid giving the evil eye, may only pretend to spit if the time and place happen to be wrong for the actual gesture. Other people, lacking a piece of wood to knock on, will playfully knock on their own heads if they happen to utter a statement that suggests some future good fortune. And otherwise perfectly sane and reasonable people will detour around a ladder, postpone business deals or trips that fall on the thirteenth of a month, or carefully date checks written on Sundays to the next day. The rationale for most superstitions such as these is that they may not help, but they won't hurt either. A news story about a sufferer from chronic hiccups, who was about to try hypnosis as a last resort, put the matter this way: "Desperate for relief, [she] already had tried surgery, shock therapy, more than 200 home remedies, chiropractic treatment, and prayer." Thus, superstitions ("home remedies") thrive side by side with modern medical science, psychology, and religion.

The "proof" that certain superstitions work seems to come

from personal experience. Case histories, such as the following, from everyday life are common in student folklore collections:

> Last December four of us were playing bridge and the first time a two, three, and four came up on an ace, one guy muttered "Wish trick". Since I considered anything worth a try, every time another wish trick came up after that I wished I would get engaged. And that same night at 11:00 Bob proposed!

*

> Whenever I play a slot machine in Nevada I leave a few coins in the pay-off tray for good luck. Money in the machine will then be attracted down there. I made my biggest winning ever when I was doing this faithfully.

*

> When my grandfather had been working all day in the fields and was really tired—when he'd come home at night, he'd stick one shoe inside the other and put it under the bed. That made it so he wouldn't toss and turn at night, and he said he'd always sleep well. I have three aunts that all still swear by this.

Many superstitions probably arose from faulty reasoning based on experiences such as these. An event is assumed to be the cause of certain later happenings—the familiar logical fallacy of *post hoc, ergo propter hoc* ("after this, therefore because of this"). In a classic account of early travel on the Santa Fe Trail, Josiah Gregg's *Commerce of the Prairies* (1844), just such an instance was described:

> There is but little rain throughout the year, except from July to October—known as the rainy season; and as the Missouri traders usually arrive about its commencement, the coincidence has given rise to a superstition, quite prevalent among the vulgar, that the Americans bring the rain with them.

The line of reasoning is no different when modern students do well on an examination and then credit their "luck" to the T-shirt they wore or the pen they used. Psychology favors them further when they retain the same fetish for later examinations. But if their luck holds, then the superstition, rather than their understanding of how their own minds work, is reinforced. Such practices are further encouraged by the human tendency to want to believe in the supernatural and be able to predict or control events.

Since individual superstitions may be generated by fallacious reasoning from personal experiences and reinforced by coincidences, it is possible that there are countless private beliefs and practices that never pass into folklore circulation at all. Nevertheless, even people's personal superstitions tend to follow traditional patterns involving luck, divination, magic, dreams, colors, numbers, and so forth. This largely explains why it is that while new collections of superstitions invariably contain many items previously unrecorded in printed collections, the existing classification schemes can readily accommodate them. Frequently, older superstitions have simply been modernized: a belief about a buggy, for example, is transferred to automobiles, or one about farming is applied to home gardening.

The Hand System of Classifying Superstitions

There are numerous collections of American superstitions, and some of them are voluminous. But although they have come from widespread sources, there is still much to be collected from more regions and more folk groups before a comprehensive study of American superstitions can be attempted. The basis for this study is at the University of California at Los Angeles in the files of Wayland D. Hand, editor of the section on superstitions in *The Frank C. Brown Collection of North Carolina Folklore* (volumes 6 and 7). Hand assembled a master file of some 200,000 individual superstitions taken from all published American collections and arranged them in one systematic sequence. Individual folklorists in most states and in several provinces of Canada have collected and published superstitions in their own regions to broaden the base of Hand's data for his planned "Dictionary of American Popular Beliefs and Superstitions." Thus, it is important to outline his classification system —as demonstrated in the North Carolina collection—as a guide to published and archived superstitions, even though much future work in the area is likely to put greater stress on the social contexts and functions of superstitions. The major collections of American superstitions published since the North Carolina collection appeared have all used some form of Hand's classification for their arrangement.

The system Hand devised for the Frank C. Brown collection contains fourteen major categories, grouped under four broad headings: *the cycle of human life, the supernatural, cosmology and the natural world,* and *miscellaneous superstitions.*

Superstitions about the Life Cycle

Superstitions related to the cycle of human life fall into the first seven categories of Hand's system as follows:

I. *Birth, Infancy, Childhood*
II. *Human Body, Folk Medicine*
III. *Home, Domestic Pursuits*
IV. *Economic, Social Relations*
V. *Travel, Communication*
VI. *Love, Courtship, Marriage*
VII. *Death and Funeral Customs*

Many items in sections I, VI, and VII correspond to three of the four kinds of ceremonies to mark changes in the life cycle (*rites de passage,* or "rites of passage") commonly practiced in primitive cultures. By means of these rituals, people "pass" safely from one stage of their existence to the next—from prelife to birth, from childhood to adulthood (at puberty), from a single to a married state, and from life to death. Folk superstitions such as putting an ax under the mother's bed to ease childbirth, having a bride wear or carry certain objects to ensure her future happiness, or guarding a corpse from cats at a wake are modern equivalents for the primitive's complex rituals at the same stages in life. For initiation to adulthood we have such formalized events as graduation, confirmation, and bar mitzvah, but few folk superstitions. A rare exception is the traditional belief that the ribbon on a diploma must not be cut or broken, but must be slipped off whole to preserve one's luck.

Numerous current superstitions associated with *birth, infancy, and childhood* (category I) display concepts and habits of reasoning also associated with primitive cultures. Although it is unreasonable to adopt a "survivals" explanation for all such items, the origins of at least some of them may be so traced. The belief in prenatal influence, for example, is essentially no different whether it exists among modern Americans or among aborigines: the pregnant mother's experiences are supposedly manifested in marks or habits of her child. If the mother is struck with something, the baby has a birthmark in the shape of that object; if she craves a particular food, that will turn out to be the baby's favorite food, too, or the baby may be "marked" in a related way. (So-called "strawberry birthmarks" are often explained from such events.) The term "harelip" for the deformity that looks like a hare's cleft lip hints at the superstition that the sight of a hare can cause a pregnant woman to bear a child with that mark. Similarly, personal names are frequently regarded with awe and surrounded with magic among primitives; modern people retain vestiges of the same attitude in such beliefs as that if an unnamed baby is sick, he will recover as soon as he is given a name, or that good luck attends a person whose initials spell a word.

Folk medicine (category II) is another area in which primitive practices may survive. In sickness, as during other crises, people almost instinctively rely on traditional cures, even if medical science has been consulted. Thus, a person may secure a salve or ointment with a doctor's prescription and then carefully apply it with the middle finger to improve its effectiveness; here magic and science combine to the detriment of neither. Or, knowing that a nosebleed may be stopped by pressing a blood vessel, a traditionally inclined person chooses "brown paper" as the compress and "under the upper lip" as the pressure point. (In the nursery rhyme "Jack and Jill" it is "vinegar and brown paper" that Jack uses to "mend his head," and some people say a brown paper bag placed against the stomach is a cure or a preventative for car sickness.) The less that medical science knows about an ailment, the more likely it is that folk remedies will survive. For this reason, hiccups, sties, warts, fever blisters, rheumatism, cancer, and the common cold are among the ailments most frequently treated with folk cures.

Typical cures for warts illustrate some characteristic patterns in folk cures. "Measuring" as a curative device is demonstrated in superstitions requiring that the number of warts be represented by knots on a string or notches in a stick. "Plugging" is used when something that has been rubbed on the warts or pricked into them is driven into a hole in a tree or buried in the ground. "Transfer" is a common device for removing warts by passing them on by means of a ritual or a saying to someone else or even to an animal or object. The same devices appear in many cures for different ailments, and all of them are based on the principle that something may be invisibly removed from the infected area and magically disposed of somewhere else. (Since warts, like colds, appear and disappear with baffling illogic, folk cures for them seem destined to live on for many generations to come.)

"Faith healers," semiprofessional folk specialists in traditional medicine, usually employ a combination of personal and religious power, sometimes in combination with certain herbs or nostrums. Their concepts of diseases and cures may reflect popular writings on medicine of many decades earlier, and they generally also display folk attitudes held by their particular regional or ethnic group. For instance, the Mexican-American *curanderos* may be called upon to treat *mal puesto* (afflictions involving magic or witchcraft) or *males natural* (natural diseases, unknown among Anglo-Americans and not treated by physicians) such as *empacho* (a form of indigestion), *mal ojo* (evil eye), *susto* (fright sickness), and *caída de la mollera* (fallen fontanel).

Just as the traditional belief systems of folk healing deserve study, so do the traditional aspects of professional medical care. For example, one common piece of hospital lore is that deaths come in threes, and there may be elaborate rules about which deaths to count and about other signs or conditions related to the deaths. Hospital taboos include not pushing a patient feet first on a stretcher and never mixing red and white flowers in a vase to be put in a patient's room. A related area of modern folklore is the way people make use of commercial medications, such as taking pills in a certain sequence or swallowing them only with beer or milk.

Superstitions associated with *home and domestic pursuits* (category III) usually concern cooking, clothing, housekeeping, and changing households. Many people, without considering themselves superstitious, will avoid such taboos as seating thirteen at a table, mending clothes while someone is wearing them, or allowing someone to enter the house, if accidentally locked out, through a window without exiting through the same route. Stirring cake batter clockwise, eating the point of a wedge of pie last, or crumpling up (rather than folding neatly) one's dinner napkin may seem meaningless habits, but to some informants they are lucky acts. Similar superstitions also survive as habits of thought in *economic and social relations* (category IV). Store owners sense—even if they are not aware of a superstition—that if the first customer of the day buys nothing, they will have bad sales all day. People walking together will avoid allowing a post or tree to come between them, perhaps not realizing that some consider it a bad luck sign or a condition that will allow wishes to come true after a dialogue is repeated that begins "Bread and butter—Come to supper." The superstitions of games and sports also fall under this category, and these constitute a rich area, especially when gambling is involved. Horse bettors, poker players, and slot-machine addicts are notoriously superstitious, but even hard-headed bridge players may think their luck is improved if they can manage to sit lined up with their partner the same way as the bathtub is positioned in the house.

Travel and communications (category V) is another "danger area" (like birth, sickness, and gambling), for which superstition may provide a safeguard. This often takes the form of auspicious days and times for beginning a trip, signs of future trips or of visitors to come, and procedures for traveling or for returning to fetch something forgotten at home. Recent superstitions about mail, telegrams, telephones, and the like conveniently fit into this category, too. These include items such as "If a letter falls to the ground when you mail it, bad luck will attend it" or "Talking on the telephone during a storm may give you an electric shock."

Superstitions of *love, courtship, and marriage* (category VI) concern aphrodisiacs and other love charms, divinations, and various practices to predict or ensure marital or sexual happiness. Although few women probably believe in divination nowadays, many will still pretend anyway to determine their future mates by consulting objects ranging from buttons (which are counted "doctor, lawyer, merchant, thief"), an apple peel pared in a whole strip (which is thrown over the left shoulder to fall in the shape of the man's initial), or a drinking straw (which is pinched into a pattern and then flattened until one of the initialed ends is intact and thus indicates the spouse's name). The taboo against trying on another person's engagement ring lest you never get married yourself is perhaps as much a matter of courtesy as an item of actual belief.

Anyone who has taken part in weddings knows the care that some brides will take to secure the required "Something old, something new, something borrowed, something blue." The suggestion that the bride might see the bridegroom shortly before the wedding is met with horror in some quarters. Other brides will even go to the extreme of being sure that they are not married while standing with their feet aligned at right angles to the floorboard in the church. After marriage, a tradition that supposedly reveals which partner is the boss in the family involves having the person fold his or her hands; the thumb that comes out on top signifies who has the power in the home, though people disagree on which thumb signifies each partner.

Superstitious *death and funeral customs* (category VII) reflect our fear of all things associated with death. A bird flying into the house, a red spider, a dog howling at night, an empty rocking chair that is moving, a picture falling off the wall—these are only a few of the signs that were once widely regarded as sure omens of a coming death and that still may occasion a good deal of anxiety. When there is a death in the house, people may stop the clocks, throw out water in flower vases, or perform other traditional acts for which there is no rational explanation, only the authority of traditional usage. Once it was bad luck to break through a funeral procession, while today it is merely bad manners (or, in many states, illegal). In any case, doing it accidentally leads one not only to a feeling of personal regret, but also to a definite twinge of uneasiness for offending the dead.

Superstitions about the Supernatural

Superstitions concerned exclusively with the supernatural are gathered in category VIII of Hand's system, *Witchcraft, Ghosts, Magical Practices.* Although the Anglo-American witch is now mostly a semicomical figure of cartoons and Halloween decorations in the urban United States, one does not have to go too far back into the backwoods or among ethnic groups to find flourishing beliefs in midnight witch-riding, conjuring, hoodoo, cursing, casting spells, haunts, shape shifting, and the like. Collections and studies of American supersitions are rich in supernatural lore, too voluminous to be summarized here. Ghost lore is still extremely active in the United States, despite the joshing that Americans reserve for British "ghost detectives" and dwellers in supposedly haunted castles. "Second sight" and other forms of supernatural communication through time or space are still trusted by some. The modern Americans' habits of carrying lucky charms, knocking on wood, crossing their fingers, and cursing things that offend them all point back to supernaturalism that is medieval, if not much more ancient.

Probably not best considered part of supernaturalism (although their popular name suggests that they *are*) are "water witches" who seek ground water sources by magical means. Such practitioners with their forked sticks or "doodlebugs" (for locating minerals) are a kind of traditional or folk scientist found in many rural counties in America and in most urban ones as well.

Folk Religion

Although Wayland Hand's extensive classification system for the thousands of isolated superstitions that were gathered in

North Carolina by Frank C. Brown cannot incorporate the much more structured nature of **folk religion,** this is an appropriate place to mention the subject in this book. Many people, perhaps most, engage in some aspects of folk religion, which comprises, in Don Yoder's words, "views and practices of religion that exist among the people apart from and alongside the strictly theological and liturgical forms of the official religion." These traditional unofficial religious attitudes and actions may range in complexity from simple aspects of prayer, veneration of religious objects, blessings, faith-promoting stories, and the like, up to elaborate folk-religious organizations such as the voodoo practiced in New Orleans, which derives from Haiti, and the Southern snake-handling cults, which take their inspiration from the literal interpretation of Biblical passages.

Folklorist William Clements has developed a useful set of distinctions to identify the traditional elements in American folk Protestantism, and, though his focus was northeast Arkansas, most of his terms could apply elsewhere. This variety of the folk church, Clements found, is oriented to the past, accepts the Scriptures literally, believes that providence works in everyday life, and strongly emphasizes evangelism. The groups' services (often held in buildings relatively isolated from mainstream churches) are characterized by informality and emotionalism. The group follows a rigorous moral code, and the church organization tends to be sectarian (split off from some orthodox congregation) and egalitarian (admitting to membership all professed believers). Clearly, many of these features may also be found among popular religious movements (such as the followings that faith healers and television evangelists enjoy), and different traits might be identified for such groups as the Unification Church, the transcendental meditators, or the American converts to Eastern religions.

Superstitions about Cosmology and the Natural World

Superstitions related to cosmology and the natural world fall into the following five categories in Hand's system:

Such *cosmic phenomena* (category **IX**) as tides, winds, rainbows, and the movements of heavenly bodies have long been studied and regarded as possible portents, often of wars or of natural disasters. The more unusual the phenomenon, the more likely it will be read as an omen. As a result, eclipses, comets, and meteors ("shooting stars") occasion more superstitions than do phases of the moon, shifting patterns of stars, and bright colors of sunsets. General superstitions of this kind, as well as those dealing with *times, numbers, and seasons,* when they are unrelated to other areas of folk belief, fall into this group. Examples include "Seeing the moon over the right [or left] shoulder is good luck"; "Sing before breakfast; cry before dinner"; "Trouble always comes in threes"; and "Nothing made of leather at Christmas time will last."

As Mark Twain pointed out, people talk about the weather, but they *do* very little about it—not even predict it with complete reliability—despite the science of meteorology, with its orbiting weather satellites. The natural result is an enormous number of *weather superstitions.* Most items in category **X** are *signs:* "If you see a dog eating grass, it is going to rain soon"; or "If it snows on Christmas day, Easter will be green." Others are *magic:* "Sit in the middle of the room and hold a glass of water in your hand and you won't be struck by lightning during a storm"; or "Sleep with a flower under your pillow and the weather will be fair the next day." Only a few are *conversions,* such as "Every flash of lightning is accompanied by a thunderbolt; if you can find one [a thunderbolt] and keep it in your house, it will never be struck by lightning."

Superstitions concerning *animals and animal husbandry* (category **XI**) or *plants and plant husbandry* (category **XIII**) include all the beliefs and practices used to enhance agricultural success. Even in an age of farm advisers in every county, government bulletins to cover all problems, and technological advances for every need, many farmers still plant by the "signs," consult almanacs, treat sick animals with home cures, and follow countless other traditional usages. One of the most whimsical animal beliefs carried to the New World from the Old is that rats may be induced to leave a building by writing them a polite note that suggests another abode nearby and stuffing it into a rat hole. Traditional ways of controlling threatening animals include "Hold your breath and bees won't sting you"; "A rattlesnake won't cross a hair rope"; "Cut off the tip of a dog's tail and carry it with you and that dog will never harm you"; and "If you see a stray dog out on your lawn, cross your fingers and hold them tight and he won't defecate there." The familiar children's rhyme "Ladybug, ladybug, fly away home . . ." is said to have been used by hop growers to spare the useful little beetles when the vines were burnt off. The most common agricultural superstitions are those that deal with the best time to perform farm work such as planting, harvesting, dehorning, castrating, and slaughtering. Some farm traditions seem to have fairly logical explanations—such as the rules for animal surgery that correlate with the times of year naturally best suited for healing (i.e., months without an "R," that is, the summer months, are sometimes taboo for castration)—while others are strictly magic—such as the belief that thanking the giver will cause a gift plant to wither and die, or the belief that only if a hen is set on an even number of eggs will they all hatch.

Fishing and hunting superstitions (category XII) exist because, like gambling, sports, sickness, crops, weather, and the like, success cannot be predicted or guaranteed. As a result, there are traditional signs for the good-luck days and places, and traditional magic for the best methodology of the hunt. Members of hunting or fishing parties may be excessively sensitive about such acts as sticking an ax into the ground (it will throw the dog's scent off) or stepping over a fishing pole (it will ruin the luck). Other sportsmen are convinced by years of experience that a big opossum will always go up a little tree and vice versa, or that the behavior of a small fish kept in a tank at home will indicate how good the fishing will be that day. Commercial fishermen have many folk signs and practices associated both with increased production and better individual protection.

As in almost every classification in the study of folklore, there remains a group of very general items that may be no better labeled than simply *"Miscellaneous."* This category (XIV) contains the lore of wishing, general good and bad luck, and a small but interesting group of modern beliefs. One of the most persistent contemporary superstitions, for example, is that to save enough of an apparently worthless item will result in some kind of reward. The items saved may be ticket stubs, cigarette packages (or the red opening-tabs from the packages), beer-bottle labels, tea-bag tabs, or the red trademark tags from Levi's. Generally the assumption is that "a million of them" (or some other large number) will be good for some charitable gift such as a seeing-eye dog for a blind person, a wheelchair for a physically disabled one, or hospital care for a poor child. Probably the publicity given to recent prize contests has done much to keep such beliefs alive. Just as American children attach some significance to finding the words "Hershey Kisses" printed three times on an opening tab or a whole Indian pictured on a Tootsie Pop wrapper, adults have traditions associated with the number of dots on an Olympia Beer label or the number of stars on a *Playboy* magazine cover. Other items for this miscellaneous category might be the beliefs that too much exposure to television or to a computer monitor may cause sterility, or that stones grow.

In this discussion of the persistence of superstitions and of their definition, classification, and folk rationalization, several theoretical aspects of superstitious behavior have also been introduced. These include faulty reasoning, coincidence, psychological predilection to believe in the supernatural, rites of passage, the theory of survival, the uncertainty of some desired ends, fear of the abnormal or of the risky, fear of the dead, modernization of superstitions, and the power of magic to persist traditionally side by side with officially maintained science and religion. Two other important theories should be mentioned.

Theories of Superstitions

The famous theory of **sympathetic magic** proposed by Sir James G. Frazer in his twelve-volume work *The Golden Bough*, although discredited by modern anthropologists, provided terminology still in use for explaining some superstitions. Frazer believed that many primitive beliefs in magic were founded on the assumption of an inherent "sympathy" between unconnected objects. This could take the form either of *homeopathic magic* (magic of similarity), based on the idea that like objects may affect each other, or *contagious magic* (magic of touch), based on the idea that objects formerly in contact with each other continue to have an invisible connection. The theory was applied beyond primitive cultures to explain many superstitions, both ancient and modern. When the witches in *Macbeth* stir up waves in their kettle to make waves rise at sea, or when a primitive person fears that his likeness in a photograph will steal his soul away, or when planting lore implies a parallel between the crescent moon enlarging and crops increasing, *homeopathic magic* is said to be at work. In each instance an event *like* the desired one is involved. But when a nail or knife that caused a wound is treated along with the wound, or when a person's footprint may be molested to harm that person, or when the spittle of someone who has delivered the "evil eye" is used in the curative ritual, *contagious magic* is said to be at work. Here each event involves something formerly *in touch* with the subject of the magic. Both kinds of sympathetic magic are involved in such rites as a curse performed with a voodoo doll made as an image of the victim that also contains bits of his hair, nail parings, or clothing. In a wart cure, if a stolen dishrag is simply buried "to rot the wart away," only homeopathic magic is used; but if it must first be touched to the wart, contagious magic is at work also. Part of the difficulty in accepting wholly Frazer's "false science" approach is that when a magical act *is* followed by the desired result, there may be nothing defective in either the logic or its application: some "superstitions," in other words, seem to be true and useful—at least part of the time. Conversely, the institutionalized religious "magic" of blessings, prayer, or good works may or may not prove effective and thus may or may not (depending on one's belief) be accepted as "true." In other words, Frazer's explanation is ethnocentric (see Chapter 15), and most folklorists using his terminology do not completely accept his underlying theory.

The theory of "**gesunkenes Kulturgut**" proposed by German scholar Hans Naumann never gained much academic support after it was introduced in the 1920s. The theory held that some modern folklore may represent surviving fragments of learned traditions (rather than only "savage" ones) that have "sunken down" from a high stratum of society among the educated to a lower level in the peasant class. (The theory was the direct opposite of that held by the "survivals" school.) "*Gesunkenes Kulturgut,*" however, is an apt explanation for certain important bodies of superstition, mainly astrology and witchcraft. In each of these areas, what were once the trusted beliefs of the best-educated people of earlier times have become present-day folk superstitions. Rulers of nations once consulted astrologers before making important decisions (some, in fact, still do), and courts of law once seriously tried and condemned witches, but only traditional practice maintains these beliefs in the United States now.

Theories concerning superstitions, like all theories of folklore, should not be formulated too rigorously or applied too mechanically without full regard for the social contexts and field data on which they are based. In many instances it is obvious that more than one theory may apply. For example, the placing of an ax under the bed during childbirth might be alternately explained as part of a *rite of passage,* as the *survival* of primitive veneration for valuable tools, as an instance of *homeopathic magic* (the sharp edge "cutting" the pain), or as a safety precaution to counter the *fear of a dangerous situation.* An alert listener can detect the theoretical basis in explanations sometimes offered for common superstitions. "Three on a match" is usually explained as a fairly recent survival from a wartime safety measure; "step on a crack and break your mother's back" involves homeopathic magic; putting a piece of the desired mineral on a "doodlebug" (miner's divining rod) draws on contagious magic and most personal validations for superstitions involve fallacious reasoning. It must also be borne in mind that explanations for superstitions, like those for proverbs, may themselves be traditional, and when such explanations become sufficiently formularized, they become legends.

It should also be remembered, as Toelken points out in the

Appendix, that some statements of alleged folk belief are merely passed on because they appeal humorously or esthetically to the group; these are, in his terms, "artistic superstitions," not the more seriously taken "religious superstitions." This is partly a matter of individual attitude—one person's religiously believed tradition may be another's whimsical saying— but other items in the *form* of folk belief are clearly not believed by anyone who repeats them, such as the following supposed cure for a cold:

> Get in bed with your hat hanging on the bedpost, and drink whiskey until you see *two* hats; then you can sleep your cold off.

Research in Superstitions

Research approaches to superstitions have generally taken the form of collecting projects, classifications, attempts at better definitions, and theoretical studies. Another promising approach, so far only touched upon, is experimentation. An experiment with superstitions might be designed to field-test a theoretical explanation, to determine the efficacy of a superstition, to study variations that occur in transmission, or for other purposes. An experiment on a very simple level that shows how coincidence reinforces belief was performed by the columnist Allan M. Trout of the *Courier-Journal* (Louisville, Kentucky) in 1960. After hearing the first katydid on July 20, Trout calculated by means of folk prognostication that the first frost would come ninety days later, on October 20. He then proceeded to write his column for that date in advance, boldly predicting the weather that the katydids had promised. What did his readers find on the morning of October 20? A light frost—the first of the season!

The katydid experiment, of course, was uncontrolled and unscientific; it demonstrated more about how superstitions arise through coincidence than about the natural causes that might underlie them. An experiment on a higher plane was reported in

1962 in the *Journal of American Folklore*. Pigeons were confined in boxes where food was delivered and colored lights were flashed in a random pattern. The birds, however, tended to react as if their own bodily movements or the appearances of the lights had a real connection with the delivery of food. They learned to respond to the supposed light patterns or to attempt to control the appearance of food by their movements; in short, they became what is termed "superstitious." The experimenters concluded that the basic conditions that may lead to superstitions are deprivation and the uncertain appearance of a desired commodity, "accidental reinforcement" of behavior which supposedly leads to success, and the continued maintenance of such behavior even without much positive encouragement. Whether such stimulus-response experimentation tells us much about the psychological state of superstitious humans is open to question.

BIBLIOGRAPHIC NOTES

Alan Dundes compared definitions of superstitions and proposed the one quoted in this chapter in his "Brown County Superstitions," *MF* 11 (1961): 25–56; repr. in *Analytic Essays in Folklore*, pp. 88–94. In "Folk Beliefs: Knowledge and Action," *SFQ* 31 (1967): 304–9, Michael Owen Jones comments on Dundes's definition and suggests a need for an improved approach that will better account for meanings and functions of superstitions and for the workings of the "folk mind."

Dundes offers the term "folk ideas" for items of traditional attitude and assumption not easily included under "folk belief" or superstition; see "Folk Ideas as Units of World View," *JAF* 84 (1971): 93–103. He has collected examples of these ideas in such articles as "The Number Three in American Culture," in his anthology *Every Man His Way* (Englewood Cliffs, N.J.: Prentice-Hall, 1968), pp. 401–24 (repr. in *Analytic Essays in Folklore*, pp. 206–25); "Thinking Ahead: A Folkloristic Reflection of the Future Orientation in American Worldview," *Anthropological Quarterly* 42 (1969): 53–72 (repr. in *Analytic Essays in Folklore*, pp. 226–38); and in an article on the primacy of sight data in American folk speech and folk belief entitled "Seeing Is Believing," *Natural History* 81 (May 1972): 8–12, 86–87.

Studies of collegiate superstitions referred to in this chapter are as follows: Fletcher Bascom Dresslar's *Superstitions and Education*, University of California Publications in Education no. 5 (Berkeley, 1907); Martha Warren Beckwith's "Signs and Superstitions Collected from

American College Girls," *JAF* 36 (1923): 1–15; Alfred Marston Tozzer's *Social Origins and Social Continuities* (New York: Macmillan, 1932), pp. 225–30, 242–66; Harold E. Driver's "A Method of Investigating Individual Differences in Folkloristic Beliefs and Practices," *MF* 1 (1951): 99–105; and Jan Harold Brunvand's "Folklore and Superstitions in Idaho," *IY* 6 (1962): 20–24 (see also a note in *WF* 22 [1963]: 202–3).

Two other notes on student superstitions are Martin L. Wine's "Superstitions Collected in Chicago," *MF* 7 (1957): 149–59 (175 items from nineteen students at Austin High School), and Charles A. Huguenin's "A Prayer for Examinations," *NYFQ* 18 (1962): 145–48 (appeals to St. Joseph of Cupertino, "The patron saint of the stupid"). Gustav Jahoda reports several other studies of student superstitions in *The Psychology of Superstition* (Baltimore: Penguin Books, 1970), pp. 31–32. An article by L. Michael Bell contains numerous folk beliefs concerning a popular soft drink collected from college students; see "Cokelore," *WF* 35 (1976): 59–65 (repr. in *Readings in American Folklore*, pp. 99–105).

Mark Graubard has compared ancient and modern attitudes toward superstitions in "Some Contemporary Observations on Ancient Superstitions," *JAF* 59 (1946): 124–33. A discussion of the truthfulness of some superstitions is E. H. Lucas's "The Role of Folklore in the Discovery and Rediscovery of Plant Drugs," *Cenntennial Review of Arts and Science* 3 (1959): 173–88. Bergen Evans's *The Natural History of Nonsense* (New York: Knopf, 1946; Vintage Books paperback, edn., 1958) debunks many popular delusions. Ray B. Browne's "Superstitions Used as Propaganda in the American Revolution," *NYFQ* 17 (1961): 202–11, illustrates the appearance of such delusions in an earlier period.

Collections of American superstitions are listed in the bibliographies of both volumes of the North Carolina collection, and Wayland D. Hand's introduction in volume 6 is a comprehensive survey of theories of superstitions and problems of research as they apply to the 8,569 items he has arranged and annotated here. Besides this invaluable work, a key European reference source is the *Handwörterbuch des deutschen Aberglaubens*, ed. Eduard von Hoffman-Krayer and Hanns Bächtold-Stäubli, 10 vols. (Berlin and Leipzig: W. deGruyter, 1927–42). Space permits listing only three other important older American collections: Harry Hyatt's *Folklore from Adams County, Illinois* (New York: Alma Egan Hyatt Foundation, 1935; 2nd rev. edn., 1965); Vance Randolph's *Ozark Superstitions* (New York: Columbia University Press, 1947; Dover Books paperback edn., 1964); and Ray B. Browne's *Popular Beliefs and Practices from Alabama*, University of California Folklore Studies no. 9 (Berkeley and Los Angeles, 1958).

Two enormous collections of American superstitions recently published in their entirety greatly broaden the base for studies in this area. Harry Middleton Hyatt's *Hoodoo-Conjuration-Witchcraft-Rootwork* was issued in five volumes by Western Publishing Company of St.

Louis, Missouri (1970–78). Newbell Niles Puckett's *Popular Beliefs and Superstitions,* including more than 36,000 items collected in Ohio, was edited for publication in three volumes by Wayland D. Hand, Anna Casetta, and Sondra B. Thiederman (Boston: G. K. Hall, 1981). The system established for the Brown collection was somewhat modified and reorganized for this work.

A good collection from Canada with bibliographic references to others is Helen Creighton's *Bluenose Magic: Popular Beliefs and Superstitions in Nova Scotia* (Toronto: Ryerson Press, 1968).

For the particular folk beliefs of Afro-American culture, begin with Newbell Niles Puckett's *Folk Beliefs of the Southern Negro* (Chapel Hill: University of North Carolina Press, 1926). An important early study is Zora Hurston's "Hoodoo in America," *JAF* 64 (1931): 317–417.

Confronting the vast materials available for classification and study, Samuel J. Sackett proposes "Using a Computer on a Belief Collection" in *WF* 29 (1970): 105–10. A reader offered a correction to Sackett's methodology in *WF* 30 (1971): 55.

In the folklore of childbirth, the curious practice of giving the husband medical care after his wife has given birth is discussed in historic and geographic perspective by Wayland D. Hand in "American Analogues of the Couvade," *Studies in Folklore,* pp. 213–29. Lucile F. Newman presents a large classified collection in "Folklore of Pregnancy: Wives' Tales in Contra Costa County, California," *WF* 28 (1969): 112–35.

A general approach to the subject of folk medicine may be made via the collection *American Folk Medicine: A Symposium,* ed. Wayland D. Hand (Los Angeles, Calif.: UCLA Center for Study of Comparative Folklore and Mythology, pub. 4, 1976). Many techniques of folk medicine (plugging, nailing, transfer, passing through, animal sacrifice, etc.) are analyzed in the twenty-three essays by Wayland D. Hand gathered in his *Magical Medicine* (Berkeley: University of California Press, 1980).

Cures using "madstones" (hair or fiber balls from the stomachs of ruminants) are discussed in a special issue of *NCFJ* 24:1 (1976). Articles on folk herbalists and their cures are found in *NCFJ* 27 (1979): 20–25, and in *TFSB* 48 (1982): 61–65.

Data on faith healing are contained in such articles as Terry M. Carbo, "The Faith Healing Beliefs of a New Orleans Family," *LFM* 2 (August 1968): 91–100, and Gopalan V. Gopalan and Bruce Nickerson, "Faith Healing in Indiana and Illinois," *IF* 6 (1973): 33–99. More analysis is given in Wayland D. Hand, "The Folk Healer: Calling and Endowment," *Journal of the History of Medicine and Allied Sciences* 26 (1971): 263–75, and Michael Owen Jones, *Why Faith Healing?* (Ottawa: Canadian Centre for Folk Culture Studies, paper no. 3, 1972). In an overview, Greg Johnson charts strategies of faith healing in "A Classification of Faith Healing Practices," *NYF* 1 (1975): 91–96. In "Faith

Healing Narratives from Northeast Arkansas," *IF* 9 (1976): 15–39, William M. Clements discusses the theology of healing among Pentacostals (from the power of the Holy Ghost) and examines some themes of faith-healing experience stories (crisis conversions, spirit baptisms, exorcisms, prophecies, etc.).

Occurrences of a curious belief concerning the human body are recorded in "Measuring for Short Growth," *HF* 7 (1948): 15–19. For instance, children may be considered undersized if their heights are not found to be seven times the length of their feet. For further data, see Barbara Ann Townsend and Donald Allport Bird, "The Miracle of String Measurement," *IF* 3 (1970): 147–62, with an additional account supplied in *IF* 4 (1971): 89–94.

Of particular interest in the general area of folk cures is Richard M. Dorson's "Blood Stoppers," *SFQ* 11 (1947): 105–18, which was reprinted with some additions as Chapter 7 of *Bloodstoppers and Bearwalkers* (Cambridge, Mass.: Harvard University Press, 1952). Another area of folk cures is presented in Frank M. Paulsen's "A Hair of the Dog and Some Other Hangover Cures from Popular Tradition," *JAF* 74 (1961): 152–68. Articles on folk veterinary medicine in Tennessee were published in *TFSB* 43 (1977): 140–48, and 44 (1978): 55–65. A related item, "Communicating with Critters," *FFV* 1 (1979): 52–59, by Elmer L. Smith, concerns various notes and verbal charms directed to insects, rats, and the like in order to repel or eliminate them.

As background for a Spanish-American pattern of faith healing and folk medicine, see Irwin Press, "The Urban Curandero," *AA* 73 (1971): 741–56. On the nature of ailments for which magical aid is sought, see Keith A. Neighbors, "Mexican-American Folk Diseases," *WF* 28 (1969): 249–59. A local study in this area is E. Ferol Benavides, "The Saints among the Saints: A Study of Curanderismo in Utah," *UHQ* 41 (1973): 373–92.

Folk practices and beliefs concerning sex are discussed in three recent articles: Eleanor Long, "Aphrodisiacs, Charms, and Philtres," *WF* 32 (1973): 153–63; George W. Rich and David F. Jacobs, "Saltpeter: A Folkloric Adjustment to Acculturation Stress," *WF* 32 (1973): 164–79; and Lydia Fish, "The Old Wife in the Dormitory—Sexual Folklore and Magical Practices from State University College," *NYFQ* 28 (1972): 30–36.

Folk beliefs and superstitions of various occupations constitute a fascinating but largely uncollected body of material. Actors' superstitions are found in Ralph Freud's "George Spelvin Says the Tag: Folklore of the Theater," *WF* 13 (1954): 245–50; Dan Gross's "Folklore of the Theater," *WF* 20 (1961): 257–63; and Wayland D. Hand's "Folk Beliefs and Customs of the American Theater: A Survey," *SFQ* 38 (1974): 23–48. Other occupational studies include Lee Allen, "The Superstitions of Baseball Players," *NYFQ* 20 (1964): 98–109; Henry Winfred Splitter,

"Miner's Luck," *WF* 15 (1956): 229–46; and two studies by Patrick B. Mullen—"The Function of Magic Folk Belief among Texas Coastal Fishermen," *JAF* 82 (1969): 214–25, and "The Function of Folk Belief among Negro Fishermen of the Texas Coast," *SFQ* 33 (1969): 80–91. Another study of fishermen's superstitions is John J. Poggie, Jr., and Carl Gersung, "Risk and Ritual: An Interpretation of Fishermen's Folklore in a New England Community," *JAF* 85 (1972): 66–72. An unusual study of urban black folk belief is David J. Winslow's "Occupational Superstitions of Negro Prostitutes in an Upstate New York City," *NYFQ* 24 (1968): 294–301.

A body of European-American beliefs and practices is described by Aili K. Johnson in "Lore of the Finnish-American Sauna," *MF* 1 (1951): 33–39 (repr. in *Readings in American Folklore*, pp. 91–98). Louis C. Jones traced "The Evil Eye among European-Americans," in *WF* 10 (1951): 11–25, but found no evidence of survival among English or Scottish stocks.

A basic study of Anglo-American supernatural folklore is George Lyman Kittredge's book *Witchcraft in Old and New England* (Cambridge, Mass.: Harvard University Press, 1929; republished New York: Russell and Russell, 1956). Patricia K. Rickels collected "Some Accounts of Witch Riding" from a black college student who had been witch-ridden—see *LFM* 2 (August 1961): 1–17, and the reprint in *Readings in American Folklore*, pp. 53–63. The major study of witch riding (or "the old hag") is by David J. Hufford, *The Terror That Comes in the Night* (AFS publications, new series, vol. 7, Philadelphia, 1982).

On the basis of an interview with a "good" witch living in Philadelphia, Jane C. Beck published "A Traditional Witch of the Twentieth Century," *NYFQ* 30 (1974): 101–16. A catalogue of American witch legends is cited in the notes to Chapter 9.

The practice of dowsing or "water witching" has attracted numerous studies; the most comprehensive is Evon Z. Vogt and Ray Hyman's *Water Witching U.S.A.* (Chicago: University of Chicago Press, 1959). A fascinating review of the book by a practicing "witch" is R. Carlyle Buley's "Water (?) Witching Can Be Fun," *IMH* 56 (1960): 65–77. Vogt also co-wrote "Some Aspects of the Folklore of Water Witching in the United States" in *JAF* 71 (1958): 519–31 with Peggy Golde; and "The Urban American Dowser," *JAF* 82 (1969): 195–213, with Linda K. Barrett. A study of dowsing in a regional context is Hilda Webb's "Water Witching as Part of Folklife in Southern Indiana," *JFI* 3 (1966), 10–29.

A "Symposium on Folk Religion," ed. Don Yoder, appeared in *WF* 33 (1974): 1–87. Steven M. Kane's "Ritual Possession in a Southern Appalachian Religious Sect," *JAF* 87 (1974): 293–302, deals with snake handling in a six-state area. Articles on Afro-American folk religion include David J. Winslow, "Bishop E. E. Everett and Some Aspects of Occultism and Folk Religion in Negro Philadelphia," *KFQ* 14 (1969):

59–80; James F. Byers, "Voodoo: Tropical Pharmacology or Psychosomatic Psychology?" *NYFQ* 26 (1970): 305–12; and Loudell F. Snow, "'I Was Born Just Exactly with the Gift': An Interview with a Voodoo Practitioner," *JAF* 86 (1973): 272–81.

William M. Clements deplores the neglect of folk religion by American folklorists in an essay published in *JFI* 15 (1978): 161–80. He proposes the list of folk-religious elements that is referred to in this chapter. Two articles on folk varieties of Catholicism appeared in *IF* 9 (1976): 147–74, and *NYF* 8, 3–4 (1982) was a special issue containing seven essays on folklore and religious belief. Just at this writing, further studies in religion in America are beginning to appear.

An early government publication, Edward B. Garriott's *Weather Folk-Lore and Local Weather Signs*, attempted to "segregate from the mass of available data the true sayings that are applicable to the United States." Material was drawn from two late-nineteenth-century collections; the work was published as U.S. Dept. of Agriculture, Weather Bureau, Bulletin No. 33—W. B. No. 294 (Washington, D.C., 1903; Superintendent of Documents Index No. A29.3:33). Another interesting older collection is W. J. Humphreys's *Weather Proverbs and Paradoxes* (Baltimore: Williams & Wilkins, 1923; 2nd edn., 1934). Louise Pound surveyed the history of attempts to make rain on the Great Plains in her article "Nebraska Rain Lore and Rain Making," *CFQ* 5 (1946): 129–42, reprinted in *Nebraska Folklore*, pp. 41–60. Background material from eighteenth-century New England for the study of a popular reference work on weather lore and other agricultural and domestic traditions is George Lyman Kittredge's *The Old Farmer and His Almanack* (Cambridge, Mass.: Harvard University Press, 1904).

Except that it becomes excessively ritualistic in its interpretations, W. W. Newell's "Conjuring Rats" in *JAF* 5 (1892): 23–32 is a good discussion of the old superstition concerning writing a note to rid a building of rats (see also "Communicating with Critters" cited earlier in these notes). Two items of recent folk belief are described in Michael J. Preston's "Olympia Beer Comes to Colorado: The Spread of a Tradition," *WF* 32 (1973): 281–83 (supposed significance of the dots on the backs of labels); and Harry Joe Jaffee's "The Stars of Playboy," *WF* 31 (1972): 122–23 (traditions about stars printed on the magazine cover).

Allan M. Trout's experiment was described in the *Courier-Journal* on October 20, 1960. The pigeon experiment was described by Arthur J. Bachrach in "An Experimental Approach to Superstitious Behavior," *JAF* 75 (1962): 1–9. In "Superstitious Pigeons, Hydrophobia, and Conventional Wisdom," *WF* 30 (1971): 1–18, Kenneth Ketner, with reference to such experiments, asserts that notions of folk groups and their supposed beliefs are useless for defining superstition. Instead he advocates study of the "psychological state of individuals" and prefers the term "conventional wisdom" to "superstition." An article that deals further with the habits of mind that permeate superstition is Eric Berne's "The Mythology of Dark and Fair: Psychiatric Use of Folklore," *JAF* 72 (1959): 1–13. Gustav Jahoda's *The Psychology of Superstition*, mentioned earlier in these notes, is the only book-length survey of modern psychological theories as they apply to folk beliefs.

15
Customs and Festivals

What Are Customs?

Possibly no other kind of American folklore has been so frequently referred to, yet so vaguely defined, so ill classified, and so little understood or studied, as folk customs have been. While few proposed definitions of American folklore would exclude customs, nowhere is there a comprehensive explication of the term, nor is it consistently employed. Tolerably rich materials are scattered through such sources as state and local historical journals, but there is no definitive folklore study of them. Customs are sometimes presented in folklore collections under such labels as "folkways," "usages," or "social institutions," or they are presented in collections together with superstitions or material folklore. Some folklore anthologies that list "customs" among their contents actually contain few or none, while others that do include customs have no special terms for them. Indexers and bibliographers of American folklore usually group customs with other "minor areas" of traditional materials. Social historians and folklorists who may be dealing with the same customs seem to be unaware of each other's publications. For all of these reasons, this chapter attempts to integrate various points of view by extracting some generally useful terms, concepts, and examples.

To begin with, it is clear that customs are closely associated with superstitions. Hence, the typical combination "Beliefs and Customs" is used in *The Frank C. Brown Collection of North Carolina Folklore* and other major collections. Like superstitions, customs involve both verbal and nonverbal elements that are traditionally applied in specific circumstances. But unlike superstitions, customs do not usually involve faith in the magical results of application. Thus, the "customs" that incorporate traditional belief in the supernatural are usually classified as "superstitions."

A **custom** is a traditional *practice*—a mode of individual behavior or a habit of social life—that is transmitted by word of mouth or imitation, then ingrained by social pressure, common usage, and parental or other authority. When customs are associated with holidays, they become *calendar customs;* and when such events are celebrated annually by a community, they become *festivals*.

Transmitting folklore is itself customary. Storytelling, ballad singing, riddle posing, game playing and prank playing, and the like all depend for their survival on traditional performance and acceptance rather than on official control. Generally, folklorists have not separated the customary contexts from folklore texts, except perhaps when studying something like quilting bees or barn raisings rather than quilt patterns or barns themselves, or searching for a "liars' contest" rather than merely for texts of tall tales. But there are more subtle behavioral patterns, integral parts of folklore performance situations, which folklorists are just beginning to study: "framing" devices that initiate and conclude folk transmissions, postural and gestural clues to meaning, audience-response codes, nonverbalized folk beliefs, and the like.

This expanded sense of the term "custom" involves the folklorist in what anthropologists term **ethnography**—the descriptive study of all traditions in a particular group or region. Ethnographic descriptions of different cultures make possible comparative studies, or **ethnology**. Since the terms "ethnography" and "ethnology" are sometimes used synonymously, especially in Europe, and both terms tend to be associated with studies of primitive cultures, the term "folklife" (from Scandinavian *"folk-liv"*) deserves the increased American usage it has had lately. **Folklife** refers to the full traditional lore, behavior, and material culture of any folk group, with emphasis on the customary and material categories. (See Chapter 19.) For verbal folklore the term **folk literature** has some currency, although whether "folklife" includes "folk literature" is not always clear. A safe generalization is that American folklorists have accepted the European concept of folklife as constituting their subject matter, and that they are borrowing from ethnography and ethnology for new field methods and theories. In both respects, customs are important data.

Not all customs are still-living folklore. Those that have become a fixed part of national behavior and are practiced unvaryingly throughout a country (or sometimes several countries) are termed *manners* or *mores*, although their origins may lie in folklore and their sustaining power may still be that of tradition. The domestic manners that characterize Americans include switching the fork from hand to hand while eating, serving certain drinks iced, and maintaining a high degree of informality in social life. Manners may involve different levels of awareness, however; we switch fork hands as a matter of course; but icing drinks is a deliberate act, and social informality may be either studied or "natural."

Mores are traditional modes of behavior that have achieved the status of moral requirements, often being institutionalized in laws. These include such practices as monogamous marriages, the patterns of family naming, and the age when adulthood begins. *Ethnocentrism* is the assumption that one's own customs, manners, and mores are the "right" ones, and that all others are scaled out in degrees of "wrongness" from this center. Ethnocentrism accounts for feelings among Americans, for example, that range from intolerance of some other culture's religion (or lack of religion) to mild annoyance at having to drive on the "wrong" side of the highway in England or being expected to bow as a greeting in Japan. That culture contacts may lead to voluntary changes as well as to hostility is demonstrated by the spread of American courtship customs throughout much of the Old World.

National manners and mores, ethnocentrism, acculturation, and related subjects are the concerns of anthropologists and especially sociologists; folklorists have been concerned mostly with customs that are both traditional and variable, being sustained informally in specific folk groups rather than nationally among the whole population. By the time traditional frontier hospitality evolved into the "Welcome Wagon" and the political barbecue became the "$500-a-Plate Dinner," these "folkways" had ceased to have much folkloristic significance, although they still might interest other students of American behavior.

Rite-of-Passage Customs

Most true folk customs in the United States are associated with special events, especially those that require "rites of passage" —birth and adolescence, coming of age, courtship and marriage, and death. They begin at once when a child is born. Boy babies are customarily dressed in blue and girls in pink, but sometimes only the first child of each sex in a family is so clothed, while later arrivals must make do with hand-me-down infantwear or may appear in other pastel shades. Father is expected to hand out cigars, a custom that may repeat itself after promotions in his occupation as well. (In Mormon-dominated Utah and perhaps elsewhere from other influences, instead of cigars a new father passes out Tootsie Rolls or bubble-gum cigars.) None of these practices is required by any authority other than local custom, which varies from region to region or even from family to family. Some families have special clothes for the baby's homecoming or christening, or heirloom furniture for the baby's room.

Celebrations of birthday anniversaries may begin as early as the first year in some families, and they may continue through one's entire life. More commonly, however, birthday parties are dropped at about high-school age, sometimes to be revived once at the symbolic age of maturity (twenty-one years) and again as an annual celebration in later middle age. Children's birthdays almost invariably are the occasion for spanking—one spank for each year, with extras "to grow on" or "for good measure." Children in some regions maintain a fairly rigid schedule of extra-punishment days before and after the birthday anniversary—"pinch day," "hit day," "kiss day," and so forth. Blowing out birthday-cake candles and wishing are standard customs, sometimes varied by naming the candles for possible marriage partners and assuming that the last candle smoking marks the mate. Birthday gifts at a party may be held over the head of the celebrating child for him or her to guess the donor or to announce the use to which that gift is to be put. For each correct guess the chid is granted a wish.

Even the birthday congratulatory song "Happy Birthday to You" may have its variations, most commonly (as shown in Chapter 11) in the form of parody verses. Other versions may be sung by the birthday person ("Happy birthday to me/ I'm sweet as can be . . .") or else turn the cheery greeting into a dismal comment, as in this one, sung to the tune of "The Volga Boatman":

> Happy birthday, happy birthday,
> People dying everywhere, not a one without a care,
> Happy birthday, happy birthday.

In many families the birthday person is allowed to rule as "King [or Queen] for the day," and in some families birthdays of pets or of favorite dolls are celebrated with the usual human traditions.

The loss of "baby teeth" provides another occasion in a child's life when folk customs are followed. The most common practice is for the child to sleep with the tooth under his or her pillow for the "tooth fairy" to buy for a quarter (prices vary). School customs (see also the Appendix) are practiced to some degree in most communities, often being channeled eventually by teachers and principals into well-regulated events. "Dress-up day" or "hillbilly day" under various names, are begun informally by students to vary the routine of regulated school dress but eventually become sanctioned and controlled by school officials and are placed on the activities calendar. One school custom remains a folk one—the designation of a certain day (often Thursday) as "queer day," when the wearing of a certain color (often green, yellow, or purple) marks the supposed homosexuals. Many unsuspecting teachers have been ridiculed behind their backs for unwittingly violating the taboo. The hazing of freshmen, initiation into clubs, and "tapping" for honorary societies are further school occasions for which the establishment has forged ersatz "traditions" to supplant or forestall folk customs, although these seldom catch on as group traditions, and when they do the participants tend to modify them back in the direction of earlier folk behavior.

Some customs are followed at school which have no real connection with school itself. The passing around of autograph books for inscriptions (see Chapter 7) often goes on there, as does the passing of "slam books"—homemade albums for the entry of negative remarks about one's classmates *and* against oneself by others. On the other side of the coin, various "friendship customs," usually involving the exchange of articles of clothing or jewelry, are equally popular. One recent practice was to give others sets of "friendship beads," tiny glass beads strung into safety pins and worn on the recipients' shoelaces.

A more elaborate adolescent custom is "legend tripping." During the years when "cruising" is popular (roughly from when one gets a learner's permit until one reaches legal drinking age), a favorite destination for nighttime drives is some locally famous site associated with a supernatural legend (see Chapter 9). Teen-agers will "cruise" to a place said to be haunted, cursed, inhabited by witches or maniacs, the scene of a terrible accident, or the like, and there retell the legends while half-hoping that something supernatural will take place. Sometimes pranks resembling initiations are performed, and often the trips are associated with drinking, drugs, sex, or vandalism. In St. Louis an unusual local variation of the cruising trip has developed called "finarking" (or "fernarking") the birds. Adolescents drive to the St. Louis Zoo on summer nights, park up close to the big bird cage there, and shout "Finark! Finark!" in an attempt to get the birds, and ultimately the whole zoo population, to screech and howl back at them. "Finarking the birds" itself has a legendary basis: some postadolescents claim that it began in the late 1930s or early 1940s, when the zoo had one exotic bird whose distinctive cry was "Finark!"

Customs associated with reaching maturity (coming of age)

are often institutionalized according to the ethnic group, educational level, or religious affiliations of the family. But the kinds of celebrations, gifts, and possible pranks provided for the confirmation, graduation, or bar mitzvah may involve folk traditions. These can include the choice of gifts, the manner of opening them, the photos that are taken (or the activities recorded and videotaped), the people invited, the dress and food deemed correct, the stories told and songs sung, and perhaps other behavioral patterns. Folklorists have largely failed to document such events, so student projects in this area would be valuable. Other possible studies might be done of practices associated with buying one's first car, going away to college, entering the military service, or reaching the legal age to drink or to vote.

Courtship and engagement begin a new round of customs that may lead to marriage, the most tradition-regulated personal ceremony in American life, or, more recently, to other arrangements of living together that may have their own folk traditions. Here, time has changed but not diminished the role of folklore. Couples formerly were granted the family parlor or porch swing for courting; today they have the automobile. Bundling as a courting custom gave way to "necking" or "petting" in the 1940s and 1950s, "making out" and "scoring" later. Ice-cream socials or church "sings" were replaced by drive-ins (both movies and restaurants). Customs of "going Dutch," "blind dates," "double-dating," "study dates," and the like depended on individual finances and desires as well as on local practices. "Going steady" with one partner became a well-entrenched dating pattern surrounded with customary devices for signaling whether one is attached or free (exchanging rings, leaving certain buttons or buckles open, placement of jewelry, etc.). But under the influence of feminism by the late 1960s women were less often willing to display signs of "belonging" to a male, and they were as likely to initiate dates as to wait to be asked. In some high schools and colleges a so-called "virgin pin" was worn, supposedly indicating by its position or shape whether a girl was or wasn't. Today the decline of a desire to "save one's virginity for marriage" has rendered the "virgin pin" obsolete;

instead, a lore of aphrodisiacs and folk birth-control methods circulates. Formally engaged couples still often have the time-payment diamond ring to advertise and seal their promises, but custom may decree the exchange of other special gifts as well.

Wedding customs begin with the "shower," often several of them, to emphasize different kinds of needed gifts. Shower parties are customarily for women only, although friends of the bridegroom may hold a "stag party" for him. Certain recreations are reserved exclusively for showers. A favorite is writing down the words of the future bride as she opens gifts. Her remarks are read aloud later as "what she will say to her husband on their wedding night."

Customs of the wedding itself are numerous and largely regulated by tradition. They include the dress of participants, the seating of guests, the choice of attendants, kissing the bride, throwing rice, playing pranks on the married couple, and decorating the car. Some of the more esoteric wedding customs originated in the Old World. The passing of the bride's shoe around in order to collect money from the guests is known in one form or another in several European countries. When the advice columnist Abigail Van Buren ("Dear Abby") once asked her readers for an explanation, she got at least half a dozen different responses: people claimed that the custom was German (money for the bride), French (for the cook), Polish (for the couple or for the first-baby's crib), Hungarian (as payment to dance with the bride), and Yugoslavian (so the husband would have to match the amount collected, give it to the bride, and thus prove he was not flat broke). The varying explanations, of course, may be regarded as part of the folklore of the custom.

Noisy harrassment of brides and bridegrooms is an old custom in the United States. First it was the "shivaree," derived from the Old World word and custom of the "charivari." A crowd of friends and neighbors would awaken a bridal couple with "rough music" and shouting, subjecting them to various indignities, and pestering them until the husband surrendered and provided refreshments. The shivaree was also known as "belling," "warmer," "serenade," "collathump," "skimmilton," and "going for a one-way ride" (dropping the groom off far from home). In 1946, a folklore journal reported that a recently married couple in Oregon was awakened and the husband dunked in a rain barrel, then forced to push his wife around in a wheelbarrow while the celebrants threw firecrackers at him; afterward he was expected to treat the crowd to refreshments. Many Americans can describe similar customs firsthand, and shivarees still occur, but the typical custom today is to decorate and sabotage the honeymoon car. Crepe-paper decorations, signs on the car, additives to the gasoline, a note in the fueltank cap ("Help, I'm being kidnapped!") are among the usual tricks. Car inscriptions may include pictures, sayings, ribald rhymes, hearts and arrows (similar to tree carvings), and such formulas as "$1 + 1 = 3$." Sometimes pranks are directed at the newlyweds' home. A favorite is removing the labels from all of their canned goods or tying bells to their bedsprings.

Once children begin to arrive, the birth customs start anew. Baby showers for the mother-to-be, for example, have as much tradition associated with them as bridal showers. The refreshments, decorations, kinds of gifts "showered" on the woman, and the games played are all likely to be suggested by folk practices. Favorite games may be based on buying baby needs (often requiring unscrambling letters that spell out "powder," "diapers," etc.) or naming the baby (sometimes asking the players to construct appropriate names out of the letters of the parents' names). Such recreations are mimeographed or photocopied and passed from mother to mother through the years. Another favorite practice at baby showers is to try the folk prognostication to determine the sex of the unborn child using observation (the way the baby is being carried or how the mother-to-be moves), magic (i.e., with a ring or needle suspended on a thread), or pseudo-science (the test with Drāno that is wet with the woman's urine).

Customs associated with death are generally fraught with suggestions of fear or superstition. Pouring water out of vases, covering mirrors, and stopping the clocks in a house in which death has occurred seem to mask some superstitious fear. Draping the furniture in the room in which a corpse lies or leaving the digging tools by the grave for some days after the burial are marks of respect—or propitiation. The custom of "telling the bees" about a death in the family lest the insects swarm and fly away is the subject of a poem by John Greenleaf Whittier (1807–1892). Sometimes the disposal of the small personal belongings of the deceased is governed by custom rather than a formal will, and many families commemorate the anniversaries of a beloved's passing by printing annual poems or notices in the classified columns of a newspaper. In some communities the funeral is organized by a traditionally appointed "arranger"; Southern and Southwestern writers have described family or community "decoration days," "memorial days," or days for "graveyard working" on which people gather at the cemetery for clean-up work and to remember those who have passed away. Special foods may be served, and the names of those who died since the last memorial day are read aloud.

Other Customs

Apart from the cycle of life and the "rites of passage," customs tend to cluster around work, recreation, or social events. Family reunions (in Utah, also "missionary reunions"), "Old Home Weeks," and "Homecomings" may be structured around special customs, foods, or entertainments. Communal-labor parties, important to frontier survival, have largely disappeared from American life, except in recent experimental communities or among such religious sects as the Amish, who have deliberately maintained them. But in the past there was a great variety of work parties—quilting bees, apple peelings, corn shuckings, ice cuttings, log rollings, house raisings, turkey drives, rabbit drives (followed by a community "rabbit dance"), and threshings.

A weekly domestic work ritual of the past is described in the following text from North Carolina, which may actually be a modern creation projected back in time and employing quaint terms and spellings:

WASHDAY RECEET

1. bilt fire in backyard to heet kettle of rain water.
2. set tubs so smoke won't blow in eyes if wind is pert.
3. shave one hole cake lie soap in bilin water.
4. sort things. make three piles. 1 pile white, 1 pile cullord, 1 pile work britches and rags.
5. stir flour in cold water to smooth, then thin down with billin water. rub dirty sheets on board, scrub hard, then bile. Rub cullard, don't bile, just rench in starch.
6. spread tee towels on grass.
7. hang old rags on fence.
8. pore rench water in flour beds
9. scrub porch with hot soapy water.
10. turn tubs upside down to dreen.

In later years the typical washday routine required only that each housewife had her clean laundry hanging on the line to dry every Monday, preferably earlier than any other woman on the block. Today we simply do the wash when we wish to, and we do it entirely inside the house. But perhaps a weekly washing of the car has to some degree substituted for the older washday custom.

Nowadays, although neighbors may willingly "pitch in" to help others in emergencies, these are spontaneous and improvised occasions, usually not traditional ones. One such communal-aid tradition, still fairly common in small-town neighborhoods, is the so-called "pound party" in which every participant brings a pound of some commodity to help set up housekeeping for a new neighbor or preacher. An urban counterpart is the Harlem "rent party." Certain occupations, such as auctioneering, livestock trading, rodeo work, and the like have rich traditional backgrounds, and many continuing folk practices are associated with them.

Most traditional American frontier amusements were lost or greatly altered in later years. No longer do we enjoy the likes of "bear baiting" or "gander pulling" as recreations. Dogfighting and cockfighting still persists illegally, while target-shooting matches ("turkey shoots," etc.) have changed their character to survive. Spelling bees, hay rides, taffy pulls, and ice-cream socials survive to some degree. Hunting and fishing are still very popular pursuits and retain some customary traces, such as marking the forehead of the hunter with the blood of his first kill or having the game divided among the participants of the hunt by a blindfolded outsider. Traditions have also developed in modern sports and children's games: choosing sides by odd or even fingers, choosing the server in tennis by spinning the racket, rallying for the serve in Ping-pong, deciding the order of play in baseball by placing hand over hand on the bat, tossing a coin for the kick-off in football.

Calendar Customs

Calendar customs in the United States cluster around a few annual events, unlike those in Europe that are linked to many more occasions. (Large collections of British folklore have been devoted to descriptions of nothing but such customs.) American tradition has retained few Old World celebrations and has originated even fewer native ones. In chronological summary, the common American calendar customs may be listed as follows: *St. Patrick's Day,* wearing green; *April Fool's Day,* playing pranks; *Easter,* dyeing eggs and wearing new clothes; *May Day,* giving "May baskets"; *Independence Day,* shooting fireworks and giving patriotic speeches; *Halloween,* "trick or treating"; *Christmas,* caroling and hanging mistletoe; *New Years' Eve,* attending a "watch party" at which there is much noisemaking and general congratulations at the stroke of midnight. Other holidays on the American calendar—whether religious, patriotic, or folk in origin—tend to have only sporadic or commercially stereotyped customs associated with them. *Valentine's Day* card exchanging is a good example, for without the elementary schools' and the merchants' emphasis of it, the custom would probably long since have died out. *Ground Hog Day* can hardly be thought of as an occasion for folk celebration, since practically the only observance of it nowadays is in newspaper feature articles. *Mother's Day* and *Father's Day* are officially established occasions only for further gift giving; but another such holiday, *Labor Day*, has become the traditional time in some regions for "closing the summer cottage" or ending the season with one last beach party.

Halloween, one of the favorite folk holidays for American children, has suffered an image problem recently as stories (some, undoubtedly, just legends) circulate annually about tainted foods being given to children. The "razor blades in apples" stories, coupled with actual crimes like the 1982 Tylenol killings, have made parents wary of sending their children out on the streets to go from door to door trick or treating on Halloween. Thus, in many communities other activities are substituted or else special hotlines or x-ray units are made available for reporting suspicious foods or checking the foods before they are eaten.

The most typical and original American holiday is certainly Thanksgiving—a combination of the traditional European peasant harvest festival and the first New England settlers' day of giving thanks to God. The Pilgrims' "first Thanksgiving" so often depicted had more of the former character than the latter, while the special meal we eat on Thanksgiving nowadays is more Victorian than colonial in its choice of foods and modes of preparation. The televised professional football games of today's holiday had their counterparts in the games and contests of early New England holidays.

Other festive gatherings in which the sharing of food promotes social interaction are not tied to a calendar date the way Thanksgiving is. Folklorist Linda T. Humphrey has proposed distinguishing from calendric events, work-centered gatherings, and fund raisings (like box socials) such "Small Group Festive Gatherings" (SGFGs) as picnics, potlucks, taffy pulls, fish fries, and cocktail parties. Sociability alone is the purpose of SGFGs, and to her list we may easily add office parties, après-ski activities, tailgate parties, wine tastings, progressive dinners (each course served in a different home), gatherings to watch television specials or to view videotapes of favorite movies, mortgage burnings, TGIF parties, sack-lunch breaks from work, and divorce celebrations.

Folk Festivals

There is little more to distinguish calendar customs from true **folk festivals,** perhaps, than the degree of community involvement in them and the elaboration of celebrations.

The religious folk dramas to be mentioned in Chapter 16 and the aspects of folk religion discussed in Chapter 14 may also be considered in the context of folk festivals. Some of the most interesting American festivals are immigrant-group seasonal traditions uniquely developed in the United States. The commercialized Mardi Gras of New Orleans, for example, is much more elaborate and sophisticated than most Old World carnival days or than the traditional celebration in some parts of rural Louisiana, where a party of masked riders travels from farm to farm singing and begging for food. The processions of the *penitente* brotherhood (carrying Christ's cross and receiving His whippings on their own backs), which originated in Spain centuries ago, differ markedly in the American Spanish Southwest, where they have evolved along new lines, even absorbing some Indian elements. The gradual change in the nature of Czech and Slovak harvest festivals as they were revived and sustained in the United States is typical of other such efforts at retention of Old World celebrations. Here, because the participants were no longer farmers, the spontaneous community ritual of Europe became a well-organized public drama with clearly defined actors and spectators. Whether there are any purely American festivals is uncertain, but probably the best case could be made for the rodeo. All others seem to have clear foreign prototypes: the county fair with harvest festivals, the circus with its ancient Roman ancestor, the family reunion with tribal and clan gatherings.

One unusual American celebration, probably derived from German festivals, is the "New Year's Shoot," as it is called in

North Carolina, or the "New Year's Sermon" of Missouri. A party of riders travels from house to house, beginning at midnight of New Year's Eve, pausing at each one for the leader or "preacher" to deliver a set speech. Afterward, firearms are discharged and the party is invited into the house for a treat. The custom has elements in it common to English "mumming," which is still found in vigorous tradition in Nova Scotia, and resembles the customs of "belsnickles and shanghais" followed in the late nineteenth century in Virginia. The procedure is also very much like the country Mardi Gras of Cajun Louisiana, and has a dim parallel perhaps in the traditional Southern holiday greeting "Christmas gift!"

The observance of Passover by East European Jews in the United States is one of the few imported festivals that has been systematically compared to its original form. The changes are characteristic of America—the traditional "search for leaven," formerly conducted with a candle and a quill, is now performed with a flashlight and brush; shopping for new clothing replaces the "visit to the tailor"; the ritual cleansing of dishes and utensils is rendered unnecessary by ownership of a special set of them for exclusive holiday use; and the careful handwork in the baking of matzoh has been automated out of existence by the invention of the matzoh machine. New quasi customs have appeared in the United States—the "Third Seder" (Passover meal) held outside the family circle, individual brand-preferences among the various commercially prepared Passover foods, new games played with the traditional old-country food (nuts), and songs sung in English (including the black spiritual "Go Down, Moses") after the Seder.

A further transplanting of holiday celebrations is exhibited in the Americanized Christmas customs that took root in Japan as early as the middle of the nineteenth century and flourished there, especially since the Allied Occupation following World War II. So pervasive is the celebration now that it is even marked on calendars issued by Shinto and Buddhist organizations, and there have been proposals either to make Christmas a new national holiday or to designate December 25 as "International Goodwill Day." Japanese merchants display Christmas decorations; families put up Christmas trees, or printed pictures of them; Christmas carols are played, parties held, and gifts exchanged. Lacking a fireplace chimney on which to attach their Christmas stockings, many Japanese children find presents placed near their pillows in the morning. Some youngsters, however, fasten their stockings on the pipe of the bathroom stove on Christmas Eve.

The term "folk festival" has been applied since the 1930s in the United States to annually sponsored public performances of folklore, generally folksongs and dances. Folklorists are increasingly attending them, studying them, planning them, and even taking part in some of them. Only on the current folk-festival stage have the folk, the folklore enthusiast, and the folklorist all met face to face and begun to try to understand one another in some depth. The oldest consecutive folk festival is the "National Folk Festival," first held in St. Louis in 1934 with strictly American performers but eventually branching out into all manner of immigrant and "ethnic" acts. Other festivals have sprung up (and some have died) faster than folklorists can make up their minds about how to regard them; these have ranged from glossy extravaganzas with celebrity performers to the rustic "Arkansas Folk Festival" in Mountain View, Arkansas, with its still largely home-grown talent and audience. Another development in the revivalist folk-festival field, and a very promising one, is the appearance of university-sponsored annual events (at the University of Chicago and the University of California at Los Angeles, for instance), where the enthusiastic collegiate folklore buff can rub elbows and share ideas with academic students of folklore and with practitioners of the genuine material itself. The Smithsonian Institution's "Festival of American Folklife," founded in 1967, has also successfully combined education with entertainment by employing folklorists and folklore students to locate talented folk artisans and performers who are brought to Washington, D.C., for the annual event.

BIBLIOGRAPHIC NOTES

Funk & Wagnalls Standard Dictionary of Folklore, Mythology, and Legend, often a good guide for separate genres of folklore, has no general headings for either customs or festivals. The index to the *Journal of American Folklore* groups "Customs, Beliefs, and Superstitions," but the articles cited are mostly about superstitions. The annual bibliographies once published by the American Folklore Society used the heading "Customs," placing under it "Festivals and Rites of Passage," but also "Social Relationships, Planting, etc." The Swiss folklorist and museum director Robert Wildhaber included a section on customs in his "Bibliographical Introduction to American Folklife," *NYFQ* 21 (1965): 259–302. He also discussed the European concept of "folklife" in his introduction.

William Graham Sumner introduced the term "folkways" in his classic book of that title (Boston, Mass.: Ginn and Co., 1907; Mentor Book paperback, 1960). He outlined the basic process of customs becoming "mores" (another term he coined) and mores becoming laws. Theodore Blegen urged historians' attention to "traditional beliefs, customs, folk art, ideas, and practices" in his *Grass Roots History* (Minneapolis: University of Minnesota Press, 1947). His section on "Pioneer Folkways" (pp. 81–102) demonstrated the approach with data from Norwegian-American immigrant life.

Paul G. Brewster edited "Beliefs and Customs" for the *Frank C. Brown Collection of North Carolina Folklore* (vol. 1: pp. 221–82). However, not only beliefs, but also material folklore are described; most of the customs that appear here are related to superstitions. Wayland D. Hand seems to have used most of the same items plus many more in volumes 6 and 7 of the same collection, "Popular Beliefs and Superstitions," in some cases citing as the only comparative reference the identical item in volume 1. Hand's article "Anglo-American Folk Belief and Custom: The Old World's Legacy to the New," in *JFI* 7 (1970): 136–55, is a good example of thorough annotation of customary lore, using as examples mainly the "dumb cake" or "dumb supper" customs.

Three chapters in Everett Dick's *Sod-House Frontier, 1854–1890* (Lincoln, Neb.: Johnsen Pub. Co., 1954) illustrate the treasury of customs to be found in some social histories. They are Chapter 20, "Sports"; Chapter 26, "Amusements"; and Chapter 35, "Crude Frontier Customs." A few special collections of customs exist: Afton Wynn's "Pioneer Folk Ways," *PTFS* 13 (1937): 190–238; Louise Pound's "Old Nebraska Folk Customs," *NH* 28 (1947): 3–31, reprinted in *Nebraska Folklore*, pp. 184–208; and "Customs," by S. J. Sackett, pp. 182–208 of *Kansas Folklore*, ed. Sackett (Lincoln: University of Nebraska Press, 1961). Norbert F. Riedl and Carol K. Buckles compiled a bibliography and an interesting study of "House Customs and Beliefs in East Tennessee" published in *TFSB* 41 (1975): 47–56. In "The Finlinson Family Reunion Tradition," *AFFWord* 4 (Spring 1974): 37–39, Jill Kelly describes a typical Mormon family celebration taking place in Oak City, Utah.

Allen Walker Read outlined the background of an American school custom in his article "The Spelling Bee: A Linguistic Institution of the American Folk," *PMLA* 56 (1941): 495–512. Iona and Peter Opie, in *The Lore and Language of Schoolchildren* (New York: Oxford University Press, 1959), give a "Children's Calendar" and describe British children's "Occasional Customs" (pp. 232–305), some of which have parallels among American children. Herbert Halpert discussed the custom of sending "chain letters" in *WF* 15 (1956): 287–89; Alan Dundes added a foreign reference and provided further examples in an article in *NWF* 1 (Winter 1966): 14–19; and Michael J. Preston traces some examples back to the 1930s in the United States and earlier in Europe in an article in *TFSB* 42 (1976): 1–14 (Preston is the only author to analyze the mathematics involved in the chain letters' promises of riches).

An essay by Julia Woodbridge Oxreider, "The Slumber Party: Transition into Adolescence," *TFSB* 43 (1977): 128–34, is a rare one taking up a traditional ritual/recreation of young American women on the threshold of maturity. She discusses games, songs, dances, and the pranks played on the first one to fall asleep.

Courtship and wedding customs in Utah were listed by Thomas E. Cheney in *WF* 19 (1960): 106, and some from the Ohio Valley were discussed by Lawrence S. Thompson in *KFR* 9 (1963): 47–50. Some modern campus courtship rituals of the kind discussed in the Appendix are the subject of Michael J. Preston's "The Traditional Ringing at Temple Buell College," *WF* 32 (1973): 271–74. Another aspect of wedding lore appears in Joyce Thompson and Phyllis Bridges, "West Texas Wedding Cars," *WF* 30 (1971): 123–26. One article on ethnic-group customs is Philip V. R. Tilney, "The Immigrant Macedonian Wedding in Ft. Wayne," *IF* 3 (1970): 3–34. E. Bagby Atwood discussed "Shivarees and Charivaris: Variations on a Theme," in *PTFS* 32 (1964): 64–71. Other discussions of the history of the term and its variations appeared in *AS* 8 (1933): 22–26, and *AS* 15 (1940): 109–10. The 1946 Oregon shivaree was described by Rex Gunn in "An Oregon Charivari," *WF* 13 (1954): 206–7.

On the customary aspects of American funerals and cemeteries, see such works as Lawrence S. Thompson's "Rites of Sepulcher in the Bluegrass," *KFR* 9 (1963): 25–28; J. Frank Lee's "The Informal Organization of White Southern Protestant Funerals: The Role of the Arranger," *TFSB* 33 (1967): 36–40; and Donald B. Ball's "Social Activities Associated with Two Rural Cemeteries in Coffee County, Tennessee," *TFSB* 41 (1975): 93–98. Kentucky family memorial ceremonies have been described in Thelma Lynn Lamkin's "Spring Hill Decoration Day," *MF* 3 (1953): 157–60, and Harry Harrison Kroll's "Licking River Revisited," *SFQ* 26 (1962): 246–51. Similar traditions from other regions are found in Ted-Larry Pebworth's "Graveyard-Working: The Passing of a Custom," *LFM* 2 (August 1961): 44–49, and Robert Cowser,

"Community Memorial Day Observances in Northeast Texas," *WF* 31 (1972): 120–21.

The following works treat various occupational customs: Henning Henningsen, *Crossing the Equator* (Copenhagen: Munksgaard, 1961); Wayland D. Hand, "The Folklore, Customs, and Traditions of the Butte Miner," *CFQ* 5 (1946): 1–25; and Donald J. Ward, "The 'Carny' in the Winter" [carnival concessions workers], *WF* 21 (1962): 190–92. Articles on traditional group work customs include William Marion Miller, "A Threshing Ring in Southern Ohio," *HF* 5 (1946): 3–13; Mrs. Arthur Turner, "Turkey Drives: South Mississippi, Greene County," *MFR* 3 (1969): 31–32; David Rhys Roberts, "Ice Harvesting," *NYFQ* 26 (1970): 114–26; and Celia M. Benton, "Corn Shuckings in Sampson County," *NCFJ* 22 (1974): 131–39. Studies of food-gathering occupations from water sources are Diane Tebbetts, "Earl Ott: Fishing on the Arkansas," *MSF* 5 (1977): 101–12, and Paul Valvo, "Clamming in the Great South Bay," *NYF* 1 (1975): 169–82.

Auctioneer's traditions are collected in William Hugh Jansen's "Down Our Way: Who'll Bid Twenty?" *KFR* 2 (1956): 113–21; Anne Marsh and William Aspinall, Jr., "Harold E. Leightley: Portrait of an Auctioneer and His Craft," *KFQ* 16 (1971): 133–50; William R. Ferris, Jr., "Ray Lum: Muletrader," *NCFJ* 21 (1973): 105–19; and Mac E. Barrick, "The Folklore Repertory of a Pennsylvania Auctioneer," *KF* 19 (1974): 27–42. Further examples of Ray Lum's lore, also reported by William Ferris, appeared in *MSF* 6 (1978): 15–26 and 43–50. A survey of Indiana auctioneering, ". . . No Two Sales the Same," was published by Phyllis Harrison in *IF* 12 (1979): 101–19. A similar form of commercial tradition was treated by Alex S. Freedman in "Garage Sale Folklore," *NYF* 2 (1976): 167–76.

Other aspects of occupational lore—still a largely unexplored field —are found in Don Boles, "Some Gypsy Occupations in America," *JGLS* 37 (1958): 103–10; Sandra Bennett, "Rodeo," *AFFWord* 2 (Sept. 1972): 1–10; and Albert B. Friedman, "The Scatological Rites of Burglars," *WF* 27 (1968): 171–79.

For three systematic and detailed presentations of a highly ritualized and illegal sporting event, see Gerald E. Parsons, Jr., "Cockfighting: A Potential Field of Research," *NYFQ* 25 (1969): 265–88; Steven L. Del Sesto, "Roles, Rules, and Organization: A Descriptive Account of Cockfighting in Rural Louisiana," *SFQ* 39 (1975): 1–14; and Charles R. Gunter, Jr., "Cockfighting in East Tennessee and Western North Carolina" *TFSB* 44 (1978): 160–69.

The American Book of Days by George William Douglas (1938); rev. ed. by Helen Douglas Compton, New York: H. W. Wilson, 1948) is a useful reference source on American holidays, their origins and celebration. George R. Stewart's chapter on holidays (pp. 222–48) in his completely engaging book *American Ways of Life* (Garden City, N.Y.:

Dolphin paperback, 1954) is the best single essay on the subject. Kelsie B. Harder's note "Just an April Fool," *TFSB* 27 (1961):5–7, describes the custom of sending April Fool letters. On another holiday see Maurice A. Mook, "Halloween in Central Pennsylvania," *KFQ* 14 (1969): 124–29, and Catharine Harris Ainsworth, "Hallowe'en," *NYFQ* 29 (1973): 163–93. The best work on a single holiday is undoubtedly Venetia Newall's *An Egg at Easter, a Folklore Study* (Bloomington: Indiana University Press, 1971), while the best general essay on the larger topic is Robert J. Smith's chapter "Festivals and Celebrations," in *Folklore and Folklife: An Introduction*, ed. Richard M. Dorson (Chicago: University of Chicago Press, 1972), pp. 159–72.

The Louisiana Federal Writers Project publication *Gumbo Ya Ya*, ed. Lyle Saxon, Edward Dreyer, and Robert Tallant (Boston: Houghton Mifflin, 1945), has much interesting information on superstitions, customs, and festivals of that state. Two general books on foreign festivals in the United States do not carefully distinguish natural survivals from self-conscious revivals, but they are, nevertheless, informative: Allen H. Eaton's *Immigrant Gifts to American Life* (New York: Russell Sage Foundation, 1932), and Helen R. Coates's *The American Festival Guide* (New York: Exposition Press, 1956). The "Festival Issue" of *WF* was 31:4 (1972); it contains studies of four regions.

Articles on individual foreign festivals in the United States have appeared with some frequency in the journal of the California Folklore Society; these include Wayland D. Hand's *"Schweizer Schwingen:* Swiss Wrestling in California," *CFQ* 2 (1943): 77–84; William Hoy's "Native Festivals of the California Chinese," *WF* 7 (1948): 240–50; Charles Speroni's "California Fishermen's Festivals," *WF* 14 (1955): 77–91; and Father John B. Terbovich's "Religious Folklore among the German-Russians in Ellis County, Kansas," *WF* 22 (1963): 79–88. In another journal, see Roslynn Plemer, "The Feast of St. Joseph," *LFM* 2 (Aug. 1968): 85–90. A similar subject treated in booklength form and fully illustrated with photographs is *The Amish Year* by Charles S. Rice and Rollin C. Steinmetz (New Brunswick; N.J.: Rutgers University Press, 1956).

Two original essays on Louisiana Cajun customary life were included in Richard M. Dorson's *Buying the Wind:* Harry Oster's "Country Mardi Gras" (pp. 274–81) and Calvin Claudel's "Folkways of Avoyelles Parish" (pp. 235–45). John Rowe described "Cornish Emigrants in America" and their traditions in *Folk Life* 3 (1965): 25–38. For another group's traditions see Norine Dresser, "'Is It Fresh?' An Examination of Jewish-American Shopping Habits," *NYFQ* 27 (1971): 153–60.

Penitente ceremonies are treated in George C. Barker's "Some Aspects of Penitential Processions in Spain and the American Southwest," *JAF* 70 (1957): 137–42; Juan Hernandez's "Cactus Whips and Wooden Crosses," *JAF* 76 (1963): 216–24; and Marta Weigle's book

Brothers of Light, Brothers of Blood (Albuquerque: University of New Mexico Press, 1976). Svatava Pirkova-Jakobson described "Harvest Festivals among Czechs and Slovaks in America," in *JAF* 69 (1956): 266–80.

Shooting the anvil, a noisy custom once commonly practiced in American communities to celebrate various holidays, was the subject of a study by Bill Harrison and Charles Wolfe in *TFSB* 43 (1977): 1–13. One blacksmith's anvil was placed atop another with gunpowder between them; ignition provided a satisfyingly ear-splitting bang. The North Carolina "New Year's Shoot" is included in Brewster's chapter in *North Carolina Folklore* (vol. 1, pp. 241–43). H. M. Belden gave a partial text of the Missouri "New Year's Sermon" in *Ballads and Songs Collected by the Missouri Folk-Lore Society*, University of Missouri Studies 15 (Columbia, 1940), p. 514. Ruth H. Cline described "Belsnickles and Shanghais," in *JAF* 71 (1958): 164–65. For information on similar celebrations in various states see Walter L. Robbins's note "Christmas Shooting Rounds in America and Their Background," *JAF* 86 (1973): 48–52. On related traditions see Charles E. Welch, Jr., " 'Oh Dem Golden Slippers': The Philadelphia Mummers Parade," *JAF* 79 (1966): 523–36, and Herbert Halpert and G. M. Story, eds., *Christmas Mumming in Newfoundland* (Toronto: University of Toronto Press, 1969).

John F. Moe in "Folk Festivals and Community Consciousness: Categories of the Festival Genre," *FF* 10 (1977): 33–40, proposes three large groupings of festivals—participatory (such as haying, marriages, and Thanksgiving dinner), semiparticipatory (such as community fairs and bluegrass festivals), and nonparticipatory (such as the Smithsonian Institution's festivals of American folklife). In an article on what he calls the "protofestival," John A. Gutowski traces the origins of a particular Midwestern community celebration as an example of an emerging festival. See *JFI* 15 (1978): 113–32. Linda T. Humphrey's essay on "Small Group Festive Gatherings" (SGFGs), referred to in this chapter, appeared in *JFI* 16 (1979): 190–201.

At the same time that many folk festivals seem to be fading out, American folklorists are finding them interesting to study. Three recent publications are Laurel Doucette's "Folk Festival: The Gatineau Valley Church Picnic," *C&T* 1 (1976): 55–62; Richard Blaustein's "The Old Time Country Radio Reunion: A Different Kind of Folk Festival," *TFSB* 47 (1981): 105–18; and James L. Evans's "Frog Jumping Contests," *MFSJ* 3 (1981): 3–28.

Beatrice S. Weinreich analyzed "The Americanization of Passover" in *Studies in Biblical and Jewish Folklore*, ed. Raphael Patai and others, Indiana University Folklore Series no. 13 (Bloomington, 1960), pp. 329–66.

John E. Baur's *Christmas on the American Frontier, 1800–1900* (Caldwell, Idaho: Caxton Press, 1961) sketches a broad view of the adaptation of European customs in the American wilderness; Elizabeth Bacon Custer, widow of General Custer, described her own Western army-camp Christmases in a manuscript edited by Walter F. Peterson as "Christmas on the Plains" and published in *TAW* 1 (Fall 1964): 52–57. David W. Plath studied "The Japanese Popular Christmas: Coping with Modernity" in *JAF* 76 (1963): 309–17. The November 1971 issue of *NCF* (19:4) contains several articles on Christmas customs and beliefs in North Carolina. Sue Samuelson's *Christmas: An Annotated Bibliography* (New York: Garland, 1982) is essential for research on this holiday. Santa Claus should bring us similar works on many other holidays. For a Mexican-American Catholic Christmas festival, see Mary MacGregor-Villarreal's "Celebrating *Los Posados* in Los Angeles," *WF* 39 (1980): 71–105.

Sarah Gertrude Knott, a founder and leading force of the National Folk Festival, described her early problems and experiences with it in "The National Folk Festival after Twelve Years," *CFQ* 5 (1946): 83–93. An address by Stith Thompson on "Folklore and Folk Festivals" delivered to the annual conference of the National Folk Festival Association in 1953 was published in *MF* 4 (1954): 5–12.

A local folk music festival and its folkloristic significance is analyzed in Barre Toelken's "Traditional Fiddling in Idaho," *WF* 24 (1965): 259–62. Gerald Weales wrote a humorous description of the 1952 Georgia Tech Homecoming Game as "an annual semi-religious festival" in his article "Ritual in Georgia," *SFQ* 21 (1957): 104–9. His observations on dress, symbols, decoration, the parade, cheers, and ecstatic responses to the game would apply easily to many other American sporting events.

16
Folk Dances and Dramas

Dances and dramas began in ritual and developed into entertainment. They have, in common with superstitions, customs, festivals, and games, significant oral and behavioral elements. Both dance and drama are essentially performances in which participants assume certain active roles, but also utter the speeches and songs, or sometimes directions, which accompany the action. Dance has been associated with drama since its ancient origins, so it may not be stretching Aristotle's definition too far to suggest that the list of six elements he proposed for the drama could fit dance almost as well: action, character, thought, language, spectacle, and music. To some degree, the student of folk dances and dramas will be concerned with all of these elements, as well as with such other aspects as structure, function, dissemination, and variation.

American folk dances and dramas have always constituted a decidedly minor field of folklore research. Folk dances in this country persist largely as a recent revival (even though a lively one), while folk dramas, replaced by commercial entertainments, are represented only in a few amateur forms or as survivals. However, even with these limitations, there are questions that remain unanswered, reference works that should be compiled, theories awaiting better analysis, and even some further collecting that might be done in the Anglo-American field. Many more opportunities for research appear if the scope is broadened to include ethnic and immigrant dances in this country.

Folk Dances

"The dance," wrote Curt Sachs, historian of the subject, "is the mother of the arts." In its basic form of a rhythmic, stylized pattern of individual or group movement performed with or without music in response to a religious or creative urge, dance has existed in every known culture, including the most primitive, and it occurs even among animals. From the movements of dancing, Sachs suggested, were derived the other means of artistic expression, all of which eventually drifted away from close involvement with worship and the cycle of life to their current connections largely with self-expression and entertainment. **Folk dances** are those dances that are transmitted in a traditional manner, whatever their origin, and that have developed traditional variants, whatever their other developments. Perhaps more than in any other field of folklore, such distinctions are extremely difficult to apply. Probably it is best, as Curt Sachs suggested, for ethnological purposes to treat all dances equally.

Gertrude P. Kurath, the leading American student of primitive dance, distinguished primitive dance from folk dance in terms of the relationship of dancing to the rest of a given culture: "Natural cultures dance from the cradle to the grave; mechanized society, for sociability and diversion." Certainly this holds true in the United States, for although we still hold dances as a matter of custom at graduations, holidays, and weddings, all of our dancing, whether folk or not, is performed for "sociability and diversion" and not as ritual. Still, the potential student of folk dance has a good deal to learn from the authority on primitive dance.

Kurath has answered very specifically the questions "What does a field worker record during the study of native dances?" and "What can a non-specialist do in the presence of unexpected festivities?" The three fundamental matters to observe, she said, are the *ground plan* (location, participants, arrangements, geometry, progression), the *body movements* (steps, posture, arms), and the *structure* (repetition, combination). Observations should be made in the above order, and the observer finally should participate in the dance he or she is describing, especially for the fullest understanding of its structure.

Complex systems of precise dance notation have been created, perhaps the most widely accepted and elaborate being the "Labanotation" invented by Rudolf von Laban in 1920. For the nonspecialist collector, the minimal technique required is simply the employment of camera or sketch pad whenever possible, and the consistent use of a standardized vocabulary for descriptions. As Kurath has shown, such a term as "step" is misleading and vague, unless the collector distinguishes such variations as the shuffle, run, trot, slide, gallop, skip, leap, jump, and hop. The last three terms can serve to illustrate just how precise dance descriptions should be, for a *leap* is springing from one foot to the other, a *jump* is springing up with both feet simultaneously and landing on both feet, and a *hop* is springing up on one foot and landing on the same foot again.

Given an interest in collecting folk dances and having established a list of questions and a vocabulary for field use, what is there for the modern student of American folk dance to observe? Regrettably, there is little in a purely traditional context. The two primary forms of Americanized folk dances—square dances and play-parties—had died out in most localities by the 1930s. A few dance *songs* were later popularized by professional folk singers, and square dancing has enjoyed a vigorous revival as an organized recreation, but neither of these developments is part of a true folk process. As a result, American folk-dance scholars must often content themselves with investigating the nature of the revival movement itself or devote themselves to discovering, analyzing, and classifying historic accounts of folk dancing. Native Americans and immigrant groups still provide opportunities for field work in dance ethnography, as do regional styles of social dancing. Even the lore of professional dance companies, which deals with dance rehearsal and performance, might be studied. None of these possibilities is without considerable folkloristic interest, and such studies ought not to be delayed longer.

Both square dances and play-parties developed from British traditions, the former from "country dances," and the latter seemingly from children's games. The terminology of early forms is badly confused. English **country dances** were usually either *rounds* (dancers standing in a circle) or *longways* (dancers in two lines facing each other). But the French, who had similar folk dances, associated the English word "country" with their term *"contre"* ("against") to produce the name *"contredanse"* for the "longways" type. The term then became Anglicized as "contradance." The country dances throughout Europe probably all represent, at least in part, inheritances via *gesunkenes Kulturgut* of such popular nineteenth-century social dances as the spirited *cotillion*, in which partners were exchanged, and the *quadrille*, a dance for four couples. Neither rounds nor longways persisted in American folk dancing proper, although both formations are found in children's games, and the still-popular "Virginia Reel" is a longways. It deserves mention that some traditional solo dancing—like clogging and tap dancing —exists, though the major folk types of American dance are the social dances for couples and larger groups. And despite the emphasis here on the older folk-dance forms, some attention should also be encouraged toward the various contemporary social dance forms such as disco and especially break dancing.

The **square dance** is an authentic American folk development of the Old World four-couple dance. The terms "New England Quadrille," "Kentucky Running Set," and "Cowboy Square Dance" indicate the principal centers of development—the Northeast, the Midwest and Southern mountains, and the Far West. The three most distinctive features of the square dance are the shuffling-gliding-running step, the handclapping done by both dancers and bystanders, and the chanted or sung "calls" giving directions for the steps. New England square dancing was rather restrained and formal, but the shuffling step or *sashay* (from French *chassé*, "dance") was already present. In the Midwest hand clapping was added, calls were formalized as part of the dance, and new figures such as "Birdy in the Cage" and "Grand Right and Left" became popular. The West introduced hybrid steps from other social dances for "sashaying," as well as the device of occasionally having boys lift their partners from the ground during the "swing." Eventually all of these movements backtracked and merged to a degree which renders it impossible to sort out the origins of such colorfully named figures as "Box the Gnat," "Georgia Rang Tang," "Dip for the Oyster," "Ocean Wave," "Shoot the Owl," "Grapevine Twist," and "Wring the Dishrag."

Play-Parties

In communities where religious influences prohibited all forms of dancing, as well as the sinful fiddle music which accompanied them, the play-party became popular as a substitute, at least according to the traditional explanation. **Play-parties** were usually organized as rounds rather than squares and were performed to songs sung by the participants themselves rather than to instrumental music and a caller. In most regions, waist swinging was forbidden, and boys held their partners by the hand instead. By such means the ban against dancing was circumvented. The terms employed for the two kinds of activities were kept carefully separated. Play-parties were "plays," "games," or even "bounce-arounds," and they were always "played," never "danced." But square-dancing parties were "hoedowns," "barn dances," "house dances," "kitchen dances," "shindigs," or even "hog wrassles." It should be emphasized that both of these kinds of activities were part of the social life of adults or adolescents of courting age, but not until recently were they held exclusively for children.

As ballroom couple-dancing became more acceptable and popular among Americans, square dances nearly died out before folklorists had a chance to collect them, and their organized revival, part of the general rise in folklore interest beginning in the late 1930s, was in full swing by the time scholars had begun to notice the form. Play-parties lasted longer in folk tradition but were not revived on a large scale. Also, the play-party song leaves more of a text to be remembered and collected than does the square-dance call. The result is that there are many more play-party songs and descriptions available in reliable folklore sources than there are accounts of square dances. The most

pressing need in square-dance studies is to uncover more published and unpublished early accounts of dances so that a better
idea of historical development may be gained. But in play-party
studies the time is ripe for a basic reference work to be compiled, along the lines of Child's great ballad anthology, in order
to organize and facilitate comparisons of the numerous play-
party texts already in print. Both endeavors would contribute to
the verification or replacement of the unproven play-party origin theory mentioned earlier.

Play-party movements and songs may seem simple and rather
repetitious, but they have been very popular in folk tradition
and have evolved into both children's games and fiddle tunes of
lasting popularity. The texts and formations themselves are not
without interest. A careful classification of play-parties would
have to take into account that a few of them are archway formations, longways, and even squares, as well as round games, and
that not all of them require only skipping around and singing—
some involve dialogue and dramatic action, choosing, kissing,
and progressive figures. Sometimes dance directions are embedded literally in the song, as in this one, called "Miller Boy":

> Happy is the miller boy, that lives by the mill;
> He takes his toll with a free good will.
> One hand in the hopper and the other in the sack,
> *The ladies step forward and the gents step back.*

The first three lines of the verse, it should be noted, contain a
traditional criticism of unscrupulous millers who extract a double toll from customers: "One hand in the hopper and the other
in the sack." And "Miller Boy" also stands up well as folk poetry; after a close study of this play-party—text, tune, and
dance—Keith Cunningham concluded that "the poetics fit the
action of the game."

In other play-parties, such as "Go in and out the Window"
and "The Needle's Eye," the dance movement is metaphori-
cally suggested. Some songs sketch a character type—"Captain
Jinks," "Old Dan Tucker," or "Cincinnati Girls"—while others
mirror frontier life—"Shoot the Buffalo," "Wait for the
Wagon," or "Weevily Wheat." A number of puzzling but

strangely effective lines and verses in old play-party songs have
yet to be explained. These include:

> Water, water, wine-flower
> Growing up so high.
> We are all young ladies,
> And we are sure to die.
>   (An American play-party derived from
>   the British children's game "Wallflowers.")
>   *
> Coffee grows in the white oak tree,
> The rivers run with brandy.
> My little gal is a blue-eyed gal,
> As sweet as any candy.
>   (The first line is the common title.)
>   *
> The higher up the cherry tree,
> The finer grow the cherries;
> The more you hug and kiss the girls,
> The sooner will they marry.
>   (From "Weevily Wheat.")

For pure, straightforward defiance of logic, however, nothing
can beat the popular line from "Skip to My Lou" that goes
"Little red wagon painted blue."

Sometimes a play-party or other dance song will tell a story
and thereby suggest an incipient ballad, or a dramatic game of
children. In the "Hog Drivers" play-party the players take the
roles of various characters. First, the hog drivers march in and
sing to a tavern keeper:

> Hog drivers, hog drivers, hog drivers are we,
> A-courting your daughter so fair and so free.
> Can we get lodging, here, oh here?
> Can we get lodging here?

To which he responds:

> I have a fair daughter who sits by my side,
> But no hog driver can get her for a bride.
> You can't get lodging here, oh here;
> You can't get lodging here.

The hog drivers then angrily sing:

> Fair is your daughter, but ugly yourself;
> We'll travel on farther and seek better wealth.
> We don't want lodging here, oh here;
> We don't want lodging here.

The conclusion of the play is that the tavern keeper's daughter whispers her choice of husband to her father, who then stops the hog drivers' march and allows the lucky young man to stay on. While this play-party is certainly related to other dramatic courtship games such as "Three Knights from Spain," it also reflects social life of eastern Tennessee and western North Carolina during the heyday of hog raising and driving in the late nineteenth century.

Another good example of a dramatic dance song is the following text collected in Edwardsville, Illinois, from an elderly woman who said it was verses for "Old Joe Clark." She sang it in a spirited manner to the tune often used for the dance song "Great Big 'Taters in Sandy Land" or "Sally Ann."

> "Hey, old man, where you been at?"
> "Down the mountainside shootin' craps."
>
> "I told you once, I told you twice,
> You can't make a livin' throwin' dice.
>
> "Get out of my house and go to town,
> Make that wooden leg jar the ground.
>
> "Sift your meal and save the bran,
> You can't make a livin' on rocky land."

The Dramatic Element in Folklore

The **dramatic element in folklore** has already been demonstrated several times in previous chapters. The Wellerism is a dramatic vignette containing both speech and action. Riddles involve two roles—the questioner's and the respondent's. In asking non-oral riddles, the poser adds a dramatic gesture to his question. Such riddle-jokes as the "knock-knocks" have separate speaking roles for each participant. The skillful narrator of folktales must impersonate many characters, and there are distinct dramatic techniques for narrating different kinds of tales —the deadpan of the tall-tale artist, the broken English of the dialect-joke raconteur, the imitative sounds of the animal-tale teller. One American fiddle tune, "The Arkansaw Traveler," has a dramatic skit associated with it. In this sketch, not to be confused with the ballad "An Arkansas Traveller" or "The State of Arkansaw" (Laws H 1), there is a dialogue between a man who gets lost traveling through the Arkansas countryside and a hill-billy fiddler that includes exchanges such as:

> Traveller: Where does this road go to?
> Fiddler: I been livin' here twenty years, and it ain't gone nowhere yet.
> Traveller: You're pretty dumb, aren't you?
> Fiddler: I ain't lost!

Most traditional ballads are dramatic, and those that are based on incremental repetition are usually related entirely in dialogue. A remarkable fluidity of dramatic form is illustrated in the American versions of "The Maid Freed from the Gallows" (Child 95). Here, a condemned girl is standing on the scaffold waiting to be hanged and repeatedly asking her relatives, and finally her sweetheart, if they have come to set her free or merely "to see me hanged on the gallow's tree." Tristram P. Coffin has observed:

> The story itself has taken a number of forms in America. It is, particularly with Negroes, popular as a drama and is also found as a children's game. It exists as a prose tale in the United States and West Indies and upon occasion has been developed as a cante fable.

Folk games, too, are often dramatic, as Chapter 18 will show. One game, "Mother, Mother, the Milk's Boiling Over," is a fairly complex playlet with ten distinct roles—mother, hired girl (or nurse), a thief (or witch), and seven children who are named for the days of the week. Each time the mother goes out, the thief distracts the hired girl and steals a child; the mother is summoned repeatedly by the cry "The milk's boiling over!" and she contrives, when the last child is gone, to win them all back, one by one, from the thief. In common with most older dramatic games, this one goes back to an English prototype. "Charades" is a popular parlor game that is entirely dramatic, while "Poppy Show" is an old amusement of little girls which consisted of arranging poppy petals between small sheets of glass and then charging one pin for a look; the showman chants:

> Pinny, pinny, poppy-show,
> Give me a pin and I'll let you know.

Folk Drama

Although the dramatic element in folklore is common, full-scale folk drama is less well known in the United States. **Folk drama** includes plays that are traditionally transmitted, usually for regular performance at such occasions as initiations, seasonal celebrations, festivals, and religious holidays. Traditional transmission, as with some folk rhymes, may in this case include handwritten manuscripts. To qualify as true drama, these performances must involve some imitation of actions (mimesis or mimicry), the assignment of roles among different players, and, of course, transmission in a folk group. What makes such pieces folkloric—whether preserved orally or in writing—is that they vary from region to region and generation to generation, that they originate in an unself-conscious folk milieu rather than from a sophisticated artistic background, and that they remain part of folk-group tradition.

One living tradition of folk drama in the United States is part of the religious pageantry of the Spanish Southwest, especially at Christmastime, but also at Easter. The Christmas play of the shepherds (*Los Pastores*) exists in the Southwest in many versions, and it has been collected and studied by three generations of American folklorists.

The traditional English Christmas drama, *The Mummers' Play*, with its masked band of begging participants, was known in the

New World in the eighteenth century. (It is further related to the New Year's "shoots" and "belsnickles" described in the previous chapter.) The drama itself, although still found in Canada, never became firmly established here as a folk custom; today's elaborate New Year's parade in Philadelphia is the only organized outgrowth of English mumming in the United States. The Philadelphia parade, which stems from traditional backgrounds, was granted official civic support in 1900. Only two instances of genuine mummers' *plays* have been recorded from American informants since then. The first was in 1909, when a text was collected in St. Louis from an immigrant from Worcestershire, England, who had taken part in it as a boy thirty-five years earlier.

The play had the familiar stock characters of the English tradition—Father Christmas, St. George, the Turkish Knight, the Italian Doctor, and others. The plot unfolds in the manner of a pageant, each grotesquely costumed character coming forth to announce himself before engaging in the simple ritualistic action, the sequence of which is suggested by the conventional identification of the parts as presentation, combat, lament, cure, and quête (the collection of a reward for the actors). In 1930 a group of Kentucky mountaineers performed a mummers' play for folklorist Marie Campbell to show her how these plays had formerly been acted. The announcer began with this revealing notice:

> We air now aiming to give a dumb show for to pleasure the little teacher for not going off to level country to keep Christmas with her kin. Hit ain't noways perfect the way we act this here dumb show, but hit ain't been acted out amongst our settlement for upward of twenty or thirty year, maybe more. I reckon folks all knows hit air bad luck to talk with the dumb show folks or guess who they air.

Few native American folk plays of any significance have developed. The use of the term for written dramas based on folk themes is misleading, but, beginning in the 1920s, a so-designated "school of folk drama" centered around the Carolina Playmakers at the University of North Carolina. Outstanding among this group's work were the plays of Paul Green, set in a regional framework, such as *In Abraham's Bosom* (1927) and *The House of Connelly* (1931). These plays, however, are literature, not folklore. Another group of outdoor dramas or pageants are sometimes billed as "folk" productions; these include *Tecumseh!* in Ohio, *The Stephen Foster Story* in Kentucky, *Vicksburg* in Mississippi, and a pageant about Joseph Smith in Palmyra, New York. Closer to the folk level are many nonliterary amateur church plays, Passion plays, parades, and small-town festivals.

A case might be made for the blackface minstrel show, the vaudeville, or the entertainments of some medicine shows, carnivals, and riverboats as American folk drama. But a better candidate is a now-obscure traveling tent comedy that still survives in some parts of the Midwest—the "Toby shows." Named for their stereotyped lead character, a red-haired, freckle-faced country bumpkin named Toby, these shows appeal to a rural carnival audience with a play based on wholesome, homespun, slapstick humor. The Toby character had emerged by 1911, and Toby shows were common throughout the Mississippi Valley and the Southwest through the 1930s. Only a few, however, were revived after World War II. The texts for Toby shows were usually based on nineteenth-century popular drama, but extemporaneous dialogue and stage business were common. At least one Toby show was reported still traveling in 1964, providing folklorists with a rare example of native folk drama in action.

Popular juvenile skits, which may derive from vaudeville or other stage comedy, are the only other shreds of possible folk drama to be found in the United States. About a dozen of these playlets are popular at children's summer camps, Boy Scout and Girl Scout meetings, Sunday school picnics, and the like, and similar original skits are sometimes composed for lodges, office parties, and family reunions. The best known of the traditional skits is probably "You Must Pay the Rent," a farcial melodrama involving the classic figures of villain, his victim (a beautiful girl), and the hero. Often this skit is performed as a monologue with the actor using a ribbon bow alternately as the girl's hair ribbon, the hero's bow tie, and the villain's drooping mustache. Another favorite skit, "Baby Can Spell," is based on the everyday humor of a small child understanding the words that adults spell out in conversations to keep secrets from him—"c-a-n-d-y," "b-a-b-y," and "s-e-x," for instance. A skit called "The Nut Buying Cider" embodies an old folk jest about a fool who tries to carry a beverage home in his hat. When the hat has been poured full, he flops it over to fill the other side. "The Balky Flivver" makes use of six children crouched down to represent an automobile's wheels, motor, and spare tire; while in "The Murder of the Lighthouse Keeper" a circular staircase is suggested simply by having all the actors run around the central figure several times—one way for up, the other for down. One of these skits, "The King of Beasts," resembles a traditional frontier prank. In the skit a group of brawny boys pull a long rope across the stage to which is supposed to be attached the "king." Instead, a small child riding a kiddy-car finally emerges tied to the end of the rope. In the old prank called "The Badger Fight," a greenhorn on the frontier would be given the honor of pulling the fierce badger out of his box to do battle with a dog. When the "greeny" pulled on the leash, a chamber pot slid into view.

Folklorist Jay Mechling has made a good case for Boy Scout campfire programs as folk drama. These have a compelling combination of darkness at the edges and flickering light within the circle, of skits and songs (some of them sexually suggestive), and of such behavior as urinating on the fire at the end of the session. Mechling sees in such performances "a ritual dramatization of male solidarity and male world view." The next question, obviously, is "What do the Girl Scouts do at camp?"

BIBLIOGRAPHIC NOTES

Curt Sachs's *World History of the Dance* (New York: Norton, 1937; Norton Library paperback, 1963) is a basic study with emphasis on the development of movements, themes, and forms from ancient to modern types of dance. The essay "Dance: Folk and Primitive" by Gertrude P. Kurath is a comprehensive survey and a scholarly article in itself, although it appeared in *Funk & Wagnalls Standard Dictionary of Folklore, Mythology, and Legend*, volume 1 (1949), p. 276–96. The sketch of the development of square dances in this chapter is based largely on this article.

Kurath published "A Choreographic Questionnaire" in *MF* 2 (1952): 53–55, and her note "A Basic Vocabulary for Dance Descriptions" was in *AA* 56 (1954): 1, 102–3. She dealt with another field technique in "Photography for Dance Recording," *FFMA* 5 (Winter 1963): 1, 4. Labanotation as a folkloristic tool was discussed by Juana de Laban in "Movement Notation: Its Significance to the Folklorist," *JAF* 67 (1954): 291–95, and in Nadia Chilkovsky in "Dance Notation for Field Work," *FFMA* 2 (Fall 1959): 2–3. A useful reference is Andrea Greenberg's "The Notation of Folk Dance: A Survey," *FF* 5 (1972): 1–10.

Kurath began a dance department in *Ethnomusicology* in 1956 (Newsletter No. 7); it is a valuable source for current bibliography. Her article "Panorama of Dance Ethnology," in *CA* 1 (1960): 233–54, is based on eighteen months of correspondence with scholars the world over; a bibliography is appended, along with a list of dance studies in progress and of dance films. An analytical article by Kurath demonstrates the possibilities of dance ethnology: "Dance Relatives of Mid-Europe and Middle America: A Venture in Comparative Choreology," *JAF* 69 (1956): 286–98.

Other professional students of folk dance are rare in the United States. The 1965 "Works in Progress" report published by the American Folklore Society listed only two besides Gertrude Kurath engaged in dance research, and both were writing historical studies. Such a work, with implications for folklore studies, is Marshall and Jean Stearns's *Jazz Dance: The Story of American Vernacular Dance* (New York: Macmillan, 1972). The situation in folk drama is no better. Five scholars are listed, but three are concerned with the use of folklore in literary drama, one is restricted to Spanish-American plays, and only one is studying general folk drama.

The American folk-dance revival movement can be traced back to the English Folk Dance Society, founded by Cecil Sharp in 1911, which merged with the Folk Song Society (founded in 1898) in 1930. An American branch was organized in 1915 and later took the name the Country Dance Society of America. Ralph Vaughn Williams outlined the history of the English societies in an article in *EM* 2 (1958): 108–12; see also the similar article by S. R. S. Pratt in *JFI* 2 (1965): 294–99. Anyone interested in these movements should study the back numbers not only of the *Journal of the English Folk Dance and Song Society* and *English Dance and Song*, but also the *Folk Dancer* and the *Folklorist*, and the American periodicals *Folk Dance Guide* and *American Squares*. *Dance Magazine* also occasionally publishes articles on folk dancing.

Books associated with the revival of square dancing are too numerous to list in detail. A typical early one was Grace L. Ryan's *Dances of Our Pioneers* (New York: A. S. Barnes, 1939). Lloyd Shaw wrote two influential works: *Cowboy Dances: A Collection of Western Square Dances* (rev. ed., Caldwell, Idaho: Caxton Press, 1952) and *The Round Dance*

Book: A *Century of Waltzing* (Caldwell, Idaho; Caxton Press, 1950). A book that features a brief opening note by folklorist Louise Pound is Cornelia F. Putney and Jesse B. Flood's *Square Dance, U.S.A.* (Dubuque, Iowa: W. C. Brown Co., 1955). Most revivalist collections do not state their sources, but David S. McIntosh's *Singing Games and Dances* (New York, 1957) published by the National Board of Young Men's Christian Associations does—his own field work in southern Illinois. An account of folk-dance revival and dance festivals in California is Virigina C. Anderson's, "It All Began Anew: The Revival of Folk Dancing," *WF* 7 (1948): 162–64.

There are few scholarly studies of square dances in American folklore journals, but an aid for such studies has been published in J. Olcutt Sanders's article "Finding List of Southeastern Square Dance Figures," in *SFQ* 6 (1942): 263–75. Sanders began by commenting on the meager list of reliable sources available for information on old-time square dancing, and the situation is little better years later. A type of needed historical work is represented by John Q. Wolf's "A Country Dance in the Ozarks in 1874," in *SFQ* 29 (1965): 319–21, and Robert D. Bethke's "Old-Time Fiddling and Social Dance in Central St. Lawrence County," in *NYFQ* 30 (1974): 164–84. Good studies of square dances in context are Thomas A. Burns and Doris Mack's "Social Symbolism in a Rural Square Dance Event," *SFQ* 42 (1978): 295–327, and Burt Feintuch's "Dancing to the Music: Domestic Square Dances and Community in Southcentral Kentucky (1800–1940)," *JFI* 18 (1981): 49–68.

The danger of an overenthusiastic folklore revival movement not having a solid background of scholarly knowledge was illustrated in an exchange published in *Western Folklore* in 1956 and 1957. A "Cowpuncher's Square Dance Call" was printed in one issue (15: 125–26) as a previously unpublished example of the "real thing" and as a contrast to the "cheap imitations" of today. But folklorist Sam Hinton pointed out later (16: 129–31) that not only had the same stanzas been several times published earlier, but they were not a dance call at all, but a poem by a known author describing a dance, and the verses could not possibly function as a square-dance call.

The pioneering book on play-parties was Leah Jackson Wolford's *The Play-Party in Indiana* (Indianapolis, 1917). It was revised by W. Edson Richmond and William Tillson and republished as volume 20 of the *Indiana Historical Society Publications*, pp. 103–326, in 1959. The discussion on page 354 of the classification of play-parties is partly drawn from Wolford's introduction in the revised edition of her book. Wolford drew all her examples from Ripley County, Indiana. B. A. Botkin collected Oklahoma play-parties for his study *The American Play-Party Song* (Lincoln: University of Nebraska, 1937; reissued, New York, 1963). A third collection is drawn entirely from another state—S. J.

Sackett's *Play-Party Games from Kansas*, in *Heritage of Kansas* 5 (Emporia, Sept. 1961). The Sackett work should be supplemented by the chapter "Dances and Games" in the same author's *Kansas Folklore* (Lincoln: University of Nebraska Press, 1961), pp. 209–25, as well as by Alan Dundes's review in *JAF* 76 (1963): 251–52, which adds several Kansas references.

Numerous play-parties from other regions have been published in *JAF*, including texts from western Maryland—54 (1941): 162–66; eastern Illinois—32 (1919): 486–96; the Midwest generally—25 (1912): 268–73, and 28 (1915): 262–89; and Idaho—44 (1931): 1–26. Richard Chase includes some square dances and play-parties in his paperback anthology *American Folk Tales and Songs* (New York: New American Library of World Literature, 1956; Dover Publications repr., 1971). The basic tool for bringing together many of the available texts is Altha Lea McLendon's, "A Finding List of Play-Party Games," *SFQ* 8 (1944): 201–34.

A good analytic review of publications on play-parties was published by Keith Cunningham in *AFFWord* 2 (April 1972): 12–23. An excellent study of the historical background of a play-party is John Q. Anderson's "'Miller Boy,' One of the First and Last of the Play-Party Games," *NCFJ* 21 (1973): 171–76 (repr. in *Readings in American Folklore*, pp. 319–23). Some interesting contextual and comparative notes on another example, published by a nonfolklorist, is Edmund Cody Burnett's "The Hog Drivers' Play-Song and Some of Its Relatives," *Agricultural History* 23 (1949): 161–68.

The dramatic dance song on page 357 was collected from Mrs. Mary Jane Fairbanks, age ninety-five, residing at the Anna Henry Nursing Home in Edwardsville, Illinois, on December 3, 1965. George Morey Miller discussed "The Dramatic Element in the Popular Ballad" in *University Studies of the University of Cincinnati*, Series 2, vol. 1, no. 1 (1905). The quotation from Tristram P. Coffin is from *The British Traditional Ballad in North America* discussed in Chapter 12. "Poppy Show" is described in W. W. Newell's *Games and Songs of American Children* and in Lady Gomme's collection of English games, both cited in Chapter 18.

Richard M. Dorson discusses *Los Pastores* in his book *American Folklore* (Chicago: University of Chicago Press, 1959), pp. 103–7. He cites the basic bibliography of Spanish-American folk drama on page 293. A translation of some scenes of the shepherd's play is given in Dorson's *Buying the Wind* (Chicago: University of Chicago Press, 1964), pp. 466–79. To Dorson's list of sources should be added John E. Englekirk's two-part article "The Passion Play in New Mexico," *WF* 25 (1966): 17–33, 105–21. An article that sets Spanish-American folk drama in a modern context is Nicolás Kanellos, "Folklore in Chicano Theater and Chicano Theater as Folklore," *JFI* 15 (1978): 57–82.

Standard works on the English mummers' play are R. J. E. Tiddy's *The Mummers' Play* (Oxford: Oxford University Press, 1923); E. K. Chambers's *The English Folk-Play* (Oxford: Oxford University Press, 1933); and Violet Alford's *Sword Dance and Drama* (London: Merlin Press, 1962). Charles E. Welch, Jr., traced the history of the Philadelphia Mummers' Parade in *KFQ* 8 (1963), 95–106; related material is cited in the notes to the previous chapter. The mummers' texts collected in the United States were published in Antoinette Taylor's "An English Christmas Play," *JAF* 22 (1909): 389–94, and Marie Campbell's "Survivals of Old Folk Drama in the Kentucky Mountains," *JAF* 51 (1938): 10–24.

James F. Hoy's "A Modern Analogue to Medieval Staging," *JAF* 90 (1977): 179–87, compares the local festival called "Biblesta" performed in Humboldt, Kansas, to the medieval English Corpus Christi processions and plays.

Information on the "school of folk drama" may be found in Robert E. Spiller and others, *Literary History of the United States*, 4th edn., rev. (New York: Macmillan, 1974), pp. 722–24, and *Bibliography*, p. 200. Charles G. Zug III evaluates this material and its relationship to traditional folk drama in an article in *SFQ* 32 (1968): 279–94.

Larry Dale Clark submitted his study "Toby Shows: A Form of American Popular Theatre" as his Ph.D. dissertation at the University of Illinois in 1963; see *Dissertation Abstracts* 24 (May 1964): 4, 858. Carol Pennepacker described "A Surviving Toby Show: Bisbee's Comedians" in *TFSB* 30 (1964): 49–52, and Jere C. Mickel published "The Genesis of Toby: A Folk Hero of the American Theater" in *JAF* 80 (1967): 334–40.

An interesting Southern black religious drama is described in Redding S. Sugg, Jr., "Heaven Bound," *SFQ* 27 (1963): 249–66.

A collection of eleven popular skits was compiled by Norris Yates as "Children's Folk Plays in Western Oregon," *WF* 9 (1951): 55–62, but these playlets are by no means peculiar to that region, nor does this article exhaust the list of such skits. Anne C. Burson drew on some satiric medical skits for her theoretical essay "Model and Text in Folk Drama" published in *JAF* 93 (1980): 305–16; she treated similar material in her "Pomp and Circumcision: A Parodic Skit in a Medical Community," *KF*, New Series, 1 (1982): 28–40. Skits, songs, and ritual behavior interact in Jay Mechling's analysis of "The Magic of the Boy Scout Campfire," *JAF* 93 (1980): 35–56.

Thomas A. Green has pioneered in redefining folk drama (or refining older definitions) in "Toward a Definition of Folk Drama," *JAF* 91 (1978): 843–50, and also in the special folk-drama issue of *JAF* (94:374 [1981]), which he edited.

17
Folk Gestures

Gestures and Meaning

Gestures are a silent language made up of movements of the body, or a part of it, used to communicate emotions or ideas. As such, they are an important aspect of informants' total perform-ances, and, as MacEdward Leach emphasized in an essay on folklore collecting, we should try to record everything, the "voice—tone and inflection—gestures, facial expressions, [and] attitudes as well as words." To retain the fullest possible report, field collectors sometimes photograph the typical gestures in-formants use, or they describe them, as in the following passage from Richard M. Dorson's discussion of black storytellers:

> When the rabbit scoots away from the fox, or John runs from the Lord, the narrator slaps his hands sharply together, with the left sliding off the right palm in a forward direction—a manual trademark of the Negro raconteur.

Gestures that accompany folktales may be stylized, like these raconteurs', or like snapping the fingers to emphasize "Just like that!" They may also be introduced from everyday behavior—shrugging the shoulders to indicate doubt, flexing a bicep to show strength, shading the eyes when looking for something, raising an imaginary gun to shoot—whatever fits the action oc-curring in the tale. However, some folktale plots include spe-cific gestures that are a necessary part of the performance. For example, Aarne-Thompson Type 924, "Discussion by Sign Lan-guage," and its subtypes concern manual-sign conversations that are sometimes mutually misunderstood but still are finished to the complete satisfaction of both parties. In a riddle joke with gestures the question is asked why a stupid fellow has hunched shoulders and a dent in the middle of his forehead. The explanation is that when you ask him a question he "goes like this" (shrugging the shoulders), and when you explain it, he "does this" (slapping the palm of one hand to the forehead). The non-oral riddles described in Chapter 6 are other traditional questions involving gestures, and among children's chants, rhymes, and songs are further gesture pieces.

Superstitions, too, often involve traditional gestures. Crossing the fingers, tossing spilled salt over the left shoulder, and knocking on wood for good luck are familiar ones, as are the actions sometimes performed to seal a pact between children—crossing one's heart, raising the right hand in imitation of courtroom swearing, and spitting on the ground. When two Americans say the same words at the same time, they may hook little fingers and say "Needles-Pins," and make a wish; Spaniards hook the same finger, but say "Cervantes." Rituals of witchcraft make use of special gestures and symbols, and some body movements are believed to have the power to cast the "evil eye" on someone else or to avert its power from oneself. An ancient one for the latter purpose is made by extending the forefinger and little finger of one hand and clenching the others —the "Devil's Horns." The sign of the cross is commonly made, outside of any formal religious context, to ward off bad luck.

A folk game involving gestures is "Rocks, Paper, and Scissors." Manual imitations of these three objects are given by several players sitting in a circle, gesturing in unison, and keeping time to a strict rhythmic beat. Penalties fall to players according to the formula that "paper covers rock, rocks break scissors, and scissors cut paper." Thus those who signed "paper" win over rock, rock over scissors, and scissors over paper. The punishment is a sharp slap on the wrist dealt by winners to losers, using the first two fingers of one hand held together, and dampened with the tongue before striking, and play continues until a player's wrist is too sore to go on.

Although gestures often accompany speech, a simple and familiar one by itself can communicate eloquently to those who know its customary meaning. Functionally, these gestures are comparable to proverbs, and even animals employ them—the friendly dog wagging its tail, for instance. Such use partly explains the long-term effectiveness of the famous United States Army recruiting poster that shows Uncle Sam pointing directly at the viewer. A profile representation of a pointing finger was once a common American direction sign, while the picture showing a forefinger laid across the lips, once posted in libraries, commanded, "Silence!" Advertisers, fashion photographers, and drama directors still make use of such well-known conventional gestures to convey desired feelings to their audiences. Many proverbial phrases contain references to gestures that have unambiguous meanings, such as "to turn up one's nose at" (scorn), "to keep a stiff upper lip" (courage), "to tear one's hair" (rage), and "to raise an eyebrow" (surprise, shock or skepticism). The very word "supercilious" derives from the Latin terms for the gesture of raising eyebrows to denote haughtiness.

Any mannerism associated with passing on oral traditions may interest the folklore collector, but not all gestures are *folk* gestures. Some are merely **autistic,** or **nervous, personal gestures;** these include drumming with the fingers, jingling change, fussing with hair or clothing, biting the lips or fingernails, and cracking knuckles. Only a few of these—such as "twiddling" the thumbs, or stroking the chin or beard—may become stereotyped signs for certain attitudes, and then begin to circulate traditionally. Closely related to autistic gestures are **culture-induced gestures**—aspects of sitting, walking, hand movements, and stance that are learned unconsciously from one's cultural surroundings and employed as a symbolic code. Other movements belong to **technical gesture systems** that are usually taught by formal methods. The military salute is a good example of this: it is described precisely, with its proper use, in military manuals, and its correct form is instilled in every new member of the group. But a traditional mock version of the salute, which turns into the derisive gesture of "thumbing the nose," can be considered a folk gesture. The saying associated with this variation goes "I salute the captain of the ship; / Pardon me, my finger slipped."

Complex systems of technical gestures are important for special uses; the best known is communication between deaf-mutes. Native American sign language constitutes another highly developed system, as do religious gestures for prayer and worship, and gestures used for communication within certain monastic orders. Many occupations require that a special gesture language be flawlessly learned and consistently performed time after time. Umpires and referees of various sports have their strict systems, as do radio and television performers, land surveyors, music conductors, traffic and airport directors, auctioneers, and even surgeons, who use some hand signals during operations to request instruments from a nurse.

These occupational gestures that are learned from manuals or special instructors have their folk counterparts in others used in the same occupations that pass on through tradition. For example, the railroad worker's operating rulebooks show only a few official hand signals, but railroad men have other gestures of their own invention used for special purposes. If an inspector or other company authority is on a train, the signal may be given with the thumbs stuck into an imaginary vest. Another is the gesture of pretending to scratch one's head a few inches out in the air to indicate that the "big heads" are approaching. Similarly, truck drivers long used the two-finger "V" sign to signal other drivers that a police patrol car is ahead. Automobile drivers picked up the same signal to warn oncoming cars of a radar speed-trap ahead.

Some systems of gesturing, such as those used for bidding in different kinds of auction sales, may have been folk gestures originally that were later regularized and formally adopted. Other systems, such as those used by a particular athletic team or coach to signal strategy, may be largely individual and secret. Whenever an occupation demands communicating in secrecy (as in professional baseball), or above the sound of loud noises (as in sawmills), or across a considerable distance (as when fencing a farm or ranch), then both systematized and informal gestures can be expected to develop.

Folk Gestures

A true **folk gesture** is one that is kept alive by tradition and that exhibits some variation in action or meaning. Most obscene gestures clearly qualify as "folk." Like customs, folk gestures tend to pattern themselves within national boundaries. An American waves good-by with his palm out; Italians keep the palm turned in. Americans "thumb" a ride, while many Europeans wave the whole hand up and down when hitchhiking. Western peoples tend to point to themselves at chest level; Orientals point to their own noses. To signify that something is "just right," a Frenchman places his right index finger tip on the right thumb tip and kisses them both, while an American forms a circle with the same two fingers, holds that hand up, and gives it a little shake. In Sicily the same idea is conveyed by pinching the cheek, in Brazil by tugging on an ear lobe, and in Colombia by pulling down a lower eyelid. Kissing, considered as a gesture, displays several variations; *where* the kiss is applied is significant—the lips, cheek, forehead, back of hand, "blown" from the fingers or palm, and so forth. A greeting that consists of two kisses rapidly applied, one to each cheek, immediately seems to identify the performer as a Frenchman, even though several other European cultures use this greeting, too. Kissing a ring, a Bible, a piece of someone's clothing, or a photograph is a widespread sign of extreme devotion.

An excellent example of a culturally significant gesture having a secret communications use was described in a news story during the Korean conflict. An American Air Force captain recounting his experiences as a prisoner in North Korea told how he was photographed with other prisoners in a mocked-up library, presumably to show the world how well they were being treated. To counter the propaganda value of the pictures, he made the sign of the "Devil's Horns' in each one, which to Americans is the "bull sign" or "baloney." To his captors, the gesture was innocuous, and the pictures were released to the press. In 1968 some members of the captured United States vessel *Pueblo* managed to repeat this trick, using an obscene gesture, when they, too, were photographed.

Gestures of greeting have become well established in different cultures and seldom change much, but the degree of formality in a social situation may allow for some variation in the greeting employed. Thus, a firm handshake is "correct" in some situations, while a hearty slap on the back or playful rumpling of the other's hair is better for others. Beginning with jazz musicians, and quickly spreading to other Americans, was an exaggerated handshake that began with a dramatic "windup" and the remark "Give me some skin, man!" and culminated with the hands or fingers barely touching. Another playful American greeting is the manual imitation of shooting a revolver at someone else, usually accompanied by a wink, and sometimes by the expression "Gottcha!" There are also mock handshakes, supposedly appropriate for different occupations: the "farmers' handshake" has the thumbs of one person turned down and being "milked" by the second person, and the "politicians' handshake" begins with great enthusiasm and ends with the two parties reaching over each other's shoulders to pick each other's pockets. Many athletic teams and other groups (probably learning to do so from black members) use complicated little palm-slapping patterns as gestures of greeting or greet others with a "high five" handshake.

Classifying and Studying Gestures

No standard system of classifying folk gestures has been adopted. Some collectors have used the parts of the body as a basis for arrangement, while others classify in terms of meanings expressed. Some collections have not been put in any special order but were simply published as random lists. A better possibility may lie in trying to establish categories based on the *nature* of different gestures. As has been shown, some are parodies of technical gestures or derivations from autistic gestures. Others imitate letters of the alphabet (forming a "C" with the hand to invite someone to have coffee with you), or they signify numbers (gestures to hot-dog salesmen in grandstands). It might be noted that even the procedure for counting on the fingers is culturally determined. Germans begin counting with the thumb, so an American tourist holding up his index finger to order a beer is actually ordering *two*.

There are gestures borrowed for general folk use from a specialized application (the prizefighters' victory sign of hands joined over the head, wagging in jubilation and triumph). Some gestures come directly to the point, such as touching a wrist watch or cupping a hand behind the ear as signals to a speaker, or holding the nose as a reaction to an idea. Other gestures are more abstract, such as that of circling the forefinger around one ear to mean "crazy" (something loose in the head?) or rubbing one forefinger held at right angles against the other toward another person for "shame" (shedding the "dirt"?). A large group of folk gestures could be classed as pantomimic—that is, they act out the intended message. We gesture and say "Chalk one up" in the air with imaginary chalk against an invisible blackboard, as if keeping score of our "goofs"; and we pretend to slash the throat with a finger to show that a certain kind of trouble has occurred or is soon expected. Other pantomime gestures are those of playing an invisible violin, for mock sympathy; mopping the brow, for great exertion; breathing on and pretending to polish the fingernails, for self-pride; and smoothing an eyebrow with a dampened little finger, used by males to denote effeminacy in other males.

Gestures can be studied historically, geographical, comparatively, and structurally, like any other kind of folklore, although very few such investigations have been made. Most published studies of gestures are physiological, linguistic, or psychological, and thus beyond the scope of this survey. Two, however deserve mention.

In 1944 a psychologist published his detailed study of the "V for Victory" campaign among the Allied nations during World War II, an outstanding instance of morale boosting by means of symbolism. To anyone who remembers the war years, the image of Winston Churchill flashing the "V" gesture with his two fingers raised immediately comes to mind. But the sign was carried much further during the war in posters, advertising, the "dot-dot-dot-dash" of Morse code, and even through allusion to the code "V" by playing or humming the first phrase of Beethoven's *Fifth Symphony* (da, da, da, **DA**). The study traced the history of the campaign, schematized the communications process involved in it, analyzed the types of symbolism found, and described the degeneration of the symbol as it was widely applied apart from its original context. More recently, of course, the "V" sign, while retaining its "victory" meaning among athletes, politicians running for office, etc., has also become a sort of peace-and-pot greeting of recognition among young people, and it has an entirely separate function in the Cub Scouts organization, calling meetings to order and signifying ideals of the group.

Archer Taylor produced the only full-length folkloristic study of an individual gesture in English in his work on the so-called "Shanghai Gesture," or thumbing the nose, also called "cocking a snook," "Queen Anne's fan," "taking a sight," and other names. After an exhaustive survey of the gesture in art, literature, news media, and oral tradition, Taylor concluded that it originated in Western Europe and had been known in Great Britain during the sixteenth century. It did not become faddish in England until early in the nineteenth century. In the United States it was first described by Washington Irving in *Diedrich Knickerbocker's History of New York* (1809), and it was well known by 1862 when Mark Twain made it the basis of his hoax in "The Petrified Man." Ezra Pound alluded to it in a poem in 1917, and since then numerous American writers and illustrators have continued to describe and picture it. Only recently, Taylor felt, has the gesture acquired an obscene connotation—the end result of its becoming increasingly more insulting as time passed.

Since 1956, when Taylor's study was published, the gesture has continued to be popular—*and* insulting. In 1959–1960, for example, which was designated World Refugee Year, some sensitive English people became alarmed when postmarks depicting the symbol for that year—an outstretched, empty hand—occasionally became imprinted on canceled letters over stamps bearing Queen Elizabeth's picture so as to show Her Majesty delivering a perfect Shanghai Gesture. In 1983, President Ronald Reagan provided news photographers with a memorable picture when he delivered the derisive gesture of sticking his thumbs in his ears and wiggling his fingers directly into the television cameras. No American needed an explanation of what he meant, and for a moment, perhaps, we were all one big folk group.

BIBLIOGRAPHIC NOTES

There are a few small collections of American gestures but almost no studies of them, although groundwork for analysis has been laid. No "Gestures" heading exists in the index to *JAF* for volumes 1 to 70 (1888–1958). Finally, in *JAF* 89 (1976): 294–309, a study appeared there: John A. Rickford and Angela E. Rickford's essay "Cut-Eye and Suck-Teeth: African Words and Gestures in a New World Guise," reprinted in *Readings in American Folklore*, pp. 355–73. A key work elsewhere is Francis C. Hayes's "Gestures: A Working Bibliography," *SFQ* 21 (1957): 218–317. Hayes's bibliography includes both foreign and English references, popular articles as well as scholarly ones, and some descriptions of specific gestures from literature and popular media. Obscure and unpublished items are included, and many entries are annotated, with their presence in four American libraries indicated.

Survey articles on gestures as folklore are rare. Charles Francis Potter's work in *Funk & Wagnalls Standard Dictionary of Folklore, Mythology, and Legend* (1, 451–53) is largely anthropological and religious in its orientation. A better survey is Levette J. Davidson's "Some Current Folk Gestures and Sign Languages," *AS* 25 (1950): 3–9; a more recent and more detailed one is Robert A. Barakat's "Gesture Systems" in *KFQ* 14 (1969): 105–21. Barakat also provides a detailed discussion of more than two hundred "Arabic Gestures" in *JPC* 6 (1973): 749–93, which may serve as a model for similar surveys in other cultures.

MacEdward Leach's comment quoted at the beginning of this chapter is from "Problems of Collecting Oral Literature," *PMLA* 77 (1962): 335–40. Richard M. Dorson described gestures of black storytellers in *Negro Folktales in Michigan* (Cambridge, Mass.: Harvard University Press, 1956), p. 24. The gestures of Austrian storytellers are discussed and pictured in Karl Haiding's, *"Von der Gebärdensprache der Märchenerzähler,"* *FFC* no. 155 (1955).

A comprehensive treatment of gestures, written by a neurologist, is MacDonald Critchley's *The Language of Gesture* (London: E. Arnold Co., 1939). Ernest Thompson Seton's book *Sign Talk* (Garden City, N.Y.: Doubleday, 1918) proposed an ingenious "universal signal code without apparatus" that borrowed gestures freely from various technical systems as well as from folk usage. An ambitious theoretical work, fully illustrated, that involves gestures in part, is Jurgen Ruesch and

Weldon Kees's *Nonverbal Communication: Notes on the Visual Perception of Human Relations* (Berkeley and Los Angeles: University of California Press, 1961).

Francis C. Hayes distinguished technical, autistic, and folk gestures in his essay "Should We Have a Dictionary of Gestures?" in *SFQ* 4 (1940): 239–45. Exactly that—*A Dictionary of Gestures*—edited by Betty J. and Franz H. Bäuml, was published in 1975 (Metuchen, N.J.: Scarecrow Press).

Articles that present occupational folk gestures are Charles Carpenter's "The Sign Language of Railroad Men," *American Mercury* 25 (Feb. 1932): 211–13, and C. Grant Loomis's "Sign Language of Truck Drivers," *WF* 15 (1956): 205–6.

Mario Pei discusses different nationalities and their typical gestures in *The Story of Language* (Philadelphia: Lippincott, 1949). Some of his findings were illustrated with photographs of people performing the gestures in "Gesture Language," *Life* (January 9, 1950), pp. 79–81. An article in German by Lutz Röhrich contains thirty-seven plates illustrating historical gestures. See "*Gebärdensprache und Sprachgebärde,*" in *Humaniora: Essays in Literature, Folklore, Bibliography Honoring Archer Taylor on His Seventieth Birthday*, ed. Wayland D. Hand and Gustave O. Arlt (Locust Valley, N.Y.: J. J. Augustin, 1960), pp. 121–49. Characteristic gestures of Spanish-speaking peoples were described in Walter Vincent Kaulfers's "Curiosities of Colloquial Gestures," *Hispania* 14 (1931): 249–64. The North Korean incident was reported in Captain Harold E. Fischer, Jr.'s "My Case as a Prisoner Was Different," *Life* (June 27, 1955), pp. 147–60. A photograph of Fischer making the gesture (which *Life* termed "the whammy sign") is found on page 157 of that issue of *Life*.

Three lists of gestures from California have appeared: Charlotte McCord described thirty collected from the Berkeley campus of the University of California in *WF* 7 (1948): 290–92; William S. King added ten more in *WF*, 8 (1949): 263–64; and Jean Cooke published a strangely mistitled list of forty more gestures from Berkeley in "A Few Gestures Encountered in a Virtually Gestureless Society," *WF* 18 (1959): 233–37. None of these notes has bibliography. Many instances of gestures used by English children are cross-referenced under "gesture" in the index to Peter Opie and Iona Opie's *The Lore and Language of Schoolchildren* (Oxford: Oxford University Press, 1959). A curiosity is Michael J. Preston's note "A Gesture Rebus," showing how two brands of whiskey are represented by folk gestures, published in *SWF* 5 (1981): 42–45.

A major study unfortunately treats only gestures in Europe and North Africa. See Desmond Morris, Peter Collett, Peter Marsh, and Marie O'Shaughnessy, *Gestures: Their Origins and Distribution* (London: Jonathan Cape, 1979). Twenty key gestures in forty sites surveyed are discussed with regard to meanings, origins, and variations. The bibliography here is impressive, and the methodology should be repeated for the United States.

Edgar A. Schuler's article "V for Victory: A Study in Symbolic Social Control," appeared in *JSP* 19 (1944): 283–99. Further developments in the uses and meanings of the V sign are illustrated in Jan Harold Brunvand, "Popular Culture in the Folklore Course," in Ray B. Browne and Ronald J. Ambrosetti, *Popular Culture and Curricula* (Bowling Green, Ohio: Bowling Green University Popular Press, 1970), pp. 59–72. Archer Taylor's "The Shanghai Gesture" was in *FFC* no. 166 (1956). Taylor added an English description of the gesture from shortly after 1810 in "The Shanghai Gesture in England," *WF* 23 (1964): 114. Wirephotos of canceled letters from England, with and without the embarrassing juxtaposition of open hand and royal nose, were distributed by the Associated Press in 1959 and printed in American newspapers.

18

Folk Games

Game Lore

Children's traditional games offer an ideal topic for folklore research. They are passed from child to child in almost pure oral tradition with little reference to print and probably negligible influence from teachers, parents, or recreation leaders. The players are naturally conservative about their texts and will strive to maintain the "right way" of playing against all variations. Thus, old games may survive, little altered, through many generations of children. Children's games also develop clear regional subtypes. When families change neighborhoods or move to other communities, the children will soon discover whether their old versions are played in the new home or whether they must adopt new ones, for seldom do newcomers succeed in converting their playmates to outside games. Finally, children are usually excellent informants—easy to locate, eager to perform, and uninhibited with their responses.

The folk games all people play, whether children, adolescents, or adults, may be based on the movements of the body (stepping, running, hopping, jumping, etc.), on simple social activities (chasing, hiding, fighting, dramatizing, etc.), on chance (the fall of dice, cards, bones, coins, etc.), or on elementary mathematics or mechanics (counting, sorting, balancing, throwing, handling equipment, etc.). These common foundation blocks may explain the similarity of certain games through long periods of time and in widespread cultures, or diffusion of folklore may better account for some similar forms. (It is the question once again of polygenesis versus diffusion from a single origin.) Only detailed studies of many versions of different games can begin to suggest answers to such questions.

By their very nature as voluntary recreations with rules fixed only by custom and tradition, folk games reveal much about the societies in which they are played and about the individuals who play them. Game preferences, the forms of games, local variations, attitudes toward play, and play behavior are all valuable cultural, sociological, and psychological data to be documented and analyzed. In such research, the nonverbal elements of games are significant along with such verbal ones as traditional sayings, rhymes, or songs associated with games. Good field work in folk games requires that one describe the action clearly and logically; secure all variations in names, rules, and texts; sketch or photograph all diagrams or equipment; and collect the full social and contextual background of the game along with the text. Useful projects in game study would include collecting the games of one family, neighborhood, school class, or season.

It is not surprising that the first American folklorists were interested in collecting and studying folk games. For example, W. W. Newell, charter member of the American Folklore Society in 1888 and first editor of its journal, had already published a classic study, *Games and Songs of American Children,* five years earlier. But this early interest declined when folklorists assumed that children had abandoned folk games. Only a scattering of articles and notes on folk games appeared in this country until Paul G. Brewster's book, *American Non-Singing Games,* published in 1953, balanced the picture Newell had given by describing the games without songs that Newell had ignored. Since then there has been increasing interest in game analysis among American scholars, and a comprehensive sociopsychological, anthropological, and folkloristic theory of play and games seems to be emerging as studies illuminate how role-playing and competition in games reveal underlying motives and reflect on other behavior.

The problem of classifying games, basic to further research, has not been completely solved. The singing or nonsinging dichotomy suggested by Newell's and Brewster's works is no better than other proposed systems that separate games of boys from those of girls, or indoor from outdoor games, or games of different age groups. One writer suggests grouping games into four classes, depending upon the elements of competition, chance, mimicry, or vertigo (motion alone, i.e., teeter-tottering). But these categories are too broad for classification purposes, and it is not clear that the last two represent games at all. A better grouping, made by anthropologists, classifies games according to their requirements for either physical skill, strategy, or chance. This has proved meaningful for studying the relationship of games to cultural and environmental factors. But for folklore purposes—especially folklore archiving—a more workable classification might be made on the basis of the primary kind of play activity involved—whether physical action, manipulation of objects, or mental activity.

First, **pastimes** (or "amusements") must be distinguished from true games. A pastime, as the name suggests, is a traditional recreation performed simply to pass the time away. It lacks what true games have—the element of competition, the possibility of winning or losing, and a measure of organization with some kind of controlling rules. Most pastimes are solo activities such as bouncing a ball, juggling, balancing oneself or an object, swinging, walking on stilts, spinning a top, operating a yo-yo, and making Cat's Cradles (string patterns on one's fingers). When two or more individuals toss a ball about, they are engaging in a mere pastime as long as they introduce no rules and no way of distinguishing a winner. Yo-yoing, top-spinning, rope-jumping, or other such activities may lead to a contest of skill or of endurance and thus turn into true games. Two people balance on a teeter-totter more commonly than just one (in the middle of the board), and sometimes two may swing together with one seated and the other standing and "pumping"; these activities, however, remain pastimes. There are also four-handed cat's cradles in which the ever-changing design in the string loop is passed back and forth from one person to another.

A solo recreation, on the other hand, may be a game—Solitare, for instance, is played against an imaginary opponent, and the player may win, or (more commonly) lose. Puzzle solving is something of a game if one thinks of "winning" by finishing the picture or word pattern in a specified time with no outside help. We even bribe ourselves to finish unpleasant or tiresome tasks by "making a game of it" or by promising ourselves a reward upon completion.

Games of Action

Games of physical action may be subdivided by the principal action involved. There are *hopping games* (Hopscotch), *chasing games* (Red Rover), *hiding games* (Hide-and-Seek), *battle games* (Prisoner's Base), and *dramatic games* (Farmer in the Dell), to list only the major kinds. At their simplest level, such games are merely outlets for high spirits and a means of getting lively exercise. They provide healthy competitions in strength and skill between individuals or teams. Games like running races, Leapfrog, Tag, Johnny on the Pony, and King on the Hill satisfy these needs, but they have other dimensions, too. In Tag, for instance, if "it" is thought of as a fearsome aggressor, possibly the Devil, the safety gained by touching iron (long used to avert evil spirits) or wood (the cross), and the truce cry "King's-X" (royal pardon plus the cross) are all readily understood. (Probably the game and the basic symbolism are pre-Christian.) Any doubts that children's games might contain such underlying themes are shaken by the actual appearance of the names "black man" or "Devil" for "it" in many games still in current circulation. Also, hopscotch patterns that have "Heaven" at one boundary and "Hell" at the other are not unusual.

Some types of hiding games illustrate the variety of play that is possible on the basis of one simple concept. In many of these all but one player hide and the person who is "it" searches; various rules govern "it's" activities while finding other players. In other games one person hides and the others search, and in one game, Sardines, the searchers join the hider one by one as they discover him or her, until all are crammed into one hiding place. Still other varieties of hiding games involve a whole team of players hiding and another team searching, or an object or objects are hidden and the players search. Truce terms and sanctuary terms differ from game to game and region to region.

Most of the active games involve a certain amount of mimicry of life situations, although it is only the most complex of these recreations that are usually called "dramatic games." Little children play a game that begins with all but one player in a "jam pile"—everyone falls down in a heap with limbs tangled. Then they cry "Doctor, doctor, we need help!" and the remaining child hurries to untangle them. The game is a simple, playful enactment of a horrible scene that might occur in accidents. In Mother, May I? the "it" player (who may be male or female) assumes the role of a demanding "mother" who allows movement toward a goal only using types and numbers of rather grotesque steps which "she" dictates, and then only if the children remember to say "May I?" and "Thank you." Cheating, however, is a regular feature of the game. The game of Fox Hunt (or Hare and Hounds) imitates hunting, with bits of scattered paper instead of a scent as the trail. The city child's counterpart game, Arrow Chase (or Chalk Walk), is an adaptation for sidewalk playing with detectivelike overtones. Nineteenth-century children, girls especially, enjoyed courtship games such as Knights of Spain or Here Come Three Dukes A-Riding, but these have mostly died out now as the more aggressive kissing and party mixer games (discussed below) flourish. Many courtship games, as well as others that involve singing, are related to the play-parties discussed in Chapter 16.

Battle games, like Cops and Robbers or Cowboys and Indians, are dramatic imitations of adult conflicts that have survived even in the age of space exploration. Children have also been reported playing a game with as old-fashioned a title (perhaps learned from TV) as Wells Fargo. Here the "Indians" are identified by strips of adhesive tape on their foreheads. When they storm the office or stagecoach, they may be "killed" by yanking the tape away.

That children are imaginative and have extremely good memories for the things that interest them is demonstrated by the fanciful forfeits sometimes proposed in games like Tappy-on-the-Icebox and the complicated dialogue preserved in one like

The Old Witch. That children have boundless stamina is shown by the hours they will spend in snowball fighting or playing a chasing game like Fox and Geese over a pattern stamped in the snow. And that children are adaptable was strikingly demonstrated after the devastating Alaskan earthquake on Good Friday 1964, when, only a few days later, the children of Kodiak were playing new games called Earthquake and Tidal Wave amid the wreckage.

Games with Objects

Games involving manipulation of objects might be classified by the objects that are used, whether "found" items like stones, sticks, and plants, or manufactured objects like marbles, jacks, balls, and knives. In these games, strategy or dexterity is usually more important than physical strength. Some of the games involve trading and winning the objects used. The most fully collected aspect of games with objects is the terminology, which may be both elaborate and lengthy. The games played with marbles, for instance, have given rise to such terms as *fudgies, stickies, changies, roundsies, clearsies, lagging, steelie, dogob, vint, one knuckle down,* and *cateye.* Jacks players use terms such as *pig pens, around the world, taps, baskets, behind the fence,* and *lefties.* All too often, collectors stop with such vocabulary, failing to document the rules and customs of play sufficiently. Thus, we have no full descriptions of knife games beyond the familiar Mumbletypeg (others include Baseball, Territories, and Chicken), and we have little data on the age groups, seasons, regions, and individual places where such games are played or about the different rules or equipment appropriate for each.

Another area of equipped folk games little studied as yet is that of variations of organized sports. Baseball or softball, for instance, in folk groups are seldom played with full teams, game officials, standard-size playing fields, and the like, Little League notwithstanding. Instead, neighborhood children will use their baseballs, bats, and gloves for games like Flies and Grounders, Scrub, Work-up, and Stickball, adapting the rules to the terrain available and to the prevailing customs. Similarly, in driveway and backyard basketball games, there is only one basket, not two, and the game may range all the way from simple basket shooting and scrambling for rebounds to elaborate spelling or mathematical contests controlled by the drops of shots into the basket. ("C-o-w" is used for a short game, "h-o-r-s-e," for a medium-length one, and "M-i-s-s-i-s-s-i-p-p-i" for a long one.) The influence of playground supervisors may be felt on group ball games such as Dodge Ball, but there are other games such as Anthony Over (or Anti Over, Rain on the Roof, etc.) played by opposing "sides" (teams) of from one on up which are completely traditional.

The survival of older folk games in play equipment now produced by manufacturers also deserves study. Checkers, Parcheesi, and other board games; Darts, Beanbags, and other target games; and most card games have traditional ancestors on their family trees. The game of Tiddlywinks, now a commercially produced one, probably had its origin in earlier play with homemade equipment. A counterpart folk game is still played by little girls in India with broken fragments of glass bangles (worn in bunches as bracelets) which they find washed out of the village dust after rainstorms and which they gamble with, attempting to win by snapping each other's bangle fragments out of a circle scratched in the ground. Marbles and Jacks, on the other hand, are folk games played now with factory-made equipment. The former, moreover, has increasingly been normalized and regulated in organized tournaments by contest officials.

Mental Games

Games of mental activity are characterized by guessing, figuring, choosing, and the like, although they usually also involve some physical action as well, and often manipulation of objects. It is difficult to classify a game like Lemonade (also called new Orleans, Dumb Trades, The Dumbies' Trade, etc.) that involves dialogue, acting, guessing, and chasing. But the heart of the game, emphasized in several of the variant names for it, is the procedure of one team acting out a kind of work and the other team *guessing* what it is. When the correct trade is named, the guessers chase the actors, and the game continues with different trades being imitated until all players have been caught. The game of Statues is a similar active-mental combination game. A leader whirls and releases each player who must then "freeze" in whatever posture the motion leaves him or her in. Sometimes each statue is "turned on" so that it can come to life and behave like the person it represents. Then the leader selects the best "statue," or the funniest, to be next leader.

A few other games of mental activity are played outdoors— Stone School on the front steps of a house, for instance, with each child advancing up through the grades (i.e., a step) by guessing which of "teacher's" hands holds a stone. But most are indoor games, called frequently *parlor games* or *party games.* Charades and Twenty Questions are two of these which eventually found their way into television "game shows," but a more complex one in folk tradition is Botticelli, often played by college students or faculty. It requires a leader to give the initials only of a personality, recent or past—real or fictional—in art, music, literature, history, etc. The group guesses at his or her identification by listing credentials that fit such figures with the same initials. Each time the leader cannot come up with the name that another player has in mind, he or she must answer truthfully a direct "yes or no" question about the person he is thinking of. Another popular guessing game is based on a kind of story riddle sometimes termed "logic problems." These are often mini-murder mysteries "solved" by spotting such slips in the story as the murderer buying a round-trip ticket for himself and a one-way for his victim, or using an icicle for a weapon that will melt without a clue. (So he thinks; it leaves a telltale puddle).

Games involving drawn diagrams are usually called *pencil-and-paper games*, although they may occasionally be played on a blackboard or even scratched into the earth or sand. Ticktacktoe is the simplest and best known, and is often played as a triple contest, each player recording the games won as well as those that went to "the old cat" as ties. Another similar game is Squares or Completing Squares; the players alternate connecting dots in a pattern, and they win a point for each square they complete and initial. Battleship is similar, but requires two diagrams containing various hidden "ships" which the players attempt to "sink" by calling out the grid coordinates where they believe the ships are located. (This game and others have been adapted for commercial sale and mass production either as table games or video games.) Another game, Hangman, ends when one player has been "hanged" by missing a guess (usually of letters in a person's name) for each line of a stick-figure drawing of a hanging man.

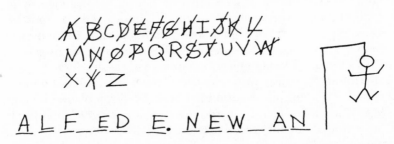

Traditional letter and number puzzles, tricks and amusements (such as those discussed in Chapter 6) occasionally come close to being games. Those played in automobiles, for example, have rules and winners—the child wins who sees a whole alphabet in initial letters of words on billboards or who sees the most distant state license plate. (No fair counting except on your own side of the car!) A similar adult amusement is the popular office game of Paycheck Poker (or Cribbage) in which the "kitty" (cash) goes to the person whose paycheck serial number represents the highest-scoring hand of cards.

Other Folk Recreations

Several kinds of folk recreations will not fit clearly into any of the above categories and must simply be grouped last. These include practical jokes, kissing games, and drinking games.

Practical jokes do not qualify as true games because, in Richard S. Tallman's definition, they consist of "a competitive play activity in which only one of two opposing sides is consciously aware of the fact that a state of play exists . . . the unknowing side is made to seem foolish or is caused some physical and/or mental discomfort." Usually practical jokes require that all participants but one be in on the joke. The unsuspecting dupe may be told that the group is going to play a game called Barnyard Chorus; each player is assigned the name of a farm animal whose sound he is to imitate loudly when a signal is given. What the dupe does not know is that everybody else will keep silent, and he alone is left calling out his animal sound—the bray of a donkey. Sometimes this trick is set up with the players blindfolded and assigned the animal sounds in pairs. Then when all of the others have found their partners and removed their blindfolds, the poor "donkey" is still lonesomely braying and stumbling around the room. Other similar practical jokes are Trip to the Dentist, during which the dupe receives a dash of pepper in his open mouth, and a mock-contest involving a nickel balanced on the forehead, which is supposedly to be flipped down into a funnel stuck into the pants. The victim receives a glass of water poured into the funnel.

Many popular practical jokes take the form of the "fool's errand"—the newcomer to a job is sent searching and asking for a variety of nonexistent tools, materials, or other items. Among the best known of these "beguilers" are the "left-handed monkey wrench," the "skyhook," and the pilot's "bucket of propwash." Other terms suggest a more advanced technical knowledge of a trade: the banker's "key to the clearinghouse," for example.

One of the most venerable pranks is the Snipe Hunt, an age-old routine which is still a successful trick on an occasional youthful camper or club member. The other hunters explain the habits of the elusive snipe—prowling nocturnally for food and responding to a soft call or whistle. The victim is to hold a bag open and make the proper sound (sometimes also hold a flashlight or lantern), while the others will fan out to drive the snipe toward him. But all the tricksters simply go home, leaving the poor hunter dolefully "holding the bag" until he realizes he has been fooled. Other old practical jokes are begun as elaborate ceremonies of initiation. In Introducing to the King and Queen, the butt of the joke is solemnly presented to a boy and girl who are seated on two chairs placed a chair's width apart and covered with a blanket or sheet. When the dupe is invited to sit between them, the royal figures rise, dropping their guest to the floor or into a tub of water.

Some practical jokes are individual gags pulled by a "trickster" on an unsuspecting audience, and only a few of these may be traditional. One prank that seems to be traditional is the "surprising drink" gambit. The prankster writes for a long time in a crowded library reading room, dipping his steel pen into a supposed well of ink (really grape juice). Suddenly he is seized with a fit of coughing so severe that it seems he will strangle unless he has a drink. Without blinking an eye, he takes up the "ink" and drinks it down. Or the trickster may carry his sample of urine (really ginger ale)) into a doctor's waiting room. He examines it critically, then remarks "Looks a little thin; I'll run it through again," and drinks. Whatever their forms, pranks and practical jokes seem to have created another traditional form, the "practical-joke story" which describes past pranks and pranksters. Any of these might be analyzed, using Tallman's adaptation of the outline developed by Oliver H. P. Ferris, in terms of The Actors (prankster or pranksters versus victim or victims) and The Action (nature, intent, and result of the prank). For some further pranks, see the discussion of school customs in Chapter 15.

Kissing games take three different forms, *chasing kiss games* (like Kiss in the Ring) in which the kiss is a reward for catching a partner; *mixing kiss games* (like Post Office) in which pairing of couples occurs temporarily during the course of the game, and *couple kiss games* (like Flashlight) in which couples are established beforehand and the game allows them to kiss each other repeatedly (partner exchanging may occur later in the game). The popularity of these three types with different age groups is roughly equivalent to the first with secondary-school pupils, the second with junior and senior high-school students, and the third with senior high-school and college students. Flashlight (or Willpower, Spotlight, etc.) illustrates the most actively companionable level of such games. "It" is seated in the center of a room holding a flashlight, and couples sit all around the darkened room. When "it" flashes the light on, he or she points it to a couple, and if they are *not* kissing, he changes places with the appropriate member. A few kissing games are more like couple amusements than true games. In Perdiddle, for instance, the boy may kiss his girl companion if he sees a car with one headlight burned out and says "perdiddle" first. If she wins, she slaps him. In Show Kiss a boy and girl attend a movie with a love plot, and every time the screen characters kiss, they do, too.

Drinking games are popular in many college- and high-school party groups, but they seldom surface for any public recognition, either by school administrators or folklorists. Only the gag sweatshirts lettered "Olympic Drinking Team" and the red-eyed students in early-morning classes allude to them. Most drinking games are transparent excuses to "chug-a-lug"—that is, to down a drink of beer or liquor in one draught. The players supply themselves with drinks and then go through a complicated routine of some kind involving numbers, a speech, a series of actions, or a rhythmic chant. Whoever misses must chug-a-lug, refill his glass, and start over. The more often one misses some requirement such as saying "Buzz" for all sevens and multiples of seven ("Buzz-buzz" for seventy-seven, etc.), the more he drinks, and the more he tends to go on missing. Among the popular drinking games are Categories, Cardinal Puff, and Colonel Powwow; in the latter two a mock title is conferred upon the player who successfully completes the game.

Studying and Analyzing Games

The first students of American children's folk games—who would have been scandalized at the idea of drinking games—believed that they were rescuing the last remaining fragments of an "expiring custom," as W. W. Newell expressed it. Newell wrote regretfully in his 1883 introduction:

> The vine of oral tradition, of popular poetry, which for a thousand years has twined and bloomed on English soil, in

other days enriching with color and fragrance equally the castle and the cottage, is perishing at the roots; its prouder branches have long since been blasted, and children's song, its humble but longest-flowering offshoot, will soon have shared their fate.

Newell's explanations of the origins of children's games were typical of late nineteenth-century folklore theories. He regarded them as belonging to the peasantry recently, but earlier descended from an upper-class source; they came, "from above, from the intelligent class." He also believed, somewhat contradictively, that some games contained survivals of ancient rites and customs. Thus, he singled out eleven for special discussion as "mythological games." The familiar London Bridge, for example, was not only "a representation of the antagonism of celestial and infernal powers," but also an enactment of the human sacrifice once practiced to placate "the elemental spirit of the land, who detests any interference with the solitude he loves, [and] has an especial antipathy to bridges." (Newell's counterpart in England, Lady Alice B. Gomme, went even further with a survivals explanation for the game London Bridge, comparing several sacrifices associated with building foundations in the "actual facts of contemporary savagery" to traditions about London associated with the game.) But despite the romanticism of Newell's attitude toward games, the frills in his writing style, and the doubtful nature of his theories, the texts and notes of American children's singing games which he published were the groundwork for later studies.

In analyses of children's games, American folklorists seem to have by-passed the stage that was so important in folktale studies—that of historic-geographic studies. There are no monographs on American games to compare with one by a Finnish scholar on the European "Game of Rich and Poor" that was done according to the classic "Finnish method" of Aarne and Krohn. Instead of this, folk-game scholars in the United States have proceeded directly from classification and annotation to studies of the meaning, function, and structure of games. Some investigators have begun simply by asking children what their games mean to them and why they like them—always an interesting line of inquiry. In general it appears that what many children like most about games is the dramatic element. They tend to identify with the situations and characters represented in games, and they especially prefer games that suit their own personalities best. Often the children's comments will be gems of analysis (or "oral-literary criticism") in themselves. One shy child wrote for a folklorist who visited her class, "The game which I love best is grean gravel because it is not plaid ruffly." Another, responding to the delight of a collector in a rare game, said quietly, "I like this one best because *you* like it."

The game preferences of American children since the 1890s have been fairly closely documented in folklore studies. One survey covering the years 1895 to 1944 for the city of St. Louis pointed out the gradual disappearance there of the older English games, the increasing influence of school games, and the occasional invention of new folk games. A more recent study extended the data in both time and space including surveys from 1896, 1898, 1921, and 1959 in Massachusetts, South Carolina, San Francisco, and Ohio, respectively. Fully 180 different games or pastimes were involved, and conclusions were drawn concerning changing boy-girl game preferences and the changes in types of games played. One interesting finding in the study was that girls have definitely tended toward the traditional male roles in games (perhaps to match the emancipation of women in American society). At the same time, boys have tended increasingly to reject roles in games that they feel smack of femininity (Hopscotch, Jacks, Jump Rope, etc.), retreating instead to the rougher masculine sports where girls could traditionally follow only as cheerleaders or spectators. Another suggestion of the study was that formal games of a traditional nature may at last be dying out as the organized and commercialized distractions of American society take over.

The structural movement in folktale studies has influenced game studies. The suggestion is made that a folktale may be described as "a two-dimensional series of actions displayed on a one-dimensional track," and a game is "structurally speaking, a two-dimensional folktale." In other words, the hero and villain "motifemes" (see Chapter 10), which are simply narrated one at a time in a folktale, are assumed as dramatic characterizations in many folk games and then acted out to a conclusion. But whereas in tales the hero always wins, in games either side may conquer. Interestingly, there are also parallels in special forms of tales and games, for example, the cumulative tale has its counterpart in a game like Link Tag, and the trickster tale is reflected in practical jokes.

Another development in game studies comes from what has been called the behavioral or contextual approach to folklore. Expressing the dissatisfaction of some folklorists with "merely collecting and annotating [game] texts and studying them within diffusionist and survivalist frameworks," and so drawing instead upon "the work of social scientists who are interested in dynamic processes," Robert A. Georges proposes using behavioral models as a device for a holistic analysis of what he prefers to call "traditional play activities." Postulating that such activities are social events involving person-to-person communication as well as cognitive experiences that are clearly recognized by all players as "play," Georges has drawn up three proposed models to represent schematically some kinds of communication and interaction that occur during play. For example:

One social entity encodes and transmits to the other(s) a message, indicating his or her desire to engage in a particular traditional play activity. (The outside arrows represent general social rules; those marked "R" are specifically "play rules" which define this particular play activity.)

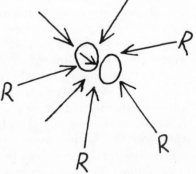

The above may seem like an overly jargonistic and complex way of representing a common situation, such as when one child says to others, "Hey, let's play Kick the Can!" It should be re-

membered, however, that such "game models" are only analytic devices drawn up in hopes of understanding the much
more complex nature of traditional play itself. They serve as
analogies or schematic representations of patterns of social interaction that constitute a clear basis for comparisons and further analysis. Also, such analyses ultimately derive from the
same basic field and reference work in folklore as did earlier
studies; as Georges puts it, his data are from "personal observation . . . participation . . . [and] printed descriptions and texts of
traditional play activities." But whether viewed from a comparative, psychological, structural, or behavioral approach, certainly folk games still offer a fertile and partly untilled field for
folklore collectors, classifiers, and analysts.

BIBLIOGRAPHIC NOTES

The "New and Enlarged Edition (1903) of W. W. Newell's *Games and
Songs of American Children* became the standard one. It was reprinted
in paperback in 1963. Lady Alice B. Gomme's important collection *The
Traditional Games of England, Scotland, and Ireland,* published in two
volumes in 1894 and 1898, was also published in paperback in 1964
(both modern editions are Dover books). The introduction by Carl
Withers for Newell and Dorothy Howard for Gomme are important
essays on game study.

Paul G. Brewster's article "Games and Sports in Sixteenth- and Seventeenth-Century English Literature," *WF* (1947): 143–56, helps to
give historical depth to studies of modern games. Brewster's work in
collecting, classifying, and annotating games has been prolific and important, especially in his book *American Non-Singing Games* (Norman:
University of Oklahoma Press, 1953), and his editing of the games in the
Frank C. Brown Collection of North Carolina Folklore (1: 29–159). A
varied and well-annotated collection in a folklore journal is Warren E.
Robert's "Children's Games and Game Rhymes," *HF* 8 (1949): 7–34.
Iona and Peter Opie's book *Children's Games in Street and Playground*
(New York: Oxford University Press, 1969) contains British children's
games, many of which have parallels in the United States.

Several scholars have proposed sweeping theories concerning games
and the impulse to play. Outstanding among them is Roger Caillois, editor of *Diogenes,* who published in that journal "The Structure and
Classification of Games," 12 (1955): 62–75, and "Unity of Play: Diversity of Games," 19 (1957): 92–121. Both articles were stages leading up
to his book *Man, Play, and Games* (New York: Free Press of Glencoe,

1961). An anthropological approach is represented in John M. Roberts, Malcolm J. Arth, and Robert R. Bush, "Games in Culture," *AA* 61 (1959): 597–605. Roberts collaborated with Brian Sutton-Smith and Adam Kendon in a special application of this theory in "Strategy in Games and Folk Tales," *JSP* 61 (1963): 185–99. Starting with the observation that "conflicts induced by child training . . . lead to involvement in games . . . which in turn provide[s] . . . learning important both to players and their societies," these scholars confirmed their hypothesis that "folktales with strategic outcomes would be found in the same cultural setting as games of strategy." They did this by comparing games and tales from several cultures, sorted on the basis of whether strategy was present, and correlating these with other data on the cultures.

Pastimes have seldom been treated in separate folklore studies. For articles on Cat's Cradle we must turn to British publications—W. Innes Pocock's article in *Folklore* 17 (1906): 73–93, 351–73; and Dorothy Howard's in the same journal, 72 (1961): 385–87. A fascinating little booklet, Kathleen Haddon's *String Games for Beginners*, first published in 1934, was still in print recently. The forty-page pamphlet contains descriptions of twenty-eight string figures from various native cultures, with instructions for learning them, and even a piece of string with which to practice. The pamphlet is published by W. Heffer and Sons, Ltd., Cambridge, England. The 1906 book by Caroline Furness Jayne, *String Figures and How to Make Them*, with an introduction by A. C. Haddon, was republished in paperback by Dover Books (New York, 1962). See also Lyn Harrington, "Eskimo String Figures," *School Arts* 50 (May 1951): 319–21, which has some good photographs although limited discussion.

Ray B. Browne's article on California jump-rope rhymes, cited in the notes to Chapter 7, analyzes the various *actions* of this popular pastime as well as the rhymes that are chanted with them. The pastime called Chinese Jump Rope, which started to be popular in the United States about 1963, has been described in Ruth Hawthorne's, "Classifying Jump-Rope Games," *KFQ* 11 (1966): 113–26, and Michael Owen Jones's, "Chinese Jumprope," *SFQ* 30 (1966): 256–63. The pastime is performed with two players holding a long elastic loop stretched between their ankles while a third player jumps in and out of it, stretching it into patterns with her toes as she does so. The same pastime with the same name (Kinesersjip) was reported from Copenhagen; see Erik Kaas Nielsen's *Det lille Folk* (Forlaget Fremad, 1965). Roger Welsch discussed a group of "Nebraska Finger Games" (mostly pastimes), in *WF* 25 (1966): 173–94.

A fascinating window into the past is opened by E. Leslie Gilliam's article "Folk-Lore of Children's Games" published in *The Peterson Magazine*, n.s. 5 (Nov. 1895): 1184–92, a reference almost impossible to come by nowadays, worthy of reprinting, if only for its excellent photographs of children at play. A similar reminiscent study is by Thomas S. Yukic, "Niagara River Playground: The Allen Avenue Gang, 1925–1946 (An Historical Glance at a Boyhood on the Niagara River)," *NYF* 1 (1975): 210–28.

A good survey of some older games is found in Mac E. Barrick's chapter "Games from the Little Red School House" in *Two Penny Ballads and Four Dollar Whiskey*, ed. Kenneth S. Goldstein and Robert H. Byington (Hatboro, Pa.: Folklore Associates, 1966), pp. 95–120. In another such article, Gilbert C. Kettelkamp's "Country School Games in the Past," *MAF* 8 (1981): 113–23, the early twentieth-century games from south-central Illinois discussed are called Blackman, Darebase, Hatball, Sowhole, and Longtown.

Various games of physical action are described in Eugenia L. Millard's "Racing, Chasing, and Marching with the Children of the Hudson-Champlain Valleys," *NYFQ* 15 (1959): 132–50. Vance Randolph and Nancy Clemens's article "Ozark Mountain Party-Games," in *JAF* 49 (1936): 199–206, describes a variety of guessing games, forfeit games, courtship games, kissing games, and active games in a regional folk culture. John Harrington Cox printed forty texts of singing games from West Virginia with bibliography and musical notation in *SFQ* 6 (1942): 183–261. Active games of city children were early collected by Steward Culin in "Street Games of Boys in Brooklyn, N.Y.," *JAF* 4 (1891): 221–37. Excellent candid photographs of New York City children playing five popular street games were published in "Youths' Concrete Joys," *Sports Illustrated* (August 17, 1959), pp. 18–22.

Some games of racial and ethnic minorities are studied in Bessie Jones and Bess Lomax Hawes, *Step It Down: Games, Plays, Songs and Stories from the Afro-American Heritage* (New York: Harper & Row, 1972); Margaret K. Brady, " 'Gonna Shimmy Shimmy 'til the Sun Goes Down': Aspects of Verbal and Nonverbal Socialization in the Play of Black Girls," *Folklore Annual* 6 (1974): 1–16; and Clement L. Valetta, "Friendship and Games in Italian-American Life," *KFQ* 15 (1970): 174–87.

A reminiscent essay on a game played with objects is J. W. Ashton's "Marble Playing in Lewiston [Maine] Fifty Years Ago," *NEF* 3 (1960): 24–27. A more rigorously statistical article along the same lines (but concerning New Zealand) in Brian Sutton-Smith's "Marbles Are In," in *WF* 12 (1953): 186–93. (This essay is reprinted in Sutton-Smith's *The Folkgames of Children*, mentioned below, pp. 455–64.) An extremely thorough study of the history of one ball game is Erwin Mehl's article "Baseball in the Stone Age," *WF* 7 (1948): 145–61, supplemented by further notes in *WF* 8 (1949): 152–56. Robert Cochran's "The Interlude of Game: A Study of Washers," *WF* 38 (1979): 71–82, describes a pitching game, somewhat like horseshoes, played by adults using metal washers about two inches in diameter.

Games based on mental activity are seldom treated separately from other games. Three exceptions are Eugenia L. Millard's article "A Sampling of Guessing Games," in *NYFQ* 13 (1957): 135–43, and two articles on games played by college teachers or students: Michael Dane Moore, "Linguistic Aggression and Literary Allusion," *WF* 38 (1979): 259–66, and John William Johnson, "Killer: An American Campus Folk Game," *IF* 13 (1980): 81–101. An interesting popular piece is Martin Gardner's "Mathematical Games. A Bit of Foolishness for April Fools' Day," in *Scientific American* 208 (April 1963): 156–66.

Practical jokes have attracted several studies. Anne Penick described six favorite pranks in "Look Out, Newcomer!" *MF* 4 (1954): 239–43. Kelsie Harder discussed Introductions to the King and Queen under the title "The Preacher's Seat," in *TFSB* 23 (1957): 38–39. The prank called Going to See the Widow has been the subject of several notes, which were consolidated and supplemented by Wayland D. Hand in *WF* 17 (1958): 275–76. An interesting example of a practical joke apparently growing out of a folktale was described by James Ralston Caldwell in "A Tale Actualized in a Game" in *JAF* 54 (1945): 50. Some pranks involving use of the telephone are discussed by Norine Dresser in *NYFQ* 29 (1973): 121–30; others concerning automobiles may be found in *NYFQ* 30 (1974): 44–65, in an article by M. Licht. A special issue of *SFQ*, edited by Richard S. Tallman and devoted to studies of practical jokes, contains a note and five extended essays on such subjects as definitions of the genre, wedding pranks, and summer-camp pranks; see the December 1974 issue (38: 251–331). Pranks are an important part of the behavior described by Robert S. McCarl, Jr., in "Smokejumper Initiation: Ritualized Communication in a Modern Occupation," *JAF* 89 (1976): 49–66.

A number of important studies by Brian Sutton-Smith, a leading student of children's games, has been printed in the AFS Bibliographical and Special series (No. 24) as *The Folkgames of Children* (Austin: University of Texas Press, 1972). Among these in his 1959 essay "The Kissing Games of Adolescents in Ohio," which furnished the terminology used in this chapter. Richard M. Dorson discussed college drinking games in Chapter 7 of *American Folklore*, pp. 265–66.

The historic-geographic study of the dramatic European "Game of Rich and Poor" was published by Mrs. Elsa Enäjärvi Haavio in *FFC* no. 100 (1932). An important early study of American children's games and the attitudes of their players was made by Jean Olive Heck, "Folk Poetry and Folk Criticism, as Illustrated by Cincinnati Children in Their Singing Games and Their Thoughts about These Games," *JAF* 40 (1927): 1–77. Leah Rachel Clara Yoffie published her study "Three Generations of Children's Singing Games in St. Louis" in *JAF* 60 (1947): 1–51; Brian Sutton-Smith's more comprehensive article along similar lines was the 1961 publication "Sixty Years of Historical Change in the Game

Preferences of American Children," reprinted in *The Folkgames of Children*, pp. 258–81. Alan Dundes, who proposed the structural approach to folktales, has applied his theories to games in "On Game Morphology: A Study of the Structure of Non-Verbal Folklore," *NYFQ* 20 (1964): 276–88, reprinted in *Analytic Essays in Folklore*, pp. 80–87, and in *Readings in American Folklore*, pp. 334–44. Robert A. Georges outlines the contextual-behavioral approach referred to at the end of this chapter in "The Relevance of Models for Analyses of Traditional Play Activities," *SFQ* 33 (1969): 1–23.

IV · MATERIAL FOLK
TRADITIONS

Essentially, the order of subjects presented in this book follows the general history of studies of American oral traditions, from the folk*lore* interest begun in the late nineteenth century to the folk*life* studies of today. These final chapters deal with material folk traditions, which constitute the largest part of the field of folklife and, in the United States, perhaps the fastest-growing branch. Material folk traditions are too diverse to be covered in a few pages, so the following chapters are mainly an outline of materials and a summary of what present studies suggest, along with some technical guidelines on recording, documenting, and analyzing material traditions. Following a short general introduction to folklife studies, the areas surveyed are folk architecture, folk handicrafts and art, folk costumes, and folk foods.

19
Folklife

Folklife and Folklore

The concept of "folklife," introduced in Chapter 15 in connection with customs and festivals, offers a promising area for original research in American folklore. Offsetting generations of literature-oriented folklore studies, the students of American folklife examine the whole range of traditional verbal lore, behavior, and material creations in folk circulation, especially the latter two categories.

A confusion in basic terminology surrounding **folklife** is immediately evident. At least in theory, the term "folklore" is synonymous with "folklife," and, in fact, many American folklorists and their publications employ the terms in this way—"folklore," in its flexible connotation taking in *all* folk-cultural products. But changing usage is evident. For example, while Alan Dundes's book *The Study of Folklore* (1965) contained chapters on verbal lore as well as on hex marks and water witching, Richard M. Dorson's *Folklore and Folklife* (1972) used both terms in the title in order to embrace the same spectrum of verbal, customary, and material folk traditions. The present textbook could be retitled *The Study of American Folklife*, taking the lead from Don Yoder, who has written, "I prefer to follow [others] in subsuming *folklore* (defining it after William Bascom as the verbal arts of a society) under *folklife*, as only one aspect of folk culture." However, an argument against this change is that American folklorists *as a group* have not yet adopted "folklife" full scale for their journals, scholarly societies, and teaching. So we follow current usage here, still defining "folklife," as Yoder says, "by default," to mean only customary and material folk traditions, even though there is good reason to substitute the word immediately and permanently for the much-abused term "folklore."

Another preliminary problem is the lack of accepted procedures and theories for American folklife studies, many of which have been simply descriptive approaches to individual artifacts or artisans. Again, Don Yoder offers guidance, identifying "three essentially different approaches": (1) Historical Folklife Studies; (2) Folklife Studies and Survivals; and (3) Folklife Studies and the Ethnographic Present. An example of the first approach is that of Theodore Blegen's documenting of the "grass-roots history" of Norwegian-American folk culture; of the second, the efforts to preserve examples of early American architecture; and of the third, questionnaire surveys of existing traditional crafts, such as quilting.

Perhaps the best direction to look in for a model of folklife studies is to Europe, especially to Scandinavia, where systematic research began. In Sweden, folklife study dates from the end of the nineteenth century with the establishment of museums of folk architecture and folk artifacts. The distinctive Scandinavian format became the open-air collection of old farmhouses and out-buildings, the earliest museum being *Skansen* park near Stockholm, which was shortly imitated in Norway, Denmark, Finland, and eventually in many central and eastern European countries. In 1937 the Swedes formally launched their term for the whole field by beginning publication of the journal *Folk-Liv* with all articles printed in English. The Swedish classification system for archiving folklife was soon widely adopted. The most convenient sources in English based on the Swedish pattern deal with Irish folklife. The official collectors' guide used in Ireland, *A Handbook of Irish Folklore* (reprinted in 1963), summarizes all the materials to be investigated, while a book like E. Estyn Evans's *Irish Folk Ways* (New York, 1957) gives a systematic discussion of the findings of fieldwork and research.

Conceptions and Misconceptions

Before the word "folklife" entered the vocabulary of American folklorists, there was a considerable number of what might be termed folklife studies done from the point of view of art history in the United States and centering on folk crafts and folk art. Some art historians continue to use the term "folk art" in the special sense of work by artists lacking formal training and reflecting everyday life. An important task of American folklife research, then, is to locate, evaluate, and synthesize these studies in order to establish a critical bibliography for the field and to determine what genuinely traditional material has already been described. The beginning student must recognize that not every publication about handicrafts or "folk art" takes a folkloristic approach; indeed, some folklorists now prefer to ignore terms like "folk" and "tradition" in their studies of objects that ordinary people create and embellish in their own individual ways. A review of two representative older publications—one a period survey and the other concerning a particular group—illustrates some of the differences between these writings and modern folklife research on similar material.

To a degree the popular interest in folk arts and crafts that arose in the 1920s and 1930s may have been a reaction against nonrepresentational modern art, but at the same time, ironically, the modern art movement claims folk art as part of its own background. In 1932 the New York Museum of Modern Art arranged an exhibition called *American Folk Art* in which two typical attitudes toward the subject were revealed in the subtitle: *The Art of the Common Man in America, 1750–1900.* The first implication was that "folk art" must be the work of "common" people, or as the text explained, "people with little book learning in art techniques, and no academic training"; the second was that the golden age of such art in America extended from the middle of the eighteenth century to the beginning of the twentieth. Further, the classification of the works by medium (oil, pastel, water-color, velvet painting, wood sculpture, metal sculpture, etc.) suggested that folk art, like academic art, should be viewed as being mainly "creative" rather than utilitarian.

That is, the artifacts chosen for display were judged significant for their decorative, not their functional, qualities. Yet many of the works illustrated were definitely useful (and, it may be hoped, effective)—weathervanes, advertising symbols (like cigar-store Indians), and signs. So it seems that once these kinds of things were admitted as "art," the door should have been opened for needlework, quilting, basketry, pottery, toymaking, and many other crafts now studied by folklife scholars, and valued (by folk and folklorists alike) for both their beauty and their utility. Unfortunately, few of these folk-art scholars pursued such crafts seriously. In any case, it seems highly doubtful that the media and period divisions of typical art histories serve any useful purpose in folklife studies.

Numerous books and articles have been based on a similar conception of American folk art, although there is much diversity in the examples to which they refer. A broader scope is found in works on folk groups and their artifacts, such as the studies of Pennsylvania German (or "Dutch") material traditions. All the distinctive forms of building, handicrafts, and decorative art in this regional-immigrant group have been the subject of attention, but the approaches and findings here are usually not applicable to other American folk groups. Few other American groups have the regional, linguistic, and general cultural unity of the Pennsylvania Germans, and few other groups go to the lengths that the Amish and Mennonites do to preserve old ways of life. The very impressive fruits of Pennsylvania German folklife studies inspire students of Anglo-American materials, but they cannot say much about what the students will find elsewhere or how they should approach it.

One basic survey in this field is Frances Lichten's *Folk Art of Rural Pennsylvania*, published in 1946. The folk art is "rural," and it flourished, according to Lichten's discussion, from the middle of the eighteenth century to about 1850. "Art" here is taken to include such disparate items as coverlets, butter molds, stove plates, and decorated barns (i.e., those bearing "hex marks"). The arrangement of items is again by medium, but here keyed to the close relationship of old-time farm life with the land—its raw materials, its crops, and its supported animals.

Such a classification brings together some odd combinations: stone houses or foundations for houses are with gravestones ("from beneath the surface of the earth"); wood houses are with cabinet-making and ornamental carving ("from the woodland"); and thatching is with basketry ("from the surface of the earth"). The book, with its many good illustrations, presents a nostalgic picture of the arts and crafts of a special group in a bygone era, but a different presentation will be required for scholars who want to begin investigating American folklife more generally, particularly if they intend to study contemporary instances of material folk tradition.

The principle of classification for folklife materials developed in Sweden and followed in Ireland and elsewhere in Europe is not by medium but by the *use* to which customs and artifacts are applied, beginning with land use, cultivation, housing, settlement, and subsistence crafts, and proceeding through furniture, domestic handwork, leisure-time handicrafts, decorative arts, representational art, musical instruments, folk toys, and the like. Basically, it is an arrangement of the whole of traditional customs and materials, ranging from the necessities of life to the pleasures.

For the purpose of a systematic presentation of the kinds of folklore, we have already dealt briefly with the customary traditions in Section III. The study of material traditions (*folk artifacts*) presents special problems, however, which are best taken up separately. When studying them, researchers will still collect, classify, and analyze data (see Chapter 2), but must also learn some new techniques. Folk artifacts must be photographed or sketched, even if they are going to be brought in physically from the field for an archive or a museum. For most field workers, then, this means the ability to make simple measured drawings and the acquisition of at least the rudiments of good documentary still photography.

Field Work: Using the Camera

Probably the best type of camera for all-around folklife field work is a good single-lens-reflex (SLR) model taking 35 mm.

film, with a built-in coupled exposure meter. Such cameras are available at a wide range of prices and with a variety of attachments and accessories. Their chief advantage is that one sights on the subject and focuses the image directly through the camera lens, thus seeing at the time exactly what will be in the picture. Since lenses in all but the cheapest SLR models are detachable and the metering system is either wholly automatic or read directly through the focusing and viewing window, this camera system offers great flexibility and ease of operation at fairly moderate costs. (The automatic electronic models are somewhat more limiting, but faster to use.) It is not necessary to master the technical details behind the inner workings of such a camera to use it well—setting the exposure, for example, is usually just a matter of lining up certain indicators in the viewfinder. But if photographers acquire the rudiments of photographic theory (as contained in the owner's manual, for example), their results will be far superior to those obtained with any fixed-focus snapshot camera. Whatever the camera used, one should practice with it and see the results at home before using it for field work.

The 35 mm. film size, of course, is the standard one for transparencies, from which color prints of publishable quality may also easily be made. Black-and white 35 mm. negatives, even on sensitive film (such as Kodak Tri-x), are also sufficiently free of "grain" (image coarseness) to make excellent enlargements. Since both slides and monochrome prints are useful for different purposes, and since 35 mm. film comes only in twenty– or thirty-six–exposure rolls, field photographers should acquire as soon as they can afford it two identical SLR camera bodies on which they may interchange their basic lenses, loading each body with a different film.

Besides the "normal" lens supplied with the camera, the two most useful extras are a wide-angle lens and a zoom-telephoto lens. The former can be used when walls, shrubbery, or topography prevent getting far enough back to take the subject in with the normal lens. One must be careful, however, with a wide-angle lens not to tip the camera off a straight vertical plane; this introduces distortion. The zoom lens offers in a single accessory a range of possibilities for magnifying a selected portion of the subject. Such shots are useful not only for bringing in distant buildings, but also for permitting close detail shots of remote features like chimney tops or cornice moldings, and with this lens the camera may even be used as a telescope to scout distant features on the landscape in order to see if they are worth hiking to, for close examination.

Both black-and-white and color films are produced with sensitivities to accommodate the existing illumination in most field conditions on relatively light days. For unusually dark conditions or subjects, the photographer should have a supplementary flash unit, such as the small electronic flash sold as an accessory with most cameras. The only other basic pieces of equipment needed are a medium-yellow filter for darkening sky tone in black-and-white photography, and a tripod for any exposures slower than $\frac{1}{60}$ of a second, particularly telephoto shots. A cable release should be used for tripod shots, or the photographer may set the camera's self-timer to take the picture, in order to avoid camera movement and achieve maximum sharpness.

Sharp, clear, and well-exposed pictures rather than artistic compositions or "trick" shots are needed for documentary purposes. Generally, one should take *many* pictures, following the reasoning that film is cheaper than travel and that the building or other artifact of interest may no longer be in existence even if one does return to the spot someday. Furthermore, black-and-white 35 mm. film and processing are inexpensive, especially if photographers learn to "roll their own" film from bulk rolls into cartridges. (Home processing of film, also cheap and simple, is the next step.) Long, medium, and close-up shots should always be taken, along with an indicator of scale in some pictures—a yardstick, ruler, pencil, hand, or person at one side of the shot for size comparison. Other "in-frame documentation" might include a meaningful inscription or sign, the informant demonstrating use of the artifact, or the tools and ingredients for a subject. For any traditional process, such as the steps of construction, a series of pictures illustrating the sequence should be taken.

Negatives, slides, and prints should be systematically filed and carefully preserved after they are processed. The 35 mm. size allows for easy printing of one full black-and-white roll on a single 8 × 10 proofsheet and subsequent filing of these proofs, plus the negatives (in strips of five or six frames), in loose-leaf binders. Photographers or their helpers should keep a log of data on all shots taken, information used to label and annotate the picture file. It is essential at the time of taking pictures to ask all persons appearing in them to sign a release form allowing possible later publication.

Studying Folklife

Folk artifacts should be measured carefully, and the materials from which they are constructed must be identified. Maps and atlases should be made up for recording the locations of finds. Sometimes it is desirable and possible to collect the artifact itself—a complex task when buildings, fencing, farm equipment, and the like are involved. Artifacts may need repairs before they can be moved or studied, and large-scale restoration and reconstruction may be necessary, using historical records or old plans as guides.

Preserving diverse material objects is much more complicated than filing manuscript sheets or tape recordings in an archive. The usual archive for manuscript folklore can adequately accept photographs, sketches, or descriptions of material traditions, but museum facilities and techniques are required for storing and displaying the objects themselves. Classification and analysis of folk artifacts require, first, that the truly traditional variations be distinguished from individual innovations that are not transmitted, and, second, that the significant traditional variations that define classes and subclasses be identified.

Students of American material folk traditions have fewer indexes and bibliographies to guide them than does the folklorist working with verbal or customary lore, although this situation is improving. They also have to become familiar with a large number of foreign folklife studies, and must search for descriptions of earlier American folk artifacts in nonscholarly publications and in local histories, diaries, collections of letters, travelers' accounts, and pioneer reminiscences. Regional literature may yield folklife data, too, such as this brief description of a log stile from Mark Twain's *Adventures of Huckleberry Finn:*

> A rail fence round a two-acre yard; a stile, made out of logs sawed off and up-ended, in steps, like barrels of a different length, to climb over the fence with, and for the women to stand on when they are going to jump onto a horse. (Chapter XXXII)

The ideal institution for carrying on folklife studies is a combination museum and research center, such as the Norwegian Folk Museum at Bygdøy, near Oslo, the Nordic Museum in Stockholm, or the Village Museum in Bucharest, Romania. There are many other examples elsewhere in Europe of such museums, but two of particular relevance for American-immigrant folklife studies are the Welsh Folk Museum at St. Fagans (near Cardiff) and the Ulster Folk and Transport Museum at Holywood, Northern Ireland. The closest American equivalent to these is the Farmers' Museum in Cooperstown, New York, a fine re-creation of an early nineteenth-century New York farm and village. Other notable American museums containing some folklife materials, also built around a village reconstruction, are Old Sturbridge Village, Massachusetts; the Stuhr Museum of the Prairie Pioneer, Grand Island, Nebraska; Old Mystic Seaport, Connecticut; and New Salem Village, Illinois. Oriented more to town life than rural folk culture are such establishments as Colonial Williamsburg, Virginia, and Greenfield Village in Dearborn, Michigan. Other notable collections are in the Shelburne Museum, Burlington, Vermont; the International Folk Art Museum, Santa Fe, New Mexico; the Norwegian-American Museum, Decorah, Iowa; the Du Pont Museum in Winterthur, Delaware; and many others. "Living Farm" museums exist near Des Moines, Iowa; Minneapolis, Minnesota; Atlanta, Georgia; and elsewhere. An accurate reproduction of "Plimoth Plantation" as it was in the early seventeenth century has been constructed in Massachusetts, and leading up to the United States Bicentennial many similar projects and existing museums received grants to establish or expand facilities. Some Canadian museums with folklife materials are Black Creek Village and Upper Canada Village in Ontario and Pioneer Heritage Park in Calgary, Alberta. To some degree in such institutions the casual visitor may observe displays of artifacts often housed in traditional buildings and see demonstrations of traditional work techniques, while a visiting scholar has access to stored collections of objects and to reference sources.

Since no unified approach to American material traditions has been established, each museum, publication, or research project tends to have its own emphasis and its own peculiarities. Many people conducting research that falls into the field of American folklife are apparently unaware of similar European studies. And even those who know the work in Europe find that European methods are not fully adaptable to American materials. For instance, here we have no single national culture, but instead a merging of numerous foreign elements. Pioneering put European Americans into a unique relationship with the wilderness continent, but technological change has been so rapid during the short history of the United States that pioneer methods and materials were either lost entirely or changed drastically before there was any interest in studying or preserving them. The social equality, political democracy, and economic opportunity of the New World, with the resulting effects on labor and crafts, were unparalleled in the Old World.

Despite these conditions, the key to studies of American folk artifacts remains the same as for all folklore—it is *tradition*. We may investigate in artifacts, as well as in texts of verbal lore or descriptions of customs, the kinds of things that are transmitted in repeated forms casually by word of mouth or by demonstration. We may attempt to discover how traditional materials originated, how changes occurred, and in what manner traditional variants related to the rest of the folk culture from which they came. We can recognize in material traditions not only survivals from the past, but also recent folk creations, and we should be prepared to admit that traditional "folk" methods of work may be followed by professional craftspeople and artists as well as by amateurs. Above all, we should not be misled in our studies by the notion that *every* artifact that is rural or old-fashioned or handmade is a piece of three-dimensional folklore, any more than we think that every amateur poem is a *folk* poem or that every picturesque remark is a *folk* saying.

BIBLIOGRAPHIC NOTES

There were appeals for many years for scholars to devote more systematic attention to American folklife. See, for example, two by Norbert F. Riedl, "Folklore vs. *Volkskunde*: A Plea for More Concern with the Study of American Folk Culture on the Part of Anthropologists," *TFSB* 31 (1965): 47–53, and "Folklore and the Study of Material Aspects of Folk Culture," *JAF* 79 (1966): 557–63. An important guide for such studies is Robert Wildhaber's "A Bibliographical Introduction to American Folklife," *NYFQ* 21 (1965): 259–302. Wildhaber mainly lists books, and he includes works on folk architecture, furniture, "imagery and popular painting," tools and utensils, wood carving, metalwork, pottery, glassware, signs, and scrimshaw.

An indication of progress in the decade since these works is W. F. H. Nicolaisen's report "Surveying and Mapping North American Culture," *MSF* 3 (1975): 35–39. This article furnishes the background of efforts to establish an American Folklore Atlas, which will begin with a pilot study of foodways. See also *Approaches to the Study of Material Aspects of American Culture*, a special issue of *FF* (12:2–3, 1979), ed. Simon J. Bronner and Stephen P. Poyser.

The volume of essays *American Folklife* (Austin: University of Texas Press, 1976), ed. Don Yoder (several times quoted in this chapter), contains important historical and theoretical statements as well as several excellent studies. Contributors discuss anthropological, esthetic, historic, and geographical perspectives; the subjects of specific studies include folk boats, coil basketry, log architecture, tollgate lore, ethnic lore, and folk customs and rituals. In particular, Warren E. Robert's report "The Whitaker-Waggoner Log House from Morgan County, Indiana" (pp. 185–27) is a model of folk architectural documentation.

Most American folklore journals did not in the past publish much on material tradition, but useful semi-scholarly articles may be found in periodicals such as *Ozark Guide, Mountain Life and Work, Antiques,* and *Hobbies.* Folklife studies are sometimes also published in the journals of historians and geographers. An important journal for studies of American material traditions is *Pennsylvania Folklife,* published quarterly under that name since 1957 but preceded by other variously titled publications of the Pennsylvania Folklife Society. Articles in this journal go beyond Pennsylvania German material, and they are generally well documented and always excellently illustrated. An important survey is Don Yoder's "The Folklife Studies Movement," *PF* 13 (July 1963): 43–56. (For further references to works on Pennsylvania German folklife, see Wildhaber's bibliography.) More recently, the journal *Pioneer America* (later renamed *Material Culture*) entered the field; the student should look here for Thomas J. Schlereth's statement "American Studies and American Things," *PA* 14 (1982): 47–66.

As an introduction to European folklife studies, besides works mentioned in this chapter, one should consult such journals as *Scottish Studies*, *Ulster Folk Life*, the Swedish *Folk-Liv*, and the English *Folk Life*. Sigurd Erixon's study "West European Connections and Culture Relations," *Folk-Liv* 2 (1938): 137–72, is a basic one. Specifically, for the British backgrounds, see Ronald H. Buchanan's "Geography and Folk Life," *Folk Life* 1 (1963): 5–15; Alexander Fenton's "An Approach to Folklife Studies," *KFQ* 12 (1967): 5–21; and the essays gathered in *Studies in Folk Life*, ed. Geraint Jenkins (New York: Barnes & Noble, 1969). Richard M. Dorson was the special editor of an issue of *JFI* (2:3 [1965]), 239–366, devoted to "Folklore and Folklife Studies in Great Britain and Ireland." R. W. Brunskill's *Illustrated Handbook of Vernacular Architecture* (New York: Universe Books, 1970) clarifies the architectural terminology and has some direct relevance to American houses, although its scope is mostly British. In "Some Similarities between American and European Folk Houses," *PA* 3 (1971): 8–14, Eugene M. Wilson surveys European antecedents for the central-passage ("dog trot") house type.

Two important essays on the role of museums in folklife research are Howard Wight Marshall's "Folklife and the Rise of American Folk Museums," *JAF* 90 (1977): 391–413, and Ormond Loomis's "Sources on Folk Museums and Living Historical Farms," *FF* Bibliographic and Special Series, no. 16 (1977).

An interesting early survey of American folklife is found in *Lewis Miller: Sketches and Chronicles. The Reflections of a Nineteenth Century Pennsylvania German Folk Artist* (York, Pa.: Historical Society of York County, 1966). Some 160 selections from a total of about 2,000 drawings and water colors are reproduced, illustrating many diverse aspects of everyday life. Perhaps a comparable effort, documented with camera and sketches, is the series called *Foxfire* (Garden City, N.Y.: Doubleday, 1 [1972], 2 [1973], 3 [1975], ed. Eliot Wigginton, a Georgia high-school teacher who inspired his students to study the folk culture of their own region and who parlayed a small periodical into book-length publications, government grants, and many spinoff *Foxfire*-like projects. Log-cabin building is covered in the original *Foxfire Book*, and a subject index is included in *Foxfire* 3.

The cultural-geography approach to American folklife materials may be seen in such works as Amos Rapoport's *House Form and Culture* (Foundations of Cultural Geography Series; Englewood Cliffs, N.J.:

Prentice-Hall, 1969) and in such regional surveys as Peter O. Wacker's *The Muconetcong Valley of New Jersey: A Historical Geography* (New Brunswick, N.J.: Rutgers University Press, 1968) and Malcolm L. Comeaux's *Atchafalaya Swamp Life: Settlement and Folk Occupations* (Geoscience and Man, vol. 2; Baton Rouge: Louisiana State University, 1972). Milton B. Newton, Jr., a geographer, has published a useful booklet as *Mélanges*, no. 2 (Museum of Geoscience publication) *Louisiana House Types: A Field Guide* (Baton Rouge: Louisiana State University, 1971). Another example of folk architecture discussed by a geographer is in Joseph E. Spencer's "House Types in Southern Utah," *GR* 35 (1945): 444–57. Two good studies of folk architecture appear in the "Material Culture in the South" special issue of *SFQ* 39 (Dec. 1975): 303–406.

Austin E. Fife was a leading advocate and practitioner of folklife studies in the West. Two of his important survey articles are "Folklore of Material Culture on the Rocky Mountain Frontier," *ArQ* 13 (1957): 101–10, and "Folklore and Local History," *UHQ* 31 (1963): 315–23. Austin and Alta Fife, together with Henry H. Glassie, edited *Forms upon the Frontier: Folklife and Folk Arts in the United States*, containing several papers on Western folk architecture and folk arts and crafts from a conference held at Logan, Utah (*Utah State University Monograph Series* 16 [April 1969]).

20
Folk Architecture

What Is Folk Architecture?

Folk architecture, sometimes called "vernacular architecture" (that which is common or native in a given area), includes all traditional nonacademic building types. In particular, these consist of cabins and houses, barns, smokehouses, wash houses, summer kitchens, spring houses, privies, stables, and other agricultural outbuildings, some taverns, shops, offices, churches and other meeting houses, and numerous minor building types such as carriage houses, sheds, garages, hunting blinds, ice houses, boat houses, mills, and covered bridges. Folk architecture, and especially folk housing, is the most basic aspect of traditional material culture, being both a three-dimensional product of folk-cultural concepts and an important continuing influence on these same concepts. The placement of the traditional buildings in relation to one another and to the landscape, their floor plans and heights, the volumes enclosed in them, the light admitted and views afforded by them, the materials of their construction and decoration, their functional qualities, and many other factors all constitute statements of certain human values, and at the same time they are pervasive forces preserving these values. Not only the physical needs for heat, shelter, storage, and uses provided by these buildings, but also the spiritual values they sustain are important to the study of traditional buildings.

Folk architecture in the United States was typified during the settlement period by the use of the most easily available local materials for building in inherited traditional forms. The teepees, wigwams, and lodges of the native Americans, the first log houses in the Eastern half of the country, the forts, dugouts, and lean-tos of explorers and homesteaders, the sod houses of the Great Plains, the adobe houses of the Southwest, and other forms all followed this principle. Henry Glassie's study, in the Appendix, of cabin types in the Southern Mountains is a prime instance of how detailed and careful the analysis of only a single kind of dwelling in one region may be. It demonstrates the application of the general theory and method for folklife field work outlined in the previous chapter and deals specifically with problems of tracing national origins of American building designs and techniques. Furthermore, Glassie's sketches and field data, map, statistics, and bibliographic documentation are all fine examples of the effective presentation of folk-architectural research. For all of these reasons, we will refer much of the following brief discussion to this base reference, which should be studied at the same time.

Architectural Form

Folk tradition may be evident in the form, the construction techniques and materials, and the uses of buildings, but it is only the first of these criteria—form—that can serve to identify genuine folk architecture and establish its types and subtypes. In other words, a log cabin is "folk" not because it is log, but because it is a traditionally laid-out cabin, "a single construction unit . . . less than two stories high" (page 532). While a true folk cabin may be made of many kinds or combinations of material (as Glassie shows), other non-folk house types (that is, nontraditional forms) might be constructed out of logs joined in traditional ways—a lavish private hunting lodge or a motel, for example. By the same token, there might be traditional or nontraditional uses of buildings, such as holding an art show in a pioneer cabin or a fiddling contest in a football stadium. Form alone defines a building itself as belonging to a culturally viable "folk" tradition.

Since form is the basic criterion, close description and measurement are the chief objects of folk architectural field work. A building under study as an artifact of folk architecture should be measured carefully along each outside wall with a long tape measure, measured again inside from the corners up to and then across each opening, and finally measured for height and for the thickness of walls. A drawn floor plan should indicate the placement of all openings, chimneys, and stairways, besides giving either an accurate indication of scale (see Glassie's floor plans) or the measurements themselves. An "elevation" drawing, also showing scale, or else a photograph can document the building's height and roof shape. It is important to remember during such field work to include all additions ("appendages") to the basic house (porch, shed, "wings," etc.) and all details of ornamentation in the documentation, but during analysis to disregard all but the essential construction unit itself in the establishment of types. The level of further details to be taken down will depend upon the needs and interests of the researcher, but a good general rule is to "keep track of everything," insofar as the time and the facilities allow.

The specific data of field observations and measurements are combined and generalized in order to describe the patterns of folk housing. Glassie speaks of the Southern cabins' *primary characteristics* (approximate height, shape, general floor plan, etc.) and their *secondary characteristics* (exact measurements, construction details, interior partitions, etc.) on page 552. In general, for all folk-architectural analysis it is the floor plan and the height of the building that are the prime considerations. The placement of doors and chimney are considered primary, but placement of windows and stairs, being more variable, are secondary to classification. One advantage of our major concern with the building's essential form rather than with the other criteria is that whatever the additions to or the condition of a structure, the form remains; asbestos shingle siding and galvanized metal roofing may effectively disguise the log and wood-shingle construction of a cabin, but they cannot hide the square shape or the gable-end chimney of the original.

It should be emphasized that the folk builders were really following traditions; they could just as well have followed a circular floor plan (like that of a Navajo hogan), built an L-shaped house, or placed the chimney centrally in the floor plan or away from a gable end; yet seldom did they vary cabin design even to the point of exceeding the typical dimensions of cabins. Nor were these sizes merely dictated by the length of available tree trunks, for approximately the same size cabins reappear in all regions, whatever their forest resources, and even in frame and adobe. Furthermore, logs were often spliced together for larger structures than cabins.

Cabin Types

Glassie's analysis (verified by other studies) reveals only two basic cabin forms beneath the many surface features and appendages that individual cabins have. These are the square cabin and the rectangular cabin, both of which have external centered gable-end chimneys and at least one dimension very close to sixteen feet. Thus, the kind of old homemade family housing most traditional in the area surveyed is characterized by a small, neatly square-cornered, single unit (or "single pen," as the log structure is called), with very specific and quite limited variations in the placement of openings. It is a conservative and functional kind of housing with little relationship to the vast areas of American landscape or any sense of separation from other family members.

The two-room Southern house types which Glassie alludes to on page 539 follow a similar strict pattern, with additions usually built only at the gable end and generally with the same traditional proportions as full cabins have. When a "double pen" house is formed by addition to the chimney end, it is a "saddlebag" house; when the addition (with a second chimney) is to the opposite end and a breezeway is left open, it is a "dogtrot" house. (Both of these house types are constructed separately, not necessarily just as additions to existing cabins.) The "dogtrot" house, despite the folksy ring of its name (also sometimes "possum trot" or "turkey trot") seems to be descended from a one-story, central-hall, two-chimney frame house type called the "hall and parlor." Another variation of the single-unit folk house is what Howard Wight Marshall termed the "stack house." It consists of two units—either square or slightly rectangular—that are stacked on top of each other. Marshall found such houses most often built on smaller lots in towns of the Midwest.

Larger traditional houses often repeat and extend the square and rectangular principles underlying cabin plans. The "I house," said to have been identified as a traditional type in states whose names begin with "I" (but also said to be shaped like an *I* at the gable ends), is two stories tall, one room deep, and two rooms wide. In New England it had a central chimney, in the Mid-Atlantic region two inside chimneys at the gable ends, and in the South usually two external gable-end chimneys. The four basic interior volumes of an "I house" are the identical square or rectangular units of traditional cabins. However, under the influence of the academic architectural model called "Georgian," "I houses" and other folk houses acquired a central hall and often Greek Revival trim (such as "return cornices"). When the roof height of a house is two stories in front and slopes down as a "lean-to" or "shed" to one story in the rear, the form is called a "salt-box" (characteristic of, and often named for, New England, but by no means original or peculiar to that region). Putting all our descriptive terminology together, we can say that a salt-box house (supposedly shaped like an old-time salt box fastened to the kitchen wall near the stove) is a central-chimney hall-and-parlor (two main rooms) "I house" with an integral rear shed consisting (usually) of three smaller rooms on the first floor. Also, from the "I house" base, a possible variation is "two-thirds of an 'I house,'" the equivalent of removing one square or rectangular unit of the floor plan, leaving only one main room (with chimney) and the "hall." Another possibility, which enlarged the house, was the "four-over-four" design, which simply doubles the house size, usually also retaining the Georgian central hall and with either central or end, internal or external chimneys, depending upon the region.

Barn Types

Some traditional barns conform to the patterning principles of American house types. A basic barn type is the double-crib design with two cabinlike units side by side, joined by one roof, and with gable ends closed and the main doors on the long side. These barns could be covered over with siding, and barns of the same proportions were built as large single units. A four-crib barn has two such structures side by side under a single roof, possibly with doors on all four sides. The transverse-crib barn of the Deep South is the evolutionary result of closing off the passage that transects the longer side of a four-crib barn. Often in transverse-crib barns there are no doors between the remaining passage that runs parallel to the roof ridge, and the stalls face each other across the middle space. Sometimes these larger barns had more than two "cribs" to a side, and often they were entirely sided over or (as with double-crib barns) could be built as one large unit. Any of these barn types (like the cabin types) might have lean-to appendages, usually extending from the long sides, but sometimes even on all four sides.

Some house and barn types, usually of regional or ethnic origin, stand apart from these general patterns. Examples are the "Cape Cod" house, an English derivative, which has two front rooms on either side of a central chimney and a row of three or more rooms along the back; the Southern "shotgun" house, possibly an African derivative via Haiti, which has a gable-end entrance and is one room wide and three or more rooms deep; and the Mormon "polygamy house," which served to provide "equal comforts" for several wives of one man. Special barn types include the "English barn," a three-bay structure with stables, hay mow, and a central threshing floor; the "bank barn," built into a hillside with a supported or overhanging bay extending out over the farmyard; and various round and polygonal barns.

Building Materials

While construction techniques and materials are not used to identify traditional architectural types, they certainly should be investigated as interesting in themselves as well as important for determining the national origins and paths of diffusion of folk buildings. American log construction (see page 537) is typified by horizontal placement of hewn logs fitted at the corners with V-notch, half-dovetail, and dovetail joints, and finished with "chinking" between the logs. The antecedents of these construction techniques are Pennsylvania German (ultimately central and eastern European), not English (where log construction is not traditional) nor Scandinavian (where logs are shaped and more tightly fitted without chinking and have their notched logs extending at the corners rather than being trimmed off square). Log buildings may have clapboard siding, either original to the construction or added at a later time. Early timber-framed buildings used older joinery techniques (like pegged laps or mortise-and-tenon joints) rather than nailing. After the Civil War, a lighter system called "balloon framing," composed of vertical studs covered with siding, was introduced.

Popular fashions in architecture tend to reject some of the functional qualities of folk architecture. Sod houses, for example, despite some obvious disadvantages, were cheap, fireproof, and well insulated. Log houses are stronger, simpler to build, and better insulated without any special materials than are most balloon-framed houses, but they are considered rustic and outmoded nowadays. As a result, people who still live in log houses often paint or shingle them as a kind of disguise. Log dwellings are sometimes preferred, however, for their same rustic quality as summer cottages or vacation resorts. Newly constructed log buildings or park structures of log often are made (for reasons of pure nostalgia) out of round logs—an earlier style later replaced in traditional building by the more efficient square-hewn logs that fit more securely together and need less chinking. The most degenerate stage of this revival is that which simply consists of false half-logs attached to the outside of a balloon-framed building.

Researching and Studying Folk Architecture

As close studies of folk architecture in specific regions are finished, it becomes possible to describe characteristic regional distributions of building types and to chart the culture contacts which they represent. Henry Glassie's book *Pattern in the Material Folk Culture of the Eastern United States* (1969) identifies the most typical house and barn types (among other artifacts) as they appear in four folk-cultural regions, the Mid-Atlantic, Upland South, Deep South, and North. There are, of course, many subregional distinctions to be made, as well as studies of the other major sections of the country where various ethnic or sectional "islands" of folk architecture may exist. The Mormon settlers of Utah, for instance, brought with them as cultural baggage mainly the forms of traditional Eastern American architecture, but these houses were constructed of local materials such as adobe, mud concrete, and various stones. Some were made by immigrant craftsmen who had been converted to Mormonism. Thus, what are called in Utah "Old Mormon Houses" may simply be variations of traditional Eastern central-hall plans constructed of locally quarried stone by a Welsh stonemason and enhanced by a modest addition of Greek Revival trim or sometimes an indigenous Utah "Alpine" decor.

While we have looked in considerable detail at some major American folk architectural forms, we have still really only scratched the surface. The principles set forth, however, should enable beginning students to start making field studies of their own. Left out of consideration here have been such technical matters as chronologies of nails and other hardware, methods of raising houses or barns and roofing them, cutting (or "riving") shingles, building stone chimneys, making adobe, and decorating the interior. We need to study the social contexts of traditional housing expressed in folk speech, folk narratives, folksongs and other genres. There are also a number of "exotic" traditional building materials, including hay bales, railroad ties, bottles (set in concrete-filled forms), and ammunition cases. Even pretentious nineteenth-century urban houses may have traditional elements associated with them, such as hand-cut scrollwork, sometimes called "Carpenter's Gothic." And in modern building the essential construction jobs such as excavating, stonework, carpentry, masonry, plastering, plumbing, and roofing could be investigated in detail for traditional elements. Practitioners of these jobs, or new ones, such as installing electrical wiring, automatic heating, or air-conditioning, may have a traditional vocabulary or retain some folk techniques in their work.

BIBLIOGRAPHIC NOTES

For American folk architecture generally, see Wildhaber's bibliography mentioned in the notes to Chapter 19. Everett Dick's *Sod-House Frontier*, cited in the notes to Chapter 15 above, includes one chapter on building and maintaining the sod house. Roger L. Welsch discussed "The Nebraska Soddy" in *NH* 48 (1967): 335–42; his extended study is *Sod Walls: The Story of the Nebraska Sod House* (Broken Bow, Neb.: Purcells, Inc., 1968). Many of the same sod-house photographs are reproduced in John L. White's "Pages from a Nebraska Album: The Sod House Photographs of Solomon D. Butcher" in *TAW* 12 (1975): 30–39. Good photographs and a bibliography accompany Tim Turner's article "Sod Houses in Nebraska," *Association of Preservation Technology Bulletin* 7 (1975); 20–37. In "The Meaning of Folk Architecture: The Sod House Example," *KF* 21 (1976–77): 34–49, Roger L. Welsch suggests that at least in part sod houses were "a response to psychological needs," such as to shut out nature and to enforce social life inside the houses. Allen G. Noble presents an annotated bibliography of sod-house scholarship in *PA* 13 (1981): 61–66.

Other Plains building materials are presented in Roger Welsch's "Sandhill Baled-Hay Construction," *KFQ* 15 (1970): 16–34, and "Railroad-Tie Construction on the Pioneer Plains," *WF* 35 (1976): 149–56. A useful "Adobe Bibliography" by Mark R. Barnes appears in the *Association of Preservation Technology Bulletin* 7 (1975): 89–101. John F. O'Conner's *The Adobe Book* (Santa Fe, N.M.: Ancient City Press, 1973), although oriented mainly to the contemporary builder of modern adobe houses, has very good practical information and fine photographic details.

Henry Glassie's notes to his study in the Appendix list numerous references on American log architecture. See also his important theoretical and regional work *Pattern in the Material Folk Culture of the Eastern United States* (Philadelphia: University of Pennsylvania Monographs in Folklore and Folklife no. 1, 1969). A useful and well-illustrated general survey is C. A. Weslager's *The Log Cabin in America from Pioneer Days to the Present* (New Brunswick, N.J.: Rutgers University Press, 1969). Peter O. Wacker and Roger T. Trindell studied "The Log House in New Jersey: Origin and Diffusion" in *KFQ* 13 (1968): 248–68, demonstrating effective use of maps, plates, and historical citations. Log cabins from the upper Midwest are illustrated in Paul W. Klammer's "Collecting Log Cabins: A Photographer's Hobby," *MH* 37 (1960): 71–77. A portfolio of excellent photographs of log buildings in Jackson Hole, Wyoming, was printed in *TAW* 1 (1964): 21–30. Another attractive nontechnical publication is Clemson Donovan's *Living with Logs: British Columbia's Log Buildings and Rail Fences* (Saanichton, B.C., Canada: Hancock House, 1974).

Two articles on log-cabin construction in *IF* 13 (1980): 46–80, are well illustrated and very systematic in their approaches. Charles F. Gritzner wrote of "Log Housing in New Mexico" in *PA* 3 (1971): 54–62, while Jennifer Eastman Attebery's topic was "Log Construction in the Sawtooth Valley of Idaho" in *PA* 8 (1976): 36–46. Going beyond articles merely on log buildings themselves, Warren E. Roberts has a comprehensive piece on "The Tools Used in Building Log Houses in Indiana," in *PA* 9 (1977): 32–61.

An article tracing one European house form as it was adapted in the United States, Albert J. Petersen's "The German-Russian House in Kansas," *PA* 8 (1976): 19–27, was reprinted in *Readings in American Folklore*, pp. 374–86. Compare Alvar W. Carlson's "German-Russian Houses in Western North Dakota," in *PA* 13 (1981): 49–60. Laszlo Kurti treats "Hungarian Settlement and Building Practices in Pennsylvania and Hungary" in *PA* 12 (1980): 35–53. The identification of the shotgun house type as an African architectural form was provided in great detail by John Michael Vlach in a two-part essay in *PA* 8 (1976): 47–70. Jay Edwards similarly traced the Louisiana Creole cottage to French, Haitian, and West African roots in an article in *LFM* 4 (1976–80): 9–40.

Stone houses of northern Utah were surveyed in an article of that title by Austin E. Fife in *UHQ* 40 (1972): 6–23. Teddy Griffith covered one community in the same region in "A Heritage of Stone in Willard," *UHQ* 43 (1975): 286–300, and Richard C. Poulsen turned to a community farther south in Utah in his study "Stone Buildings of Beaver City," *UHQ* 43 (1975): 278–85. On Utah folk architecture in general, see Jan Harold Brunvand, "The Architecture of Zion," in *TAW* 13 (1976): 28–35.

Noting a nine-by-eight-foot shelter built by transients is Ted Daniels's "A Philadelphia Squatter's Shack: Urban Pioneering," *PA* 13 (1981): 43–46.

For studies in American traditional house designs beyond the simplest forms, see William R. Ferris, Jr., "Mississippi Folk Architecture: A Sampling," *MSF* 1 (1973): 71–83; James R. O'Malley, "Functional Aspects of Folk Housing: A Case for the 'I' House, Union County, Tennessee," *TFSB* 38 (1972): 1–4; Alice Reed Morrison, "Rediscovering Roots through a Material Artifact: An Indiana I-House," *IF* 12 (1979): 146–64; Richard Pillsbury, "Patterns in the Folk and Vernacular House Forms of the Pennsylvania Culture Region," *PA* 9 (1977): 12–31; Henry Chandlee Forman, *Early Nantucket and Its Whale Houses* (New York: Hastings House, 1966); and Henry Glassie's brilliant study *Folk Housing in Middle Virginia: A Structural Analysis of Historic Artifacts* (Knoxville: University of Tennessee Press, 1975). Glassie's influence is apparent in such recent works as Howard Wight Marshall's *Folk Architecture in Little Dixie: A Regional Culture in Missouri* (Columbia: University of Missouri Press, 1981).

In common with Marshall, William Lynwood Montell and Michael Lynn Morse discuss barns and other farm outbuildings as well as houses in their *Kentucky Folk Architecture* (Lexington: University Press of Kentucky, 1976). Barns have also been studied in such works as Wilbur Zelinsky's "The New England Connecting Barn," *GR* 48 (1958): 540–53; Henry Glassie, "The Variation of Concepts within Tradition: Barn Building in Otsego County, New York," in *Man and Cultural Heritage: Papers in Honor of Fred B. Kniffen, Geoscience and Man 5*, ed. H. J. Walker and W. G. Haag (Baton Rouge: Louisiana State University School of Geoscience, 1974), pp. 177–235; Glassie's "Barns across Southern England: A Note on Transatlantic Comparisons and Architectural Meanings," *PA* 7 (1975): 9–19; Allen G. Noble's "Barns as Elements of the Settlement Landscape of Rural Ohio," *PA* 9 (1977): 63–79; Theodore H. M. Prudon's "The Dutch Barn in America: Survival of a Medieval Structural Frame," *NYF* 2 (1976): 123–42; and two essays by Roger L. Welsch: "The Nebraska Round Barn," *JPC* 1 (1967): 403–9, and "Nebraska's Round Barn," *NH* 51 (1970): 49–92. A fine survey of barn types (including ethnic examples, round barns, and polygonal barns), barn construction details, and barn-building tools and materials appeared in a special section by Lee Hartman, "Michigan Barns, Our Vanishing Landscape," *Michigan Natural Resources* 45 (March–April 1976): 17–32. Alvar W. Carlson provides a "Bibliography on Barns in the United States and Canada" in *PA* 10 (1978): 65–71.

David R. Lee and Hector H. Lee document the "Thatched Cowsheds of the Mormon Country" in *WF* 40 (1981): 171–87; these simple structures found in parts of Utah, Idaho, and Nevada are used to protect livestock from rain, snow, and cold. In a supplementary note, Charles S. Peterson compared such cowsheds to the pioneer bowery, and the "Old Tabernacle" of the Mormons to "The Grove" erected in Nauvoo, Illinois, and to "speaking stands" used by Brigham Young during the Western trek—see *WF* 41 (1982): 145–47.

In a unique folklife study, John M. Vlach made a detailed survey of two Parke County, Indiana, covered bridge builders' works (36 out of Indiana's 130 examples) which was published in *IF* 4 (1971): 61–88.

21

Folk Crafts and Art

Folk Crafts

The artifacts of American folk design and creation are an engaging and worthwhile subject for study, but a unified theoretical basis for such study is difficult to formulate. Perhaps even more than with other types of folk tradition, it is extremely problematic to categorize the artifacts themselves as being "folk" or "non-folk" and their production as being "craft" or "art." How can one distinguish the impulse to create and to decorate objects as essentially any different in a *folk* sense from a "higher" *art* sense? Where does a utilitarian *craft* leave off and an *art* begin? The usual assumptions underlying studies of folklife are not much help. **Folk crafts,** for instance, are usually thought of as amateur labor resulting in traditional homemade objects that are primarily functional. But these items may also be made by professional or semiprofessional artisans well aware of their creative abilities, and often the artifacts are decorative as well as useful.

Fencing, for example, is a necessary stage in settlement; and pioneer fences, like houses, were at first made from the nearest resources of the local region. Thus, we find stone fences, wooden fences, hedges, and ditches to be common in different parts of the country. The proper construction techniques for each type were traditionally passed on, along with such variant names as "snake fence," "worm fence," or "zigzag fence" for those made of interlocking split rails. The simplest fences, usually also the earliest, were rows of the waste material generated from clearing land for cultivation—brush, stones, or stumps (generally interwoven into a "rip gut" or "bull" fence). Such fences were fairly functional but were unattractive and wasteful of land, because their meanders prevented cultivation to the edge of the cleared plot. Later, as time permitted and esthetic considerations prevailed, more attractive rail or "post and rider" fences were put up, and these were often contracted for with local builders or carpenters. Solid, well aligned, and often painted, wooden fencing is still a high-prestige consideration for many property owners, both rural and suburban, so the folk fence may be considered simultaneously as an adjunct to architecture, a useful craft, and a commonplace work of art. When barbed wire became readily available for fencing, devices employing the levering principle were invented for tightening the strands, and rock-filled frames were made for supporting posts in hard ground where they could not be implanted.

Gates and stiles in fences range from the level of just removing some rails or leaving a small crack to slip through, to elaborate arrangements that permit opening the gate from horseback or in a buggy and that have an automatic self-closing feature. American fence and gate makers demonstrated their taste and ingenuity in the uses to which they put old wagon wheels. Some are lined up in rows as the fence itself; others appear as the pivot point of a gate or are just fastened to the gate as decoration. The theme is carried indoors when a wagon wheel is used as a chandelier or its hub alone becomes a lamp base. Form and function are barely distinguishable here. Western cattle guards (which occasionally also use old wagon wheels as the "wings" to span the area between road and fence) are other folk artifacts that demonstrate both ingenuity and considerable variation. Blocking ranch animals' passage along a roadway (no one is sure exactly *why* they work!), cattle guards are made of wood rails, metal pipes, or other materials, either with or without a pit; they can be elaborate or very simple, and sometimes are simply represented by stripes painted on the pavement.

Stands for rural mailboxes show similar patterns of development. The basic needs to support the box at a suitable level and to identify its owner can be solved simply by nailing the box to a post and painting a name on it. But people have gone to great lengths to improve on this solution with handcrafted, and often quite decorative, traditional devices made of welded chain links, bent pipes, driftwood, and other materials. A favorite American mailbox stand is the plywood Uncle Sam who is painted red, white, and blue and holds the box in his hands. Another is the old piece of discarded farm equipment—milk can, cream separator, wagon wheel, hand plow, or the like—or a pot-bellied stove. The last sometimes appears supporting a box marked "mail," the smoke pipe marked "newspapers," and the door to the stove itself marked "bills." A variation on the "joke" mailbox has an extra receptacle for mail mounted on a pole some ten or more feet high; it is marked "Air Mail."

Folk Art: Problems in Identity

In folklife studies, **folk art** is usually thought of as the purely decorative or representational items produced by traditional means. But much folk art is very close to handicraft and it is difficult to distinguish the two fields. Stenciling, for example, was once a favorite decorative medium for house floors and walls, and it is often displayed or pictured as an early American "folk art." But except for the original creative cutting of the design in the stencil pattern, the application of it to a surface was a mere mechanical matter of moving it along, holding it down, and applying paint to the cutout opening. Fancy sewing, quilting, rug hooking, and weaving also satisfy the creative urge and go beyond just holding textiles together or making bodies, beds, or floors warm; they might be considered both folk craft and art. If a "craft" piece, like a duck decoy or a quilt, is shelved or hung as decoration, then it would seem to have become "art."

As with building trades and handicrafts, mere amateur status does not define the folk artist, for traditional creations have come from many professional artists—portraitists, carvers, calligraphers, metal workers, and the like. In fact, only artisans or artists producing things solely for their own or their family's use can, strictly speaking, be called amateurs. But the vast majority of such creators are specialists who produce only one kind of artifact and then sell or barter it with others; professionalism is the rule, not the exception, in folk crafts and arts.

The particularly loose terminology of many folk-art studies further confuses the matter of definitions. We find "primitive art," "popular art," "schoolgirl art," "provincial art," and several other terms in use for essentially the same materials. The most consistent use of the term "folk art" (see Chapter 19) is for untrained ("nonacademic") representational artists, primarily painters, who worked with traditional subjects in traditional styles. Some, but not all of them, were itinerant artists, but *none* of them (at least it has never been proved) painted bodies on canvases all winter and traveled around adding the heads of their customers in the summer. This notion is merely a folk legend of considerable tenacity.

More broadly conceived by folklorists, American folk art can take in a variety of miscellaneous decorative traditions. In a drowsy schoolroom, for instance, children may amuse themselves by tracing repetitious looped patterns on scratchpaper or on flyleaves of books. Others like to carve a checkerboard pattern down the length of a new pencil and all the way around it. Some people fold long paper chains out of gum wrappers or one-dollar bills. Others specialize in carving wooden chains or a "ball in cage" from one piece of wood. Cattails, dried milkweed pods, and other weeds may be gathered and painted for decorations.

A prolific source of folk crafts and art, already touched on in discussing rural mailboxes and the re-use of old wagon wheels, is what W. F. H. Nicolaisen calls "distorted function"—adaptation of old artifacts for new purposes. Just as older bits of verbal lore (such as sea chanteys) may later reappear as entertainment (i.e., be sung in a folk-music concert), outmoded or leftover pieces of raw material or equipment may find a new use (i.e., a piece of rain guttering converted into a planter). Similarly, plastic bleach jugs, tin cans, and milk cartons are turned into baskets, banks, or toys. Wreaths are woven of wool, feathers, or human hair and may be fashioned of coat hangers and plastic bags. One may even see a modern wreath formed out of plastic holders for "six packs" of canned soda or beer twisted into patterns and stapled onto old wooden gravemarkers as decorations. The enhancement of "found objects" also produces folk art. In one Western sawmill, for example, the "chopper sawyers," whose job it is to cut knots out of second-grade to fourth-grade lumber, specialize in decorating knots with a pencil or pen and sending their artwork down the line for the other men to admire. The drawings may be animal figures, caricatures of fellow workmen, or scenes.

However simple these creations may seem, they are certainly more valid as instances of genuine folk art than are, say, pieces of ersatz tole painting (decorated tinware), fake plastic scrimshaw (whale-ivory decorating), or Navajo-like sand-painting designs produced by professional artisans or by amateurs from factory-made kits. The colors and design of an artifact do not make it authentic as folk art, no matter how closely these follow a folk prototype; the traditional construction and use of an artifact, however, *do* establish it as "folk." Folklife specialist Roger Welsch has even gone so far as to suggest that the brilliant autumn color of a prominent tree in a Nebraska small town— much appreciated by the residents and closely watched each year—is perhaps an object of "folk art" for that community.

Folk Art: Studies and Examples

Another American folklorist who has given these matters a great deal of thought, Michael Owen Jones, in a study of Kentucky chairmakers, proposed this definition of art in general, which describes *folk* art insofar as the individual creator works within a group or regional tradition that is transmitted informally:

> skill in the making or doing of that which functions as (among other things) a stimulus to appreciation of an individual's mastery of tools and materials apparent in what he has made, the output of that skill; and the activity manifesting the use of that skill. . . . [Art] is something thought to be special (usually because of the skill required), generating an appreciative, contemplative response in the percipient.

In practice, Jones's informants recognized both the functional and the esthetic qualities of well-made objects; one man referred to the "beauty part" and the "lasting part." Following this lead, we may use the terms "craft" and "art" synonymously when studying traditional artifacts. Consequently, the goals for field work in folk artifacts (in common with those for folk architecture) require several different kinds of data: careful description and picturing of the items themselves, facts about the raw materials used and the stages of construction, information about how the skills were acquired and to what uses the finished items are put, psychological profiles of the builders and the users, and statements by the individual makers and their community regarding the "esthetic" appeal of the finished products. However, these are the ideal dimensions of a study, which are seldom realized.

Traditional handcrafted devices for home, farm, and ranch are numerous, and many are still being constructed and are in regular use. Outside the house proper, there are weathervanes, whirligigs, door knockers, wells, and yard ornaments to investigate. Another interesting category is the identification devices for dwellings, including signs for family and residence names (especially on ranches and summer cottages). Some people handmake items that have long since been replaced by factory-produced ones—wooden scoop shovels, lawn furniture, and garden tools are examples.

In a rare study of a homemade rural piece of folk technology, the Central Western hay derrick was investigated by Austin and James Fife in research that considered the classification and distribution of the objects, the need for them, and their probable history. When they realized that light rainfall in the region allowed for the year-round outdoor storage of hay, Great Basin pioneer farmers created devices to stack their hay into high, compact formations that would shed what rain did fall. First they just dragged the hay up by means of a rope rigged to a "flagpole," but soon they constructed more complex derricks with pivoted booms and sometimes even wheels for moving them from job to job. Neighbors borrowed ideas from one another as the hay-derrick idea spread through the region, and so successful was this traditional manufacture that only recently have any mass-produced devices begun to replace the home-made ones.

Similar studies might be made of traditional fruit-boxing equipment, berry pickers, rat traps, harvesting tools (corn knives, husking pegs, etc.), rope twisters, bits, spurs, rawhide equipment, scarecrows, and other agricultural artifacts. Home-made hunting, fishing, and camping equipment may also be tra-ditional. These include shelters, boats, traps, animals calls, fishing lures, some trout flies, decoys (used for ducks, geese, swans, and even fish), and camp lanterns, all of which are com-mercially produced in great variety but which also linger in some folk forms. A good example of a recent folk invention in this category is the fishing lure made from the aluminum snap-top of a beer or soft-drink cap. This appeared in the West for steelhead fishing only about one year after the pop-top bever-age can was introduced to the market.

Household or domestic arts and crafts, sometimes subsumed under the inaccurate label of "women's art," form another large category of material for documentation and study. While it is true that certain clichéd themes of art were stressed in the "fe-male academies" of the eighteenth and nineteenth centuries (still-life paintings, pastoral scenes, memorial pictures, etc.) and that crafts like needlework are almost entirely the province of women, not every such work can be positively identified as a woman's production. Conversely, American women and men did occasionally cross over and engage in art or craft work that was not usually associated with their respective sex. Just *who* painted all the early American decorated fireplace screens, window shades, furniture, and kitchenware, for example, is not at all clear, although in many instances it may be guessed (as one art historian put it) that "anonymous was a woman." Most stitched samplers, embroidered bed rugs, and woven coverlets were certainly made by women, though men were also known to do some kinds of needlework in special circumstances (such as when they went to sea for long periods). Women also occa-sionally invaded such "hard" crafts as carpentry or blacksmith-ing.

Some of the old subsistence crafts like spinning, dyeing, braiding, soapmaking and candlemaking, and quilting are practiced nowadays solely as recreational pastimes. Among them, only quilting has been the subject of much study, perhaps partly because the picturesque names for the many colorful quilt patterns provide both linguistic and artistic matter for consideration. As Austin Fife has pointed out, these names may be simply *descriptive* ("Turkey Tracks"), or they may be *romantic* ("Steps to the Altar"), *Biblical* ("Jacob's Ladder"), *ancestral* ("Grandmother's Fan"), *exotic* ("Arabic Lattice"), or *evocative of the pioneering experience* ("Road to California").

A large number of professional crafts with formal apprenticeships provided useful objects for the home and farm through much of the nineteenth century. The list includes woodworking, cabinetmaking, furniture making, blacksmithing and other metalworking, glazing and glass blowing, pottery, basketry, and broommaking. Such production has largely been transferred to factories now, although small-scale individual-shop manufacture does continue and, in the case of some crafts like stained-glass making, has begun to flourish again in recent years. The other side of the picture—traditional aspects of modern manufacturing—is represented by a skill such as sheet-metal working (producing downspouts and gutters, air conditioning and heating ducts, and the like). With its background in the traditional tinkers' trade, this industrial craft, studied by David Shuldiner, retains some aspects of the old folk practices, and the same is probably true of other modern industries.

Turning to a surviving traditional craft, basketry stands out as a prime example. Although baskets have been largely replaced as everyday containers by cartons, bottles, bags, and the like, whatever baskets are still made almost invariably are folk products. There are several good practical reasons for the continuing production of baskets: they are durable, inexpensive, light for their strength, reusable, and may be constructed in a variety of pleasing shapes and handy sizes. American baskets are usually made of splints (or "splits") of pliant wood, such as white oak or ash, woven around bent wood hoops or ribs. Different sizes and shapes of baskets are made for marketing, for food harvest or storage, or for use as picnic baskets, magazine baskets, laundry baskets, fishing creels, or pack baskets. Afro-American basketry is of the "coil" type, made from bundles of "sweet grass" and long-leafed pine needles coiled around and upward to form the bottom and sides, and sewn together with thin strips made from fronds of palmetto trees.

Folk pottery making, once widely practiced in the United States, is a more complex and diversified craft involving chemistry and physics, special equipment, numerous designs, and different marketing traditions. The investigator must study the raw materials (clays and glazes), equipment (wheels, mills for grinding materials, kilns), the potter's shop layout, decorative elements (colors, shapes, handles, lids, inscriptions, etc.), and the great variety of artifacts produced, which include syrup jugs, whiskey jugs, pickling crocks, bowls, mugs, plates, and churns. The few truly traditional potters that remain (apart from native American potters) are in the South.

The craft of barrelmaking no longer exists with individual "coopers" turning out the entire barrel, but traditional work methods persist in the remaining modern cooperages which supply the relatively few wooden vessels of staves and hoops that are still in use. While barrels and kegs were once commonly employed for flour, crackers, nails, lard, gunpowder, wine, beer, and many other commodities, and coopers also made tubs, buckets, and churns, nowadays the principal use for barrels in the United States is for aging bourbon whiskey. The industry's need for tight, charred, white-oak barrels keeps the craft alive, and modern coopers face the same problems of shaping their staves, "raising" a barrel, fitting the hoops and heads, and assuring its tightness as their predecessors did.

The traditional craft of handmaking skis in the United States would provide for an interesting study. It would require a great deal of searching through early accounts of life in northern parts of the country, including Alaska, and making careful distinctions between skis and snowshoes, both of which were frequently called "snowshoes" in some regions in the nineteenth century. A character called "Snowshoe" Thompson, for example, wore long, homemade skis when he carried mail in the California mountains in 1856. A Colorado minister in the 1860s wrote in his autobiography:

> I made me a pair of snow-shoes, and, of course, was not an expert. . . . [They] were of the Norway style, from nine to eleven feet in length, and ran well when the snow was just right, but very heavy when they gathered snow. I carried a pole to jar the sticking snow off.

A man who settled in Boise, Idaho, in 1869 referred to home-made skis in his reminiscences as "Idaho snowshoes." Were such skis made in other regions, and were they called "snow-shoes" or something else there? Does the term "Norway style" indicate that Norwegians taught others to make skis in this country? What materials and techniques were used to make skis? How were they employed? The answers to such questions might well be found in a thorough research project.

Folk toys existed in the past and still exist in great variety. They are made both by parents and by children themselves. Some are made from natural materials (willow whistles, corn-stalk "fiddles," apple-head dolls, burr baskets, and dandelion chains), while others begin with manufactured items (clothespin dolls, spool window-rattlers and "tanks," and tobacco-can "harmonicas"). A whole family of toys is made simply from folded paper—"cootie catchers" (a toy for the mock capture of "cooties" from a person's scalp), airplanes, noisemakers, and hats—while toy weaponry forms another large class (slingshots, hairpin launchers, peashooters, and rubber-band guns with spring-clothespin triggers). Some children make an effective— and dangerous—substitute for fireworks by screwing a machine bolt halfway into a nut, filling the cavity with tips cut from wooden "kitchen matches," and then screwing a second bolt in from the other end. The device is thrown into the air so it will come down on a sidewalk or pavement, and when a bolt head strikes, the whole arrangement blasts apart with a loud report.

Musical instruments of folk construction have benefited from the widespread interest in folk music in this country and, thus, have received considerably more study than many other kinds of material tradition. A number of very simple instruments are found in Afro-American tradition—a "rattler," made of bottle tops loosely nailed to a paddle, "quills," or the panpipe, fashioned of hollow reeds tied together; the "diddly bow" (or "bow diddly"), a single string stretched along a board, broom, or house wall (sometimes also called a "jitterbug"); and the slightly more elaborate washtub bass. Much more highly developed, both physically and musically, from African roots is the American five-string banjo. The unfretted fifth string on the folk banjo contributes a drone sound in some strumming styles and takes a more active role in finger-picking. Another distinctive American instrument is the Southern-mountain plucked dulcimer. Enjoying a revival today, the plucked dulcimer is not to be confused with the much rarer (and usually German or east European) hammered dulcimer. The plucked dulcimer derives from the European family of folk instruments that includes the Norwegian *langeleik,* the Swedish *humle,* the German *Scheitholt,* and the French *espinette des vosges,* all instruments with drone strings that are played while being rested horizontally on a table or on the lap. The American mountain dulcimer generally has three strings—a melody string and two drones—and is shaped in graceful curves along the sides, with sound holes (often heart-shaped) on the top surface. Traditionally, the dulcimer is played with a quill or "feather pick."

Aspects of purely decorative and representational American folk art already mentioned include whittling, needlework, stenciling, and painting. Other examples are scrimshaw (carving and decorating objects of whale bone or ivory), tattooing, gravestone carving, and what have been called "dendroglyphs" (patterns, inscriptions, and pictures carved on trees), particularly common on the white bark of birches and aspens. Folk artisans sometimes make special "art" objects, such as face jugs and figurines by potters and toy furniture or miniature farm equipment by woodworkers. In Afro-American folk art, alligators, heads, and grotesque skulls are found in clay sculpture and wood carving. Even the making of snowmen and other snow sculpture may be considered a folk art form.

Just as musical expression has been identified at folk, popular, and art levels, comparisons might be made of such forms as portraiture, still life, the grotesque, or caricature as they appear in folk art, popular art, and "high" art. Or a historical subject, such as "Custer's Last Stand," might be compared in American folk expressions, in popular media such as magazine illustrations or Currier and Ives prints, and in serious academic art. Some scholars, however, argue against the utility of identifying such "levels" of art, and they prefer to drop the terms "folk art" and "primitive art" in favor of something like Michael Owen Jones's formulation "units or structures of expressive behavior learned and manifested primarily in situations of firsthand interaction." Still, some kind of esthetic and comparative evaluations of art levels seems necessary, if only to provide a good foundation for supporting or rebutting such provocative generalizations as these from an art historian:

> Folk art is naïve, crude, clumsy and old-fashioned, popular art often skillful and technically apt, though vulgar, subject to superficial and rapid transformation, but incapable of achieving either more radical change or finer discrimination. Genuine art is used up, disintegrated, and simplified by folk art; it is watered down, botched and bowdlerized by popular art.

BIBLIOGRAPHIC NOTES

The following are general older surveys of American handicrafts, all containing some illustrations and useful descriptions, although their analyses are out of date: *Hands That Built New Hampshire,* published by the Works Project Administration Writers' Program (Brattleboro, Vt., 1940); Ella Shannon Bowles, *Homespun Handicrafts* (Philadelphia, 1931; reissued, New York: Benjamin Blom, 1972); Allen H. Eaton, *Handicrafts of the Southern Highlands* (New York: Russell Sage Foundation, 1937; paperback reprint, New York: Dover Publications, 1973); Rollin C. Steinmetz and Charles S. Rice, *Vanishing Crafts and Their Craftsmen* (New Brunswick, N.J.: Rutgers University Press, 1959); and Erwin O. Christensen, *American Crafts and Folk Arts,* America Today Series, no.4 (Washington, D.C.: Robert B. Luce, 1964).

Mamie Meredith collected "The Nomenclature of American Pioneer Fences" in *SFQ* 15 (1951): 109–51. Two studies with more depth are H. F. Raup's "The Fence in the Cultural Landscape," *WF* 6 (1947): 1–12, and E. C. Mather and J. F. Hart's "Fences and Farms," *GR* 44 (1954):

201–23. A unique fence, "the lopped tree fence," was described by Mary Catharine Davis in *SFQ* 21 (1957): 174–75. Patricia Mastick writes of "Dry Stone Walling," the construction technique that proceeds without mortar between the stones, in an article in *IF* 9 (1976): 113–33, based on interviews with an Indiana master of the form. James F. Hoy's *The Cattle Guard: Its History and Lore* (Lawrence: University Press of Kansas, 1982) is an unusual book-length study of a familiar kind of Western folk technology.

The Fifes's hay-derrick study was published in *WF* 7 (1948): 225–39, with addenda in *WF* 10 (1951): 320–22. A distributional study of a particular type of homemade hair- or rope-twister is Fred Kniffen's "The Western Cattle Complex: Notes on Differentiation and Diffusion," *WF* 12 (1953): 179–85. On a related craft, see Robert and Martha Cochran, with Christopher Pierle, "The Preparation and Use of Bear Grass Rope: An Interview with Robert Simmons, Mississippi Folk Craftsman," *NYFQ* 30 (1974): 185–96. An interview with a Finnish "tie-hacker" of McCall, Idaho, was published by H. J. Swinney in *WF* 24 (1965): 271–73. On traditional blacksmithing techniques, see Mody C. Boatright, "How Will Boatright Made Bits and Spurs," *JAF* 83 (1970): 77–80, and John M. Vlach, "The Fabrication of a Traditional Fire Tool," *JAF* 86 (1973): 54–57, which deals with a black craftsman who is the subject of Vlach's 1981 book *Charleston Blacksmith: The Work of Philip Simmons* (Athens: University of Georgia Press). Vlach surveyed "Afro-American Folk Crafts in Nineteenth Century Texas" in *WF* 40 (1981): 149–61. A special double issue of *SFQ* (42:2–3, 1978) concerned Afro-American material culture (basketry, pottery, fifes and flutes, wood carving, etc.)

The Colorado skiing minister quoted in this chapter was the Reverend John L. Dyer, whose autobiography, *The Snow-Shoe Itinerant*, was published in Cincinnati in 1890. "Idaho snowshoes" were described by Thomas Corwin Donaldson in *Idaho of Yesterday* (Caldwell, Idaho: Caxton Press, 1941).

Three studies that relate folk craftsmanship to larger-scale production are Carlos C. Drake, "Traditional Elements in the Cooperage Industry," *KFQ* 14 (1969): 81–96; Robert S. McCarl, Jr., "The Production Welder: Product, Process and the Industrial Craftsman," *NYFQ* 30 (1974): 243–53; and David Shuldiner, "The Art of Sheet Metal Work: Traditional Craft in a Modern Industrial Setting," *SWF* 4 (1980): 37–41.

Several books offer general illustrated surveys of household and farm crafts. Jared van Wagenen, Jr., in *The Golden Age of Homespun* (New York: American Century Series, 1963), provides "a record of the lore and the methods by which our forebears lived upon the land" in upper New York State from the Revolution to the Civil War. Several works by Eric Sloane are beautifully illustrated with line drawings of museum pieces. These include *American Yesterday* (New York: W. Funk, 1956); *The Seasons of America Past* (New York: W. Funk, 1958);

Diary of an Early American Boy: Noah Blake, 1805 (1962; repr. Ballantine paperback, 1974); *A Reverence for Wood* (1965; repr. Ballantine, 1973); and *A Museum of Early American Tools* (1964; repr. Ballantine, 1974).

In "An Indiana Subsistence Craftsman," *PA* 8 (1976): 107–18, Willard B. Moore documents the work of a part-time craftsman, not well known in his community, who makes and repairs various artifacts for personal or local use—gambrel sticks (to hang hogs for butchering), well drops (to retrieve lost buckets from wells), clevises (to secure chains), corn knives, foot-adze handles, sledge runners, wheels, and the like. "Flag and Rush Industry of Savannah, New York," by Hugo Freund and Amy Rashap, shows the use of swamp plants (of the cattail family) as gaskets in barrels and the folk industry that supplies them (in *NYF* 7 [1981]: 1–46).

Special studies of particular crafts are becoming increasingly more common in American folklore journals. See, for example: Mac E. Barrick, "Pennsylvania Corn Knives and Husking Pegs," *KFQ* 15 (1970): 128–37; Laurence Clayton, "How Litt Perkins Treats Hides and Makes Leather Goods," *WF* 40 (1981): 162–71; and three articles on basketmaking—Henry Glassie, "William Houck, Maker of Pounded Ash Adirondack Pack-Baskets," *KFQ* 12 (1967): 23–54; Howard Wight Marshall, "Mr. Westfall's Baskets: Traditional Craftsmanship in Northcentral Missouri," *MSF* 2 (1974): 43–60 (reprinted in *Readings in American Folklore*, pp. 168–91); and Glenn Hinson, "An Interview with Leon Berry, Maker of Baskets," *NCFJ* 27 (1979): 56–60.

Kentucky's Age of Wood, by Kenneth Clarke and Ira Kohn (Lexington: University Press of Kentucky, 1976), deals with many artifacts traditionally made of the same material. Other articles on craftsmen in wood include Sylvia Ann Grider and Barbara Ann Allen, "Howard Taylor, Cane Maker and Handle Shaver," *IF* 7 (1974): 5–25; James R. Dow, "The Hand Carved Walking Canes of William Baurichter," *KFQ* 15 (1970): 138–47; Frank Reuter, "John Arnold's Link Chains: A Study in Folk Art," *MSF* 5 (1977): 41–52; and three articles on woodworkers and carvers in *IF* 13 (1980): 1–45.

Beulah M. D'Olive Price describes "Riving Shingles in Alcorn County" in *MFR* 6 (1972): 108–14, while David J. Winslow's topic is "New York Duck Decoys" in *KFQ* 17 (1972): 119–32. Two essays on traditional boatbuilding are Howard Wight Marshall and David H. Stanley, "Homemade Boats in South Georgia," *MFR* 12 (1978): 75–94, and Malcolm L. Lomeaux, "Origins and Evolution of Mississippi River Fishing Craft," *PA* 10 (1978): 73–97.

Southern American folk-pottery tradition is discussed in Charles G. Zug III, "Pursuing Pots: On Writing a History of North Carolina Folk Pottery," *NCFJ* 27 (1979): 35–55. John A. Burrison's interest in Southern pottery, expressed in "Alkaline-glazed Stoneware: A Deep-South

Pottery Tradition" *SFQ* 39 (1975): 377–403, flowered into his book *Brothers in Clay: The Story of Georgia Folk Pottery* (Athens: University of Georgia Press, 1983).

A general list of household handicrafts was given in the article by Afton Wynn cited in the notes to Chapter 15. Paul Brewster included information on quilt patterns, dyeing, and folk toys in volume 1 of *The Frank C. Brown Collection of North Carolina Folklore*. For related studies, see Annie Louise D'Olive, "Folk Implements Used for Cleaning," *MFR* 2 (1968): 125–34, and Annelen Archbold, "Percy Beeson, a Kentucky Broommaker," *MSF* 3 (1975): 41–45.

There are many books on quilt patterns, most of them offering instructions for making quilts and providing historical notes. A good one is Carrie A. Hall and Rose G. Kretsinger's *The Romance of the Patchwork Quilt in America* (Caldwell, Idaho: Caxton Press, 1936; reissued, New York [n.d.]). Carrie Hall's large collection of quilt patches and patterns is deposited in the Museum of Art at the University of Kansas in Lawrence. Commenting on a list of quilt-pattern names submitted by Paul Brewster to *CFQ* 3 (1944): 61, Wayland D. Hand pointed out the interplay of folk and commercial patterns fostered by companies that sold quilt battings wrapped with advertising for their own lines of quilt patterns: see *CFQ* 3 (1944): 151–52. Useful for further studies are Andrea Greenberg's survey "American Quilting," in *IF* 5 (1972): 264–79, and a bibliography of American quilt making compiled by Susan Roach and Lorre M. Weidlich and published in *FFemC* 3 (Spring 1974): 17–28. For the work of individual artisans, see Joanne Farb, "Piecin' and Quiltin': Two Quilters in Southwest Arkansas," *SFQ* 39 (1975): 363–75.

Quilt studies continue to flourish, perhaps in part because quilting has a secure status as a revival craft in urban environments, although the focus of most studies is rural or small town. *Kentucky Quilts and Their Makers*, by Mary Washington Clarke (Lexington: University Press of Kentucky, 1976), offers a compact history and analysis. Recent articles include Sandra K. D. Stahl, "Quilts and a Quiltmaker's Aesthetics," *IF* 11 (1978): 105–32; Elizabeth Smith Schabel, "The Historical Significance of Patchwork Quilt Names as a Reflection of the Emerging Social Consciousness of the American Woman," *TFSB* 47 (1981): 1–16; and Geraldine N. Johnson, "'More for Warmth Than for Looks': Quilts of the Blue Ridge Mountains," *NCFJ* 30 (1982): 55–84.

Two works on other textile crafts are Gerald L. Pocius, "Hooked Rugs in Newfoundland: The Representation of Social Structure in Design," *JAF* 92 (1979): 273–84, and Ann Williams, "The Alexander Family 'Kentucky Beauty': The Unraveling of a Coverlet Draft" [about weaving], *NCFJ* 29 (1981): 94–105.

Michael Owen Jones has written a number of important studies of American furniture making, such as "The Study of Traditional Furniture: Review and Preview," *KFQ* 12 (1967): 233–45: "'They Made

Them for the Lasting Part': A 'Folk' Typology of Traditional Furniture Makers," *SFQ* 35 (1971): 44–61; and "'For Myself I Like a *Decent*, Plain-made Chair': The Concept of Taste and the Traditional Arts in America," *WF* 31 (1972): 27–52. Jones's work in these and other articles is incorporated into his book *The Hand Made Object and Its Maker* (Los Angeles: University of California Press, 1975). A lengthy study of a family of rural and urban chairmakers is Warren E. Roberts's "Turpin Chairs and the Turpin Family: Chairmaking in Southern Indiana," *MJLF* 7 (1981): 57–106.

American folk toys have been included in general books on folk crafts but have had little individual scholarly treatment. A popular, nostalgic book that deals largely with simple folk toys is Robert Paul Smith's *How to Do Nothing with Nobody, All Alone by Yourself* (New York: W. W. Norton, 1958). An article describing a small local industry for manufacturing copies of folk toys is Henry B. Comstock's "Folk Toys Are Back Again," in *Popular Science* (March 1960): 144–47. Two instruction books on folk-toy making are Joan Joseph's *Folk Toys around the World and How to Make Them* (New York: Parents Magazine Press in cooperation with the U.S. Committee for UNICEF, 1972), and Dick Schnache, *American Folk Toys: How to Make Them* (Baltimore: Penguin Books, 1973).

Andrea Koss studied the making of apple-head dolls in an article in *IF* 12 (1979): 38–54. In "The Cooties Complex," *WF* 39 (1980): 198–210, Sue Samuelson discusses children's play centering on an imaginary invisible germ or bug but fails to mention the folded paper toy known as a "cootie catcher." Donald B. Ball writes of "The 'Spoke Gun' and 'Match Gun': Examples of Two Southern Folk toys" in *TFSB* 42 (1976): 181–83. A broader view of folk toys is taken in Mark I. West's "Meaning in the Making: The Toys of Young Folk," *TFSB* 48 (1982): 105–10.

Roger Welsch discussed "The Cornstalk Fiddle" (a toy, not an instrument) in *JAF* 77 (1964): 262–63 (repr. in *Readings in American Folklore*, pp. 106–7). Another widely distributed folk noisemaker is described by John C. McConnell in "The Dumbull or Srauncher," in *TFSB* 25 (1959): 89.

Louise Scruggs gave a brief and sketchy "History of the 5-String Banjo" in *TFSB* 27 (1961): 1–5. More detailed studies are Gene Bluestein's "America's Folk Instrument: Notes on the Five-String Banjo," *WF* 23 (1964): 241–48; C. P. Heaton's "The 5-String Banjo in North Carolina," *SFQ* 35 (1971): 62–82; and Jay Bailey's "Historical Origin and Stylistic Developments of the Five-String Banjo," *JAF* 85 (1972): 58–65. Information on an even simpler class of traditional stringed instruments is given by David Evans in "Afro-American One-stringed Instruments," *WF* 29 (1970): 229–45. Charles Seeger submitted "The Appalachian Dulcimer" to a full historical treatment in *JAF* 71 (1958): 40–51; and S. E. Hastings reports on one notable old instrument in his article "Construction Techniques in an Old Appalachian Mountain Dulcimer," in *JAF* 83 (1970): 462–68. A good regional survey is Charles W. Joyner's "Dulcimer Making in Western North Carolina: Creativity in a Traditional Mountain Craft," *SFQ* 39 (1975): 341–61. Other useful information on dulcimer playing in the Southern mountains is found in the following popular works: John F. Putnam's "The Plucked Dulcimer," *MLW* 34 (1958): 7–13; Putnam's booklet *The Plucked Dulcimer and How to Play It* (Berea, Ky.: Council of the Southern Mountains, 1961); and Jean Ritchie's *The Dulcimer Book* (New York: Oak Publications, 1963). L. Allen Smith reports on his comprehensive and systematic study in "Toward a Reconstruction of the Development of the Appalachian Dulcimer: What the Instruments Suggest," *JAF* 93 (1980): 385–96.

S. J. Sackett discussed "The Hammered Dulcimer in Ellis County, Kansas," in *JIFMC* 14 (1962): 61–64. A study of the folk use made of a commercial musical instrument is A. Doyle Moore's "The Autoharp: Its Origins and Development from a Popular to a Folk Instrument," in *NYFQ* 19 (1963): 261–74.

There are numerous books and publications on folk art, using either that term or one of the others listed in this chapter. Two important exhibition catalogues that are available are *The Abby Aldrich Rockefeller Folk Art Collection: A Descriptive Catalog, by Nina Fletcher Little* (Colonial Williamsburg, Va., 1957), and Agnes Halsey Jones and Louis C. Jones, *New-found Folk Art of the Young Republic* (Cooperstown, N.Y.: New York State Historical Association, 1960). Among well-illustrated works on nonacademic representational and decorative art are Janet Waring, *Early American Stencils on Walls and Furniture* (1937; reprinted by Dover Publications, New York, 1968); Jean Lipman, *American Primitive Painting* (London and New York: Oxford University Press, 1942); Henry J. Kauffman, *Pennsylvania Dutch American Folk Art* (1946; rev. and enlarged edn., New York: Dover Publications 1964); Alice Ford, *Pictorial Folk Art: New England to California* (London and New York: Studio Publications, 1949); and Nina Fletcher Little, *American Decorative Wall Painting 1700–1850* (Sturbridge, Mass., and New York: Old Sturbridge Village and Studio Publications, 1952).

An important picture book on American folk crafts and art is Erwin O. Christensen's *The Index of American Design*, published by the Smithsonian Institution (Washington, D.C., 1950). The index was part of the Federal Art Project of the 1930s and is now housed in the National Gallery of Art. It includes photographs and drawings of designs, weathervanes, utensils, costumes, and pictorial art. Some good examples of its riches are used as illustrations in Duncan Emrich's article entitled "America's Folkways," in *Holiday*, 18 (July 1955): 60–63 and following.

Jean Lipman's book *American Folk Art in Wood, Metal, and Stone*

(New York: Pantheon, 1948) is another well-illustrated survey volume, as is her work done in collaboration with Alice Winchester, *The Flowering of American Folk Art (1776–1876)* (New York: Viking Press, 1974). The book *America's Arts and Skills*, published by the editors of *Life* (New York, 1957), although neither wholly art nor folk, contains some folk art and is magnificently illustrated. It surveys American popular art and design from colonial times to the present, as do several similar works produced to commemorate the United States Bicentennial.

Kenneth L. Ames's *Beyond Necessity: Art in the Folk Tradition* (Winterthur, Del.: Winterthur Museum, 1977), part of the catalogue of an exhibit, sought to dispel some "myths about folk art" and bring the thinking of art historians closer to that of modern folklorists. The dialogue was continued (in what some called "the shootout at Winterthur") in a conference published as *Perspectives on American Folk Art* (Winterthur Museum, 1980), ed. Ian M. G. Quimby and Scott T. Swank. Henry Glassie was much quoted here, and American folklorists were represented in person by Roger Welsch, Marsha McDowell, Kurt Dewhurst, John Michael Vlach, and Michael Owen Jones, all of whom contributed strong papers that are required reading for anyone working in this field.

Two articles on the work of individual painters are John Michael Vlach's "Quaker Tradition and the Paintings of Edward Hicks: A Strategy for the Study of Folk Art," *JAF* 94 (1981): 145–65, and Simon J. Bronner, "'We Live What I Paint and I Paint What I See': A Mennonite Artist in Northern Indiana," *IF* 12 (1979): 5–17.

American women's folk art, a long-neglected topic, was treated in two 1979 publications—Mirra Bank, *Anonymous Was a Woman* (New York: St. Martins), and C. Kurt Dewhurst, Betty MacDowell, and Marsha MacDowell, *Artists in Aprons: Folk Art by American Women* (New York: E. P. Dutton)—both well illustrated but only the latter with any in-depth discussion of the topic and with a large bibliography.

Some byways of folk art are charted in articles such as Geoffrey Cortelyon and Kathleen Green's study "Pop Owen," concerning an amateur artist in rural New York State, in *KFQ* 28 (1972): 293–304; Alan B. Govenar's "Leonard L. 'Stoney' St. Clair, Tattooist," *JOFS* 3 (1975): 9–14; Charles L. Perdue, Jr.'s "Steve Ashby: Virginia Folk Artist," concerning a black creator of various "constructions," in *FFV* 2 (1980–81): 53–66; and E. N. Anderson, Jr.'s "On the Folk Art of Landscaping," *WF* 31 (1972): 179–88. Kenneth S. Goldstein published an important article concerning his discovery, "William Robbie: Folk Artist of the Buchan District, Aberdeenshire" in *Folklore in Action*, pp. 101–11.

Michael Owen Jones has published a number of thoughtful studies of methodology and analysis of American folk arts and crafts, beginning with "Two Directions for Folkloristics in the Study of American Art," *SFQ* 32 (1968): 249–59. Jones's other work has appeared in *SFQ* 36

(1972): 43–60; *JPC* 4 (1970): 194–212, and 6 (1973): 794–818; *KFQ* 16 (1971): 39–48; and *WF* 30 (1971): 77–104, and 32 (1973): 19–32. A related essay is Elizabeth Mosby Adler's "Direction in the Study of American Folk Art," *NYF* 1 (1975): 31–44.

Three studies of the whalers' art of ivory carving are the following: Marius Barbeau, "All Hands Aboard Scrimshawing," *The American Neptune* 12 (1952): 99–122 (reprinted by the Peabody Museum of Salem, [Mass.], 1966); Walter K. Earle, *Scrimshaw: Folk Art of the Whalers* (Cold Spring Harbor, N.Y.: Whaling Museum Society, Inc., 1957): and Edouard A. Stackpole, *Scrimshaw at Mystic Seaport* (Mystic, Conn.: The Marine Historical Assoc., 1958). A brief note on a domestic art/craft form is Ila A. Wright's "Hair Watch Chains and Flowers," *WF* 18 (1959): 114–17.

American gravestones as folk art have been treated in a number of illustrated books of various degrees of scholarly merit and in such articles as Phil R. Jack's "Gravestone Symbols of Western Pennsylvania," in *Two Penny Ballads and Four Dollar Whiskey*, ed. Kenneth S. Goldstein and Robert H. Byington (Hatboro, Pa.: Folklore Associates, 1966), pp. 165–73, and Beulah M. D'Olive Price, "The Customs of Using Portrait Statues as Gravestones," *MFR* 3 (1969): 58–64, 112–20. See also Thomas A. Zaniello, "American Gravestones: An Annotated Bibliography," *FF* 9 (1976): 115–37; Donald B. Ball, "Wooden Gravemarkers: Neglected Items of Material Culture," *TFSB* 43 (1977): 167–85; and Warren E. Roberts, "Tools on Tombstones: Some Indiana Examples," *PA* 10 (1978): 107–111, with a follow-up by Roberts in *PA* 12 (1980): 54–63.

The journal *AFFWord* published a series of articles on cemeteries and their decoration, beginning with the issue (vol. 1) for July 1971; the traditions touched on included Papago, Mormon, Chinese, Polynesian, and Mexican-American. Sara Clark described "The Decoration of Graves in Central Texas with Seashells," in *PTFS* 36 (1972): 33–43.

Black American folk art has had some special study in such works as William R. Ferris, Jr., "Vision in Afro-American Folk Art: The Sculpture of James Thomas," *JAF* 88 (1975): 115–31 (which expands upon a 1970 article), and David Evans, "Afro-American Folk Sculpture from Parchman Penitentiary [Miss.]," *MFR* 6 (1972): 141–52. Both writers provide good bibliographic guidance for background reading in this area.

Designs carved on aspen trees by Western sheepherders and vacationers were first documented with photographs by Ansel Adams and Paul Hassel in *TAW* 1 (Spring 1964): 37–45. Since then such studies have appeared as Jan Harold Brunvand and John C. Abramson, "Aspen Tree Doodlings in the Wasatch Mountains: A Preliminary Survey of Traditional Tree Carvings," in *Forms upon the Frontier*, ed. Austin Fife, Alta Fife, and Henry H. Glassie, Monograph Series 16:2 (Logan: Utah State

University, 1969), pp. 89–102; James B. DeKorne, *Aspen Art in the New Mexico Highlands* (Santa Fe: Museum of New Mexico Press, 1970); and Kenneth I. Periman, "Aspen Tree Carvings," *SWF* 3 (1979): 1–10. Other obscure folk-art expressions are depicted and discussed in general in Avon Neal and Ann Parker, *Ephemeral Folk Figures: Scarecrows, Harvest Figures, and Snowmen* (New York: Clarkson N. Potter, 1969).

The closing quotation in this chapter is from Arnold Hauser's "Popular Art and Folk Art," *Dissent* 5 (Summer 1958): 229–37, reprinted in *The Philosophy of Art History* (New York: Knopf, 1959), p. 347.

22
Folk Costumes

Traditional costumes hold a prominent place in European folk-life research, and consequently they are often featured there in publications, archives, museums, and folk festivals. Vestiges of folk costume still linger in the everyday life of some rural regions in almost all European countries, and many city people occasionally put on national or regional garb at festive occasions. Americans have become familiar with these and other foreign folk costumes through folksong and -dance groups from abroad, publications and television broadcasts, and travel. We easily recognize certain clichés of clothing as being nationally symbolic—the German in *lederhosen*, the Scot in kilts, and the Russian in a fur cap and high boots, for example. But we tend to assume that the United States really has no distinctive costume traditions, recognizing, perhaps, only a comical American tourist stereotype of a man in shorts, a loud sport shirt, sandals or tennis shoes, and a baseball cap, with a camera dangling around his neck; or an Indian chief with beaded buckskins and full headdress.

The few studies of traditional American clothing that have appeared give the impression that native Indian dress and vestiges of European costume among religious sects constitute the whole subject. In the *Journal of American Folklore*, for example, all of the major references to costume in the published index refer to that of Indian tribes. Most of the monographs and book-length studies have dealt with sectarian costumes, usually those of Pennsylvania-German Protestant groups. But there are many other traditional aspects of clothing in the United States that deserve study.

Despite the pervasive influence of international fashion and the easy accessibility of ready-made mass-produced clothing, some traditional influences continue to be apparent both in *what* Americans wear and *how* they wear it. While we have never had a peasant class with distinctive folk attire, and mobility and mass communications have wiped out many regional clothing styles, some folk-group differentiation is effected as much by costume choices as by folk speech, customs, beliefs, or other forms. Examples include special clothing, such as a tennis or ski "outfit"; holiday costumes, such as for Halloween or the custom of wearing green on St. Patrick's Day; and "dressing up" for special occasions, such as first communion or marriage. Just as with folk music, where traditional material mingles with commercialism, fashion leaders have borrowed ideas from folk practice and exploited them. For instance, a style called "folkloric" has been introduced which (supposedly) took elements from European peasant costumes to produce and market for the middle-class masses. But since there is considerable published work on cycles in the history of fashionable and popular styles, we will confine ourselves here to outlining only some possibilities in traditional American dress, very few of which have been studied so far.

Folk-costume research involves identifying and classifying details of *traditional* dress and adornment among the standardized general aspects, relating these traditions to the larger structure of folk-group behavior, and interpreting the meanings of these patterns. Probably in clothing research we will have even greater problems sorting out folk, popular, and elite influences than with any other aspect of folklore. Clothing manufacture, after all, is a gigantic international industry which is quick to respond both to the dictates of "high fashion" or to hints of future fads in current folk practices. So rapid are these changes that to cite specific examples risks dating this chapter. I take a chance mentioning just two styles prominent in store displays at the time of this writing. These are platform shoes, dictated by fashion despite their awkwardness and even health hazards, and, and in a style based on traditional practice, "cut-off" shorts with ragged unhemmed lower edges, now available as ready-made garments.

Historical Study

One useful avenue of approach to American folk-costume research is the historical, tracing the development of today's clothing styles out of the medley of national and ethnic styles that settlers brought to the New World. We may identify historical differences and developments in costume according to age, sex, national origin, region, occupation, economic and social status, and whether people are dressing for every day or a special occasion.

The first settlers, of course, came to the New World wearing the ordinary clothes of their homelands and bringing whatever fine clothes they could, according to their wealth and social status. Colonial costume, as historical research reveals, preserved considerable diversity in dress, depending upon the national origins, religions, occupations, and other cultural traits of the settlers. Soon, however, modes of dress more appropriate for a frontier society developed, influenced by the physical environment, the available raw materials and means of production, and to some extent by the Indians' example.

The characteristic frontiersmen's outfit—a distinctive American costume—was made from the typical native material, buckskin, right down to the moccasins. The trousers were close-cut without cuffs, but sometimes had long fringes down the sides; the upper garment was a tunic, slit part way down the front and laced, with a sort of cape-shawl shoulder piece. The sleeve edges and cape were also fringed. A coonskin or other fur hat topped the rig, and a belt—usually worn with buckle to the rear to prevent sun glare or snagging—completed it. The explanations offered for the fringing on the outfit sound suspicious. One is that the longer the fringes, the better the rain water would drip off a man. Another story is that the fringes were there to provide a ready source of buckskin thongs for tying. Cases are also on record of mountain men deriving nourishment, or at least believing that they did, from chewing the fringes from their clothing. Probably the fringe came first as a mere decorative device, and its various practical uses developed later and were orally transmitted.

The settlers that followed the trail blazers on the Great Plains and beyond were farmers from "back East" who wore the homemade clothing common to all of the settlements. As Francis Parkman described them in *The Oregon Trail*, from his observations in 1846, the men wore broad-brimmed hats, and "their long angular proportions [were] enveloped in brown homespun, evidently cut and adjusted by the hands of a domestic female tailor." The women wore homespun or "linsey-woolsey" dresses, sometimes supplemented by an apron or a shawl, and sunbonnets. A fine description of part of the process of a family making most of its clothing is included on the Library of Congress recording "Jack Tales Told by Mrs. Maud Long of Hot Springs, N.C." (AAFS L47):

> It would be on a long, winter evening when, after supper, all of us were gathered before the big open fire, my mother taking care of the baby or else the baby was in the cradle very near to mother, and she would be sewing or carding.
>
> My father would be mending someone's shoes or maybe a bit of harness. The older girls were helping with the carding or the sewing. And all of us little ones would either have a lapful or a basket full of wool out of which we must pick all the burrs and the Spanish needles and the bits of briars and dirt against the next day's carding.
>
> For my mother wove all of this wool that had been shorn from the backs of our own sheep—raised there on the farm that was in the heart of the Great Smoky Mountains in North Carolina—into linsey-woolsey, for hers and our dresses, or into blue jeans for my father's and brothers' suits, or into blankets to keep us warm, or into the beautiful patterned coverlets, to say nothing of all the socks and stocking and mitts and hoods that it took for a large family of nine children. And so she needed every bit of the wool that she could get ready.

As settlers became adjusted to the Far West, they modified their costume. Mark Twain described himself in miner's garb in *Roughing It*, only a year after he had arrived there in 1861 as a typical greenhorn, as "rusty looking . . . coatless, slouch hat, blue woolen shirt, pantaloons stuffed into boot-tops, whiskered half down to the waist, and the universal navy revolver slung to my belt." The blue or red color of the shirt was evidently a traditional touch; an 1859 guidebook for overland travel stated that "the shirt [should be] of red or blue flannel, such as can be found in almost all the shops on the frontier." Bandanna handkerchiefs, too, were until recently made only in blue or red, and the L. L. Bean Company of Freeport, Maine, long-time outfitter of hunting, fishing, and camping parties, long advised in its catalogue "A good blue flannel shirt cannot be beaten for all around wear."

The changes in Mormon pioneer dress during the first thirty-odd years of settlement in the West illustrate a unique case of adaptation of important styles. The Saints numbered among them Midwesterns and Easterners, as well as many European converts, all of whom brought elements of their clothing traditions with them to Utah when they first began to arrive there in 1847. But in their eagerness to become "real Americans," most immigrants quickly discarded peasant styles. (One exception may be the Mormon pioneer men's "barn-door trousers," possibly developed from north European peasant breeches; these had a front-buttoned flap, somewhat like that on the traditional sailors' pants.) The American fashions of the time influenced women to substitute pasteboard, folded newspapers, or wooden slats for starch and the whalebone stiffeners used in bonnets and skirts. The climate in the mountain settlements dictated warmer clothing—including quilted petticoats—than was common back East. The desire for adornment on clothing was filled partly by weaving straw flowers out of native grasses and making dyes from wild plants. Special religious rituals and beliefs led to the everyday wearing of sacred underclothing ("Temple Garments") and to robes used exclusively in temple ceremonies. Unlike several other American sects, however, the Mormons developed no uniform outer clothing as a mark of membership and piety, although a women's work costume with wide pants, a short skirt, and wide-brimmed straw hat ("The Deseret Costume") was proposed at one time. Currently in Utah many of the ethnic groups, whether Mormon or not, are returning to national costumes for festive occasions, and the Mormon women and girls have a strong preference for long "Pioneer style" dresses to wear for church or going out. A Latter-day Saint (LDS) splinter group, the Order of Aaron, has adopted a conservative sectarian costume for general everyday use.

Occupational Dress

Most early American occupational groups had traditional costume elements, such as a leather apron for a cobbler or blacksmith, a miller's smock, or the nineteenth-century farmer's outfit with its heavy shoes, vest, suspenders, and wide-brimmed hat (later replaced by denim bib-overalls, and still later by matching pant and shirt sets in green, blue, or gray). Merchant sailors of all nations tended to have some distinctive garb, just as different navies of the world still do. American loggers wore checkered shirts, pants that were "stagged" (cut off above the cuffs), sometimes a sash around the waist, and always hob-nailed and well-greased boots. The cowboy's distinctive outfit, much improvised upon, has become a national symbol. Originally it was characterized by the smooth leather (later sometimes fur) "chaps," a dull-colored shirt set off by a red scarf, vest, gunbelt, gloves, high-heeled boots, and wide-brimmed hat. Some of the cowboy-hat styles first associated with different parts of the West are still named for these regions and sell better in some places than others. The first cowboy trousers were usually of brown or naturally colored canvas, but the blue Levi's were introduced by the 1860s, and the copper rivets at stress points arrived in 1872 or 1873, although cowboys declined to accept them until about the 1890s. Other occupational traditions in dress may be distinguished, as well as the prestige values of different modes, as suggested in such verses from folksongs as this:

> I would not marry the farmer,
> He's always in the dirt;
> I'd rather marry the railroader
> Who wears the striped shirt.

Immigrant Dress

The later immigrants to the United States and Canada from
southern and eastern Europe repeated even more rapidly the
earlier settlers' practice of discarding native styles in preference for Westernized fashions. They sensed at once as they
mingled with their new countrymen how clearly one's clothes
projected a personal image, identifying the outsider as a for-
eigner. M. E. Ravage, a Romanian-Jewish immigrant, arrived in
New York City in 1900; he commented frequently on his awareness of clothes making the man in his book *An American in the
Making* (1917). He soon discovered that many of his fellow Ro-
manians mixed their clothing styles as badly as they did their
languages; some he saw were "clad in an absurd medley of Ru-
manian sheep-pelts and American red sweaters." *Real* Americans, he felt, showed more taste and "obvious wealth (judging
from their clothes)." It amused him to recall that in his home
village of Moldavia "none but young ladies of marriageable age
wore gloves; for any one else the article would have been regarded as silly dandyism." But in New York, he wrote, "even
teamsters and street laborers wore gloves at their work, to preserve, I supposed, their dainty hands." After many rebuffs during his first job-seeking, Ravage mustered up the courage to ask
a potential employer what was lacking in him:

> He looked me over from head to foot, and then, with a con-
> temptuous glance at my shabby foreign shoes (the alien's
> shoes are his Judas), he asked me whether I supposed he
> wanted a greenhorn in his store. . . . In order to have a job
> one must have American clothes, and the only way to get
> American clothes was to find a job and earn the price.

Ravage finally managed to break out of this vicious circle by
borrowing money and some articles of clothing to create a better appearance and win a position. With his first earnings he
purchased a new suit, new shoes, and derby hat; thus (in about
three months' time) began to evolve an "American in the making." Ironically, now, descendants of immigrants with experiences like this have formed folksong and -dance groups and like

to put on a semblance of national costume. And when I traveled in Romania in the early 1970s American tourists were often judged conspicuous for their shoes (usually tennis sneakers), and embroidered Romanian "peasant shirts" were popular souvenir items. The Romanian villagers were often anxious to trade parts of their folk costumes for Western blue jeans or panty hose.

Researching Folk Costumes

Besides historical developments in traditional dress and the special garb of a few nationality or sectarian groups, other possibilities exist for research in traditional American costumes. Standardized uniforms (as for monastic orders, military units, or bands) are not folk costumes, but probably less formal dressmarkers indicating one's role or status are, such as the medical student's lab coat, the chef's tall white hat, the motorcyclist's leather jacket, or the ballet dancer's favorite well-worn warm-up clothes. The sense of what constitutes "dressing up" in what were once referred to as "Sunday go-to-meeting" clothes, and which occasions call for such garb, would seem to be a traditional matter with variation from one period to another and from region to region. Or people may deliberately "dress down" to show rejection of society's clothing standards and to signal their alliance with like-minded individuals, whether "hippies," "freaks," "punks," defenders of the ecology, or others. (These examples illustrate that even within nonconformity there is conformity with another set of standards. Some dissident youth—often dedicated antimilitarists—favor old military uniforms as their badge of rebellion.) Patchwork and embroidered decoration on denim clothing and the modification of jeans and bib overalls into other garments has developed as a modern clothing craft of great variation and popularity. The supposed and actual dress of homosexuals might be studied. The degree of belief and practice involved with lucky clothing, for which basketball coaches are notorious, is another open question, as is the symbolic use of certain garments. For example, the native American coonskin hat was an effective political trademark for Senator Estes Kefauver of Tennessee, then briefly a fashion in children's wear. The popularity of "Come as you are" or period-dress parties could be studied, as could the visual clichés of pioneer costume concocted for use in local historical parades and pageants. Even *not* wearing something—going braless, shoeless, and tieless—constitutes a statement about a tradition made via one's mode of dress, and there are traditional associations between the age of a person and what he or she wears. Some metaphoric proverbial language refers to clothing: "to give the shirt off one's back," "to bet one's boots," "to throw one's hat in the ring," "if the shoe fits, wear it," "to wear the pants in the family," and "to beat the socks off someone" are examples. Perhaps a good begining for costume research would be simply to inventory one's own wardrobe to see what traditional elements are present, then to look more closely at one's friends and acquaintances for a time, to see what their clothes seem to be saying about them and to what degree these are traditional statements or are made by some traditional means.

BIBLIOGRAPHIC NOTES

Since there are very few studies in American folk costume, two survey articles by Don Yoder that refer to what little bibliography there is are especially valuable. One is "Sectarian Costume Research in the United States," in *Forms upon the Frontier*, ed. Austin Fife, Alta Fife, and Henry H. Glassie, Monograph Series, 16:2 (Logan: Utah State University Press, 1969), pp. 41–75; the other is Yoder's chapter "Folk Costume," in *Folklore and Folklife: An Introduction*, ed. Richard M. Dorson (Chicago: University of Chicago Press, 1972), pp. 295–323. Robert Wildhaber's bibliography (mentioned in the notes to Chapter 20) has a short section on costume and textiles. Some studies of *customs* (see Chapter 15) touch on *costumes* as well.

The following are general histories of American dress that contain good illustrations and some discussion: Douglas Gorsline, *What People Wore: A Visual History of Dress from Ancient Times to Twentieth-Century America* (New York and London: B. T. Batsford, 1952); R. Turner Wilcox, *Five Centuries of American Costume* (New York: Scribners, 1963); and Edward Warwick, Henry C. Pitz, and Alexander Wyckoff, *Early American Dress: The History of American Dress*, vol. 2 (New York:

B. Blom, 1965). Many illustrated works on American occupations and trades (cattle raising, railroading, seafaring, farming, etc.) are good sources of information on distinctive forms of work costume and uniform.

The article "Fashion on the Frontier" by Hazel Stein in *SFQ* 21 (1957): 160–64, is poorly documented and of slight scholarly value. Much better is Fairfax Proudfit Walkup's study "The Sunbonnet Woman: Fashions in Utah Pioneer Costume," *UHR* 1 (1947): 201–22, which is carefully documented and well illustrated.

A rare book-length study of an American costume tradition, Melvin Gingerich's *Mennonite Attire through Four Centuries* (Breiningsville, Pa.: The Pennsylvania-German Society, 1970), is highly detailed and very well illustrated.

The decoration of students' shirts and jeans with embroidery is the subject of Patricia Kemerer Downey's article "Current Trends in Decorative Embroidery: Folklore or Fakelore," *TFSB* 42 (1976): 108–24. Fifty illustrations of stitches and designs are included here; the conclusion, however, is that this does not represent true folklore, a finding that might well be disputed from the evidence presented.

The advice quoted in this chapter about buying red or blue shirts for Western travel was given in Randolph B. Marcy's *The Prairie Traveler: A Handbook for Overland Expeditions* (1859: republished by West Virginia Pulp and Paper Company, 1961). This book contains other interesting references to clothing and food for Western living, as well might other such works. The quotation from L. L. Bean is from the Spring 1966 catalogue. In 1976 an executive of L. L. Bean wrote me, "Traditionally red-blue is worn out of doors and these colors do not show dirt as do tans."

23
Folk Foods

Folk foods are the only traditional product to be quickly and wholly consumed, usually in a short time after preparation. Folk songs and stories may be forgotten, traditional houses deteriorate and burn down, and folk costumes eventually wear out or are discarded; but only folk foods disappear regularly with such speed and completeness. The study of folk foods, therefore, should include the entire process of traditional food handling and consumption: what is eaten, how and when it is eaten, food preparation and preservation, seasoning and serving food, ethnic and regional foods, religious food taboos and other requirements, food terms and beliefs, kitchens and cookware, table manners, and so forth. Such studies, as with most folklife subjects, are far more advanced in Europe than in the United States; European foodways specialists have prepared atlases of food traditions, studies of national and festival foods, films on food preparation, and, since 1979, have gathered at international conferences of "Ethnological Food Research" or "Ethnogastronomy" in order to plan and coordinate such research. (Other suggested names for folk-foods research are "Folk Cookery" and "Ethnocuisine.") It is clear that anything as basic as eating, with so many traditional attitudes and techniques associated with it, highly deserves serious study. Eventually, American folklorists got the message and began to produce good folk-foods research of their own.

Historical Study

As with American folk costume, a historical approach to national food traditions is a good place to start, although only a brief sketch is possible here. The first settlers took some hints from the Indians about how to use the resources of the new land. As we have seen in earlier chapters, native American culture had a negligible influence on settlers in terms of verbal folklore; but for solving the practical problem of subsisting in a wilderness, it contributed more. For example, the very term "Indian corn" that the Englishmen used for *maize* (the Spanish-derived word for it) indicated a debt to the natives, as do the Indian-derived names for some corn dishes, such as corn *pone, hominy,* and *succotash*. Traditionally, in the Northern states the European peasant staple-food oat or wheat porridge was modified into corn mush (called hasty pudding); in the South corn was traditionally preferred processed into hominy (by treating the whole kernels with lye) or coarsely ground and cooked in salted water as grits and eaten with butter or gravy.

White trappers and hunters learned from the Indians how to prepare lightweight survival rations like pemmican and "jerked" beef. The "Mountain Men" of the Western fur trade developed tastes for the Indians' favorite wild meats—both cooked and raw—and even for dog meat. A rendezvous feast of buffalo meat has been described in these terms:

> . . . the Mountain Men often began their repast by drinking some of the blood, which reminded them of warm milk. Then the liver was eaten raw, flavored with the contents of the gall bladder. If the cow buffalo was pregnant they savored one of the trappers' most exotic luxuries: the raw legs of unborn calves. . . . After these delicacies, the trappers were ready for their feast. This always included the hump ribs, which were pulled away by hand and the fat meat gulped down, while grease dripped over the face and clothing. These might be alternated with strips of the tenderloin, partially roasted or boiled, or by chunks of the tongue. Another prized portion was the "fleece," the inch-thick layer of fat that lay just beneath the buffalo hide. Scarcely less tempting were the intestines, or *boudins,* which were roasted, in the fire until puffed with heat and fat, then coiled on a blanket and gulped down without chewing. On such an occasion two trappers would start on the opposite ends of a pile of intestines and work their way toward the middle, each eating faster and faster to get his share, and shouting to the other to "feed fair."

In the Northeast, as late as the 1850s, Henry David Thoreau learned from an Indian companion how to make tea from the "creeping snowberry"; it was "better than the black tea which we had brought," he wrote in *The Maine Woods*. Thoreau mused in his journal in 1859: "I think that a wise and independent self-reliant man will have a complete list of the edibles to be found in a primitive country or wilderness. . . . He will know what are the permanent resources of the land and be prepared for the hardest of times."

If not from Indian lore or systematic study of the wilderness, at least from their own ingenuity and desperation, the tamers of the American frontier sooner or later ate every kind of meat that the land offered. An examination of the literature of early Western exploration and travel turned up reports of eating not just the standard fare of game animals, but also badgers, coyotes, insects, lizards, prairie dogs, skins and pelts (either as soup or simply chewed upon), wolves, many other beasts, and even, in extreme circumstances, human beings. One Western army veteran wrote that when his unit was out of provisions and forced to devour the mules one by one, a bit of extra flavor could be added to the unseasoned meat by burning the mule steaks on the outside and sprinkling gunpowder over them.

Among these vanguards of the frontier, the diet prescribed by available resources and field expediency became, to a degree, traditional. From such practices perhaps we might trace at least part of some modern American's continued passion for hunting wild game and for liking meat cooked rare and served in large portions. Also, the early use of such a variety of animals for food probably underlies the current humorous folklore of mock recipes for preparing tough or undesirable game. The cook is directed to put the meat on a plank, season it well, cook it carefully and slowly, and then to discard the meat and eat the plank. Related items are the jesting recipe for "Shadow Soup," which is supposedly made from only the shadow of a fowl that is hung over the cooking pot, and the "Stone Soup" of traditional folktales.

The food of typical frontier occupations developed along traditional lines, limited by what was most readily available and what could be preserved easily. Native folksongs contain some records of these menus. In "The Buffalo Skinners" (a parody of "Canaday I O"), for example, the singer complains,

> We lived on rotten buffalo hump and damned old iron-wedge bread,
> Strong coffee, croton water to drink, and a bull hide for a bed.

In another version the fare is "old jerked beef, croton coffee, and sour bread." ("Croton water" is probably a reference, surviving from the older song, to water coming from the Croton River in Westchester County, New York, first tapped for the New York City water supply in 1842; various early references to "Croton water" show that there was some difference of opinion then about its drinking qualities and appearance. One writer referred to the New York City town pumps, located at street corners, "so that no person who is athirst need perish. . . . If he stand in need of physic at the same time, the pump will furnish that also." Perhaps the suggestion in the song is just "river water," or the cathartic "Croton oil" may be implied.)

The housekeeping of a "Lane County [Kansas] Bachelor" is described in a song of that title that is also known as "Starving to Death on a Government Claim."

> My clothes are all ragged, my language is rough,
> My bread is case-hardened, both solid and tough . . .
>
> The dishes are scattered all over the bed,
> All covered with sorghum, and government bread.
> Still I have a good time, and I live at my ease,
> On common sop sorghum, an' bacon an' cheese.

What the bachelor yearned for in the song was a comfortable home elsewhere and three square meals every day, prepared by someone else:

> Farewell to Lane County, farewell to the West,
> I'll travel back East to the girl I love best,
> I'll stop at Missouri and get me a wife,
> And live on corn dodgers, the rest of my life.

"Corn dodgers" (a term applied to a variety of corn-meal cakes) represent relative luxury in other songs, too, but the long-term bad effect of the unbalanced diet is pictured in "The State of Arkansas" or "An Arkansaw Traveler":

> He fed me on corn dodger that was hard as any rock,
> Till my teeth began to loosen and my knees began to knock.
> And I got so thin on sassafras tea I could hide behind a straw,
> You bet I was a different lad when I left old Arkansaw.

Another popular folksong that pictures the crudeness of bachelor life on the frontier is directed as a warning to young ladies not to marry Kansas boys, Cheyenne boys, Mormon boys, boys of many other places, and, in the following version, "Texan Boys":

> Come all ye Missouri girls and listen to my noise;
> You must not marry these Texan boys.
> For if you do your portion will be
> Cold Johnnycake [corn bread] and venison is all you'll see. . . .
>
> When the boys get hungry they bake their bread.
> They build up a fire as high as your head,
> Shovel up the ashes and roll in the dough;
> The name that they give it is dough, boys, dough!

On the nineteenth-century American sailing ships, as described in R. H. Dana's *Two Years before the Mast*, the diet was a tiresome repetition of meals consisting mostly of weak tea, tough salt beef, and hard biscuits. The shipboard meat barrels were picked over for the officers' meals first, so the ration that reached the crew was bad enough to inspire a chant, called "The Sailor's Grace," which began "Old horse! old horse! what brought you here?" A rare treat was "scouse," made of pieces of salt beef boiled up with pounded biscuits and a few potatoes. Pudding, or "duff," made of flour, water, and molasses, with a little dried fruit added for Christmas, was an occasional dessert treat.

American cowboys and loggers ate a little better than this, although still without much variety. A local song from Maine describes the food supplies of a typical camp in these terms:

They tote in all their flour and pork
    their beans, oat, peas, and straw,
Their beef it comes from Bangor, boys,
    and some from Canada;
They haul it to our good cook Lou
    who cooks it in a pot
And serves it on the table
    when it is nice and hot.

Staples of the cowboy diet were similar, although not usually stewed. The Westerners consumed large meals of fried steak, sourdough biscuits, and strong coffee, with canned or dried foods included if available. Although one verse of the widely sung "Old Chisholm Trail" declared "Oh it's bacon and beans 'most every day, I'd as soon be a-eatin' Prairie hay," the cowboys appreciated their cooks' good efforts and got what they could when they could from the countryside to vary the diet. They traded beef for vegetables, fruit, or melons whenever possible, hunted up wild birds' eggs, tried to shoot game, and, if nothing else were available, just referred to their bacon as "fried chicken" and gulped it down. There seems to be no truth to the story that in logging and cow camps the men took turns being amateur cooks, each being replaced whenever a man complained, and the complainer taking over. (One punchline of this story is "That tastes like moose turd pie, and by God I *like* it!")

The Dutch oven (a cast-iron kettle with a heavy lid), which allowed controlled baking to be done by an open fire or over a bed of coals, saved cowboy cookery from the tyranny of the frying pan and the stewing pot. A good-food company was sometimes referred to as "strictly a Dutch-oven outfit," and its cook could be counted on to prepare dried-apple pies regularly, and other kinds of treats when supplies were on hand. (The term "Dutch oven" is probably a national slur, like "Dutch treat.") Sourdough cookery, about which a whole book might be written concerning both its cowboy and many other Western specialists, provided a staple for the menus of all meals, only occasionally varied with salt-rising bread. The latter, one cowboy commented, "tasted mighty good, but smelled something like old dirty socks."

American men's cooking in their own work camps always concentrated on solid fundamentals that stuck to the ribs. As women settled on the frontier they began to exercise their talents to supply the frills, often having no more to work with than the foods that would keep or could be gathered from the land. Their traditional recipes were passed on from mother to daughter or exchanged with neighbors. Frontier men had already learned to settle for substitutes when supplies ran out—"Horsemint tea" for coffee, or shredded red-willow bark for tobacco. But it took women to invent a way of stretching the coffee supply by baking corn meal in molasses and stirring it into the grounds. Another method was to burn coffee dregs for re-use, and, in fact, nearly every berry, grain, weed, or seed which could be roasted and ground seems to have been tried at one time or another as a substitute for coffee. Sweetenings, always in short supply and expensive, were another challenge to housewives. Sugar, maple sugar, sorghum, and honey were used when readily available, and when they were not, the cook fell back on corncob syrup to stretch the supply of sweetening, or watermelon syrup to replace it. Other ingenious culinary gimmicks included "Lengthened Eggs" (with milk and flour) for breakfast omelets, "Mock Strawberries" made from chunks of peaches and apples, and "Casserole of Rabbit," which was designed to make something worthwhile out of those pesky creatures. (The recipe was revived during the Dust Bowl period.)

It was with the "Nothing-in-the-house Pies" that the early American housewife showed her best form, and some of her creations are still favorites. These were either concocted from otherwise insipid fruits—green currants or elderberries, for instance—or from unlikely ones such as grapes. The out-and-out "mock" pies required the greatest daring—crushed crackers could be made to taste like an apple filling, with the proper seasoning, and cream pie flavored with either vinegar or field sorrel might pass for lemon. One mock mincemeat pie was made from green tomatoes, and another from rolled crackers and raisins properly seasoned. It is apparent in such examples that the frontier settlers were intent upon serving the status foods associated with Eastern or Old World menus, even in preference to some of the succulent wild fruits and berries that the new land provided. (By the same reasoning, few white settlers really seemed to relish the Indian foods they tried, and ate them only during periods of shortage.) In some families there was a traditional pie-top design, often a monogram, that was cut or punched into the top crusts as a last flourish—another pie tradition still preserved by some cooks.

Apart from frontier food traditions, they are many other historical foodways that might be studied, only a few examples which can be cited here. These include wild-food gathering (greens, mushrooms, honey, maple sap), traditional food processing (molasses-making, moonshining), and several kinds of food preservation (smoking, pickling, salting, drying, canning, and freezing, plus boiling fruit down into "butter" or drying it as "leather"). Studies of American festival foods need to be done, including those eaten for birthdays, weddings, or other special occasions. Ethnic foodways among a few groups have been largely maintained, but in most immigrant groups are relegated to special occasions; studies so far also suggest that there is little interpenetration of ethnic recipes, even in situations of intermarriage.

Regional Foods

The development of regional food specialties and preferences deserves study. The identification of baked beans with Boston, one kind of clam chowder with New England and another with Manhattan, black-eyed peas and fried chicken and many other foods with the South, corn-on-the-cob with the Midwest, and Mexican specialties with the Southwest are partly traditional matters, especially in a day and age in which any region's food can be delivered to any other region with ease, and in which one can declare that chicken cooked anywhere (and in several ways) is "Southern fried."

A unique instance of food regionalizing is the "Cincinnati Chili Culinary Complex" described by folklorist Timothy Lloyd. Served now in dozens of chain-operated chili parlors, Cincinnati Chili ingredients typically include such spices as cinnamon, allspice, and bay leaves, presumably because the original recipe was invented by a Greek cook who wanted something different in the way of chili but tasting familiar (to him) as a meat dish. Even more unusual is the terminology of serving chili combinations: there is "a bowl of plain," two-way (served over spaghetti, as are all subsequent "ways"), three-way (cheese added), four-way (onions added), and five-way (beans added). The protocol of ordering requires that one state the highest "way" involved, then possibly subtract lower-ranking ingredients: thus, *never* "three-way with onions," but *possibly* "four-way, no cheese." Chili, of course, is loaded with regional and personal quirks in preparation all through the South and Southwest, and it deserves a full study by a food specialist with an iron stomach.

The varying names for similar foods in different regions have folkloristic overtones, too. When the columnist Allan M. Trout of *The Courier-Journal* of Louisville, Kentucky, described a traditional stew made at hog-killing time, his readers wrote in to say that it was called "Pluck" (or "Pluck and Plunder") "All Sorts," "Scrapple," "Liver Mush," "Giblets," and "Monroe County Stew." (Other regional names for it are "Cowboy Stew," "Son of a Bitch [or Gun]," "Forest Ranger Stew," "Boss-Man Stew," and "Mother-in-Law Stew.") Doughnuts are variously termed "Fried Cakes," "Sinkers," "Crullers," and "Ginger Nuts," in different parts of the country. Green beans may be called "String Beans" or "Snap Beans," and pancakes appear on menus across the land as "Hotcakes," "Griddle Cakes," "Flapjacks" or "Wheat Cakes." Some similar situations occur with soft drinks ("soda," "pop," "soda-pop," "tonic," etc.). Also from our regional cooks have come terms like "Hopping John," "Snickerdoodle," "Hush-Puppies," "Apple Slump," "Cinnamon Flop," "Red-Eye Gravy," and "Red-Flannel Hash."

The Folk Meal

The basic characteristics of the American folk meal seem to be large quantities, great variety, and the use of regional specialties. This is true whether it is a family meal, a "company meal," or the fixin's for a special festival or gathering that is described. Descriptions of the varied offerings at gargantuan American feasts have been a commonplace of our literature since the Pilgrims' "First Thanksgiving," and the following two are merely a pair of less familiar examples. From Kentucky, this is given as an everyday meal at about the turn of the century:

> The meat was fried old ham, with red gravy. Also on the table were chicken and dumplins, corn, beans, sweet potatoes, okra, candied apples, sliced tomatoes, potato salad, miscellaneous pickles and relishes, hot chess pie topped with whipped cream, and chocolate pie with deep meringue.

And this one is from Oregon from a novel set in 1905:

> The supper was all everyday victuals, but there were plenty of them. There was fried deerliver with onions, a little greasier than it needed to be; beefsteak, excellent cuts but infernal cooking, with all the juice fried out and made into flour-and-milk gravy; potatoes, baked so the jackets burst open and showed the white; string beans, their flavor and nutritive value well oiled with a big hunk of salt pork; baked squash soaked in butter; a salad of lettuce whittled into shoestrings, wilted in hot water, and doped with vinegar and bacon grease; tomatoes stewed with dumplings of cold bread; yellow corn mowed off the cob and boiled in milk; cold beetpickles, a jar of piccalilli, and a couple of panloads of hot sourdough biscuits. For sweets there were tomato preserves, peach butter, wild blackcap jam, and wild blackberry and wild crabapple jelly. For dessert there was a red-apple cobbler with lumpy cream, and two kinds of pie, one of blue huckleberry, and the other of red. The country fed well, what with wild game and livestock and gardens, milk and butter and orchards and wild fruits; and no man was every liable to starve in it unless his digestion broke down from overstrain.

The same American tendency to dream of much good eating is reflected in traditional songs such as "Big Rock Candy Mountain," the metaphorical suggestions of "Pie in the Sky" (labor organizer and martyr Joe Hill's famous parody of "In the Sweet By and By"), and in stanzas from hillbilly favorites such as the following:

Bile 'em cabbage down;
Bake 'em hoecake brown.
The only song that I can sing,
Is "Bile 'em cabbage down."

*

Gonna buy me a sack of flour,
Bake me a hoecake every hour,
Keep that skillet good and greasy all the time.

Other appearances of this theme occur in the phrase "chicken every Sunday" and the political slogan "A chicken in every pot."

"Playing with Your Food"

"Playing with your food" represents a fairly strong American taboo that is, in fact, frequently broken. For example, some people eat a chocolate-cream sandwich cookie by "screwing apart" the two halves and licking off the filling; the principle here is "best first." But "best last" is the game when the frosted end of a wedge of cake is set aside, possibly also with the rest of the frosting and filling. (Similarly, some people will eat all around the yolk of an egg that is fried "sunny side up" and eat this part last.) Mashed potatoes with gravy may be sculpted into a miniature volcano (or well?) and then manipulated until the gravy flows as the food is eaten.

Another sort of food recreation is represented in various playful recipes for special cakes, the simplest and most common of which is for "Upside-Down Cake." Sometimes this is a matter of ingredients, as with "Tomato Soup Cake" and "Sauerkraut Cake" (in which relatively small amounts of the "odd" ingredient are used). In another set of funny directions we find "Wacky Cake" (in which the moist ingredients are placed atop mounds of the dry ones), "1-2-3-4 Cake" (in which the portions of the first four ingredients are in units from one to four), and "Scripture Cake" (in which Bible verses are referenced where the necessary ingredients are mentioned). And, recalling the urban legends of Chapter 9, the recipe for "Red Velvet Cake" contains the surprising addition of a large dollop of red food coloring as the cook's supposed "secret."

Researching Folk Foods

Modern American foodways offer a real challenge to the folklife scholar: while there are traditional qualities in virtually every aspect of eating and drinking, the most obvious factors influencing these acts are now commercial and professional ones. For instance, ethnic and regional tastes are reflected in many of the fast-food chains (e.g., Taco Bell and Kentucky Fried Chicken) and even in TV dinners; mixtures of traditions are apparent in such restaurant names as "Mexican-American Smorgasbord" or "Der Wienerschnitzel" (which serves no actual "schnitzels," but mostly varieties of hot dogs). The foods people prefer for breakfast, while mainly of commercial origin, group themselves in traditional ways: Continental breakfasts, hot versus cold foods, meat versus cereals, fruit and sweets for breakfast, pie for breakfast, side dishes of potatoes or grits, and so forth. The names, timing, and foods considered appropriate for other meals and snacks, as well as for camping or picnics, could be studied. Foods for backpacking range from the commercial freeze-dried products to homemade jerky and pemmican; "natural" or "organic" food devotees, similarly, may either produce their own foodstuffs or buy them in special shops. The concept of "soul food"—including both what is eaten and how it interrelates with other traditional aspects of a subculture, would be a useful piece of research, as would the idea of eating "lighter" or more "natural" foods.

Kay Cothran viewed "participation in tradition" in food preferences of Deep South (pineywoods) "cracker culture." The four categories of foods she identified were (1) those appropriate whenever eating itself is; (2) those that follow "situational food rules" (e.g., curative foods); (3) foods to be avoided in certain circumstances (e.g., just after childbirth); and (4) things *never* to be eaten (some regarded by her informants as "nigger foods"). Such food rules could be studied much closer to home, and the results would likely involve taboos against talking with one's mouth full or wasting food, and attitudes toward mixing certain foods in one meal or even mixing them up on one plate.

Probably any American could add something to the following list of other prospective subjects for studies of traditional eating and drinking in the United States: folk speech references to food, such as "in apple-pie order," "not worth his salt," "to eat crow," and "in a stew"; traditions of the "potluck" or "pitch-in" dinner; varieties of alcoholic mixed drinks and ice-cream sundaes; dandelion and other homemade wines; rhymed recipes; "Tuna Wiggle," "Barf on a Board," and other traditional names for institutionalized cooking; "Adam and Eve on a Raft," "CB" (meaning "cardboard" for the "to go" containers), and other hashslingers' terms; hobos' recipes; and superstitious food taboos. No folklorist need starve for ideas when so many juicy tidbits remain.

BIBLIOGRAPHIC NOTES

The study of American foodways (ethnocuisine, ethnogastronomy, etc.) got a good early start among folklorists but was a long time developing, finally coming into its own recently as a viable subspecialty of research. The only full-length article on food published early in *JAF* is John G. Bourke's "Folk-Foods of the Rio Grande Valley and of Northern Mexico," in *JAF* 8 (1895): 41–71. A good indication of progress is the "Special Food Issue" of *KFQ* with five articles edited and introduced by foodways specialist Jay Anderson, *KFQ* 16 (1971): 153–214; it contains studies of foodways research, Indian foods, soul food, and the organic-foods movement, plus a report on an international ethnological food research symposium.

Thirty-three papers representing the proceedings of the Third International Conference on Ethnological Food Research, which met in Cardiff, Wales, in 1977, provide a good cross section of approaches. See Alexander Fenton and Trefor M. Owen, eds., *Food in Perspective* (Edinburgh: John Donald, 1981). Among American folklorists attending the conference whose papers are published here are Jay Anderson, Roger L. Welsch, and Don Yoder. American anthropologist Robert J. Theodoratus presented a paper on Greek immigrant cuisine in America, which is also relevant to this chapter.

A special issue of *JAC* (2:3, 1979) offered a "Focus on American Food and Foodways," ed. Kay Mussell and Linda Keller Brown. The most useful articles to folklorists are Angus K. Gillespie's "Toward a Method for the Study of Food in American Culture" (pp. 393–406) and Charles Camp's "Food in American Culture: A Bibliographic Essay" (pp. 559–70); however, the latter does not list this chapter and its notes!

Cookbooks and popular works on American foods may be useful in research. *The American Heritage Cookbook and Illustrated History of American Eating & Drinking* (New York: American Heritage Publishing Co. and Simon and Schuster, 1964), for example, is well written, informative, and also magnificently illustrated in both black and white and color. A similar publication is *American Cooking*, by Dale Brown (New York: Time-Life Books, 1968), particularly its chapter "Two Hundred Years in the Kitchen," pp. 184–99.

The description of mountain men eating buffalo meat quoted in this chapter is from Ray Allen Billington's *The Far Western Frontier, 1830–1860* (New York: Harper, 1956; Harper Torchbook paperback edition, 1962), p. 51. Martin Schmitt surveyed Western food traditions in "'Meat's Meat': An Account of the Flesh-eating Habits of Western Americans," *WF* 11 (1952): 185–203. My note on a Western tradition of "Mock Recipes for 'Planked' Game" appeared in *WF* 2 (1962): 45–46, and a similar item of food jokelore is described in Mac E. Barrick's "Texas Chicken" [fried fatback], *NCFJ* 27 (1979): 88–92.

Three articles concern the preparation of sweetenings by folk methods: William E. Lightfoot, "'I Hardly Ever Miss a Meal without Eating Just a Little': Traditional Sorghum-Making in Western Kentucky," *MSF* 1 (1973): 7–17; Nora Leonard Roy, "Maple Sugaring in Southern Indiana: A Descriptive Study of the Technology of Four Maple Sugar Makers," *IF* 9 (1976): 197–234; and Suzanne Stiegelbauer, "A Folk Craft as a Folk Art: An Example of Cane Syrup Production in East Texas," *MFR* 12 (1978): 118–30. Sylvie Howbart describes "A Hog Killing in Eastern North Carolina," *NCFJ* 28 (1980): 42–55, while Howard Wight Marshall takes the process further in "Meat Preservation on the Farm in Missouri's 'Little Dixie,'" *JAF* 92 (1979): 400–17. Another food-preparation study is Marlene Schroeder's "George DeMeyer: Belgian-American Wine-Maker," *IF* 11 (1978): 193–200.

The frontier folksongs referred to in this chapter appear in many collections. Several of these texts are from H. M. Belden's *Ballads and Songs Collected by the Missouri Folk-Lore Society*, University of Missouri Studies 15 (Columbia, 1940). Logger's stew is described in "The Depot Camp" quoted in "Folksongs from Maine," *NEF* 7 (1965): 15–22. Roger L. Welsch gives a number of folksong references to frontier foods, plus other interesting data, in his article "'Sorry Chuck': Pioneer Foodways," *NH* 53 (1972): 99–113 (repr. in *Readings in American Folklore*, pp. 152–67). The food of sailors and cowboys was compared in my own article "Sailors' and Cowboys' Folklore in Two Popular Classics," *SFQ* 29 (1965): 266–83. Edward Everett Dale's *Frontier Ways:*

Sketches of Life in the Old West (Austin: University of Texas Press, 1959) has chapters on "Cowboy Cookery" (pp. 25–42) and "Food on the Frontier" (pp. 111–31). An extended study of the former topic is Ramon F. Adams's *Come an' Get It: The Story of the Old Cowboy Cook* (Norman: University of Oklahoma Press, 1952; reissued, 1972). Rose P. White discussed that staple of Western cooking in "The Sourdough Biscuit" in *WF* 15 (1956): 93–94; Peter Tamony explored the terminology, mystique, and history of "Sourdough and French Bread" in his Western Words section of *WF* 32 (1973): 265–70. A revealing project which suggests other possibilities with other groups is Charlie Seemann's paper "Bacon, Biscuits, and Beans: Food of the Cattle Trails as Found in American Cowboy Songs," *AFFWord* 4 (Oct. 1974): 24–39.

Three early notes in *JAF* concerned recipes for substitutes. These were "Traditionary American Local Dishes," *JAF* 13 (1900): 65–66; "Some Homely Viands,'" *JAF* 13 (1900): 292–94; and "Blood-Root 'Chocolate,'" *JAF* 19 (1906): 347–48. Miriam B. Webster's "Maine Winter Menus: A Study in Ingenuity," *NEF* 1 (1958): 7–9, has some similar recipes, as do several of the works on pioneer foods mentioned previously.

A query for variant terms and shapes for doughnuts was published by Charles Peabody in *JAF* 18 (1905): 166, but apparently no responses were ever printed. The subject may be pursued, however, in several studies of folk dialect.

B. A. Botkin has sections on regional foods in *A Treasury of New England Folklore* (New York: Crown, 1947) and *A Treasury of Southern Folklore* (New York: Crown, 1949). Southern traditional recipes were discussed by George W. Boswell in two articles appearing in *MFR* 5 (1971): 1–9, and *MSF* 3 (1975): 13–20. Early American recipes from New York and elsewhere in the East are given in articles by Janet R. MacFarlane in *NYFQ* 10 (1954): 135–40 and 218–25, and in *NYFQ* 11 (1955): 305–9. The latter contains one rhymed recipe.

In a study of "Children's Food Preferences," *NYF* 5 (1979): 189–96, A. J. Lamme III and Linda Leonard Lamme summarize the results of a questionnaire given to 1,000 children at the 1976 Smithsonian Festival of American Folklife—cake and ice cream, corn, peanut butter and jelly sandwiches, and cereal led the choices here. In "The Cincinnati Chili Culinary Complex," *WF* 40 (1981): 28–40, Timothy Charles Lloyd traces the history and varieties of this regional speciality. A query by the editor of *PA* on "Sliced Tomatoes for Breakfast" (vol. 9, 1977, 11) asks for information on the eating of sliced fresh tomatoes instead of grits or potatoes with eggs and meat as a breakfast dish. A (somewhat) related item is a note and reply entitled "Were Tomatoes Considered Poisonous?" *PA* 11 (1979): 112–13; while some early references describe the eating of tomatoes, others seem to reflect suspicions about them, so the point is still moot.

The description of a Kentucky meal in this chapter is quoted from Allan M. Trout's *Greetings from Old Kentucky, Volume Two* (Frankfort, Ky., 1959), p. 71. A food item from another Southern state is described in James W. Byrd's "Poke Sallet [a dish made of pokeweed greens, bacon drippings, and eggs] from Tennessee to Texas," *TFSB* 32 (1966): 48–54. Paul Brewster includes cooking, preserving, and beverage making in volume 1 of the *Frank C. Brown Collection of North Carolina Folklore*, edited by a committee of specialists (Durham, N.C.: Duke University Press, 1952–64), pp. 266–75.

The description of the Oregon meal in this chapter is quoted from H. L. Davis's novel *Honey in the Horn* (New York: Harper, 1935; Avon paperback ed., [n.d.]), p. 19. Some Utah folk foods are included in Jan Harold Brunvand, *A Guide for Collectors of Folklore in Utah* (Salt Lake City: University of Utah Press, 1971), pp. 118–19. Marjorie Sackett has discussed Kansas folk recipes in *Kansas Folklore*, ed. S. J. Sackett (Lincoln: University of Nebraska Press, 1961), pp. 226–38; in *MF* 12 (1962): 81–86; and in *WF* 22 (1963): 103–6.

Ethnic American foodways offer many good subjects for study. Three fine examples of published work are Don Yoder's articles "Sauerkraut in the Pennsylvania Folk-Culture," *PF* 12 (Summer 1961): 56–69; "Schnitz·in the Pennsylvania Folk-Culture," *PF* 12 (Fall 1961): 44–53; and "Pennsylvanians Called It Mush," *PF* 13 (Winter 1962–63): 27–49. Other studies are Elaine J. Abboud and Jean A. Sarrazin, "New Orleans Lenten Recipes: A Multi-Ethnic Sampling," *LFM* (April 1970): 55–69; Janet Langlois, "Moon Cake in Chinatown, New York City: Continuity and Change," *NYFQ* 28 (1972): 83–117; and Craig Soland, "How to Make a Sve-te-Saba [Serbian food]," *AFFWord* 3 (Spring 1974): 1–7. Marjorie Sackett investigates "the recipe as a measure of the extent to which neighboring cultures influence each other" in her note "Folk Recipes as a Measure of Intercultural Penetration," *JAF* 85 (1972): 77–81.

Since 1971, when the journal began publication, *AFFWord*, the organ of the Arizona Friends of Folklore, has periodically had an "Ethno Cuisine" section. The subjects have included Western cooking techniques (Dutch ovens, the goat roast, pit barbecue), food specialties (flour tortillas, son-of-a-bitch stew, cactus jelly), ethnic foods (Norwegian, Serbian, Flemish, Mexican, German of Transylvania), playful recipes (wacky cake), and even pseudo-recipes or food hoaxes (rattlesnake steak).

A good example of modern foodways research merging with recent folklore theory is Kay L. Cothran's thought-provoking article "Talking with Your Mouth Full: A Communications Approach to Food Rules," *TFSB* 38 (1972): 33–38. An extended summary of an important piece of European food research is provided by Roger L. Welsch in *KFQ* 16 (1971): 189–212; the work is Gunter Wiegelmann's *Alltags- und Fest-*

speisen: Wandel und gegenwartige Stellung [Daily and Festival Foods: Migration and Present Situation] (Marburg: N.G. Elwert Verlag, 1967).

An imaginative project that yielded fine results is reported in Carter W. Craigie's "The Picnic Experience," *TFSB* 45 (1979): 161–65; he drew on oral and written accounts of picnics in Chester County, Pennsylvania, from 1870 to 1925 to show how formalities of everyday life were relaxed and new social-interaction patterns developed while people were attending picnics. Similar studies might be done of backyard barbecues, brown-bagged lunches, company parties, clam bakes, fish fries, and so forth. In a brief but suggestive note, Melissa Caswell Mason writes of "Food and Food-related Metaphors in Folkspeech" such as "You said a mouthful!" in *FMS* 6 (1982): 29–33.

The major recent publication on American folk foodways is the special issue of *WF* (vol. 40, 1981) edited by Michael Owen Jones, Bruce Giuliano, and Roberta Krell. A prologue, thirteen articles, and an epilogue take up such diverse topics as playing with food, food aversions, customs relating to food portions, carnival food, compiled cookbooks, and food-related speech.

APPENDIX
Putting It All Together:
Research in American Folklore

Using the Book

Understanding and participating in the study of American folklore, for most beginning students, require more than simply reading *The Study of American Folklore*, although having done that, you have made an excellent start. But as a learning experience, reading about scholarship—especially in folklore—is inferior to *doing* it. (This is why most instructors in college folklore courses assign a research project.) As detailed and comprehensive as the summaries of folklore types and studies are in this textbook, they are still *only* summaries of representative materials. Folklore does not occur in real life packaged into the tidy definitions and subtypes of the preceding chapters; nor do folklore studies line up on the library shelves in the neat order of these bibliographic notes. Thus, in order to bring together into a workable methodology the many ideas about studying American folklore discussed in this book, you need to decide what sort of research you want to do and then draw on sections of the book that can help you. The four sample studies in this appendix, along with this brief introduction to them, demonstrate how materials and concepts introduced here may be applied in a scholarly manner by folklorists, whether trained professionals or beginning students.

Because American folklore and its study are presented here (as the Preface points out) in a systematic manner, finding a specific term, a definition, an example, or a bibliographic reference is a simple matter of consulting the appropriate chapter or looking in one of the indexes. Whether a chapter concerns proverbs, folksongs, games, gestures, or foodways, it begins with definitions and categories and concludes with a discussion of scholarly approaches. But because the major chapters focus on *genres* (types of folklore), theories and methods of folklore research are scattered through the book. To offset this situation (which is an advantage when classifying a folklore collection), the first three chapters introduce folklore and its study, and the Glossarial Index gathers all references to primary definitions.

As you gain practice using this text, you will note instances of similar ideas presented separately as they pertain to different categories of American folklore. For example, the fundamental issue of what constitutes "folk" tradition is introduced in theoretical terms in Chapters 1 ("The Field of Folklore") and 3 ("Folk Groups"); but the same question is also treated in relation to proverbs in Chapter 5, to songs in Chapter 11, to folklife in Chapter 19, and to folk crafts and art in Chapter 21. A similar strategy is followed with reference to the question of how religious belief relates to "folk" ideas; this is discussed in Chapter 8 in connection with myth and in Chapter 14 as an aspect of the study of superstition. Approaches to folklore analysis are also treated in more than one chapter of the book, as a glance at such headings in the Glossorial Index as "Contextual analysis," "Structural analysis," or "Style" reveals.

A question that readers should pose to themselves as they use this book is what each separate folklore genre really has in common with other folklore genres. Folklore, after all, never exists in a vacuum but lives in company with other kinds of folklore and other aspects of culture and behavior. The proverb and the riddle, for example, are both conversational genres of oral folklore that seem to be nearly mirror images of each other. Both forms are expressed verbally in concise phrases, sentences, or rhymes, but the proverb clarifies a situation and offers a comment upon it, while the riddle confuses or baffles listeners. Proverbs often contain metaphors, but these are *clear* figures of speech that are readily understood; riddles, on the other hand, are based on unclear metaphors demanding some kind of thoughtful solution. Proverbs apply to recurrent life situations—occasions for which tradition furnishes a ready response—but riddles are divorced from particular social contexts and function mainly as wit-teasers or demonstrations of cleverness.

If we compare other genres to these, we see that the traditional gesture is more like the proverb, being a visual (rather than oral) summary statement about "how things are," although there are also gesture riddles (as shown in Chapter 6). Traditional pranks are related functionally and structurally to riddles, although these "practical jokes" (as that term suggests) also have things in common with narrative jokes, especially "tall tales." These suggestions are only hints of the discussions American folklorists have engaged in through papers and publications concerning the forms and functions of folkloric genres, and genre study is only one kind of folklore scholarship.

Your Own Folklore Projects

One of the most useful features of this book for locating relevant published studies in American folklore, which is sometimes frustrating to students, is the section of bibliographic notes appended to each chapter. To conserve space, very few references are given more than once—at the point most appropriate to a particular folklore genre—in the book, and journal titles are usually abbreviated. But it is not difficult to use these references as guides to your own college library's resources. The problem of using bibliographic notes productively is related to the problem of using the library efficiently, and there are some simple ways to get started. One could, for instance, mark on the list of journal abbreviations in the front of this book the major folklore periodicals that the library owns and then check the basic reference works available for various categories of lore. Which proverb dictionaries, what ballad indexes, and how many basic regional collections of American folklore does your library have? Another useful exercise is to select a subcategory of folklore (something fairly specialized like tongue-twisters, pictorial folktales, greenhorn pranks, water witching, or apple-head dolls), and then to see how many references listed in this textbook are in your library and how many *more* references you can locate using the bibliographies or other sources mentioned either in this book or in outside sources. When using the bibliographic notes, keep two things in mind: (1) the items are always presented in the same order as subjects in the chapter itself; and (2) the annotations give you some idea of the possible value of the references listed to your project. (This last feature is especially important if you use Interlibrary Loan to get publications not found in your library.)

The nature of your research will depend somewhat on the kind of course for which this book is being used as a text. In an English-department folklore course, for example, you may be studying the use of American folklore in literature; in a course taught in an anthropology department, the emphasis may be more on whole cultures and social systems. For either a literary or anthropological approach (and for several other common viewpoints), there are good references cited in the Bibliographic Notes to Chapter 2.

Very likely, the project you select to work on in American folklore will be chosen because of some connection to your own life, such as your region, your college major, your job, your hobbies, or your family. *Family folklore* is an especially rewarding area for one's earliest attempts at folklore research, and there are several good publications to guide you. Notice first the references to the family as a context for folklore transmission in Chapter 3, then the more extended discussion of family stories in Chapter 9 (with the major bibliographic entry at that point); there are further mentions of family traditions in the chapters on folk speech, customs, and food. Or *modern folklore* might be the focus of your interest: Can you find discussions and references to Xeroxlore, computer folklore, and (this is the easy one) urban legends in this book? For references to the *folklore of a particular occupation or recreation* you would probably need to consult Chapter 3 (for the group), Chapter 14 (for folk beliefs related to that subject), Chapter 15 (for customs of the field), and perhaps others as well. Beginning a study of the *folklore of a particular ethnic group or region* would involve a similar search through the book—here the most recent published collection or bibliography would be the main thing to seek.

College folklore has long been one of the most popular topics for student research because it offers the obvious advantages of being easily available and close to the interests of many researchers themselves. In studying college folklore that you have collected, you gain not the benefit once traditionally claimed for taking American folklore courses —learning to know your grandparents—but rather you learn to know *yourself* a little better. This should not suggest that *you* are more worthwhile than your ancestors, but only that starting with the present and the familiar in folk studies is a good way to prepare yourself for moving back to the lore of the past or outward to less familiar traditions in other subcultures. As an introduction to the study of college folklore there is no better guide than Barre Toelken's essay here with its associated footnotes. But in the text you should also note the mention of traditional parodies of course names in Chapter 4 and the discussion of college students' superstitions in Chapter 14.

Learning from the Sample Studies

Sample studies in American folklore have been included in this book since the first edition in 1968, and these have been revised and replaced as necessary to keep them viable as teaching aids and interesting to new generations of readers. Each study is both a scholarly interpretation of some facet of American folklore and a model for the kind of research you might want to do in a related area. (My *Readings in American Folklore* selections are also well-written and representative studies.) The four sample studies in this edition, all original and unpublished elsewhere, are each generally about a different type of lore—oral, customary, material, and musical.

The first study, by the author of this book, begins with a short review of American urban legend studies and then examines an international horror story that circulates orally and in print in this country. Students could easily apply the essay's methods to another of the dozens of urban legends that are well known in modern tradition. The second sample study is Toelken's survey and analysis of recent American college folklore. This study exposes the wealth of folklore in students' lives and suggests possibilities for further projects. Henry Glassie's essay on Southern mountain cabins proceeds from field work in material tradition and the description of the social/cultural setting to the crucial stage of classification. Thus, it demonstrates a process that any scholar uses in organizing the data represented by a mass of collected materials. Finally, David Evans, in discussing "Structure and Meaning in the Folk Blues," shows how text and music may be analyzed technically by a specialist, and then how the findings of each study may be interpreted culturally. Even students lacking expertise in musical analysis should appreciate blues and blues-influenced popular music better after reading this essay.

The Baby-Roast Story as a
"New American Urban Legend"
by Jan Harold Brunvand

Although it is not possible from present evidence to trace a reliable history of the baby-roast legend, comparative and analytical study allows us to gain a better idea of its background, people's motives for telling it, and the meanings it has for storytellers and audiences. Material from the mass media as well as oral tradition, and ideas from technology (how microwaves cook food) and psychology (the oven as a symbol), also prove useful in understanding this piece of modern folklore.

Students could compare versions of "The Baby Roast" that they have heard with those cited here to see if the themes remain consistent or if further variations would modify the conclusions. Another good exercise would be to elicit comments on the legends—as Betty J. Belanus, quoted in this study, did—to determine how common the attitudes she described may be. Following the model of this study, students could gather and compare examples of a different urban legend from print and oral tradition. What subtypes do the variants fall into? What patterns of detail, or clichés of wording, are evident? May truth be distinguished from fantasy, and may the traditional nature of the stories be established by comparison with other folk plots and motifs? Finally, does the array of data you have assembled allow you to make a preliminary structural, functional, or psychological analysis of the legend?

The urban legend came into its own during the past two decades as a topic for research in American folklore. After beginning to collect "urban belief tales" (as they were then called) in the 1940s and 1950s, American folklorists from the 1960s on have become intrigued with analyzing the history, variety, persistence, and widespread acceptance as literal truth of such bizarre yet plausible modern narratives as "The Death Car," "The Hook," "The Kentucky Fried Rat," "The Snake in the Blanket," "The Spider in the Hairdo," and "The Runaway Grandmother." Drawing on publications in this area by my fellow folklorists, I wrote the first scholarly book on the subject in 1981; it dealt with some thirty-six classic stories of this type and was entitled *The Vanishing Hitchhiker: American Urban Legends and Their Meanings*. Three years later, using stories and clippings sent in by readers, supplemented by my own wider study of the genre, I published a sequel, *The Choking Doberman and Other "New" Urban Legends*.[1] With these two books, American urban legends may be said to have arrived as a subject of serious study, although this in no way diminishes their appeal simply as entertaining stories nor exhausts the possibilities of research. The present essay looks closely at one urban legend discussed in my first book in the light of information gathered more recently.

As a preliminary, however, we must consider some problems in terminology for urban-legend studies. The term "urban" itself is the first difficulty, because many of the stories involved are *modern* without specifically concerning cities. In fact, the suburbs more often than the inner cities are the scenes depicted in urban legends. Second, "legend" may not be the most accurate term, since a number of these items are often told as mere unverified *reports* (that is, rumors) rather than as plotted narratives, and not all of them are universally believed. (Belief is assumed to be a hallmark of the legend.) Most American folklorists, however, are content to refer to stories like "The Boyfriend's Death" and "Red Velvet Cake" or even to the less structured reports like "Alligators in the Sewers" and "The Procter & Gamble Trademark" as legends, recognizing that there is usually *some* narrative content to these traditions and that at least *some* people tell them as true. Substitutes for the term "urban" that have been suggested include "modern," "adolescent," and "mercantile," but "urban legend" is still the most common label for this kind of folk story.

Other difficulties arise with the "Americanness" and "newness" of urban legends collected and studied in the United States. *The Vanishing Hitchhiker* identified international variants of "American urban legends" but gave the overwhelming impression of a largely native folkloric product. As for the modernity of the stories, the word "new" in the subtitle of my sequel is within quotation marks, because the antiquity that was established for a few stories in the first book was much more impressive for several studies in the second book. Also, as folklorists in other countries have studied urban legends, their age and international character have become well established.[2]

A last problem with terminology lies in the names assigned to individual legends by folklorists. Sometimes an arbitrary label like "The Solid Cement Cadillac" or "The Mouse in the Coke" suggests that these stories are static entities with consistent content whereas they are really fluid oral narratives that are always changing as they are performed by oral storytellers in reconstructions based on traditional motifs. Further, the supernatural nature of "The Vanishing Hitchhiker" legend (in which a ghost haunts the roadside) is untypical of the rest of this narrative tradition, since no other urban legend has any consistent supernatural content. "The Choking Doberman"—a crime story—is a more appropriate piece to represent modern oral narratives, although not all urban legends are necessarily horror stories and certainly not all urban legends may be traced to such ancient roots as this one has.

The subject of the present study is horrible enough, however. It is the widespread urban legend about the pet or baby that is put into an oven—most recently a microwave oven—and is killed there by being cooked alive or exploded. It is probably a story that most readers have either heard or read about at some time. In reviewing past scholarship plus newly gathered data on this legend, we may understand better how research in verbal folklore proceeds, by what means modern oral narratives are disseminated, and what conclusions are possible about them as a result of research.

In *The Vanishing Hitchhiker* the legend that I am calling here "The Baby-Roast" was described as a modernization of an earlier "pet in the oven" tradition which had possibly originated in people's realistic accounts of their pets accidentally getting into household clothes driers or gas ovens. I suggested that the older legends (going back to the 1950s) about cooked pets had simply been updated to become microwave-oven stories and then had merged with other modern legends about babysitters to result in a new legend—"The Hippie Baby-Sitter"—known in American folklore since the early 1970s. This modern American legend, I surmised, had eventually spread to Europe and then, by some means, had even become known in Nigeria, as a tale quoted from an African student seemed to show. In the notes to the chapter I referred to a possible "Brazilian" (it should have been "Argentinian"!) analogue for the story published in 1951. I concluded that "the distribution of the cooked baby story is doubtless more extensive in time and space than we can now demonstrate."

Rather than repeating *The Vanishing Hitchhiker* material (which the reader may easily locate on pages 62–65 and 72–73), the following encapsulated versions of the two main branches of this tradition from a recent book of apocryphal stories will introduce them. The source is Paul Dickson and Jospeh C. Goulden's amusing anthology called *There are Alligators in Our Sewers and Other American Credos: A Collection of Bunk, Nonsense, and Fables We Believe:*[3]

The Poodle in the Microwave

A woman bathes her pet poodle and, in a hurry to dry it, decides to pop the animal in her new microwave oven for a few seconds. The poodle explodes.

The Baby and the Turkey

A baby-sitter waits until the parents have left and then takes LSD. Shortly thereafter she follows the instructions given to her: Put the turkey in the oven and put the baby to bed. She dutifully puts the baby in the oven and the turkey in bed.

A longer version of the cooked-baby legend is given in English folklorist Paul Smith's collection *The Book of Nasty Legends*[4] as follows:

The Roast Dinner

An American couple, living outside New York, went out for dinner one evening leaving their baby son in the care of a teenage baby-sitter and her boyfriend. When they returned from the dinner the boyfriend was gone and the girl appeared to be acting rather strangely. They asked the girl if everything was all right to which she replied that everything was fine and that they had stuffed the turkey and put it in the oven.

The wife was rather puzzled by this remark as she did not remember having a turkey in the house and they began to realize that something was certainly wrong. Fearing the worst, they ran upstairs to check on their son but he could not be found anywhere. In desperation they started to search the house. In the kitchen the husband noticed a funny smell and that the oven was switched on. When he looked inside to see what was burning he found the baby in the roasting dish all set out like a turkey and surrounded by roast potatoes and all the trimmings. It transpired that the baby-sitter and her boyfriend has been using 'Angel Dust', a powerful drug, and had roasted the baby while on a 'trip'.

The language in this text—"to which she replied," "set out like a turkey," and "it transpired"—betray it as an authorial retelling, and a British one at that, of presumably an American oral legend. Smith cites no specific source for the story except to mention that "versions . . . have been reported in the United States since about 1970." He offers no analysis beyond that the story is "related to older folk narratives dealing with similar incidents." Both of these published sources, which are popular rather than folkloric in nature, present the legends as being foolish whimsy and more like jokes than serious matters of concern— just "fables we believe." The professional comedian Robin Williams made a similar joke out of the story in 1978 in his parody of the children's television program "Mr. Rogers' Neighborhood": "Welcome to my neighborhood. Let's put Mr. Hamster in the microwave oven. O.K.? Pop goes the weasel!"[5]

A good example of how such legends are sometimes told and received as the truth in real life is the following excerpt from a reader's letter dated July 22, 1983—still a written version, but a much folksier one:

> I was told this story by my friend Jerry B . . . who worked as a recording secretary in the emergency room at Parkland Hospital in Dallas, Texas. As I understand it, his job involved writing down what materials were used during the hectic, hurried treatment of emergency victims, such as sponges, gauze, and tape, and to take statements from the patients as soon as they were in any condition to give them.
>
> According to Jerry, he was working the evening shift one day, in 1976 or '77, when they brought in a middle-aged woman in a state of extreme hysteria but otherwise apparently unharmed. Unable to calm her by other means, the doctor on duty put her under heavy sedation. When she started to come around several hours later, Jerry went in, and as gently as he could, asked her for a statement. This sent her into a frenzy only slightly less severe than the first. Again they sedated the woman. Another tactful attempt two or three hours later had the same effect, with less severity still. Predictably, the third attempt to elicit her story was successful.
>
> "I was washing Pepper," said the woman through her barely controlled sobbing and sharp intakes of breath, "and I

was late for the dentist and I was afraid to leave him under the air conditioner wet like that so I toweled him off but he was still damp and everything so I thought . . . well I didn't want him to catch cold or anything . . . and . . . well" (She is fast losing control.) ". . . so I put him in the microwave, and I just put it on *warm*, but Pepper 'sploded!!" Here she breaks down completely and must be sedated again. Pepper, of course, turns out to be her pet poodle.

You may imagine my chagrin when I read your versions of that same story, and realized that I had been duped by my friend. He even went so far to say that *Newsweek* had carried a filler on the story. I am usually skeptical of such stories, but this one sucked me in completely, being told by someone I trusted, as a firsthand account.[6]

Evidently, this storyteller performed "The Pet in the Oven" as a hoax story, although the emergency room is a frequent setting for telling "true" stories about either horrible or hilarious accidents involving exploding toilets, superglue, skiing mishaps, and the like.

Even more likely a story than "The Pet in the Oven" to be narrated in a completely serious manner and to give rise to worried discussion by listeners concerning its pros and cons is "The Baby-Roast" legend, often known as "The Hippie Baby-Sitter." Here, for example, is a version with commentary collected in 1971 by a student of folklorist Lydia Fish at the State University College in Buffalo, New York, William J. Kreidler, another of whose texts from an undergraduate term paper was quoted in *The Vanishing Hitchhiker*. (As indicated there [page 65], Professor Fish in a published note "took the first official scholarly notice [of this story] in the United States . . . in 1971.") Kreidler's informant was in nurses' training in Boston, Massachusetts, when she heard the story:

It seems these people hired a really freaky college girl to baby-sit. They had a little baby; it must have been less than seven months old.

The mother called in the middle of the evening—they were at a play and it was intermission. The girl told her everything was fine, she had just stuffed the turkey and was going to put it in the oven. The lady knew she didn't have a turkey, and I guess she thought the girl sounded strange, so she told her to wait, they would come home right away.

They called the police who went to the apartment and they found that the girl had stuffed the baby and was going to bake it. I don't know if they saved the baby, but I do know the girl was on some kind of drug.

I'm sure this is a true story. One of the nurses told it to me when I was working in the hospital one night. She heard it from a friend of hers who worked in Bellevue where I think it happened.

Another of Professor Fish's students in Buffalo in 1971, Janet Hilinski, part of whose term paper was also quoted in *The Vanishing Hitchhiker,* wrote out her own version with comments as she remembered it from her hometown tradition in Orchard Park, New York:

Some parents left their baby with a neighborhood teenage girl while they attended a party. The girl had previously taken LSD and she began hallucinating. Thinking the baby was a turkey, she prepared it for roasting and put it in the oven.

The mother called from the party to check and see how things were going at home. The girl sounded normal and she mentioned that she had just put the turkey in the oven.

Later that evening the mother realized that they did not have a turkey at home. Her husband agreed that they should go home and find out was was going on. When they returned, they were horrified to find their baby in the oven, and the baby-sitter gone.

I first heard this tale over the phone from a girlfriend who said she heard it from a neighbor whose cousin (or sister) had read it in the paper. I think we both believed it at the time. This was in 1967 or '68, when the weird effects of LSD were being widely circulated; thus it did not seem too outrageous.

Later, in 1970, when I was a senior at Orchard Park High School, a girl in my home economics class brought it up again. Most of the class had already heard of it. The teacher was so interested in it, that the entire period was spent exchanging weird tales. I think most of us believed them.[7]

The folk versions more than the pop versions I have quoted underscore themes that are fairly consistent in this modern-legend tradition. The reliability of the stories, for instance, is frequently buttressed by some reference to a knowledgeable friend of a friend or to an alleged published reference to the event. The settings in which the stories are told or with which they are associated are often more or less "official" places, such as a hospital or school; the precise locale may directly suggest the theme of the story, such as an emergency room (with its accident victims) or a home-economics classroom (with its ovens) did here. In "The Pet in the Oven," the implied reason for the mistake is the foolishness of the pet owner, while in "The Hippie Baby-Sitter" the warning is directed against either an eccentric personality type, a young person, a drug user, or, most often, all three. The baby-sitter legend often seems to imply that the parents, by going off to a party, to a restaurant, or to the theater, are neglecting their child; then the surrogate parent who is left in charge harms the child. The tellings of both legends often lead directly to discussions of their possible authenticity or of the lessons they contain.

Betty J. Belanus, a folklorist trained at Indiana University, pursued this latter point in a 1979 graduate research paper on microwaved-pet stories concerning the free association people engage in after telling modern legends.[8] Confirming that the folk *do* perceive "messages" in their lore, Belanus collected discussions of the "drug" and "hippie" themes in the legend, people's speculations about the actual dangers of microwaves, and even conversations inspired by the stories concerning what kind of person would have a poodle for a pet and would shampoo and dry it regularly. (Poodles were described by some of her informants as "lap dogs" wearing "diamond choke collars" and with "painted toenails" and "yappy barks"; only a "silly society woman," it was stated, would own one and refer to it as "the dear little thing.") Belanus also reported that people recalled personal experiences (though sometimes second-hand ones or something remembered from published sources) that involved pets getting into household appliances.

Indeed, mail I have received provides good evidence that the cooked-animal theme is as much a part of personal narratives as it is of urban legends, though there is often a possibility that people *think* they are relating a true story when they are only repeating a tradition. A possible case in point is this story sent to me by a reader in Minnesota:

> When my mother was about six or seven years old (she was born in 1930), she was playing with a pet cat in the pasture behind her house. At the time my mother lived in Deatsville, Alabama, a small town about thirty miles north of Montgomery. While playing with the cat, the animal fell in the "branch" or stream running through the pasture. My mother retrieved the cat from the water, and took it inside the house. Once inside, my mother decided to dry the cat in the oven.

As you might guess, the cat was forgotten and was "dried" to death.

My correspondent supplied her mother's address so that I could write to her for verification of the event. (I wanted to know how it was that the cat failed to utter any sound loud enough to call attention to its fate. Was it perhaps dead from drowning already?) Unfortunately, my letter was never answered.

Other personal narratives about pets getting into scrapes involving home appliances are told by people who stand close enough to the incident to establish its truth. This one came from a reader in Portage des Sioux, Missouri:

A friend of mine was doing her laundry. Like most house-wives, she put a load in the washer and went upstairs to make the beds. Down again to put in another load and upstairs to do the dishes. Somewhere along the line her daughter's cat got in the dryer to sleep because it was warm. Imagine her surprise when she opened the dryer. All the clothes had to be pitched, but the hardest part was telling her daughter what happened to her cat when she came home from school.

My acceptance of this story is based not only on the fact that Missouri is the "Show Me" state and that the source this time is a friend, not merely a friend of a friend, but also that at the very time I was writing this essay one of our family cats, Bingley, a gray and white striped male troublemaker, did truly climb into the warm clothes drier between loads. Bingley did not get shut in, however, and so I have not made a personal narrative out of the incident. The point for folk-legend research about such experiences is that they may easily become traditionalized as they are repeated from person to person and from generation to generation, and such a process possibly underlies the whole cooked-pet cycle of stories.[9]

Another direction that the folk tradition may go, I have noticed, is toward developing "one liners" that treat the basic story motif as a joke. For instance, a letter to the editor of *Newsweek* began: "I was amazed by your article 'Is SAT a Dirty Word?' . . . Intelligence is more important than memory. I've known people who knew every general involved in World War II but didn't have enough common sense not to dry their dog in the microwave."[10] Or, even more succinctly, a successful writer of romance novels who is the mother of five boys was quoted as saying "My seven-year-old's antics, such as drying the cat in the microwave, can be distracting!"[11]

Joking aside, microwave radiation is nothing to fool with, and certainly some uneasiness about the potential dangers of microwaves to living creatures underlies the popularity of these legends in the United States. What we commonly term "microwaves" are concentrated into a single frequency in a microwave oven and cause foods to heat by activating the molecules of water present in them. A similar heating effect is induced under certain conditions by the microwaves used for radio and television transmissions or in radar. Microwaves—whether in small appliances or large installations—have been connected to such diverse health problems as simple burns, cataracts, sterility and other sex-related problems, cancer, and potential genetic disorders. The whole subject was carefully and chillingly studied by Paul Brodeur in a series of articles in the *New Yorker* that grew into his book *The Zapping of America: Microwaves, Their Deadly Risk, and Cover-Up*. Brodeur had concerns of much greater magnitude than exploding poodles to deal with, though he did hint at a body of "folklore, based on a mixture of intuition, observation, and apprehension" that he found had developed during World War II, taking such forms then as what he termed "black humor, scuttlebutt, and quasi-medical practice."[12]

Another writer on microwave ovens also alluded to "numerous adverse effects from exposure to radiation from microwave ovens" but discounted the reports (specifying them only as the "tingling of skin," burns, and interference with pacemakers) because they were unverified. The closest that this source came to a microwaved-pet reference was the mention of "silkworm-cocoon cooking" as a possible commercial use for microwave ovens, but nothing is said about the possibility of the creatures exploding when zapped.[13] However, as cooks are often warned, potatoes and other completely encased foods *will* explode when they are microwaved unless holes are punched through their skins to allow steam to escape during cooking. Whole eggs, too, will explode if microwave-cooked; scrambled eggs are okay. Poodles, cats, and babies should probably keep clear of these appliances; in fact, Brodeur warns against merely watching food cook through the glass door of a microwave oven!

Although many references in oral tradition to supposed published accounts of cooked- and microwaved-pet stories cannot be verified, this does not mean that none has *ever* appeared in newsprint. Sometimes press mentions of such incidents are merely reports of folklore studies (such as this one), which an inattentive reader may later recall as a genuine news item. For instance, the *Des Moines Tribune* for April 26, 1978, in a story about Thelma C. Johnson of Sioux City, Iowa, and her personal collection of urban legends, printed this: "Told to Johnson

four or five times in the span of one week [was the story] about a cat that
had been drenched in a rain storm. The children who owned the animal
tried to dry it out—by placing it in a microwave oven. The cat is said to
have exploded all over the kitchen."[14] A similar piece of hearsay that
got into print in 1983 was a San Francisco law student's description to
an inquiring reporter of "the cat in the microwave case" in which, he
understood, "the person sued the microwave company for a defective
latch on the door and won."[15]

An actual lawsuit involving a microwaved cat in Warwick, Rhode Island, was reported by United Press International in September 1980. I
have clippings from the *Muncie* [Indiana] *Star* and the *Chicago Tribune*,
which name the convicted man as well as the judge and the defense
lawyer, and state the amount of the fine ($200).[16] Although this inci-
dent is undoubtedly authentic (and surely was widely reported in the
press that week), part of the UPI wording for the story also has the ring
of legend: "The singed cat," it reads, "had its claws imbedded in the
oven's grill when they opened the door." The unsuccessful appeal of
this case was reported in some detail in Murray Loring's "Cats in
Court" column, which described how "from the smallest state in these
United States" came "one of the most flagrant and outrageous cruelty
cases, involving a feline."[17] The appeal was denied and dismissed by the
Supreme Court of Rhode Island (*State* v. *Tweedie*, April 27, 1982) and
the judgment was confirmed. Dr. Loring's discussion, however, omits
the description from the published appeal record of exactly how the cat
died, a passage that is interesting in terms of the folklore involved
though it might have been too gruesome for the pages of *Cats Magazine*. Two things are evident here: first, the cat did *not* explode; second,
the official account of its death differs from what the newspapers said.
In crisp, unemotional legal style, it reads: "The record reflects that a
scratching noise was heard coming from the oven. As the door was
opened the rear legs of the cat fell out. The cat was alive but died
shortly after."[18]

Probably there are many other suffering-pet news stories that have
not come to my attention, though I happen to have two more from the
spring of 1983. On April 14 the *Ogden* [Utah] *Standard-Examiner* carried an Associated Press story about a Montana State University fraternity member putting a kitten that was frozen inside a block of ice into a
punch bowl; on June 3 the *Skagit Valley* [Oregon] *Herald* carried an AP
story about a teen-ager in Lillooet, British Columbia, sentenced to six
months in jail and two years attendance at Alcoholics Anonymous
meetings for killing a cat in a microwave oven. Modern life, we can see,
may sometimes be as horrifying as legend.

Returning to the baby-roast legends, we find that they consistently include three themes that are never part of the pet tragedies: parental neglect, treating the child as food, and drug-induced behavior. Even a short text written out by a fourteen-year-old Midwestern girl has these three typical elements (and little else):

> A girl went to some people's house to babysit their baby. The mother asked her to put a roast in the oven around an hour before they came home. The parents came to find the baby buttered and prepared like you'd do a roast and in the oven cooked. The babysitter was tripping on LSD.[19]

The two further American variations on the cooked-baby stories that I have collected are the mother that returns home because of a strong sense of danger—arriving just in time to save her baby—and a "group of hippies," high on drugs, roasting a baby in a grotesque ceremony. Versions in which the baby is *microwaved* rather than being merely roasted are not numerous, though they are known since the mid-1970s. One reference to this tradition appeared in "The Straight Dope" column of the Chicago weekly paper *Reader* (February 3, 1984). Columnist Cecil Adams responded to a reader's query about microwaved-baby legends by summing up my discussion of them in *The Vanishing Hitchhiker* and admitting that he could find no evidence that such an actual event had ever occurred.[20]

Most unfortunately, something resembling the microwaved-baby legend *did* occur in Michigan in 1982.[21] On December 18 the *Detroit Free Press* carried a small item datelined Hastings, Michigan, stating that "a baby who police say might have been burned in a microwave oven was placed under court protection." The victim was identified as a ten-week-old girl who had been in a Grand Rapids hospital since October 31 and had suffered burns that required amputation of part of her right foot and several fingers from her left hand. The *Lansing State Journal*, on January 21, 1983, carried a longer story (headlined "Baby Burned, Mom Charged") concerning the incident. Doctors had concluded that the child's burns were caused by radiation, but the mother claimed that she had only heated a bottle of formula in her microwave oven while the child was lying nearby on an ironing board. Various experts testified that the oven was not faulty, and while the court was considering the case further the baby was put into a foster home. On July 21, 1983, the *Lansing State Journal* reported (" 'Microwave' baby returns to mother") that the baby had been returned home from foster care as a ward of the court. Later the mother was sentenced to five years' probation and ordered to perform one hundred hours of community service. No news story that I have seen has clarified how just *part* of a body could be burned by microwaves as long as the oven-door safety lock was operating properly.

There have been other news stories about cruelty to children, sometimes involving burns and ovens, and the Michigan case is cited only as a recent and representative example. What should be noted here are the ways that the reported case is *different* from the baby-roast urban legend. There is no baby-sitter, the child is neither prepared as food or killed, no drugs or other mind-influencing substances are mentioned, and—most striking of all—the specific names, places, and dates (some of which I have omitted) are included. The news story, then, is not an urban legend, though it may remind readers of a legend; and possibly the events described may even have been influenced by an urban legend. Some readers of such stories in the mass media may later believe that they once read about a case "just like" the baby-roast story that someone tells them. Such a quotation in one of these Michigan news items as a policeman's comment that the baby's toes had been cooked "through and through" comes rather close to the style of a modern horror legend, and it is just the kind of dramatic detail that a reader might well remember.

Following the appearance of *The Vanishing Hitchhiker* in an English paperback edition in Spring 1983,[22] I soon began to hear from readers throughout Great Britain and in Australia and New Zealand about urban legends they had heard. It became clear then that the cooked-pet story was well known in these countries in forms very similar to the American versions. I received letters about cats trapped in "spin dryers," old ladies' poodles being washed and then microwaved, and in several instances I encountered the notion, not well known in the United States, that the pet's owner had successfully sued the microwave-oven manufacturer for selling a hazardous product. But although an English book on urban legends had mentioned "current microwave oven myths" as a general topic as long ago as 1978,[23] the only cooked-baby story sent to me from an English-speaking country was an Australian report of a supposed news item about it being an *American* incident. The following is from a letter dated July 17, 1983:

> This was a newspaper report anything up to six years ago. As I recall, it was in "The News" and datelined somewhere in the U.S.A. . . .
>
> Hospital staff are watching a ?-month-old baby in their care. His fourteen-year-old babysitter put him into the microwave oven and turned it on "to see what would happen."

The doctors are unsure of what damage has been done, as a microwave cooks from the inside out.[24]

That the American "Hippie Baby-Sitter" legend had quite early migrated to Europe, however, is shown by a letter from Switzerland dated December 27, 1983:

> I first heard a version of "The Hippie Baby-Sitter" in Geneva about ten years ago [i.e., about 1973]. Not having heard of "urban legends" I took it at face value. In the local tale the baby-sitters were Geneva University students who had freaked-out on dope. When the mother phoned home to check, she was told that the baby had been "smeared with mustard" and was all ready for the oven. Luckily the parents got back in time to save the child.[25]

We recognize here the familiar pattern known in the United States since the early 1970s: mother absent, child cooked as food, and baby-sitter taking drugs.

The Nigerian version that I collected from a student in 1979 (as she remembered it from 1976) seemed at the time nothing more than a transplanted American legend. As the text reads in *The Vanishing Hitchhiker*, the mother telephoned home from work to check on her baby-sitter, who appeared to be doing her job well. But when the mother returned home in the evening, she found that the sitter had roasted the baby. Also reminding us of urban-legend tradition in the United States is the association of this story with particular sections of the city (Calabar, Nigeria) and with particular friends of friends who presumably knew the facts of the case. What is *different* in the story, however, is that the baby-sitter's misbehavior is caused not by drugs or malice but by simple misunderstanding of the mother's orders. The baby's mother had used an expression (given in the Efik language) for "sit him up" (that is, "get him out of bed"), which the sitter, a novice at her job, interpreted as a homophonous expression meaning "cook the baby." Her error, then, lay in conscientiously following the mother's instructions exactly as the baby-sitter had understood them. The warnings given in this story, then, are against careless choice of words and thoughtless interpretation of orders rather than against eccentric or drug-induced behavior.

The version of the legend from Buenos Aires mentioned in *The Vanishing Hitchhiker* has features reminiscent of the American stories, but surprisingly it was circulated in 1949, some twenty years *before* the legend had been collected by folklorists in the United States. Paulo de

Carvalho-Neto reports it in this fashion, in his book *Folklore and Psychoanalysis,* referring to it as if it were an actual event or, as he puts it, a "pathological case which occurred under the influence of the Evil Mother":

> A young married couple hires a servant since the wife is pregnant and almost due. The baby is born. A few weeks later the husband and wife go to the movies one evening, leaving the baby in the servant's care. Until that time she has always been reliable. *According to one version,* on their return she receives them ceremoniously dressed in the wife's bridal gown and tells them she has prepared quite a surprise for them. She bids them come into the dining room to serve them a special meal. They enter and find a horrifying spectacle. In the middle of the table, placed there with great care, they see their son on a large platter, roasted and garnished with potatoes. The poor mother goes insane at once. She loses her speech and no one has heard her utter a single word since then. The father, *according to several versions,* is a military man. He pulls out a revolver and shoots the servant. Then he runs away and is never heard from again.[26] [Italics added]

Marie Langer's 1951 book *Maternidad y sexo* had originally published the account that is summarized above. Langer described this particular baby-roast story in her psychiatric study *not* as being one of her actual clinical cases but rather as a "modern myth" or rumor which, as she wrote, had been rampant in Buenos Aires during June 1949, especially among servants, taxi drivers, and barbers. In the space of a single week in Buenos Aires she collected nine versions of the story that differed only in details. The one that she quoted (and which was repeated in Carvalho-Neto's book) was merely "the most complete version of this strange story that was making the rounds."[27] Langer also commented that the story "was accepted as truth by people generally capable of critical judgment."[28] In other words, it was in every respect typical of an urban legend.

"The Evil Mother" mentioned by Carvalho-Neto is a Freudian concept explained by him as "the son's image of the mother resulting from the castration complex" (page 43, note). Langer introduced the baby-roast story as she had heard it in 1949 into her chapter on the unconscious image of the evil mother (*madre mala*)—the opposite of the ideal of a wholly *good* mother that is cherished by both children and adults. In Langer's opinion, a "suppressed unconscious situation" based on "infantile anxieties" concerning the actual "goodness" of mothers could generate stories depicting grossly evil mothers; these stories, then, might circulate in oral tradition and even lead to neuroses. She compared instances of evil parents (both mothers and fathers) in myths and fairy tales (including "Hansel and Gretel") to the similar theme in the modern "rumor," without mentioning that the recent story really depicts more a *neglectful* than an evil parent. The servant, however, in wearing the mother's bridal gown assumes the role of the real mother, and both women in the story react to the loss of "their" baby by losing their minds.

Interpreting the baby-roast legend in psychological terms is tempting, especially with regard to the core idea of putting a child into an oven. As a doctor in the Columbia University College of Physicians and Surgeons wrote in a letter to *Psychology Today* in 1980, "One discovers the same theme in fairy tales. For example, the wicked witch attempted to cook Hansel and Gretel in the oven."[29] According to orthodox Freudianism, the stove or oven, as well as many other images of rooms and containers encountered in dreams or folklore, all symbolically represent female genitalia; this means that, as one analyst put it, "the womb is the 'stove' inside which the child is 'baked.' "[30] This symbolic meaning recurs in other examples of folklore, such as the familiar "Pattycake" rhyme or the euphemistic phrases, "to put a bun in her oven" and "to have one in the oven" (i.e., to be pregnant).[31] The Jungian psychologist Erich Neuman cited further oven-as-womb proverbial sayings as part of his argument for "the thoroughgoing identification of the oven with the Feminine."[32]

Before accepting an absolute oven/womb equivalency in the folk stories, however, it is well to remember that the two abandoned children in the fairy tale did *not* finally perish in the oven (only the witch did). We would also have to explain how or why the act of roasting or microwaving a baby might reasonably be equated with returning it to the womb. Possible symbolism aside for the moment, the tale of Hansel and Gretel has a completely different plot and certainly cannot be taken as the historical prototype for our modern legend.

Although at least the *threat* of cooking Hansel in the oven is a standard part of the international tradition of "Hansel and Gretel,"[33] commentators on the story have generally refrained from calling this detail a sexual symbol. Max Lüthi, for example, in *Once upon a Time: On the Nature of Fairy Tales*, sees the witch only as "a personification of evil . . . [who] perishes by her own devices." This illustrates, Lüthi says, how "evil consumes itself."[34] Jack Zipes in *Breaking the Magic Spell: Radical Theories of Folk and Fairy Tales* is more specific. He interprets the witch as a symbol of "the entire feudal system or the greed and brutality of the aristocracy"; her destruction by the clever children, he says, illustrates how the European peasants might have learned "to *act* to improve their lot."[35] Even the psychiatrist Bruno Bettelheim, in his well known work *The Uses of Enchantment: The Meaning and Importance of Fairy Tales,* emphasizes the "starvation anxiety" and "oral regression" (poor family, abandoned children, eating the witch's house, threat of the oven, etc.) rather than a sexual theme.[36] Despite Zipes's contention that Bettelheim usually follows Freudianism as a "straitjacket theory" (p. 162), Bettelheim here eschews a strictly Freudian symbolic reading. In fact, he nearly ignores the oven. Although an oven does undeniably symbolize a womb in other folkloric manifestations, I am no readier than Bettelheim was to say that it positively does so either in "Hansel and Gretel" or "Baby-Roast." Certainly, however, some symbolic meanings and neurotic behavior are involved in the baby-roast legend.

The theme of mental illness, as suffered by the servant and mother in the Argentinian version of the story, is mentioned specifically in a report of a Middle Eastern version sent to me by Dr. Seyfi Karabaş of Ankara, Turkey. He wrote on September 15, 1980 (quoting a friend of his): "These baby-sitters may do terrible things. For example, one of them, a woman discharged prematurely from the mental hospital, almost roasted the poor baby in the oven. She thought it was a turkey." When I asked Dr. Karabaş to inquire further into the story, he replied (November 4, 1980), "If and when I can catch my friend I will try to find the owner of the oven in which a baby almost got roasted. I discussed it with her on the phone and she is positive that this negative event took place."[37] There is also an allusion to a Swedish instance of a mentally ill woman roasting her baby. According to this source, in about the early 1950s a story was current in Sweden "about a young mother who, psychotic after childbirth, serves the baby roasted to her husband."[38]

Yet another similar legend has circulated far away from the other known texts. This version of "The Girl Who Cooked the Baby" was collected in the South Pacific area of Micronesia on the island of Yap by folklorist Roger E. Mitchell in 1971 and published two years later.[39] The story, told by a forty-five-year-old man in Yapese through a translator, begins with the observation that the older children in Micronesia are often left to care for their younger siblings while the mothers work in the gardens. But the story soon begins to sound very much like the Nigerian version, when the mother instructs her daughter, "While I'm in the garden, you be sure to make your brother hot." After some deliberation, the girl concludes that in order to comply with her mother's orders she must indeed cook her little brother, so she puts the child into a pot with some food and builds up the fire. When the mother returns, the daughter tells her mother, "I did what you told me. You told me to heat my brother and so I cooked him because that's how we can get hot." The mother beats her daughter, breaking her arms and legs, and throws her into a stream. The daughter drifts along in the stream singing a mad song about her deeds (somewhat like Ophelia in *Hamlet*!) until she drowns. Mitchell's note mentions that "this little tale is considered a true happening on Yap, and some informants dislike to tell it, since it is offensive to the girl's living relatives."

Other versions of this Micronesian tale, however, establish it as being a traditional plot—one resembling the African and Argentinian stories—rather than an account of a bizarre local happening. (Even so, Mitchell's field notes mention another Yap informant's version of the same story with the notation "The family is still alive, the story well known, and it would be embarrassing if it was published in a book.")

Two unpublished Micronesian versions in Mitchell's collection are filed in the Indiana University Folklore Archive; both were recorded in 1970, and both resemble the Yap versions in having the person who cooks the baby being severely punished and cast out to wander away and die. The first of these, from Satawan Atoll in the Truk district, is the more detailed. Here an older son, named Lipok, is told by his parents to cook an octopus and tend to the baby while they go out to gather taros to complete the meal. The tale continues:

> He didn't know whether they were referring to the baby or the octopus because he didn't find the octopus. He thought that maybe they were referring to the baby. . . . So he killed the baby and he went out and gathered some breadfruit leaves, very big ones, came back and wrapped the baby in them. Then he put it on the fire. When it was cooked, he took it down and put it where they stored their food.

After telling this story the informant commented that the expression "to have the ear of Lipok" had become proverbial among his people for getting something wrong or mixed up. The second archived text in Mitchell's collection is from Ulithi Atoll in the Yap District. Here an older son cooks his brother simply because "he was tired of doing the same thing, so he put his brother in their pot and cooked him."

Confirming that the Micronesian "Girl Who Cooked the Baby" legends of 1970–1971 are not just recent importations from abroad revised into local traditions, Mitchell cites several analogues published in the older anthropological literature. The two closest versions were those published by Wilhelm Müller from Yap in 1918 and a Papuan (New Guinea) version published by Annie Ker in 1910.[40] Here are summaries, slightly edited, as provided by Dr. Mitchell:

> *Müller:* Fathali was a lame girl to whom mother said she should remain with her younger sister. Fathali said, "Then I will cook her." "Certainly not," said mother. Fathali repeated she'd cook her. "Therefore good then," answered the mother, annoyed. She inspected the child and went to the field to work. When she came home, she asked where the child was. "I have cooked her," answered Fathali; and when mother took cover from pot, child lay within. [Her mother strikes her, breaking her leg; Fathali tells the neighbors what has happened, jumps into the sea, and is covered with black mud which hardens into a stone that is still seen today.]

> *Ker:* The parents went to the gardens and left two daughters to bathe their brother and cook some food so he could eat. Older daughter: "Mother said to stay and cook brother. Let us obey her." Younger disagreed, but older prevailed. They cooked the brother. Parents returned, and drove them out.

These five versions of the baby-roast legend available from the South Pacific range in time from 1910 to 1971 and fall into two main subtypes. The first type has the distinctive features of the parents' orders being misunderstood; such is true of the Papuan version of 1910, the Trukese of 1970, and the Yap text of 1971. The second subtype contains the alternate theme of the baby-sitter cooking the infant in anger; this occurs in the Yap text of 1918 and the Ulithian version of 1970. It is clear as well that the Nigerian version of 1976 matches the first subtype while the Argentinian one of 1949 seems to stand apart (along with the Swedish and Turkish versions) in that the child-cooking there is the result of the servant's mental illness.

In pursuing what is evidently an international story cycle about cooked babies, the *Motif-Index of Folk-Literature* provides a little help, but *only* a little. Mitchell classified his texts under the general heading of Motif S10. *Cruel Parents,* but this is too general to be useful, especially when we consider that the story is mainly *not* about a cruel parent but about a foolish (or insane) behavior of a surrogate parent. Motif K1461. *Caring for the child: child killed,* has some relevance, but the only two instances that Stith Thompson cites for it are far from our legends. (The first, Rune No. 31 of the Finnish epic *The Kalevala,* concerns a man who becomes crazed from being rocked too much as a baby and who later tortures and kills [but *not* by cooking] a baby that is left in his charge. The second, a story collected in the 1930s from Indians of the Chaco region of Argentina, concerns a trickster in the shape of a fox that deceives a mother into leaving and then kills her baby left in its care by sucking out its insides.)[41]

Another promising motif reference is S112.6. *Murder by roasting alive in oven or furnace,* for which Thompson supplies two examples: a motif-index of Jewish legends that lists various fiery-furnace scenes (no babies, no sitters) and a Tongan tale in which a man's concubines (but no babies) are pushed into an oven and burned to death.[42] Still another unrelated, though faintly similar item to our modern legend is the Greek myth about how the goddess Demeter nursed the human baby Demophoön for its parents, trying to grant it immortality by annointing it with ambrosia and putting it into a fire; but its mother, failing to understand, intervened. While this story does have a baby and a sitter, there is no oven and no murder.[43]

As for the particular *cause* of the baby roasting—that is, the psychology involved—motif J2460. *Literal obedience,* contains the key idea and proves to be a widely known concept. The submotif J2460.1. *Disastrous following of misunderstood instructions,* in fact, is precisely what occurs in several versions discussed above. Thompson's sole example of the theme is a Chinese tale in which a person is told to burn the land (in order to clear it for planting) and then to sow the seed; but he does just the opposite: he sows the seed first, then burns the land.[44] While there is no baby, no oven, and no cooking in this story, it does contain the idea of reversed instructions found in such baby-roast legends as the Papuan (bathe the baby and cook the food), the Trukese (cook the octopus and tend the baby), and some American ones (put the turkey in the oven and the baby in bed). In the Chinese story the *order* of instructions is reversed, while in the baby-roast stories the *actions* to be performed on the two creatures or objects are reversed.

What the *Motif-Index* provides in this instance is clear exposure of the common international concern with basic themes of our legend— cruelty, deception, choosing carefully those who will tend babies, mental illness, and tragically foolish misunderstanding of orders. Viewed as a complete tale rather than a mere collection of motifs, versions of the baby-roast plot are strikingly similar over a wide extent of time and space, although not nearly so universal as the Jungian theory of "archetypal" origins drawing from common patterns in a "collective unconscious" would predict. In fact, the situation for this tale is somewhat like that for the world-wide stories about witches and ogres who threaten children. As Thompson wrote in connection with "Hansel and Gretel," the versions are such that "one is frequently puzzled to know whether we are dealing with a borrowing or with an independent invention."[45]

The argument for the borrowing of the baby-roast legend from one culture to another—especially for many modern versions—lies in the repetition of specific details within similarly patterned texts. Time and again the parents have gone to a party, a play, or a film. They leave some ambiguous instructions for the baby-sitter and later telephone home to check on her. The child is served to them as food (often a turkey) and is appropriately garnished (frequently stuffed or with potatoes on the side) by someone who is either literally insane or temporarily "crazed" (i.e., by youthful naïveté, language problems, jealousy, or drugs). The Jungian writer Marie-Louise von Franz, however, offers a possible psychological model, similar to Marie Langer's, for the independent formation of such stories:

> When something strange happens it gets gossiped about and handed on, just as rumours are handed on, then under favourable conditions the account gets enriched with already-existing archetypal representations and slowly becomes a story.[46]

But whether such stories were independently invented or just widely borrowed from a common original, the modern person's trust in the urban legends about cooked pets and babies seems to hinge on faith that such "strange" things can and *have* happened, this belief being "enriched" by the lurking fears which the supposed happenings symbolically project.

The historical origin and the dissemination routes of the baby-roast legend remain something of a puzzle, but the adaptations of the plot to fit different cultures are clear. These range from references to the child-care and food-gathering customs of Micronesia, to problems of modern working mothers in Nigeria, to anxieties about drugs, "hippies," and microwave ovens in Europe and America. Underlying all versions of the legend are both a concern about the parents' appropriate role in child rearing and a sense of guilt for leaving the job to others.[47] While the folks are away the infant's caretaker foolishly, childishly, insanely, or jealously destroys his or her charge. Shoving the baby into the oven may well be taken as an equivalent for returning it to the womb or "putting it back where it belongs," just as serving it up as food for the parents is a way of trying to return it to its place of origin.

As Alan Dundes suggests, the psychological device of projection allows people (via their folklore, in this instance) "to attribute to another person or to the environment what is actually within themselves."[48] Thus, the sins of the baby-sitters in the baby-roast legends may represent suppressed fears or desires in the minds of the parents and storytellers. Surely, these urban legends convey some of the same guilt feelings that Dundes identified in the dead-baby joke cycle—in particular, as he put it, "a protest against babies in general."[49] But while Dundes postulated such trends as legalized abortion efforts and easier access to reliable methods of contraception in our time as underlying reasons for guilt, the baby-roast legends focus on changing child-care practices of modern parents. The descriptions in this cycle of popular American legends of drug-crazed hippies (who were earlier failures of child rearing) thrusting babies left in their charge into gas or microwave ovens may really symbolize unconscious anxieties, shared widely with people in other cultures, about the manner in which parents tend to their children. More specifically, these legends are about the manner in which American parents believe that they *fail* to tend to them personally nowadays, in contrast to the practices of the past. Earlier in the legend cycle such disastrous neglect or ignorance resulted merely in deaths of substitute children—pet cats or dogs—but eventually the legends explicitly described the deaths of children themselves.

Epilogue—Another Version of "The Baby Roast"

After the above study was completed, I received a letter dated May 15, 1985, containing the following version from Beatrice Faust of North Carlton, Victoria, Australia. She refers to her experience with various horror stories about abortions performed late in pregnancy and the supposed results—both physical and psychological. One such story, Ms. Faust recalls, involved cooking a baby, and it is similar to baby-roast legends in being an unverified account that assumes the mother's insanity and describes the baby being prepared as food. Ms. Faust had believed the story at the time she heard it; but, becoming aware of the urban legends about cooked babies, she wondered now if this might have been a traditional legend or perhaps a fabrication. My guess is that it is yet another example of a specific local adaptation of "The Baby

Roast," made consistent with attitudes and social problems of the time and place in which it was told:

> I do not have the leisure to write down all the abortion legends that I have heard but I shall offer you a variant of the roasted baby story that I heard from a female social worker attached to one of Melbourne's two major maternity hospitals:
>
> "The woman had a history of mental illness when she became pregnant for the fourth or fifth time. Her social worker referred her to a consultant gynecologist with a view to having her aborted. At the time, abortion was legal under precedent law in Victoria, but illegal under statute law. The gynecologist did what many doctors do still: he procrastinated. The Christmas vacation intervened and after that the pregnancy was too advanced to be terminated by then practiced techniques. In due course, the baby was born and the unwilling and unbalanced mother took it home where she roasted it for the family's midday Sunday meal."
>
> The story was told to me in about 1964 by a social worker who claimed that it happened to a patient at her hospital but not directly under her care. She attributed the experience to "someone else in this department," i.e., an immediate colleague. I never heard any corroboration. The implication was that the woman had been quietly institutionalized because it was too dreadful a case to be brought to court and because the (masculine) medical mafia did not want to see one of their members embarrassed by bad publicity.

If nothing else, this example illustrates how important it is *always* to accept new versions of old stories into our studies. Apparently the last word on "The Baby Roast" has not yet been written.

NOTES

[1] (New York: W. W. Norton, 1981 and 1984, respectively.)

[2] International conferences on modern legends were held at the Centre for English Cultural Tradition and Language, University of Sheffield, England, in July 1982 and 1983; at least two sessions on urban legends were held during the Eighth Congress of the International Society for Folk Narrative Research in Bergen, Norway, in June 1984. (I read papers on the topic at the first Sheffield conference and at the ISFNR Congress.)

[3] (New York: Delacorte Press, 1983), pp. 137, 145.

[4] (London: Routledge and Kegan Paul, 1983). Smith also gives stories about a chef's microwaved innards and an old lady's microwaved Persian cat on pp. 64–65. See also n. 47.

[5] "The Robin Williams Show," *Time* (October 2, 1978), p. 86.

[6] Letter from Marcus W. Muirhead, Air Dept., V-4 Div., USS Iwo Jima.

[7] Both student papers from State University College, Buffalo, were sent to me by Professor Fish in 1979 with permission to quote from them.

[8] This paper is discussed in *The Vanishing Hitchhiker* (pp. 64–65, 72); the published version appeared in *Kentucky Folklore Record* 27 (1981): 66–75.

[9] Another example of a "folklorized" personal-experience story is given in *The Choking Doberman*, pp. 71–73.

[10] Quoted in the appendix to *The Choking Doberman*, p. 216.

[11] Kathryn Falk, *Love's Leading Ladies* (New York: Pinnacle Books, 1982), p. 23, quoting Parris Afton Bonds.

[12] (New York: W. W. Norton, 1977), p. 14.

[13] Helen J. Van Zante, *The Microwave Oven* (Boston: Houghton Mifflin, 1973), p. 153.

[14] A copy of this news story, plus many other interesting reports of urban legends in her area, was sent to me by Mrs. Johnson.

[15] Quoted from the *San Francisco Chronicle* in the appendix to *The Choking Doberman*, p. 215.

[16] Thom Tammaro of Ball State University sent me the Muncie clipping of September 28, 1980, and Elaine Viets of the *St. Louis Post-Dispatch* sent me the September 26, 1980, *Tribune* clipping.

[17] *Cats Magazine* (November 1982), p. 19.

[18] State v. Tweedie, R.I., 444 A.2d 855; the quoted message is on p. 857.

[19] Carolyn Eastwood, "Folklore among Adolescents," *Indiana English Journal* 11, no. 2 (Winter 1976–77): 40–46; text on p. 43. Other sources of published oral texts are given in *The Vanishing Hitchhiker*, pp. 72–73.

[20] This clipping was sent to me by Catherine Collins of the *Chicago Tribune*.

[21] I am grateful to John R. Halsey, State Archaeologist in the Michigan History Division in Lansing, and to Todd Marsh of Center Line, Michigan, for sending me clippings about this case.

[22] (London: Picador division of Pan Books).

[23] Rodney Dale, *The Tumour in the Whale: A Collection of Modern Myths* (London: Duckworth, 1978), pp. 72–73.

[24] From Dianne Smerdon of Eden Hills, South Australia.

[25] From Carl Freeman of Geneva.

[26] (Coral Gables, Florida: University of Miami Press, 1972), pp. 43–44; this is a translation of the second (1968) edition of his book published in Spanish.

[27] Langer's chapter also appeared as "Le 'Mythe de l'enfant rôti' " [trans. Madelaine Baranger], *Revue Française de Psychoanalyse* 16 (1952): 509–517.

[28] Her book is subtitled *Estudio psicoanalitico y psicosomatico* (Buenos Aires: Editorial Nova, 1951); see pp. 98–99. No English edition has appeared.

[29] *Psychology Today* 14, no. 4 (September 1980), p. 6.

[30] Gerhard Adler, *The Living Symbol: A Case Study in the Process of Individuation* (New York: Pantheon, 1961), p. 157. See also Sigmund Freud, *A General Introduction to Psycho-Analysis* (New York: Liveright, 1935), p. 139.

[31] See Beryl Rowland, "The Oven in Popular Metaphor," *AS* 45 (1970): 215–22.

[32] Erich Neuman, *The Great Mother, an Analysis of the Archetype* (New York: Pantheon, 1955), p. 286.

[33] "Hansel and Gretel" is folktale Type 327A, discussed in Stith Thompson's *The Folktale* (New York: Dryden, 1946), pp. 36–37.

[34] (Bloomington: Indiana University Press, Midland paperback ed., 1976), p. 64.

[35] (Austin: University of Texas Press, 1979), p. 32.

[36] (New York: Knopf, 1976), pp. 159–66.

[37] Dr. Karabaş is a member of the Department of Humanities at the Middle East Technical University in Ankara.

[38] Mentioned by Bengt af Klintberg in a review of *The Vanishing Hitchhiker* published in *Arv: Scandinavian Yearbook of Folklore* 37 (1981): 188–89.

[39] Roger E. Mitchell, "Micronesian Folktales," *Asian Folklore Studies*, vol. 32 (Nagoya, Japan: Asian Folklore Institute, 1973), Tale 54, pp. 156–58, note p. 257. I am grateful to Dr. Mitchell not only for providing a copy of this publication but for sending me summaries of other texts discussed in relation to his published one.

[40] The two original sources, unavailable to me, are Wilhelm Müller, *Yap*, vol. 2, *Ergebnisse der Südsee-Expedition 1908–1910* (Hamburg: Friederichsen, 1918), and Annie Ker, *Papuan Fairy Tales* (London: Macmillan, 1910).

[41] See Stith Thompson's *Motif-Index*, new enlarged and rev. ed., 6 vols. (Bloomington: Indiana University Press, 1955–58). There are, of course, plenty of world folk narratives concerning cruel parents, as Elizabeth Tucker, for one, shows in her article "The Cruel Mother in Stories Told by Pre-Adolescent Girls," *IFR* (1981): 66–70; few if any of these bear any relationship to the baby-roast legend. For the ancient Finnish example, see Francis Peabody Magoun, Jr., trans., *The Kalevala*

(Cambridge, Mass.: Harvard University Press, 1963), Rune no. 31, esp. pp. 225–26. For the Argentinian example, see Alfred Métraux, *Myths of the Toba and Pilaga Indians of the Gran Chaco*, Memoir Series, vol. 40 (Philadelphia: American Folklore Society, 1946), p. 133.

[42] These are in Dov Noy, "Motif-Index of Talmudic-Midrashic Literature," (diss., Indiana University, 1954), and Edward Winslow Gifford, *Tongan Myths and Tales*, Bernice P. Bishop Museum Bulletin No. 8 (Honolulu, 1924), pp. 189–90.

[43] See Robert Graves, *The Greek Myths* (London: Penguin, 1955), p. 90.

[44] David Crockett Graham, *Songs and Stories of the Ch'uan Miao*, Smithsonian Miscellaneous Publications, vol. 123, no. 1 (Washington, D.C., 1954). Material collected from 1921 until the early 1930s.

[45] *The Folktale*, pp. 36–37.

[46] Marie-Louise von Franz, *An Introduction to the Psychology of Fairy Tales*, 2d. ed. (Zurich: Spring Publications, 1973), p. 14.

[47] A Russian story mentioned without a citation by Paul Smith has the baby cooked in a different way but preserves the theme of parental neglect: "The Tale is related of a mother bathing her baby in a tub of warm water. Placing the tub on top of the apparently unlit stove, the mother goes out and stands gossiping with a neighbor for some time. On returning indoors she is horrified to discover the draught of the open door has rekindled the fire and cooked the baby in the tub." See *Nasty Legends*, note p. 65.

[48] "Projection in Folklore: A Plea for Psychoanalytic Semiotics," in *Interpreting Folklore* (Bloomington: Indiana University Press, 1980), p. 37.

[49] "The Dead Baby Joke Cycle," *WF* 38 (1979): 145–57.

The Folklore of Academe

by Barre Toelken

Barre Toelken, longtime director of the Folklore and Ethnic Studies program at the University of Oregon, recently became director of the Folklore Program at his undergraduate alma mater, Utah State University. Drawing on a wide range of examples from his own student and faculty experiences at these universities and others, Toelken presents a convincing argument for the serious evaluation of the modern folklore of academe. He discusses the oral and customary traditions of, as he calls them, the "academicians on both sides of the podium." His collecting methods and his discussion of diffusion, structure, function, and other matters illustrate principles introduced throughout this book. In addition, several types of folklore only mentioned earlier in passing are set here in their proper group context and then analyzed. As a result, this study should encourage readers to attempt a further "careful folkloristic scrutiny of their own culture."

At first, many people are inclined to equate folklore with illiteracy, or at least with a lack of literary sophistication. Indeed, in the belief that folklore was rapidly dying out with the spread of literacy and urbanization, American folklorists of the early twentieth century spent much of their time combing the backwoods, rural communities, cultural niches, and less frequented byways of the country—places where cultural backwardness, illiteracy, and folklore were believed to coexist—looking for the vestigial remains of an ancient traditional inheritance. And, of course, they found plenty of old folklore, for there was no lack of it in the places where they sought it.[1] The same collectors might have been astounded to discover what the readers of this book by now have learned: that folklore also comes into being contemporaneously; that it seems to have nothing at all to do with backwardness, illiteracy, or rural domicile; that there may be a greater quantity of it now than ever before (since it seems to thrive best among close groups of people with an intense awareness of their own shared identity—and of these groups we have plenty); and that folklore is as much at home in the big city as in the remote village.

This book has provided numerous examples of living folklore; but even so, there still may exist some doubt about how far the idea of modernity in folklore can be carried. Certainly, some may feel, it does not include ourselves—educated, liberated, academic freethinkers that we are—does it? Interestingly enough, a close look at the ongoing oral and gestural traditions, customs, and beliefs we have shared avidly ever since grade school indicates that even those institutions designed to "draw us out" (L. *educare*) from ignorance and illiteracy became themselves the living contexts in which folklore could, and did, thrive. We may see several important lessons in this. One is that some unwritten folk traditions may be just as important as written expressions— even in some cases more central to daily existence: a student may get through high school semiliterate, but hardly is it possible to get through without assimilating a tremendous range of customs, gestures, specialized jargon terms, games, jokes, legends, beliefs, dances—all learned from other students, not from books.

Another observation is that some kinds of folklore are interdependent with written forms or exist mostly in writing (autograph and yearbook verses, Rugby-club song pamphlets, graffiti): neither writing nor oral tradition seems to threaten each other's existence. Finally, we may suspect that the great and continued abundance of things in print in a literate culture like ours (a situation intensified for students because of textbooks, written assignments, tests, printed records, and the like) actually may cause people to express many of their most personal, as well as their ongoing shared (traditional), concerns orally or gesturally. In folklore, closely related people use channels and modes of expressions already recognized by the members of their group, their "culture," as efficient and enjoyable ways of sharing familiar, sometimes emotionally charged, situations. Such groups, whether they are literate or not, exhibit a cohesiveness and a sense of identity better expressed in the informal but formularized oral exchanges and "performances" that have been developed through, and polished by, the formative processes of tradition.[2]

The cultural elements that bind students together in such close, identifiable groups have little to do with formal public schoolboard policies, student codes, or college catalogues. Even less are they learned from the directives of dean, professor, teacher, or principal (though they may exist in defiance of those orders). They are not directly derived from official activities with formalized rules, though they may often take place there (traditional cheers at intercollegiate football games, for example). Rather, they grow out of a shared cluster of live experiences, common fears, hopes, and frustrations that have been experienced in common by a substantial number of the group's membership—emotions that are difficult, if not impossible, to express in crisp essay form (though they may appear anonymously on desk tops and lavatory walls).[3] Students, whether in school or at the university, can be seen as members of a distinct folk group, the members of which are separately literate but communally aliterate. That is to say, while they may know how to read, their cultural expressions (insofar as they reflect the shared academic experience) do not ordinarily come forth through the agency of the *printed* word. We will find that in these groups, traditional materials are far from dead or even anemic; in point of fact, the folklore of academe is widespread and viable, and reveals with great vividness the traditional concerns of academicians on both sides of the podium, expressed in many of the same genres as folklore is found to take among other folk groups.

In the present essay, I will provide a general survey of the topics and genres of high-school and college folklore (mostly the latter), based on my own observations as a member of both student and faculty camps, as well as on surveys made in high-school and college classes. The study is thus partial and general in many regards, which means that it will serve only as a background against which some comments and suggestions can be made about the function of folk beliefs among literates. The student who carries the subject further into particular issues in academic lore will want to focus on a more restricted topic, should use extensive and carefully gathered field data, and will need to be attentive to the specific contexts in which the traditional expressions normally occur.[4] The careful reader of this essay will notice that there are regional variations in the materials cited, and that there is a considerable and continual change in the appearance and function of academic customs through time. The student will do well to take this dynamic state of flux as a basic component of academic folklore as well as of folklore in general.

The primary distinction between faculty and students goes much deeper than the superficial fact that schools are places where the less informed go to study with the more informed. The faculty at any school or college not only share in a "great enterprise" that accords them a certain status not attached to income, but they often see themselves somewhat heroically aligned against a common foe that is willing to use the most devious tactics to win out. Their stories and legends abound in accounts of what other faculty members do, or have done, to quiet a noisy class, to wake up a sleeping student, or to turn away the amorous advances of a charmer in the front row. According to one typical story, an angry professor throws a piece of chalk at a sleeping boy to wake him up, but it enters his wide-open mouth, lodges in his throat, and nearly chokes him to death (in some versions, the student is still recovering in a nearby hospital while the professor has been assigned to other duties). Another professor is visited by a young woman who announces with a blush that she will do anything for a good grade in his class. "Anything?" he asks in mock disbelief. "Yes, anything. I have to get a good grade in here, or I can't stay in my sorority." "*Anything?*" he asks again, closing the door. "Anything," she says, eyes downcast. Then, whispering into her ear, he says, "Well, then, why don't you try studying?" Still another professor gains traditional fame when he becomes upset that so many students are bringing tape recorders to class; he sends an assistant in his place who plays tape-recorded lectures to them. Widespread attitudes about arrogant students and about the shabbiness of their own lot are revealed in the professors' cynical proverblike descriptions of their profession ("casting fake pearls before real swine").

Common in both the United States and England is the story of Professor Jenkins, a teetotaler, who is a visiting lecturer on leave from a religious college. At a reception given by the department chairman in his honor, sherry is passed around, at which Professor Jenkins exclaims, "Why, I'd as soon commit adultery as take a drink of wine!" "So would we all, Mister Jenkins," says his host, "so would we all." A Milton professor is supposed to have walked into his classroom on the first day and asked all the young women in the front row to cross their legs. "Now that the gates of Hell are safely closed," he says, "we may begin our discussion of *Paradise Lost.*" The reader can no doubt supply many more examples of the same sort, for they are not restricted in their circulation to the conversations that take place between faculty members. Yet faculty members usually tell them to illustrate "our difficult situation," while the students usually tell them to show what odd folks the faculty are.[5] Judging from their folklore, faculty members see themselves as benevolent patriarchs whose words are needed, but most often unheeded, by their naïve clients; they reveal a faith in their unfortunate attractions to the opposite sex, but demonstrate a remarkable dedication—in their own estimation bordering on raw heroism—to keeping a proper professional distance from their numerous besiegers.

When not beset by amorous students, the professors of tradition turn their attention to the vampiric hordes of congenital liars who swoop down on them in every class just before each vacation and after every exam with vivid accounts of near-deadly accidents, family tragedies, dying grandmothers, and doctors' appointments. In spare moments they brood about being caught in the "publish or perish" system, and many in desperation succeed in doing both.[6] However, if we look closely at the implied meanings suggested by the imagery of professors' narratives and customs, we may get a more sobering view of a group of people who, as a class, experience a sense of power over younger people, especially women. The discrepancy between what the members of a folk group are conscious of and not conscious of in their traditional expressions provides us with one of the most interesting ongoing areas of study in folklore: a barometer for cultural psychology.

Suggestive of a fear shared by many academicians that people "off campus" believe students and professors do not live in a real world of sweat and work, is the heavy use of terms and metaphors suggestive of labor, technology, and exactitude. The folk speech of academe is liberally spiced with terms like "social *science*," "human *engineering*," and "music *clinic*." Books are "*tools* of the trade"; advanced degrees are "*union cards*"; we hear of the "*mechanics*" of writing and about the "*technical* aspects" of dramatic composition. We teach "*workshops*" in poetry and in fiddling; we speak of "*tension*" and "*torsion*" in our literary criticism; we entertain "visiting *firemen*" instead of official observers or candidates for academic positions; our librarians use "*trucks*" on which they push books around, and place the books in "*stacks*" and "*decks*" more often than on floors and shelves. Even in the modern world of computer communication, the work is characterized by terms like "*hardware*," "*terminals*," "*slaves*," "*master*," "*the guts*," and "*garbage* in, garbage out."

The student, on the other hand, tells stories about fellow students who were able to outsmart the teacher, relates "real" instances of eccentricities among instructors, reminisces about obscene remarks made by professors in class, recalls the petty actions and philosophies of prudish deans from previous years (no red dresses allowed on campus, no patent leather shoes, no girls to sit on boys' laps without the interposition of telephone book or pillow), and describes in gleeful detail what other students will do or have done for a grade.[7]

One friend has a music professor who climbed out of the grand piano the first day of class; another friend knew someone who witnessed the "Gates of Hell" remark in Milton class (except that it was really four years ago in Professor Chumleigh's class, not two years ago in Professor Svendsen's); someone else has it on good authority (i.e., heard from a friend) that an English professor concluded a mid-campus conversation with a student by asking "Which way was I going when we stopped?" and, on being told, answered, "Oh, then I *have* eaten lunch!"

Just last year, one hears from reliable friends, an easily embarrassed biology teacher who was frightened of discussing sex in mixed company got rid of all the women in class by writing an obscene word on the board before taking roll, or by asking an intentionally ambiguous question: "Can you tell me, Miss, what part of the body expands to three times its normal size when properly stimulated?" After the young woman leaves, the professor asks the class innocently, "What's so bad about the pupil of the eye?"[8]

Their own folk traditions reveal that students express themselves as people unfairly beset by a system that imposes on its prisoners too many unwanted oddball instructors and too much unneeded homework; students are served a constant diet of obscenity in class and inedible food in the dormitory (rumor has it that flies avoid the garbage cans in back of the dorm). They get poor grades because "the curve" was unfair (a phenomenon attributed in student legends to the erratic correction practices of the professor, who often enlists the aid of his infant children, or to the flagrant display of sexuality by some attractive person in the front row).

Students' lore and language suggest that a certain amount of paranoia is thus obligatory, and that a modicum of silent rebellion against their oppressors is justifiable and appropriate. They describe the inevitable paperwork in the academic bureaucracy as a "hassle," implying that the whole process is put into action only as a purposeful and arrogant infringement on student freedom. Students "cut class" whenever the situation permits, do only enough work to satisfy the minimum requirements, and engage in public activities that challenge the naïve and reactionary ideas they are certain their teachers passionately believe in. Their code of behavior permits, even encourages, them to make academic gains through wit, stealth, or late and reluctant spurts of studying ("outfoxing the prof," "cribbing," "cramming"), but prohibits, or at least devalues, the exercise of personal charm, amiability, or good looks ("brown-nosing"). Protracted and serious academic work is not entirely taboo, but must be rhetorically downplayed if the student is to escape being labeled a "drudge" or a "nerd." On a higher place in the scale of values (at least according to the oral tradition) are those who are well known for their popularity, good looks, or talent in sports (though in some quarters the last category is often labeled with the denigrating synecdoche "jocks"). It is of greatest importance to realize that while the folklore of academe continually features such elements as these, the items themselves may not match the particular tastes and beliefs of any single student. The existence of hundreds of ways to cheat on an exam is not to be taken as proof that all students try to cheat; rather, it is a strong indication that the subject of cheating, of the unpredictability of exams, is an enduring one among those who are continually threatened by their existence. The beliefs and stories tend to bring to the fore the anxieties and the concerns more accurately than they represent "normal" student behavior. Academic folklore expresses the concerns and anxieties of both teachers and students, and since each group defines itself emotionally by contrast to the other, a knowledge of both sets of folk traditions is required to make sense of either one. And an awareness of the poetic and hyperbolic in human expression is necessary to understand fully how these beliefs function.

In addition to the jargon and beliefs of academe, there exists a seemingly endless supply of narrative materials and songs in the oral tradition of school and campus. Especially the legend (a story told as true, with all the accompanying features of believability in style, content, and source) is alive and well on campus, and the texts are an accurate indicator of the fact that students pass on not only the narrations of their own group, but those of the larger culture as well. Legends confined to academic subjects are easily collected (some of the professor anecdotes mentioned above would be good examples), as well as stories that have circulated all over the country. The modern legend, sometimes referred to as the urban belief tale or the urban legend or the *sage*, features an incident that is just odd or striking enough to merit passing on to others, but it is usually one which would never be believed by the listeners unless there were some believable corroboration built into the narrative. Legends now in circulation across the United States that are also common currency on college campuses include the cement-truck driver who fills an assumed rival's car with concrete, the new car for sale cheap because it carries an ineradicable death smell, the fifty-dollar Porsche being offered for sale by the angry wife of a man who has run off with his secretary, the woman forced to pay an outlandish price for a recipe by the snooty chef of a famous hotel restaurant, the old lady with damp poodle who blows him up by trying to dry him out in her new microwave oven, the three elderly ladies who sit down in an elevator when a black man (later identified as a well-known sports star) gets on with his Doberman and orders it to "Sit!"

These and others are known and actively passed along as true, or plausible, stories by both faculty and students. In addition to these are legends that have themes particularly applicable to high-school and college situations; these are so widely popular as to be current virtually everywhere one can find students. One version of the *Vanishing Hitchhiker* legend (Motif E332.3.3.1.), for example, depicts a student driver who picks up a wet young woman hitchhiker in the night rain. He drops her off at her home, letting her wear his sweater to keep warm, and when he returns the next day to retrieve it he is told by her mother that the girl died in an accident after the prom some twenty years before and that someone has reported picking her up at that spot on the anniversary of the accident every year thereafter. Trying to check out the story, the young man visits the graveyard and finds her tombstone—with his sweater wrapped around it. Modern readers or hearers of this legend may recall that at least two "pop-rock" songs of the 1960s and 1970s used the same motif, but they may not be aware that the legend is also told in Hawaii, where it is often the goddess Pele who appears as the hitchhiker, or told in Utah, where it is usually one of the Three Nephites bringing a message to a Mormon driver. Not long after the eruption of Mount St. Helens in Washington State in 1980, there occurred a rash of legends telling of a prophetic young hippie hitchhiker who foretold the disaster and then disappeared from the back seat. Folk traditions can be seen to have a local frame of reference that binds the teller to his or her audience through their shared associations and values; just as important is the fact that folklore also has an international dimension that can usually be discovered only by arduous and continual research.[9]

Given the dating customs of high-school and college students, given the ubiquity and the emotionally symbolic employment of the automobile in American culture, it is no surprise to find that there are a great number of legends that feature the anxieties of young lovers in their car on lovers' lanes. Salt Lake City high schoolers in the 1950s and 1960s watched carefully for the Hopping Lady of Memory Grove, the unfortunate and apparently jealous wraith of an unmarried woman whose legs had grown together. She was often seen hopping about a small memorial park scratching on the windows of parked cars, attacking their occupants if their windows were open (one's car could be made Hopping Lady–proof only by parking it crossways in the road and blinking its high beams a certain number of times on the house believed to have been that of the woman before her death; students, however, differed in their understanding of which house was the proper one, thus allowing apprehensions about parking in the darkened grove to remain at high pitch).[10] Both high-school and college students know about the couple parking on Lovers' Lane who hear an announcement over the radio that a maniac with a hook on his arm is loose in the area (they later find a hook and arm cup on the door handle), or about the young girl stranded all night in the car while her boyfriend goes for gasoline (after listening to scratching, dripping, or scraping all night she is rescued by policemen who fail to keep her from looking back and seeing her boy-friend's body suspended upside down over the car). Young men report telling such stories to their dates in order to encourage them to move over closer; young women report telling them as a means of expressing fears or insecurities about dating or "petting"; parents seem to use such stories to instill a warning about careless parking or behavior. Yet, even though these stories have such pragmatic capacities, they are still told as actually having happened, usually nearby. Clearly, if such oc-currences had actually taken place, they would have appeared in the *local* papers. But these stories are told all over the country, a fact that should indicate to us that the narratives have developed lives of their own. We do not need to prove that "it" really happened right here in Springfield; neither do we need to debunk the story. What makes these legends folklore is that they are being passed around as narrative ex-pressions of real shared values and concerns.[11]

Less structured than these legends but just as current are the count-less brief anecdotes told by students about their teachers and profes-sors.[12] Some of these may simply be narrative recollections of something that actually happened in class—not whole legends but ac-counts of a remarkable occurrence that the teller realizes will be inter-esting to his audience. Most often, these are told in the first person, and they highlight some particular idea of importance to the group. In time, such an anecdote may be passed on to others, features in it may be ac-centuated, and it may emerge later as a full-blown legend or it may continue to circulate as a rumor (based on shared attitudes, beliefs, or suspicions—such as we see in the "information" we sometimes hear about the miraculous carburetor, or alligators in the sewers). Since here the story *qua* story is less important than the "information" it im-parts, we may call these items traditional incidents, memorates, or leg-end cores.[13] For example, without any narrative to give it dramatic structure, we hear simply that there is a professor on campus who writes equations on the board so fast that a graduate assistant must fol-low and erase the board behind him. Since the assistant erases faster than anyone can take notes, most of the material is irretrievably lost.

Another professor writes on the board with his right hand and erases as he goes with his left; anyone who cannot take immediate notes or memorize quickly is lost. But since the professor has given the same final examination for the past twenty-three years, everyone always gets an A. One professor is known to wear the same suit every day for the whole year; another always wears mismatched socks; one wears a trench coat in class; another leaves the room while lecturing and comes back fifteen minutes later still talking, but on another subject. A philosophy professor asks only "Why?" on the final exam and gives an A to the student who answers "Because." One professor lectures only to the best-looking young man in the class, looks only at him, checks out the success of every joke by noting his response, and directs all major points to him (of course, the young man nods constantly throughout the lectures to indicate to the professor and the other students that he understands everything perfectly). One day, late in the term, the young man is absent. The professor enters, opens his books and notes, looks out over the class to the empty seat and in puzzlement asks, "Where *is* everybody today?" This last instance is closer to legend format because of its tendency toward a story line, but one often hears it told as a fragmentary anecdote, with a stress on the last line. What makes these items folklore? First of all, folklore does not indicate that an anecdote is false, only that it is in circulation. But what makes these items decidedly folklore, whether they actually happened anywhere or not, is that they have become recurrent in performance among the members of a particular group sharing particular values: they have become a formularized part of the expressive system of the academic scene, and their narration helps to socialize new members into the values and attitudes of the on-going culture of that scene.

Although music plays a smaller role on campus than it did in years past, it is still in use enough to make a good subject for folkloristic analysis. In contrast to the often tacky official anthems imposed on students by their predecessors of fifty or a hundred years ago are the many songs that circulate almost exclusively in oral tradition among the "Greeks," the participants in beer busts, and the members of specialized clubs (e.g., the Foresters, the Engineers, the rugby team). Songs that remain in oral circulation are mainly humorous or risqué, preferably both. While such songs are normally not sung where folklorists may collect them or deans sneak in and hear, students themselves are in a position to participate in them, collect them, and provide informed analytical commentary on their meaning and function. As is the case in much of folklore, the insider often understands the expression quite differently than would an outsider. A parent listening to the songs sung after a rugby game might conclude on the basis of their content and vocabulary that the college population had suddenly become fanatic proponents of the most degraded sexual fantasies. The rugby players themselves, being no more degraded than anyone else in the culture, would experience the same songs as humorous expressions of physical aggressiveness and conquest—feelings parallel to the motivations for playing the game. Neither parent nor team member would necessarily feel inclined to explicate the poetic dimensions of folk sexual hyperbole for the benefit of a scholarly audience, but that in itself is no reason to suppose the subject is not a rewarding one that could add considerably to our appreciation of human expression. The songs given below are not the most powerfully expressive examples of college songs, but they testify to the various ways in which the "official" songs of sorority or club life can be augmented and undercut by anonymous—let us say vernacular—expressions that do not come from, or get into, the official handbooks:

> Violate me in the violet time
> In the vi-o-lest way that you know;
> Ravish me savagely, simply lavish me
> On me no mercy bestow;
> For the best things in life are the obvious, oblivious;
> Oh, give me a man who is lewd and lascivious.
> Oh, violate me in the violet time
> In the vi-o-lest way that you know.

Many songs are sung by the members of one fraternity in order to cast a good-natured slur on the members of another. Such rivalry songs are common on all campuses, and, as one would expect of traditional songs, considerable variation comes into play. Representative are the following:

> A garbage can, a garbage can,
> Upon a field of blue,
> A closer look revealed to me
> The crest of Sigma Nu.

> Adam was a beta boy,
> Job went Sigma Chi,
> Moses was an S A E
> but Jesus was a Phi.

I am a dirty D G,[14]
A dirty little D G,
I spread a reign of terror where I go;
My chief delight is stirring up a fight
And I beat little kids on the head til they're dead.
For I am a D G, a dirty little D G,
I put poison in my mother's shredded wheat;
I am a blotch on the family's scotch,
And I eat—raw—meat.

The Greek system also serves as nucleus for a number of collegiate practices and stories (both legends and memorates) about those practices. "Goat Week," "steals," initiation ceremonies, as well as corollary customs among other student groups make up a considerable part of college folklore, although these items may not be shared by all inhabitants of academe. In addition to the usual formal induction ceremonies of exclusive groups, which may feature special gowns, midnight rituals, exhausting tasks, subordination to authority (and other ancient ingredients of threshold rites), there are legendary accounts of a more shocking and (sometimes) humorous nature. Student folklore collections mention such experiences as having to down fourteen raw eggs in fifteen minutes, being paddled with a variety of instruments, having to eat mentholatum sandwiches, playing hair-pulling games with fellow pledges, and being treated to dinners secretly loaded with laxatives. One Western sorority holds its initiation ceremony in the basement of a nearby church. There, blindfolded pledges grope into toilet bowls to encounter bananas, face inquisitions about their private sex lives, receive obscene nicknames, after which they are required to enact the giving of birth to a nation (or to imitate the flushing of a toilet). Finally, they are placed one by one in a coffin, shut briefly in, and are then allowed out into the light, "reborn" as active members of the chapter.[15]

Nearly every fraternity or club has or has had a brother who was able to perform a more obscene act in public than his rival in another fraternity (the penis in the popcorn box is a common one; "mooning" is another);[16] many groups tell of a former president who was kidnaped (either by pledges or by rivals) and left handcuffed, nude, tied to a tree in the wilderness, to the gatepost of a nearby university, or suspended from a construction derrick; many fraternities and clubs tell of having had a horse shot in their basement during a dance or vacation (the animal develops rigor mortis before it can be removed, and thus has to be dismembered); most groups have had at least one dance or party where the centerpiece on the head table was a hand (head, foot, etc.) borrowed from the medical-school anatomy lab (Motif N384.0.1.1.). While such incidents may or may not have been actual events, they are so commonly found in oral tradition that they can be seen as live dimensions of the psychological atmosphere of a college setting. Indeed, some of these stories can be shown to have a considerable antiquity, but that does not keep modern narrators from passing them on as recent oral history. The widespread story of the initiate who dies of fright when he is whipped or stroked with a cold towel (which he believes is a knife) has been traced back to British university tradition of the late 1700s.[17] But it is as timely now as it was then, for it dramatizes the fear people have of initiatory experiences, threshold anxieties, the power of their own imaginations. In these and in other examples of student folklore we may observe the embodiment in narrative form of many private and social "repressions"—actions or words that a student might consider taboo or socially dangerous if actually performed or stated in the normal course of daily events but that may be released safely as verbal or pictorial expressions with anonymous origins.[18]

In this sense, much of folk narrative may provide a kind of vicarious experience that tradition bearers actually prefer over "real" experience. For example, during the 1970s, when many students were familiar with the use of LSD, a legend about the dangers of the drug circulated widely: six students were found totally blind on the side of a hill, where, under the influence of LSD, they had spent the afternoon staring at the sun. Each legend contained the name of the university the students had attended, and after the story got into the newspapers several times, there was a rash of denials by the universities concerned. Various journalists did local research on the story, but no one was able to come up with the "real" occurrence. It may or it may not have happened, but for thousands of student-legend narrators, it allowed for the expression of fears and concerns that would have been considered "uncool" among those who felt they needed to demonstrate their familiarity with the drug scene. Beyond all these aspects of folk narrative, we need to acknowledge that many of these stories are interesting, exciting, funny, and engaging; they make good entertainment, and this may be as important a reason for their continuance as any functional aspect brought forth by scholarly analysis.

The currency of fraternity and sorority lore hit a peak in the 1950s and 1960s. Then—as students in general took a more radical view of their relation to the world about them—in the 1970s, Greek membership fell at many universities; and with the diminution of Greek presence and centrality in the social milieu, fraternity folklore seemed to be dying out. In the 1980s, however, along with a swing toward conservatism on the part of many college students, the Greek system is once more on the rise: the songs of Rush again fill the autumn air at most colleges and universities.

Other campus groups have their own esoteric lore. Members of such clubs as the Foresters tell of outlandish pranks played on their campus rivals (often the Engineers). In the usual style of the legend, the incidents are said on the best authority to have happened in the recent past; they consist of details about bricking up the entrance to the Engineering Building one day when the students were all in class, engaging in gun battles with the campus police in order to lure them away from the scene of some other outrageous prank (like rolling a huge log down Founders' Hill at some offensive old building), leading well-fed bovines into the offices of unpopular faculty members at night, and so on. In reality, a good many pranks—including head shaving, practiced on captured opponents—do occur during the friendly rivalry of such clubs, and there is ample reason to believe some of the more spectacular stories about pranks played during the club's "Mythic Age"; nonetheless, even the casual collector of such legends and anecdotes will begin to perceive a general thread of repetition on campuses across the country that testifies to the traditional diffusion of the stories as narratives, not as eyewitness accounts. Moreover, the continued existence of the stories, whether or not they convey absolutely accurate information, shows us that the *custom* of playing pranks under certain traditional circumstances is still alive and well in the student world. A recent film, *Salamanders: A Night at the Phi Delt House*, set in a fraternity situation, can be seen as an indication of how alive and lively all such traditions remain today.[19]

For an interesting example of ritual on campus, one might investigate local variations of the pinning or engagement ceremony.[20] The young woman who intends to reveal her engagement arranges the details with a few trusted friends in the dormitory or sorority house where she lives. During the evening meal, certain signals (often the passing of candy) are given that such a ritual will take place, but—if the plans are tightly kept—no one knows who the lucky person is. Tension and anticipation mount. After the meal everyone gathers in a darkened room or at the bottom of a staircase, where a friend of the young woman passes a plate with a burning candle on it to the group. Often the candle is surrounded by candies, cookies, rosebuds, fruits, even vitamin pills. Sometimes the candle is decorated with a bow or a small flower with an engagement ring attached, or sometimes the ring is actually placed over the tip of the candle. The plate is passed slowly and reverently around the circle while everyone sings an appropriate love song. On the third pass, the engagee reveals herself by blowing the candle out, whereupon her surprised friends rush in at her with noisy congratulations. It is significant to note that very few people today make any association between this ritual and the older traditional associations of the candle, ring, rosebuds, fruits, the chanting circle of women, and the blowing out of the candle.[21] Rather, these old elements have probably been retained because the next previous generation "did it" that way, and no one wants to be the person to change a warm-hearted and supportive ritual such as this. The modern college woman does not need to see the custom as a modern version of an ancient fertility ritual but probably does want to see it as a socially acceptable and pleasant way to "break the news" to friends. Nonetheless, elements in the ritual are actually ancient, even though the enactment of the ritual is functional in modern times, and thus both dimensions are important to our understanding of the tradition.

Both the engagement and the means of its revelation are of importance to the young woman; as in many such cases, the person turns to a well-known traditional ritual instead of to invention, for the group inheritance often has more stability to offer than an isolated individual can muster alone. In studying these materials, as with all folklore that comes from the past, we must constantly keep in mind that the functional properties ascribed to a belief or custom by those who practice it today are not necessarily the same as those that might have occasioned a similar ritual in another age. An unwillingness to understand ongoing developments and accommodations in tradition can lead to embarrassing theoretical conclusions, as many folklorists at the turn of the century discovered.[22] Unwillingness to discover ancient roots of modern ceremonies may lead to the equally false conclusion that we have developed all the really meaningful rituals only within the last few years.

An important group of traditional academic beliefs and customs that have both modern applications and strong links with the primitive past are those that cluster about the taking of exams. In response to a questionnaire passed out to a number of folklore classes in the 1960s, more than four hundred out of six hundred students reported (some in wonderful detail) that they engaged in special customary behavior during final exam week in order to influence their performance or their professors' perception of it.[23] Probably the most common of these had to do with manipulations of clothing or grooming styles, such as growing beards, or wearing "grubby" clothes—not simply informal dress, but intentionally rumpled and dirty items, often those which had been worn on previously successful exams. Other practices included eating raw meat, fasting, abstaining from sex, taking a good-luck toy or amulet to the exam, wearing lucky undergarments, hoping the hardest exam would fall on a lucky date (usually the seventh, fourteenth, twenty-first, or twenty-eighth), not combing or setting hair. Nowadays, with beards more common on campus, men report shaving their beards before exam week, and other magical customs are still very much in practice: a picked-up penny indicates luck on a coming exam; a number seven in the exam identification code is a lucky omen; wearing lucky clothes will affect the outcome of the exam favorably. Students carry lucky pens; wear lucky rings, lucky socks, shoes, or hat; bring a religious medallion; sit in a lucky seat; dress "sloppy"; and even shake or knock loudly on the desk before starting the exam (these last, incidentally, were collected in 1983 from students of law at a major university). Clearly, some kind of body magic or invocation of nonstandard rules is intended here, although students remain fairly adamant about not calling these practices "superstitions" (mostly, one assumes, because that term has usually been used to denote the foolish beliefs of *others*, not one's own perfectly normal behavior during times of stress). They do admit, however, that these practices are not simply ways of saving time during the press of exam week; these are methods undertaken with the direct purpose of affecting one's ability to "ace" (or at least survive) the exam.

It probably need not be explained that practices such as fasting, eating certain foods while abstaining from others, abstinence from sex, wearing of ritualized clothing, carrying lucky amulets and similar items, not washing or shaving (or at least altering the normal grooming pattern noticeably) are customs found more or less typically among a number of so-called primitive cultures, who attempt by such measures to affect their futures by ensuring a good hunt or a successful engagement with the enemy. It would be possible, thus, if one were to ignore the caveat above, to see the modern student as little more than a literate savage. The observances are strikingly similar, and they may very well suggest to us that, faced with certain kinds of shared pressure or anxiety, human groups are likely to attempt to affect the future by magical means requiring the suspension or downplaying of mere practical modes of behavior and by placing in the foreground special or magical qualities of the situation in dramatically satisfying ways. Since the situation itself is emotionally charged, the means of coping with it must be appropriately pregnant with emotional meaning. We may note these similarities between the student and the ancient tribesman without assuming that they are identical: after all, the traditions and the worlds in which they operate will remain distinguished by the simple fact that the primitive hunter is usually faced with hunger—if not starvation—if the hunt does not succeed, and in many cases he believes he is killing a relative who is ritually offering its flesh as food. The student, on the other hand, is faced at most with embarrassment, taking the exam over, failing a class, or competition among friends and colleagues. In both cases, obviously, tradition has much to offer the lonely individual.

One of the most widespread of student beliefs up until recently was the almost religious adherence to the obligatory wait for a late professor. One form of the code allows a wait of five minutes for an instructor, ten minutes for an assistant professor, fifteen minutes for an associate professor, and twenty for a full professor. At some universities the custom is ten minutes for all ranks except professor—twenty for a professor. In some cases students were confused because they did not fully understand the difference in the ranks or in the jargon that describes them, but the custom was firmly established in its general form: after the obligatory wait, students could safely leave class without fearing the professor would come along and count them late. In the above-mentioned poll of college-student lore, the responses about this practice illustrated well some generally accepted folklore theories. Out of more than six hundred students polled during the 1960s, only one reported never having heard of a rule for waiting; not surprisingly, it was found that this student lived off campus, was unaffiliated with any campus group, ate and studied off campus, and was, in short, not a participating member of the folk group (although she was indeed a student in the technical sense that she registered for classes, attended them, did the work, and received grades). Although other students gave a number of different answers on the obligatory length to wait, more than 78 percent gave essentially the same answer: ten minutes for a non-Ph.D., fifteen for a Ph.D. This illustrates that at that time a specifically formulated belief was held by a sizable majority; the rest of the members of the folk group were aware of the belief and were in the habit of observing it, but were not agreed on the details—a condition that may be typical of the acceptance/practice rate for any traditional belief and one that, regularly measured over a large enough sample of a folk group and over a substantial range of time, could reveal the rate of development or deterioration of a particular traditional item within the expressive system of the group. As might be expected, among those who knew the belief, the more impressionable, more anxious freshman and sophomores exhibited a higher rate of belief in the obligatory wait than did students in the upper classes, which may suggest that as students matured and became more "agnostic" about the rules of college life, they either found out that there was no obligatory waiting period dictated by their college or continued to believe there was but declined to observe it.[24] Most of the students who gave the most common answer (ten minutes/fifteen minutes) were, as one would expect, complete members of the folk group: they not only registered for and attended classes together, but they ate and studied on campus, thus participating as fully as possible in the specialized community of academe and sharing continuously in its specialized pressures.

When asked why they observed the waiting period, the students generally answered that they understood it to be a college rule (though they admitted they had heard it only from each other) and that their observance of it would provide them with a structured mode of conduct that released them from responsibility in the event they did leave the classroom. The first part of their answer indicates the uncritical aspect of their belief—an element found organically in superstition; the second part shows that they did have, however, a good sense of how this particular belief functioned for them within their culture. In the 1970s, a mere ten years after these figures were first obtained, students reported that although they still recognized the custom, they felt less obliged to honor it. Many phrased the newer situation thus: ten minutes and no more for most profs; twenty minutes for one you respect. In the 1980s, some students responded that they know and practice the custom, but it is now the upperclassmen who are the more conservative adherents—or at least they are the ones who can articulate an answer on the matter when questioned. Further studies of this custom at particular colleges and universities would reveal far more on this matter than this brief survey has been able to produce. Even though folklorists must exercise caution when getting explanations of customs from informants who are believers, they should never on that account ignore the fact that the informants can supply comment on the function of a belief or custom which would otherwise be unavailable to the collector. Moreover, as the above instances indicate, talking with informants over time about the same beliefs can provide us with a more accurate notion of the viability and currency of a belief.

In the closer investigation of academic folklore, students should keep in mind a number of distinctive categories that will enable them to see more clearly and thus to evaluate more reliably the functions, the actual working characteristics, of the various traditional modes and genres. In addition to the basic division between faculty and students, one ought to consider local particularities at specific schools and colleges, age and sex of the informants, and possible changes in the currency of the materials collected (old traditions remaining in memory but not in practice versus viable current traditions in wide use among most members of a group). This last consideration is an important one for modern folklore theory, for although a number of students have demonstrated the modern degeneration of older traditions,[25] there has been comparatively little emphasis on the dynamic development of newer forms and newer items within traditional genres. The incredible rise and spread of urban legends and the continued currency of academic tradition would certainly indicate that while some kinds of folklore may die out or get confused in their usage, others are constantly arising and providing current groups of people with patterned modes of expression.

Sometimes the situation remains the same, a shared evaluation stays constant, but the means of expressing it require updating. When a college class was asked in 1967 what word they used to denote a fellow student who curries favor with the teacher, students under thirty years of age usually answered "brown-nose" or "brownie," the males understanding the term as metaphor for an offensive anatomical contact between inferior and superior, the females taking it as a reference to Brownie Scouts working for merit badges. Of students aged thirty to forty-five, the men almost all answered "brown-nose," but women nearly all gave "apple polisher." Of students over forty-five, men and women gave "apple polisher" almost without exception (occasionally an older parent admitted learning the more "modern" term "brown-nose" from teen-aged children). Without further extensive comparative and regional data, a conclusion cannot be drawn from this, but some preliminary hunches and hypotheses may be possible. The term "brown-nose" seems to have come into use comparatively recently, apparently having been used by men first. The term, by 1967, might not have been "taboo" for younger women, but many apparently were unaware of the original imagery (which seems to have come from a derisive army song about soldiers who try to become too chummy with officers). By the 1980s, both sexes at the university use "kiss ass" and "butt-kiss" with an openness that indicates the disappearance both of restraints on women's vocabulary and on the public use of terms that a few years ago would have been considered offensive. It is to be remembered that the same students who feel at ease using such terms among their own folk group, where the vocabulary is current, would not use the terms in front of Grandma Jorgensen during a family reunion (similarly, Grandma Jorgensen, who may have put in a lifetime as a midwife, will not use many of her terms in front of her grandsons or other menfolk). The esoteric-exoteric factor in folklore continues to function as it always has; it is the insider who best knows the beliefs and customs as well as the nuances of their usage in performance.

For instance, it is the insider who knows the difference between current forms of expression that *talk* about belief and the actual practice of a belief. On most of the same campuses where the obligatory wait was a serious part of campus belief, there was also in existence some interesting means of discovering a virgin: statues stood up or spoke when she walked by, fixed gates would close, stone animals twitter and roar, paintings and statues of angels would blow horns or flap wings ("and the last time it ever happened was in 1930, when Shirley Temple visited campus"). "Beliefs" of this sort were widespread, but did anyone actually seriously believe them? If not, why were they phrased as beliefs? There are two considerable differences between the fifteen-minute wait and the belief that the Pioneer Mother statue will stand up when a virgin walks by, one of them more subtle than the other. Most obvious is the fact that the virgin test is known to be simply a jocular way of commenting on the supposed rarity of virgins on campus; no one actually believes the Founder will whistle when one walks by. This is a reflection of an attitude, phrased as a belief the very basis of which is that the statue has never been seen to move, ergo, there are no virgins on campus. This is hyperbole, not belief, while the custom of the obligatory wait, even though people might occasionally have laughed about it, was considered serious. Even students who had reservations about it would probably have observed it, but certainly no one has found the student who, just in case it might be so, watches the Pioneer Mother carefully as his true love walks by. The insider knows that one is a belief and the other is not, but only masquerades as a belief for the sake of humorous overstatement.

But the more subtle difference between the two expressions might escape the insider (while it will not have escaped the notice of the modern sensitive reader): while the obligatory wait is for everyone, the virgin test is for women, for everyone *assumes* that "the virgin" referred to is female. Whose business is it to wonder if any woman on campus, or all of them, are virgins? What accounts for the ongoing concern about this matter which lasted for so long that even among educated people from coast to coast at the most advanced universities, men were snickering and wondering about the rarity of female virginity? Since we know that we joke about many of the things that strike us at the deepest levels of anxiety and uncertainty, we may suggest that the virgin test "hyperbole" was more than just a witty use of language, but rather a revealing expression of male concerns over the rapidly developing status of women at universities for the 1940s onward. The movement of women into domains previously thought of as male and rapid changes in women's habits (smoking, drinking, voting) have often brought out charges that sexual promiscuity was also somehow involved. While sensible college men of the 1940s and 1950s would not have said such things consciously, many of their forms of humor indicate that they shared some of the some malaise as their male colleagues in the culture off campus. And it would have been strange if it had not been so: for all the lamenting about the ivory tower's ability to seal its occupants off from what passes in street philosophy as "the real world," the dwellers in academe have also remained members of their larger cultures as well and have responded to the same undercurrents that touched everyone (even though their sometimes elite vision of academe let them feel they were somehow above it all). In this matter, as in so many of the instances mentioned previously in this essay, the folklorist must try to employ both the insider's help with interpretation and the outsider's use of comparative and analytical scholarship.

Graduating students wear black robes at commencement exercises because they have become customary and are thus the only thing available; yet a cynical "belief" circulating among some college women that these are black robes of mourning, imposed as an outward show of penance and punishment for those who have not succeeded in finding a mate during their four years at college. An incautious anthropologist/folklorist from another culture might easily use traditional items such as these, bolstered by the testimony of some insiders, to show that in spite of technological advances, Americans are highly superstitious, that they prize virginity but believe it does not exists, that they believe some statues can speak or move when presented with miraculous phenomena, that they value marriage so highly that they force unsuccessful candidates for matrimony to walk, to the accompaniment of a dirge and in robes of mourning, to an open field, where they are chastised by senile priests who tell them they are now to become the servants of their more successful former colleagues.[26]

Such a statement would strike us as humorous, unless it were put forward as a serious theory to explain the American national character; then we would treat it as ludicrous and full of errors. As a parody of college attitudes held by some, such a charade would be thought clever; as an *explanation* of college attitudes, it would fail. The reader might indeed marvel that such a far-out example of potential misunderstanding is brought forth here, but some reading into early folkloristic and anthropological researches shows that many theories about other groups of people have been constructed on the same inability to distinguish what might be called *artistic superstition* (beliefs that are passed along because they—or the way they were stated—may appeal somehow humorously, esthetically, psychologically to the group and the attitudes it needs to express) from *religious superstition* (beliefs and customs that are taken seriously and are considered to one degree or another obligatory to members of the group). Since the term "superstition" is justifiably going out of fashion (because it carries the connotation of erroneous or ignorant belief, especially the mistaken views of others), perhaps a better set of terms here would be "traditional imagery" (where the image or its expression acts as a touchstone, a reference point, a dramatic foregrounding, of values shared by a group of people) and "traditional belief" (where belief, or its expression, actualizes some seriously taken set of values which must appear in thought and custom in order for the world to seem normal and for the individual to be able to navigate in that world with a minimum of threat). Neither of these forms of traditional expression, none of the other genres mentioned in this essay, should be seen in any way as backward or ignorant. Rather they should be taken as testimony that the folk groups of academe function as other folk groups do—with an internal dynamism that is expressed in oral and gestural traditions shared by most full members of the group.

As is the case with other folk groups, there is in academe a tendency to exaggerate and intensify certain symbolic traditions. Immigrants far from their original homes, surrounded by strange peoples, often foreground a few selected foodways or family customs or gestures which function as ritual forms of identification and stability. Ethnic groups, often under pressure of prejudice from outsiders, will elevate even the simplest shared ingredient of their lives to the status of sacrament: soul food, for example. College students, often away from parents for the first extended period, perched on the edge of adulthood, anxiously anticipating their entry into a real world of competition, failure, and success, engage in a number of exaggerated traditions which speak to the pressures and stresses of their psychological position. The prim behavior, compulsive grooming, and impeccable dress of Rush Week anticipate in hyperbolic forms the presumed necessary behavior in adult polite society, just as the later beer busts, hell weeks, toga parties, and pig dances enact an orgiastic rejection of these same rules of acceptable behavior in the opposite extreme. This double vision of behavior, acted out in traditions of some antiquity, expresses the psychological dilemma of the college student in particular: old enough to drink, work, fight in wars on the one hand, dependent on money from state or parent, dependent on the tastes of overbearing professors, dependent on the vagaries of a changing job market on the other. Independent adults they may be, but their arrested youth allows them, in the words of one cynical professor, to have their parents and eat them, too.

Nowhere is this schizophrenia more evident than in the hundreds of drinking games in which students compete with each other to see who can drink himself into oblivion first. Games such as Pig, Thumper, Quarters, Caps, Categories, Fuzz-Buzz, Cardinal Puff, Snaps, Matches, 99, Chugs, Funnel, Tap Run, Straw Races, Shotgun, Hi Bob, Love Boat, Prince of Whales, Zoom Schwartz Pigfigliano, Spoons, and Salute (the variety of names is itself a testimony to the intense interest in providing ritual situations for heavy drinking) are mostly structured ways of simply getting drunk together. But why get drunk together? And why do people enjoy it more (or seem to) when using a traditional game, when one could probably drink alcohol faster just by consuming it doggedly? And why, if the university is where people come to train their minds, has drinking itself, and the traditional games in which drinking is the central aim, become such an intensely developed activity? The students themselves say they play these games "to have fun and get drunk," but this does not even start to answer our questions. Perhaps the relaxation afforded by drinking helps to take the edge off the stresses of academe. If so, this would indicate that academe is a more stressful place than we have imagined, and we might suggest that folklore within this folk group provides us with some indicators of how and why this might be the case. Also, we notice that the drinking games usually offer the same kind of meaningless competition that the students find themselves engaged in in class. Perhaps the orgiastic exaggeration of such competition in the pursuit of unconsciousness provides students with a subtle (and cynical) symbol of a meaningful source of anxiety in their daily lives. There may be a number of explanations, but I think the least likely one would be the simple observation that students are all becoming alcoholics, for that also overlooks the strong component of tradition, shared values, ritual, and formulaic language: features of folklore that are obviously central to the issue.

The view of academic folklore offered here is of necessity general and relatively superficial. In following some of these topics further in their own specific research, students will find that careful folkloristic scrutiny of their own culture will lead not only to valuable considerations about the operation of folklore in general, but to the realization that their own traditions include complexes of customary belief and expression that are significant and absorbing in and of themselves. Most important, students will find that folklore is far from dead, even far from tired, and certainly far from being buried by the purveyors of mass folkiness. Folklore is more than the chance survival of antique oddments: it is the informal but vital form of human expression that embodies most powerfully those social, psychological, biological, and artistic elements lying at the heart of cultural experience.

NOTES

[1] See, for example, the editor's introductory remarks in Dundes, *The Study of Folklore*, pp. 1–3.

[2] For a more exhaustive exposition of this concept, see Barre Toelken, *The Dynamics of Folklore* (Boston: Houghton Mifflin, 1979), esp. pp. 23–149.

[3] See Jan Harold Brunvand, "Desk-Top Inscriptions from the University of Idaho," *NWF* 1 (Winter 1966): 20–22; also Allen Walker Read, *Lexical Evidence from Folk Epigraphy in Western North America: A Glossarial Study of the Low Element in the English Vocabulary* (Paris: privately printed, 1935; repr. as *Classic American Graffiti* Waukesha, Wisc.: Maledicta Press, 1977).

[4] In addition, the student should also consult Daniel R. Barnes, "Some Functional Horror Stories on the Kansas University Campus," *SFQ* 30 (1966): 312–31; L. Michael Bell, "Cokelore," *WF* 35 (1976): 59–65 (repr. in *Readings in American Folklore*, pp. 99–105); Michael L. Crawford, "Legends from St. Mary-of-the-Woods College," *IF* 7 (1974): 53–75; Martha Dirks, "Teenage Folklore in Kansas," *WF* 23 (1963): 89–102; Dorson, *American Folklore*, esp. pp. 254–67: Dorson, "The Folklore of Colleges," *American Mercury* 48 (1949): 671–77; Susan Martin Fagan, "Ten Words for a Dollar—a New Campus Custom," *WF* 40 (1981): 337–43; Sylvia Ann Grider, "*Con Safos:* Mexican-Americans, Names, and Graffiti," *JAF* 88 (1975): 132–42 (repr. in *Readings in American Folklore*, pp. 138–51); Grider, "Dormitory Legend-Telling in Progress: Fall 1971–Winter 1973," *IF* 6 (1973): 1–32; James Gary Lecocq, "The Ghost of the Doctor and a Vacant Fraternity House," *IF* 6 (1973): 191–204; Marilyn Ruth Schlesinger, "Riddling Questions from Los Angeles High School Students," *WF* 19 (1960): 191–95; Terrance L. Stocker and others "Social Analysis of Graffiti,"

JAF 85 (1972): 356–66; Betty Suffern, " 'Pedro' at California," *WF* 18 (1959): 326; and Francis Very, "Parody and Nicknames among American Youth," *JAF* 75 (1962): 262–63.

⁵ A convincing delineation of the in-group versus outsider complex as it relates to the study of folklore is given by William Hugh Jansen, "The Esoteric-Exoteric Factor in Folklore," *Fabula: Journal of Folktale Studies* 2 (1959): 205–11 (repr. in *The Study of Folklore*, pp. 43–51).

⁶ An engaging account of the methods used by some academicians is given by Alan Dundes in "Chain Letter: A Folk Geometric Progression," *NWF* 1 (Winter 1966): 14–19.

⁷ For traditional narratives and beliefs about cheating on examinations, see Lew Girdler, "The Legend of the Second Blue Book," *WF* 29 (1970): 111–13.

⁸ Brunvand discusses such items briefly in two notes on "Sex in the Classroom," *JAF* 73 (1960): 250–51, and 75 (1962): 62–63.

⁹ Many such legends are taken up by Brunvand in *The Vanishing Hitchhiker: American Urban Legends and Their Meanings* (New York: Norton, 1981) and in *The Choking Doberman and Other "New" Urban Legends* (New York: Norton, 1984).

¹⁰ A complex of related stories is reported from the New Orleans area in Mary C. Senn, "Mona Lisa, Is That You?" *LFM* 5 (1983): 27–30, and E. O. Chambers, "The Mona Lisa Legend of City Park, New Orleans," *ibid.*, 31–39.

¹¹ Linda Dégh and Alan Dundes both discuss functions and meanings of such stories in their contributions to *American Folk Legend: A Symposium*, ed. Wayland D. Hand (Berkeley and Los Angeles: University of California Press, 1971).

¹² See Bruce Jackson, "The Greatest Mathematician in the World: Norbert Wiener Stories," *WF* 31 (1972): 1–22, and James T. Bratcher, "The Professor Who Didn't Get His Grades In: A Travelling Anecdote," *PTFS* 36 (1972): 121–23.

¹³ Linda Dégh and Andrew Vázsonyi, "The Memorate and the Proto-Memorate," *JAF* 87 (1974): 225–39.

¹⁴ Delta Gamma.

¹⁵ Inside informants on these and other esoteric customs of the campus tongs have asked to remain anonymous, for obvious reasons.

¹⁶ See Anonymous, "Scatological Lore on Campus," *JAF* 75 (1962): 260–62.

¹⁷ Alexander Hobbs, "Downie's Slaughter," *Aberdeen University Review* 45 (1973): 183–91.

¹⁸ William R. Bascom discusses this and other related concepts in "Four Functions of Folklore," *JAF* 67 (1954): 333–49 (repr. in *The Study of Folklore*, esp. pp. 287–91).

¹⁹ George Hornbein, Marie Hornbein, Tom Keiter, and Kenneth Thigpen, *Salamanders: A Night at the Phi Delt House*, 14 minute color film, 16 mm (State College, Pa.: Documentary Resource Center, 1982).

²⁰ As Michael Preston has done in "The Traditional Ringing at Temple Buell College," *WF* 32 (1973): 271–74.

²¹ Even those who are familiar with the old song "Blow the Candles Out" do not immediately associate the metaphor—used there to denote sexual intercourse—with their own practice. For a discussion of several fruits and flowers in connection with the process of sex in traditional metaphor, see Barre Toelken, " 'Riddles Wisely Expounded,' " *WF* 25 (1966): 1–16.

²² Richard M. Dorson mentions a few of them in "The Eclipse of Solar Mythology," *JAF* 68 (1955): 393–416 (repr. in *The Study of Folklore*, pp. 57–83).

²³ The statistical observations here and throughout the essay are based on a number of questions given to a total of 627 students at four Western U.S. colleges: the Universities of Oregon and Utah, Portland State, and Reed College. The classes in which these questions were given were of different sizes, and students did not all answer all questions; thus the statistics are not reliable for anything beyond indicating a tendency or demonstrating that a particular item was known or practiced. For high-school customs, I am indebted to numerous public-school teachers, including Rob Roy, Lily Uno Havey, Ray Schofield, and Walt Bolton, among many others. Students and colleagues who have helped compile many of the materials discussed in this essay include Penelope Diumenti, Saundra Keyes, Carolyn Middlemiss, Lee Newcomer, Brenda Russell, Ralph Wirfs, Polly Deemer, JoZell Johnson, Becky Reynolds, and archivists Susan Fagan and Janet Cliff.

²⁴ To be sure, many professors make their own rules about how long a class should wait before abandoning the room; however, in most cases, the professors themselves give the traditional formula—depending on their degree—and pass it on to their classes saying, "At this university it is the custom to wait . . ." I have conducted an ardent, but thus far fruitless, search for the college or university that prescribes in its written codes how long a class must wait for a tardy professor.

²⁵ For example, see Herbert Passin and John W. Bennett, "Changing Agricultural Magic in Southern Illinois: A Systematic Analysis of Folk-Urban Transition," *Social Forces* 22 (1943): 98–106 (repr. in *The Study of Folklore*, pp. 314–28).

²⁶ Such a study would not have taken into account the recent developments in graduation custom: shorts and other sportswear worn underneath the robe; flower leis on Hawaiian graduates; models, cartoons, and signs attached to the mortarboard or the robe; bottles of champagne carried secretly and popped off during the long commencement speech. These newer elements would certainly not support the image suggested superficially by the black robes and solemn music.

Further studies of the folklore of academe, mostly recent, are William H. Beezley, "Better Ag Than Fag!—and Other Carolina Jokes,"

NCFJ 29 (1981): 112–19; George W. Boswell, "Irony in Campus Speech," *TFSB* 45 (1979): 154–60; Donald Brenneis, " 'Turkey,' 'Wienie,' 'Animal,' 'Stud': Intragroup Variation in Folk Speech," *WF* 36 (1977): 238–46; Oliver Finley Graves, "Folklore in Academe: The Anecdote of the Professor and the Transom," *IF* 12 (1979): 142–45; Carolyn Hunter, "Folklore on the Prudish Campus, or Watch Out for the Dean of Women," *SWF* 1 (1977): 11–29; James P. Leary, "The Notre Dame Man: Christian Athlete or Dirtball?" *JFI* 15 (1978): 133–45; Melissa Caswell Mason, "Sorority Serenading: Its Pretext and Defense," *FMS* 1 (1977): 51–52; Roger E. Mitchell, "Campus Drug Lore and the Sociology of Rumor," *MJLF* 8 (1982): 89–108; and Vance Randolph, "A Survival of Phallic Superstition in Kansas," *Psychoanalytic Review* 15

The Types of the Southern Mountain Cabin*

by Henry Glassie

Henry Glassie, one of the first systematic tillers of the field of material folk traditions in the United States, especially folk architecture, has trained a generation of students in this field. An early master's degree recipient of the now-defunct American Folk Culture Program at Cooperstown, New York, and a University of Pennsylvania Ph.D. in folklore, Glassie supports his considerable field-work experience in the Southern Appalachians and elsewhere with a solid theoretical basis and an excellent grounding in the international bibliography of folklife scholarship. Glassie is presently professor of folklore and American civilization at the University of Pennsylvania.

*This paper is a survival from an earlier day in folkloristic studies of architecture. Its basic historical assertions, that there are two Southern Mountain cabin forms, one English (the square), one Irish and west British (the rectangular); and that log construction has a Germanic provenance, have held together fairly well over the period since the article's composition. Other things have changed. Much more information is in, both European and American, and the paper's cultural conclusions can be refined. Many people have turned and are continuing to turn to folk architectural—or "vernacular" architectural—research. The static, classificatory mode of vision presented as the "methodology" of the piece has been replaced by more dynamic and true, tougher, deeper approaches to man-made realities. And most importantly, the period of collection and annotation has passed. Studies of material manifestations of culture have caught up. Data have accumulated. It is time to talk about bigger matters, matters of structure and functions, meanings and values. The reader wishing to become more up to date, bibliographically and conceptually, is referred to my own overly recondite but earnest book, *Folk Housing in Middle Virginia: A Structural Analysis of Historic Artifacts* (Knoxville: University of Tennessee Press, 1976); see pp. 43–46, 51, 75, 80–85, 88, 104–6, 117–8, 148–52, 200–3 for later thinking on the cabins; see pp. 223–27 for more recent writings on folk architecture; see Chapter 3 for field methods, Chapters 3–5 for more modern ways to the analysis of form, Chapters 6–8 for more speculative and probing interpretive possibilities.

The essentially simple system that Glassie offers for placing in order widely varying artifacts demonstrates effectively how theoretical concepts in folklore may arise out of a bewildering mass of data. An excellent student project along similar lines would be to measure, describe, and catalogue a collection of other folk artifacts, such as folded paper toys, homemade rural mailbox stands, or snowmen. Or, if cabins still exist in their locality, students could visit and measure them in order to learn how closely they fit the formal types that are described by Glassie. Other kinds of American folk architecture appropriate for study are suggested in Chapter 20.

Glassie's fine drawings not only clarify his explanations, but also show what a "collection" of buildings may consist of apart from open-air folk museums. However, even simple line sketches or clear photographs of folk structures may serve to document them for a usable record.

The study of which this paper is part began in 1961 as a rambling field survey of the folk architecture of the upland South, stretching from eastern Pennsylvania through western Arkansas.[1] From this large area a smaller one emerged which seemed to be central to the understanding of the traditional architecture of those areas initially settled from either Pennsylvania or the tidewater South. This area (Fig. 1) is only a part of the Southern Appalachian region; it includes the Blue Ridge from northern Virginia to northern Georgia, including the Great Smokies and their foothills; the southern and central valley of Virginia; and the eastern escarpment of the Alleghenies in Virginia and West Virginia. It does not include the Cumberlands, the southwestern limits of the Southern Mountains, and most of the Tennessee Valley, as these Appalachian areas received less direct Pennsylvania German influence and are a part of a different architectural complex, which is comparatively Southern in orientation. This area is not lacking in either historical or topographical continuity, but it has been established not by geography but by architecture: there are folk-architectural elements common in the areas adjacent to the one under study but rare or peripheral within it; examples include the flue-curing tobacco barn,[2] square- and diamond-notched corner timbering on log buildings,[3] and the dog trot house.[4] It is no accident that this is the same area that continues to yield up an amazing quantity of European-American folklore, for just as songs and tales which were probably common in other areas may now be found with regularity only in the mountains, construction techniques and building forms (including the cabins with which this paper deals) once usual but now rare in southeastern Pennsylvania and the coastal South remain common and vital in the Southern Mountains.

FIGURE 1.   AREA OF THE SOUTHERN MOUNTAIN FOLK ARCHITECTURAL
COMPLEX.

It is only within this area that the field survey was intense and systematic; however, those areas which contributed to the mountain culture and to which the mountain culture contributed were also sampled.
All kinds of structures—not only houses, barns, and other outbuildings, but fences, bridges, and haystacks as well—were entered in the
field notes.

Once a ponderous bulk of field material has been accumulated the
problem of what to do with it arises; to let it lie unorganized in a closet

would be selfish. The usual collections of American folksong or tale include all of the items (or at least those that are intuitively folk) which were collected. The great amount of field material available to students of folk architecture and necessary for their study to be significant normally precludes the publication of a description, drawings, and photograph of each building. Students, therefore, must order their examples into reasonable types, and, after the conclusion of their field work, the establishment of these types is the first, the most important, and the most often misdirected step of their study.

The study of American material folk culture is so young that a well-classified study could be of value, and one of the few solid works on American folk architecture, Charles H. Dornbusch's *Pennsylvania German Barns*,[5] is simply a classification. Generally, the folklorist goes beyond this stage and, by adding bibliographical notes at the heads or feet of his collectanea, suggests the spatial and temporal patterns which include his material. It may be that the study of some aspects of folklife —Child ballads, for instance—is moving past the "collection, classification, and annotation phase," but the study of material culture in America has not, and cannot for many years.

The following treatment of the cabins observed within the area sketched above is offered in order to give some idea of how folk architecture may be classified and annotated. The characteristics that most cabins share will be considered first, and then the formal, historical, and distributional aspects of the cabins which separate them into two basic types—the square and the rectangular—will be outlined.[6]

These two basic house types are classified as cabins because both are composed of a single construction unit and both are less than two stories high.[7] Americans often find it difficult to say "cabin" without prefixing it with "log,"[8] but, because house types can move through environmental zones with the same facility that tale types can, cabins were built of stone in Pennsylvania,[9] of brick in Virginia,[10] of log in Texas,[11] of frame in Louisiana,[12] of mud in Ireland,[13] of adobe in Utah.[14] Further, in areas where log construction was common, such as the Southern Mountains, it was employed not only on cabins, but also on bridges and turkey traps and buildings ranging from a four-by-six-foot corncrib to barns and mills measuring over fifty feet in length.[15]

In the building traditions of Scotland and Ireland, houses less than two stories high had the floor joists of the loft framed in at the top of the wall or at the plate—the horizontal beam at the top of the wall on which the rafters of the roof rest. A few Southern Mountain cabins were similarly constructed (Fig. 2A), but the great majority had the

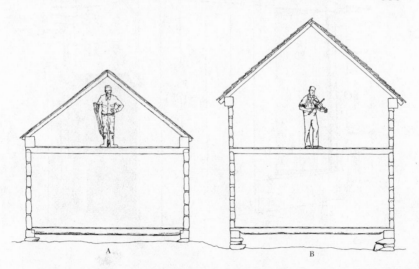

FIGURE 2.   CROSS SECTIONS THROUGH SOUTHERN MOUNTAIN CABINS.
A. Half-dovetailed, rectangular log cabin situated south of Del Rio, near Nough, Cocke County, Tennessee (May 1966). B. V-notched, square log cabin situated near Woodville, Rapahannock County, Virginia (May 1963).

floor joists of the loft framed in three to five feet—two, four, or, usually, three logs in cabins of log—below the plate, affording considerably more headroom (Fig. 2B). Some one-story houses were so constructed in England, particularly in those areas in which stone construction predominated.[16] But they were not usual in the English colonies of the New World,[17] and it seems likely that the height of the usual mountain cabin is the result of Pennsylvania German influence, for the characteristic German cabins in Pennsylvania were constructed in the same manner.[18]

The cabin loft is usually unheated, though a small fireplace has been observed in a few (Fig. 5C); it is used for the storage of trunks, medicinal herbs, dried fruits, smoked meat, and odd "plunder" such as old harness and license plates; formerly the spinning was often done in the loft. Only the older children sleep in the loft; their parents sleep in a low bed in a corner of the ground-floor room. The room generally contains, in addition to the bed, a table, a cupboard, a bench, perhaps a "boughten" couch (used at night as a bed, just as the bed serves as a

FIGURE 3. BOXED-IN STAIRS IN SOUTHERN MOUNTAIN CABINS.

A. From the square cabin pictured in Fig. 7A; situated south of Fletcher, near Hood, Green County, Virginia (July 1963). B. From a V-notched square cabin situated between Free Union and Boonesville, Albemarle County, Virginia (August 1964).

couch during the day), and a great many chairs (usually mule-eared slat-backs with seats woven of hickory splints or strips of inner tube) which spill out the front door onto the porch or into the bare front yard. The interior walls are whitewashed, papered (ceiling as well as walls) with newspaper, or covered with planed boards usually nailed on vertically. On the walls are hung clothes and firearms, framed oval daguerreotypes of stern and startled ancestors and bright prints (acquired, probably, as a part of a bargain package from WCKY or WWVA) of The Last Supper or Christ in the Garden.[19] In a few cabins the loft is reached via a ladder, and in a very few the floor is an earth one, such as was very common in Ireland and throughout Britain.[20] But, usually, a "boxed in" late medieval[21] stair leads to the loft. The stair, which often has the cabin's only closet under it, is built in a corner or along one wall, usually that opposite the fireplace (Fig. 3). And the floor is almost always composed of boards nailed over "sleepers"— logs hewn flat only on the top—framed in between the sills—the large squared beams placed at the bottom of the front and rear walls (Fig. 2).

Both of the mountain cabin types have an external chimney in the center of one gable end (Fig. 4). External chimneys were not unknown in Switzerland,[22] and it is conceivable that this continental tradition trickled through Pennsylvania and Maryland into the northwestern valley of Virginia;[23] the predominance of the external chimney in the Southern Mountains, however, is owed to English influence. The external chimney was primarily a Mediterranean tradition[24] and was taken at an early date, possibly with the Normans,[25] from France to England (Fig. 4A, B). Though found in many sections of England, it is most common in the West Midlands and on both sides of the Welsh border.[26] It became standard in the coastal regions of the South (Fig. 4C) during the earliest period of settlement and was carried from the Chesapeake Bay westward by settlers of English background and contributed to the predominantly German and Scotch-Irish architectural tradition in the upland areas of Maryland and Virginia. The chimneys in the Tidewater were brick; in the mountains they usually are of "rock" mortared with mud (Fig. 4E, F), although a few, particularly in eastern Tennessee, were built entirely of brick, and many were built of stone to the top of the fireplace, or to the shoulders (Fig. 4D), with the remainder of brick. The fireplace (Fig. 5) had a shallow "firebox" to throw the heat out into the room, and, like hearths throughout the British Isles,[27] an iron pole was placed across it (Fig. 5A) or a swinging crane was placed at one side on which kettles were hung. The cabin chimney does not have a built-in bake oven, for the mountain people, like the

A   B   C

D   E   F

FIGURE 4. EXTERNAL CHIMNEYS IN ENGLAND, THE TIDEWATER, AND THE
SOUTHERN MOUNTAINS.

A. Sussex, England; after W. Galsworthy Davie and E. Guy Dawber,
Old Cottages and Farmhouses in Kent and Sussex (London: Bastford,
1900), plate 49. B. Gloucestershire, England; after Charles Holme, ed.,
Old English Country Cottages (London, Paris, New York: Studio, 1906),
p. 85. C. Tidewater chimney situated in Port Royal, Caroline County,
Virginia (July 1963). D. From a V-notched rectangular cabin situated
southwest of Millboro Spring, Bath County, Virginia (July 1964). E.
From a weatherboarded rectangular log cabin, situated south of Marion, Smyth County, Virginia (July 1964). F. From a vertical boarded
rectangular frame cabin situated in Dunn's Rock Community, Transylvania County, North Carolina (August 1964).

Irish and Scots and unlike the English and central Europeans,[28] traditionally do not bake in ovens but rather make bread in a pot, on a flat
board, stone, or skillet, or in a bed of ashes beside the fire.

The basic cabin types share with the other Southern Mountain house
types certain characteristics of construction. Until World War I—the
great folk-cultural watershed—most of the cabins were built of horizontal log, though a few of the oldest cabins extant are of frame. In the
past half century most have been built of frame and only a few of log.
Southern Mountain log construction (Fig. 6L–N) is characterized by
logs, usually hardwood, hewn flat on the front and back, or, less commonly, split in half and then hewn on the outside.[29] Although the logs
employed in the construction of outbuildings are often left in the
round, less than 3 percent of the over five hundred log houses surveyed
within this area were built of unhewn log.[30] Wide interstices were left
between the logs, which were "daubed with mud," "chinked" with
mud and stones, shingles or rails, or covered with boards. The interstices were often finished off with a layer of lime plaster. Two major
methods were used to join the logs at the corner. Both were used
throughout the area, but one—V-notching (Fig. 6K, N)—predomi-
nates in Virginia, and the other—half-dovetailing (Fig. 6G, L, M)—in
Tennessee and North Carolina. These two types of corner-timbering
are closely related: both are notched on only the bottom of the log, and
in both the ends of the logs are cut off flush producing a box corner
(Fig. 6E).

Log construction was unknown in England[31] and, except for military
construction,[32] in the English colonies.[33] It was employed during the
seventeenth century by the Swedes on the Delaware, and the early

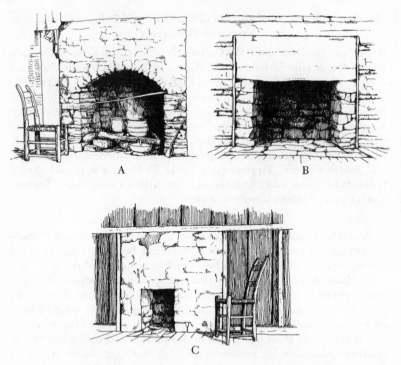

A   B

C

FIGURE 5.   FIREPLACES OF SOUTHERN MOUNTAIN CABINS.

A. After Morley, *The Carolina Mountains* (Boston and New York: Houghton Mifflin, 1913), facing p. 186. B. From a V-notched rectangular log cabin, situated east of Etowah, Henderson County, North Carolina (June 1963). C. From the loft of the frame square cabin pictured in Fig. 7B, situated between Crozet and Whitehall, Albermarle County, Virginia (August 1964).

scholars, hindered by a sketchy picture of European traditions, guessed that American log construction had its source in the tiny settlement of New Sweden.[34] Scandinavian log construction (Fig. 6A–C) is characterized by logs, usually pine, left in the round, or hewn to a square or hexagonal shape; by the absence of interstices between the logs; by the fact that the logs are notched on the top or both sides of the log; and by the fact that the ends of the logs extend a uniform distance beyond the corner of the building.[35] On each point, then, Scandinavian log work is markedly different from the American tradition.

Log construction in Europe is not confined to Scandinavia; it is also common in some of the several areas from which the Pennsylvania Germans came. In Switzerland and Germany, dovetailed log construction with box corners (Fig 6D), as well as construction of the Scandinavian type (Fig. 6F), is usual.[36] Similar dovetail construction was also known—but known rarely—in Scandinavia.[37] However, the Scandinavian and Swiss-German dovetailing lacked the chinked interstices so characteristic of American construction; and it is in Bohemia, western Moravia, and Silesia (now northwestern Czechoslovakia) that log construction of exactly the American type can be found (Fig. 6G–I).[38] Immigrants came to Pennsylvania from these areas, and although it is difficult to state why from a distance of 250 years, their construction (not that of the numerically dominant Swiss, and surely not that of the little group of Swedes who were becoming acculturated Englishmen) came to predominate in Pennsylvania, and from Pennsylvania it was carried, beginning in 1732, into the Southern Appalachian region.

In central Europe, southeastern Ireland, and the Scottish Highlands, the small houses often had hipped roofs; but in the mountains, as in medieval England, eighteenth-century Scotland, and northern and western Ireland,[39] the small houses have gable roofs. The cabin's gable roof is formed with simple rafters butted at the edge—the "comb"—either on each other or on a plank ridge pole; both of these roof-framing methods were common in medieval England; the latter was usual in Scotland and Ireland, the former in Germany and throughout the American colonies.[40] Over the rafters, horizontal roofing boards were nailed, and to them were nailed split shingles, called "shakes"[41] in the North but just "boards" in the mountains. Such split shingles were very common in England until the end of the fourteenth century; at the time of the first settlement of America they were still being employed in southern England and the English planted areas of Ireland.[42] They remain common in central Europe,[43] and were employed until the mid-nineteenth century throughout the eastern United States[44] and nearly to the present in the Southern Mountains. The gable ends of the cabin were not built up of succeedingly smaller logs,[45] as was usual in Scandinavia, but are covered with vertical boards (fig. 9D), as in central Europe and Southeastern Pennsylvania,[46] or, more commonly, with horizontal, overlapping weatherboards (Fig. 7C, 9B) nailed to vertical studs framed between the top log in the end wall and the end pair of rafters.

The cabins, like the other mountain house types, were often enlarged by traditional additions. These additions may be viewed either as appendages to a basic type or as creating new types.[47] Cabins very

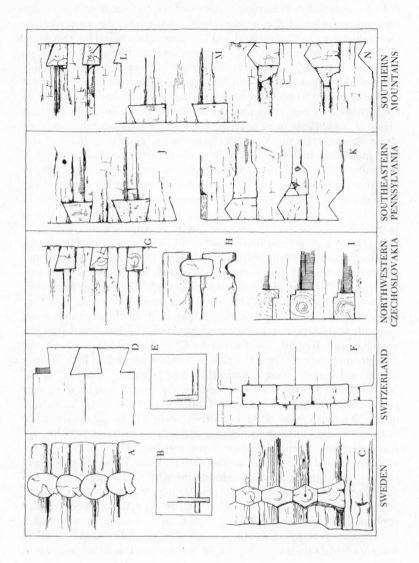

often have a shed or lean-to addition, which almost always serves as a kitchen; it is usually built onto the rear of the cabin (Figs. 7C, 9B–D), but may also be placed on one end (Fig. 7B). This form of addition is distinctly British; it is particularly common in western England[48] and was usual in the early English colonies.[49] Frequently, a front porch (Fig. 9B, 9D, 10C) balances the rear shed and provides what, in the summer, amounts to an additional room. Much less usual than shed additions or porches, are ells, gabled wings added at right angles to the rear of the cabin. A rare form of addition, which has been observed only at the southern end of the North Carolina Blue Ridge, consisted of a separate cabin built immediately behind the original cabin so that their ridges were parallel. These additions should be considered appendages to a basic type, not altering the classification of the example, for houses did not become consistently built as a whole composed of a

FIGURE 6.   HORIZONTAL LOG CORNER-TIMBERING.

A. After Boëthius, *Studier i den nordiska timmerbyggnadskonsten*, Fig. 117, p. 126. B. View from above of the corner of a log building with the ends of the logs extending beyond the plane of the wall, as is usual in Scandinavian tradition. C. After Erixon in *Folkliv*, 1937:1, plate II, 1, p. 18. D. After *Schweizer Volkskunde* 47:5–6 (1957): Fig. 5, p. 73. E. View from above of the corner of a log building with the ends of the log cut off flush producing a box corner, as is usual in central European and American tradition. F. From a photograph taken in the Canton of Zug, by Henry H. Glassie, Sr., in the autumn of 1964. G. After *Slovenský Nárdodopis* 9(1961): p. 522. H. After *Český Lid* 50:4 (1963): photos after p. 224. This corner-timbering is comparable to V-notching. Several outbuildings, though no houses, have been observed in the North Carolina Blue Ridge constructed with exactly this form of corner-timbering. I. After *Etnographica* 3–4 (1961–62), plate 60. J. Full-dovetail corner-timbering from a house near Pine Grove, Schuylkill County, Pennsylvania (July 1962). Full-dovetailing appears also in the northwestern valley of Virginia. K. V-notching from a house situated near Mount Nebo, Lancaster County, Pennsylvania (July 1963). L. Half-dovetail corner-timbering from a house near Bald Creek Community, Yancey County, North Carolina (June 1963). Half-dovetailing is found commonly also in central Pennsylvania. M. Half-dovetail corner-timbering from a house situated near Zionville, Watauga County, North Carolina (July 1963). N. V-notching from a house situated between Rock Oak and Rio, Hardy County, West Virginia (June 1964).

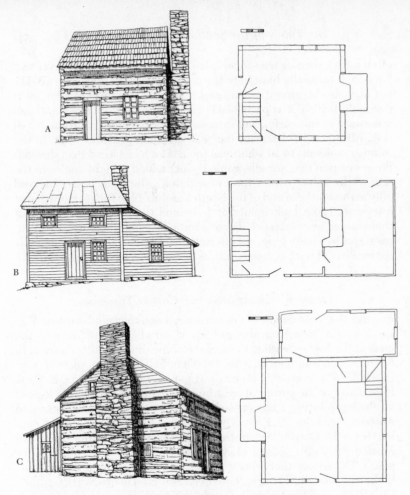

FIGURE 7. SOUTHERN MOUNTAIN CABINS OF THE SQUARE TYPE.

A. V-notched cabin situated south of Fletcher, near Hood, Greene County, Virginia (July 1963). By May 1966 this cabin had fallen to ruins. B. This cabin was built of balloon (light, sawed, nailed together) frame covered with vertical boards. When the shed was added to the chimney end, both parts were covered with weatherboards. It is situated between Crozet and Whitehall, Albemarle County, Virginia (August 1964). C. V-notched cabin with rear shed addition situated north of Boones Mill, Roanoke County, Virginia (August 1965). The rear door was apparently cut through when the shed was added, for it swings outward rather than in. This is the largest square cabin that has been observed in the Southern Mountains.

cabin in combination with any one of these features. The addition of a gabled room onto the end of the existent house was the most usual form of addition through most of Europe; in some parts of Ireland it was thought to mean death to add elsewhere.[50] Gabled end additions were often made onto mountain cabins; the resultant two-room house types —two types depending upon whether the addition was made onto the chimney end or the end opposite the chimney—came to be constructed commonly as wholes throughout the South, so, while these types were an important part of the survey of mountain architecture, they lie outside the narrow scope of this paper.

The two basic cabin types which share the characteristics discussed thus far, now will be established.

The Square Cabin

The floorplan of the square cabin is roughly sixteen feet square, though the square proportions are more significant than any specific size. The most usual dimensions are 16' × 16' and 16' × 18'; other dimensions include 14' × 16', 15' × 15', 15' × 17', 18' × 18', 21' × 21'. It has a gable roof and an external chimney in the center of one gable end. Only very rarely is it partitioned into two rooms (Fig. 7C). The front door is located near the center of the front wall or is displaced on the front wall away from the chimney end of the house (Fig. 7A). Occasionally, there is a second door in the gable end opposite the chimney (Figs, 7A, 11B). Characteristically, there is no rear door. It very often has a shed addition on the rear (Fig. 7C) and occasionally on one end (Fig. 7B); ell additions are not usual. There may be a second large external chimney built onto the addition. Front porches are not very common.

It has often been written that the sixteen-foot unit—the bay—originated during the Anglo-Saxon period as a response to the stabling requirements of oxen,[51] and it is possible that the square proportions are the result of the squaring off of the Neolithic British hut circle.[52] Be that as it may, it is enough to say that the sixteen-foot bay had become traditional by the Tudor period and that it was employed commonly in the construction of English cottages, many of which were composed of one room, roughly sixteen feet square, with a loft above (Fig. 8A).[53] The most usual one-room house throughout the English colonies consisted of the traditional single bay.[54] The small square cabin is no longer commonly found in the Tidewater of the South, but a few examples have been observed up on the coastal plain (Fig. 8B) and into the Piedmont, from where it was carried into the Virginia Blue Ridge. The only

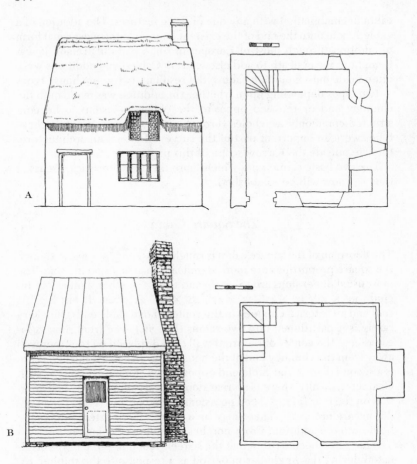

FIGURE 8.   ANTECEDENTS OF THE SQUARE CABIN.

FIGURE 8.   ANTECEDENTS OF THE SQUARE CABIN.

A. Square stone English house; after Wood-Jones, *Traditional Domestic Architecture in the Banbury Region*, Fig. 51. B. Frame cabin of the type found in the coastal regions of the South; situated between Orchid and Gum Spring, Louisa County, Virginia (July 1963). This cabin was built into the end of a large frame house subsequent to its initial construction.

difference between the Tidewater-Piedmont and the Blue Ridge examples are that the pitch of the roof on the mountain cabin is less than that found farther east, and the loft higher; that the eastern examples occasionally have internal rather than external gable end chimneys (as in Fig. 8A); and that the mountain cabin is usually log with a stone chimney, whereas the Piedmont examples are usually weatherboarded frame with a brick chimney (Fig. 8B). Folk-architectural patterns, however, are not simple, and in the Piedmont of southern Virginia and northern North Carolina the square cabin is often of log, and several frame square cabins have been found in the mountains (Fig. 7B).

The square cabin is extremely common all along the eastern slopes of the Blue Ridge in Virginia. It is found only occasionally in the valley of Virginia and the Blue Ridge of Tennessee. It is also found occasionally in the Cumberlands and the Tennessee Valley, and, of either log or frame, in both the piney woods and river bottoms of the Deep South.

The Rectangular Cabin

The most usual dimensions of the rectangular cabin are 16′ × 22′ and 16′ × 24′; others include 14′ × 23′, 15′ × 20′, 15′ × 24′ 16′ × 26′, 17′ × 24′, and 18′ × 23′. It has a gable roof with an external chimney in the center of one gable end. It may consist of only one room but is frequently divided by a light partition into two rooms, the larger of which contains the fireplace and front door (Figs. 9C, 11D). Rarely there are two internal partitions producing a narrow central passage (Fig. 9D). The front door is located near the center of the front wall or is displaced on the front wall toward the chimney end of the house (Fig. 9A). There is characteristically a rear door in line with the front door. Shed additions are common; they are almost always built onto the rear (Fig. 9B–9D). Ell additions and front porches are more common than they are on square cabins. There is not usually a large chimney built onto the addition.

When the Scotch-Irish arrived in America, it was natural that they should build cabins of the type they had known in northern and western Ireland.[55] The cabins of Ulster, Connaught, and west Munster were composed of a single construction unit, measuring in the vicinity of 12′ × 20′, 13′ × 19′, 13′ × 22′, 14′ × 24′, or 18′ × 27′. They were usually partitioned into two rooms, the larger of which contained the hearth and front door; had an internal gable end chimney; and had opposed front and rear doors (Fig. 10A).[56] The traditional stone and mud con-

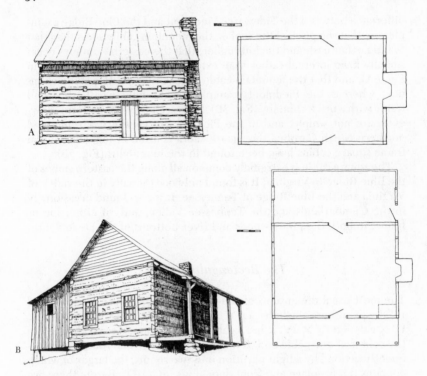

FIGURE 9.   SOUTHERN MOUNTAIN CABINS OF THE RECTANGULAR TYPE.

A. Half-dovetail cabin located west of Allen Gap, Greene County, Tennessee (August 1964). This is one of the few observed mountain cabins that has an earth floor. Like many other early log houses, this cabin has been converted into a tobacco barn. B. Half-dovetail cabin with front porch and rear shed additions situated in the Shelton Laurel area north of Marshall, Madison County, North Carolina (June 1963). In the front corner at the fireplace end of the cabin, there is a trap door in the loft floor to give access via a ladder to the loft.

struction of the Scotch-Irish[57] proved impractical in the New World forests, and these folk quickly adopted the log construction of their German neighbors. As a result, cabins very similar to those in Ireland may be found—though they are far from common today—in southeastern Pennsylvania and north-central Maryland built either of stone (Fig. 10B) or log (Fig. 10C). Although somewhat similar cabins may be found in southern Ireland,[58] Scotland,[59] England,[60] and, particularly,

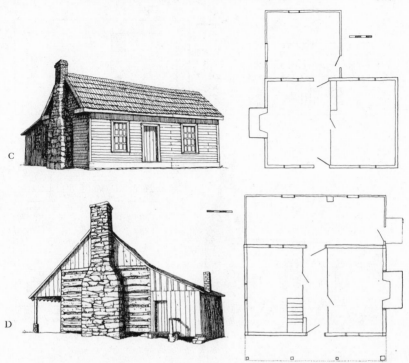

C. Weather-boarded frame cabin with late rear shed addition, situated west of Allen Gap, Greene County, Tennessee (May 1966). A cupboard is built into the partition. This cabin has Greek Revival trim of the type very common in the rural North during the second quarter of the nineteenth century (see Talbot Hamlin, *Greek Revival Architecture in America* [New York: Dover, 1964; reprint of 1944], generally pp. 258–310) but rare in the Southern Mountains. While built by a carpenter who had some awareness of the non-folk architectural mainstream of his period, this is a perfect example of the rectangular cabin type. D. V-notched cabin with front porch and rear shed additions situated north of Fairfield, Rockbridge County, Virginia (July 1963).

Wales,[61] it seems that the Ulster-Connaught, gable-chimney cabin, with only a change to the English-Tidewater external chimney, became the rectangular cabin type of the Southern Mountains.[6] This hypothesis is buttressed by two major formal characteristics the rectangular cabin shares with the cabins of northern and western Ireland, but that are not

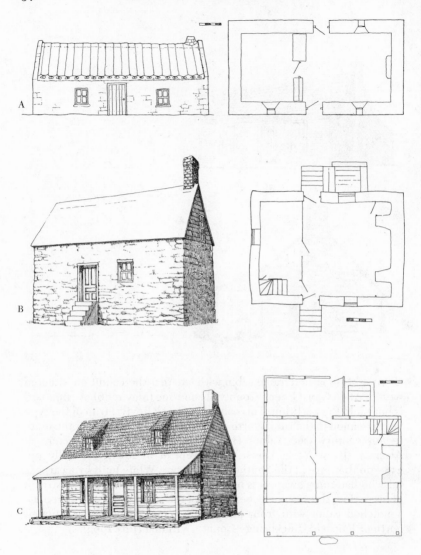

typical of the essentially English square cabin. The first is that this cabin, while one construction unit, is, like the Irish and Scottish, often divided by a light partition into two rooms, the larger of which contains the fireplace. In the mountain cabins these partitions are almost always built of vertical boards and are whitewashed. The second characteristic is the opposed front and rear doors. Such opposed doors may be found widely in western Europe[63] but are usually part of a complex structure, such as the Welsh longhouse;[64] whereas, in Ireland, as in the mountains, they are found on one-room houses. These doors represent a survival from the period when the gable-chimney house type sheltered the farmer, his family, and his cattle; they facilitated the movement of stock and probably served to produce a draft for threshing and fire building.

The rectangular cabin appears most commonly in those areas in which the Pennsylvania influence was greater than that of the Tidewater. It is found occasionally through the valley of Virginia and the eastern Alleghenies, and is very common among the Blue Ridge of North Carolina and Tennessee and into the upland Piedmont of North Carolina.

The great majority of the cabins observed within the area of this study conformed very neatly to one of these two basic types. There are, however, a number that vary from the basic type in some significant feature. The most usual variant is of precisely the form of one of these types except that it lacks the chimney. These are very recent cabins,

FIGURE 10.   ANTECEDENTS OF THE RECTANGULAR CABIN.

A. Stone cabin with internal gable end chimney from County Kerry, Ireland; after Ó Danachair in *Ulster Folklife* 2 (1965): Fig. 1, p. 25. The partition is formed by a dresser and a cupboard. B. Stone cabin with internal gable end chimney, located west of Monkton, Baltimore County, Maryland (August 1965). C. V-notched log cabin with internal gable end chimney, front porch and rear shed additions, situated between Kingsville and Bel Air, Harford County, Maryland (July 1962). During the spring of 1966 this house partially burned. Some folklorists wish their informants to be sociopolitically aware; graffiti scribbled on the plastered wall of this cabin reflect the attitudes of the American countryman better than any "protest song": "Balto Co Politicians to do dam dirty work / cominist unions / UnGodly people They are a discrase to our cuntry / all so aganst non union people / Dont want the poor old time people to make a living / money hogs."

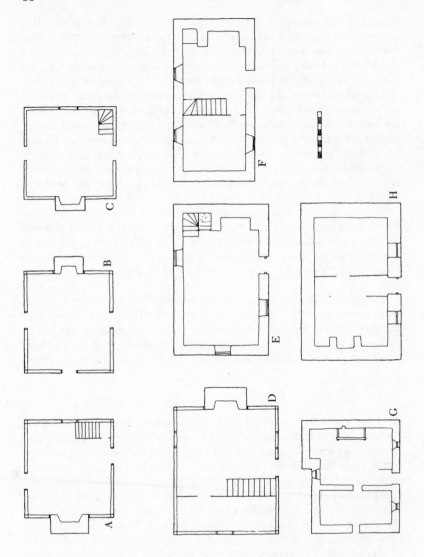

usually—but not always—frame, which have a stove for heating and cooking rather than the traditional chimney. The stove is served by a narrow brick flue usually built against the inside or outside of one gable wall. Another area of variation is in the doors. The square cabin typically has no rear door, although a few were observed that did have one; this rear door was not always in line with the front door (Fig. 11A), but in a few cases it was (Fig. 11B). This could be the result of influence from the Scotch-Irish rectangular cabin, although square cabins in the English-Tidewater tradition did occasionally have rear doors (Fig. 11C).[65] Similarly, a very few of the observed examples of the rectangular cabin had no rear door (Fig. 11D). A few of the observed rectangular stone cabins with internal gable end chimneys in southeastern Pennsylvania also lacked the rear door (Fig. 11E, F). In southern Ulster and ad-

FIGURE 11.   GROUND FLOOR PLANS OF VARIANT CABINS WITH THEIR ANTECEDENTS.

A. V-notched square log cabin situated between Whitehall and Crozet, Albemarle County, Virgina (May 1966). A frame addition was built onto the end of this cabin opposite the chimney, but it has since fallen in. B. Half-dovetail square log cabin situated in the Shelton Laurel area, north of Marshall, Madison County, North Carolina (June 1963). Note that this cabin has three doors but no windows. C. Frame cabin after Forman, *Tidewater Maryland Architecture and Gardens*, p. 67. D. Half-dovetail rectangular log cabin situated betwen Earlysville and Free Union, Albemarle County, Virginia (August 1964). Of all observed Southern Mountain cabins this was the most difficult to classify: it lacks a rear door like the square cabin; it is more square (four feet longer than wide) than the usual rectangular cabin and more rectangular than the usual square cabin. It is situated in an area in which square cabins are very common. Probably it is a rectangular cabin that has been influenced by the square cabin. E. Stone cabin situated southeast of Honey Brook, Chester County, Pennsylvania (May 1966). F. Stone cabin situated north of West Chester, Chester County, Pennsylvania (October 1965). G. From County Londonderry, Northern Ireland; after McCourt in *Gwerin* 3:4 (1961): Fig. 1, p. 169. At the rear of the kitchen is a "bed outshot," a feature that does not seem to have been transplanted to America; for it, see Caoimhin Ó Danachair's "The Bed Outshot in Ireland," *Folk-Liv* 19–20 (1955–56): 26–29; and Desmond McCourt's "The Outshot House-Type and Its Distribution in County Londonderry, *Ulster Folklife* 2 (1956): 27–34. H. From County Wicklow, Ireland; after Ó Danachair in *Béaloideas* 5 (1935): facing 211.

jacent Leinster,[66] the gable-chimney houses, possibly as a result of English influence,[67] often had no rear door (Fig. 11H). Further, the tradition of the opposed doors has been moribund in other parts of Ulster since before 1800 (Fig. 11G),[68] so that the American rectangular cabins lacking the rear door may represent a minor strain in the northwestern Irish gable-chimney house tradition rather than a nontraditional, individual innovation.

The proportions of the floorplans of the cabins—square or rectangular—very rarely presented a problem. The rectangular cabins were always twenty or more feet in length and almost always over five feet longer than wide. In the valley and Blue Ridge of Virginia a few cabins were measured which, while they appeared to be square cabins, were slightly more rectangular than usual. All of them were roughly sixteen feet long but were less than sixteen feet in width; almost all of them measured 17' × 14', and none was more than three feet longer than wide. In England the single bay houses were generally about sixteen feet in length but were often less wide than long,[69] so that these cabins follow in the English tradition and should be regarded as variants of the square cabin, particularly because all of their other characteristics—absence of the rear door, displacement of the front door away from the chimney end of the house—are the same as those of the square rather than the rectangular cabin.

From a study of this kind, two sets of conclusions may result. The first is methodological. For analysis any example or type must be broken down into its components; houses, while they appear as wholes, are combinations of separable parts. The mountain cabins are relatively simple house types, but any attempt to understand the cabin's history by considering only, as has been usual, its construction[70] or only the shape of its floorplan would yield a faulty picture. Once the components of a type have been recognized, they must be grouped into primary and secondary characteristics. For the mountain cabins the primary characteristics that define the type are approximate height, shape and general size of floorplan, placement of doors and chimney, and form of roof. The secondary characteristics, which do not help to define the type but which are still culturally significant, are exact height, construction of walls, type of roof framing and covering, precise size of floorplan, interior partitions, placement of windows and stairs, and types of appendages.

The second set of conclusions is cultural. Both mountain cabin types reflect some English influence in the external chimney and, possibly, some Pennsylvania German influence in the usual height. One is basically English in origin; the other is basically north Irish. The techniques used to construct the cabins were mainly Pennsylvania German (in log examples) and Anglo-American (in frame examples). To place these two types in a larger folk-architectural context, the other Southern Mountain house types to which a European provenance can be surely assigned (some of which are more common than the cabins) are all English. The types of the Southern Mountain barns, fences, and outbuildings are mostly Pennsylvania German or derived from German originals, with a few of English origin. Southern Mountain folk architecture is, then, predominantly Tidewater-English and Pennsylvania German; [71] yet the majority of the mountain people are of Scotch-Irish ancestry, and those Southern Mountain folk cultural elements that have received attention—most notably songs—seem to be a part of a north British, north Irish tradition. Architecture, therefore, tends to balance the picture of the mountain culture and indicate that the search for the origins of other elements of the Southern Mountain folk culture—such as pottery, tales, vehicles, food, quilt patterns, dance tunes, and firearms—should be carried on in central Europe and southern England as well as in the Lowlands of Scotland and northern and western Ireland.

NOTES

[1] An earlier form of this paper was read before the American Folklore Society in Denver, Colorado, November 20, 1965. I am indebted to Professors Fred Kniffen, E. Estyn Evans, and Bruce Buckley for help at various stages of the project.

[2] The flue-curing tobacco barn is common through the southern Virginia and North Carolina Piedmont immediately east of this area; see: John Fraser Hart's and Eugene Cotton Mather's "The Character of Tobacco Barns and Their Role in the Tobacco Economy of the United States," *Annals of the Association of American Geographers* 51 (1961): 288–93.

[3] Square-notched corner-timbering is common in the valley of Virginia north of this area through the Virginia and North Carolina Piedmont, and is found also in eastern Kentucky. A few, generally late examples have been observed within this area, particularly in the Smokies. Diamond-notched corner-timbering is common east of this area in Virginia and North Carolina; only one diamond-notched building has been observed within the area. For these types see: Fred Kniffen's and Henry Glassie's "Building in Wood in the Eastern United States: A Time-Place Perspective," *The Geographical Review* 56 (1966): 53–65.

[4] This type is found in the northern North Carolina Piedmont, in southeastern Kentucky, in the mountains of Alabama, the Tennessee

Valley and throughout the Deep South. Very few examples have been observed in the Blue Ridge of North Carolina and Tennessee. For this type see Edna Scofield's "The Evolution and Development of Tennessee Houses," *Journal of the Tennessee Academy of Science* 11 (1936): 229–40, and Martin Wright's "The Antecedents of the Double-Pen House Type," *Annals of the Association of American Geographers* 48 (1958): 109–17. The conclusions of both of these papers are questionable, but both present good material on the type.

⁵ The Pennsylvania German Folklore Society 21 (1956) (Allentown, 1958).

⁶ A bibliography of material on Southern Appalachian cabins would include the following, which while their quality is very uneven, contain an interesting note or two, and most include valuable photographs: Henry Howe's *Historical Collections of the Great West* (New York and Cincinnati: George F. Tuttle, 1857), 2, pp. 193–94, 262, 308; Frederick Law Olmsted's *A Journey in the Back Country* (New York: Mason Brothers, 1860), pp. 230–31, 237–38: James Lane Allen's "Through Cumberland Gap on Horseback," *Harper's New Monthly Magazine* 73 (June 1886): 61–62; John Fox, Jr.'s *Blue-Grass and Rhododendron* (New York: Charles Scribner's Sons, 1901), pp. 10–11; Ellen Churchill Semple's "The Anglo-Saxon of the Kentucky Mountains: A Study in Anthropogeography," *The Geographical Journal* 17 (1901): 596–98; Samuel Kercheval's *A History of the Valley of Virginia* (Woodstock, 1902), pp. 151–52; John Water Wayland's *The German Element of the Shenandoah Valley of Virginia* (Charlottesville: author, 1907), pp. 190–91; Margaret W. Morley's *The Carolina Mountains* (Boston and New York: Houghton Mifflin, 1913), pp. 184–85; John Preston Arthur's *Western North Carolina: A History (from 1730 to 1913)* (Raleigh, 1914), pp. 258–60; John C. Campbell's *The Southern Highlander and His Homeland* (New York: Russell Sage, 1921), pp. 73, 87–89, 143, 195–97; James Watt Raine's *The Land of Saddle-Bags* (New York: Council of Women for Home Missions and Missionary Education Movement of the United States and Canada, 1924), pp. 13, 74, 208–10; Horace Kephart's *Our Southern Highlanders* (New York: Macmillan, 1926), pp. 76, 82, 110–11, 216–17, 314–17, 322–23; Robert Lindsay Mason's *The Lure of the Great Smokies* (Boston and New York: Houghton Mifflin, 1927), Chapter 9; Margaret A. Hitch's "Life in a Blue Ridge Hollow," *The Journal of Geography* 30 (1931): 312, 315; Mandel Sherman's and Thomas R. Henry's *Hollow Folk* (New York: Thomas Y. Crowell, 1933), pp. 1, 5, 49–50; J. Wesley Hatcher's "Appalachian America," in *Culture in the South*, ed. W. T. Couch (Chapel Hill: University of North Carolina Press, 1935), pp. 382, 387; Jack Manne's "Mental Deficiency in a Closely Inbred Mountain Clan," *Mental Hygiene* 20 (April 1936): 269–70; Allen H. Eaton's *Handicrafts of the Southern Highlands* (New York: Russell Sage, 1937), pp. 41–43, 47–54, 256–57; Laura Thornborough's *The Great*

Smoky Mountains (New York: Thomas Y. Crowell, 1937; Knoxville: University of Tennessee Press, 1962), pp. 95–96; Edwin E. White's *Highland Heritage* (New York: Friendship Press, 1937), pp. 31–32; Clark B. Firestone's *Bubbling Waters* (New York: Robert McBride, 1938); pp. 8, 12, 17, 47, 84; Works Projects Administration, *North Carolina: A Guide to the Old North State* (Chapel Hill: University of North Carolina Press, 1939), p. 124; Works Projects Administration, *Tennessee: A Guide to the Volunteer State* (New York: Viking, 1939), pp. 155–56; Works Projects Administration, *West Virginia: A Guide to the Mountain State* (New York: Oxford University Press, 1941), p. 161; Charles S. Grossman's "Great Smoky Pioneers," *The Regional Reviews* 7:1, 2 (July–August 1941): 2–6; Alberta Pierson Hannum's "The Mountain People," in *The Great Smokies and the Blue Ridge*, ed. Roderick Peattie (New York: Vanguard, 1943), pp. 140–41; Elizabeth Skaggs Bowman's *Land of High Horizons* (Kingsport, Tenn.: Southern Publishers, 1944), pp. 36–37; Muriel Earley Sheppard's *Cabins in the Laurel* (Chapel Hill: University of North Carolina Press, 1946), pp. 52–53, 67, 156–57; J. Paul Hudson's "Appalachian Folk Ways," *Antiques* 57 (May 1950): 368–69; Inez Burns's "Settlement and Early History of the Coves of Blount County, Tennessee," *East Tennessee Historical Society Publications* 24 (1952): 54–55; North Callahan's *Smokey Mountain Country* (New York: Duell, Sloan, and Pierce, and Boston: Little, Brown, 1952), pp. 9–11; Wilma Dykeman's *The French Broad* (New York and Toronto: Rinehart, 1955), pp. 52–53: Esther Sharp Sanderson's *County Scott and Its Mountain Folk* (Huntsville, Ala.: author, 1958), pp. 56–57; Marion Pearsall's *Little Smoky Ridge* (University: University of Alabama, 1959), pp. 25, 82–86; Harriet Simpson Arnow's *Seedtime on the Cumberland* (New York: Macmillan, 1960), pp. 256–76; Joseph S. Hall's *Smoky Mountain Folks and Their Lore* (Asheville, N.C.: Great Smoky Mountains Natural History Association, 1964), p. 48.

[7] There are two-story one-room houses in the Southern Mountains; these have floor plans of the same proportions as the cabins but usually have larger dimensions. They seem to be the result of the English tradition of the two-story one-room house; for examples, Rowland C. Hunter's *Old Houses in England* (New York: John Wiley, and London: Chapman and Hall, 1930), plate 16: the references under footnote 53; Henry Chandlee Forman's *Early Manor and Plantation Houses of Maryland* (Easton, Maryland: author, 1934) p. 189; J. Frederick Kelley's "The Norton House, Guilford, Conn.," *Old-Time New England* 14 (January 1924): 122–30; and Arthur Kyle Davis's *Traditional Ballads of Virginia* (Cambridge, Mass.: Harvard University Press, 1929), facing p. 244.

[8] In 1803, a traveler in the Alleghenies, Thaddeus M. Harris, distinguished between cabins and houses on the basis of their construction: a "log cabin" has round logs, a "log house" hewn logs. Harris has been

consistently followed by historians. Even if his distinction did represent a traditional usage, it does not hold within the area of this study, where one-room houses of hewn log, round log, or frame are generally "cabins." For a much more important reason than this, however, his distinction must be abandoned: house types cannot be established or named even partially on the basis of their construction. Within the area of this study the smallest houses and outbuildings were built of hewn log, whereas in the Deep South even a large two-story house might be built of round logs. For an example, see Wilbur Zelinsky's "The Log House in Georgia," *GR* 43 (1953): 174–75, 177 fig 3.

[9] Eleanor Raymond's *Early Domestic Architecture of Pennsylvania* (New York: William Helburn, 1931), plates 72–77.

[10] A one-room brick house of exactly the same proportions as the square mountain cabin of log or frame was observed in Middleburg, Loudoun County, Virignia (August 1964).

[11] Fred R. Cotten's "Log Cabins of the Parker County Region," *West Texas Historical Association Year Book* 29 (1953): 96–104; Seymour V. Connor's "Log Cabins in Texas," *The Southwestern Historical Quarterly* 53 (1949): 105–16. Cotten's paper represents a careful, local, untheoretical study of the type needed currently in folk architectural studies.

[12] Fred Kniffen's "Louisiana House Types," in *Readings in Cultural Geography*, ed. Philip L. Wagner and Marvin W. Mikesell (Chicago: University of Chicago Press, 1962; reprinted from *Annals of the Association of American Geographers* 26 [1936]: 179–93), pp. 159–61, 164. This is the classic culturogeographic study of architecture.

[13] Patrick Duffey's "The Making of an Irish Mud Wall House" (with comment by Pádraig MacGréine), *Béaloideas* 4 (1933): 91–92.

[14] J. E. Spencer's "House Types of Southern Utah," *GR* 25 (1945): 450.

[15] Charles Morse Stotz's *The Early Architecture of Western Pennsylvania* (New York: William Helburn, 1936), pp. 269, 276–77, reports a mill built of logs measuring 54′ 9″. In the Southern Mountains and central Pennsylvania, several log barns have been measured that are over seventy feet in length.

[16] M. W. Barley's *The English Farmhouse and Cottage* (London: Routledge and Kegan Paul, 1961), p. 106.

[17] Thomas Tileston Waterman's *The Dwellings of Colonial America* (Chapel Hill: University of North Carolina Press, 1950), p. 245. For examples of one-story houses with the joists of the loft framed in at the plate from both the North and South, see Addision F. Worthington's *Twelve Old Houses West of Chesapeake Bay*, The Monograph Series (Boston: Rogers and Manson, 1931), and Ernest Allen Connally's "The Cape Cod House: An Introductory Study," *Journal of the Society of Architectural Historians* 19 (1960): 47–56.

[18] Robert C. Bucher's "The Continental Log House," *PF* 12 (Summer 1962): 14–19.

[19] The interiors of the cabins in the Southern Mountains and in Ireland seem to be very similar, particularly in such matters as furnishings, the use to which the loft is put, and the whitewashing and decorating of the walls. For a few of the many good descriptions of Irish interiors, see Dorothy Hartley's *Irish Holiday* (Dublin: Browne and Nolan 1938), pp. 238–48; Robert Lynd's *Home Life in Ireland* (London: Mills and Boon, 1909), pp. 17–19, 30, 291; Robin Flower's *The Western Island or The Great Blasket* (New York: Oxford University Press, 1945), pp. 43–47; and Eric Cross's *The Tailor and Ansty* (New York: Devon-Adair, 1964, originaly published in 1942), Chapter 2.

[20] For assorted references to earth floors in folk houses in Ireland and Britain, see Walter Gregor's *An Echo of the Olden Time from the North of Scotland* (Edinburgh, Glasgow: John Menzies, and Peterhead: David Scott, 1874), pp. 18, 36; Peter F. Anson's *Scots Fisherfolk* (Banffshire: Saltire, 1950), pp. 14–15; J. C. Atkinson's *Forty Years in a Moorland Parish* (London: Macmillan, 1891), p. 19; A. K. Hamilton Jenkin's *Cornish Homes and Customs* (London and Toronto: J. M. Dent, 1934), pp. 17, 36–37; Thomas Roscoe's *Wanderings and Excursions in South Wales* (London, n.d., probably c. 1855), p. 43; Edward MacLysaght's *Irish Life in the Seventeenth Century: After Cromwell* (London: Longmans Green, 1939), pp. 111, 333.

[21] Nathaniel Lloyd's *A History of the English House* (London: The Architectural Press, and New York: William Helburn, 1931), p. 451. For good American examples see Don Blair's *Harmonist Construction*, Indiana Historical Society Publications, 23 (Indianapolis: Indiana Historical Society, 1964), pp. 67–70, plate VI.

[22] C. Gillardon's "Das Safierhaus," *Schweizerisches Archiv für Volkskunde* 48 (1952): pp. 201–32.

[23] An early log house was observed between Broadway and Edom, Rockingham County, Virginia, which had an external chimney different in profile from the usual English-Tidewater chimney and like the few published photos of the Swiss chimneys (June 1964).

[24] Sigurd Erixon's "West European Connections and Culture Relations," *Folkliv* 2 (1938): 165–66.

[25] Cf. C. F. Innocent's *The Development of English Building Construction* (Cambridge: Cambridge University Press, 1916), p. 269; Margaret Wood's *The English Mediaeval House* (London: Phoenix, 1965), Chapter 20.

[26] Barley *op. cit.*, pp. 98, 112, 145, 156, 221; Joscelyne Finberg's *Exploring Villages* (London: Routledge and Kegan Paul, 1958), pp. 134–36; Sir Cyril Fox's "Some South Pembrokeshire Cottages," *Antiquity* 16 (December 1942): 307–19.

[27] Arthur R. Randell's *Sixty Years a Fenman*, ed. Enid Porter (London:

Routledge and Kegan Paul, 1966), p. 65; Michael J. Murphy's *At Slieve Gullion's Foot* (Dundalk: Tempest, 1945), pp. 23–24; Kevin Danaher's *In Ireland Long Ago* (Cork: Mercier, 1964), pp. 20–21; F. Marian McNeill's *The Scots Kitchen: Its Traditions and Lore with Old-Time Recipes* (London and Glasgow: Blackie, 1937) Chapter 4, particularly p. 49; Alwyn D. Rees's *Life in a Welsh Countryside* (Cardiff: University of Wales, 1950), pp. 43–44.

[28] Caoimhín Ó Danachair's "Bread," *Ulster Folklife* 4 (1958): 29–32. For the English tradition, see George Ewart Evans's *Ask the Fellows Who Cut the Hay* (London: Faber and Faber, 1962), Chapter 4. For the Pennsylvania German tradition, see Amos Long, Jr.'s "Bakeovens in the Pennsylvania Folk-Culture," *PF* 14 (December 1964): 16–29. Some of the traditional mountain recipes may be found in *Mountain Makin's in the Smokies* (Gatlinburg, Tenn., Great Smoky Mountains Natural History Association, 1957).

[29] The traditional log construction must not be confused with the non-folk "rustic" log construction of which hunting lodges and park structures are built. This type of construction, based vaguely on Scandinavian rather than American traditions, may be found in Chilson D. Aldrich's *The Real Log Cabin* (New York: Macmillan, 1928); William S. Wicks's *Log Cabins and Cottages: How to Build and Furnish Them* (New York: Forest and Stream 1929); *Building with Logs*, Miscellaneous Publication No. 579 U.S.D.A. Forest Service (Washington, D.C., 1945); William E. Petty and Clayt Seagears's "Log Cabin" *The New York State Conservationist* 6 (December–January 1951–52): 20–21. Such construction is to traditional log work as a Brooklyn folknik is to a traditional ballad singer from Newfoundland.

[30] The approximate number five hundred represents those houses on which the log construction could be examined. The majority of the log houses of the Southern Mountains are covered over with boards or asbestos, and their construction cannot be inspected. Only a little over 30 percent of the log buildings surveyed within this area are houses; most are barns and other outbuildings.

[31] H. L. Edlin's *Woodland Crafts in Britain* (New York: Batsford, 1949), pp. 136–37.

[32] Stuart Bartlett's "Garrison Houses along the New England Frontier," *The Monograph Series* 19 (1933): 33–48; also in *Pencil Points* 14 (June 1933): 253–68.

[33] Harold R. Shurtleff's *The Log Cabin Myth*, ed. Samuel Eliot Morison (Cambridge, Mass.: Harvard University Press, 1939). His thesis is stated on pp. 3–8, 51–56, 186–87, 209–15.

[34] This idea was put forth by Henry C. Mercer in "The Origin of Log Houses in the United States," *Collection of Papers Read before the Bucks County Historical Society* 5 (1924): 568–83, and in *Old-Time New England* 18 (1927). It was followed with reservation by Shurtleff (p. 209),

but has been wholeheartedly adopted by both historians and architectural historians. It appears, for example, in these two standard and generally excellent texts: James Marston Fitch's *American Building* (Boston: Houghton Mifflin, 1948), p. 8, and Hugh Morrison's *Early American Architecture* (New York: Oxford University Press, 1952), pp. 12–13, 504–6. For a more complete treatment of log construction, see Kniffen and Glassie, *op. cit.*

[35] For Scandinavian log construction, see Sigurd Erixon's "The North-European Technique of Corner Timbering," *Folkliv* (1937): 13–60; Gerda Boëthius's *Studier i den nordiska timmerbyggnadskonsten från vikingatiden till 1800-talet. En undersökning utående från Anders Zorns samlingar i Mora* (Stockholm: Fritzes, 1927), pp. 50–91.

[36] Richard Weiss's *Häuser und Landschaften der Schweiz* (Erlenbach-Zurich and Stuttgart: Eugen Rentsch, 1959), pp. 40–43, 54–57.

[37] Kristofer Visted and Hilmar Stigum's *Vår Gamle Bondekultur* (Oslo: J. W. Cappelens, 1951), 1, p. 54.

[38] There are many articles on and photographs of northwestern Czechoslovakian log construction scattered through the Czech folklife journals: *Slovenský Nárdodopis, Český Lid, Sborník Slovenského Národného Muzea Etnografia,* and *Etnographica.*

[39] Innocent, *op. cit.*, p. 90; Alan Gailey's "The Peasant Houses of the South-West Highlands of Scotland: Distribution, Parallels and Evolution," *Gwerin* 3 (1962): 227–42; E. Estyn Evan's *Irish Heritage* (Dundalk: W. Tempest, 1963), pp. 58–60, 84–85. For roof types, see Aymar Embury II's "Roofs!" *The Monograph Series* 18:1 (1932): pp. 250–264.

[40] Innocent, *op. cit.*, pp. 13–14, 82–85; I. F. Grant's *Highland Folk Ways* (London: Routledge and Kegan Paul, 1961), pp. 144, 149; Alan Gailey's "Two Cruck Truss Houses near Lurgan," *Ulster Folklife* 8 (1962): 57–59; Morrison *op. cit.*, p. 27.

[41] Bradford Angier's "Shake Roof," *The Beaver* 293 (1963): 52–53.

[42] Innocent, *op. cit.*, pp. 184–85; Harry Batsford and Charles Fry's *The English Cottage* (London, New York, Toronto, and Sydney: Batsford, 1950), pp. 20, 65; W. H. Crawford's "The Woodlands of the Manor of Brown Low's-Derry, North Armagh, in the Seventeenth and Eighteenth Centuries," *Ulster Folklife* 10 (1964): 60.

[43] H. Bichsel's "Das Schindeln," *Schweizer Volkskunde* 30 (1940): 1–3; Stefan Apáthy's "Sindliarstvo v okolí Bardejova," *Slovenský Nárdodopis* 2 (1954): 65–93.

[44] Marcus Whiffen's *The Eighteenth Century Houses of Williamsburg* (Williamsburg, Va.: Colonial Williamsburg, 1960), p. 69; J. Frederick Kelley's *The Early Domestic Architecture of Connecticut* (New York: Dover, 1963, reprint of 1924), pp. 49, 84–85, 133–34; Henry C. Mercer's *Ancient Carpenters Tools* (Doylestown, Pa.: Bucks County Historical Society, 1960), pp. 11–14 (also in *Old-Time New England* 15–19).

⁴⁵ A few minor outbuildings in the North Carolina–Tennessee Blue Ridge were constructed with purlin roofs in this manner. The Walker Sisters' cabin in the Smokies, which is pictured in several of the publications listed under footnote 6, was also built with a purlin roof, but this survey uncovered no other examples.

⁴⁶ G. Edwin Brumbaugh's "Colonial Architecture of the Pennsylvania Germans," *Pennsylvania German Society Proceedings* 41 (1933): 23, plates 14, 23–26.

⁴⁷ Cf. Sidney Oldall Addy's *The Evolution of the English House* (London: Swann Sonnenschein, 1898), p. 42.

⁴⁸ Barley, *op. cit.*, pp. 115–16, 134; Raymond B. Wood-Jones's *Traditional Domestic Architecture of the Banbury Region* (Manchester: Manchester University Press, 1963). p. 218.

⁴⁹ Henry Chandlee Forman's *The Architecture of the Old South* (Cambridge, Mass.: Harvard University Press, 1948), pp. 37, 90–93, 147–49; Norman M. Isham and Albert F. Brown's *Early Connecticut Houses* (New York: Dover, 1965; reprint of 1900), p. 268.

⁵⁰ E. Estyn Evans's *Irish Folk Ways* (New York: Devin-Adair, 1957), pp. 41, 45.

⁵¹ Addy, *op. cit.*, pp. XXII–XXIII, 66–69, 200; Allen W. Jackson's *The Half-Timber House* (New York: McBride, Nast 1912), pp. 4–5; Reginald Tumor's *The Smaller English House 1500–1939* (London: Batsford 1952), p. 12.

⁵² At Skara Brae, a Neolithic settlement in the Orkneys culturally related to East Anglia, have been found several houses which seem to be transitional between round and square. The one in the best state of preservation, house number 17, is internally seventeen feet square, but the outer wall, which varies from three to eight feet thick, gives it a round appearance. See V. Gordon Childe's *Ancient Dwellings at Skara Brae* (Edinburgh, 1956), and Childe's *The Dawn of European Civilization* (New York: Alfred A. Knopf, 1958), p. 333.

⁵³ Batsford and Fry, *op. cit.*, pp. 16, 36, 87; Barley, *op. cit.*, pp. 46, 48, 59, 142–43, 162–63, 250, fig. 36 Coningsby (B); Wood-Jones, *op. cit.*, Chapter 8 and pp. 197, 199; Sydney R. Jones's *English Village Homes and Country Buildings* (London: Batsford, 1947), pp. 89–90, plan A; Anthony N. B. Garvan's *Architecture and Town Planning in Colonial Connecticut* (New Haven, Conn.: Yale University Press, 1951), pp. 82, 105–6.

⁵⁴ Morrison, *op. cit.*, pp. 21, 65–67, 136; Henry Chandlee Forman's *Virginia Architecture in the Seventeenth Century* (Williamsburg, Va.: Virginia 350th Anniversary Celebration Corporation, 1957), pp. 23, 37–39; Forman's *Architecture of the Old South*, pp. 15, 36–41, 113, 121; Frances Benjamin Johnston and Thomas Tileston Waterman's *The Early Architecture of North Carolina* (Chapel Hill: University of North Carolina Press, 1947), p. 26.

[55] Some early historians—Charles A. Hanna's *The Scotch-Irish* (New York, 1902), 1, p. 163, for example—maintained that the Scotch-Irish culture was purely Scottish and that the period the Lowland Scots spent in Ulster did not affect them. In this regard it is interesting to note that the Scotch-Irish cabin is Irish, not Scottish.

[56] For the gable-chimney Irish house, see Åke Campbell's "Irish Fields and Houses: A Study of Rural Culture," *Béaloideas* 5 (1935): 57–74; Campbell's "Notes on the Irish House," *Folkliv* 2–3 (1937): 205–34; Canoimhin Ó Danachair's "Three House Types," *Ulster Folklife* 2 (1956): 22–26; Ó Danachair's "The Combined Byre-and-Dwelling in Ireland," *Folk Life* 2 (1964): 58–75; E. Estyn Evans's "The Ulster Farmhouse," *Ulster Folklife* 1 (1955): 27–31; Evans's "Donegal Survivals," *Antiquity* 13 (June 1939): 209–20; Evans's *Irish Heritage*, Chapter 7; Evans's *Irish Folk Ways*, Chapter 4; and the references under footnotes 66 and 68.

[57] Caoimhín Ó Danachair's "Materials and Methods in Irish Traditional Building," *The Journal of the Royal Society of Antiquaries of Ireland* 87 (1957): 61–74.

[58] Kevin Danaher's "Old House Types in Oighreact Ui Chonchubhair," *The Journal of the Royal Society of Antiquaries of Ireland* 68 (1938): 227–29, plate XXVIII, 1.

[59] Colin Sinclair's *The Thatched Houses of the Old Highlands* (Edinburgh: Olive and Boyd, 1953), "Dailriadic Type." John Dunbar's "Some Cruck-framed Buildings in the Aberfeldy District of Perthshire," *Proceedings of the Society of Antiquaries of Scotland* 90 (1956–57): 82; Grant, *op. cit.*, Chapter 7.

[60] Basil Oliver's *The Cottages of England* (New York: Charles Scribner's Sons, and London: Batsford, 1929), pp. 23–24; Addy, *op. cit.*, pp. 38–41.

[61] Iorwerth C. Peate's *The Welsh House* (Liverpool: Hugh Evans, 1946), pp. 88–111, plate 36; Sir Cyril Fox's and Lord Raglan's *Monmouthshire Houses* (Cardiff: National Museum of Wales, 1953) 2, 43 ff.; Fox's and Raglan's *Monmouthshire Houses* (Cardiff: National Museum of Wales, 1954) 3, 38, 40; Fox, *op. cit.*, pp. 307–14.

[62] Cf. E. Estyn Evans's "Cultural Relics of the Ulster Scots in the Old West of North America," *Ulster Folklife* 11 (1965): 34

[63] Peate's *The Welsh House*, p. 144.

[64] For the Welsh long-house, see the following articles in I. Ll. Foster and L. Alcock, eds., *Culture and Environment Essays in Honour of Sir Cyril Fox* (London: Routledge and Kegan Paul, 1963); J. T. Smith's "The Long-House in Monmouthshire, A Reappraisal," pp. 389–414; P. Smith's "The Long-House and the Laithe-House: A Study of the House-and-Byre Homestead in Wales and the West Riding," pp. 415–37; and Iowerth C. Peate's "The Welsh Long-House: A Brief Re-appraisal," pp. 439–44.

[65] For examples, see Henry Chandlee Forman's *Tidewater Maryland Architecture and Gardens* (New York: Bonanza, 1956), p. 67; Henry Lionel Williams and Ottalie K. Williams's *Old American Houses 1700–1850* (New York, 1957), p. 71.

[66] Caoimhín Ó Danachair's "Old Houses at Rathnew, Co. Wicklow," *Béaloideas* 5 (1935): 211–12.

[67] Cf. Evans's "The Ulster Farmhouse," p. 29.

[68] George Thompson, Desmond McCourt, and Alan Gailey's "The First Ulster Folk Museum Outdoor Exhibit: The Magilligan Cottier House," *Ulster Folklife* 10 (1964): 29; Desmond McCourt's "Cruck Trusses in North-West Ireland," *Gwerin* 3 (1961): 168–73.

[69] See Addy, *op. cit.*, pp. 32–34; G. E. Fussell's *The English Rural Labourer* (London: The Batchworth Press, 1949), pp. 10–12; and the references in note 53.

[70] Mercer's "The Origin of Log Houses" (see note 34) guessed that because log construction was Swedish, the whole cabin must be Swedish, and he had been generally followed. A somewhat more modern view, which still fails to completely separate construction and form, holds that the Southern Appalachian cabin is a Pennsylvania German log house that has undergone some change through Tidewater influence; see Henry Glassie's "The Appalachian Log Cabin," *MLW* 39 (Winter 1963): 5–14, and Fred Kniffen's "Folk Housing: Key to Diffusion," *Annals of the Association of American Geographers* 55 (December 1965): 561.

[71] Unfortunately the only works on mountain architecture to which the reader can be referred are my own: "The Smaller Outbuildings of the Southern Mountains," *MLW* 40 (Spring 1964): 21–25; "The Old Barns of Appalachia," *MLW* 40 (Summer 1965): 21–30; "The Pennsylvania Barn in the South," *PF* 15 (Winter 1965–66): 8–19; 15 (Summer 1966): 12–25; "Southern Mountain Houses: A Study in American Folk Culture," Master's thesis, American Folk Culture Program, Cooperstown, State University of New York College at Oneonta, 1965.

Structure and Meaning in the Folk Blues

by David Evans

The following essay on blues structure and meaning was written for the second edition of this book in order to provide a sample of folk-music analysis in a performance context. It has been corrected and updated for this edition. David Evans brings to bear his many years of experience in field work and study upon eight examples of folk blues collected by himself from black performers. The resulting study gives rich insights into blues performance styles, the context of blues singing, the interplay with commercial musical trends, and attitudes of blues singers toward their traditional art. Particularly important in this essay is Evans's rebuttal of racist arguments put forward by earlier writers on blues.

Students with some musical training could benefit from playing out on a piano or guitar the full musical transcription sample that Evans provides of one stanza of Example 5. Good aural examples of blues are the commercial recordings Evans lists of folk- and popular-blues performances. Students wishing to try their own musical transcription and analysis projects might begin with relatively simple examples from their own culture, such as children's chants and game songs, parody songs, or college drinking songs. (A song performance may be recorded and the context and style usefully *described* without a full technical transcription being prepared.) A nonmusical project inspired from this essay might be reviewing the past interpretations of blues referred to by Evans in the light of more recent writings on Afro-American music and folk culture. A dialogue between black and white students about what makes the stereotypes of blues singing seem fresh and appealing might also be worthwhile.

David Evans is professor of music at Memphis State University and director of graduate-degree programs in ethnomusicology (regional studies). He received two degrees in folklore and mythology from the University of California, Los Angeles: an M.A. in 1967 and the first individual Ph.D. awarded by UCLA in 1976. He has done field work in black folk music since 1964, and has published his findings in a number of folklore journals and in two books: *Tommy Johnson* (London: Studio Vista, 1971), a study of a folk blues singer, and *Big Road Blues: Tradition and Creativity in the Folk Blues* (Berkeley: University of California Press, 1982). He has also produced several record albums of his field recordings of blues and other types of folk music. The photographs accompanying his essay are by his wife, Cheryl Evans.

Since the beginning of the twentieth century over fifty thousand performances of blues have been recorded or collected on paper. The bulk of this vast documentary enterprise has been carried out by commercial phonograph companies, beginning in 1920. Even before this, in 1912, blues had begun appearing in sheet-music form. In origin, however, blues were a noncommercial form of folksong performed by Southern blacks. This folk-blues tradition has continued to the present time, carried on by mostly obscure performers little known outside their own communities, while the rest of the world has come to know the blues mainly through its more commercialized forms popularized by phonograph records and other mass media.[1]

Such a broad variety of settings is indicative of the extraordinary importance blues have had for black Americans. These songs have commented on almost every major aspect of daily life for blacks as well as a great number of personal and topical subjects of special interest to individual singers. For many years blues were one of the few forms of artistic expression available and open to large numbers of blacks. As a result, many of the finest musical and lyrical creations of black culture in America have been expressed through the medium of the blues.

There have been many thousands of blues singers in all sorts of community settings from Southern plantations and small farm areas to towns and urban ghettos. Some of the more popular commercial performers have made a good living as professional musicians, but the great majority of blues singers have been semiprofessional at best, having to supplement what little money they might make from music with income from other, steadier forms of work.

Despite the humble status of most black blues singers, the form of music they created has exerted enormous musical influence both among blacks themselves and in a much wider community. By the end of World War I, blues had become the predominant form of black secular folk and popular music. Even earlier than this they had begun to enter the Southern white folk-music tradition. By the 1920s they had become an important part of commercial "hillbilly" music, and they have continued to influence various forms of "country and Western" music.[2] Also by the 1920s, blues had entered the mainstream of American popular music. Many white vaudeville singers performed blues, and instrumental blues formed a large part of the repertoire of dance orchestras. Blues were fundamental to the development of jazz and swing music during the 1920s and 1930s, and still, today, whenever jazz musicians want to return to their musical roots, they generally turn to the blues. In the 1950s blues again affected American popular music through the medium of rock 'n' roll. For the first time large numbers of American whites began listening to authentic black blues singers. White rock 'n' roll singers like Elvis Presley also featured blues in many of their performances. British and American rock groups like the Rolling Stones and the Grateful Dead gave young people yet another strong taste of the blues in the 1960s, and popular singers and composers continue to use the blues form for a large number of their songs. Blues are now known internationally and can be heard as part of the popular music of many countries. Thus, although blues began and have continued as a form of regional black American folklore, they have also gained world-wide recognition and helped to change the course of popular music both in America and abroad.

With so many recorded examples and such a long history, blues naturally exhibited a great variety of characteristics, making it difficult to arrive at a concise definition. Nevertheless, there are certain traits that recur in the majority of blues, so that the form is capable of being described and one can recognize a blues and distinguish it from other song forms. The following traits are the most characteristic and distinctive ones for the blues, especially the folk blues.

Blues singers themselves generally describe the blues as a worried feeling, a description that differs little from the long-time standard English usage of the word. Indeed, blues songs deal with a wide range of life's problems as they are experienced by generally lower class blacks. But blues, despite their name, can also treat life's joys and successes. Basically, blues celebrate life itself with all its ups and downs, treating their subjects dramatically and often with striking imagery. Their style is lyric rather than narrative, stressing the subject's emotional dimension from a first-person point of view. They are usually sung in a highly emotional and animated manner, as if the singer were describing his personal feelings and experiences. Most singers, in fact, claim to have experienced or at least witnessed the things that they sing about. But their subjects are also typical, even universal, experiences, well known to their audiences. Thus not only can blues function as self-expression, catharsis, and therapy for the singer, but they also fulfill the same needs for the audience. In fact, if they fail to fulfill these wider needs, the singer will find himself without an audience.

All of the subjects that blues singers deal with are potential problem areas of life. For the most part blues singers are content to describe the dimensions of their subjects, taking the situation as given and not likely to be altered significantly in the long run. No real solutions to major problems are proposed in the blues. At the same time, however, small temporary successes and failures are constantly noted, often in a highly exaggerated manner. Self-pity and grandiose fantasy, abuse and praise alternate throughout blues lyricism. The man/woman relationship is by far the most important subject in the blues, probably because this area of life is most susceptible to daily fluctuation. Blues are also frequently sung in a social context of dancing and partying where relationships between the sexes are being formed, broken, strengthened, or strained. A closely related theme is travel and wanderlust. Blues singers often express an intention to "leave town" or "catch the first thing smoking," presenting themselves as victims of mistreatment or unfaithfulness by a lover. Sometimes the singers claim to be returning to a faithful lover back home or a former lover, an "old-time used-to-be." Sometimes travel or hoboing is undertaken simply for its own sake, the consequence of the singer having "a rambling mind." The more active blues singers, in fact, frequently are ramblers, going from town to town in search of musical jobs and better times. Additional themes in the blues are farming and its problems, industrial work, poverty, alcohol and drugs, sickness and death, gambling, voodoo and magic, crime and prison, the color hierarchy within the black community, natural disasters, racism, and topical events that affect the singer and his community. Often the man/woman and travel themes are worked into other themes.

The majority of blues utilize a twelve-measure stanza structure like that printed below in Example 5. The verses usually have an *AAB* patten, the first line being repeated once while the final line adds to or comments upon the first two. Usually the lines rhyme or display assonance. Each line of text lasts approximately two and one-half measures and is followed by an instrumental response lasting about a measure and a half. The most common accompanying instruments in the folk blues are the guitar, piano, or harmonica, usually played by the singer himself, to which may be added one or more instruments played by others. Female singers accompany themselves less often. The accompaniment usually creates or suggests a standardized harmonic pattern. This consists of a chord based on the tonic note for the first four measures (line 1). Although the vocal melody of line 2 is usually the same as that of line 1, the harmony of the accompaniment switches to a chord based on the subdominant for measures 5 and 6, returning to the tonic for measures 7 and 8. For the third line the accompaniment moves to the chord based on the dominant for measure 9, changes to the subdominant for measure 10, and returns to the tonic for measures 11 and 12. Many folk blues, however, depart somewhat from this standardized pattern, often by adding or subtracting a few beats from the twelve measures or altering the harmonic pattern of the accompaniment. Examples 1, 4, 5, 7, and 8 below all contain slight modifications of this sort in some of their stanzas. Other blues utilize two-line, four-line, and other patterns. Eli Owens's "Ways Like the Devil" (Example 6), for instance, is made up of four-line stanzas formed by repeating the final line of the standardized *AAB* pattern. Charlie Taylor's "Annie Lee" (Example 2) also has a final four-line stanza, while Bessie Mae Charleston's "Water Boy" (Example 3) with its long moaning lines could be considered almost free form. Improvisational variation, in fact, both in the vocal melody and the instrumental accompaniment, could be considered a regular feature of the blues. In some cases singers actually employ alternate strains in some of their stanzas or a quite different accompaniment part, particularly when playing instrumental choruses or (borrowing the jazz term) "breaks."

Several stylistic features of blues performance serve to create a type of musical tension that matches the lyric tension or ambivalent mood so characteristic of blues texts with their celebrations of life's vicissitudes. For one thing, the instrumental phrase at the end of each line serves as "response" to the "call" of the vocal. Often the instrument also punctuates the vocal lines with notes or phrases that answer other notes or phrases in the singing. In creating this pattern of call and response, the performer frequently develops a rhythmic tension between the voice and accompaniment or between two or more musical lines in the accompaniment. This tension often takes the form of duple and triple rhythms performed simultaneously. A further melodic tension is found in the use of neutral tones or "blue notes." The most common of these occur at the third and seventh degrees of the scale and are pitched approximately midway between the major and minor of those degrees. In staff notation blue notes are often indicated by arrows (↑ and ↓)

printed above the note on a staff or above a sharp or flat in the key signature to indicate that the note is slightly raised or lowered. From the
point of view of the blues singer, of course, blue notes are not tension-
producing per se but are rather a normal part of the blues scale. They
do, however, create a sense of melodic tension when they are sounded
against the notes of an instrument played in a Western scale (which
lacks blue notes). And if the performer wants to produce blue notes on
an instrument of Western origin, such as a guitar, piano, or harmonica,
he must use special playing techniques like "choking" or "worrying"
the guitar strings or "bending" notes on the harmonica.

As noted earlier, the blues developed around the beginning of the
twentieth century as a form of folksong among mostly rural lower-class
blacks, but it soon became popularized and commercialized, especially
in the cities. Popular blues, as exemplified by the majority of blues issued on commercial phonograph records, usually contain original
lyrics composed by the performer or a professional songwriter, unless
the piece is a re-creation of some earlier commercially recorded blues.
They also tend to adhere closely to the AAB or some other standardized
stanzaic pattern. Their lyrics are usually thematic in the sense that from
listening to the text it is possible for one to reconstruct a coherent story
or visualize a scene clearly. Each blues, then, treats one particular
aspect of one of the typical blues themes.[3] The earliest folk blues, on
the other hand, relied mainly on traditional verses that the singers
would recombine in a number of different ways in the processes of
learning and composing their songs.[4] The traditional verses and stanzas
served as formulaic building blocks that could be recombined in a limit-
less number of ways to construct new texts. These traditional elements
are still used by many folk blues singers in composing and performing
their songs. The texts of these blues are often nonthematic in the sense
that a single theme is not maintained throughout and the listener cannot reconstruct a coherent story or visualize a single scene clearly. On
the other hand, as the commercial recording of popular blues has increased over the years, many folk blues singers have been influenced
by blues that they hear on records and have begun to compose blues of
their own in the manner of the more commercialized pieces. Thus some
folk blues today continue to be nonthematic textually, while others are
thematic. The following examples illustrate the variety of approaches
to composition that can be found in folk blues.

"Monday Morning Blues" is a good example of the more modern
type of folk blues modeled on the thematic approach of popular blues.
Its singer and composer, Ira Coney, was born in 1933 and has been

more influenced in his style and repertoire by phonograph records than have the other artists represented here, all of whom were born around the beginning of the century and compose blues in older styles. Indeed, his "Monday Morning Blues" borrows much of its melody and text from a commercial recording made in 1946 by Lowell Fulson, "Trouble Blues" (Big Town 1074). The scene that Coney's text describes is easy to visualize, as it is presented in the form of a dialogue between the singer and his woman. In fact, the text comes close to being a narrative in its logical sequencing of stanzas, but it lacks the sequence of scenes or episodes that characterizes a narrative text in the strict sense. The continuity between stanzas is aided by Coney's spoken remarks (in italics), and even his guitar helps in presenting the song's message, as Coney makes the strings "moan" by bending them and playing many blue notes. Although most of the verses are traditional and used by other blues singers in different combinations, the song as a whole is obviously a very deliberate and carefully worked-out composition. Coney even has a story about how he came to compose this piece: "We have a lot of rough weekends, you know. I be feeling bad some Monday mornings, have to get up and go to work. So I thought that over, and so I put one together on that. It goes something like this right here."

> *Example 1.* "Monday Morning Blues." Ira "Tiny" Coney,
> vocal and guitar.[5]

1. Now now, when I wake up some Monday mornings, blues and trouble around my bed.
   Now, when I wake up some Monday mornings, blues and trouble around my bed.
   You know, I never will forget the words I heard my baby said.
   What'd she say?

2. She say, "I'm gonna leave you in the morning, and your crying won't make me stay."
   Yes, I'm gonna leave you in the morning, and your crying won't make me stay."
   "Only thing I can say, little girl, that I'll meet you again some day."
   When I told her that, it hurt her. She had to moan one time. She said . . .

[Guitar chorus—guitar moans.]

All right!

3. *When I told her,*
    I said, "If you is got to go, I hope to meet you again some day.
    Oh, if you is got to go, I hope to meet you again some day.
    Oh, when I do, little girl, you'll be changed of your evil way."

Charlie Taylor's "Annie Lee" shows yet another form of influence from popular blues. In fact, it is loosely based on a record of the same title (Aristocrat 2301) made by Robert Nighthawk (Robert Lee McCollum) in 1949. Taylor sticks more or less to Nighthawk's melody, while his brother attempts to imitate the record's guitar part, but the singer makes the song his own by departing considerably from the text of the record. This is done by composing original lines in a stream-of-consciousness manner, sacrificing the ending rhymes in order that the song's composition may be simultaneous with its performance. This is a compositional technique that Taylor and many other folk-blues singers favor, though it is rarely recorded commercially, since such pieces often betray the looseness of hasty improvisation and are so highly personal as to be obscure in the meaning. Taylor's piece, however, is a well-structured folk blues, and by basing it on a popular record he can be certain of gaining the audience's interest. The text is thematic, clearly presenting a scene of the singer begging Annie Lee to return to him, though at the same time he appears to be having second thoughts about the relationship. The scene is not developed, however, by having the stanzas follow each other in a logical sequence. In fact, from a purely logical standpoint the song would make better sense if the stanzas were sung in reverse order. As the text stands, Taylor says in his opening stanza that he is going to quit calling Annie Lee, but then he goes on to sing about her for another five stanzas. In the song's final line he states that he is going to talk about Annie Lee and then ends his singing abruptly, letting the guitars finish out the line. But by using this reverse logic Taylor is able to increase the song's dramatic power enormously, letting the singer's plight gradually unfold to its full dimensions rather than stating the problem's outlines at the beginning and then filling in the details. Taylor opens the song with statements about how he loves Annie Lee and is constantly calling her (Stanzas 1–2). Then he appears to be addressing her directly, begging her to return (Stanza 3). Next we learn that the singer has been "running around," probably the cause of Annie Lee's leaving him (Stanza 4). Finally we are told that she is not nearby but that the singer must call her on the telephone and that she is so far away that they are not likely ever to get back together again

(Stanzas 5–6). By gradually building up to this dramatic climax, Taylor is able to increase the sense of tension in his song. He does this even further by shifting between addressing the song to Annie Lee and to his predominantly male audience ("boys"). This alternation must be viewed as symbolic of the tension between the singer's devotion to Annie Lee (begging her and calling her name) and the audience's ideal of unconcerned masculine behavior (letting her go). This basic tension is not resolved in the song, as is true of most folk blues, but the performance itself helps to define the dimensions of a typical problem and make such problems more bearable by providing a catharsis for both the singer and his audience. This process is all the more remarkable when one considers the fact that the text was composed spontaneously and that its structure was developed unconsciously.

> *Example 2.* "Annie Lee." Charlie Taylor, vocal and guitar; Willis Taylor, guitar.[6]

1. Annie Lee, Annie Lee, darling, I swear I keep on calling
   Miss Annie Lee.
   I said, I'm calling Miss Annie Lee, darling; I swear I call
   Miss Annie the whole night long.
   I'm gonna quit calling Miss Annie Lee, now darling; I think
   I'll let Miss Annie Lee even go.

2. I love Miss Annie Lee, darling; I loves her all the time.
   I said, I love Miss Annie Lee, boys now; I swear I love Miss
   Annie Lee, boys, all the time
   I'm gonna stop talking about Miss Annie Lee now; I ain't
   gon' say no more.

3. I'm begging Miss Annie Lee. Annie Lee, pleas ma'am,
   come back home.
   I said, I'm begging Miss Annie Lee now, darling. Annie
   Lee, please ma'am, come back home.
   I want you to come back now, darling; baby, please don't
   leave no more.

4. I love Miss Annie Lee, darling; she keep me crying, boys,
   all night long.
   I said, I love Miss Annie Lee, boys now; I swear she keeps
   me crying all night long.

I'm gonna quit my way of running around, boys now; won't
have to cry no more.

5. I'm gonna call Miss Annie Lee. I'm gonna call up over the
telephone.
I'm gonna call Miss Annie Lee, boys. Believe I'll call up
over the telephone.
I'm gonna call up to Atlanta, boys now. Lord, let Miss
Annie Lee even go.

6. Looka here, Miss Annie Lee, what are you trying to do?
Go on and leave me, Miss Annie Lee. Say, you ain't gonna
leave me no more.
I says, I love Miss Annie Lee, boys, love Annie Lee the
whole night long.
I'm gonna talk about my loving Annie Lee now. Yeah . . .

The two blues that we have examined so far are both thematic. Both
suggest a clear and consistent scene in the minds of listeners. They also
display the original creative powers of their composers, "Monday
Morning Blues" through its tightly constructed combination of sung
text, spoken comments, and guitar figures, and "Annie Lee" through
its spontaneous dramatic development of a scene from life. Many other
folk blues contrast with these by utilizing almost exclusively traditional
textual elements, combining them in such a manner that nonthematic
texts are produced. As we have observed, most of the earliest folk blues
were traditional and nonthematic, and today this approach is mainly
used by older performers, having been largely supplanted by original
thematic composition among younger singers under the influence of
more than fifty years of commercially recorded blues.
A number of prominent writers on blues have criticized the reliance
on traditional verse material by folk blues singers. Samuel Charters, for
instance, has labeled these traditional elements "undistinguished,"
"overly familiar," "conventional," and "derivative."[7] Paul Oliver has
stated of them that "for the minor singer with small creative talent they
are an indispensable substitute for original thought; for the more in-
ventive bluesman they are sometimes too easy a solution for the verse
problems posed by his own song."[8] Such assertions, however, often fail
to take into account the fact that artfully constructed blues can be created from traditional elements combined in an original manner. Often
the traditional verses contain remarkable poetic imagery, and many

Bessie Mae Charleston and Mott Willis PHOTO BY CHERYL EVANS

blues singers must be applauded for their excellent taste in selecting these verses and keeping them alive in tradition.[9] Originality of composition cannot in itself be said to have greater merit than borrowing from tradition. Instead, each piece must be judged objectively on its own merits. The examples that follow all rely heavily, almost exclusively, on traditional textual elements, yet they display some remarkable poetic qualities.

Some traditional blues, although textually nonthematic, do present a general consistency of mood or setting while their specific subject shifts in successive stanzas. Bessie Mae Charleston's "Water Boy" is an example of such a blues.[10] It is the lament of a prisoner on a chain gang, drawing heavily on the tradition of verses developed by countless singers in Southern jails, prison farms, and levee camps.[11] The moaning and long, gradually descending lines of the melody serve to link this blues with the unaccompanied hollers sung by black workers in these and other settings, a style which can be traced back to the slavery period.[12] Charleston, in fact, normally sings this piece unaccompanied, though on this recording a friend strummed simple guitar chords behind her singing. After setting the scene of the chain gang in Stanza 1, she goes on in the rest of the song to depict three different incidents in the typical daily life of a prisoner. Each incident involves water in some form (rain, ice, drinking water). Normally one might think of water as something soothing in the context of a chain gang, but in each of the last three stanzas a mood of dissatisfaction is actually expressed, culminating in the singer's grumbling against the water boy, who has a lighter task than the other prisoners. The imagery of Stanza 3 is especially striking. This song, then, displays a well-developed structure, even though it is not thematic in the manner of the first two examples.

Example 3. "Water Boy." Bessie Mae Charleston, vocal; Mott Willis, guitar.[13]

1. Mmmm, captain, captain, mmmmmmmmmm.
   If I had a' listened what my mother said,
   I wouldn't a' been wrestling with the ball and chain.
   Mmmmmmmmmm, mmmmmmmmmm, mmmmmmmmmm,
   mmmmmmmmmm.

2. Captain, captain, it's started raining.
   I asked for shelter.
   "Pick up your pick and shovel, just keep on working."
   Mmmmmmmmmm, mmmmmmmmmm.

3. Aaaaaaaaah, ooooh.
   I asked for a pillow. He gave me a block of ice.
   Mmmmmmmmmmm, mmmmmmmmmmm, mmmmmmmmmmm,
   mmmmmmmmmmm.

4. Water boy, water boy, pass your water 'round.
   If you ain't got no water, set your bucket down.
   Mmmmmmmmmmm, mmmmmmmmmmm.

Many other nonthematic folk blues lack even the degree of textual consistency found in "Water Boy." Often such blues jump from one subject to another and even make contrary statements in successive stanzas. These characteristics have led many writers to label such blues "incoherent" and the products of poor compositional skills on the part of their singers. As early as 1911 the folklorist Howard W. Odum noticed this tendency in many blues, attributing it to the mingling of stanzas that originally belonged to two or more separate songs, each of which was presumably a more coherent composition.[14] Odum failed to realize that the singers were actually drawing from a mental reservoir of traditional lyrics that they could use in building any number of songs, and that most of these traditional lines and stanzas did not belong to any particular song in the singers' repertoires. A few years later another folklorist, Dorothy Scarborough, sought a racial explanation for this practice, stating: "The colored mind is not essentially logical, and the folksong [i.e., blues] shows considerable lack of coherence in thought. Unrelated ideas are likely to be brought together, as stanzas from one song or from several may be put in with what the singer starts with, if they chance to have approximately the same number of syllables to the line."[15] Although some writers have attempted to defend this textual inconsistency,[16] the overwhelming opinion in print has been negative. Charters has called one example "confused."[17] John Fahey has noted "disconnection, incoherence, and apparent 'irrationality' of the stanzas" as an outstanding characteristic of the blues of singer Charley Patton.[18] Stephen Calt states that another singer is "struggling with two separate stories" and characterizes folk blues in general as "jumping capriciously from subject to subject."[19] Even some blues singers themselves have criticized the lack of apparent continuity in many folk blues, such as Brownie McGhee, who states: "I always believed in telling a story without getting lost on three or four different subjects."[20]

While many of the blues to which these writers refer are indeed superficially inconsistent, a closer examination reveals that they are hardly products of illogical or confused minds but rather that they often reveal a tight underlying poetic structure. Let us look at "It Won't Be Long," a blues by Charley Patton that Fahey has called an example of "extreme incoherence" and "non-sensical."[21] Patton was one of the greatest and most influential of the early Mississippi folk-blues singers. Born sometime in the 1880s, he is one of the few representatives of the first generation of blues singers to make commercial recordings. He recorded this piece at his first session in 1929, taking the tune and most of the lyrics from the common repertoire of traditional elements.[22] Mengelwood, in Stanza 2, was a logging camp a few miles outside of Memphis.

> *Example 4.* "It Won't Be Long." Charley Patton, vocal and
> guitar.[23]

1. I believe sweet mama gonna do like she said, baby.
   I believe sweet mama gonna do like she said, baby.
   She gon' cook my supper, Lord, put me in her bed.

2. You ever go to Memphis, stop by Mengelwood, baby.
   You ever go to Memphis, stop by Mengelwood, baby.
   You Memphis women don't mean no man no good.

3. She's got a man on her man, got a kid on her kid, baby.
   She's got a man on her man, got a kid on her kid, baby.
   Done got so bold, Lord, won't keep it hid.

4. Ah, rider, ain't gonna be here long, baby.
   Well, ah, rider, ain't gonna be here long, baby.
   Well, ah, rider, daddy ain't gonna be here long.

5. I believe sweet mama sure was kind to me, baby.
   I believe sweet mama sure was kind to me, baby.
   She's up at night like a police on his beat.

6. I'll tell you something; keep it to yourself, baby.
   I'm gonna tell you something; keep it to yourself, baby.
   Please don't tell your husband, Lord, and no one else.

7. She is a long tall woman, tall as a cherry tree, baby.
   Got a long tall woman, tall as a cherry tree, baby.
   She gets up 'fore day and she puts that thing on me.

Although the song is ostensibly addressed to the singer's "baby," it would be a mistake to view this as a unifying element in the text. This is simply a literary convention of the blues and has no more semantic significance than the interjection "Lord" in the last line of several stanzas. The key element to an understanding of this text is the second stanza with its implied contrast between the women of Memphis and Mengelwood. Although the precise basis for the contrast is not made clear in this stanza, the remainder of the stanzas, in fact, can be grouped into two sections depicting contrasting relationships with women. Stanzas 1, 3, and 4 form the first section, while Stanzas 5, 6 and 7 form the other. Stanzas 1 and 5 both describe women who treat the singer right, but in 1 the singer is obviously visiting the woman at her home, while in 5 the woman is walking out at night, evidently to visit the singer. Stanzas 3 and 6 continue the contrast. Stanza 3 describes a woman who openly consorts with two husbands and two boy friends ("a man on her man, a kid on her kid"), while Stanza 6 is the singer's plea to his woman not to tell her husband or anyone else about their relationship. The final contrast consists of the singer's bidding farewell to a woman in Stanza 4 and a woman discreetly (" 'fore day") coming to visit the singer in Stanza 7. Patton does not make clear which woman he prefers, for both apparently treat him well (Stanzas 1 and 5). Stanza 2 does not make clear which woman is from Memphis and which is from Mengelwood. This ambiguity is probably deliberate, for the function of Stanza 2 is not to identify the "actors" but to set the framework of contrast into which the other stanzas can fit. The basic message of this blues that the singer presents to his audience is a dilemma. One type of woman entertains many men openly and is visited for brief periods by the singer. Another type of woman sneaks away from her husband at night to visit the singer secretly (presumably returning to her husband before he awakes). Both types of woman are capable of satisfying the singer, yet there is a note of uneasiness expressed in Stanza 2 that some women "don't mean no man no good." In fact, it is obvious to anyone that both types of relationship that Patton describes can lead to trouble. Ambivalence and contrast, then, are at the heart of this blues, and its text is well structured to express this fact.

It is impossible to know whether Charley Patton consciously conceived of the contrastive structure of the text of "It Won't Be Long." This type of structure is common in folk blues that make use of traditional textual elements, but the singers are rarely articulate about their processes of composition except usually to say that their songs just "come to them" or are "in the air."[24] The chances are, however, that contrastive structural patterns are an unconscious product of the singer's imagination. Many of the blues that employ traditional elements are composed at the time of performance with the singer spontaneously calling forth verses and stanzas from his mental storehouse and setting them to his chosen melody and instrumental accompaniment. A blues of this sort is never repeated the same way again, although all of its separate elements are used by the singer in other performances. Since such performances are unique and not planned in advance, whatever structure they display must be considered unconscious.

Roosevelt Holts's "I'll Catch the Train and Ride" is a good example of a spontaneously composed blues constructed from traditional elements. This was the first piece I recorded from Holts in a four-day series of sessions with him. All of its textual and musical elements were used by him in various other blues during this period except for the first stanza, though he also used this stanza in blues recorded on other occasions. Like the previous example, it displays a contrastive structure. Stanza 1 is an expression of regret by the singer for his lifestyle, while the next stanza is a ringing affirmation of the free, rambling life

Roosevelt Holts PHOTO BY CHERYL EVANS

style. The third and fourth stanzas also present contrasting images, one of loneliness and the other of intimacy. In addition to *contrast,* this blues displays another important structural principle of traditional nonthematic blues: the *association* of related ideas. The two contrastive pairs of stanzas are linked to form a tightly constructed blues by the association of ideas of catching a train in Stanza 2 and drifting like a ship in Stanza 3. (The music of Stanza 2 is printed here as an example of the standardized twelve-measure *AAB* stanza pattern.)

Example 5. "I'll Catch the Train and Ride." Roosevelt Holts, vocal and guitar.[25]

1. Crying, Lord, have mercy, baby, on my bad-luck soul.
   Lord, have mercy, baby, on my bad-luck soul.
   Well, that Good Book teach you, gonna reap just what you sow.

2. Well, I'll drink my whisky, I'll catch the train and ride.
   Lord, I'll drink my whisky, I'll catch the train and ride.
   Yeah, when I find me a sweet little woman, I'm gonna pin her to my side.

3. Well, I'm drifting, I'm drifting like a ship out on the sea.
   Lord, I'm drifting, I'm drifting like a ship out on the sea.
   Well, I ain't got nobody in this world to care for me.

4. Well, the sun's going down; know what you promised me.
   Lord, the sun going down; know what you promised me.
   Well, you promised me something the poor boy really need.

Not all blues that use traditional elements are composed at the time of performance. Some of them are largely or entirely set pieces, offering little or no room for improvisation at the time of performance. Their relatively fixed form may be due to the fact that they were learned from other performers whose creations have been respected and left intact, or they may simply represent combinations of traditional elements created by their current performers which constitute for them satisfactory finished products, ones that they see no need to alter in subsequent performances. In the latter case the structure of such pieces may be developed consciously by the composer, although an unconscious process is equally possible.

An example of a relatively fixed blues made up of traditional lyrical and musical elements is Eli Owens's "Ways Like the Devil," also called

Eli Owens PHOTO BY CHERYL EVANS

by him "Commissary Blues." Owens stated that the piece properly contained four stanzas, though in five performances recorded in the span of five days he never sang a complete version. Nevertheless, he sang only four different stanzas altogether, so that these can probably be considered the ones that belong in a complete version by him. This piece is probably such a stable item in Owens's repertoire because he associates it with another blues singer, Harrison Lee Bridges, from whom he learned it in the 1920s in Oak Vale, Mississippi. Owens respected Bridges as a musician and has apparently been reluctant to change the piece. In Stanza 1 of the version transcribed below the term "monkey men" means fools, especially in the sense of men who put complete trust in the fidelity of their women. Stanza 3 should be interpreted in the sense that the singer's woman has run up a large bill at the commissary where he trades. Many employers on large plantations, levee camps, and lumber camps used to operate a general store or "commissary" where their employees could obtain food and other goods on credit against their payment at the end of the work period. Many black workers often found themselves broke or in debt to the company store at "settlement time," frequently through such causes as low wages, high prices at the store, a dishonest boss, or extravagant purchases on credit (in this case made by the singer's woman).

Example 6. "Ways Like the Devil." Eli Owens, vocal and guitar.[26]

1. I got ways like the devil born in the lion's den.
   I got ways like the devil born in the lion's den.
   Well, my daily occupation, taking women from the monkey men.
   Yeah, my daily occupation, taking women from the monkey men.

2. Don't the moon look pretty shining down through the tree?
   Don't the moon look pretty, woman, shining down through the tree?
   Oh, I see my baby when she don't see me.
   Yeah, see my baby when she don't see me.

3. I went to the commissary laughing, where I come away crying.
   Went to the commissary laughing, where I come away crying.
   Well, that dog-gone woman, she done took up all my time.
   Yeah, that dog-gone woman, she done took up all my time.

[Guitar chorus.]

In two of his other versions Owens inserted the following stanza after the first stanza above:

> My baby got ways like a fox squirrel in a tree.
> My baby got ways like a fox squirrel in a tree.
> Oh, she see me coming, she go hide from me.
> Yeah, she see me coming, she go hide from me.

Adding this stanza, we again have a blues that displays a contrastive structural pattern. The stanzas numbered 1 and 3 above represent the song's outer framework. In the first stanza the singer boasts about how he can steal women away from their foolish husbands or lovers, while in the final stanza the singer himself has been made a fool of by his woman, quite likely with the consent of his boss who runs the commissary, the "other men" in this case. The two interior stanzas present images involving a tree, but they contrast scenes in which the singer and his woman look on each other unobserved. This blues, then, deals with the problem of trust and faithfulness, doing so with a nonthematic text and a contrastive structural pattern.

The last two examples above were both constructed out of traditional textual and musical elements. One was put together at the time of performance, and the other was a relatively stable item in the performer's repertoire. Some traditional blues, however, represent a compromise of sorts between these two approaches to composition in that they contain some elements that constitute a stable *core* that does not vary from one performance to another, while the other elements are added to the core at the time of performance. Usually a blues core consists of a vocal melody, an instrumental part, and a single stanza or line of text. To this are added additional stanzas sung to the same melody and accompaniment, chosen during the performance itself. The line or stanza of text that belongs to the core usually contains a striking image or figure of speech that helps to make the core memorable both to the singer and his audience. In fact, many blues cores become traditional fixed musical/lyrical combinations, utilized by a number of blues singers, each of whom adds his own set of traditional stanzas to the core during performance.

"Canned Heat Blues" by John Henry "Bubba" Brown is an example of a blues constructed from a core. In this case the core consists of the piece's melody, guitar part, and the line "canned heat's a' killing me." Brown learned this blues core from Tommy Johnson in Jackson, Mississippi, who composed and recorded, "Canned Heat Blues" in 1928 (Victor V-38535).[27] "Canned Heat" is a type of cooking fuel made by the Sterno Company. During Prohibition some people drank this cheap and readily available alcoholic substance along with such other unwholesome products as denatured or rubbing alcohol ("alcorub"), hair tonic, liquid shoe polish, and extract of Jamaica ginger. Tommy Johnson was addicted to canned heat and these other drinks and spread their use along with his song to many others in Mississippi over the course of a long blues-singing career that lasted until his death in 1956. His recipe for preparing the drink has been described by his brother:

> That canned heat, you know, it was red. It was in those little old cans. When you open it, take the top off the can. He'd strike him a match and burn it, burn the top of it. And he'd put it in a rag and strain it. It's got juice in it. Squeeze the juice out of it into a glass. And then get him some sugar and put it in there. And then some water. And there he'd go.[28]

Canned heat and similar substances not only produced inebriation, but often they also produced a permanent disability known colloquially as the "limber leg" or "jake leg" (after Jamaica ginger).[29] The effects of such drinks became the theme of many other blues besides Johnson's, indicating that the subject was well known to blues singers.[30] Remarkably, Tommy Johnson himself did not seem to suffer any consequences from his lifelong addiction. He died of a heart attack at the age of sixty![31]

Although the version of "Canned Heat Blues" that Tommy Johnson recorded commercially in 1928 was a thematic blues, "Bubba" Brown says that in person Johnson would sing "most anything" in it. Evidently he means that Johnson performed the song's core, adding to it additional stanzas at the time of performance, probably to produce a nonthematic blues. Certainly this is the practice that Brown himself follows, as his two versions printed below demonstrate. Other singers who learned the piece from Johnson also perform the song's core while adding other stanzas different from those on Johnson's recorded version.[32] Brown's first version is as follows. He states that some of his verses besides the core verse were ones that Johnson sometimes sang in this piece.

> *Example 7.* "Canned Heat Blues." John Henry "Bubba" Brown, vocal and guitar.[33]

> 1. Oh well, I drink so much canned heat 'til I walked all in my sleep.
> Says, I drink so much canned heat, I walked all in my sleep.

Says, I had to drink that canned heat. Lord, I didn't have
nothing else to eat.

2. Says, my dog, he jumped a rabbit, and he run him a solid
   mile.
   Says, my dog jumped a rabbit, and he run the rabbit a solid
   mile.
   Well, he seen he couldn't catch the rabbit; he sit down and
   cried just like a child.

3. Says, I'm going to Memphis, from there to Baltimore.
   Says, I'm going back to Memphis, boys, from Memphis
   back to Baltimore.
   'Cause when I was around your place, you drove me 'way
   from your door.

4. Says, now I done drinked so much canned heat until that
   canned heat's a' killing me.
   Well, I done drinked so much canned heat, babe, 'til
   canned heat's a' killing me.
   I'm gonna get me a train; I'm going back to Memphis,
   Tennessee.

5. Says, and my dog, he jumped a wild fox, and he run him
   'round in front of my door.
   And my dog, he jumped a wild fox; he brought him right in
   front of my door.
   I says, "Just looky here, dog, don't run no chicken-eater
   up here no more."

The above text apparently does not develop a single theme. In fact, it
seems to contain three different themes: the singer's drinking and
health problem, his desire to travel, and his dog's inability to hunt
properly. This text, then, might seem to confirm Brown's observation
that "Canned Heat Blues" was a song in which one could sing "most
anything." Yet, though the stanzas do not represent a single definite
underlying story or scene, they do maintain a consistency of mood,
somewhat in the manner of "Water Boy" (Example 3). The singer depicts himself as addicted to canned heat and ruining his health (Stanzas
1 and 4). This and the fact that his friends (or possibly his lover) have
driven him away (Stanza 3) can be taken as the reasons for his desire to
travel (Stanzas 3 and 4). The stanzas about the singer's dog (2 and 5)

again present an image of a lack of success. Possibly the dog is even to be taken as symbolic of the singer himself, in which case we might compare Stanzas 3 and 5, in which the singer and the dog are driven away from their companion's door. The general mood of this piece, then, is one of regret and self-pity.

A little over a month later Brown recorded another version of "Canned Heat Blues," this one very different in mood though still employing the same core.

> *Example 8.* "Canned Heat Blues." John Henry "Bubba"
> Brown, vocal and guitar.[34]

1. Says, I tell you baby, canned heat's a' killing me.

2. Well, I drinked so much canned heat 'til it made me weak in my
     knee.
   Says, I drinked so much canned heat 'til it made me weak all in my
     knee.
   Well, I'm gonna drink my canned heat just as long as I can live.

3. Says, I'm going to Memphis, from there to Birmingham.
   Says, I'm going to Memphis, from there back to Birmingham.
   'Cause I'm gonna make my home way down in good old Alabam'.

4. Says, I drinked so much canned heat 'til it made me weak all in my
     knee.
   Says, I drinked so much canned heat 'til it made me weak all in my
     knee.
   I'm gonna drink my canned heat; you can say just what you please.

Here the mood is not one of regret and self-pity but rather one of boasting and determination to survive. The travel theme in Stanza 3 seems more of an affirmation of a life style of drinking and rambling than a desire to escape or a feeling of rejection. These two examples, then, of "Canned Heat Blues" by the same singer show that a blues core is a very flexible compositional device that can be used to help generate texts that are otherwise very different from each other. Although most folklorists would probably consider these pieces to be variants of each other or of a common song type, the pieces obviously can have quite different meanings.

The eight examples printed above should demonstrate the flexibility and variability in folk blues. They can be thematic or nonthematic; de-

liberately composed prior to performance, improvised during performance, or partly improvised and partly composed deliberately (the core
technique); and they can be either original compositions of the singer,
arrangements of traditional material, copies of phonograph records, or
even combinations of material from all of these sources. Folk blues also
may or may not be the direct personal expressions of their singers or
composers, though from their vivid first-person style of delivery they
usually appear to be such. Most of the blues printed here, however, did
not represent the current or the former conditions of their singers.
"Bubba" Brown was never a canned-heat drinker or a rambler. In fact,
he retired on a pension after working thirty years for the same company. He associated "Canned Heat Blues" with his friend and fellow
blues singer Tommy Johnson, whose music Brown greatly admired. Although Roosevelt Holts sang "I'll drink my whiskey, I'll catch the train
and ride," he was a teetotaler at the time of recording, and if he rode
anywhere, it would have been in his Chrysler. Bessie Mae Charleston
was definitely never a chain-gang prisoner, and in her song, in any case,
she adopts the persona of a male convict. Charley Taylor's "Annie
Lee," although highly personal in style, was ultimately a reworking of a
phonograph record of the same title. Eli Owens lived in town at the
time of recording, nowhere near a commissary, nor was he in the habit
of stealing women from "monkey men." In any case, he learned his
song from another singer. And Ira Coney, despite the picture of marital
dissolution in his "Monday Morning Blues," was a happily married man
and father of nine who performed the piece in front of his wife and family.

Most blues singers employ a variety of the approaches to learning,
composition, and performance described above, relying to a greater or
lesser extent in each individual performance on such factors as originality, tradition, personal experience, improvisation, and so forth. No
folk-blues singer familiar to me uses only one of these approaches exclusively. Yet the singers do recognize one criterion that should be
common to all blues: that they tell the truth.[35] Obviously this truth need
not be literal or autobiographical.[36] Instead the performer must sing
something that is true to life, something that represents a typical experience or thought for people in the singer's community or audience. All
of the texts printed above are filled with such typical experiences or
thoughts. Thus, even if the words of a folk blues represent a fantasy for
their singer, they are reality for someone else close to the singer or a
fantasy in which others can easily share. Folk blues do not deal with
unique or remote experiences that only the singer could understand or

with the experiences of people unlike the singer and his audience. These songs, then, serve as a means of self-expression for the blues singer but also indirectly for the audience around him. The blues singer becomes their spokesman, the organizer of their thoughts, opinions, and fantasies.

If the folk-blues singer must be conscious of his audience, we should look again at the contexts of these songs. Of all the social situations for blues performance described at the beginning of this article, probably the most common are the house party and the gathering at the local juke joint. These situations are usually characterized by dancing, drinking, a great deal of noise besides the music, and a variety of other distractions from the music, such as conversation, gambling, and watching the dancers. In some of the larger affairs there may even be two competing sources of music, one of which may be a record player, juke box, or radio. In any case the blues singer must compete with his context as well as perform within it. The attention span of people in this kind of audience tends to be short. Frequently they do not listen closely to an entire performance even if they are in close enough range to the singer to hear it clearly. Thus only one or two stanzas of a song might actually register on a typical member of a folk-blues audience. If a song is well structured as a total composition, this fact is not likely to be perceived during its performance except possibly by the blues singer himself. Under these circumstances, then, such devices as nonthematic composition, improvisation, and textual structures based on the principles of contrast and association of related ideas prove to be great advantages for the blues singer in reaching his audience and fulfilling his function as their spokesman. They provide the singer the opportunity to develop ideas succinctly, appeal to a variety of interests, and express contrasting sides of common problems, thus maximizing his appeal to various members of his audience. The blues singer can have something for everyone. Frequently members of the audience will respond to an individual line or stanza with a shout of encouragement or agreement with the singer or banter directed toward a statement expressed in one of the verses.[37] Rarely are comments made on the song as a whole.

But folk blues are not always sung under such hectic circumstances. Charley Patton's "It Won't Be Long" (Example 4) was sung in a commercial recording studio, while the other examples printed here were sung in the singer's or a neighbor's home, either with an audience of family and friends or strictly for the collectors. In fact, these pieces would have been difficult to record at a juke joint or house party because of the noise, crowded conditions, and sometimes rowdy behavior of the participants.[38] Although the conditions of the natural context can influence the content of a blues performance, and although some of these conditions were lacking in the examples presented here, these examples still give a true picture of the variety of styles used by folk-blues singers in composing and performing their songs, for the singers are so used to performing under hectic circumstances that they simply retain the same approaches in more relaxed ones. It is only when singers begin to become more self-conscious about their roles as popular artists for a mass audience or when they realize that they can reach a mass audience with their thoughts through phonograph records and other mass media that they make a major shift in their approach to composition and performance. Records can be contemplated by their audience at leisure and under controlled circumstances, and a popular singer on a stage performing through a public-address system can be heard over the noise of his surroundings. Under these conditions blues usually contain thematic texts with a single idea more fully developed than in the folk blues. Popular blues texts are usually more original and deliberate compositions than folk-blues texts, which are frequently traditional and improvised at the time of performance. These developments must not be taken as indications of progress, however. They simply represent equally suitable responses to different social circumstances.

NOTES

[1] For a good history of the blues, see Paul Oliver, *The Story of the Blues* (London: Barrie & Rockliff, 1969). Blues singers themselves discuss their music and careers in Paul Oliver, *Conversation with the Blues* (New York: Horizon, 1965), and Robert Neff and Anthony Connor, *Blues* (Boston: David R. Godine, 1975). Blues recordings through 1966 are listed in two important discographical works: John Godrich and Robert M. W. Dixon, *Blues & Gospel Records 1902–1943*, 3rd edn., rev. (Chigwell, Essex: Storyville, 1982), and Mike Leadbitter and Neil Slaven, *Blues Records: 1943–1966* (London: Hanover, 1968). The earliest substantial collection of folk blues was made by Howard W. Odum early in this century in Mississippi and Georgia and published in "Folk-Song and Folk-Poetry As Found in the Secular Songs of the Southern Negroes," *JAF* 24 (1911): 255–94, 351–96. This article was reprinted with few changes in Howard W. Odum and Guy B. Johnson, *The Negro and His Songs* (Chapel Hill: University of Noth Carolina Press, 1925). For a more recent large collection of folk blues, see Harry Oster, *Living*

Country Blues (Detroit: Folklore Associates, 1969). Some early blues sheet music has been reprinted in *Blues, an Anthology,* ed. W. C. Handy, with a historical and critical text by Abbe Niles, rev. Jerry Silverman (New York: Mcmillan, 1972). Collections of blues texts from commercial phonograph records are printed in Paul Oliver, *The Meaning of the Blues* (New York: Collier, 1963); Eric Sackheim, *The Blues Line, a Collection of Blues Lyrics* (New York: Grossman, 1969); Stefan Grossman, Hall Grossman, and Stephen Calt, *Country Blues Songbook* (New York: Oak, 1973); A. X. Nicholas, *Woke Up This Mornin': Poetry of the Blues* (New York: Bantam, 1973); Jeff Todd Titon, *Early Downhome Blues: A Musical and Cultural Analysis* (Urbana: University of Illinois Press, 1977); Jeff Todd Titon, *Downhome Blues Lyrics* (Boston: G. K. Hall, 1982); and Michael Taft, *Blues Lyric Poetry: An Anthology* (New York: Garland, 1983).

² On black-white interchange in the blues, see Tony Russell, *Blacks, Whites and Blues* (New York: Stein and Day, 1970).

³ On the folk/popular distinction in the blues, see David Evans, "Folk, Commercial, and Folkloristic Aesthetics in the Blues," *Jazzforschung* 5 (1973): 11–32, and David Evans, *Big Road Blues: Tradition and Creativity in the Folk Blues* (Berkeley: University of California Press, 1982), pp. 16–105. On the attitudes and activities of the songwriters, commercial record companies, and their blues artists, see W. C. Handy, *Father of the Blues* (New York: Collier, 1970); Perry Bradford, *Born with the Blues* (New York: Oak, 1965); "Quality in 'Blues,'" *The Metronome* 39 (Sept. 1923): 140; "Origin of 'Blues' Numbers," *Sheet Music News* 2 (Oct. 1923): 8–9, 41; Robert M. W. Dixon and John Godrich, *Recording the Blues* (New York: Stein and Day, 1970); Mike Seeger, "Who Chose These Records? A Look into the Life, Tastes, and Procedures of Frank Walker," in *Anthology of American Folk Music,* ed. Josh Dunson and Ethel Raim (New York: Oak, 1973), pp. 8–17; David Evans, "An Interview with H. C. Speir," *John Edwards Memorial Foundation Quarterly* 8 (1972): 117–21; Lester Melrose, "My Life in Recording," in *The American Folk Music Occasional,* ed. Chris Strachwitz and Pete Welding (New York: Oak, 1970) pp. 59–61; Norman Cohen, "'I'm a Record Man': Uncle Art Satherly Reminisces," *John Edwards Memorial Foundation Quarterly* 8 (1972): 18–22; Kip Lornell, "Living Blues Interview: J. B. Long," *Living Blues* no. 29 (Sept.–Oct., 1976): 13–22; Charles Keil, *Urban Blues* (Chicago: University of Chicago Press, 1966), pp. 69–95; Mike Leadbitter, *Crowley, Louisiana Blues* (Bexhill-on-Sea, England: Blues Unlimited, 1968); and Mike Leadbitter and Eddie Shuler, *From the Bayou* (Bexhill-on-Sea, England: Blues Unlimited, 1969).

⁴ These processes are identified and described in David Evans, "Techniques of Blues Composition among Black Folksingers," *JAF* 87 (1974): 240–49. For a more detailed discussion see David Evans, *Big Road Blues,* pp. 41–48.

⁵ Recorded near Portal, Georgia, January 15, 1976, by David and Cheryl Evans.

⁶ Recorded in Crystal Springs, Mississippi, August 31, 1970, by David Evans.

⁷ Samuel Charters, *The Bluesmen* (New York: Oak, 1967), pp. 73, 133, 134, 209.

⁸ Paul Oliver, *Screening the Blues: Aspects of the Blues Tradition* (London: Cassell, 1968), pp. 90–91.

⁹ On poetic imagery in the folk blues, see especially Odum and Johnson, pp. 269–96; Sterling A. Brown, "The Blues As Folk Poetry," in *Folk-Say, a Regional Miscellany: 1930*, ed. B. A. Botkin (Norman: University of Oklahoma Press, 1940), pp. 324–39; Sterling A. Brown, "The Blues," *Phylon* 13 (1952): 286–92; Samuel Charters, *The Poetry of the Blues* (New York: Oak, 1963); Oster, pp. 61–95; Stephen Calt, "The Country Blues As Meaning," in Grossman, Grossman, and Calt, pp. 8–35; and Paul Garon, *Blues and the Poetic Spirit* (London: Eddison, 1975).

¹⁰ For analyses of other blues of this sort, see Charters, *The Poetry of the Blues*, pp. 23–26.

¹¹ For an important study of the Southern black prison song tradition, see Bruce Jackson, *Wake Up Dead Man: Afro-American Worksongs from Texas Prisons* (Cambridge, Mass.: Harvard University Press, 1972). For prison blues, see Oliver, *The Meaning of the Blues*, pp. 231–58; and Oster, pp. 305–46.

¹² On the "holler" tradition, see Harold Courlander, *Negro Folk Music U.S.A.* (New York: Columbia University Press, 1963), pp. 80–88. On the relation of the holler to the blues, see Charters, *The Bluesmen*, pp. 27–28; Oliver, *The Story of the Blues*, pp. 17–25; Oster, pp. 11–13; John A. Lomax and Alan Lomax, *Folk Song U.S.A.* (New York: New American Library, 1966), p. 70; Alan Lomax, *The Folk Songs of North America* (Garden City, N.Y.: Doubleday, 1960), p. 573; and David Evans, *Big Road Blues*, pp. 41–48.

¹³ Recorded near Crystal Springs, Mississippi, July 14, 1971, by David and Cheryl Evans.

¹⁴ Odum, "Folk-Song and Folk-Poetry," pp. 260, 268.

¹⁵ Dorothy Scarborough, *On the Trail of Negro Folk-Songs* (Cambridge, Mass.: Harvard University Press, 1925), p. 272.

¹⁶ Francis Lee Utley noted the "masterful poetic logic" of one such blues in "The Genesis and Revival of 'Dink's Song,'" in *Studies in Language and Literature in Honor of Margaret Schlauch*, ed. Mieczysław Brahmer, Stanisław Helsztyński, and Julian Kryzyżanowski (Warsaw: Polish Scientific Publishers, 1966), pp. 457–72. Oster, pp. 76–87, also attempts to explain several such blues.

¹⁷ Charters, *The Bluesmen*, p. 121.

¹⁸ John Fahey, *Charley Patton* (London: Studio Vista, 1970), p. 60.

¹⁹ Calt, pp. 20, 21.

[20] Barry Elmes, "Living Blues Interview: Sonny Terry & Brownie McGhee," *Living Blues* no. 13 (Summer 1973): 20. For other similar opinions of blues singers see Bruce Iglauer, Jim O'Neal, and Bea Van Geffen, "Living Blues Interview: Lowell Fulson," *Living Blues* no. 6 (Autumn 1971): 18; and Charters, *The Poetry of the Blues,* p. 20 (quoting Furry Lewis).

[21] Fahey, pp. 60, 63.

[22] Related blues by Memphis groups are "Minglewood Blues" (Victor 21267; recorded 1928) by Cannon's Jug Stompers, reissued on *Cannon's Jug Stompers,* Herwin 208, 12" double-LP; and "New Minglewood Blues" (Victor 23266; recorded 1930) by Noah Lewis's Jug Band, reissued on *The Great Jug Bands,* Origin Jazz Library 4, 12" LP.

[23] Recorded in Richmond, Indiana, June 14, 1929; issued on Paramount 12854; reissued on *Charley Patton, Founder of the Delta Blues,* Yazoo L-1020, 12" double-LP.

[24] David Evans, *Tommy Johnson* (London: Studio Vista, 1971), pp. 91, 99; David Evans, "Booker White," in *Nothing but the Blues,* ed. Mike Leadbitter (London: Hanover, 1971), pp. 253–54; Valerie Wilmer, "Blues People: Fred & Roosevelt," *Jazz Journal* 19 (Aug. 1966): 24; Al Wilson, "Robert Pete Williams, His Life and Music," *Little Sandy Review* 2 (July 1966): 21; Oster, p. 4.

[25] Recorded in Bogalusa, Louisiana, August 24, 1970, by David Evans. Issued on *Roosevelt Holts and His Friends,* Arhoolie 1057, 12" LP.

[26] Recorded in Bogalusa, Louisiana, August 26, 1970, by David Evans. Issued on *South Mississippi Blues,* Rounder 2009, 12" LP.

[27] Johnson's version is printed and discussed in Evans, *Tommy Johnson,* pp. 56–58, 93–94. For more information on Brown, see David Evans, "Bubba Brown: Folk Poet," *MFR* 7 (1973): 15–31.

[28] Evans, *Tommy Johnson,* p. 57.

[29] See Kelsie B. Harder, "The Jake Leg," *TFSB* 27 (Sept. 1961): 45–47 and John P. Morgan and Thomas C. Tulloss, "The Jake Walk Blues: A Toxicologic Tragedy Mirrored in American Popular Music," *Annals of Internal Medicine* 85, no. 6 (Dec. 1976): 804–8.

[30] Among the other blues on this theme are Tommy Johnson's "Alcohol and Jake Blues" (Paramount 12950; recorded 1930; no known copy extant); Ishman Bracey's "Jake Liquor Blues" (Paramount 12941; recorded 1930); Keghouse's "Canned Heat Blues" (Vocalin 1239); "Sloppy" Henry's "Canned Heat Blues" (Okeh 8630; recorded 1928); Will Shade's "Better Leave That Stuff Alone" (Victor 21725; recorded 1928); Willie "Poor Boy" Lofton's "It's Killing Me" (Decca 7010; recorded 1934) and "Jake Leg Blues" (Decca 7076; recorded 1934). Bracey and Lofton were friends of Tommy Johnson, although their songs are unrelated except in theme. Many songs on the "jake leg" theme are reissued on *Jake Walk Blues,* Stash ST-110, 12" LP.

[31] Evans, *Tommy Johnson*, pp. 85–87.

[32] K. C. Douglas, "Canned Heat," issued on *K. C. Douglas, a Dead-Beat Guitar and the Mississippi Blues*, Cook 5002, 12" LP (recorded 1956); K. C. Douglas, "Canned Heat," issued on *K. C. Douglas, Big Road Blues*, Bluesville BV 1050, 12" LP (recorded 1961); Houston Stackhouse, "Canned Heat," issued on *Mississippi Delta Blues*, vol. 1, Arhoolie ST 1041, 12" (recorded 1967).

[33] Recorded in Los Angeles, California, June 9, 1967, by David Evans and Marina Bokelman. Issued on *The Legacy of Tommy Johnson*, Matchbox SDM 224, 12" LP.

[34] Recorded in Los Angeles, California, July 17, 1967, by David Evans and Marina Bokelman.

[35] Evans, "Folk, Commercial, and Folkloristic Aesthetics in the Blues," 13–15; Charters, *The Poetry of the Blues*, pp. 11–14; Oliver, *Conversation with the Blues*, pp. 23–25.

[36] On the question of "autobiography" in blues see Rod Gruver, "The Blues As Dramatic Monologues," *John Edwards Memorial Foundation Quarterly* 6 (1970): 28–31; Jeff Titon, "Autobiography and Blues Texts: A Reply to 'The Blues As Dramatic Monologues,'" *ibid.* 6 (1970): 79–82; and Rod Gruver, "The Autobiographical Theory Re-Examined," *ibid.* 6 (1970): 129–31.

[37] On the role of the audience at blues-singing events, see William Ferris, Jr., *Blues from the Delta* (Garden City, N.Y.: Anchor Press, 1978), pp. 101–56.

[38] On this point, see David Evans, "Fieldwork with Blues Singers: The Unintentionally Induced Natural Context," *SFQ* 42 (1978): 9–16.

Glossarial Index

General Index